W9-AQM-368

Second edition

CENTURY 21® TYPEWRITING

D. D. Lessenberry
Professor of Education, Emeritus
University of Pittsburgh

T. James Crawford
Chairman
Department of Administrative Systems and Business Education
Graduate School of Business
Indiana University

Lawrence W. Erickson
Assistant Dean
Graduate School of Education
University of California, Los Angeles

Lee R. Beaumont
Professor of Business
Indiana University of Pennsylvania

Jerry W. Robinson
Senior Editor
South-Western Publishing Co.

ISBN: 0-538-20800-7
Library of Congress
Catalog Card Number: 76-6643
6 7 8 9 H 4 3 2 1 0 9 8

Complete course

T80

Published by South-Western Publishing Co.

Cincinnati West Chicago, Ill. Dallas Pelham Manor, N.Y.
Palo Alto, Calif. Brighton, England

Contents

Cycle 1 Lessons 1–75

Basic Typing Operations

Cycle 2 Lessons 76–150

Personal/Professional Typing

Cycle 3 Lessons 151–225

Developing Typewriting Production Power

phase 7
Improving typing competence

phase 8
Office communication skills

phase 9
Data communication skills

Cycle 4 Lessons 226–300

Simulated Office Typing

phase 10
Improving basic/production skills

phase 11
Functional office simulations

phase 12
Specialized office simulations

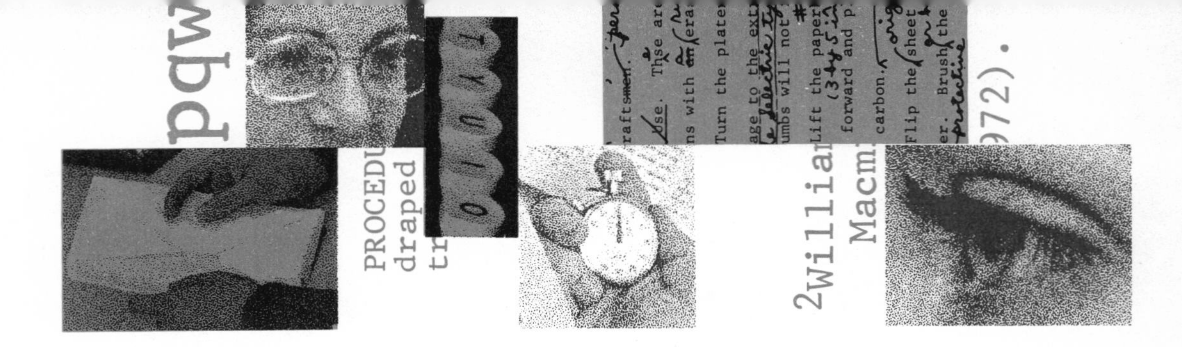

Preface

Given appropriate amounts of the right kinds of practice, almost everyone can learn to type. All students do not learn at the same rate, however, or reach the same level of skill at the same time. A primary goal of this new edition of *Century 21 Typewriting,* therefore, is to provide a sequence of learning materials and activities that will help every student reach optimal skill levels within the limited time available for learning to type. Some of the unique features specifically designed to achieve this purpose are described here.

Technique emphasis

Efficient technique patterns of keystroking, spacing, shifting, and returning the carriage (or carrier) are essential conditions of learning to type with speed and accuracy. In *Century 21 Typewriting* these technique elements are kept vividly before the student by special drawings, goals, cues, and drills. Other important techniques are presented and reinforced as needed for the extension of the skill.

Controlled repetition

The value of repeating keystroking sequences in a variety of word settings cannot be overestimated in developing keyboard mastery. To assure the needed repetition and variety, however, practice materials must be carefully designed. In this textbook the keyboard learning materials and basic skill building drills are scientifically structured and computer checked to assure proper amounts and variety of repetitive practice.

Delayed figure/symbol typing

To assure adequate mastery of the letter keyboard and basic typewriting techniques, the introduction of figure keys is delayed until Lessons 26–30. To develop optimum control of the figure keys, symbol presentation is delayed until Lessons 36–40. Postponing the introduction of top–row reaches until the easier reaches are mastered results in improved control of both the letter and figure/symbol keyboards.

Goal setting

Practice done with a specific purpose in mind has been shown repeatedly to result in improved performance. For this reason, goals are provided for many of the learning activities. At strategic times, a specific goal is stated as the *minimum* level of acceptable performance. At other times, three levels of goals are given (acceptable, good, and excellent). Often the goals are student selected (totally individualized), based on the individual student's immediate past performance. Separate goals are provided for techniques, speed, and control.

Triple-controlled copy

Copy difficulty has a vital effect on the speed with which students type. Copy of low syllable intensity, low average word length, and high common–word content is easier to type than copy of the opposite composition. In building skill, students need practice on copy selections of varied difficulty. Measurement activities, on the other hand, should be on copy of standard difficulty to provide dependable measures of real skill growth. In this textbook, materials are deliberately written at different levels of difficulty for different skill–*building* purposes; whereas, materials are carefully controlled at a standard (average) level of difficulty for skill–*measurement* purposes—once students have built the skill to a level sufficient to handle copy of average difficulty without undue stress or frustration.

Speed/control building

The student cannot effectively practice for speed and control at the same time. Therefore, practice goals and directions specify different levels of practice for different writings. In one writing the student is asked to stress speed; in another, improved control; and in still another, technique at an in–between (optimum) level of performance. A variety of materials and individualized practice procedures is provided, each designed to fit the specific purpose of the practice activity.

Skill-transfer activities

All studies of the copy sources from which typists work indicate that both personal and office papers are frequently prepared from handwritten copy, rough draft, and copy containing figures and commonly used symbols. In this textbook these kinds of copy are introduced early and emphasized systematically in an activity called "skill–transfer typing." In this activity, the student is encouraged by timing and rate comparisons to transfer as much of the straight–copy skill as possible to the typing of script, rough draft, and statistical copy.

Related communication skills

The primary purpose in learning to type is to be able to apply the skill—in school, at home, on the job. Applying the skill effectively involves more than mere typing; it involves the application of accepted guides for dividing words, spelling, capitalizing, expressing numbers, punctuating, spacing with punctuation marks and symbols, and grammar. It often requires composing at the typewriter, too. This textbook includes a systematic review of related English skills and provides many opportunities for students to compose as they type.

Problem typing

Problem typing is presented in simple–to–complex order: easy processes and formats before more difficult ones; model copy before semiarranged and unarranged copy; short, easy problems before longer, more challenging ones. Applications include personal, personal–business, and business papers—all adapted from real–life typing situations. The basic typing operations (centering, letters, tables, reports, and business forms) are emphasized. They are then reinforced in expanded recurring cycles to develop skill maturity.

Production power building

Extended–time production activities on a series of problems (involving planning, arranging, typing, proofreading, and correcting) are emphasized in the final third of first–year work and throughout the second year. A well–tested four–step plan of production skill development is employed: (1) learning/problem solving, (2) skill building, (3) sustained production, and (4) production measurement. Timed and time–limit activities are featured.

Office simulations

Following intensive production skill–building activity, the final fifty lessons of the book present a series of simulations of various office typing jobs. This sampling of work situations adds practical realism to the job tasks and provides the student an opportunity to explore various fields in which typing is a required skill. In these simulations, students do more than type–they plan, they decide, they look up needed information, they organize, and they arrange, type, and correct their work just as they are expected to do in a real business office.

D. D. Lessenberry, T. James Crawford
Lawrence W. Erickson
Lee R. Beaumont, Jerry W. Robinson

The diagram above shows the parts of a manual (nonelectric) typewriter; the diagram on page 2 shows the parts of an electric typewriter.

Since all typewriters have similar parts, you will probably be able to locate the parts on your typewriter from one of these diagrams. However, use the instructional booklet that comes with your machine if you have it, as it will identify the exact location of each operative part.

1 Carriage return lever: used to return carriage to left margin and to move paper up

2 Left platen knob: used to push carriage to the right

3 Variable line spacer: used to change writing line setting permanently

4 Left carriage release: used to release carriage so it moves freely to left or right

5 Line-space selector: used to move paper up 1, 2, or 3 lines for single, double, or triple spacing

6 Automatic line finder: used to change line spacing temporarily, then refind the line

7 Paper guide: used as a permanent guide for inserting paper

8 Paper guide scale: used to set paper guide at desired position

9 Left margin set: used to set left margin stop

10/14 Paper bail rolls: used to hold paper against platen

11 Paper bail: used to hold paper against platen

12 Card/envelope holders: used to hold cards, labels, and envelopes against platen

13 Printing point indicator: used to position carriage at desired point

14 (See 10)

15 Right margin set: used to set right margin stop

16 Paper table: supports paper when it is in typewriter

17 Platen (cylinder): provides a hard surface against which typebars strike

18 Paper release lever: used to allow paper to be removed or aligned

19 Right carriage release: used to release carriage so it moves freely to left or right

20 Right platen knob: used to turn platen as paper is being inserted

21 Aligning scale: used to align copy that has been reinserted

22 Line-of-writing (margin) scale: used when setting margin and tab stops and in horizontal centering

23 Ribbon carrier: positions and controls ribbon

24 Tabulator: used to move carriage to tab stops that have been set

25 Tab set: used to set tabulator stops

26 Backspace key: used to move printing point to left, one space at a time

27 Right shift key: used to type capitals of letter keys controlled by left hand

28 Space bar: used to move printing point to right, one space at a time

29 Left shift key: used to type capitals of letter keys controlled by right hand

30 Shift lock: used to lock shift mechanism so that all letters are capped

31 Ribbon control: used to select ribbon typing position

32 Margin release key: used to move carriage beyond margin stops

33 Tab clear: used to clear tabulator stops

Know your typewriter: manual

300b ▶45 Measure production skill: forms and tables

1. Type the 3 problems for 30'; correct errors as you type. If you complete the problems before time is called, retype Problem 1 on plain paper as page 2 of an interoffice memo, beginning with ¶ 1.

2. Compute *n–pram*; compare with score you achieved on 240b, page 376.

Problem 1 [LM p. 215]
Interoffice memorandum

	words
TO: All Department Chiefs FROM: Alice M. Oliver, Chief Administration	12
Office DATE: November 13, 19-- SUBJECT: Reducing Postage Costs (¶ 1)	22
Positive steps must be taken to minimize the impact of the postal rate increase	36
scheduled to be implemented on December 31. As a key step, please take	52
immediate action to purge all mailing lists of duplicates, returns, and in-	67
correct addresses. Wherever possible, use titles rather than individual	81
names on all mailing lists. This technique can also produce substantial	96
savings by reducing costly address changes. (¶ 2) As further measures,	109
instruct your clerical personnel to (1) batch all mail to a common address	124
in a single envelope so that several letters can go for the price of one;	139
(2) use the smallest possible envelope that will accommodate the enclosures	154
to reduce the possibility of the enclosures shifting and bursting the en-	169
velope; and (3) use special postal services, such as special delivery,	183
certified, registered, and insured mail, only when absolutely necessary	196
since fees for these services are scheduled to increase significantly.	211/222

Problem 2 [LM p. 217]
Invoice

To:	Star Electronics Company	Date	December 2, 19--	8
	3200 Old Canton Road	Our Order No.	M-45597	14
	Jackson, MS 39126	Cust. Order No.	84503-Y	19
		Shipped Via	UPS	20
Terms:	Net			21

Quantity	Description	Unit Price	Total	
20	Combination wrench sets	17.89	357.80	29
50	Flex-head ratchets, 15 mm drive	5.10	255.00	38
20	Micrometers, 0.25 mm	7.95	159.00	46
100	Socket wrenches, 8-way	5.95	595.00	53
25	Torque wrenches	7.65	191.25	61
			1,558.05	63

Problem 3
Table
Reading position; DS the items. Use the current year for Column 3 and the previous year for Column 2.

R. W. SIMPSON TOOL CO., INC. 6

Financial Highlights for Fiscal Years 19-- and 19-- 16

Highlight	19--	19--	Change	26
Net sales	$234,880,700	$248,034,000	+ 5.6%	40
Depreciation	8,359,400	8,652,000	+ 3.5%	52
Net income	10,082,200	9,437,000	− 6.4%	63
Cash dividends	3,910,000	4,133,000	+ 5.7%	75
Capital expenditures	7,990,800	6,081,000	−23.9%	87
Shareholders' equity	113,203,000	117,618,000	+ 3.9%	100
Dividends per common share	1.72	1.80	+ 4.7%	112
Common shares outstanding	2,045,639	2,117,237	+ 3.5%	124
Book value per share	53.06	55.71	+ 5.0%	136
Shareholders at year end	6,124	6,300	+ 2.9%	148
Employees at year end	7,514	7,935	+ 5.6%	159

The diagram above shows the parts of an electric typewriter; the diagram on page 1 shows the parts of a manual (nonelectric) typewriter.

Since all typewriters have similar parts, you will probably be able to locate the parts on your typewriter from one of these diagrams. However, use the instructional booklet that comes with your machine if you have it, as it will identify the exact location of each operative part.

1 Carriage return lever (not on electric)

2 Left platen knob: used to push carriage to right (except on single element typewriters—Adler, Olivetti, Royal, Selectric, and Sperry/Remington)

3 Variable line spacer: used to change writing line setting permanently

4 Left carriage release: used to release carriage so it moves freely to left or right (except on single element typewriters)

5 Line-space selector: used to move paper up 1, 2, or 3 lines for single, double, or triple spacing

6 Automatic line finder: used to change line spacing temporarily, then refind the line

7 Paper guide: used as a permanent guide for inserting paper

8 Paper guide scale: used to set paper guide at desired position

9 Left margin set: used to set left margin stop

10/14 Paper bail rolls: used to hold paper against platen

11 Paper bail: used to hold paper against platen

12 Card/envelope holders: used to hold cards, labels, and envelopes against platen

13 Printing point indicator: used to position carriage (or element carrier) at desired point

14 (See 10)

15 Right margin set: used to set right margin stop

16 Paper table: supports paper when it is in typewriter

17 Platen (cylinder): provides a hard surface against which type element or bars strike

18 Paper release lever: used to allow paper to be removed or aligned

19 Right carriage release: used to release carriage so it moves freely to left or right (except on single element typewriters)

20 Right platen knob: used to turn platen as paper is being inserted

21 Aligning scale: used to align copy that has been reinserted

22 Line-of-writing (margin) scale: used when setting margin and tab stops and in horizontal centering

23 Ribbon carrier: positions and controls ribbon at printing point (not shown—under the cover)

24 Tabulator: used to move carriage (carrier) to tab stops

25 Tab set: used to set tabulator stops

26 Backspace key: used to move printing point to left, one space at a time

27 Right shift key: used to type capitals of letter keys controlled by left hand

28 Space bar: used to move printing point to right, one space at a time

29 Left shift key: used to type capitals of letter keys controlled by right hand

30 Shift lock: used to lock shift mechanism so that all letters are capped

31 Ribbon control: used to select ribbon typing position (not shown—under cover)

32 Margin release key: used to move carriage (carrier) beyond margin stops

33 Tab clear: used to clear tab stops

34 Carriage return key: used to return carriage to left margin and to move paper up

35 ON/OFF control: used to turn electric typewriters on or off

Know your typewriter: electric

299b, continued

Problem 2
Leftbound report with side headings

words

UNLOCKING THE SECRETS OF COSMIC ENERGY 8

(¶ 1) New theories about energy, matter, and the origin of the universe are developing as a result of the discovery of amazing celestial objects. Among these celestial bodies which are under study by astrophysicists are quasars, pulsars, and black holes. 22 37 53 58

Quasi-Stellar Radio Sources (¶ 2) Quasars, which are thought to be the same size as large stars, emit energy as light and as radiowaves at all wavelengths equivalent to that of a thousand galaxies and produce more energy in a given volume than any other object in the sky. Quasars are very difficult to observe because they are receding at tremendous velocities--up to 92 percent of the speed of light--billions of light years from the earth. Understanding their energy processes, however, could be a key part of developing theories about the structure of matter itself. 79 94 109 125 140 155 171 177

Pulsating Stars (¶ 3) Pulsars are spinning stars, with diameters of only about ten miles, that generate beams of directional energy that sweep across space like a lighthouse beacon with minutely exact regularity. When the beam flashes across the earth, it appears as a pulse. Pulsars are extremely dense, rotating neutron stars with intense magnetic fields. They are formed from the collapsed remnants of supernovae explosions. One of the major problems under study by astrophysicists is the detailed process by which these stars collapse. 195 211 225 241 256 271 286 288

Black Holes (¶ 4) Black holes are former stars that have an exceptionally powerful gravitational field. This field is so strong that it literally sucks up matter like a powerful vacuum cleaner. A black hole converts mass into enormous energy and does so more efficiently than any other process known today. For this reason, black holes have been called the ultimate source of cosmic energy. 304 319 333 347 362 369

(¶ 5) The information gathered by astrophysicists about these celestial objects can result in great economic benefit. These stars exhibit much more efficient ways of producing energy than anything known to civilization today. If the secrets of these stars can be unlocked, they may open the way to a new era of inexhaustible cosmic energy. 383 399 414 430 435

Problem 3
Topbound report

Type the material in ¶s 2 and 3 of 298d, page 457, as a topbound report.
Heading: WHAT YOU NEED TO KEEP A JOB (5 words)

300

300a ▶5 Conditioning practice

twice SS; repeat difficult lines

Jack questioned my belief that new taxes might jeopardize our venture.
In 1976, they produced 439,094 units as compared with 265,833 in 1975.
On June 1, the price of Item 37692 will increase 5% (from $80 to $84).
If the attorney delays his report, the men may demand a special audit.
| 1 | 2 | 3 | 4 | 5 | 6 | 7 | 8 | 9 | 10 | 11 | 12 | 13 | 14 |

Type E

Lever-arrow set

Olivetti manual

If margin stop is to be moved inward:

1. Move carriage to desired position.

2. Pull appropriate margin lever forward.

If margin stop is to be moved outward:

1. Move carriage to existing margin stop.

2. Move appropriate margin lever forward and hold it in the forward position.

3. Depress carriage release button and move the carriage to desired position.

4. Release margin lever.

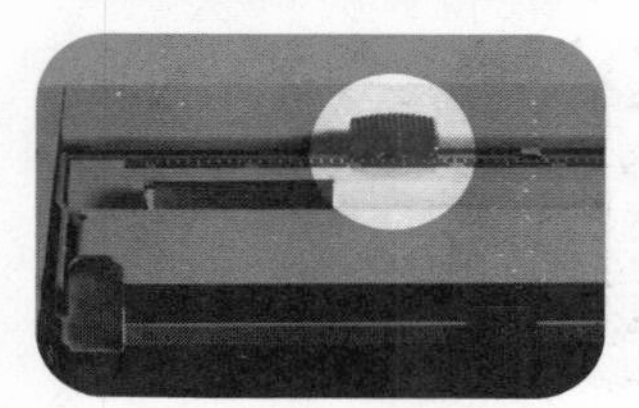

Type A

Push-button set

Adler, Olympia, Remington, Royal 700/870 manuals, Smith–Corona

1. Press down on the left margin set button.

2. Slide it to desired position on the line–of–writing (margin) scale.

3. Release the margin set button.

4. Using the right margin set button, set the right margin stop in the same way.

Type B

Push-lever set

Single element typewriters, such as Adler, Olivetti, Royal, Selectric, Sperry/Remington

1. Push in on the left margin set lever.

2. Slide it to desired position on the line–of–writing (margin) scale.

3. Release the margin set lever.

4. Using the right margin set lever, set the right margin stop in the same way.

Type C

Magic margin set

Royal 470/560/970

1. Pull left magic margin lever forward.

2. Move carriage to desired position on the line–of–writing (margin) scale.

3. Release the left margin lever.

4. Using the right magic margin lever, set the right margin stop in the same way.

Type D

Key set

IBM typebar, Olivetti electric

1. Move carriage to the left margin stop by depressing the return key.

2. Depress and hold down the margin set (IBM reset) key as you move carriage to desired left margin stop position.

3. Release the margin set (IBM reset) key.

4. Move carriage to the right margin stop.

5. Depress and hold down the margin set (IBM reset) key as you move carriage to desired right margin stop position.

6. Release the margin set (IBM reset) key.

General information for setting margin stops is given here. If you have the manufacturer's booklet for your typewriter, however, use it because the procedure for your particular model may be slightly different.

299b ▶45 Measure production skill: report manuscripts

1. Type the 3 reports for 30′; correct errors as you type. If you complete the reports before time is called, start over.

2. Compute *n–pram*. Compare with score achieved on 233b, page 368.

words

Problem 1
Unbound report with footnote

BRIDGING THE COMMUNICATIONS GAP 6

Communication--or the lack of communication--is a big issue 19
today. Many citizens charge that their elected leaders have lost 32
touch with them; workers in industry say that they are considered 45
as only cogs in a machine. The younger generation complains that 58
no one listens to them; members of the older generation grumble 71
that they are being ignored. 77

To bridge the communications gap, leaders of government at 89
all levels are taking to the radio and television to explain their 102
actions and ideas to the people. In many communities and schools, 116
joint groups of people of all ages meet to study current problems 129
and exchange ideas. A great effort is being made in industry to 142
tell workers what they want to know. 150

Great emphasis is placed by business executives on communica- 162
tions skills. They demand office workers who can do something 174
more than type, take dictation, and run office machines. They are 188
willing to pay premium wages to those who are skilled in communi- 200
cations. Your success in the business world may well depend upon 214
your ability to express ideas clearly and concisely. As Wolf and 227
Aurner point out, success in business depends "upon your success 240
as a communicator; upon your ability to issue, transmit, and ful- 253
fill messages; upon your attaining proficiency and profit through 266
words that produce appropriate actions."[1] 274

278

---

[1] Morris Philip Wolf and Robert R. Aurner, _Effective Communica- 294
tion in Business_ (6th ed.; Cincinnati: South-Western Publishing 310
Co., 1974), p. 8. 314

1 Arrange work area

Begin each lesson by arranging your desk or table as shown.

- Typing paper at left of typewriter
- Front frame of typewriter even with front edge of desk
- Book at right of typewriter and elevated for easy reading
- Rest of desk clear of unneeded books and other materials

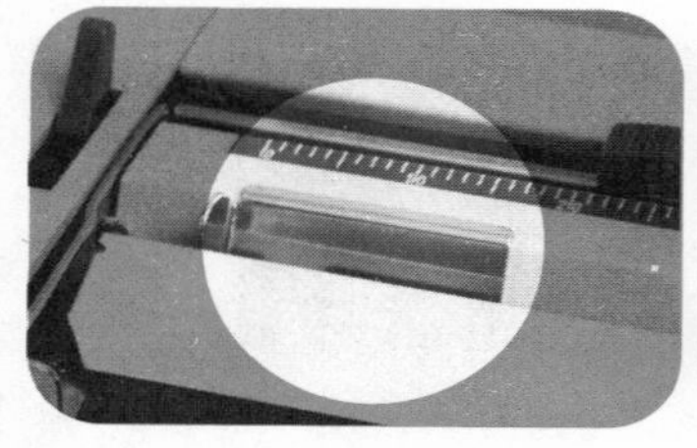

2 Adjust paper guide

Move **paper guide (7)** left or right so that it lines up with 0 (zero) on the **paper-bail scale (11)** or the **line-of-writing** or **margin scale (22).**

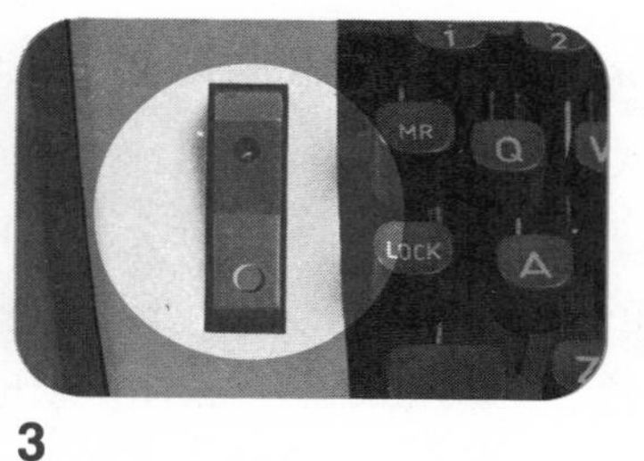

3 Adjust ribbon control

Set **ribbon control (31)** on black to type on upper part of ribbon.

4 Insert typing paper

Take a sheet of paper in your left hand and follow the directions and illustrations at the right and below.

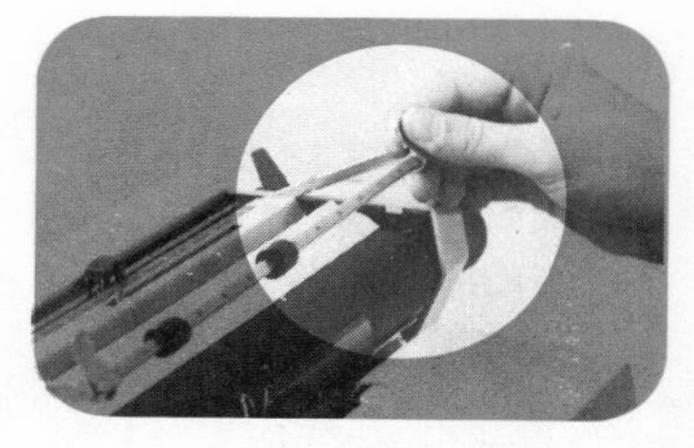

1. Pull **paper bail (11)** forward (or up on some machines).

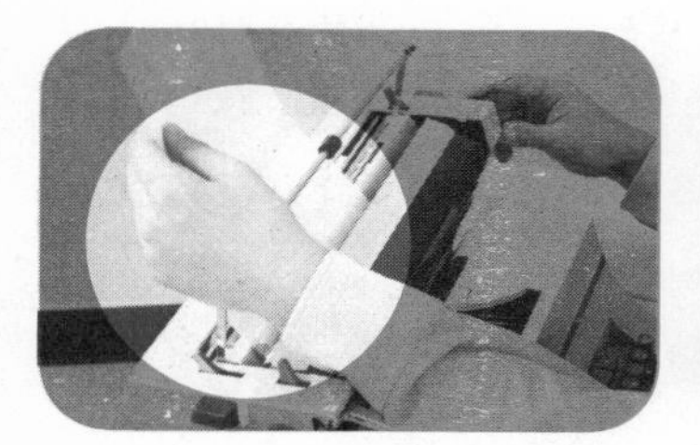

2. Place paper against paper guide, behind the **platen (17).**

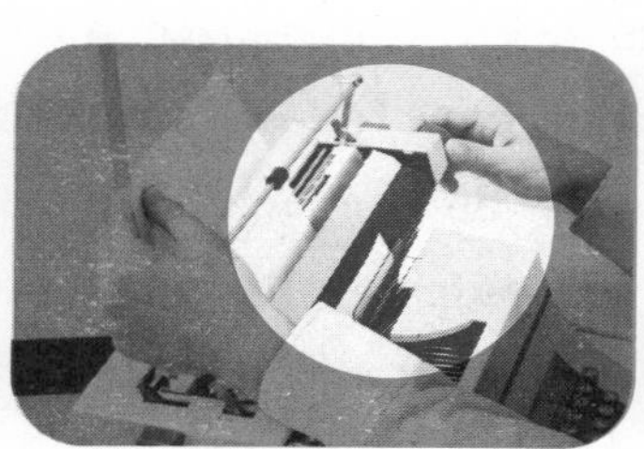

3. Twirl paper into machine, using **right platen knob (20).**

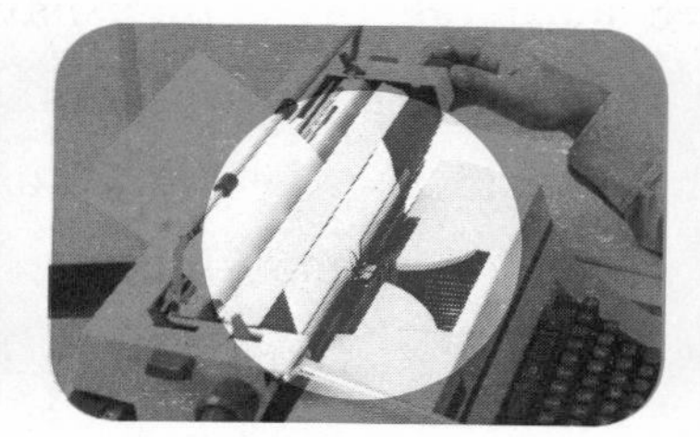

4. Stop when paper is about 1½ inches above **aligning scale (21).**

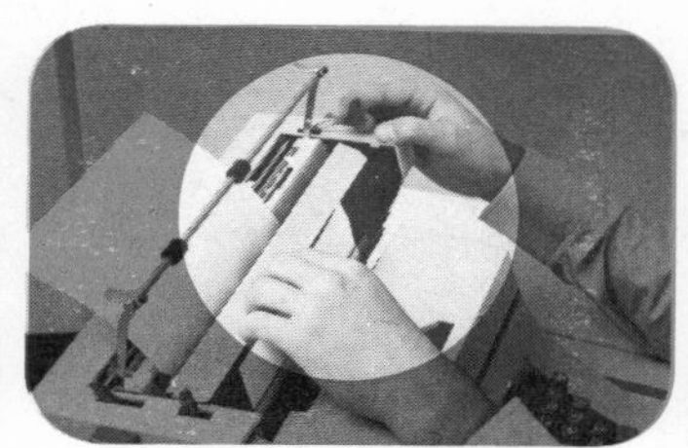

5. To straighten paper, pull **paper release lever (18)** toward you.

6. Straighten paper, then push paper release lever back.

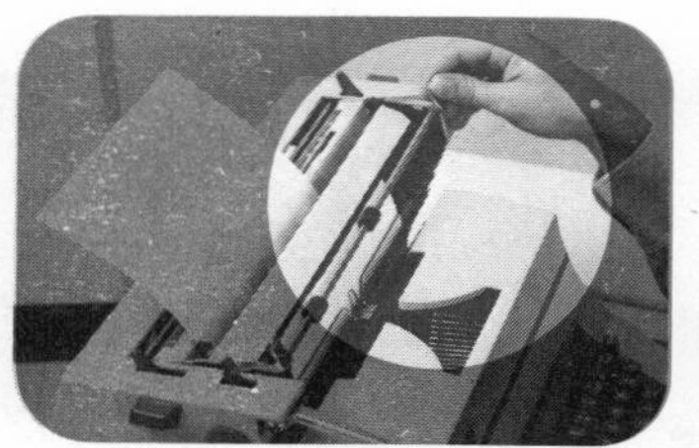

7. Push paper bail back so that it holds paper against platen.

8. Slide **paper bail rolls (10/14)** into position, dividing paper into thirds.

9. Properly inserted paper.

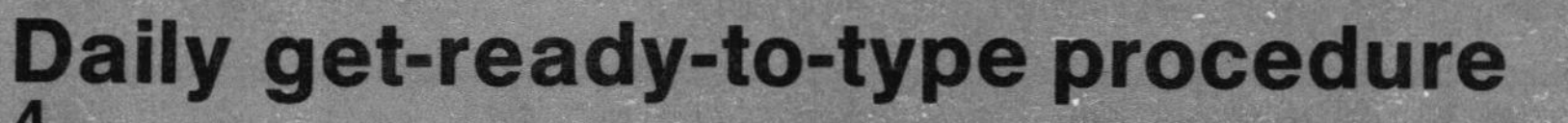

298d ▶17 Measure basic skill: straight copy

1. Two 5′ writings on ¶s 1–3 combined.

2. Record *gwam* and errors on better writing. Compare with scores achieved in 266c, page 358.

3. As time permits, type a 1′ writing on each ¶.

all letters used | A | 1.5 si | 5.6 awl | 80% hfw

	gwam 1′	5′	
It is often more difficult to keep a job than it is to find one.	13	3	61
The bases for the selection of office workers are chiefly objective	27	5	63
in nature. Office workers are chosen on the basis of their ability to	41	8	66
type a given number of words a minute, to take dictation and transcribe	55	11	69
a mailable letter, to operate standard office machines, and to achieve	70	14	72
a passing score on a standardized test of general knowledge. Based on	84	17	75
these tests, only those with the best skills are selected.	95	19	77
Only a small number of those who lose their jobs do so because they	14	22	80
lack the proper skills to do a good job. A number of studies have been	28	25	83
made which indicate that poor work habits and bad personality traits are	43	28	86
two of the major reasons given by employers for the firing of office	56	30	89
workers. These include the failure to adapt to the work situation, a	70	33	91
lack of cooperation, the inability to get along with other employees,	84	36	94
and frequent absences from work for reasons other than illness.	97	38	97
Employers today expect a great deal more from their office workers	13	41	99
than clerical ability. They seek employees who will display a sincere	28	44	102
interest in their jobs, who will take pride in their work, and who will	42	47	105
persevere until the tasks they have been assigned to do have been com-	56	50	108
pleted. They also seek workers who can follow directions exactly and	70	52	111
use their time to the best advantage, who are on the job unless they are	85	55	114
ill, and who possess the ability to get along well with others.	97	58	116

gwam 1′ | 1 | 2 | 3 | 4 | 5 | 6 | 7 | 8 | 9 | 10 | 11 | 12 | 13 | 14 |
5′ | 1 | 2 | 3 |

299

299a ▶5 Conditioning practice

twice SS; repeat difficult lines

Vic King quickly explained the hazardous job of atomic waste disposal.
The population of the city rose from 52,804 in 1967 to 83,456 in 1977.
The temperature on May 17 rose from 20° C to 35° C (68° F. to 95° F.).
When it is time for the women to go, he will take them to the airport.

| 1 | 2 | 3 | 4 | 5 | 6 | 7 | 8 | 9 | 10 | 11 | 12 | 13 | 14 |

5
Set line-space selector

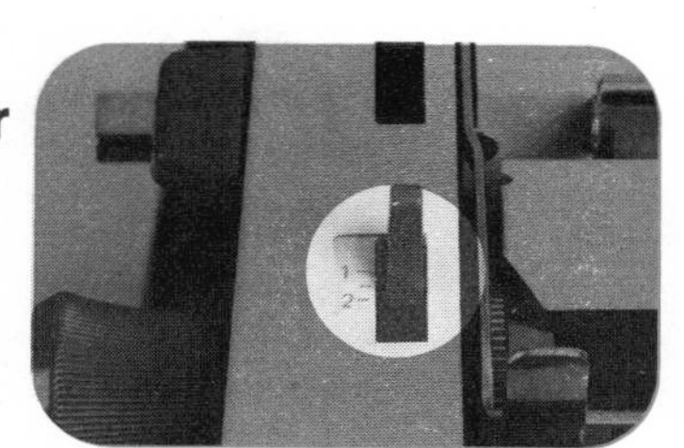

Set **line-space selector (5)** on "1" to single-space (SS) the lines you are to type in Phase 1 lessons.

When so directed, set on "2" to double-space (DS) or on "3" to triple-space (TS).

Single-spaced (SS) copy has no blank line space between lines; double-spaced (DS) copy has 1 blank line space between lines; triple-spaced (TS) copy has 2 blank line spaces between lines.

```
1 Lines 1 and 2 are single-spaced (SS).
2 A double space (DS) separates Lines 2 and 4.
3              1 blank line space
4 A triple space (TS) separates Lines 4 and 7.
5
6              2 blank line spaces
7 Set the selector on "1" for single spacing.
```

6
Plan and set margin stops

Study the following information, then set margin stops for a 50-space line as directed on page 3 for your typewriter.

Typewriters have at least one **line-of-writing scale (22)** that reads from 0 to *at least* 110 for machines with *elite* type, from 0 to *at least* 90 for machines with *pica* type.

The spaces on the line-of-writing scale are matched to the spacing of the letters on the typewriter—elite or pica, as shown above right.

When 8½- by 11-inch paper is inserted into the typewriter (short side up) with left edge of paper at 0 on the line-of-writing scale, the exact center point is 51 for elite, 42½ for pica machines. For convenience, *use 50 for elite, 42 for pica center.*

To have typed material centered horizontally, set left and right margin stops the same number of spaces from center point of paper (50, elite center; 42, pica center).

A warning bell on the typewriter rings 6 to 11 or more spaces before the right margin stop is reached, so add 3 to 7 spaces (usually 5) before setting right margin stop.

The diagrams at right indicate margin stop settings for 50-, 60-, and 70-space lines, assuming the paper is inserted with the left edge at 0 on the line-of-writing scale and that 5 spaces are added to right margin for ringing of the bell.

`You can type 12 elite characters in a horizontal inch.` (2.54 centimeters)

`You can type 10 pica characters in a horizontal inch.`

inches: 1 | 2 | 3 | 4 | 5

centimeters: 1 | 2 | 3 | 4 | 5 | 6 | 7 | 8 | 9 | 10 | 11 | 12 | 13 | 14

Elite type is smaller than pica type. As a result, there are 12 elite spaces but only 10 pica spaces to an inch.

Elite center

Pica center

Elite

	Left edge	Center point	Right edge
	0	50	102
50-space line	25 (−25)	+25, +5	80
60-space line	20 (−30)	+30, +5	85
70-space line	15 (−35)	+35, +5	90

Pica

	Left edge	Center point	Right edge
	0	42	85
50-space line	17 (−25)	+25, +5	72
60-space line	12 (−30)	+30, +5	77
70-space line	7 (−35)	+35, +5	82

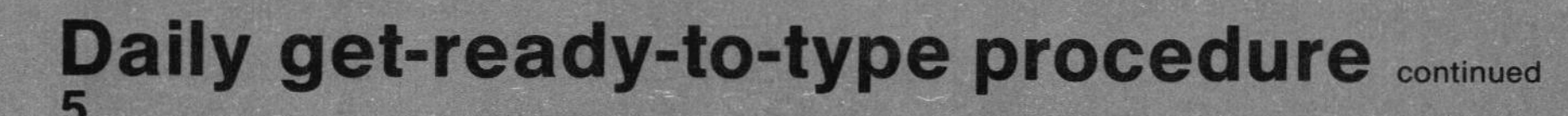

298

298a ▶5 Conditioning practice

twice SS; repeat difficult lines

As expected, Jacob Gray memorized his lines quickly for the new revue.
Will you please call me at 465-3921 or 465-8580 on May 17 at 2:30 p.m.
Part 2470-36 will measure exactly 50.80 cm by 68.58 cm (1′8″ by 2′3″).
If they wish us to do so, we will rush the keys for the trucks by air.

| 1 | 2 | 3 | 4 | 5 | 6 | 7 | 8 | 9 | 10 | 11 | 12 | 13 | 14 |

298b ▶11 Basic skill building

two 1′ writings on each line of 298a

298c ▶17 Measure basic skill: statistical copy

1. Two 5′ writings on statistical ¶s 1–3 combined.
2. Record *gwam* and errors on better writing. Compare with scores you achieved on 239c, page 375.
3. As time permits, type a 1′ writing on each ¶.

all letters/figures used | A | 1.5 si | 5.6 awl | 80% hfw |

	gwam 1′	5′
The median or average pay of secretaries, stenographers, and typ-	13	3
ists has been rising steadily. In 1962, for example, the average pay	27	5
was $3,936; in 1966, it was $4,419; in 1970, it was $5,668; and, in	40	8
1975, it was $7,162. During the period 1970 to 1975 alone, the average	55	11
pay increased $1,494 or 26.4%. Salaries, of course, vary from region	69	14
to region. In 1975, secretaries received an average pay of $159 a week	83	17
in the South, $188.50 in the West, and $167 in the north.	95	19
Some individuals who enter the job market for the first time do not	14	22
realize that there is a vast difference between gross pay and take-home	28	25
pay. Take, for example, a clerical worker in an eastern state, with no	42	27
dependents, who earned $7,600 in 1975. Of this sum, $917 was paid in	56	30
federal taxes; $152, or 2%, was paid in state income taxes; another $152	71	33
was paid to the local municipality; $466.60 was paid into Social Secu-	85	36
rity; and $380, or 5%, was contributed to a company retirement fund.	99	39
A total of $2,067.60 was deducted, leaving a take-home pay of $5,532.40.	113	42
As a rough estimate, experts suggest that you budget 25% of your	13	44
take-home pay for housing, 20% for food, 12% for clothing and personal	27	47
care, 10% for a car or transportation, and 8% for medical fees. This	41	50
leaves 25% for recreation, savings, and other expenses. For a clerical	56	53
worker with a net pay of $5,552.40, this is equal to $1,388 for housing,	70	56
$1,110 for food, $666 for clothing, $555 for a car, and $444 for medical	85	59
bills, leaving a remainder of $1,389.40.	93	60

gwam 1′ | 1 | 2 | 3 | 4 | 5 | 6 | 7 | 8 | 9 | 10 | 11 | 12 | 13 | 14 |
5′ | 1 | 2 | 3 |

phase 1 lessons 1–25

Learning to typewrite

uio

asdf

unit 1 lessons 1–15

The letter keys

Almost everyone can learn the very useful skill of typewriting. Just how well you learn, however, depends upon you: your interest, your effort, your ability to follow directions—both written and oral.

To achieve the best results in typewriting, you must read, listen, observe, and practice meaning-fully. Make *improvement* the goal of each practice effort.

Before you can put the typewriter to practical use, you must become skilled in operating the keyboard and basic service keys: space bar, the return, shift keys, tabulator, and so on.

In Phase 1 (25 lessons), you will learn:

1. To operate the letter keys and basic service keys by touch.
2. To type words, sentences, and paragraphs with continuity and good techniques.
3. To type from typewritten, handwritten, and rough–draft copy.

1

1a ▶ Get ready to type

1. Study the **Know-your-typewriter** information given on pages 1-3.
2. Follow the **Daily get-ready-to-type procedure** on pages 4-5.

1b ▶ Take good typing position

1. Study the illustrations of correct typing position shown below.

2. Observe each of the points as you take good position at your typewriter.

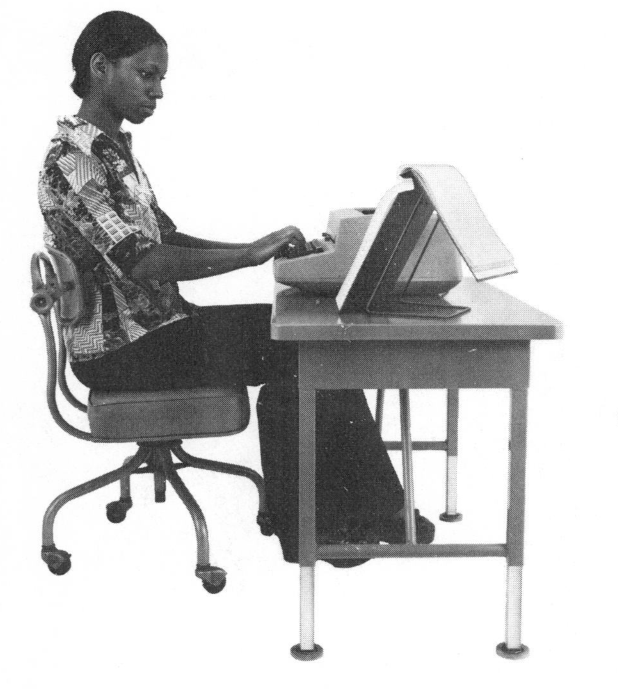

eyes on copy

fingers curved and upright; wrists low

forearms parallel to slant of keyboard

sit back in chair; body erect

textbook at right of machine and elevated for easy reading

table free of unneeded books

feet on floor for balance

297b ▶45 Measure production skill: letters

Type the 4 letters for 30′ on plain paper; correct errors as you type. If you finish all letters before time is called, start over.

Compute *n-pram*: total acceptable words + ½ unacceptable words ÷ 30. Compare *n-pram* with score achieved on 227b, page 360.

Problem 1
Block, open

	words
May 1, 19-- Mrs. Gloria C. Gleason Director of	9
Personnel Clark Manufacturing Co. 985 Main	18
Street Hartford, CT 06103 Dear Mrs. Gleason	27
Subject: Policy H-8698 (121-30-4527) (¶ 1)	34
Thank you for your letter of April 24 concerning	44
the medical care policy cited above covering	53
Mr. Dennis T. Barkley and his dependents. (¶ 2)	62
Before we can add Mr. Barkley's grandmother	71
to his coverage, we must have a sworn state-	79
ment from him advising us that she is com-	87
pletely dependent on him for support, that	96
she is claimed as a dependent on his income tax,	106
and that she resides at the same residence.	115
(¶ 3) We will process Mr. Barkley's change in	123
dependent coverage as soon as we receive his	132
statement. Sincerely yours Scott D. Fitzsim-	141
mons District Manager (97)	145/**166**

Problem 2
Modified block, mixed

May 5, 19-- Mrs. Patricia C. Johnson, Head	9
Business Education Department Roosevelt	17
High School 5600 Oakland Avenue St. Louis,	25
MO 63110 Dear Mrs. Johnson (¶ 1) Stellar	33
Computer Services will have vacancies for	41
three clerk-typists to begin work on June 15.	50
(¶ 2) The duties of these employees will be to	59
type all kinds of correspondence, file, answer	69
the telephone, and operate standard office	77
machines such as calculators and copiers. The	87
employees will be trained to operate the key-	95
punch machine and the computer console. They	105
should be able to type a minimum of 50 gross	114
words a minute with a high degree of accuracy.	123
(¶ 3) If you have any students who may be	130
qualified for these jobs, will you please ask	140
them to send a letter of application directly to	149
me. Sincerely yours L. P. Bradshaw Assis-	159
tant Director (119)	162/**186**

Problem 3
Modified block, indented ¶s, mixed

	words
May 17, 19-- Edison & McNeil, Inc. 109 E. Jef-	9
ferson Blvd. South Bend, IN 46606 Attention	18
Mr. T. Carl Ackerman, Purchasing Agent	26
Ladies and Gentlemen (¶ 1) On April 1, at	33
your request, we submitted bids for the manu-	42
facture of a number of special-purpose tools in	52
metric sizes. As you suggested, we prepared a	61
separate bid for each different item. Copies of	71
these bids are enclosed. (¶ 2) Production sched-	79
ules for the second half of this year must be	88
plotted soon, and we must know the contracts	97
to which we are committed so that we can make	106
the proper plans. For this reason, we are anx-	116
ious to know which, if any, of our bids were ac-	125
ceptable, as well as the number of contracts	134
awarded to us. (¶ 3) Will you please write or	142
call me no later than June 1 and let me know	151
what disposition has been made of our vari-	160
ous bids. If no final action has been taken as	169
yet, will you please indicate the approximate	178
date on which we can expect a decision. Sin-	187
cerely yours R. W. SIMPSON TOOL CO., INC.	195
George T. Albertson Marketing Director En-	204
closures (156)	206/**229**

Problem 4
AMS style

July 8, 19-- CERTIFIED MAIL Mr. Daniel V.	8
DiCicco 1401 Canterbury Road New Haven,	16
CT 06518 CLAIM P 33 172 (POLICY DA-628 509)	25
(¶ 1) Thank you for sending us the information	33
necessary to consider your claim for disability	43
under your Policy DA-628 509. (¶ 2) The en-	50
closed check for $1,000 is in payment for the	60
period April 15 to June 30. In your letter of May	70
17, you indicate that your disability began on	79
April 7. However, in his statement of May 6,	88
Dr. Jon Greenwalt, your physician, indicates	97
that your sickness began on April 15. If Dr.	107
Greenwalt's statement is in error, will you	115
please ask him to correct it. (¶ 3) In order to	124
receive your disability payments, it will be	133
necessary for you to submit Form 5836-A each	142
month. Upon receipt of this form, your check	151
will be mailed to you automatically. A supply	161
of these forms is enclosed for your use. (¶ 4) If	170
you have any further questions regarding your	179
disability payments, please write or call us.	188
PHYLLIS T. GILBERT, CLAIMS EXAMINER En-	196
closures (160)	198/**213**

1c ▶ Place fingers in home-key position

1. Locate on the chart **asdf** (home keys for left hand) and **jkl;** (home keys for right hand).

2. Locate the home keys on your typewriter. Place fingers of your left hand on **asdf** and of your right hand on **jkl;** *with your fingers well curved and upright (not slanting).*

3. Remove your fingers from the keyboard; then place them in home-key position again, curving and holding them *lightly* on the keys.

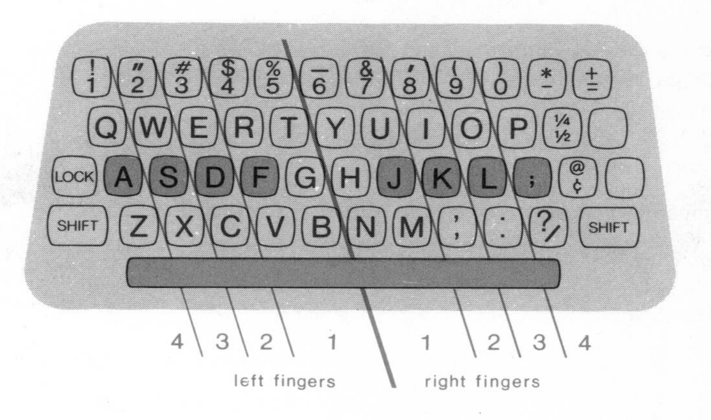

1d ▶ Learn to strike keys and space bar

Study the keystroking and spacing illustrations; then type the drill as directed.

On electrics, strike keys as on manual typewriters, except use less force.

Strike the key with a quick, sharp finger stroke; snap the finger slightly toward the palm of the hand as the keystroke is made.

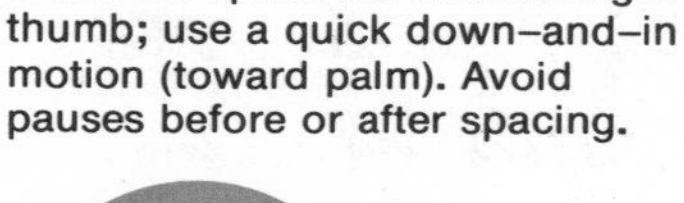
Strike the space bar with the right thumb; use a quick down-and-in motion (toward palm). Avoid pauses before or after spacing.

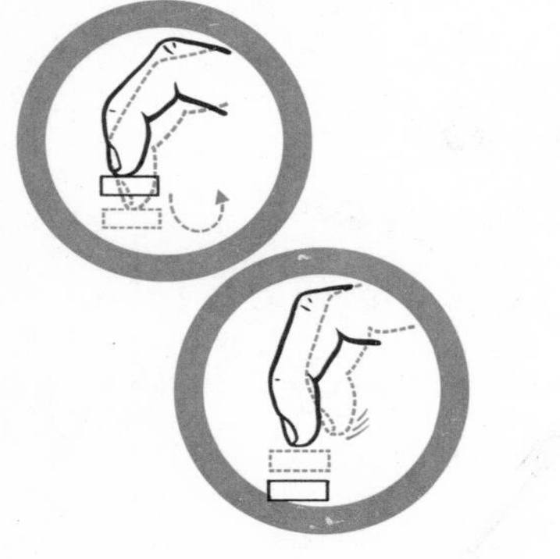

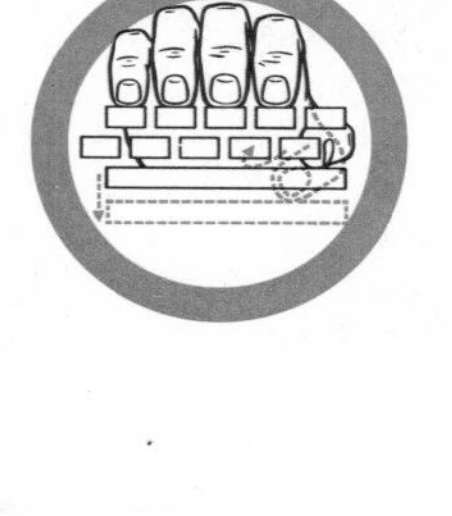

Space once

Type **ff** (space) **jj** (space) twice as shown: 1 `ff jj ff jj`

On same line, type **dd** (space) **kk** (space) twice: 2 `dd kk dd kk`

On same line, type **ss** (space) **ll** (space) twice: 3 `ss ll ss ll`

On same line, type **aa** (space) **;;** (space) twice: 4 `aa ;; aa ;;`

1e ▶ Return the carriage (or element carrier)

The **return lever (1)** on a manual typewriter or the **return key (34)** on an electric is used to space the paper up and make the return to the beginning of the new line.

1. Study the illustrations at the right; then make the return *3* times (triple-space) at the end of your typed line.

2. Turn to page 8 to see how your typed line should look.

Manual return

Move the left hand, fingers bracing one another, to the carriage return lever and move the lever inward to take up the slack; then return the carriage with a quick inward flick-of-the-hand motion. Drop the hand quickly to typing position without letting it follow carriage across.

Electric return

Reach with the little finger of the right hand to the return key, tap the key, and return the finger quickly to its typing position.

296d ▶17 Measure basic skill: script

1. Two 5′ writings on ¶s 1–3 combined.
2. Record *gwam* and errors on better writing. Compare with scores achieved on 226d, page 359.
3. As time permits, type a 1′ writing on each ¶.

all letters used	A	1.5 si	5.6 awl	80% hfw

	gwam 1′	5′
Few of us can achieve financial success without some kind of	12	2	58
financial planning. The individuals who realize the goal of pru-	25	5	61
dent spending and saving are those who establish a financial plan	38	8	63
or budget. In essence, a budget helps an individual live within	51	10	66
his income. It helps him to determine how much he can spend and	64	13	69
how much he can save. It also helps him to determine what he can	77	15	71
and must have so that he will not squander his money recklessly.	90	18	74
The initial step in setting up a budget is to ascertain just	12	20	76
how much money you will have available in a given period. This in-	25	23	79
cludes cash on hand, net wages, and any income from other sources.	39	26	82
The next step is to estimate your expenses. These include all	52	28	84
fixed payments such as rent, taxes, and savings, and variable pay-	65	31	87
ments which may vary from month to month such as those for food,	78	34	89
clothing, utilities, recreation, and the cost of driving a car.	90	36	92
Keeping records is a vital part of budgeting. At the outset,	12	39	94
it is essential that you keep a detailed record of all income and	26	41	97
expenditures. After a few months, these transactions should be	38	44	99
reviewed to find out how much was spent in the various categories.	52	46	102
Since little change can be made in the fixed payments, you must	65	49	105
focus your attention on the variable items to ascertain how you	78	52	107
can change your spending habits to balance the budget or to make	91	54	110
the most effective use of your money.	98	56	111

297

297a ▶5 Conditioning practice

twice SS; repeat difficult lines

Jack F. Davis will probably summarize the steps in quilling next week.
We will hold special meetings on May 2, 5, 6, 7, 8, 9, 13, 14, and 20.
They need $382,765 (40%) for salaries and $181,813 (19%) for supplies.
They will check the price of the item when they go to the city in May.

| 1 | 2 | 3 | 4 | 5 | 6 | 7 | 8 | 9 | 10 | 11 | 12 | 13 | 14 |

1f ▶ Check your typing

Your typed line should look like the line at the right. The **printing point indicator (13)** of your typewriter should be under the first **f**.

```
ff jj ff jj dd kk dd kk ss ll ss ll aa ;; aa ;;
```

Return 3 times to triple-space (TS)

1g ▶ Type home-key letters

Type the lines once as shown, leaving one blank line space between lines (DS). With the **line-space selector (5)** set on "1," operate the return lever or key twice at the end of the line to double-space.

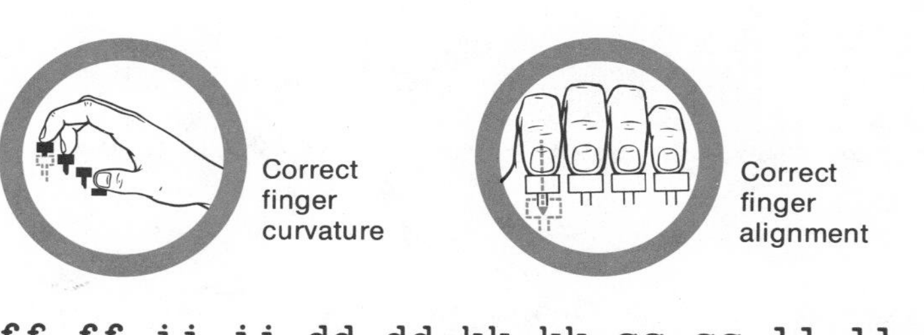


```
ff ff jj jj dd dd kk kk ss ss ll ll aa aa ;; ;; fj
```
DS
```
f j fj d k dk s l sl a ; a; fj dk sl a; fj dk sl a
```
DS
```
a;a fdsa jkl; asdf ;lkj a;sldkfj a;sldkfj a;sldkfj
```
TS

1h ▶ Type words and phrases

Type the lines once as shown (DS). If time permits, retype them.

Space with right thumb

Use down-and-in motion

Spacing cue: Space once after words and after **;** used as punctuation. At the end of the line, however, return without striking the space bar.

```
a a ad ad lad lad all all as as ask ask fall falls
```
DS
```
a fad; a fad; as a lad; as a lad; all ads; all ads
```
DS
```
a; a fall; a fall; a jak; a jak; ask dad; ask dad;
```
TS

1i ▶ End of lesson

1. Raise **paper bail (11)** or pull it toward you. Pull **paper release lever (18)** toward you.

2. Remove paper with your left hand. Push paper release lever back to its normal position.

3. Depress **right carriage release (19)**; hold **right platen knob (20)** firmly and move carriage so that it is approximately centered.

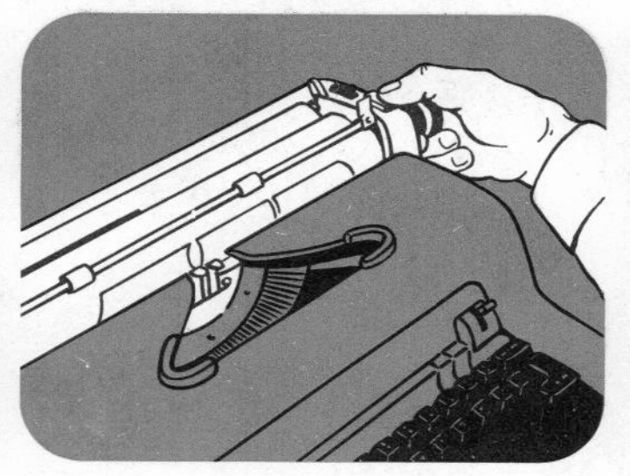

4. Turn *electrics* **off.**

296c ▶17 Measure basic skill: rough draft

1. Two 5′ writings on ¶s 1–3 combined.

2. Record *gwam* and errors on better writing. Compare with scores achieved on 232c, page 367.

3. As time permits, type a 1′ writing on each ¶.

all letters used | A | 1.5 si | 5.6 awl | 80% hfw

	gwam 1′	5′
Many of us are faced with the necessity of acquiring money so that	13	3
we can meet our desires and needs. We expend a significant amount of	27	5
time acquiring a skill, a trade, or a porfession so that we will possess	41	8
saleable personal qualities to offer in the world of business. Through-	55	11
out life, most people strive to better their positions so that they can	69	14
earn more money. Earning money is vital in our system of economics,	83	17
but how we expend it canbe just as important.	92	18
Many of us, no matter how much cash they earn, expend more than	13	21
they earn. There are forever in debt and are harrassed constantly by	26	24
money worries. On the other hand, there are poeple with small incomes	41	27
who are not harassed with problems of money and who find it possible	55	29
to save some. Many of us donot earn enough salary to procure all the	82	35
of our basic needs plus the lusuries we want. To get the most frm our	97	38
money available, we must plan our buying and spending carefully.	111	41
Wise spending is a problem of making chioces and decisions. Often,	13	43
we must choose between buying an item we desire or buying an item we	27	46
need. These are normally choices between luxuries and necessitys. Of	41	49
course, we are faced every day with deciding whether or not to buy a	55	52
certain product or another ofthe same kind as well as selecting between	69	55
two widely dissiminlar products. We are faced also with the choice of	83	57
using our money now or saving it and spending it at a date later.	97	60

The difference lies in the wise expenditure of their monetary resources.

2

2a ▶ Get ready to type

Refer to pages 4-5 if necessary.

1. Arrange work area.
2. Insert paper (straighten if necessary).
3. Adjust paper guide.
4. Set line-space selector on "1" for single spacing.
5. Set ribbon control on black (to type on upper part of ribbon).
6. Set left margin stop (center of paper – 25 spaces).
7. Move right margin stop to right end of scale.

2b ▶ Review keystroking, spacing, and carriage (or element carrier) return

Keystroke

Curve fingers of your left hand and place them over **asdf**
Curve fingers of your right hand and place them over **jkl;**
Strike each key with a quick, snap stroke; release key quickly.

Space

To space after letters, words, and punctuation marks, strike the space bar with a quick down-and-in motion of the right thumb. Do not pause before or after spacing stroke.

Return

Manual: Reach to lever and return the carriage with a quick flick-of-the-hand motion.
Electric: Reach the little finger to return key, tap the key, and release it quickly.

type the line once as shown

```
f ff j jj d dd k kk s ss l ll a aa ; ;; a;a fjf a;
```

Return 3 times to triple-space (TS)

2c ▶ Improve home-key stroking

once SS as shown;
DS between 2-line groups

Note: If you are typing on an electric machine, strike each key with a light tap with the tip of the finger; otherwise, keystroking technique is the same as for a manual typewriter.

Space once

```
ff jj dd kk ss ll aa ;; fj dk sl a; a; sl dk fj a;
ff jj dd kk ss ll aa ;; fj dk sl a; a; sl dk fj a;
```
DS
```
a; al ak aj s sl sk sj d dl dk dj f fl fk fjdksla;
a; al ak aj s sl sk sj d dl dk dj f fl fk fjdksla;
```
DS
```
ja js jd jf ka ks kd kf la ls ld lf jfkdls;a jf kd
ja js jd jf ka ks kd kf la ls ld lf jfkdls;a jf kd
```
TS

2d ▶ Type home-row words and phrases

once as shown;
then at slightly faster pace

```
ad ad sad sad lad lad all all fall fall as as asks
ad ad sad sad lad lad all all fall fall as as asks
```
DS
```
a lad; as a lad; ask a lad; a sad lad; a sad fall;
a lad; as a lad; ask a lad; a sad lad; a sad fall;
```
DS
```
all fall; a fall fad; all lads fall; ask all dads;
all fall; a fall fad; all lads fall; ask all dads;
```
TS

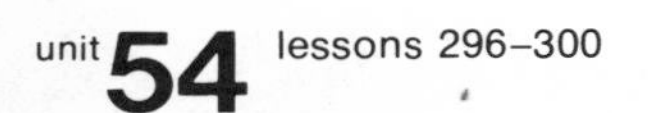

unit **54** lessons 296–300

Measuring basic/production skills

Learning goals

1. To measure speed and accuracy in typing rough draft, script, statistical, and straight copy.

2. To measure production skill in typing letters, reports, tables, and business forms.

296

296a ▶5 Conditioning practice

twice SS; repeat difficult lines

alphabet	Using a bulldozer, Jason's expert workmen quickly leveled the factory.
figures	Please send them 15 copies of Form 3-874 and 20 copies of Form 6-9510.
fig/sym	On 5/30/76, Parek & Olson offered bonds at 6 3/4%, 8 1/2%, and 9 1/4%.
fluency	They may want to change the sign when they take title to the business.

| 1 | 2 | 3 | 4 | 5 | 6 | 7 | 8 | 9 | 10 | 11 | 12 | 13 | 14 |

296b ▶11 Improve skill transfer: straight copy; statistical copy; rough draft

1. Two 1′ writings on each ¶.

2. Additional 1′ writings on more difficult ¶s to increase speed and accuracy.

all letters/figures used

HA	1.6 si	5.8 awl	75% hfw

	gwam 1′
Less than sixty years ago, the typical American family bought very	13
few goods on credit. A family could assume a mortgage to buy a home;	27
but the use of credit to acquire other goods and services, particularly	42
luxuries, was frowned upon. Today, the consumer who does not use credit	56
or procure merchandise on the installment plan is rare indeed.	69
The rise in the use of credit by consumers has been amazing. To	13
illustrate: Consumer credit outstanding in 1950 was $21.5 billion;	27
in 1965, it was $89.8 billion; and, in 1975, it was $184.3 billion--an	41
increase of approximately 760% in a period of 25 years. The increase	55
in installment loans was dramatic--from $14.7 billion in 1925 to $152	69
billion in 1975.	72
Since there is all ways a danger that a persin may go too far	13
into debt, individuals must learn to use credit wisely. They should	27
learn to exercise restraint and to re sist the idea of making expen-	41
sive puechases when they can not afford to do it. By planning properly	55
and budgeting judiciously, a smart man will be capable of getting more	68
of the many things he wants in life--through credit.	79

2e ▶ Type with continuity

1. Type Line 1 twice single-spaced (SS); then double-space (DS).

2. Type Line 2, then Line 3, then Line 4, in the same way.

3. Check your completed copy with the model. Do you have 4 pairs of single-spaced lines with double spacing between the 2-line groups? If not, retype the drill.

Continuity goal: To keep carriage (carrier) moving without pausing after keystrokes or spacing.

```
ff jj dd kk ss ll aa ;; fj dk sl a; fj dk sl a; fj
ff jj dd kk ss ll aa ;; fj dk sl a; fj dk sl a; fj

as as all all lad lad ask ask dad dad fall fall as
as as all all lad lad ask ask dad dad fall fall as

a lad; a lad; a fad; a fad; ask dad; ask dad; fall
a lad; a lad; a fad; a fad; ask dad; ask dad; fall

a jak; a fad; ask dad; a flask; all fall; all lads
a jak; a fad; ask dad; a flask; all fall; all lads
```

1 **ff jj dd kk ss ll aa ;; fj dk sl a; fj dk sl a; fj**

2 **as as all all lad lad ask ask dad dad fall fall as**

3 **a lad; a lad; a fad; a fad; ask dad; ask dad; fall**

all letters learned 4 **a jak; a fad; ask dad; a flask; all fall; all lads**

2f ▶ End of lesson

Remove paper

Center carriage

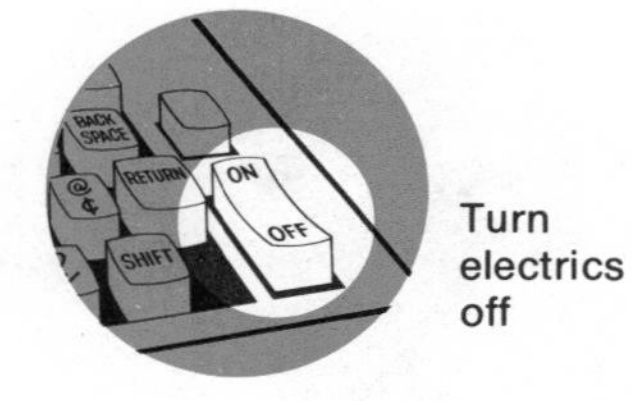

Turn electrics off

3

3a ▶ Get ready to type

Follow steps on pages 4-5.

3b ▶ Conditioning practice

each line twice SS (once slowly, then faster); DS between 2-line groups

Goals

- recall home-key locations
- quick, sharp keystroking
- down-and-in spacing
- return without pausing

all letters learned

fj fj dk dk sl sl a; a; a;sldkfj a;sldkfj a;sldkfj

all fall ad lad fad as ask asks all ads ask a lad;

a jak; all fall; all lads fall; as a dad; as a lad

Triple-space (TS) between lesson parts.

293b-295b, continued

Job 4 [LM p. 205]
Medical letter
modified block; mixed
3 cc's

May 8, 19-- Mr. Anthony C. Burton, Director State Department of Disability Determination 102 Saint Philip Street Baton Rouge, LA 70801 Dear Mr. Burton Subject: Michael Alan McClure (¶ 1) It has been determined that Michael Alan McClure is, at this time, physically unfit for physical labor of any kind by reason of ventricular hypertrophy, with complications. (¶ 2) Mr. McClure has been under our care for approximately two years. When first admitted, he underwent resection of an aortic valve for aortic stenosis and aortic insufficiency and a resection of an ascending aortic aneurysm. A Starr-Edwards prosthetic valve and a Teflon tube aortic graft were used as replacements. (¶ 3) Following his discharge from the medical center, Mr. McClure was left with residual pain, numbness, and weakness in the right lower extremity. Varying types of exercises were prescribed, all of which provided slow improvement in the numbness and weakness of the right leg. Six weeks ago, however, he was treated in our emergency room as a result of an episode of tachycardia with shortness of breath and dizziness. (¶ 4) A summary of laboratory tests made on April 17 shows an EKG which reveals left ventricular hypertrophy and a chest x-ray which shows pulmonary vascular congestion. Mr. McClure continues to have a Grade V pansystolic murmur over the left precordium, as well as a Grade IV diastolic murmur. (¶ 5) In light of his physical condition, Mr. McClure would be classified as totally disabled. If you would like any further information about his condition, I will be happy to furnish it. Sincerely yours Dennis T. Showalter, M.D. Chief of Medical Services

---

Job 5 [LM p. 207]
Interoffice memorandum
1 cc on plain paper

TO: All Medical Staff Members DATE: May 19, 19--

FROM: Dennis T. Showalter, Chief Medical Services SUBJECT: Monthly Staff Conference

The ~~regular~~ monthly meeting of the Medical Staff will be held on June 1 at 7:30 p.m. in the conference room. The agenda for this meeting will include:

1. Administrative Processing of Patients
2. Control of Dangerous Substances
4.~~3~~. Plans for Expansion
3.~~4~~. Scheduling of the Operating Room

If you have any additional ~~items~~ topics you wish to ~~have~~ discuss~~ed~~ at the meeting, please submit them in writing to my office by May ~~29~~ 24.

3c ▶ Learn new keys: h e o

1. Find new key on illustrated keyboard chart.
2. Locate new key on your typewriter keyboard.
3. Study reach-technique illustration for new key.
4. Watch finger make reach to new key a few times.
5. Type reach-technique drill.

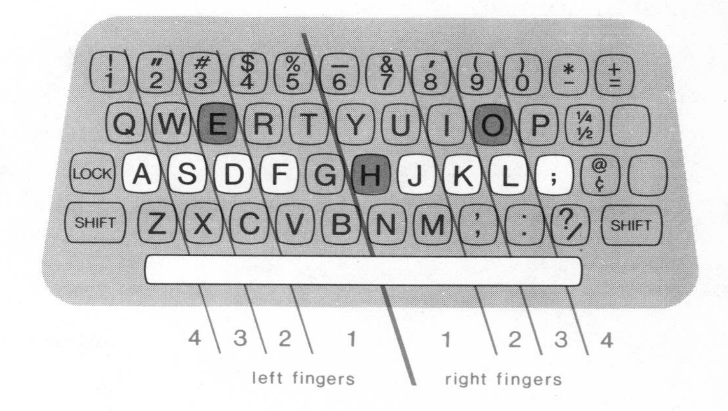

Reach technique for h

Reach to *left* with *right first* finger.

h hj hj ha ha had had had

h h hj ah ah has has half

DS

Reach technique for e

Reach *up* with *left second* finger.

e e ed ed led led el jell

e ed ed eel eel keel keel

DS

Reach technique for o

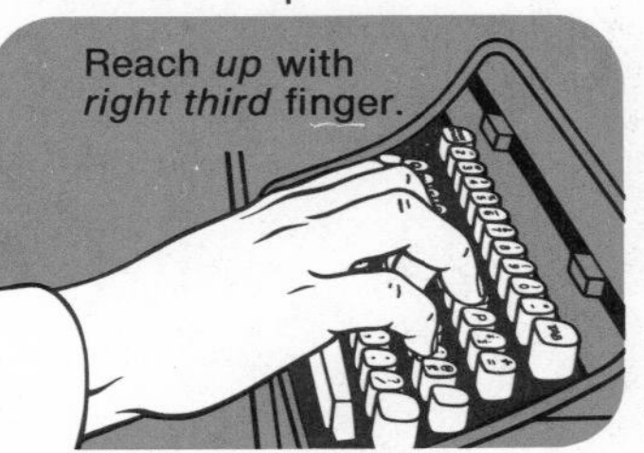

o o ol ol do do so so old

o of of odd odd loss loss

TS

3d ▶ Improve keystroking technique

each line 3 times SS (slowly, faster, slowly); DS between 3-line groups

Do not type line identifications.

h ah ha ha has has had had half half hall hall shall

e el led led lake lake sale sale fell fell jell jell

o ol do do so so oak oak old old sold sold fold fold

h/e/o he she foe odd ode oh hoe shoe sole hole hose joke

3e ▶ Type with continuity

each line twice SS (slowly, then faster); DS between 2-line groups

Technique cue: Fingers curved and upright.

Goals

1. Strike keys with quick, snappy strokes.
2. Space with a down-and-in motion of right thumb.
3. Make return quickly and start new line.

he has; he has; she sold; she sold; a joke; a joke

do so; do so; so old; so old; sold hose; sold hose

he had; he had; he fell; he fell; odd joe; odd joe

has old jade; had a jell sale; he held a shoe sale

293b-295b, continued

Job 3
Report of operation

Type the heading lines as illustrated; SS the lines of the procedure.

LASALLE MEDICAL CENTER

REPORT OF OPERATION

PATIENT NUMBER: 372,194

NAME: Roche, Robert C.

DATE OF OPERATION: 4/12/77

PROVISIONAL DIAGNOSIS: Diseased tonsils

FINAL DIAGNOSIS: Same

OPERATION: Tonsillectomy; adenoidectomy

SURGEON: Jon C. Wilcox, M.D. ASSISTANTS: Juan Martinez, M.D.
L. T. Schultz, R.N.

PROCEDURE: Under local anesthesia, the patient was prepared and draped in a supine position. The left hypertrophied tonsil was re-

PROCEDURE: Under local anesthesia, the patient was prepared and draped in a supine position. The left hypertrophied tonsil was retracted medially and a superficial incision was made along the anterior and posterior tonsillar pillar. Connective tissue of the tonsil was dissected free with a Freer elevator. A snare wire was drawn into the cannula, and the tonsil was removed in the usual fashion. In a similar manner, the opposite tonsil was removed. After this procedure was completed, both tonsillar fossae were injected with a mixture of Depo-Medrol, Depo-Cer-O-Cillin, and 2% Xylocaine. Inspection of the nasopharynx revealed adenoidal tissue. Using curved adenoid curettes and LaForce adenotomes, the adenoidal tissue was removed. The remaining tissue was packed with a sponge to control bleeding. The mouth and throat were suctioned. After a few minutes, the sponge was removed. Approximate blood loss: 30 cc's. One figure-of-eight suture was placed in the left posterior tonsillar pillar. The patient tolerated the procedure well.

4

Time schedule

A time schedule for the parts of this lesson and lessons that follow is given as a guide for your minimum practice. The figure following the triangle in the lesson part heading indicates the number of minutes suggested for the activity. If time permits, however, retype selected lines from the various drills of the lessons.

4a ▶5 Get ready to type

Follow steps on pages 4-5.

4b ▶8 Conditioning practice

each line twice SS;
DS between 2-line groups

Goals

First time: Slow, easy pace, but strike each key quickly.

Second time: Faster pace; move from key to key quickly; keep carriage (carrier) moving.

Technique cues

1. Keep fingers well curved.
2. Try to make each key reach without moving hand or other fingers forward or downward.

home keys	all jaks; all ads; fall ads; ask a lad; add a dash
h/e/o	do so; she fell; a hoe; has sold; as a joke; ah so
all letters learned	of so do he she oak sold kale jell joke jade shall

4c ▶12 Learn new keys: t i left shift key

1. Find new key on chart above.
2. Find new key on keyboard.
3. Study reach illustration.
4. Watch finger make reach.
5. Type reach–technique drill.

Reach technique for t

t tf tf to to the the the
t to to dot dot told told
DS

Reach technique for i

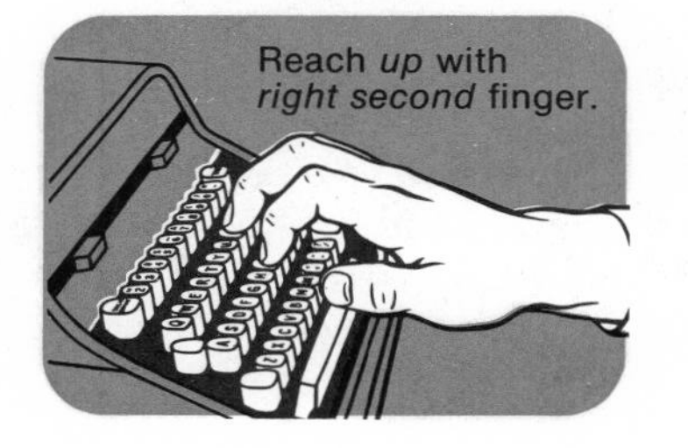

i i ik ik if if fish fish
i is is did did dish dish
DS

Control of left shift key

Reach *down* with
left little finger;
shift, type, release.

J Ja K Ka L La Jake Lakes
Hal Hal Oak Oak Jake Jake
TS

LaSalle Medical Center
2010 TULANE AVENUE
NEW ORLEANS, LA 70112

PATIENT NAME (LAST, FIRST)	Roche, Robert C.
OCC.	Student
EMP.	
HOSPITAL NUMBER	372,194
ADDRESS (IF DIFFERENT FROM SUBSCRIBER'S)	
HOME PHONE	482-4639
SUBS. NAME	Charles P. Roche
ADDRESS	2815 Pauger Street
CITY & STATE	New Orleans, LA 70119
TWP. & CO.	
OCC.	Lineman
EMP.	Louisiana Power & Light Company
NEAREST REL.	Charles P. Roche
REL. TO PAT.	Father
HOME PHONE	482-4639
WORK PHONE	370-8720
DRS ATT	Dr. Jon C. Wilcox
DRS REF	Dr. C. G. Black
ROOM NO.	412
RATE	$75

BIRTH DATE	AGE	SEX	M. S.	RELIGION	HOW ADMITTED	DATE ADM.	TIME AM	PM	DATE DIS.	TIME AM	PM
4/2/64	13	M	S	Catholic	Father	4/11/77	8:30		4/13/77		1:30

BC	COMMERCIAL	COMP.	INDIV.	GROUP	B/C GROUP NO.	B/C AGREEMENT NO.		MALE SELF 1	MALE HUS. 2	MALE SON 3	FEMALE SELF 4	FEMALE WIFE 5	FEMALE DAUG. 6
Blue Cross				X	9001-A	141 01 2242				X			

PROVISIONAL DIAGNOSIS

Diseased tonsils

FINAL DIAGNOSIS

Diseased tonsils

COMPLICATIONS

None

OPERATIVE PROCEDURES

Tonsillectomy; adenoidectomy

DISCHARGE SUMMARY

This young man has a history of recurrent tonsillitis manifested by fever, difficulty in swallowing, and adenopathy of the neck on a current or recurrent basis of four or more times per year. He has been treated by Dr. C. G. Black and was referred to me for evaluation. The patient hears adequately and breathes through his nose adequately. He has no otorrhea or otalgia. The patient has no history of bleeding tendencies and usually responds to antibiotics.

Tonsils were huge, almost meeting at the midline. There were nodes in the neck, bilaterally, which were nontender. The patient was taken to the operating room for a tonsillectomy and adenoidectomy. His postoperative course was unremarkable. He was discharged to his home on Tylenol liquid for pain. The family was told that if he had any bleeding to bring him to the emergency room immediately. He is scheduled to return in a week for a follow-up examination.

Jon C. Wilcox, Attending Physician

4d ▶15 Improve keystroking technique

each line 3 times SS
(slowly, faster, slowly);
DS between 3-line groups

Goals
- curved, upright fingers
- finger-action stroking
- quick return with your eyes on textbook copy

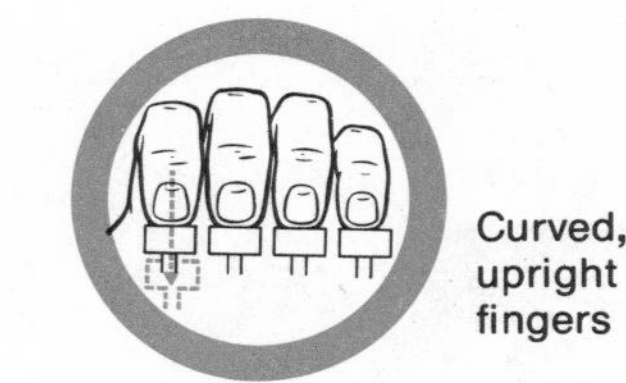

Curved, upright fingers

Finger-action stroking

```
t               to to toe toe the the dot dot lot lot jet jet lets
i               is is if if did did aid aid die die fish fish laid
left shift      Hal Lake had a jade sale; Jake Oakes led all fall;
t/i/left shift  Hal did it; he is at Oak Lake; Kate said it is so;
```

4e ▶10 Type with continuity

each line 3 times SS
(slowly, faster, slowly);
DS between 3-line groups

Continuity goal: Avoid pauses or breaks as you type.

all letters learned

```
dot it; fell the oak; it is too old; it is his jet
she has told it; he is to see it; if the fish die;
Joe felt ill; he is at Oak Lake; he is to see Jeff
```

5

5a ▶5 Get ready to type

Follow steps on pages 4-5.

5b ▶8 Conditioning practice

Type each line of 4e, above, twice: first, at an easy pace to review keystroking patterns and to improve technique; second, to increase your speed.

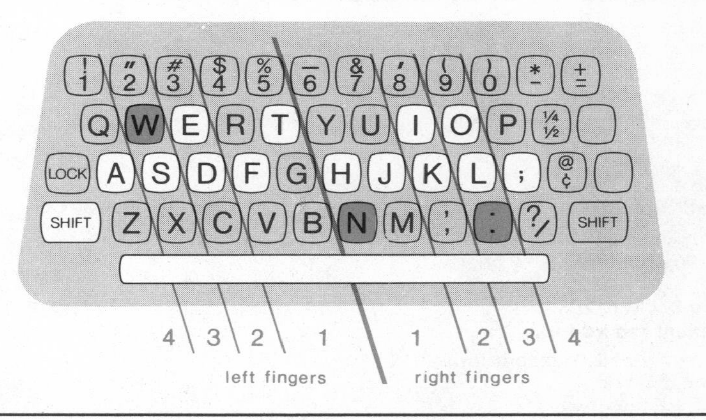

5c ▶12 Learn new keys: n w . (period)

Reach technique for n

Reach technique for w

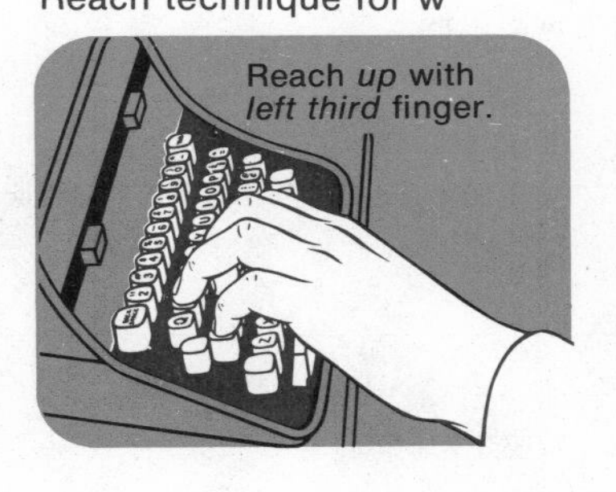

Reach technique for . (period)

Reach *down* with *right third* finger; space twice after . at end of sentence.


```
n nj nj an an and and and
n nj an end end lend lend
                       DS
w ws ws wow wow wish wish
w ws we wit wit with with
                       DS
.l .l ft. ft. hdkf. hdkf.
.l It is Ike.  It is Ike.
                       TS
```

unit **53** lessons 293–295

Medical office typing

Learning goals

1. To develop an understanding of the duties of a clerk–typist in a medical office.

2. To improve production skills by typing representative jobs found in a medical office.

293-295

293a-295a ▶5 Conditioning practice

twice SS;
repeat difficult lines

alphabet	In January, six inches of snow very quickly paralyzed many big cities.
figures	Check pages 45, 73, 80, and 92 in the 1975-1976 edition of the manual.
fig/sym	Mary won bonuses of $3,241, $4,567, and $5,890 on sales of $1,690,327.
fluency	He plans to have a major sale during the first five days of the month.

| 1 | 2 | 3 | 4 | 5 | 6 | 7 | 8 | 9 | 10 | 11 | 12 | 13 | 14 |

293b-295b ▶45 Production typing

In these lessons, you will work as a clerk–typist in the Administration Office of the LaSalle Medical Center, 2010 Tulane Avenue, New Orleans, LA 70112.

Job 1
Medical form
Type the medical form at the right as an unbound manuscript.

Job 2 [LM p. 203]
Patient record form
Type the patient record form on page 449.

CONSENT FOR ADMISSION TO LASALLE MEDICAL CENTER

Date ______________________________

I do hereby consent to hospital care, diagnostic examinations and procedures, and to such medical, surgical, and anesthetic procedures as may be deemed necessary or advisable by the doctors named below or others as designated by them in the treatment of my case. I acknowledge that no guarantee has been made to me as the result of such examinations or treatment.

I consent to the release of information for this admission to my insurance company for the completion of my hospitalization claim.

This information has been fully explained to me, and I certify that I understand its contents.

TS

Name of patient ______________________ Signature ______________________

DS

Signature of
nearest relative ______________________ Relationship ______________________

DS

Witness ______________________________

TS

Doctors: Referring ______________________________________

Attending ______________________________________

5d ▶13 Improve keystroking technique

each line 3 times SS (slowly, faster, slowly); DS between 3-line groups

Keystroking cue: Keep the fingers curved and upright (not slanting); move the fingers, *not* the hands.

Spacing cue: Space once after . following an initial or an abbreviation; twice, at end of sentence.

n an an and and end end lend lend in in ink ink done

w wit wit with with wish wish we we owe owe law laws

. J. L. Oaks left to ski. Lt. Heald sold his skiff.

n/w/. Jane and Keith now know. Ken will win in the end.

5e ▶12 Type with continuity

type drill twice; repeat if time permits

Continuity cue: Return without pausing; start new line quickly.

third row
he is; to do; did owe; the law; she told; his wish
It is his wish. He is to do it. I did that show.

bottom row
an; an; a fan; a hand; all land; and all; hall fan
Hal and Nan had a fall ad. Jan and Hans had land.

third and bottom rows
he owns it; an old fan; she wants it; own the land
Ken skis on the new lake. Jane owns all the land.

6

6a ▶4 Get ready to type

Follow steps on pages 4-5.

6b ▶3 Recall

Typing position: Recall these features of good typing position:

- body erect; sit back in chair
- feet on floor (for balance)
- fingers curved, upright
- wrists low and relaxed
- forearms parallel to keyboard
- eyes on copy in book

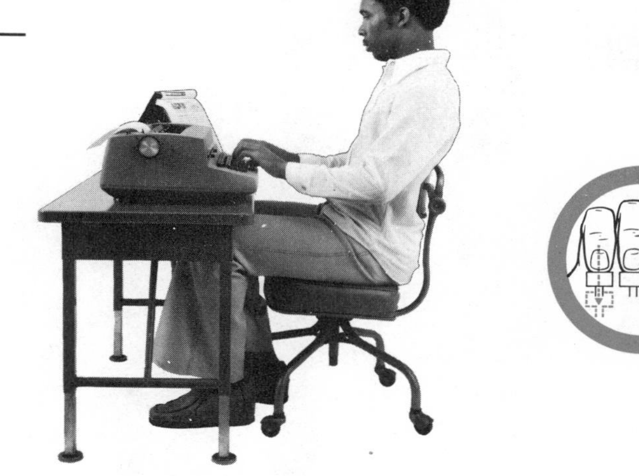

Finger position. Position your hands and arms so that your fingers are in an *upright* (not a slanting) position over the home keys. Keep fingers curved and upright as you type.

6c ▶8 Conditioning practice

each line twice SS (slowly, then faster); DS between 2-line groups

Practice goal: Eyes on copy as you type and make return.

home row has half; ask all; a fall ad; shall ask; adds all;

e/o/t to the; do the; of the; to do; to do so; she took;

i/w/n I was. I wish. Jan is in. Nan and Law will ski.

290c-292c, continued

Job 5 [LM p. 201]
Power of attorney

1 cc on
plain paper

Know all Men by these Presents,

THAT I, WILLIE T. GREEN,
do make, constitute and appoint GUY C. MILES, of the City of Birmingham, County of Jefferson, State of Alabama,
true and lawful attorney for me and in my name
to negotiate for the purchase of the oil painting known as "Freedom Rings" by Henry C. Bates

with power also of attorney or attorneys under - - - - - - - - - - - - - - *for that purpose to make and substitute, and do all lawful acts requisite for effecting the premises, hereby ratifying and confirming all that the said attorney or substitute or substitutes shall do therein by virtue of these presents.*

IN WITNESS WHEREOF, I *have hereunto set* my *hand and seal the* fourteenth *day of* November *in the year of our Lord one thousand nine hundred* and (spell out year)

Signed, Sealed and Delivered in the Presence of

.... (SEAL)

.... (SEAL)

.... (SEAL)

State of Alabama
County *of* Jefferson } *ss.*

This fourteenth *day of* November *A. D. 19*....., *personally appeared before me,* a Notary Public, in and for said County and State,
the above named WILLIE T. GREEN, whose name is subscribed to the foregoing instrument *and acknowledged the foregoing Power of Attorney to be* his *act and deed, and desired the same might be recorded as such according to law.*

Witness my hand and Official *seal, the day and year aforesaid.*

....

6d ▶10 Check spacing technique

each line 3 times SS;
DS between 3-line groups

Goals, line by line

1. Quick down–and–in motion of right thumb.

2. No pause before or after spacing stroke.

3. Right thumb on or close to space bar.

1 he she is his it at did odd an in do so of off all

2 the tie an than aid oak own if it she sit fit fish

3 she did|of all|owns it|odd fish|in town|an old oak

Do not type the color dividers.

6e ▶18 Check keystroking technique

each line 3 times SS;
DS between 3-line groups

Goals, line by line

1. Fingers curved and upright over home keys.

2. Without moving hands up to third row.

3. Without moving hands or other fingers down.

4. Reduce time between letters and words.

5. Steady, even pace (no pauses).

6. Avoid pausing for shifting and punctuating.

all letters learned

1 ask dad; a lad had; all halls; fall ads; all fall;

2 we did sell jade; if she owes it; he was to do it;

3 Nan and he need a loan. Jan is a fan of the Nats.

4 it is his wish to do it; she did own the lake land

5 John filed the test list. Hank lost an oil lease.

6 Half that field is his; L. K. owns the whole lake.

6f ▶7 Check shift-key and return technique

each line once SS on a separate line; repeat if time permits

Goals

1. To shift without moving hand down.

2. To return without pausing at end of one line or at beginning of next line.

1 Jane is to ski with Hans.

2 Neil had a skiff at Kent.

3 Keith lent a hand to Nat.

4 Lil went to sit with Jan.

5 I know Ike has a new tie.

6 Kit will talk with Niles.

7 Nate and Ken saw the doe.

8 Jess is to ask Jean Lane.

9 Ned saw Kate at Oak Lake.

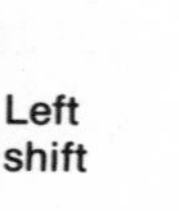

Left shift

Manual upright

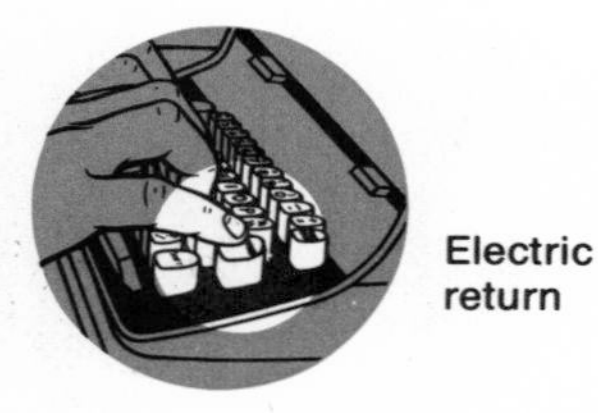

Electric return

Manual underslung

290c-292c, continued

Job 4 [LM pp. 197–200]
Partnership agreement

Use legal paper, if available; if not, use the 11" ruled paper provided in the workbook; make 1 cc. The illustration below shows the solution, in pica type, on 8½" × 11" paper.

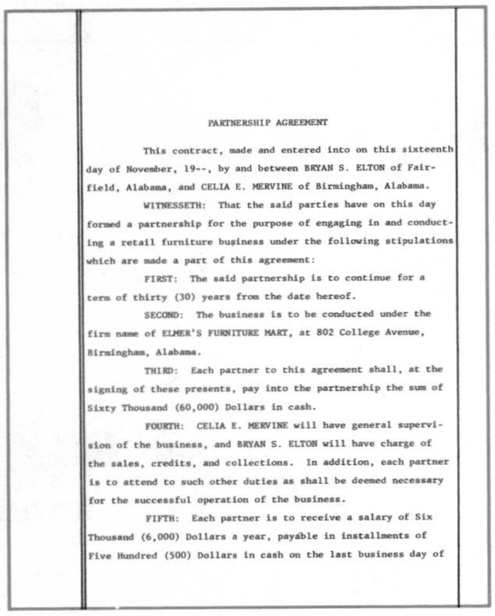

PARTNERSHIP AGREEMENT

This contract, made and entered into on this sixteenth day of November, 19--, by and between BRYAN S. ELTON of Fairfield, Alabama, and CELIA E. MERVINE of Birmingham, Alabama.

WITNESSETH: That the said parties have on this day formed a partnership for the purpose of engaging in and conducting a retail furniture business under the following stipulations which are made a part of this agreement:

FIRST: The said partnership is to continue for a term of thirty (30) years from the date hereof.

SECOND: The business is to be conducted under the firm name of ELMER'S FURNITURE MART, at 802 College Avenue, Birmingham, Alabama.

THIRD: Each partner to this agreement shall, at the signing of these presents, pay into the partnership the sum of Sixty Thousand (60,000) Dollars in cash.

FOURTH: CELIA E. MERVINE will have general supervision of the business, and BRYAN S. ELTON will have charge of the sales, credits, and collections. In addition, each partner is to attend to such other duties as shall be deemed necessary for the successful operation of the business.

FIFTH: Each partner is to receive a salary of Six Thousand (6,000) Dollars a year, payable in installments of Five Hundred (500) Dollars in cash on the last business day of each month. At the end of the fiscal period, the net profit or loss after salaries have been allowed is to be shared equally.

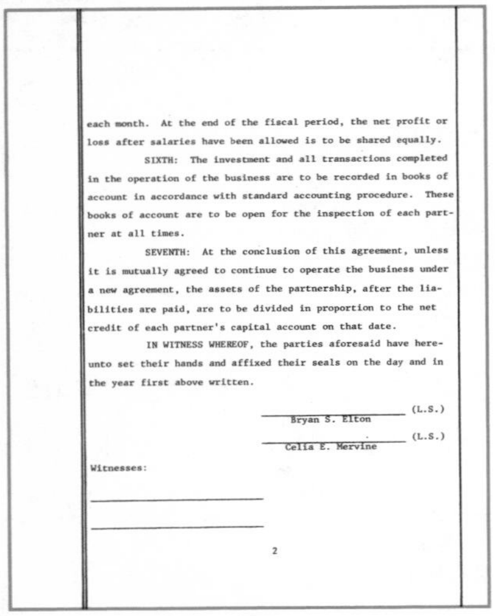

SIXTH: The investment and all transactions completed in the operation of the business are to be recorded in books of account in accordance with standard accounting procedure. These books of account are to be open for the inspection of each partner at all times.

SEVENTH: At the conclusion of this agreement, unless it is mutually agreed to continue to operate the business under a new agreement, the assets of the partnership, after the liabilities are paid, are to be divided in proportion to the net credit of each partner's capital account on that date.

IN WITNESS WHEREOF, the parties aforesaid have hereunto set their hands and affixed their seals on the day and in the year first above written.

________________ (L.S.)
Bryan S. Elton

________________ (L.S.)
Celia E. Mervine

Witnesses:

____

____

2

PARTNERSHIP AGREEMENT

(¶ 1) This contract, made and entered into on this sixteenth day of November, 19--, by and between BRYAN S. ELTON of Fairfield, Alabama, and CELIA E. MERVINE of Birmingham, Alabama. (¶ 2) WITNESSETH: That the said parties have on this day formed a partnership for the purpose of engaging in and conducting a retail furniture business under the following stipulations which are made a part of this agreement: (¶ 3) FIRST: The said partnership is to continue for a term of thirty (30) years from the date hereof. (¶ 4) SECOND: The business is to be conducted under the firm name of ELMER'S FURNITURE MART, at 802 College Avenue, Birmingham, Alabama. (¶ 5) THIRD: Each partner to this agreement shall, at the signing of these presents, pay into the partnership the sum of Sixty Thousand (60,000) Dollars in cash. (¶ 6) FOURTH: CELIA E. MERVINE will have general supervision of the business, and BRYAN S. ELTON will have charge of the sales, credits, and collections. In addition, each partner is to attend to such other duties as shall be deemed necessary for the successful operation of the business. (¶ 7) FIFTH: Each partner is to receive a salary of Six Thousand (6,000) Dollars a year, payable in installments of Five Hundred (500) Dollars in cash on the last business day of each month. At the end of the annual fiscal period, the net profit or loss after salaries have been allowed is to be shared equally. (¶ 8) SIXTH: The investment and all transactions completed in the operation of the business are to be recorded in books of account in accordance with standard accounting procedure. These books of account are to be open for the inspection of each partner at all times. (¶ 9) SEVENTH: At the conclusion of this agreement, unless it is mutually agreed to continue to operate the business under a new agreement, the assets of the partnership, after the liabilities are paid, are to be divided in proportion to the net credit to each partner's capital account on that date. (¶ 10) IN WITNESS WHEREOF, the parties aforesaid have hereunto set their hands and affixed their seals on the day and in the year first above written.
TS

________________________(L.S.)
Bryan S. Elton
DS

________________________(L.S.)
Celia E. Mervine
DS

Witnesses:
TS

____
TS

____

7

7a ▶3 Get ready to type

Follow steps on pages 4-5.

Curve your fingers and position them upright (not slanting) on home keys. Keep your wrists low and relaxed.

7b ▶7 Conditioning practice

each line twice SS;
DS between 2-line groups

First time: Slow, easy pace; work for quick, snappy keystrokes.

Second time: Faster pace; move from key to key quickly; keep carriage (carrier) moving steadily.

Spacing summary: Space once after **;** and once after **.** at the end of an abbreviation or following an initial. Space twice after **.** at the end of a sentence. *Do not* space after any punctuation mark that ends a line.

all letters learned	a;sldkfj fjdksla; hj ed ol tf ik nj ws .l Lt. Hahn
n/w/.	It is new. I saw J. N. knew. He is now with Lew.
easy words	it is do of he she the then than and own town wish

7c ▶12 Learn new keys: r right shift c

1. Find new key on chart above.
2. Find new key on keyboard.
3. Study reach illustration.
4. Watch finger make reach.
5. Type reach–technique drill.

Reach technique for r

r rf rf or or for for for

r or or ore ore risk risk

DS

Control of right shift key

Reach *down* with
right little finger;
shift, type,
release.

F; F; Do Al A. E. Dane F;

Flo Flo Sid Sid Todd Todd

DS

Reach technique for c

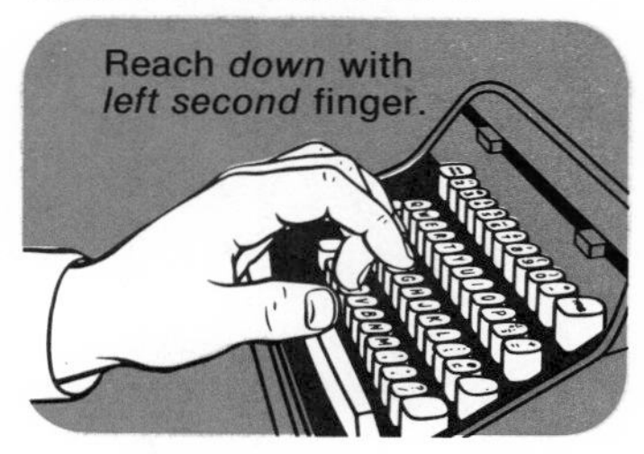

c cd cd cot cot dock dock

c c cod cot cot sick sick

TS

290c-292c, continued

Job 3
Leftbound manuscript with side headings

Green & Hazard
Attorneys-at-Law
LONG BEACH, CALIFORNIA 90802

LAST WILL AND TESTAMENT OF JOSEPH PHILIP LEAR

I, JOSEPH PHILIP LEAR, a resident of the City of Los Angeles, State of California, declare this to be my Last Will and Testament, and revoke all former Wills and Codicils.

FIRST: I direct that my just debts and funeral expenses be paid.

SECOND: I declare that I am married, and my wife's name is JOANNE DAVIS LEAR; I have two children now living, JOHN TH[illegible]S LEAR and RALPH CHARLES LEAR.

THIRD: I give, devise, and bequeath all property, real and personal and wherever situated, to be divided into equal portions, one third to my wife, JOANNE DAVIS LEAR, one third to my son JOHN, and one third to my son RALPH. In the event my wife does not survive me, then her portion is to be divided equally between my sons.

FOURTH: I appoint as Executrix of my Will my wife, JOANNE DAVIS LEAR, to serve without bond. In the event she is unable or unwilling to serve, or to complete such service as Executrix, then it is my wish that CHRISTOPHER OWENS, a long-time friend of mine, shall be appointed as Executor.

This Will and Testament is subscribed by me on the sixteenth day of June, 19--, at Los Angeles, California.

__________________(L.S.)

The foregoing instrument, consisting of one page, was subscribed on the date which it bears, by the testator, JOSEPH PHILIP LEAR, and at the time of subscribing was declared by him to be his Last Will and Testament; and we, at the testator's request and in his presence and in the presence of each other, have signed such instrument as witnesses.

________________residing at________________

________________residing at________________

Legal document with a backing sheet

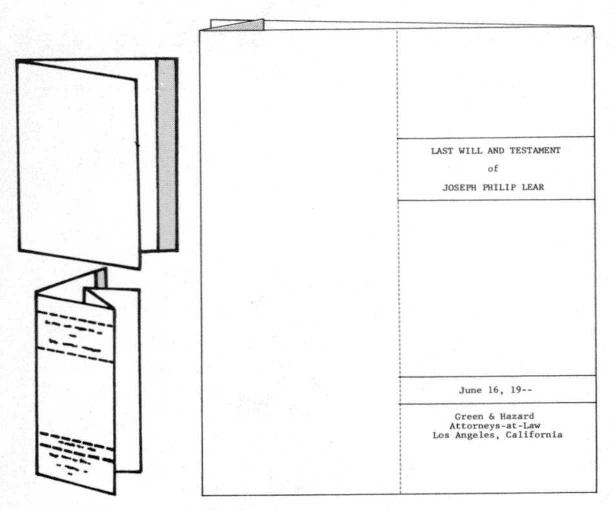

Folding a legal document

Endorsement on backing sheet

TYPING LEGAL DOCUMENTS

Typewritten Legal Forms (¶ 1) Legal documents may be typed with double spacing on standard 8 1/2- by 11-inch paper. Many legal documents, however, are typed on legal paper, which is 8 1/2 by 13 or 14 inches with a double rule at the left margin and a single rule at the right margin. Type within the ruled lines, leaving a space or two between the ruled lines and the typing. If the paper does not have vertical rulings, use a left margin of 1 1/2 inches and a right margin of 1/2 inch. (¶ 2) All pages of a legal document should have a top margin of 2 inches and a bottom margin of approximately 1 inch. The top and bottom margins are often modified to fit material to a page. The first page is not numbered; subsequent pages are numbered 1/2 inch from the bottom of the page with the number centered between the marginal rules. Since legal documents are used frequently in a court of law as evidence, each document must be typed and proofread carefully to insure that it is absolutely correct.

Printed Legal Forms (¶ 3) Printed legal forms of deeds, leases, affidavits, wills, and other commonly used legal instruments are available. Type the required information in the blank spaces provided, using the variable line spacer to insure that the typewritten material is on the same lines as the printed material.

Backing Sheets (¶ 4) A legal document may be bound in a manuscript cover or a blue backing sheet (legal back), a sheet somewhat heavier and about 1 inch wider and 1 1/2 inches longer than the sheet on which the document is typed. The typed document is inserted under a 1-inch fold at the top of the backing sheet, and it is stapled in place. (¶ 5) In some law firms, a description (called the endorsement) of the legal paper is typed on the outside cover, or the backing sheet may have a printed endorsement which usually includes the name of the document and the name and address of the law firm. The completed document and the backing sheet are then folded in a special way for convenient storage in a safe deposit box or for filing in special filing cabinets. In modern legal practice, legal documents are usually stapled to a backing sheet and filed without folding and without an endorsement on the backing sheet.

Abbreviations (¶ 6) Two abbreviations used frequently in legal documents are "L.S." and "ss." "L.S." is the abbreviation for the Latin phrase locus sigilli and is used in place of a seal. The letters "ss." are the abbreviation for the Latin word scilicet, which means "namely."

7d ▶15 Improve keystroking technique

each line 3 times SS
(slowly, faster, slowly);
DS between 3-line groups

r or or for for rid rid rod rod work work risk risks

right shift Todd Wills laid the tile; then Sid Foss washed it.

c cold cold colt colt cost cost lock lock wick wicks

r/right shift/c Chris Reis checks clocks. Dr. Farj checks hearts.

7e ▶13 Type with continuity

type drill twice;
repeat if time permits

Technique cue
Reach with the fingers, *not* the hands.

Do not type the color dividers.

third row
1 he is|to do|if she|to the|we did|that is|work with
2 Reid is to do all the work; Joe has said it is so.

bottom row
3 a fan|and hand|can call|lacks cash|can land|a cask
4 Dan can flash a cash call. Nan lacks half a sack.

third/bottom
5 can do|in for|and sons|low cost|is rich|work jeans
6 Rick knew he won the clock. He had seen the list.

8

8a ▶3 Get ready to type

Follow steps on pages 4-5.

8b ▶7 Conditioning practice

Type 7e, above, once as follows:

Lines 1-2: To develop quick, snappy upward reaches.

Lines 3-4: To make finger-action reaches to bottom row.

Lines 5-6: To increase speed on easy words and to slow down slightly for harder ones.

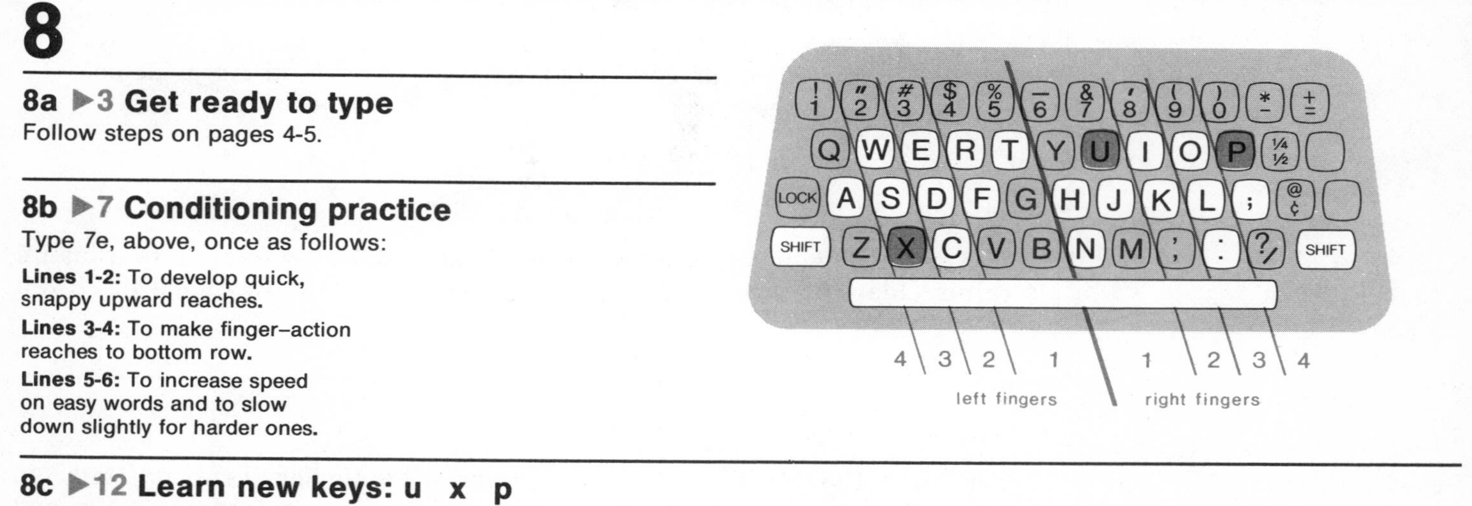

LOCK
SHIFT
SHIFT
4 3 2 1 1 2 3 4
left fingers
right fingers

8c ▶12 Learn new keys: u x p

Reach technique for u

Reach *up* with *right first* finger.

Reach technique for x

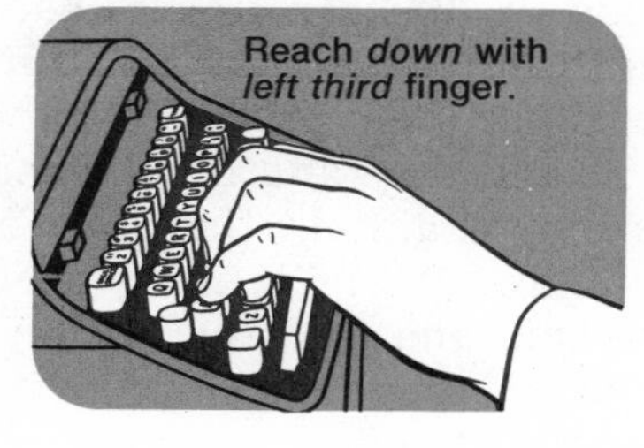

Reach *down* with *left third* finger.

Reach technique for p

Reach *up* with *right little* finger.

u uj uj us us due due due
u uj sue sue use use just
DS

x xs xs ox ox six six six
x xs ox fix fix flex flex
DS

p p p; p; pan pan apt apt
p p; pen pen nap nap kept
TS

290c-292c ▶37 Production typing

You have been hired as a clerk–typist in the office of Miles & Powell, Attorneys–at–Law, 210 North 20th Street, Birmingham, AL 35203.

Since accuracy is of the utmost importance in typing legal documents, proofread all work carefully to insure that it is free from error.

Job 1 [LM p. 193]
Legal letter
Modified block; mixed punctuation. Indent the legal notice 5 spaces from side margins. Make 2 cc's with a blind carbon copy to Ms. Celia E. Mervine.

November 12, 19-- The Birmingham Courier 602 North 18th Street, Birmingham, AL 35202 Ladies and Gentlemen (¶ 1) Please publish the following notice in the classified section under "Legal Notices" on November 17, 19--:

NOTICE OF INTENTION TO FILE CERTIFICATE TO CONDUCT
BUSINESS UNDER ASSUMED OR FICTITIOUS NAME

Notice is hereby given that there will be filed in the Office of the Secretary of State of Alabama and in the Office of the Prothonotary of Jefferson County on December 1, 19--, a certificate of registration under the provisions of the Act of the Legislature of the State of Alabama, approved May 24, 1945, as follows:

1. The name and address or addresses of all persons interested in said business are:

Bryan S. Elton	Celia E. Mervine
R.D. 2	3329 Carol Drive
Fairfield, AL 35064	Birmingham, AL 35217

2. The name, style, or designation under which said business will be carried on or conducted, and the location of its principal place of business, are:

ELMER'S FURNITURE MART
802 College Avenue
Birmingham, AL 35209

(¶ 2) The invoice for this advertisement should be addressed to Elmer's Furniture Mart in care of this office. Yours very truly Raymond L. Powell Attorney-at-Law

Job 2 [LM p. 195]
Legal letter
modified block; mixed punctuation; 1 cc

December 2, 19-- Mr. R. T. Parker Director of Public Services City Hall 710 North 20th Street Birmingham, AL 35203 Dear Mr. Parker (¶ 1) Mr. and Mrs. Ray Woods of 100 Stratford Road have consulted us concerning the maintenance of Valley Lane from Stratford Road to South Street. This portion of Valley Lane abuts their property and has been used as a public thoroughfare for many years. Mr. and Mrs. Woods have advised us that the City has recently refused to maintain the Lane even though it continues to be used as a public wayfare. (¶ 2) We have checked the records and indices of the City of Birmingham and find that Valley Lane is shown on the General Plan as a public street. Under these circumstances, the City is responsible for the maintenance of Valley Lane. (¶ 3) On behalf of Mr. and Mrs. Woods, therefore, I hereby request that the City institute a program to repair and maintain Valley Lane properly. Sincerely yours MILES & POWELL Guy C. Miles Attorney-at-Law

8d ▶14 Improve keystroking technique

each line 3 times SS (slowly, faster, slowly); DS between 3-line groups

Practice cue: Keep eyes on copy as you type and make return.

u	us us use use due due sue sue cut cut fur fur just
x	ax ax ox ox fox fox fix fix six six flex flex hoax
p	pen pen pan pan nap nap apt apt lap lap kept keeps
u/x/p	Pru will pick six cups. Rex paid our dues at six.

8e ▶14 Type with continuity

each pair of lines twice (slowly, then faster); repeat if time permits

Continuity cue: Avoid pauses between keystrokes and after spacing.

1 he is due|she is apt|six of us|fix the pen|for fun
2 Dru just said that four of us could use her house.

3 she is next|up to par|put it up|kept a cup|with us
4 Don Fox can pick up six packs of tax cards at two.

5 it is just|take a nap|a lax law|can keep|which pad
6 Paul kept the pen next to the pad on his new desk.

9

9a ▶3 Get ready to type

Follow steps on pages 4-5.

9b ▶7 Conditioning practice

Type 8e, above, as follows: first, Lines 1, 3, and 5 to improve typing of easy words and word groups; then, Lines 2, 4, and 6 at a slightly slower pace to keep the carriage (carrier) moving *steadily*.

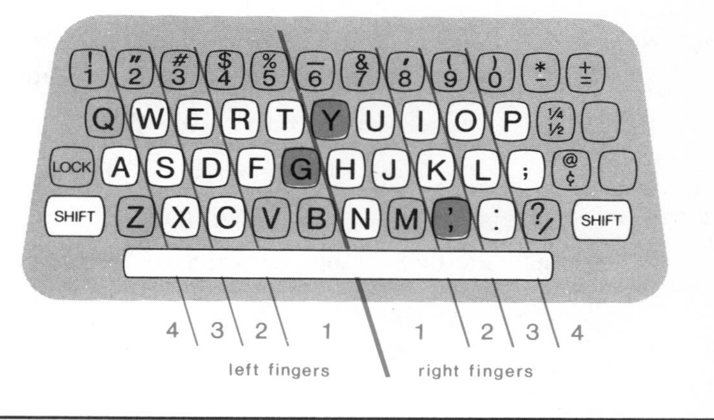

9c ▶12 Learn new keys: y g , (comma)

Reach technique for y

y y yj yj lay lay pay pay
y yj dye dye sky sky play
DS

Reach technique for g

g gf gf go go dig dig dig
g gf got got fog fog flag
DS

Reach technique for , (comma)

Reach *down* with *right second* finger; space once after , used as punctuation.

, , ,k ,k Ike, Kit, and I
ski, a ski, kit, in a kit
TS

unit **52** lessons 290–292

Legal office typing

Learning goals

1. To increase production skill by typing typical jobs in a legal office.

2. To type statistical copy at higher speeds and with improved control.

290-292

290a-292a ▶5 Conditioning practice

twice SS; repeat difficult lines

alphabet	Jack, the expert, zoomed along a curvy freeway leading to a busy quay.
figures	Please check the correct prices of Items 408, 871, 925, 973, and 2658.
fig/sym	Jones & Black offered a discount of $365 (10% and 2%) on Order 59874A.
fluency	The women will not do the work if they do not receive their pay today.

| 1 | 2 | 3 | 4 | 5 | 6 | 7 | 8 | 9 | 10 | 11 | 12 | 13 | 14 |

290b-292b ▶8 Improve basic skill: statistical copy

290b: A 5′ writing for control. Find errors and *gwam*.
291b: Two 1′ writings on each ¶, first for speed; second for control.
292b: A 5′ writing for control. Find errors and *gwam*. Compare with scores in 290b.

all letters/figures used | HA | 1.6 si | 5.8 awl | 75% hfw |

	gwam 1′	5′	
At some time in our lives, many of us utilize the services of a law-	14	3	56
yer when we make a will, settle an estate, acquire property, or require	28	6	59
representation in lawsuits. The number of lawyers in the nation has	42	8	62
increased rapidly. In 1960, for example, there were 285,933 lawyers;	56	11	64
by 1970, there were 324,818 lawyers or one for every 626 individuals.	70	14	67
Most lawyers are engaged in general practice, but a sizable number spe-	84	17	70
cialize in one branch of law, such as corporate, patent, or criminal law.	99	20	73
Aside from attorneys, numerous other individuals are engaged in	13	22	76
providing a variety of legal services. In 1950, there were 235,000 of	27	25	78
these individuals. This number grew to 310,000 in 1960 and to 405,000	41	28	81
in 1970--an increase of practically 75% in a span of 20 years. In the	55	31	84
3-year interval between 1970 and 1973, the number rose from 405,000 in	70	34	87
1970 to 468,000 in 1973--an average yearly growth of 31,000 employees.	83	36	90
There are many good jobs for typists in the legal field, and it is	13	39	92
anticipated that the demand for legal typists will escalate during the	28	42	96
1980's. In 1975, there were over 150,000 law firms in the nation with	42	45	98
approximately 205,000 clerks, typists, and stenographers in their employ.	57	48	101
Since over 85% of all law firms are one-man operations with but a few	71	51	104
clerical assistants, they hire only typists of the highest caliber.	84	53	106

gwam 1′ | 1 | 2 | 3 | 4 | 5 | 6 | 7 | 8 | 9 | 10 | 11 | 12 | 13 | 14 |
5′ | 1 | 2 | 3 |

9d ▶14 Improve keystroking technique

each line 3 times SS
(slowly, faster, slowly);
DS between 3-line groups

Technique goal: Type with quick, snappy keystroking.

y pay pay say say yes yes yet yet dye dye play plays

g go go got got rug rug tug tug sign sign good goods

, it is, it is, he is, he is, is due, is due, and is

y/g/, Hugh has gone, you say. Yes, Gayle has gone, too.

9e ▶14 Type with continuity

each pair of lines twice
(slowly, then faster);
repeat if time permits

Continuity goal: Type easy words with speed; space quickly after each word.

1 to pay, did go, sign it, and say, for you, saw you
2 Jay can pay for the sign. This rug is new, I see.

3 to do, and do, go with, the work, is right, in the
4 Karl, the clerk, was here. He did the work right.

5 he is to pay; she is to go, too; she did it right;
6 Faye did her work right; she has gone for the day.

10

In this lesson and the remaining ones of this unit, the time for the Conditioning Practice is changed to 8 minutes. In this time you are to make machine adjustments, get ready to type, and type the lines.

10a ▶8 Conditioning practice

each line twice SS
(slowly, then faster);
DS between 2-line groups

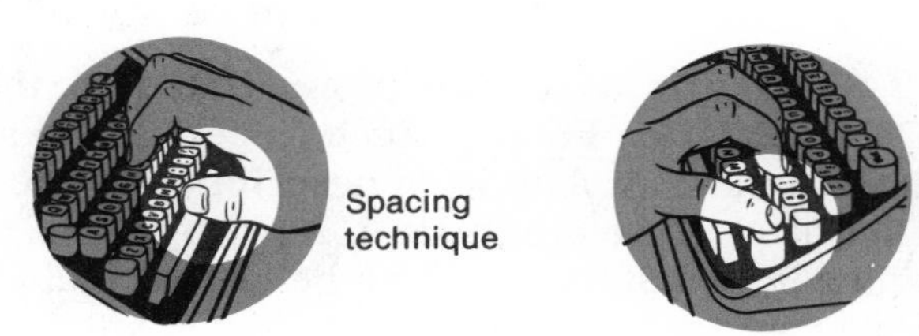

all letters learned hj ed ol tf ik ws nj rf uj cd p; xs yj gf a;sldkfj

y/x/p/g fix it, he got it, pay her, six pens, you sign it,

easy sentence Keith is to fix the sign; then I shall pay for it.

10b ▶7 Check shift-key technique

once as shown

Goal: To use each of the shift keys without wasting time or motion.

Shifting cues
1. Depress the shift key.
2. Strike the letter key.
3. Release shift key quickly.

Abbreviations such as U.S. and N.Y. may be typed solid (without internal spacing).

left shift Hal Oakes; Kate Hauss; P. J. Kahle; Oak Hills Hall

right shift Dr. Wilkes; St. Charles; Fort Worth; Rholff Court;

both shifts Lars J. Houck; Dr. Keith G. Sayle; U.S. Air Force;

284b-289b, continued

Job 6
Office procedures manual
Starting on Line 7, type the material at the right as pages 9 and 10 of a leftbound manuscript. SS and indent enumerated items 5 spaces from side margins; double space between items. Make 1 cc.

PROGRAM DOCUMENTATION PROCEDURES

(¶ 1) All programs written by personnel of the Systems Division must be fully documented. Each program will be assigned a Charge Number and a Library Name. The Charge Number will be used on the JOB Control Card each time the program is run. The Library Name must be unique within the DOS Library. It is limited to eight (or fewer) alphabetic characters. (¶ 2) The documentation package for each program will consist of a Program Card which contains data about the program in a machine processable form; a Documentation Folder which will include the information outlined below; a sheet of Operating Instructions; and the Source Deck for the program. A program will not be considered completed until all parts of this package have been prepared. (¶ 3) A Program Card will be punched for each program in accordance with the following format:

COLUMNS	INFORMATION
1-10	Charge number of the program.
11-18	Library name assigned to the program.
19-21	Programmer's Employee Code.
22	Language in which the program is written (F-Fortran, C-Cobol, A-Assembly, R-RPG, P-Pl/I, S-Sort/Merge).
23-28	Date the program was completed or last modified.
29-31	Total effort spent in writing, testing, and documenting the program (in man-hours).
32-80	Descriptive title of the program.

(¶ 4) All printed information related to the program should be filed in a Documentation Folder. Each folder should have, as a minimum, the following information: 1. A written description of the program. 2. Layout forms for all files used in the program. 3. A listing of the source language statements. 4. All other information that may be useful, including program flow charts, system flow charts, and any source documents. (¶ 5) The programmer will be responsible for developing a set of Operating Instructions that can be used by the computer operator whenever the program is run. These instructions should include the following information: 1. A heading which consists of the charge number and library name of the program; the date the program was completed; the name of the programmer; and the description title of the program. 2. A description of any file handling that may be necessary. 3. Any additional remarks or instructions that may help the operator, including the explanation for any programmed halts or pauses. (¶ 6) The original copy of the Source Deck will be turned in as part of the documentation. The cards will be kept in a central program file and will be removed only when the program is being run or modified. (¶ 7) When a programmer has completed a program, including the testing and debugging, he must submit the documentation for that program to the Assistant Director for Systems. Once the documentation has been approved, the Program Card, Documentation Folder, and Source Deck will be filed. The Operating Instructions will be given to the computer operator.

10c ▶8 Check space-bar technique

type drill twice;
space with down-and-in (toward palm) thumb motion

Goal: To type words without pausing before or after spacing stroke.

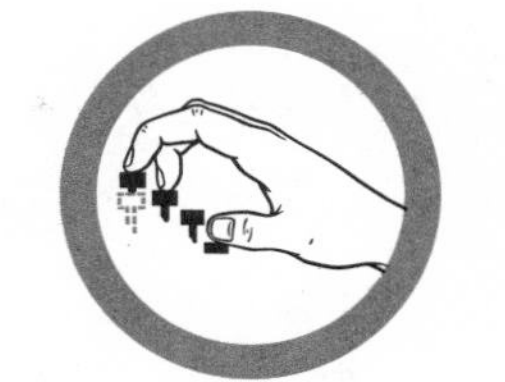
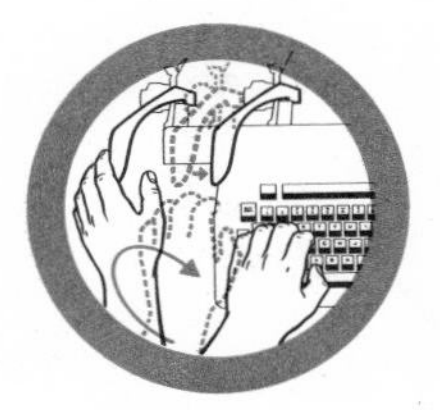

```
the end|as so|hit the|or run|and do|in no|pay your
I was told he hit a long, high fly to right field.

say it|pay it|pay for|say yes|dye it|lay it|try to
If you say yes, I shall try to play the role well.
```

10d ▶10 Check keystroking technique

type drill twice

Goals, line by line
1-2. Without moving hands upward.
3-4. Without moving hands downward.
5-6. Without moving elbows in or out.

home/third
```
1 low key|to put|top row|wish it|good work|just laws
2 It is a just law for us who work at the lake site.
```

home/bottom
```
3 an ax, all land, can call, a hack, a sax, and flax
4 Jan lacks cash.  Cal has a sax.  Nan can add cash.
```

third/bottom
```
5 fix the net|not as yet|want to cite|call the plant
6 Ned is to call the plant.  Ceil is to land at six.
```

10e ▶17 Check carriage (carrier) return technique

1. Each line once untimed.
Goal: To return without pausing at line endings and beginnings.

2. Two 30–second (30″) writings on each line.
Goal: To reach end of each line as "Return" is called.

3. A 1-minute (1′) writing on each line without the call of the return.
Goal: At least 14 gross words a minute (*gwam*).

all letters learned

return without looking up

		words in line*	gwam 30″
1	It is up to us to try it.	5	10
2	Jane can do this work, I know.	6	12
3	Len is to work with us at the lake.	7	14
4	Clyde will fix their gold urn if he can.	8	16
5	Keith is to pay the six girls for their work.	9	18
6	Frank said it is right for us to do the work well.	10	20

| 1 | 2 | 3 | 4 | 5 | 6 | 7 | 8 | 9 | 10 |

* **How typewritten words are counted**
Five strokes are counted as one standard typewritten word. The figures in the first column at the right of the drill sentences show the number of 5-stroke words in each of the lines. The scale beneath the copy shows the word-by-word count (5 strokes at a time) for each of the lines.

To determine words-a-minute rate
1. List the figure at the end of each complete line typed during a writing.
2. For a partial line, note from the scale the figure directly below the point at which you stopped typing.
3. Add these figures to determine the total gross words typed (the same as *gwam* for a 1′ writing).

284b-289b, continued

Job 4 [LM p. 183]
Interoffice memorandum
1 cc

TO: L. P. Bradshaw, Assistant Director DATE: March 21, 19--

FROM: R. L. Caruso, Systems Analyst SUBJECT: Payroll Program

~~Enclosed~~ Attached is a typewritten copy of the pay roll Program requested by Searle & Alden, Inc. ~~The~~ This program ~~catalogs the~~ identifies each hourly ~~wage~~ employee by ID Number, ~~registers~~ records the total number of hours ~~employed~~ worked during a ~~given~~ pay-roll period, ~~calculates~~ computes the ~~worker's~~ employee's gross wages at $2.75 ~~each~~ an hour, ~~subtracts~~ deducts 20% for taxes, and ~~sets forth~~ records the net wage.

(¶) With minor additions or changes, this program can be adapted to: (1) compute the wages of hourly employees with any given wage and (2) compute the net wages based upon multiple deductions of varying percentages.

(¶) If this program meets the requirements of Searle & Alden, complete documentation will be provided.

Job 5 [LM pp. 185–190]
Message/reply memos
2 cc's, 1 cc on plain paper; address envelopes for COMPANY MAIL; see page 311 for directions, if necessary.

TO: **Mr. L. P. Bradshaw Assistant Director Room 732 April 5, 19--** (¶ 1) **We are considering the use of sheet microfilm for storing reports. Each form, 1/2″ x 5 3/4″ negative card, can hold up to 60 pages which can be viewed on a desk-top reader. If needed, full-size copies can be reproduced quickly and easily.** (¶ 2) **May I have your reaction to the adoption of sheet microfilm? F. C. Cohen, Chief of Records**

Compose and type a reply for Mr. Bradshaw to the message of April 5 from Mr. Cohen. Date the reply April 8. Mr. Cohen is located in Room 510. Tell him that his suggestion to use microfilm for the storage of reports sounds interesting. Ask him what he considers to be the major advantage of using microfilm. Also ask him what means are used to retrieve reports once they are filed.

TO: **Mr. L. P. Bradshaw Assistant Director Room 732 April 12, 19--** (¶ 1) **Compactness is the major advantage of using microfilm. Microfilm sheets of 1,000 reports of average length would fit into a regular shoe box. To facilitate retrieval, each negative card is coded by number and by the title and date of the reports.** (¶ 2) **If you wish, we can make a detailed study of this proposal. F. C. Cohen, Chief of Records**

Compose and type a reply for Mr. Bradshaw to the message of April 12 from Mr. Cohen. Date the reply April 16. Tell him that his proposal to use a microfilm storage system appears to have considerable merit. Ask him to send his detailed study as soon as it has been completed.

11

11a ▶8 Conditioning practice

each line twice SS;
DS between 2-line groups

First time: Easy, controlled pace to develop good stroking.

Second time: Faster pace; move from key to key and from word to word quickly.

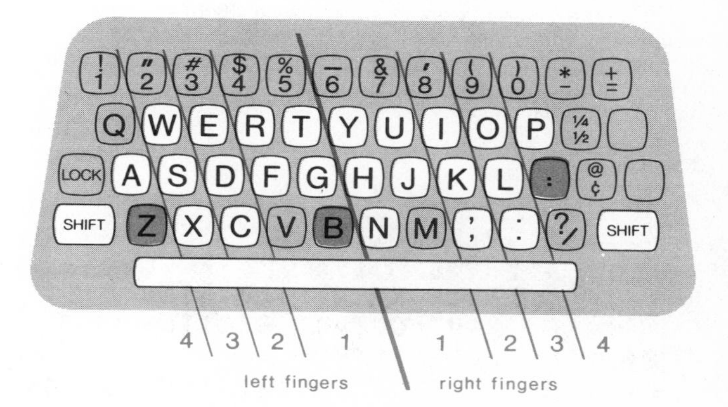

4 3 2 1 1 2 3 4
left fingers
right fingers

all letters learned	Jeff plans to go with Ray Ruhl to the dock at six.
y/g/u/p	a gyp, pays up, get us, you pay, sign up, gold urn
easy sentence	Kent paid the eight girls to aid us with the work.

| 1 | 2 | 3 | 4 | 5 | 6 | 7 | 8 | 9 | 10 |

11b ▶12 Learn new keys: b : (colon) z

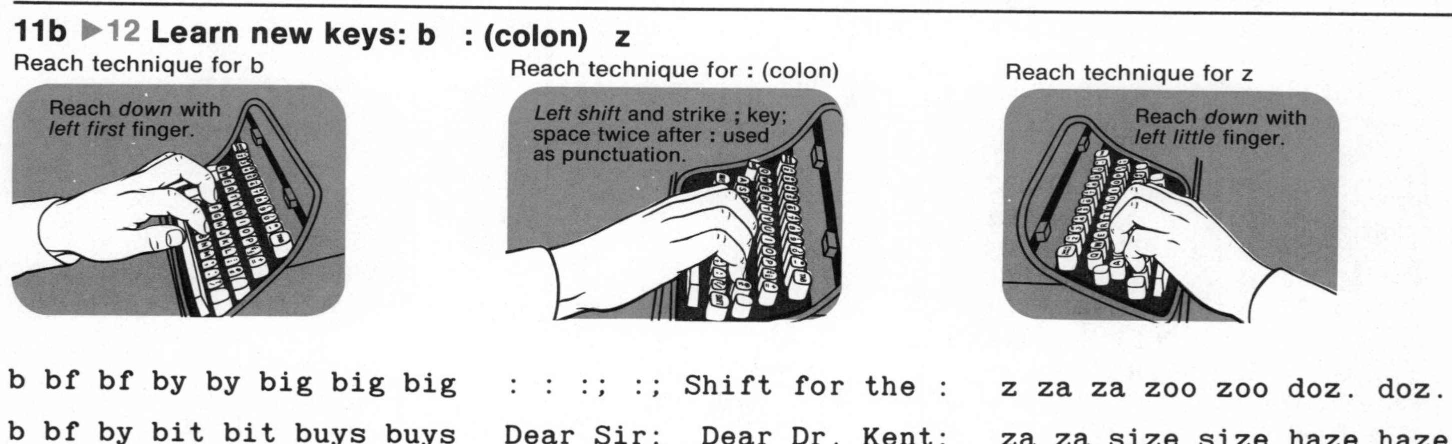

Reach technique for b
Reach down with left first finger.
Reach technique for : (colon)
Left shift and strike ; key; space twice after : used as punctuation.
Reach technique for z
Reach down with left little finger.

b bf bf by by big big big
b bf by bit bit buys buys
DS

: : :; :; Shift for the :
Dear Sir: Dear Dr. Kent:
DS

z za za zoo zoo doz. doz.
za za size size haze haze
TS

11c ▶15 Improve keystroking technique

each line 3 times SS
(slowly, faster, slowly);
DS between 3-line groups

b	by by but but rub rub cub cub box box buy buy born
: (colon)	:; :; :p: Read: Type: Date: To: Dear Dr. Kahn:
z	z zag zag zip zip zoo zoo jazz jazz prize oz. doz.
b/:/z	Zoe read: Zeb bet Liz a big jazz band would play.
all letters learned	Zach Dye will win a big cup for just six ski acts.

284b-289b, continued

Job 3
Computer program

1. Type the COBOL computer program from the Coding Form below on plain paper *exactly* as shown. Each individual block on the form is equal to one horizontal typewritten space.

2. Top margin: 1½"; left margin: 6 for pica type; 15 for elite. Heading: PAYROLL PROGRAM. Note: The zero (0) is typed with a diagonal through it (Ø) so that the terminal or keypunch operator will not mistake it for the letter "O."

3. Proofread the program carefully to insure that it is spaced and punctuated exactly as shown.

COBOL Coding Form

SEQUENCE (PAGE) (SERIAL) | CONT. | A | B | COBOL STATEMENT

```
ØØ1Ø1Ø IDENTIFICATION DIVISION.
ØØ1Ø2Ø PROGRAM-ID.   PAYROLL.
ØØ1Ø3Ø ENVIRONMENT DIVISION.
ØØ1Ø4Ø INPUT-OUTPUT SECTION.
ØØ1Ø5Ø FILE-CONTROL.
ØØ1Ø6Ø     SELECT PRNTFILE ASSIGN TO PRINTER.
ØØ1Ø7Ø     SELECT CARDFILE ASSIGN TO CARD-READER.
ØØ1Ø8Ø DATA DIVISION.
ØØ1Ø9Ø FILE SECTION.
ØØ11ØØ FD  PRNTFILE                    LABEL RECORDS ARE OMITTED.
ØØ111Ø Ø1  PRNT-REC.
ØØ112Ø     Ø3  FILLER                  PICTURE X.
ØØ113Ø     Ø3  ID-NO-OUT               PICTURE X(6).
ØØ114Ø     Ø3  GROSS                   PICTURE $(6).99.
ØØ115Ø     Ø3  TAXES                   PICTURE $(6).99.
ØØ116Ø     Ø3  NET-PAY                 PICTURE $(6).99.
ØØ117Ø FD  CARDFILE                    LABEL RECORDS ARE OMITTED.
ØØ118Ø Ø1  CARD-REC.
ØØ119Ø     Ø3  ID-NO-IN                PICTURE X(6).
ØØ12ØØ     Ø3  HOURS                   PICTURE 99V9.
ØØ2Ø1Ø     Ø3  FILLER                  PICTURE X(71).
ØØ2Ø2Ø WORKING-STORAGE SECTION.
ØØ2Ø3Ø 77  TOTAL-PAY                   PICTURE S9(5)V99 COMPUTATIONAL-3.
ØØ2Ø4Ø 77  TOTAL-TAXES                 PICTURE S9(5)V99 COMPUTATIONAL-3.
ØØ2Ø5Ø PROCEDURE DIVISION.
ØØ2Ø6Ø BEGIN-JOB.
ØØ2Ø7Ø     OPEN INPUT CARDFILE, OUTPUT PRNTFILE.
ØØ2Ø8Ø     MOVE ' ID.NO.    GROSS    TAXES  NET PAY' TO PRNT-REC.
ØØ2Ø9Ø     WRITE PRNT-REC AFTER ADVANCING 6 LINES.
ØØ21ØØ READ-CARDS.
ØØ211Ø     READ CARDFILE AT END GO TO END-OF-JOB.
ØØ212Ø     MOVE SPACES TO PRNT-REC.
ØØ213Ø     MOVE ID-NO-IN TO ID-NO-OUT.
ØØ214Ø     MULTIPLY 2.75 BY HOURS GIVING TOTAL-PAY ROUNDED.
ØØ215Ø     MULTIPLY Ø.2Ø BY TOTAL-PAY GIVING TOTAL-TAXES ROUNDED.
ØØ216Ø     SUBTRACT TOTAL-TAXES FROM TOTAL-PAY GIVING NET-PAY.
ØØ217Ø     MOVE TOTAL-PAY TO GROSS.
ØØ218Ø     MOVE TOTAL-TAXES TO TAXES.
ØØ219Ø     WRITE PRNT-REC AFTER ADVANCING 1 LINE.
ØØ22ØØ     GO TO READ-CARDS.
ØØ3Ø1Ø END-OF-JOB.
ØØ3Ø2Ø     CLOSE CARDFILE, PRNTFILE.
ØØ3Ø3Ø     STOP RUN.
```

11d ▶15 Build response patterns

each pair of lines twice (once at easy pace, then faster); repeat if time permits

Continuity goal: To speed up the typing of short, easy words.

balanced-hand words
an ox|by us|fur rug|cut it|fix it|big fox|the jays
Ken is to go by bus to the town to do work for us.

balanced-hand words
and the|did the|he held|with us|then she|the girls
Leith paid for the fur, but it is a bit too tight.

balanced- and one-hand words
if no|at the|on the|get it|was to|pay you|the safe
It is up to you to set the date to start the test.

balanced- and one-hand words
for you|to get|the ink|the date|they are|with zest
He read the text to us; then he drew the big gear.

| 1 | 2 | 3 | 4 | 5 | 6 | 7 | 8 | 9 | 10 |

12

12a ▶8 Conditioning practice

each line twice SS; DS between 2-line groups

First time: Easy, controlled pace to refine stroking patterns.

Second time: Faster pace; work for continuity of keystroking.

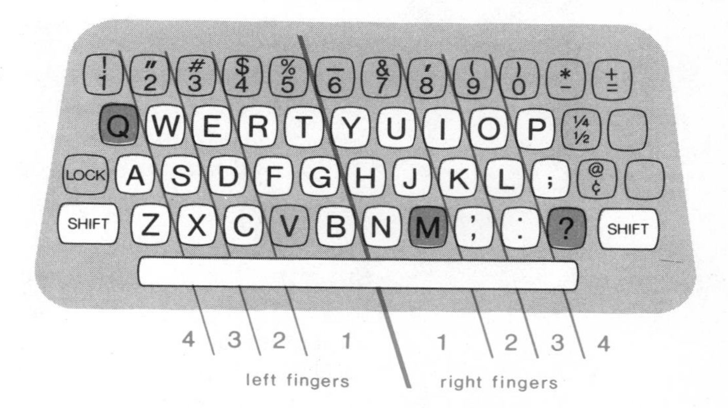

all letters learned
Zip can go with Lex Bir to ski in just a few days.

b/:/z
Type these words: be, by, but; zeal, zest, prize.

easy sentence
She is to aid us with their work for half the pay.

| 1 | 2 | 3 | 4 | 5 | 6 | 7 | 8 | 9 | 10 |

12b ▶12 Learn new keys: m q ? (question)

Reach technique for m

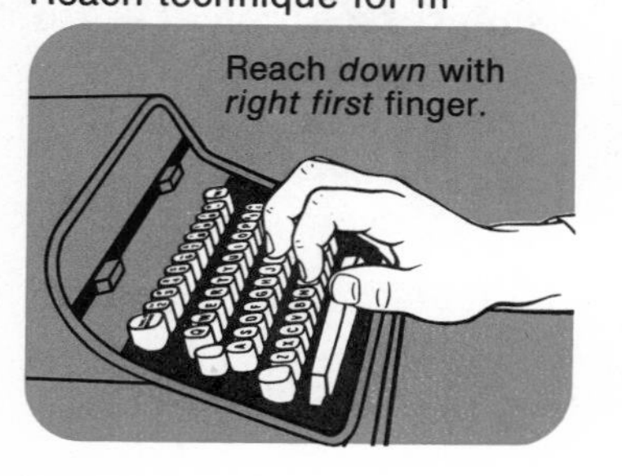

m m mj mj me me am am man
m mj man man may may make
DS

Reach technique for q

q q qa qa quit quit quite
q qa qt. qt. quote quotes
DS

Reach technique for ? (question)

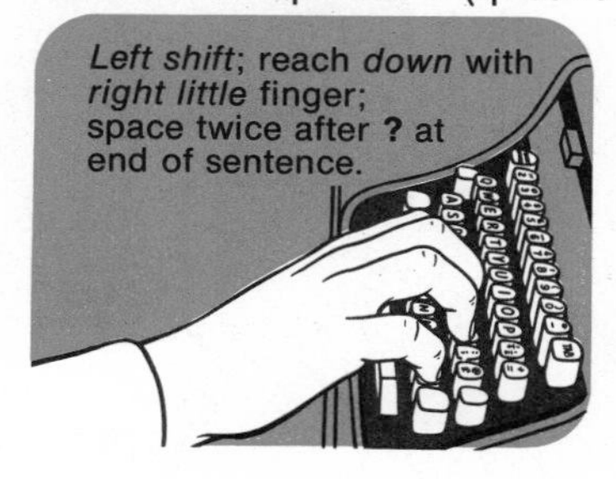

Left shift; reach *down* with *right little* finger; space twice after **?** at end of sentence.

? ?; ?; Who? When? How?
?; ?; Is he? Is he next?
TS

284b-289b, continued

Job 2 [plain paper]
Model copy of two-page letter
Type the letter at the right as a model copy for duplication in the modified block style with mixed punctuation.

April 23, 19--

DS

Dear Subscribers

We are pleased to announce that a new program has been installed under our Disc Operating System for your convenience. This program, known as Rapidpic, has the ability to create two-dimensional flowcharts from debugged FFORTRAN, FCOBOL, and ASSEMBLY programs in source form without modification.

These steps must be followed to run Rapidpic:

1. Remove all Control statements from the deck. This includes the JOB, OPTION, all EXEC, /* and /& statements. The COBOL options and FFORTRAN options cards must not be included in the deck.

2. Punch the following jobstream:

```
//JOB jobname ppuuu accounting information
//EXEC RPFPxxxx
  (Rapidpic option card)
  (Your source program)
/*
/&
```

Substitute a job name for "jobname," your Accounting Code (ProjectID and UserID) for "ppuuu," and the appropriate accounting information. "RPFP" is an abbreviation for "Rapidpic Flowcharting Program." Substitute one of the following for "RPFPxxxx": RPFPBAL for an ASSEMBLY Program; RPFPCOB for an FCOBOL Program; or RPFPFORT for an FFORTRAN Program.

A Rapidpic option card must precede your source deck. Its format is as follows:

COLUMN	ASSEMBLY	FFORTRAN	FCOBOL	REMARKS
1-56	Title	Title	Title	Free form title of program.
60	Blank	Blank	"C"	The "C" suppresses the Data Name Cross Reference in COBOL.
75	"A"	Blank	Blank	The "A" suppresses printing of comments in ASSEMBLY.
77	"A"	Blank	Blank	The "A" suppresses remarks in the ASSEMBLY flowchart.
78	"("	"("	Blank	Must be present for ASSEMBLY and FFORTRAN programs.
79	"8"	"8"	"8"	Required for all programs.

All unused columns from 57 through 80 inclusive must be blank. Your program follows the option card, with all Job Control statements removed, including CBL and FTC cards. A "/*" (end-of-file) and "/&" (end-of-job) card must follow your program deck.

If you have any questions about the operation of Rapidpic, please call or write Bruce E. Beaumont, our Assistant Director for Systems.

Sincerely yours Jeff C. Mattocks Director

12c ▶15 Improve keystroking technique

each line 3 times SS (slowly, faster, slowly); DS between 3-line groups

Spacing cue: Space once after **?** *within* sentence; twice after **?** at *end* of sentence, except at the end of a line.

m	man man map map amp amp am am them them form forms
q	quit quit quay quay quiz quiz torque torque clique
?	Can he type these words: zoo? haze? zone? bronze?
m/q/?	Is Quim quite quick? Will he make my squash team?
all letters learned	Jean Bux typed quite fast; Rick Maze won his goal.

12d ▶15 Type with continuity

type the drill twice; repeat if time permits

Continuity goals, line by line

1-6. Steady, unhurried pace.

7-8. Speed up keystroking on easy words.

m/q	1	am quick|may quit|main squad|quote him|same clique
	2	James may quit my squad to tour the quaint mosque.
b/g	3	by half|go buy|zoo cage|big box|gold key|game ball
	4	Berle may bring the big book he bought last night.
y/w	5	we may|why try|two yen|may dye|new style|say which
	6	Kyle will pay the two new boys when they are done.
easy sentences	7	I am to work with them if I am right for the work.
	8	Al is to go to the firm for the pay due the girls.

| 1 | 2 | 3 | 4 | 5 | 6 | 7 | 8 | 9 | 10 |

13

13a ▶8 Conditioning practice

Type Lines 1–6 of 12d, above, once as shown. Keep fingers curved and upright on home keys. Type with quick, snappy keystrokes and at a steady pace.

If time permits, type a 1′ writing on Lines 7–8 combined.

Goal: At least 16 *gwam*.

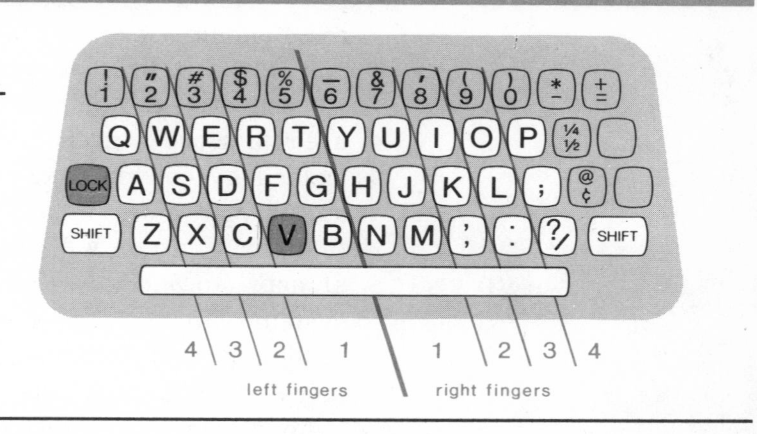

13b ▶7 Learn new keys: v shift lock

Reach technique for v

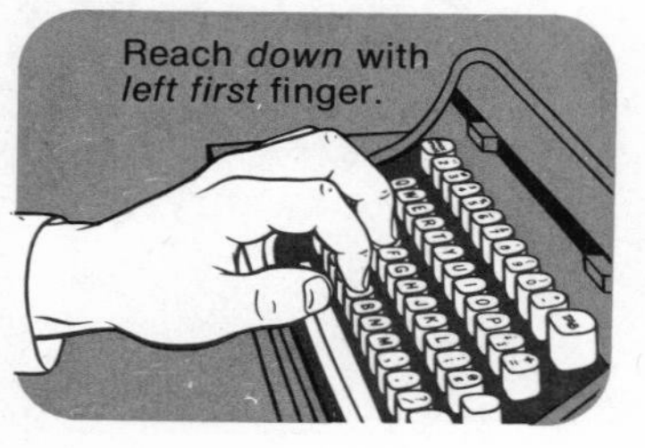

Reach technique for shift lock

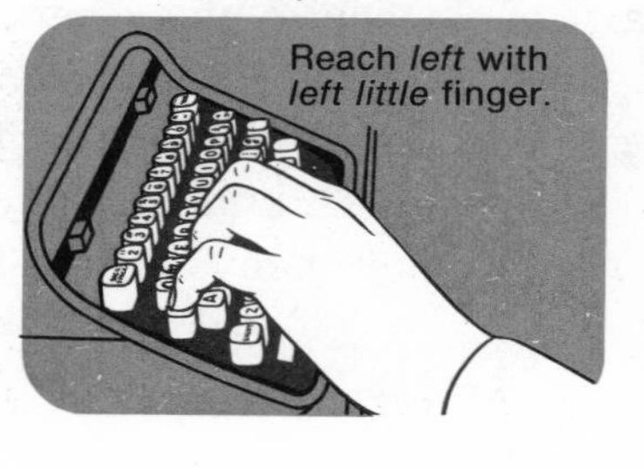

Note

Depress the **shift lock (30)** and leave it down until the ALL-CAP combination has been typed. Operate the shift key to release the shift lock to return to regular capital-and-lowercase typing.

Be sure to release the shift lock to type the word "and" in the tryout drill for the shift lock at the left.

v vf vf vie vie five five

vf vf view view cove cove

DS

Type: CPA, CPS, and AMS.

Type: NBC, ABC, and CBS.

TS

284b-289b ▶45 Production typing

In these lessons, you will work as a clerk–typist for Stellar Computer Services, Inc., 1422 Francis Street, St. Louis, MO 63106. Stellar provides on–site and remote computer services for its subscribers. It also publishes a quarterly magazine called the STELLAR PRINTOUT.

Job 1
Manuscript for magazine article

Type the article at the right as an unbound manuscript with footnotes. SS and indent the quoted ¶ 5 spaces from the side margins.

THE WONDERFUL WORLD OF THE LASER (¶ 1) "Ray guns" are nothing new to science fiction fans. For years, heroes in science fiction have used ray guns to stun the villain, to disintegrate huge boulders, and to blast their way through massive prison walls. Once but a figment of imagination, the ray gun is becoming a reality in the form of the laser. (¶ 2) The laser, an abbreviation of the phrase "Light Amplification by Stimulated Emission of Radiation," is a device that emits an extremely intense beam of energy in the form of light rays. Electrons around a positive atomic nucleus are first increased in energy and then stimulated causing them to release the excess energy as laser beams. (¶ 3) Although the laser has a great many possibilities, its development remains, to a great extent, in the experimental stage. Theoretically, for example, it is possible for a single laser beam to carry thousands of radio, television, or telephone messages simultaneously. Its inability to penetrate adverse atmospheric conditions, however, has limited its range to very short distances. It has been reported, though, that there are probably more physicists and engineers working on the problems of transmitting information by laser than on any other single project in the field of laser application.[1] As a result, many scientists believe that laser beams will become the primary method of electronic communications before the close of this century. (¶ 4) In the field of business, the laser has many possibilities. It has been used to weld a great variety of metals, including some which cannot be welded by conventional methods, to cut hard metals and other substances, and to drill holes as small as 1/1000″ in diameter. Kahn and Wiener report that the laser will also have important applications in the field of data storage: (quoted ¶) IBM has already developed a memory-storage system using an eight-colored laser beam to store as many as one hundred million bits of information on a square inch of photographic film. Even more impressive is the "Data Device" reported by an Air Force scientist, John F. Dove, at Griffiss Air Force Base, Rome, New York. He reports that by using a laser beam to reduce the size of the data signals submitted, an entire library of 20,000 volumes can be stored on an 8- by 10-inch piece of nickel foil, thus storing in one inch what would go on ten miles of magnetic tape. The device measures three by four feet by six inches, was developed for $125,000, and cost (sic) about $50,000, some twenty times cheaper than the cost of many storage systems.[2]

---

[1] Stewart E. Miller, "Communication by Laser," Scientific American, January, 1966, p. 19.

[2] Herman Kahn and Anthony J. Wiener, The Year 2000 (New York: The Macmillan Company, 1967), p. 100.

13c ▶9 Improve keystroking technique

each line 3 times SS
(slowly, faster, slowly);
DS between 3-line groups

v	vote vote love love dove dove have have view views
shift lock	Did you OK this show for ABC? for NBC? or for CBS?
v/shift lock	I have seen Val Voss on five WLW and KVO TV shows.

13d ▶11 Type with continuity

type drill twice

Continuity cue: Keep the hands quiet; let the *fingers* do the typing.

home/third	for us|it was|the squid|we took|they are|jute rope Faye told us she took the file to the youth group.
home/bottom	an ad; a van; can land; a mask; has flax; all can; Ann Lanz has a bad hand. Shall Nan sack all cash?
third/bottom	in it, we can, fix them, pay him, to have, by size Vic can give you the vote count to prove his case.

| 1 | 2 | 3 | 4 | 5 | 6 | 7 | 8 | 9 | 10 |

13e ▶8 Know your typewriter: tabulator

To clear tab stops
1. Move carriage (carrier) to extreme left.
2. Depress **tab clear (33)** and hold it down as you return carriage (carrier) all the way to the right to remove all tab stops. *Some typewriters have a Total Tab Clear mechanism that clears all stops at once.*

To set tab stops
Move the carriage (carrier) to the desired position; then depress the **tab set (25).** Repeat this procedure for each stop needed.

Tabulating technique
Manual: Depress and hold the **tabulator bar (24)** [right index finger] or **key** [right fourth finger] down until the carriage has stopped.

Electric (and some manuals): Tap the **tab key (24)** [little finger] or **bar** [index finger] lightly; return the finger to home-key position at once.

Drill procedure
1. Clear all tab stops, as directed above.
2. Begin Line 1 at the left margin.
3. Set tab stop for Line 2 five spaces to right of left margin stop.
4. Set tab stop for Line 3 five spaces to right of first tab stop; and so on for Lines 4 and 5.
5. Type the drill once DS as shown.

Margin ▼		I shall learn to use the tab key or bar right now:
Indent 5	——▶ Tab once	I shall clear all the tab stops as I am told;
Indent 10	————▶ Tab twice	I shall set new stops each five strokes;
Indent 15	——————▶ Tab three times	I shall then use my tab key or bar,
Indent 20	————————▶ Tab four times	but for just four of my lines.

283c ▶25 Improve basic skill: rough draft

1. A 5′ writing on ¶s 1–3 combined.
2. Three 1′ writings on each ¶.
3. A 5′ writing on ¶s 1–3 combined with a goal of increased speed and fewer errors.

all letters used | HA | 1.6 si | 5.8 awl | 75% hfw

	gwam 1′	5′	
The technicological advances made during the past 70 years have been	13	3	48
really amazing. We progressed from man power to atomic power, from the	27	5	50
shop to factories that are automated, from manuel computation to the com-	41	8	53
puter, and from the horse buggy to complex space craft. The progress in	54	11	56
the area of technology has been indeed greater in this century than in	68	14	59
any other period of time.	71	14	59
There are many fine positions in technical areas for an apt typist.	13	17	62
Many of the new and unusual space companies hire those who are skillful	28	20	65
typists. Offers also may come from companies that work in areas such	42	23	68
as computer services, electronics, or scientific research. Not only are	57	26	71
jobs like these interesting, they pay good money for those who qualify.	71	28	73
You must be excellent typist with high standards of neatness and	13	31	76
speed to qualify for a job ina technical firm. One qualification is	27	34	79
the skill to type numbers and other comples material properly and to	41	37	82
solve problems in typing placement. In as much as one mistake in a	55	39	84
technical report can result in a serious loss of time, materials, and	69	42	87
money, all technical reports must be typed and proofread with great care.	83	45	90

284-289

284a-289a ▶5 Conditioning practice

Weber analyzed the cost of manufacturing the expensive quilted jacket.
Note that Model 95642 will be replaced by Model 18370 on September 30.
The net amount due on Invoice 8103-A is $756 ($945 less 20% discount).
Did she ask one of the girls who work for her to mail the check to us?

| 1 | 2 | 3 | 4 | 5 | 6 | 7 | 8 | 9 | 10 | 11 | 12 | 13 | 14 |

13f ▶7 Learn to type paragraphs

1. Clear all tab stops; then set a tab stop for a 5-space paragraph (¶) indention.

2. Use double spacing (DS) and indent Line 1 of ¶.

3. Type the ¶ as shown; work for continuity of typing.

4. Two 1′ writings on the ¶; determine 1′ *gwam.*

all letters used | VE | 1.0 si | 4.5 awl | 95% hfw |

	gwam 1′
Tab ⟶ Do not quit as soon as you have reached your	9
first goal. Size up the next one. You can reach	19
it, too; but you must do all the work you have to	29
do in just the right way each day.	36

gwam 1′ | 1 | 2 | 3 | 4 | 5 | 6 | 7 | 8 | 9 | 10 |

Copy difficulty

The ease with which a paragraph can be typed is influenced by three major factors:

1. *Syllable intensity* (si) or average number of syllables per word.

2. *Stroke intensity* or average word length (awl).

3. *Percent of high-frequency words* (hfw).

Careful control of these three factors—si, awl, and hfw—makes it possible to show the difficulty of the copy selections in this book as:

VE Very easy
E Easy
LA Low average
A Average
HA High average
D Difficult

Difficulty index

VE	1.0 si	4.5 awl	95% hfw
	1 Syllable intensity	**2** Average word length	**3** High-frequency words

14

14a ▶8 Conditioning practice

each line twice SS (slowly, then faster); DS between 2-line groups

Technique goal: Keep your eyes on the copy as you type and return.

alphabet Have my long quiz boxed when Jack stops by for it.

v/? Have we used these words: vote? view? five? gave?

easy sentence Chris may go with us to the town down by the lake.

| 1 | 2 | 3 | 4 | 5 | 6 | 7 | 8 | 9 | 10 |

14b ▶5 Check space-bar technique

once as shown; space with down-and-in (toward palm) thumb motion

Goal: To type words and punctuation marks without pausing before or after them.

try to; pay me; my age; of your; all told; and was
Try to pay me the wage that is now due if you can.

by then, off the, buy it, or put, use the, low key
If she is off work by then, we can fly to my lake.

unit **51** lessons 283–289

Technical office typing

Learning goals

1. To develop production skill by typing materials of a technical nature.

2. To type rough draft at higher speeds and with improved control.

283

283a ▶5 Conditioning practice

twice SS; repeat difficult lines

alphabet	As the quarterback objected, the Gems were penalized five extra yards.
figures	The chart shows that 7.68 squared is 58.9824; its reciprocal, .130208.
fig/sym	The men's case (Item 5139-074) is 21″ x 15″ x 7″ and sells for $21.98.
fluency	They may see the bright lights if the airplane flies over the islands.

| 1 | 2 | 3 | 4 | 5 | 6 | 7 | 8 | 9 | 10 | 11 | 12 | 13 | 14 |

283b ▶20 Improve typing techniques

1. A 1′ writing on each line. Strive for accuracy. Find *gwam*.

2. Additional 1′ writings on difficult lines as time permits.

Response patterns

word	If he is to do all that is to be done, he must work as hard as he can.
stroke	Unfortunately, departmental production dropped considerably yesterday.
combination	The senior pilot explained the aerodynamics of the experimental model.

| 1 | 2 | 3 | 4 | 5 | 6 | 7 | 8 | 9 | 10 | 11 | 12 | 13 | 14 |

Finger position

first row	Vance Zimmerman, a bomb expert, can examine the many boxes in the van.
home row	Dad asked Jake to stack the salad plates; Jeff washed all the glasses.
third row	Were you there when the new reporter wrote a witty story on etiquette?

| 1 | 2 | 3 | 4 | 5 | 6 | 7 | 8 | 9 | 10 | 11 | 12 | 13 | 14 |

Stroking

adjacent keys	We might consider a contract to prepare a new safety series for radio.
double letters	All the books and supplies needed will be shipped to your office soon.
direct reaches	My survey of prices charged this summer reported many great decreases.
left hand	After we were briefed, we agreed to erect a new water treatment plant.
right hand	Jon Youngman bought Polly Killion a pink nylon blouse trimmed in mink.
balanced-hand	Both auditors will help us do the special analysis for the firm today.

| 1 | 2 | 3 | 4 | 5 | 6 | 7 | 8 | 9 | 10 | 11 | 12 | 13 | 14 |

14c ▶17 Check carriage (carrier) return technique

1. Type each line once.

Goal: To return without pausing at line endings and beginnings.

2. Two 30" writings on each line.

Goal: To reach end of each line as "Return" is called.

3. As time permits, type a 1' writing on each line without the call.

Goal: At least 16 *gwam*.

all letters used

		words in line	gwam 30"
1	Jane is to do the work for us. (return without pausing)	6	12
2	Did the eight girls sign it, too?	6½	13
3	He may fix the big dam by the lake.	7	14
4	Is it all right for me to lend a hand?	7½	15
5	I may go to the dock if it is all right.	8	16
6	Vic is the man to make the land map for us.	8½	17
7	He may go with us to the zoo by the big quay.	9	18

| 1 | 2 | 3 | 4 | 5 | 6 | 7 | 8 | 9 |

14d ▶8 Check shift-key technique

each line twice

Goal: To make each shift-key reach without wasting time or motion.

Shifting cues

1. Depress shift key.
2. Strike letter key.
3. Release shift key quickly.

left shift Most of us have to work: Miss, Mr., Mrs., and Ms.

right shift Gib, Sue, and Vi went with Dr. Dye to St. Charles.

both shifts Ms. Burns gave a tea for Dr. and Mrs. Frye in May.

shift lock USC played in the NIT; UCLA copped the NCAA crown.

14e ▶12 Type paragraph with continuity

1. Clear all tab stops; then set a tab stop for a 5-space ¶ indention.

2. Type the ¶ as shown; then type two 1' and two 2' writings.

Goal: 15 *gwam*.

Note: To clear a single tab stop without canceling others, tab to the stop and operate the *tab clear*.

all letters used | VE | 1.0 si | 4.5 awl | 95% hfw |

	gwam 1'	2'	
Tab → If I try for high speed, I must try to build	9	5	23
good form, too. It just works out that the quick	19	10	28
move is a part of good form. So next time I must	29	15	33
go for the prize of speed with good form.	37	18	37

gwam 1' | 1 | 2 | 3 | 4 | 5 | 6 | 7 | 8 | 9 | 10 |
2' | 1 | 2 | 3 | 4 | 5 |

280c-282c, continued

Blind carbon copy notation

At times it is desirable to type a notation on only the carbon copy of a letter—not on the letter itself. This notation, known as a *blind* carbon copy notation, is typed at the left margin a double space below the last typed line.

> Insert a heavy piece of paper *between* the ribbon and the original or first sheet. Type the notation, such as
>
> bcc Ms. Toni P. Marshall
>
> This notation will appear on the carbon copy but not on the letter.

Job 4 [LM p. 179]
Letter with blind carbon copy notation
modified block; indented ¶s; mixed; 2 cc's

November 1, 19-- Mr. James T. Cooke 378 Peach Orchard Road, Waterbury, CT 06712 Dear Mr. Cooke (¶ 1) Welcome to the Hartford District of the Centennial Insurance Company. (¶ 2) It is our company's policy to notify the local district when policyholders are transferred into its territory so that we may offer them any service they may require on their insurance--in your case, Life Insurance Policy No. 20 353 478. (¶ 3) Your local representative is now Ms. Toni P. Marshall, who is located at 137 Grand Avenue in Waterbury (Telephone: 348-7100). She will call on you within the next few weeks. In the meantime, if we can be of any service to you, please write or call Ms. Marshall or this office. Cordially yours Marcia Charneco District Manager bcc Ms. Toni P. Marshall

Job 5
Quarterly report
Center in reading position.

CENTENNIAL INSURANCE COMPANY

Hartford District

Life and Health Insurance Issued

Quarter Ending December 31, 19--

Representative	Life	Health	Total
Melvin Moody	$ 295,106	$ 219,356	$ 514,462
Lois Hlavac	268,459	199,986	468,445
Toni Marshall	239,560	178,875	418,435
David Marcum	210,679	165,482	376,161
Chris Morton	199,706	146,593	346,299
Lisa McCord	178,459	130,721	309,180
Bruce Deveaux	170,362	120,831	291,193
Henry Kendall	152,486	105,296	257,782
Ann Crafton	136,187	99,568	235,755
Robert Chase	106,549	98,747	205,296
TOTAL	$1,957,553	$1,465,455	$3,423,008

15

15a ▶8 Conditioning practice

each line twice SS
(slowly, then faster);
DS between 2-line groups

alphabet	Buck Zahn will vex the judge if he quits my group.
n/z	Zeal and zest of the men in my zone won the prize.
easy sentence	He may do all the work if he works with good form.

| 1 | 2 | 3 | 4 | 5 | 6 | 7 | 8 | 9 | 10 |

15b ▶9 Check control of service keys

once as shown

Goals, line by line

1-2. Down-and-in motion (toward palm); do not pause before or after spacing.

3-4. Type capital letters without pausing before or after shifting.

5-6. Use shift lock for ALL-CAP items; release lock for typing lowercase letters.

7-8. Clear all tab stops; set new stop at center of paper. Tab and return quickly.

space bar	1	I knew it was my job to do my best in all my work.
	2	Try in the right way, and you can reach your goal.
shift keys	3	Jayne Storm is to go to the dance with Paul Quinn.
	4	Rex Quig used gal. and qt.; J. M. Poe, ft. and in.
shift lock	5	ALL CAP such items as these: NSA, NBEA, and NASA.
	6	ALL CAP book names, too: THE OLD MAN AND THE SEA.
tabulator and return	7	Tab ⟶ At the end of the line, I
	8	will keep my eyes on the book.

15c ▶8 Check keystroking technique

once as shown;
repeat if time permits

Goals, line by line

1-2. Without moving hands upward.

3-4. Without moving hands downward.

5-6. Quiet hands and arms.

7-8. Continuity of keystroking.

home/third	1	It will add to your risk if they rush to the lake.
	2	Peg says it is a tour all eight girls should take.
home/bottom	3	Max has had a small bash. All ads can flash cash.
	4	Alf has had a van all fall, and Cal has had a cab.
third/bottom	5	These men have caught six snakes for the town zoo.
	6	Can the two men come by to quote on the new plans?
alphabet	7	Jay Witz asked me if Val Price got the quaint box.
alphabet	8	Did Jane Glick buy the quartz pin Wes Fox gave me?

| 1 | 2 | 3 | 4 | 5 | 6 | 7 | 8 | 9 | 10 |

280c-282c, continued

Job 3 [LM pp. 173–178]
Invoices

Type an invoice, similar to the one illustrated, to each of the addressees listed below. Make 1 cc.

CENTENNIAL Insurance Company
Property and Casualty Division

Hartford District:
984 Main Street
Hartford, Conn. 06103
203-116-0904

INVOICE 70412

Date: October 3, 19--

To: Mr. Jerome C. Carlton
503 Lakeview Drive
Meriden, CT 06450

Renewal Date	Policy Number	Property and Coverage	Amount	Premium
11/3/19--	M31100686	Boat Policy ($100 deductible)		207.85
		Motor launch	50,000	
		Bodily injury	100,000	
		Property damage	200,000	

Invoice: **70412** Date: **October 3, 19--**
To: **Mr. Jerome C. Carlton, 503 Lakeview Drive, Meriden, CT 06450**
Renewal Date: **11/3/19--** Policy Number: **M31100686**

Property and Coverage	Amount
Boat Policy ($100 deductible)	
Motor launch	**50,000**
Bodily injury	**100,000**
Property damage	**200,000**

Premium: **207.85**

Invoice: **70427** Date: **October 7, 19--**
To: **Wickham Department Store, 710 New Britain Avenue, Hartford, CT 06106**
Renewal Date: **11/15/19--** Policy Number: **CL737650**

Property and Coverage	Amount
Department Store (710 New Britain Avenue)	
Public liability	**750,000**
Fire	**1,000,000**

Premium: **1,263.50**

Invoice: **70438** Date: **October 17, 19--**
To: **Mrs. Lucy T. Taylor, 486 Colonial Avenue, Waterbury, CT 06708**
Renewal Date: **11/20/19--** Policy Number: **RE229679**

Property and Coverage	Amount
Homeowners Policy ($100 deductible)	
Dwelling (486 Colonial Avenue)	**40,000**
Household contents	**15,000**
Liability	**50,000**
Medical	**1,000**

Premium: **138.25**

15d ▶10 Check keystroking speed

1. Two 1′ writings on each of the ¶s.

Goal: 16 *gwam.*

2. A 2′ writing on the 2 ¶s combined.

Goal: 14 *gwam.*

*Charts for recording your speed scores appear on Laboratory Materials (LM) pp. 3, 4.

all letters used | VE | 1.0 si | 4.0 awl | 95% hfw

	gwam 1′	2′
If I am to win, I must not quit now. I must	9	5
type on, one right move at a time. If I can work	19	10
on and not give up, I will learn.	26	13
So I will size up the job, and I can make it	9	17
next time. Now I see that it is how I do my work	19	22
that will help me reach the goal.	26	26

gwam 1′ | 1 | 2 | 3 | 4 | 5 | 6 | 7 | 8 | 9 | 10 |
2′ | 1 | 2 | 3 | 4 | 5 |

15e ▶15 Individualize your practice

each line once;
then retype selected lines according to your needs

Technique emphasis: Position the fingers curved and upright over the home keys; strike each key with a quick, snap stroke. Space quickly. Hold hands and arms quiet, with wrists low and relaxed.

Each sentence includes at least 4 uses of the letters that sentence is designed to emphasize. Thus, the sentences provide an intensive review of the keyboard.

Enrichment material for Unit 1 appears on LM pp. 5–8.

a/b Beth Brach is our best aide; she can do a big job.

c/d Did Clay Cole check the due date on the cost card?

e/f Ed Fish feels that one file for each firm will do.

g/h Greg is great with weights; Garth, with the rings.

i/j If it is a large jet, Jim will just jump with joy.

k/l Kate Blake keeps all kinds of lists for Mr. Block.

m/n Man is known more for his mind than for his might.

o/p To cop the prize post, you must plan your trip up.

q/r Be quick to run our queer quartz rock to the quay.

s/t Stu said to be sure to ask the terms of that sale.

u/v Our votes have been pledged but give us your view.

w/x Rex Dow filed the tax of the new wax works at six.

y/z Yes, Liz, you won the prize by your zeal and zest.

| 1 | 2 | 3 | 4 | 5 | 6 | 7 | 8 | 9 | 10 |

280c-282c, continued

Job 2 [LM pp. 169–172]
Form letters

1. Type the form letter at the right (modified block; indented ¶s; mixed) to the owners of Policy No. 25 401 328 and Policy No. 27 563 872.

2. Obtain the name and address of the policyholder and the name of the company representative from the list prepared in Job 1. Provide an appropriate salutation.

October 8, 19--

Dear

Subject: *Your Policy (add number)* ~~Paid-up Policy~~

It is a pleasure ~~We are pleased~~ to inform you that your *recent* ~~monthly~~ premium payment was the *final* ~~last~~ one and that your policy is now paidup. Although *you* ~~it~~ will not be *required* ~~necessary~~ to pay any *further* ~~more~~ premiums, your policy will continue to provide *full* ~~complete~~ protection.

If you have any questions abuot the *value* ~~valuation~~ of your policy or if you would like to *consider* ~~buy~~ additional insurance conerage, please call your local centennial *representative* ~~man,~~ (Mr. Mrs. Miss) ______________________. (Mr. Mrs. Miss) _______________ is a *trained* specialist ~~in~~ insurance, and (he she) will be *happy* ~~glad~~ to answer ~~all~~ your questions and *provide* ~~proffer~~ any service you may need.

If you ~~should~~ cahnge your address in the future, *please* let us know. In thisway, we can keep your records on your policy up-to-date.

Thank you for your *confidence in Centennial* ~~kind patronage.~~ ~~If you need any additional insurance coverage in the future, be sure to call or write us.~~

Sincerely yours,

Marcia Charneco
District Manager

If we can be of any further service to you in the future, please let us know. It will be our pleasure to serve you.

unit **2** lessons 16–20

Improving typing motion patterns

Learning goals

1. To improve keystroking skill.
2. To refine the operation of basic service keys.
3. To increase speed of typing sentences and paragraphs.
4. To learn to use the backspace and the margin release keys.

Machine adjustments

1. Paper guide at *0.*
2. Ribbon control on black.
3. Margin sets: 50–space line.
4. Line–space selector on *1* for drills.
5. Line–space selector on *2* for paragraphs.

16

16a ▶7 Conditioning practice

each line 3 times SS;
DS between 3-line groups

First time: Even pace; note awkward letter sequences; practice these as time permits.

Second time: Faster pace; work for improved stroking patterns.

Third time: Push for higher speed; space quickly after words; keep carriage moving.

alphabet	Rex Glanz packed my bag with five quarts of juice.
v/?	Who got the prize: Vic? Bev? Van? Marv? or Verna?
fluency	The girls did their work then spent all their pay.

| 1 | 2 | 3 | 4 | 5 | 6 | 7 | 8 | 9 | 10 |

16b ▶7 Improve tabulator and return technique

each line once

1. Clear all tab stops. (See page 24.)
2. Set tab stop for Line 2 five spaces right of left margin stop.
3. Set 3 additional tab stops 5 spaces apart.
4. Begin Line 1 at left margin.

Goal: To tabulate and return without pausing at beginning or end of line.

I must get ready to type in the same way each day:

Indent 5	Tab once →	First, I clear my desk of all unneeded items.
Indent 10	Tab twice →	Next, I twirl paper into the typewriter.
Indent 15	Tab three times →	Then, I adjust the machine quickly.
Indent 20	Tab four times →	Finally, I turn to the lesson.

16c ▶6 Improve shift-key and shift-lock technique

each line twice SS
(slowly, then faster);
DS between 2-line groups

Goals
- to shift, type, and release quickly
- to use shift lock and to release it quickly

left shift	Is Mary Hall in Oakland? Marla Parks, in New York?
right shift	Ceil, Elaine, and Vince work for Bozy Toy Company.
both shifts	Ask Mrs. Given to call Ms. Zelda Lamb on Thursday.
shift lock	I bought two books: TO RACE THE WIND and SYMBOLS.

280c-282c ▶35 Production typing

In this unit, you will work as a clerk–typist in the Hartford district office of the Centennial Insurance Company, 984 Main Street, Hartford, Conn. 06103.

Follow directions carefully. Make carbon copies when directed to do so; address envelopes when appropriate. Correct errors neatly.

Job 1
List of paid-up policies

From the worksheet at the right, type a list of the policies that were paid up in September. Type the list according to number, beginning with the lowest number. Use the headings shown, but do not type the ruled lines. Center the material in reading position. Make 1 cc.

POLICIES PAID UP IN September, 19--

POLICY NO.	INSURED	REPRESENTATIVE
26 840 912	Mrs. Leslie C. Reilly 158 Woodland Street Hartford, CT 06105	Mr. Melvin Moody
25 406 498	Miss Rose M. O'Hara 36 Goshen Road Manchester, CT 06040	Mr. Bruce Deveaux
26 593 021	Mr. Edwin S. Kent 807 Sixth Street Middletown, CT 06457	Mrs. Lisa McCord
25 401 328	Mrs. R. L. Steinberg 6840 Roslyn Street New Britain, CT 06052	Mr. Chris Morton
27 563 872	Dr. Lois A. Hlavac 139 Brookfield Avenue Bristol, CT 06010	Miss Robin Norton
25 309 207	Mr. Peter C. Denver 32 Crestview Circle Hartford, CT 06117	Mrs. Ann Crafton
27 391 486	Mr. Robert L. Chase 19 Station Avenue Torrington, CT 06790	Mr. John Monroe
26 103 208	Mr. Lance P. Ramsey 1120 Hughes Street Hartford, CT 06106	Mr. David Marcum
26 465 220	Ms. Celia A. Costlow 1007 Bay Avenue New Britain, CT 06053	Mr. Henry Kendall

16d ▶17 Guided writing: sentences

1. Each sentence once without timing; easy, controlled pace with quick speedup on short, easy words.

Goal: To increase speed from sentence to sentence.

2. A 30" writing on each sentence.

Goal: To reach the end of the line as "Return" is called.

3. A 1' writing on each of Lines 1–5 without the call of the return.

Goal: At least 18 *gwam*.

all letters used

		words in line	gwam 30"
1	I must do the drill at a fast rate.	7	14
2	If you are to go, send the fee today.	7½	15
3	Could he come back to fix the big clock?	8	16
4	Ryan will return the big boat to the dock.	8½	17
5	Jen may envy me but she does not let it show.	9	18
6	Mark is to give the boys a hand and to pay them.	9½	19
7	Zeke is to handle their squad if the pay is right.	10	20

| 1 | 2 | 3 | 4 | 5 | 6 | 7 | 8 | 9 | 10 |

16e ▶13 Goal typing: paragraphs

The paragraphs are marked with special signals to identify your practice goals.

Goals
1' ▼ 15 ■ 19 ● 23

▼ acceptable
■ good
● excellent

Follow this practice plan:

1. A 1' writing on ¶ 1; determine *gwam*.

2. With your *gwam* as a base, select from the goals in the copy the first one to the right of your base rate.

3. Three 1' writings on ¶ 1, trying to reach or exceed your new goal rate. *As soon as you reach your new goal, try for the next higher goal rate.*

4. Type ¶ 2 in the same way.

Goals

1. At least 15 *gwam*.

2. At least 4 *gwam* increase over your base rate.

all letters used | VE | 1.2 si | 4.6 awl | 97% hfw |

	gwam 2'
I now know how to type; I know where all the	4
letters are. I am also able to type each of them	9
without looking. Before long I shall be a typist.	14
My next step is to develop good form so that	19
I can cut the waste time. This is quite a job, I	24
realize; however, if I keep trying, it could help.	29

gwam 2' | 1 | 2 | 3 | 4 | 5 |

Word counts. Each paragraph (¶) is marked with a 4–word count shown in figures and with an in–between count of 2 words shown by a dot (·) to aid you in noting your 1-minute *gwam* goals.

The figures in the 2' *gwam* column at right of ¶s and the scale beneath ¶s are used to determine 2' *gwam*: figure at end of last complete line typed + figure beneath last word typed in a partial line.

unit **50** lessons 280–282

Insurance office typing

Learning goals

1. To improve production skill by typing typical jobs found in an insurance office.
2. To type script and rough-draft copy at higher speeds and with improved control.

280-282

280a-282a ▶5 Conditioning practice

twice SS; repeat difficult lines

alphabet	Jeanne Powers drove the truck quickly through a maze of six obstacles.
figures	Machines with serial numbers 290371-984 and 285061-375 will be traded.
fig/sym	The vote was 103 (47%) "yes"; 79 (36%) "no"; and 37 (17%) "undecided."
fluency	Iris told the workers to throw the eight bushels of corn on the truck.

| 1 | 2 | 3 | 4 | 5 | 6 | 7 | 8 | 9 | 10 | 11 | 12 | 13 | 14 |

280b-282b ▶10 Increase script speed: progressive script

1. A 1′ writing on each ¶; find and compare *gwam*.
2. Two 1′ writings on each of the slower ¶s to increase speed on more difficult copy.

all letters used

¶				
¶ 1	E	1.2 si	5.0 awl	90% hfw
¶ 2	A	1.5 si	5.6 awl	80% hfw
¶ 3	D	1.7 si	6.0 awl	70% hfw

gwam 1′

Six boys were on their way to school in Quentin's car when a tire 13
blew out. Quentin did not have much money, so the boys discussed it 27
and agreed to share the cost of having the tire fixed. In this way, it 41
did not cost any one of them too much. In simple terms, this is the 55
way insurance works. A great number of people put a little of their 69
money together to help pay for the losses of a few people. 81

All of us face many risks in our personal or business lives. We 13
may lose our property by fire, storms, floods, and many other natural 27
disasters. Our property may be taken or damaged by vandals or rioters. 42
Accidents in our homes or places of business may cause injury to other 56
people and result in costly legal action. To help protect us against 70
the chance of loss, we often turn to insurance companies for help. 83

Insurance companies are organized for the purpose of assuming the 13
risks for certain types of hazards. For a small payment, known as the 27
premium, the company agrees to reimburse a business or individual for 41
specified kinds of losses or injuries. The risks that can be insured 55
must be sufficiently numerous to make the law of averages operate. When 70
this is so, the yearly losses can be predicted with amazing accuracy. 84

17

17a ▶7 Conditioning practice

each line 3 times SS (slowly, faster, slowly); DS between 3-line groups

```
alphabet  Jo Fox made five quick plays to win the big prize.
c/v       Can Victor come to work at five? Calvin, at seven?
fluency   She is to go to the city by bus to sign the forms.
          | 1 | 2 | 3 | 4 | 5 | 6 | 7 | 8 | 9 | 10 |
```

17b ▶7 Learn to use backspace key and margin release

use exact 50-space line: center − 25; center + 25

Line 1 (backspacer)

1. Type first incomplete word in Line 1 as shown.

2. Backspace and fill in the missing letter.

3. Type other incomplete words in the same way.

Line 2 (margin release)

1. Depress **margin release** or **bypass (32)** and backspace 5 spaces into left margin.

2. Type Line 2 twice: type until carriage locks (ignore ringing of bell); then depress margin release (bypass) and complete the line.

Backspacer
To position the carriage to fill in an omitted letter, depress the **backspace key (26).** Locate the key on your typewriter.

Electric
Make a light, quick stroke with the little finger. Release the key quickly to avoid a double back-space. Hold the key down when you want repeat backspacing.

Manual
Straighten the little finger slightly and reach it to the backspace key with minimum hand motion. Depress the backspace key firmly; release it quickly.

```
1        ja z, up n, un il, jac et, val e, ac uire, vol mes
2  DO:   Move right margin stop to end of scale after the drill.
```

17c ▶13 Improve keystroking technique: response patterns

Word response
Short, balanced-hand words (as in Lines 1–2) are so easy to type they can be typed as words. Think and type them at high speed.

Letter response
Many one-hand words (as in Lines 3–4) are not so easy to type. Such words may be typed *letter by letter* with continuity.

Combination response
Normal copy (as in Lines 5–6) includes both word- and letter-response sequences. *Use high speed for easy words, lower speed for more difficult ones.*

Lines 1-6: Once from dictation; then once from copy only.

Lines 7-9: 1′ writing on each line. Compare *gwam*.

```
word         1  do so go to of or ox if is it us an am ah he me by
response     2  it is|do so|to us|if he|of us|an ox|or by|to do it

letter       3  as in we on be no at up ax my oh ex pi are you was
response     4  at no|be in|as my|be up|as in|at my|ax him|was you

combination  5  so as of no go at if on am up or we us my to be by
response     6  if no|to be|is up|of no|is my|go up|is in|am up to

word         7  I am to go to the dock, and he is to work with me.
letter       8  As you saw up at my mill, my rate was up on water.
combination  9  If we are to be in the city, we may see them then.
                | 1 | 2 | 3 | 4 | 5 | 6 | 7 | 8 | 9 | 10 |
```

277b-279b, continued

Job 5
Model copy of program

Prepare a model copy of a 4–page program, similar to the one at the right, based on the following information:

Page 1: The New Century Club of Buffalo, New York, will present a fashion show and dinner at the Algonquin Lodge at 7:30 p.m. on Friday, April 16, 19—.

Page 2: The dinner menu will consist of: tomato juice; tenderloin beef tips and mushrooms over rice pilaf; tossed green salad with French or Italian dressing; buttered peas and carrots; rolls and butter; strawberry torte; coffee, tea, or milk; nuts and mints.

Page 3: The narrators for the fashion show will be Susan Allen and Dennis Seaman; the models for women's fashions will be: Renee Parks, Sandy Gordon, Beverly Adamson, and Ruth Bertolotti; the models for men's fashions will be: Tom Radovich, Michael Ogden, Earl Lescova, and Glenn Martin; the director of the show is Margaret Harrison; the organist is William Delmont; fashions will be provided by the Kensington Department Store of Buffalo, New York.

Page 4: The officers of the New Century Club are: Nancy Hartman, President; Thomas McGuire, Vice President; William Donaldson, Secretary; Samantha Smithley, Treasurer; and David Aultman, Historian. The officers of the club wish to thank all those who helped make the event a successful one and to salute those in attendance for their generous support which enables the New Century Club to continue its support to the Mid-Town General Hospital.

Learn to type spread headings

1. Backspace from center once for each letter, character, and space *except the last letter or character* in the heading. Begin to type where the backspacing ends.

2. In typing a spread heading, space once after each letter or character and 3 times between words.

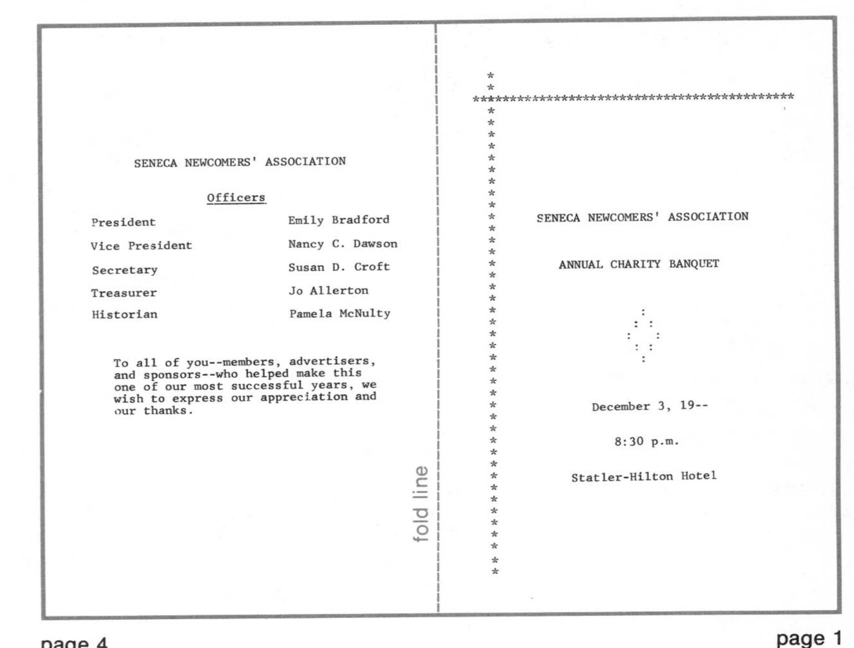

SENECA NEWCOMERS' ASSOCIATION

Officers

President	Emily Bradford
Vice President	Nancy C. Dawson
Secretary	Susan D. Croft
Treasurer	Jo Allerton
Historian	Pamela McNulty

To all of you--members, advertisers, and sponsors--who helped make this one of our most successful years, we wish to express our appreciation and our thanks.

fold line

SENECA NEWCOMERS' ASSOCIATION

ANNUAL CHARITY BANQUET

December 3, 19--

8:30 p.m.

Statler-Hilton Hotel

page 4 page 1

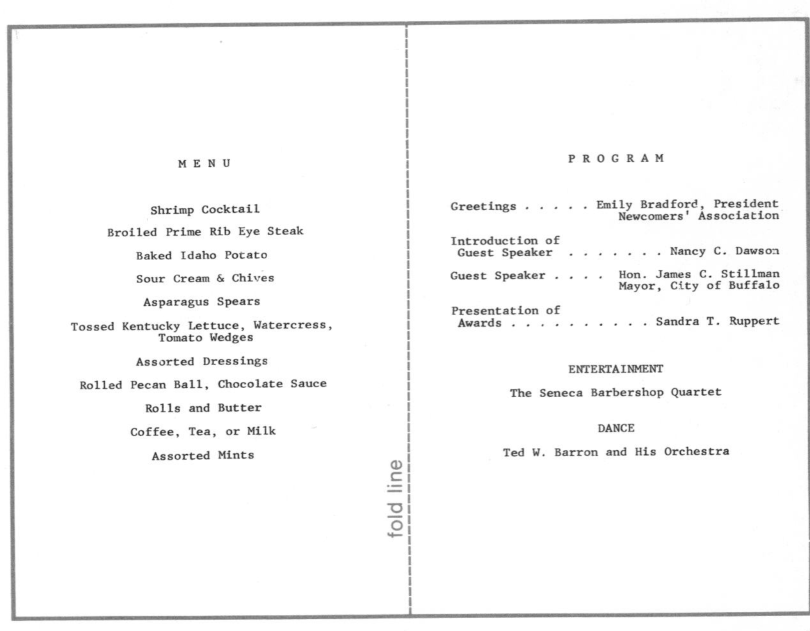

M E N U

Shrimp Cocktail

Broiled Prime Rib Eye Steak

Baked Idaho Potato

Sour Cream & Chives

Asparagus Spears

Tossed Kentucky Lettuce, Watercress, Tomato Wedges

Assorted Dressings

Rolled Pecan Ball, Chocolate Sauce

Rolls and Butter

Coffee, Tea, or Milk

Assorted Mints

fold line

P R O G R A M

Greetings . . . . . Emily Bradford, President Newcomers' Association

Introduction of Guest Speaker . . . . Nancy C. Dawson

Guest Speaker . . . . Hon. James C. Stillman Mayor, City of Buffalo

Presentation of Awards . . . . Sandra T. Ruppert

ENTERTAINMENT

The Seneca Barbershop Quartet

DANCE

Ted W. Barron and His Orchestra

page 2 page 3

17d ▶23 Guided writing: sentences

1. Lines 1–10 once as shown.

Goal: To discover improved stroking patterns for one-hand and balanced-hand words.

2. A 30″ writing on each line of each pair (Lines 1–10).

Goal: To type the second line at the same rate as the first.

3. As time permits, type a 1′ writing on each of Lines 5–10.

Goal: 20 *gwam* on odd-numbered lines; 18 *gwam* on even-numbered lines.

all letters used

		words in line	gwam 30″
1	Al owns the kale field by the lake. (return without pausing)	7	14
2	Did you base the case on the facts?	7	14
3	Title to the land is held by the city.	7½	15
4	Name the city you are to visit in May.	7½	15
5	Max paid for half the jam he got for us.	8	16
6	It is up to you to work with care, also.	8	16
7	Sign the form and pay the man for the work.	8½	17
8	She was a good queen; she cut the tax rate.	8½	17
9	Did any of the girls wish to visit the firms?	9	18
10	Of all the girls, Jaye read at the best rate.	9	18
11	Virla is to go with them to the quay by the zoo.	9½	19
12	The water in the zoo lake is bad for their fish.	9½	19
13	When she got such a profit, she paid for the land.	10	20
14	You may enter the city meet if you pay these fees.	10	20
15	She is to do social work for the city when they wish.	10½	21
16	He may save the tax if you sign the rate form by six.	10½	21

| 1 | 2 | 3 | 4 | 5 | 6 | 7 | 8 | 9 | 10 | 10½ |

18

18a ▶7 Conditioning practice

each line 3 times SS (slowly, faster, slowly); DS between 3-line groups

alphabet Vic, a big prize, joins my flight squad next week.

b/v Bev and Bob have served at the voting booth today.

fluency Is he to do all the field forms for the usual pay?

| 1 | 2 | 3 | 4 | 5 | 6 | 7 | 8 | 9 | 10 |

18b ▶20 Guided writing: sentences

Repeat 17d, above, as follows:

1. Lines 9–16 once as shown.

Goal: To improve keystroking patterns on the balanced- and one-hand words.

2. A 30″ writing on each of Lines 9–16.

Goal: To type the second line at the same rate as the first.

3. As time permits, type a 1′ writing on each of Lines 11–16.

Goal: 21 *gwam* on odd-numbered lines; 19 *gwam* on even-numbered lines.

277b-279b, continued

Job 3
Office procedures manual
Type the copy as a leftbound manuscript. List the numbered items in ¶ 4 in appropriate form.

PHOTO OR THERMAL PROCESS COPIERS (¶ 1) There are a number of machines available that will copy typewritten or printed material from an original copy. These machines operate on a principle of xerography (light) or thermography (heat) to transfer the material from the original to special copy paper or plain paper. A few of these machines will produce copies in colors. The machines used most commonly, however, will produce only copies in black and white. (¶ 2) Photo and thermal copy machines are especially useful in making additional copies of documents such as customers' orders and bills of lading. They may be used also when additional copies of correspondence and reports are required. Considerable time is saved by reproducing copies from the original, and the danger of errors which may be made when material is retyped is eliminated. (¶ 3) Although some copiers have been designed to reproduce as many as 100 copies per minute, their use as duplicators has been restricted to a great extent by the cost. If only 1 to 10 copies of typewritten material are required, however, time and labor may be saved by reproducing the copies required on a copy machine. This procedure eliminates the necessity for making carbon copies and frees the typist from the tedious task of correcting errors on multiple carbon copies. (¶ 4) The preparation of materials for copy machines is quite simple: 1. Be certain that the type is clean and that the ribbon will produce dark print. 2. Type the material to be copied on bond paper unless special paper is required. 3. If you make an error, it is best to erase the error and correct it. If you use correction tape, which merely masks the error, it is possible the original error may show through on the copy, particularly if a thermal copier is used.

Job 4 [LM p. 167]
Model copy of sales circular
Arrange the material attractively as a model copy for duplication on a company letterhead. SS and indent the duplication processes given in ¶ 2.

REPRO-QUIK DUPLICATING SERVICES (¶ 1) REPRO-QUIK provides fast, economical duplication of any material--reports, forms, bulletins, programs, sales letters, memorandums, menus, price lists, circulars, etc. We can plan and produce attractive copies from data you provide or reproduce materials from your own originals. The cost depends upon the complexity of the material, the duplication process selected, the number of colors desired, and the number of copies required. (¶ 2) You can select the duplication process which best meets your needs: SPIRIT DUPLICATION. A quick, economical process for reproducing up to 300 copies in purple, blue, red, black, and green at a cost as low as $.75 per 100 copies. STENCIL DUPLICATION. Up to 5,000 copies in black, red, blue, green, and yellow can be reproduced quickly at a cost as low as $1 per 100 copies. THERMAL OR XEROGRAPHIC DUPLICATION. Immediate or overnight service is available for one-color copies at a cost as low as $.02 per copy. We specialize in reproducing mail labels on pressure-sensitive paper. (¶ 3) We will sort, fold, collate, and staple documents into program or booklet form at no additional cost. Colored paper (green, blue, yellow, or pink) is available at a slight additional cost. We will produce material on your letterhead or on 3-hole punched paper at no extra charge. (¶ 4) Let us help you solve your duplicating problems. No job is too big or too small for REPRO-QUIK. Just write or call us for an estimate. You will be pleasantly surprised how much you can save by using our duplicating services.

18c ▶10

Improve keystroking technique: awkward reaches

type drill twice

Lines 1-3: Adjacent-key sequences, such as *er*, *oi*, *ew*, and *op*, need special attention. Think each letter vigorously; strike each key precisely.

Lines 4-6: Make a direct, quick reach from *n* to *y*, *c* to *e*, and *u* to *n*, and the like, without pausing at home-key position between strokes.

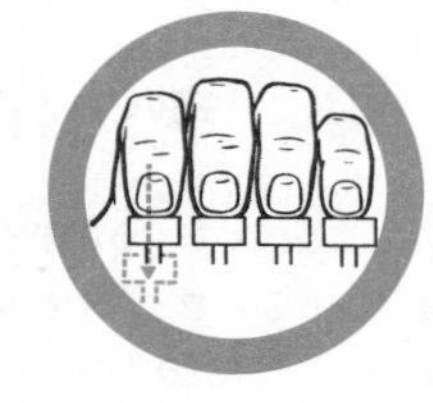
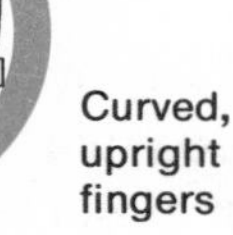

Curved, upright fingers

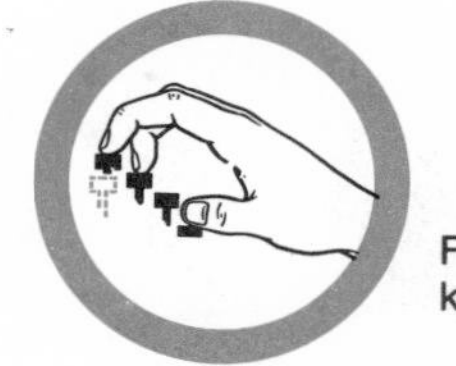

Finger-action keystroking

adjacent keys
1 red here over error suit guide oil soil point copy
2 new view went well asks fast says same leads lends
3 Please read her news report as a basis for action.

consecutive finger reaches
4 any many face pace piece effect under until amount
5 much must sums assume why buys true trip part sort
6 Any special effort to perfect my technique counts.

| 1 | 2 | 3 | 4 | 5 | 6 | 7 | 8 | 9 | 10 |

18d ▶13

Goal typing: paragraphs

1. A 1′ writing on ¶ 1; determine *gwam*.

2. Select from the goals in the ¶ the next speed *above* your base rate.

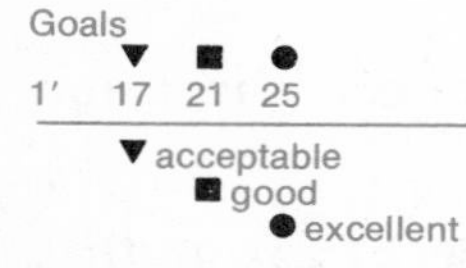

Goals
1′ ▼ 17 ■ 21 ● 25

▼ acceptable
■ good
● excellent

3. Three 1′ writings on ¶ 1, trying to reach or exceed your new goal rate.

4. Type ¶ 2 in the same way.

Goal: At least 17 *gwam* on each ¶.

all letters used | VE | 1.2 si | 5.0 awl | 96% hfw |

gwam 2′

It is important for me to learn to force two — 4
to four letters close together in time. If I can — 9
cut the time between them, my skill will increase. — 14
The size of the word and the sequence of its — 19
letters may determine just how fast I can move to — 24
handle it. To cut time should get next attention. — 29

gwam 2′ | 1 | 2 | 3 | 4 | 5 |

19

19a ▶7

Conditioning practice

each line 3 times SS (slowly, faster, slowly); DS between 3-line groups

alphabet Jacques Voltz kept the new forms by the tax guide.
q/w Lewis Quick will work the squad if Wes Quim quits.
fluency If she turns the handle to the right, it may work.

| 1 | 2 | 3 | 4 | 5 | 6 | 7 | 8 | 9 | 10 |

19b ▶15

Goal typing: paragraphs

Three 1′ and three 2′ writings on ¶s 1–2 combined of 18d, above; determine *gwam* on each.

Goals
At least 18 *gwam* on the 1′ writings;
at least 16 *gwam* on the 2′ writings.

277b-279b, continued

Job 2
Office procedures manual

Type the copy as a leftbound manuscript. SS and indent enumerated items 5 spaces from side margins; DS between items.

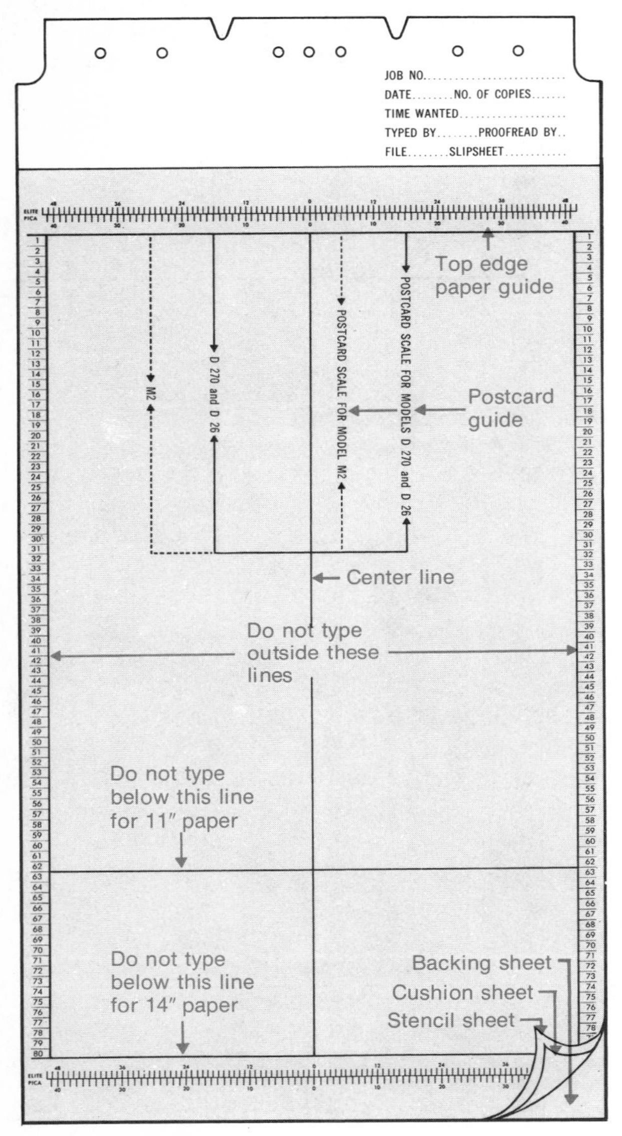

Guides for stencil

THE STENCIL DUPLICATION PROCESS

(¶ 1) Thousands of copies of typed material can be reproduced in a short time through the use of the stencil duplication process. A stencil consists of three basic parts: the stencil sheet, the backing sheet, and the cushion sheet. When a typewriter key strikes the stencil sheet, it "cuts" an impression in the shape of the type. The cushion sheet is placed between the stencil and the backing sheet to absorb the impact of the striking keys. A film sheet may be placed on the top of the stencil sheet if darker print is desired. This film also protects the stencil sheet from letter cutout when the type face is extremely sharp.

(¶ 2) Before typing the stencil, follow these steps:

1. Type a model copy of the material to be reproduced. Check it for accuracy of form and typing. Be certain that you place the copy on the page so that it will be within the stencil guide marks.
2. Clean the typewriter type thoroughly.
3. Adjust the ribbon lever to stencil position.
4. Insert the cushion sheet between the stencil sheet and the backing sheet.
5. Check the touch control to see that it is set at a point that will assure the sharpest outlines without cutting out the characters.
6. Place the top edge of the model copy at the corner marks of the stencil to see where to type the first line of the copy. The scales at the top and sides of the stencil will help you position the copy correctly.

(¶ 3) Insert the stencil assembly into the typewriter and align it correctly, exactly as you would a sheet of paper. Use a firm, uniform, staccato touch as you type. On some machines, the period and comma keys and keys with parts completely closed (such as "a," "d," "o," "p") must be struck more lightly, whereas capitals and certain letters such as "m" and "w" must be struck with greater force.

(¶ 4) If you make an error, it can be corrected easily with correction fluid. If there is a film over the stencil, this must be detached until you resume typing. Use a glass burnisher or a smooth paper clip to rub the surface of the error on the stencil sheet. Place a pencil between the stencil sheet and the cushion sheet and apply a light coating of the correction fluid over the error. Let it dry and then make the necessary correction, using a medium touch.

19c ▶8
Improve space-bar technique

each line 3 times SS (slowly, faster, slowly); DS between 3-line groups

Goal: Keep thumb resting lightly on space bar.

```
y/n/m  by my try pay day may any many forty twenty gladly
       Twenty of us may go by the city lake today to ski.

:/,/?  Date:  To:  From:  File:  should head my new form.
       Did Clay, Glenn, and Randy go to Rome? or to Bern?

       | 1 | 2 | 3 | 4 | 5 | 6 | 7 | 8 | 9 | 10 |
```

19d ▶20
Guided writing: sentences

1. Lines 1–10 once as shown.

2. A 1′ writing on each of Lines 1–8.

Goal: To type the second line of a pair at same rate as the first line.

3. As time permits, type a 1′ writing on each of Lines 5–10.

Goal: 21 *gwam*.

all letters used

		words in line	gwam 30″	gwam 20″
1	It is up to me to shape my own world.	7½	15	22
2	As a people, we shape our own future.	7½	15	22
3	I keep the antique urn by the big chair.	8	16	24
4	Let me get the picture into sharp focus.	8	16	24
5	He kept a quantity of forms for us to use.	8½	17	25
6	They are members of the cast of this play.	8½	17	25
7	Pamela may handle the six title forms for us.	9	18	27
8	Did you forward the case to the state office?	9	18	27
9	I am told the profit of the auto firms is down.	9½	19	28
10	Joy sent for a dozen pens and a box of pencils.	9½	19	28
11	Dick is to make a visit to the eight island firms.	10	20	30
12	We have seated a jury of five men and seven women.	10	20	30
13	She is to go to work for an auto firm in the spring.	10½	21	31
14	To get the right job is a real chore for each of us.	10½	21	31

| 1 | 2 | 3 | 4 | 5 | 6 | 7 | 8 | 9 | 10 |10½|

20

20a ▶7
Conditioning practice

each line 3 times SS (slowly, faster, slowly); DS between 3-line groups

```
alphabet  Bev aims next to play a quick game with Jud Fritz.

x/c       Cora cannot expect to excel on the next city exam.

fluency   Their key to the problem is to cut profit by half.

          | 1 | 2 | 3 | 4 | 5 | 6 | 7 | 8 | 9 | 10 |
```

20b ▶10
Guided writing: sentences

A 1′ writing on each even-numbered line of 19d, above; determine *gwam* on each.

Goal: 20 *gwam* on each line.

277b-279b ▶45 Production typing

You have been hired as a clerk–typist by REPRO–QUIK, Inc., 261 Delaware Avenue, Buffalo, NY 14202, a company that provides a variety of repro–graphic services.

Study and follow the job directions carefully. Strive for error–free copy.

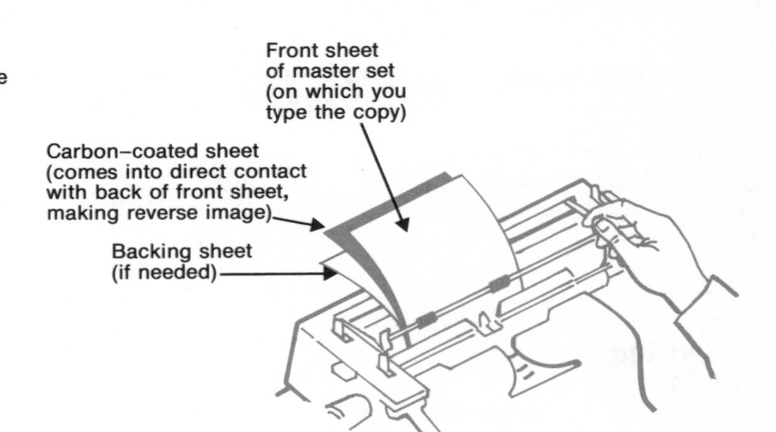

Job 1
Office procedures manual
Type the copy as a leftbound manuscript. SS and indent enumerated items 5 spaces from side margins. DS between items.

THE SPIRIT DUPLICATION PROCESS

(¶ 1) The spirit duplication process is used for reproducing copies quickly at a low cost when the appearance of the copy is not of primary importance. As many as 300 copies can be reproduced from a single master, although the usual number of copies from a single master ranges from 11 to 150. (¶ 2) The spirit master set consists of two basic parts: the master sheet and a sheet of special carbon that can be used only once. A backing sheet may also be used to obtain a better consistency of type. If a specially prepared master set is not available, simply place the carbon paper between the master sheet and the backing sheet, with the glossy side of the carbon sheet toward you. When you type, the carbon copy will be on the back of the master sheet. (¶ 3) Follow these suggestions for better masters:

1. Prepare a model copy of the material to be typed. Leave at least a one-half inch margin at the top. Check the model copy for accuracy of form and typing.
2. To avoid "fuzzy" type and filled-in characters, clean the type and use a thin ribbon. If the ribbon is too heavy, the master may be typed with the ribbon indicator in the "stencil" position. This procedure makes it difficult to proofread the copy, however.
3. Use a firm, even stroke on a nonelectric machine; type capitals a little heavier than usual and punctuation marks a little lighter. On electric type-writers, a lower setting on the impression control lever usually provides better copies.
4. If you make an error, scrape off the incorrect letter or word on the reverse side of the master sheet with a razor blade or knife. Then, rub a correction pencil over the scraped area.
5. Before correcting the error, tear off an unused portion of the carbon and slip it under the part to be retyped; remove the torn portion as soon as you have corrected the error.
6. Proofread the copy and correct any errors you may have missed before you remove the master from the typewriter.

20c ▶15 Check machine parts control

type each pair of lines twice

Lines 1-2: Clear all tab stops; set stop at center of paper; make return and tab to begin Line 1.

Line 9: Type incomplete word, then backspace and fill in missing letter.

Line 10: Use margin release and back-space 5 times into left margin to start line.

tabulator and return
1 Tab ——→ I make the return quickly
2 and begin the line without pausing.

space bar
3 I will try to boost my speed only if I find a way.
4 I will gladly pay any of the men to lay the brick.

shift keys
5 Kevin and Paul lost the first set to Alan and Sol.
6 Is Meg Spitz a charter member of Alpha Kappa Club?

shift lock
7 Was that news report carried by NBC, CBS, and ABC?
8 Francis read MARKINGS and THE GREENING OF AMERICA.

backspace key 9 j st, qu lt, ele t, ind x, e tra, let ers, fulfi l

margin release key 10 It is how you type, not just how much, that counts most now.

20d ▶18 Check keystroking speed

1. Two 1′ writings on Line 1, then on Line 2. Determine *gwam* on each.

Goals: 16 *gwam* on Line 1; 20 *gwam* on Line 2.

2. Two 1′ writings on each of the two ¶s. Determine *gwam* on each.

Goal: At least 18 *gwam*.

3. A 2′ writing on each of the two ¶s. Determine *gwam* on each (use first rate column).

Goal: At least 16 *gwam*.

4. A 2′ writing on ¶s 1–2 combined. Determine *gwam* (use second rate column).

Goal: At least 17 *gwam*.

alphabet Max Goff will zip his mail to Denver by quick jet.

fluency Rick is due by six and may go to the city with me.

| 1 | 2 | 3 | 4 | 5 | 6 | 7 | 8 | 9 | 10 |

all letters used | VE | 1.2 si | 4.9 awl | 95% hfw |

	gwam 2′	2′
If you are moving with more control now than	4	4
you were last week, you can be quite certain that	9	9
you have shown growth in typing. You can develop	14	14
as fast as you desire if you will work with zest.	19	19
For the next several days, put a little more	4	24
effort into your work; then check the increase in	9	29
speed. You will find that just a bit more effort	14	34
day by day can result in a much higher skill.	19	38

gwam 2′ | 1 | 2 | 3 | 4 | 5 |

276c ▶25 Improve basic skill: straight copy

1. A 5′ writing on the ¶s. Find *gwam*.
2. Two 2′ writings on each ¶ to increase speed. Find *gwam*.
3. A 5′ writing on the ¶s to measure improvement. Find *gwam*.

all letters used | HA | 1.6 si | 5.8 awl | 75% hfw |

	gwam 2′	5′	
Reprographics is a term so new that it has not yet found its way	6	3	60
into many of our dictionaries. In a narrow sense, the term includes	13	5	63
only the mechanics of duplicating copies of all kinds of documents. In	21	8	66
a broad sense, however, the term involves all the steps required in the	28	11	69
reproduction of materials in some graphic form. This includes planning	35	14	72
and organizing the data to be reproduced as well as deciding the most	42	17	74
practical and efficient means of duplication.	47	19	76
There are numerous factors to be considered when you plan and orga-	7	21	79
nize material for duplication. A significant factor, of course, is cost.	14	24	82
The objective is to select a duplication process that will produce the	21	27	85
lowest feasible cost per copy. The appearance of the copy in terms of	28	30	87
clarity and eye appeal must be considered. Format, size, and makeup of	35	33	90
the copy are also of primary importance. Since the time available to	42	36	93
do the job may affect quality and cost, time is a vital factor.	49	38	96
There are several kinds of duplicators that can be used to make	6	41	99
multiple copies. The spirit duplicator is the least expensive means for	14	44	101
runs of several hundred copies and can produce copies with as many as	21	46	104
five colors. The mimeograph machine can produce thousands of copies in	28	49	107
color at a low cost. If cost is not a major factor, however, the offset	35	52	110
duplicator can produce copies of finer quality. Xerographic or thermo-	42	55	113
graphic copies can be used if just a few exact copies are desired.	49	58	115

gwam 2′ | 1 | 2 | 3 | 4 | 5 | 6 | 7 |
5′ | 1 | 2 | 3 |

277-279

277a-279a ▶5 Conditioning practice

twice SS; repeat difficult lines

Government funds subsidized the expressways linking Queens to Jamaica.
Eliminate Items 825, 934, 1068, 1739, 2465, and 3701 from the catalog.
In the off-season, they perform out-of-doors in out-of-the-way places.
He named a special panel to study the problem of the acid in the lake.

| 1 | 2 | 3 | 4 | 5 | 6 | 7 | 8 | 9 | 10 | 11 | 12 | 13 | 14 |

unit **3** lessons 21–25

Improving typewriting speed/control

Learning goals

1. To improve typing techniques.
2. To improve speed/control on sentence and paragraph copy.
3. To learn to type from handwritten and rough-draft copy.
4. To learn to center headings.

Machine adjustments

1. Paper guide at *0*.
2. Ribbon control on black.
3. Margin sets: 50-space line.
4. Line-space selector on *1* for drills; on *2* for paragraphs and problems.

21

21a ▶7 Conditioning practice

each line 3 times SS (slowly, faster, slowly); DS between 3-line groups

alphabet Bev saw a quick lynx jump down from that zoo cage.

space bar try sky say play any many rainy fancy fifty eighty

fluency It is their duty to lend a man a hand if they can.

| 1 | 2 | 3 | 4 | 5 | 6 | 7 | 8 | 9 | 10 |

21b ▶15 Improve keystroking technique: response patterns

Lines 1-6: Each line once from dictation.

Lines 7-9: Two 1′ *speed* writings on each line; compare *gwam*.

Goals: To speed up on easy words and to type difficult ones with continuity.

word response
1 an and end did due air own she six men may but big
2 and may|the jam|for six|but she|did own|an end cut

letter response
3 my get him few you war oil far pin act him age mop
4 you set|oil car|get him|bad pun|few kin|set my tax

combination response
5 due bad big age man oil own act sir set but ago no
6 for you|due him|and get|may set|zoo fee|she saw us

word 7 She is to pay the eight men for the work they did.
letter 8 I see you set my rate after you saw my data cards.
combination 9 Quig may be the best, but my men will not give up.

| 1 | 2 | 3 | 4 | 5 | 6 | 7 | 8 | 9 | 10 |

21c ▶8 Learn to type from script (handwritten) copy

1. Type the ¶s once without timing to become familiar with typing from script.
2. A 1′ writing on each ¶; determine *gwam* on each.
Goal: At least 17 *gwam*.

	gwam 1′	2′
This copy is written with pen and ink; it is	9	4
called script. I may be able to type it about as	19	9
fast as I can type copy that is shown in print.	28	14
I must read with care to do this, since each	9	19
letter may not be exactly formed. I also have to	19	24
decide on the spacing to use after punctuation.	28	28

lessons 276–300

Specialized office simulations

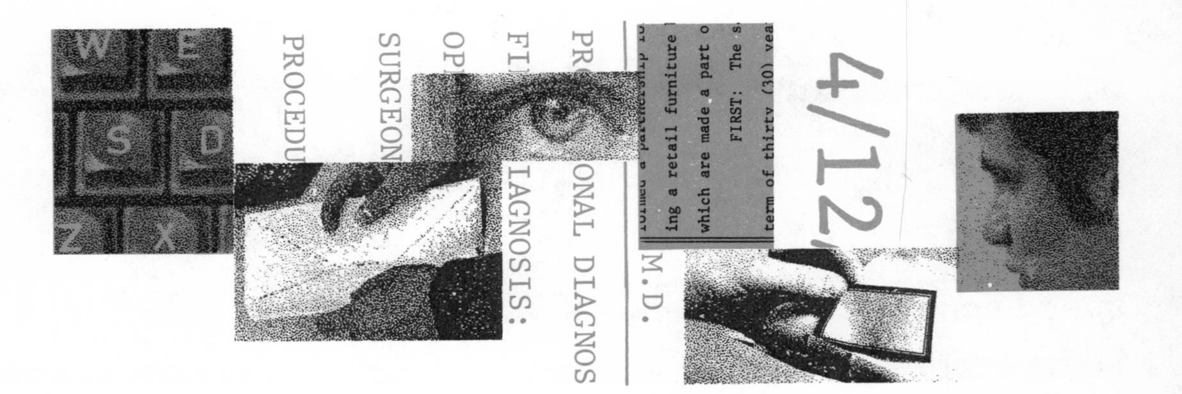

Learning goals

Phase 12 provides realistic practice on typical tasks performed by typists in specialized offices which require the application of basic knowledge, skills, and concepts previously learned.

As you type the material, strive to:

1. Plan, organize, and complete your work with a minimum of supervision.

2. Increase your speed and accuracy in typing production material.

3. Produce typewritten materials that are attractive and free from error.

Machine adjustments

1. Line: 70 for drills and timed writings.

2. Spacing: SS sentence drills; DS ¶s; space problems as directed.

lessons 276–279

Reprographic office typing

276

276a ▶5 Conditioning practice

twice SS; repeat difficult lines

alphabet	Sit back, relax, and enjoy the view and the amazing aquatic performer.
figures	For further information, call 672-3928 between 8:30 a.m. and 4:15 p.m.
fig/sym	The total (as of June 30, 1975) was $12,450,800--an increase of 26.5%.
fluency	The price of the item will depend on the quantity and quality desired.

| 1 | 2 | 3 | 4 | 5 | 6 | 7 | 8 | 9 | 10 | 11 | 12 | 13 | 14 |

276b ▶20 Improve speed/control: sentence guided writings

1. A 15″, 12″, and 10″ speed spurt writing on each sentence.

2. A 1′ writing on each sentence at a speed you can type without error.

		gwam 15″	12″	10″
double letters	The letter will tell the supplier to send the cotton goods by express.	56	70	84
short words	I feel if it is to be, it will be; if it is not to be, it will not be.	56	70	84
long words	Changing technology frequently necessitates operational modifications.	56	70	84
direct reaches	Did your secretary receive a carbon copy of my annual progress report?	56	70	84
left hand	Wages and prices were affected to a great extent by increased tariffs.	56	70	84
right hand	In my opinion, it is poor policy to use nonunion help at my pulp mill.	56	70	84
balanced-hand	If the men fix the dial on the panel box, they will finish their work.	56	70	84

| 1 | 2 | 3 | 4 | 5 | 6 | 7 | 8 | 9 | 10 | 11 | 12 | 13 | 14 |

21d ▶20 Guided writing: paragraphs

Select a practice goal:

1. Type a 1′ writing on ¶ 1; determine *gwam*.

2. Using the *gwam* as a base, add 4 *gwam* to determine your *goal* rate.

3. Choose from Column 1 of the following table the speed nearest your goal rate. At the right of that speed, note the ¼′ points in the copy you must reach to maintain your goal rate.

gwam	Q1	Q2	Q3	Time
16	4	8	12	16
20	5	10	15	20
24	6	12	18	24
28	7	14	21	28
32	8	16	24	32

4. Note from the word-count dots and figures above the lines in ¶ 1 the checkpoint for each quarter minute. [Checkpoints for 24 *gwam* are 6, 12, 18, and 24.]

Practice procedure

1. Two 1′ *speed* writings on ¶ 1 at your goal rate guided by the quarter-minute calls: *one*, *two*, *three*, *time*.

2. Type ¶ 2 in the same way.

3. A 2′ writing on ¶s 1–2 combined without the guides.

4. A 3′ *control* writing on ¶s 1–2 combined without the guides.

Speed level of practice
When the purpose of practice is to reach out into new speed areas, use the *speed* level. Take the brakes off your fingers and experiment with new stroking patterns and new speeds.

Control level of practice
When the purpose of practice is to type with ease and control, drop back in rate 2 to 4 *gwam* below the speed level and emphasize *control* (good techniques; improved accuracy).

To determine *gwam* for 2′ and 3′ writings: Use appropriate column at right for completed lines; use appropriate scale below ¶s for partial line.

all letters used | E | 1.3 si | 5.2 awl | 90% hfw

	gwam 2′	3′
When I explore new typing speed zones, I try	4	3
my best to control every move I make. Every move	9	6
must be made quickly and in a correct manner. By	14	10
making this a major objective, I can find success.	19	13
When I lower the typing speed, there is more	24	16
time to attend to my work habits. If I lower the	29	19
speed two to four words a minute, I will increase	34	23
control and cut the number of copy mistakes, also.	39	26

gwam 2′ | 1 | 2 | 3 | 4 | 5
3′ | 1 | 2 | 3

22

22a ▶7 Conditioning practice

each line 3 times SS (slowly, faster, slowly); DS between 3-line groups

alphabet Glenda saw a quick red fox jump over the lazy cub.

shift keys Klaus and I were in St. Paul for a week in August.

fluency The firm also owns the big sign by the town field.

| 1 | 2 | 3 | 4 | 5 | 6 | 7 | 8 | 9 | 10 |

22b ▶20 Guided writing: paragraphs

Repeat 21d, above.

274c-275c, continued

Problem 5
Leftbound report with footnote

words

THE OFFICE IN THE FUTURE 5

What ~~is in~~ *does* the future *hold* for ~~persons~~ *those* who wish to ~~follow~~ *pursue* careers 18

as office ~~employees?~~ *workers?* Experts predict that there will be amazing 30

changes in the ~~business~~ office of the future. Video Telephones *(l.c.)*, al- 42

ready in ~~some~~ *limited* use, will be~~come~~ common place. All ~~correspondence~~ *messages* will 54

be ~~sent~~ *transmitted* through the air by ~~electrical~~ *electronic* means and will be reproduced on 70

recieving sets in either the home or the office. ~~Letters~~ *All correspondence* will be 86

filed in the ~~storage area~~ *memory bank* of a central computer. To retreive a letter, 100

an individual will merely ~~punch~~ *type* the number of the letter into a con- 113

sole and ~~it~~ *the letter* will appear on ~~his TV~~ *a video* screen. If it is ~~desired,~~ *needed,* a paper 129

copy can be made on a ~~regular~~ *special* copier. 136

Will automation eliminate the ~~necessity~~ *need* for the office worker? 148

Far from it. ~~Instead of being eliminated, the demand for office workers~~ 160

~~will increase by millions as business expands.~~ However, these workers, 173

will need to work and study to keep up with the rapid ~~technological~~ 184

advances *in technology*. As more ~~sophisticated~~ *complex* equipment is ~~utilized,~~ *put in use,* they must learn 201

to be ~~proficient~~ *experts* in its use. Above all, they must ~~expand~~ *grow* with the ~~many~~ 213

changes and, if they are to succeed, use their ~~abilities~~ *talents* to create new 227

and ~~better~~ *more efficient* ways to work. 232

"Employment of office workers is expected to increase rapidly through the mid-1980s."[1]

236

---

[1] U.S. Department of Labor, Occupational Outlook Handbook (Washington, D.C.: Government Printing Office, 1974), p. 86. 249 259 265

22c ▶15 Improve keystroking technique: response patterns

Lines 1-6: Once from dictation.

Lines 7-9: Two 1′ *speed* writings on each line; compare *gwam*.

Goal: To type with smooth, but variable, rhythm on Line 9.

word response
1 they form firm them lend hand half with also signs
2 they did | for them | with us | he also | half of | the sign

letter response
3 care card save rest read base only ever upon cases
4 my area | face up | in fact | only him | you save | tax base

combination response
5 they jump lend gave half free land serve into quiz
6 the rate | they save | with care | he reads | she did only

word 7 Sign the form for the city to pay the eight girls.
letter 8 You gave only a few facts in my case on oil taxes.
combination 9 Lana gave a talk on the state of art in the world.

| 1 | 2 | 3 | 4 | 5 | 6 | 7 | 8 | 9 | 10 |

22d ▶8 Learn to type from rough-draft copy

Rough draft
Typewritten copy that is corrected with pen or pencil is called *rough draft*. Some common marks that proofreaders use for correcting copy are shown at the right. Study them before typing the rough-draft copy shown below.

Proofreader's marks

∧	insert	#	add space	¶	paragraph
∽	transpose	⁀	close up	lc /	lowercase
℘	delete	⊙	insert period	⊐	move right
Cap or ≡	capitalize	∧,	insert comma	⊏	move left

Practice procedure

1. Type ¶s 1–2 once without timing to become familiar with typing from rough draft.

2. A 1′ writing on each ¶; determine *gwam* for each.

Goal: At least 14 *gwam*.

	gwam 1′	2′
The ease ∧(with) which I can hand(el) rough draft	9	4
depends largely upon ~~on~~ how rough ∧(the) corrected copy	19	9
is. ≡this copy is(#)quite easy compared to so me⊙	28	14
¶ To handle rough draft well ∧, I must learn how	9	19
(lc) To use correction ∧(marks) ~~symbols~~.(#)I must ∧(also) be alert to	19	24
⊐changes by reading ahead in(#)the copy I am typing.	29	28

23

23a ▶7 Conditioning practice

each line 3 times SS (slowly, faster, slowly); DS between 3-line groups

alphabet Jeb Dietz could have Wes Kopf fix my antique ring.
shift lock Read these books: THE RIGHT JOB and EASY WRITING.
fluency Both of us may aid the busy auditor with the work.

| 1 | 2 | 3 | 4 | 5 | 6 | 7 | 8 | 9 | 10 |

23b ▶8 Type from rough-draft copy

1. A 1′ writing on each ¶ of 22d, above; determine *gwam*.
Goal: At least 15 *gwam*.

2. Two 2′ writings on the 2 ¶s combined; determine *gwam*.
Goal: At least 14 *gwam*.

Problem 2 [LM p. 165]
Interoffice memorandum

words

TO: All Department Heads FROM: D. C. Kearns Director of Administration 12
DATE: June 9, 19-- SUBJECT: Central Purchasing (¶ 1) Effective July 1, a 23
central purchasing office will be established within the Administrative Branch. 39
This office will purchase all common supplies and equipment used by all 53
departments. (¶ 2) Requests for supplies and equipment should be sub- 66
mitted to the Administrative Division on a purchase requisition at least 90 81
days prior to the date desired. The purchase requisition should include a 96
detailed description of the goods, the quantity to be ordered, and the 110
desired delivery date. If possible, it should also include the name and 125
address of a firm from which the goods may be purchased, the catalog num- 139
ber, and the price of each item. Emergency purchases required within a 153
period of less than 90 days must include a complete justification for the 168
emergency action. 172

Problem 3 [LM p. 165]
Purchase order

words

To: R. W. Simpson Tool Co., Inc. Purchase Order No. 23306-F 7
200 East Market Street Date August 7, 19-- 15
Indianapolis, IN 46204 Terms Net 20
Ship Via Coastal Van Lines 24

Quantity	Cat. No.	Description	Price	Total	words
20	8R1297	Combination wrench sets	17.89	357.80	33
20	8R3922	Drive tool sets	15.50	310.00	41
50	8R6022	Flex-head ratchets, 12 mm drive	5.10	255.00	52
15	8T3101	Micrometers, 0.25 mm	7.95	119.25	62
				1,042.05	64

Problem 4
Table
reading position;
DS items

words

MUIR MANUFACTURING CO. 5

Financial Highlights 9

(1967-1976) 11

Year	Total Sales (Millions)	Net Income (Millions)	Earnings Per Share (Dollars)	words
				29 / 36
1976	$201.6	$12.1	$2.08	41
1975	186.7	10.6	2.01	45
1974	177.8	10.3	1.94	49
1973	171.0	10.1	1.86	54
1972	166.1	9.9	1.80	58
1971	165.3	9.8	1.80	62
1970	160.5	9.6	1.75	66
1969	145.9	7.3	1.60	70
1968	143.2	8.6	1.65	74
1967	141.7	7.1	1.59	77

23c ▶15 Improve keystroking technique

type drill at least twice

Lines 1-3: Keep fingers upright over keys. Think vigorously adjacent-key sequences (*er*, *re*, *tr*, *rt*, *po*, *op*, *ui*, *oi*, and *io*).

Lines 4-6: Make *direct* reaches for consecutive strokes by same finger (*hy*, *ce*, *mu*, *un*, *gr*, *rv*, *ce*, *bt*, *un*, *nu*, *um*, *yn*, *br*, and *hu*). Bypass home-key position.

Lines 7-9: Use short, quick strokes for double-letter sequences such as *ll*, *oo*, *ss*, *ee*, *ff*, and *tt*. Strike key twice in quick succession.

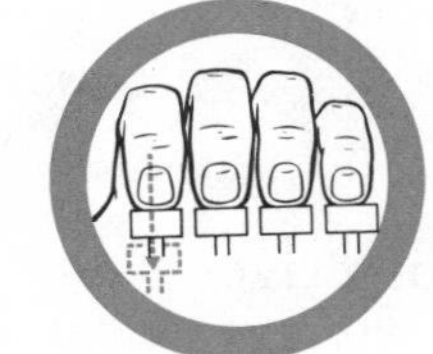

Curved, upright fingers

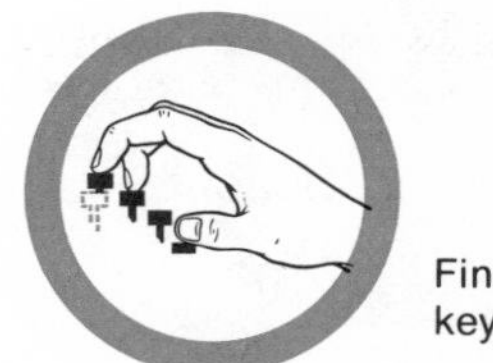

Finger-action keystroking

adjacent keys
1 term mere sort trip ever very post shop easy suits
2 going points credit reports proper serious periods
3 Vera did buy a top coin last night at an art sale.

consecutive direct reaches
4 why ice nice cent once much fund pound group curve
5 pieces recent except obtain doubts country numbers
6 Lynn found a gold nugget; it brought a huge price.

double letters
7 full took food loss issue seems steel offer little
8 fill still sheet three unless matter happen accept
9 Jessica is sorry that all her efforts seem wasted.

| 1 | 2 | 3 | 4 | 5 | 6 | 7 | 8 | 9 | 10 |

23d ▶20 Guided writing: paragraphs

Type a 1′ writing on ¶ 1; determine *gwam*. Add 4 *gwam* to set a new goal rate; then type additional writings as follows:

¶ 1: Two 1′ guided *speed* writings at your goal rate.

¶ 2: Two 1′ guided *speed* writings in the same way.

¶s 1-2: Two 2′ *speed* writings on ¶s 1–2 combined; determine *gwam* on the better writing.

¶s 1-3: A 3′ unguided *control* writing on ¶s 1–3 combined; determine *gwam*; circle errors.

Goals
1′ writing: At least 20 *gwam*.
2′ writing: At least 19 *gwam*.
3′ writing: At least 18 *gwam*.

all letters used | E | 1.3 si | 5.2 awl | 90% hfw |

	gwam 2′	3′
As you type, read the copy carefully; but do	4	3
more than that. Think each word, also. Focusing	9	6
on a word may aid in stroking easy words as units.	14	10
You must realize that some words have letter	19	13
sequences that are hard to type. These are often	24	16
traps for a new typist who does not yet know them.	29	20
Your major purpose now should be to learn to	33	22
type the easy words faster and to lower the speed	38	26
for hard ones. Learn to vary your speed expertly.	43	29

gwam 2′ | 1 | 2 | 3 | 4 | 5 |
3′ | 1 | 2 | 3 |

274c-275c, continued

Problem 4 [LM p. 161]
Purchase requisition

				words
Deliver to:	T. M. Stacy	Requisition No.	4872-3	4
Location:	Shop 3	Date	June 28, 19--	8
Job No.	T-431	Date Required	August 5, 19--	12

Quantity	Description	words
100	Grease seal driver sets	18
500 ft.	Insulated primary wire, 18 gauge, white	27
40	Master disconnect switches, 12 volt	35
300 ft.	Seamless copper tubing, 1 cm diameter	44
300 ft.	Seamless copper tubing, 2 cm diameter	53

Problem 5
Table
reading position; DS items

MUIR MANUFACTURING CO.

Production of 940C Assembly During 19--

Month	Total	Acceptable	words
			5
			13
			21
January	1,311	1,245	25
February	1,296	1,213	29
March	1,340	1,273	33
April	1,487	1,413	37
May	1,165	1,107	40
June	1,272	1,196	43
July	1,198	1,162	47
August	1,254	1,191	50
September	1,376	1,334	55
October	1,395	1,325	59
November	1,274	1,223	63
December	1,099	1,033	70
Total	15,467	14,715	75

Test 2

Problem 1 [LM p. 163]
Business letter
modified block with indented ¶s; mixed

words

April 12, 19-- Bolton & Paulsen, Inc. 7 Bull Street Savannah, GA 31401 Atten- 15
tion Mr. J. T. Mills, Sales Manager Ladies and Gentlemen (¶ 1) On April 28
6, 19--, we were forced to discontinue production on our 73Y29 assembly 43
because the assembly did not meet quality control standards. After exhaus- 58
tive investigation, we found that the cause of the trouble was your DV-830 73
coupling. (¶ 2) Tests made by our Quality Control Division revealed that 86
your couplings measure 4 cm x 3.8 cm. The specifications under which the 101
couplings were ordered provided for 4 cm x 4 cm couplings with a tolerance 116
of not more than ± .1 cm. A random sample of 10,000 couplings received 130
under our Order CP-50794 indicates that all of them are defective. (¶ 3) 144
Fortunately, we have sufficient couplings of the correct size to continue 159
production for 30 more days. In the meantime, will you please take action 174
to replace the defective couplings. Yours very truly MUIR MANUFACTURING 188
CO. Susan C. Boston Director of Purchasing (151) 197/208

24

24a ▶7 Conditioning practice

each line 3 times SS (slowly, faster, slowly); DS between 3-line groups

alphabet	Van glazed my floors with wax after Jeb Peck quit.
space bar	I heard him say for us to stay on the beaten path.
fluency	To do the work right is the duty of all the girls.

| 1 | 2 | 3 | 4 | 5 | 6 | 7 | 8 | 9 | 10 |

24b ▶8 Type from script (handwritten) copy

1. Each line once untimed to explore stroking patterns and to improve skill when typing from script copy.

2. Each line twice with the 20″ call of the guide. Try to complete each line as "Return" is called.

Goal: At least 20 *gwam.*

		gwam 20″
1	Art is to test the six cars.	17
2	You and I are to set the rate.	18
3	Al gave us the facts of the case.	20
4	Pam was to get the big case of jam.	21
5	Jim works at the big mill on the lake.	23
6	Zoe gave me the cards for the oil tests.	24
7	The queen sat in the red chair at my right.	26

24c ▶15 Individualize your practice

each line once, noting awkward combinations; repeat those lines that caused you difficulty

Emphasized letters are used a minimum of 4 times in the line.

a/b	Alma Borbon has broken a swim record at that club.
c/d	Daily practice did cause increases in their speed.
e/f	Flo offered to finish the entire report by Friday.
g/h	Hugh Briggs is handling the funds for both groups.
i/j	In my judgment, Jill is just the girl for the job.
k/l	Kyle is willing to check the books of Kohler, Inc.
m/n	He designed some of those modern mailing machines.
o/p	It is company policy to share part of its profits.
q/r	Her request requires a quick reply of top quality.
s/t	This clerk surely types over forty words a minute.
u/v	Marv ought to review fully various musical events.
w/x	Will the six women explain this tax law next week?
y/z	Roz was truly puzzled by a young boy in the plaza.

| 1 | 2 | 3 | 4 | 5 | 6 | 7 | 8 | 9 | 10 |

274c-275c ▶40 Production skill measurement

1. Type the problems in each test for 30'; correct errors as you type. Since only usable problems will count, proofread and correct each page before you remove it from the typewriter.

2. If you finish before time is called, start over.

Test 1

words

Problem 1 [LM p. 159]
Block style letter, open

April 3, 19-- Darlington Manufacturing Company 1601 Ninth Street Tulsa, OK 74120 Ladies and Gentlemen (¶ 1) Your order No. C-53492 of March 9 for special electronic components is now being processed. We are very sorry that your order has been delayed by a strike at the plant of one of our major suppliers. We were forced to discontinue production for several days until we were able to find another source of supply. (¶ 2) Your order will be shipped to you no later than April 11. To express our appreciation for your patience, we shall pay the additional costs in shipping the order by air express. (¶ 3) You will be interested in the enclosed advance copy of a new supplemental price list. If you act quickly, you will be able to build your inventory of standard parts at reduced prices. We can guarantee prompt shipment of these items immediately upon receipt of your order. Sincerely yours Stanley F. Pajak Director of Sales (153)

14 27 41 56 71 85 100 116 130 145 161 176 184/**197**

Problem 2
Unbound report

CREDIT AND THE CONSUMER (¶ 1) Credit has played a vital role in the growth of our nation. Most of us are unable to pay cash for expensive items such as automobiles and refrigerators. This financial barrier was broken into small, periodic payments by the use of installment credit. As a result, the market for goods grew very rapidly. The huge demands of the consumer enabled producers to exploit the economics of mass production which, in turn, led to lower prices and goods of better quality. (¶ 2) As a consumer, you must learn to use credit wisely. Although credit is a valuable asset, there is always a danger you may go too far into debt. You must learn to exercise reasonable restraint and to resist the temptation to buy that expensive car when you really cannot afford to do so. By careful budgeting, you can determine just how much money you can afford to allot monthly for credit purchases. Careful planning will help you keep out of financial trouble and will help you to get more of the many things you want in life--through credit.

14 29 45 60 75 90 103 118 133 148 163 177 193 208

Problem 3 [LM p. 161]
Interoffice memorandum

TO: J. Murray Strock, Legal Counsel FROM: Susan C. Boston, Director of Purchasing DATE: June 3, 19-- SUBJECT: Defective Components (¶ 1) On February 17, 19--, we ordered 10,000 couplings from Bolton & Paulsen, Inc., 7 Bull Street, Savannah, GA 31401. Payment for the couplings was made on March 24. (¶ 2) After the couplings were received, it was found that they did not meet the specifications set forth in the order. We have made several attempts to have the couplings replaced, but Bolton & Paulsen refuse to do so. (¶ 3) Attached are the order and all correspondence relating to this matter. Will you please review this material to determine what legal steps we can take to solve the problem.

12 22 36 50 64 79 94 107 123 132/**148**

24d ▶20 Guided writing: paragraphs

Type a 1′ writing on ¶ 1; determine *gwam*. Add 4 *gwam* to set a new goal rate; then type additional writings as follows:

¶ 1: Two 1′ guided *speed* writings at your goal rate.

¶ 2: Two 1′ guided *speed* writings in the same way.

¶s 1-2: Two 2′ *speed* writings on ¶s 1–2 combined; determine *gwam* on the better writing.

¶s 1-3: A 3′ unguided *control* writing on ¶s 1–3 combined; determine *gwam*; circle errors.

Goals
1′ writing: At least 22 *gwam*.
2′ writing: At least 21 *gwam*.
3′ writing: At least 19 *gwam*.

all letters used | E | 1.3 si | 5.2 awl | 90% hfw

	gwam 2′	3′
Be sure to take good position at the machine	4	3
when you type. Balance is vital, for it will cut	9	6
tension. Try to stay in this same alert position.	14	10
If you are working toward a high speed, keep	19	13
the carriage moving. Put your mind in charge and	24	16
let it direct each motion needed to type the copy.	29	19
Speed is often a question of timing now. If	33	22
you can adjust your speed to the character of the	38	26
copy, you should expect to extend your speed zone.	43	29

gwam 2′ | 1 | 2 | 3 | 4 | 5
3′ | 1 | 2 | 3

25

25a ▶7 Conditioning practice

each line 3 times SS (slowly, faster, slowly); DS between 3-line groups

alphabet Virgil Quin has packed twenty boxes of prize jams.
shift keys Has Donna gone to St. Paul? and Vic, to Las Vegas?
fluency The girls go by bus to visit the six island firms.

| 1 | 2 | 3 | 4 | 5 | 6 | 7 | 8 | 9 | 10 |

25b ▶8 Check keystroking speed: sentences

two 1′ *speed* writings on each sentence; determine *gwam* on each

Goals
Line 1, 25 *gwam*.
Line 2, 20 *gwam*.
Line 3, 23 *gwam*.

word Pay them for the sign work they do if it is right.
letter Test awards are based only upon faster base rates.
combination It is great for him to be able to get such a wage.

| 1 | 2 | 3 | 4 | 5 | 6 | 7 | 8 | 9 | 10 |

274-275

274a-275a ▶2 Conditioning practice

once SS;
repeat Line 3

Six days of hazy weather have delayed a ski jumping contest in Quebec.
We served 1,428 meals on May 30; 2,569 on June 1; and 3,708 on June 2.
Some of the items on display may not be sold during this special sale.

| 1 | 2 | 3 | 4 | 5 | 6 | 7 | 8 | 9 | 10 | 11 | 12 | 13 | 14 |

274b-275b ▶8 Measure basic skill: straight copy

a 5′ writing;
find *gwam* and errors

all letters used | A | 1.5 si | 5.6 awl | 80% hfw |

	gwam 5′	
Although there is usually a great demand for office workers, it is	3	61
not always easy to find just the right job. Set your sights on a job	5	64
that pays a good salary, offers pleasant working conditions, and pro-	8	66
vides opportunities for promotion. The first step in finding a good	11	69
job is to locate job vacancies. Your instructors and your guidance	14	72
counselor may be able to help you do so. You can also scan the want	16	75
ads in the newspaper and visit state or private employment agencies.	19	77
When you locate a job vacancy that interests you, you are faced	22	80
with the challenge of selling yourself to the employer. You can do so	25	83
through a letter of application, a personal data sheet, and an inter-	27	86
view. Your letter and personal data sheet should be neat, attractive,	30	88
and typed without error. The letter should arouse interest and create	33	91
a desire on the part of the employer to hire you. Your personal data	36	94
sheet must reflect that you have the skills and ability to do the job.	39	97
If you receive a call to report for an interview, it means that	41	99
the company was impressed by your letter and personal data sheet and	44	102
wants an opportunity to size up your personal traits. Look your very	47	105
best when you go for the interview; be sure to avoid extremes in attire	50	108
and grooming. Listen carefully to the questions asked in the course of	53	111
the interview. Your answers should be direct, honest, and polite. If	56	113
you make a favorable impression, the chances are the job will be yours.	58	116

gwam 5′ | 1 | 2 | 3 |

25c ▶20 Check keystroking speed: paragraphs

1. Two 1′ *speed* writings on each of the ¶s; determine *gwam* for each; record the best of the 6 writings.

Goal: At least 24 *gwam.*

2. Two 2′ *control* writings on ¶s 1–3 combined; determine *gwam* on each writing; record the better rate.

Goal: At least 22 *gwam.*

3. Two 3′ *control* writings on ¶s 1–3 combined; determine *gwam* on each writing; record the better rate.

Goal: At least 20 *gwam.*

all letters used | E | 1.3 si | 5.2 awl | 90% hfw

	gwam 2′	3′
Establish a daily work goal; then keep it in	4	3
mind while you practice. Work toward it by doing	9	6
expertly all that is within your power to try now.	14	10
You do not attain success easily or quickly.	19	13
It costs much time and effort. There is no magic	24	16
road to success, now or ever. It means hard work.	29	20
It is a good feeling to complete whatever we	33	22
start to do. A major sign of our success lies in	38	26
what we learn through the maze of vexing problems.	43	29

gwam 2′ | 1 | 2 | 3 | 4 | 5
3′ | 1 | 2 | 3

25d ▶15 Learn to center headings

Get ready to center

1. Insert paper with left edge at *0.*

2. Move left margin stop to *0;* move right margin stop to right end of scale.

3. Clear all tab stops; set a new stop at horizontal center of paper: elite, 50; pica, 42.

How to center

1. Tabulate to center of paper.

2. From center, backspace *once* for each *2* letters, spaces, figures, or punctuation marks in the line:

Backspace once:
◀1 1 1 1 1
GU | ID | ES | space T | 0 space
and so forth.

3. Do not backspace for an odd or leftover stroke at the end of the line.

4. Begin to type where backspacing ends.

Drill 1

Center on a separate line each heading at the right. TS after the first one; DS after each of the others.

Drill 2

Reset left margin stop for a 50–space line. Insert a plain sheet of paper. Space down about 9 lines. Center the heading

GUIDES TO TYPING SUCCESS

TS and set a new tab stop 5 spaces to right of left margin. Type as much of the three ¶s of 25c as you can in the time remaining.

GUIDES TO TYPING SUCCESS
TS
Daily Work Goals
DS
Time, Effort, and Hard Work
DS
Finish What You Start

Enrichment material for Unit 3 appears on LM pp. 9, 10.

273

273a ▶5 Conditioning practice

twice SS;
repeat difficult lines

Karl adjusted a few valves to equalize pressure in the oxygen chamber.
Tour 631 departs June 29; Tour 745 on July 6; and Tour 892 on July 10.
John ("Buzz") Kenton is 6'9" tall; Ralph ("Skip") Cutler is 7'1" tall.
Perhaps they will have a special sale on these items during the month.

| 1 | 2 | 3 | 4 | 5 | 6 | 7 | 8 | 9 | 10 | 11 | 12 | 13 | 14 |

273b ▶45 Compose a letter of application

Compose at the typewriter a letter of application, similar to the one at the right, for one of the following jobs which have been advertised in your local newspaper:

Clerk-typist
Stenographer
Bookkeeping clerk
Keypunch operator

Use your home address for the return address and the letter style you prefer. Address the letter to Mr. Sean A. McPherson, Personnel Director, Associated Department Stores, Inc., 4800 Sixth Street, your city, state, and ZIP Code.

In the letter, tell Mr. McPherson:

1. You are replying to the advertisement in the newspaper.

2. When you will be graduated from high school and available for work.

3. Why you believe you are qualified to fill the position. Include your major field, the specific courses you have taken, and any special skills you possess, plus your work experience.

4. You are enclosing a personal data sheet.

Give any other information you think will strengthen your application.

After you have composed the letter, make any needed pencil corrections, and retype the letter in good form.

5517 Elmwood Avenue
Philadelphia, PA 19143
May 2, 19--

Mr. Sean A. McPherson, Personnel Director
Associated Department Stores, Inc.
4800 Sixth Street
Philadelphia, PA 19120

Dear Mr. McPherson:

Your advertisement in the Philadelphia Inquirer indicates that you have a vacancy for a stenographer. If you are looking for a young woman with a solid background in secretarial skills, your search is over.

On June 4, I shall complete my studies at Roosevelt High School. My general field of study has been business education. This program includes courses in general business, machines, business correspondence, typewriting, shorthand, and office practice. In addition, I shall complete the required general courses such as English and mathematics.

I can type 65 words a minute on straight-copy material and take dictation at a rate of 120 words a minute, and I can apply these skills in the production of letters, reports, tables, and other business papers. I have been active in school organizations. Last year I was secretary of the student government association and was elected to the National Honor Society. This year I am President of the Future Business Leaders of America. The enclosed personal data sheet will give you additional information.

When you consider my skills, work experience, and participation in school activities, I feel sure you will agree that I possess the qualifications to succeed in a stenographic position. May I come for an interview at a time that is convenient for you? If you wish to call me, my telephone number is 349-5621.

Sincerely yours,

Beverly A. Dorman

Beverly A. Dorman

Enclosure

Statistical typing and basic applications

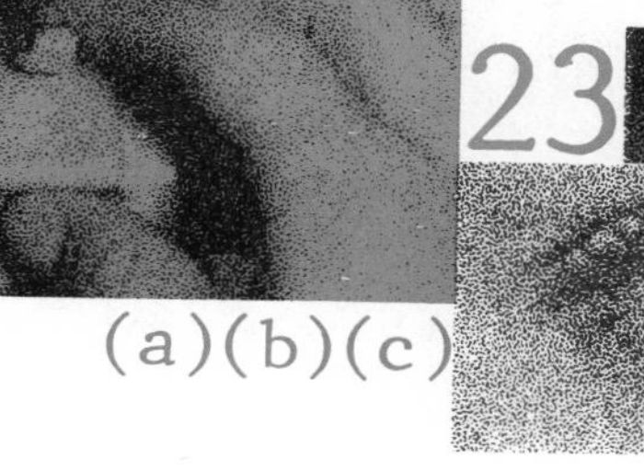

Learning goals

In the 25 lessons of this phase, you will:

1. Learn to type figures and basic symbols by touch and with good techniques.
2. Increase speed/control on straight copy, script, rough draft, and statistical copy.
3. Apply your basic skills in preparing simple personal and business papers.

Machine adjustments

1. Paper guide at *0*.
2. Ribbon control on *black*.
3. Left margin set at center − 30 for 60-space line; right margin set at right end of scale.
4. Line-space selector on *1* for drills; on *2* for ¶s; as directed for problems.

Up to now most copy has been shown in typewriter type. In Phase 2 much of the copy is shown in printer's type. Continue to type it line for line as shown, unless otherwise directed.

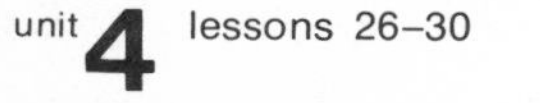

unit 4 lessons 26–30

The figure keys

26

26a ▶7 Conditioning practice

each line 3 times SS (slowly, faster, slowly); DS between 3-line groups

alphabet Jack Waven dozed off as he quietly prepped for his big exam.

letter l as 1 The 11 men and 111 boys fly to Rome on July 1 on Charter 11.

fluency Nell did sign the usual title forms for the eight box firms.

| 1 | 2 | 3 | 4 | 5 | 6 | 7 | 8 | 9 | 10 | 11 | 12 |

26b ▶12 Improve technique: service keys

each pair of lines twice

Line 1: Clear tab stops; set new stop at center of paper; return and tab to begin Line 1.

Line 7: Type an incomplete word as shown; then backspace and fill in missing letter.

Line 8: Set right margin stop: center + 30. Depress margin release key; backspace 5 spaces and start the line. When carriage locks, depress margin release key and complete the line.

tabulator and return
1 Tab ——————→ Tab to the stop; type the line
2 quickly; then return and begin the new line without pausing.

space bar
3 Penny will be very happy if you delay your party until July.
4 I may boost our sales price if they raise the oil tax again.

shift keys and lock
5 Tony Chiodi and Jay Ribolt play Ivan Yates and Nick Billson.
6 Jill works for USAFI in Cologne; Karen, for NASA in Houston.

backspacer
7 e pect scho l so th wor h thi d din er s ace ac ount p zzled

margin release
8 There is no better time than now to do all your work in the right way.

unit **48** lessons 272–275

Employment activity typing

Learning goals

1. To provide typing experiences typical of those you will encounter when applying for a job.

2. To measure speed and accuracy on straight–copy material.

3. To measure ability to type letters, reports, and forms and tables.

272

272a ▶5 Conditioning practice

twice SS; repeat difficult lines

alphabet The board will fight the complex request to raze or move the junkyard.

figures The rate increased in 1963, 1964, 1968, 1970, 1972, and again in 1975.

fig/sym Model 80-C sells for $4, Model 63-B for $7, and Model 21-A for $19.75.

fluency Does the original study show the total quantity of materials required?

| 1 | 2 | 3 | 4 | 5 | 6 | 7 | 8 | 9 | 10 | 11 | 12 | 13 | 14 |

272b ▶45 Compose a personal data sheet

Compose at the typewriter a data sheet similar to the one at the right. Arrange the material attractively on the page. Include information under each of these principal categories:

1. *Personal data*: age, place of birth, height and weight, etc.

2. *Education*: name of high school, major field, and perhaps something about your scholastic achievement.

3. *School Activities*: school activities in which you have participated or any honors you have earned.

4. *Work Experience*: any work experience you have had, including part-time jobs.

5. *References*: three references other than relatives. Indicate that you have permission to use the names as references.

After you have composed the data sheet, make any needed pencil corrections and retype the data sheet in good form.

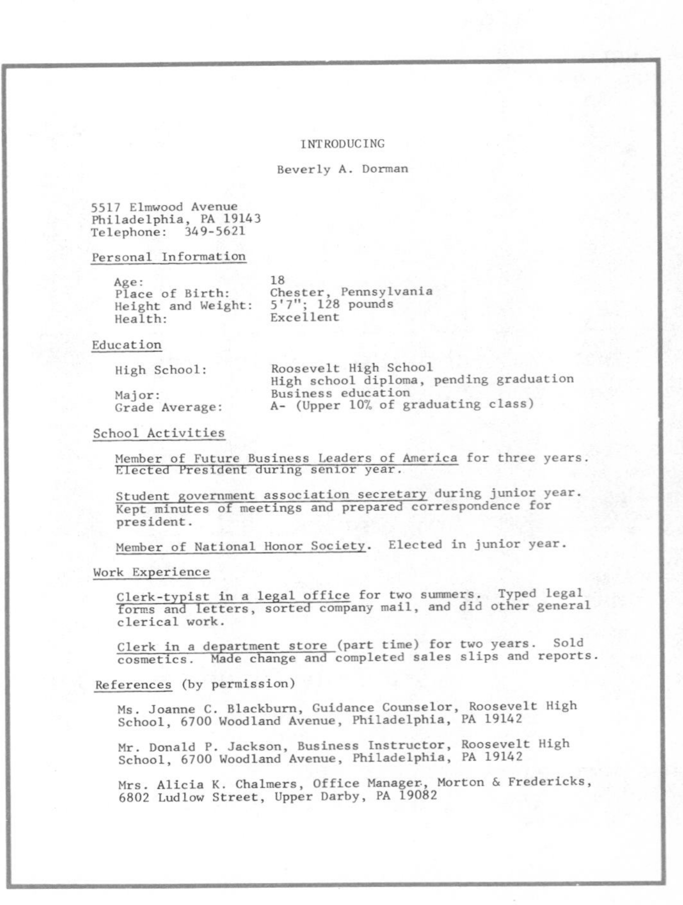

INTRODUCING

Beverly A. Dorman

5517 Elmwood Avenue
Philadelphia, PA 19143
Telephone: 349-5621

Personal Information

Age:	18
Place of Birth:	Chester, Pennsylvania
Height and Weight:	5'7"; 128 pounds
Health:	Excellent

Education

High School:	Roosevelt High School High school diploma, pending graduation
Major:	Business education
Grade Average:	A- (Upper 10% of graduating class)

School Activities

Member of Future Business Leaders of America for three years. Elected President during senior year.

Student government association secretary during junior year. Kept minutes of meetings and prepared correspondence for president.

Member of National Honor Society. Elected in junior year.

Work Experience

Clerk-typist in a legal office for two summers. Typed legal forms and letters, sorted company mail, and did other general clerical work.

Clerk in a department store (part time) for two years. Sold cosmetics. Made change and completed sales slips and reports.

References (by permission)

Ms. Joanne C. Blackburn, Guidance Counselor, Roosevelt High School, 6700 Woodland Avenue, Philadelphia, PA 19142

Mr. Donald P. Jackson, Business Instructor, Roosevelt High School, 6700 Woodland Avenue, Philadelphia, PA 19142

Mrs. Alicia K. Chalmers, Office Manager, Morton & Fredericks, 6802 Ludlow Street, Upper Darby, PA 19082

26c ▶7 Learn new keys: 4 and 8

each tryout drill twice SS

Reach technique for 4

Reach *up* with *left first* finger.

Reach technique for 8

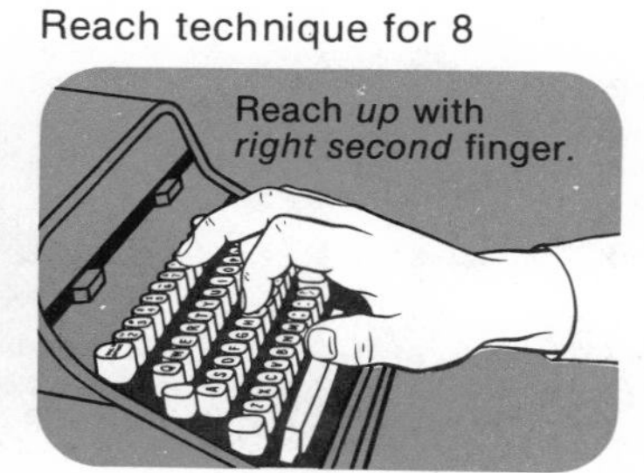

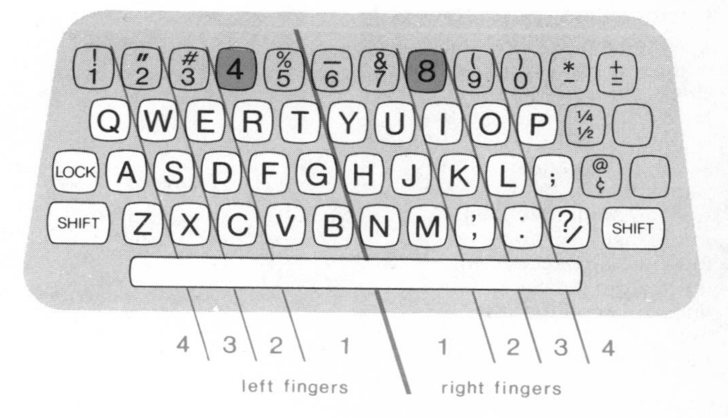


```
4f 4f 4 4 f4f f4f 444 Claim 44

8k 8k 8 8 k8k k8k 888 Space 88
```

26d ▶9 Improve figure control

type twice, using the letter l for 1

Goals: Keep wrists low; fingers curved, upright, and relaxed; try to make each reach without moving the hand forward.

4 Only 4 of the 144 girls got 41 of the 44 quiz answers right.
Did the 14 boxes Joe shipped on May 4 weigh just 144 pounds?

8 The April 18 assignment covers pages 11 to 18 and 81 to 188.
Mr. Marx gave the March 8 exam which covered pages 18 to 88.

4/8 Posted scores were: April 11, 48 to 44; April 18, 88 to 84.
Review Figures 44 and 48 on pages 414 and 418, respectively.

26e ▶15 Guided writing: sentences

1. Each line once without timing: easy, controlled pace; reduce time between strokes.

Goal: To improve stroking patterns on balanced- and one-hand words.

2. Each line once with the 20″ call of the guide.

Goal: To reach end of line as "Return" is called.

3. As time permits, one 1′ writing without the call, beginning with Line 1.

Goal: At least 25 *gwam*.

all letters used

		words in line	gwam 20″
1	Only a few of the men were checked.	7	21
2	Neither of us can fix the foreign motor.	8	24
3	Adjust your speed to fit the different words.	9	27
4	Gaining speed is partly a question of saving time.	10	30
5	This course gives you a chance to build a strong skill.	11	33
6	Capital letters should rest on the line, not above or below.	12	36
7	I am coming along in my ability to type words of different sizes.	13	39

| 1 | 2 | 3 | 4 | 5 | 6 | 7 | 8 | 9 | 10 | 11 | 12 | 13 |

268b-271b, continued

Job 7
Memorandum of agreement

Type the memorandum as a leftbound manuscript with side headings. Make 2 cc's. Main heading: MEMORANDUM OF AGREEMENT; secondary heading: September 6, 19--. List the numbered items in the last ¶ DS and indented 5 spaces from the left margin. Leave 3 blank lines between the last ¶ and the lines for the signatures.

A meeting between Gemini International, Inc., and Local 482 of the International Clerical Union was ~~conducted~~ held on Sept. 6, 19--, to discuss the ~~conditions~~ arrangements for negotiating the labor agreement between the two parties which ~~ends~~ expires on Dec. 31. ~~Representing~~ Present for the Company ~~was~~ were Mark D. Cameron, President, and Lawrence L. Pastore, Director of Labor Relations. Representing the Union ~~was~~ were William U. Grant, President, and Keith A. Goodson, Business Manager.

~~Both sides~~ The parties agreed to the following general conditions under which the negotiations will ~~take place~~ be conducted.

<u>Site of Meetings</u> The meetings will be ~~conducted~~ held in Suites 908 and 910 of the Hotel Ambassador. Costs of the meeting site will be shared equally by the Company and the Union.

<u>Dates and Times of Meetings</u> The meetings will take place each weekday beginning on October 30 from 9 a.m. to 4 p.m. By mutual agreement, changes may be made in dates and times.

<u>Agenda for Meetings</u> Fifteen (15) days prior to the ~~initial~~ first meeting, the Union shall submit to the Company ~~their~~ its proposals for changes in the contract. Areas for discussion will include, but will not be limited to, the following. Either party may ~~suggest~~ propose additional matters for discussion upon ~~24~~ 48 hours' notice. 1. Rights of the Parties; 2. Union Membership and Checkoff; 3. Grievance Procedures; 4. Arbitration; 5. Hours of Work; 6. Holidays and Vacations; 7. Seniority; 8. Employee Benefits; 9. Length of the Agreement; ~~and~~ 10. Rates of Pay.

Mark D. Cameron

William U. Grant

27

27a ▶7
Conditioning practice
each line 3 times SS (slowly, faster, slowly); DS between 3-line groups

alphabet Joel Knox led a big blitz which saved the play for my squad.

figures Try these figures: 1, 4, 8, 14, 18, 48, 84, 11, 44, and 88.

fluency It is their wish to buy land maps of the eight island towns.

| 1 | 2 | 3 | 4 | 5 | 6 | 7 | 8 | 9 | 10 | 11 | 12 |

27b ▶7
Learn new keys: 3 and 7
each tryout drill twice SS

Reach technique for 3

Reach technique for 7

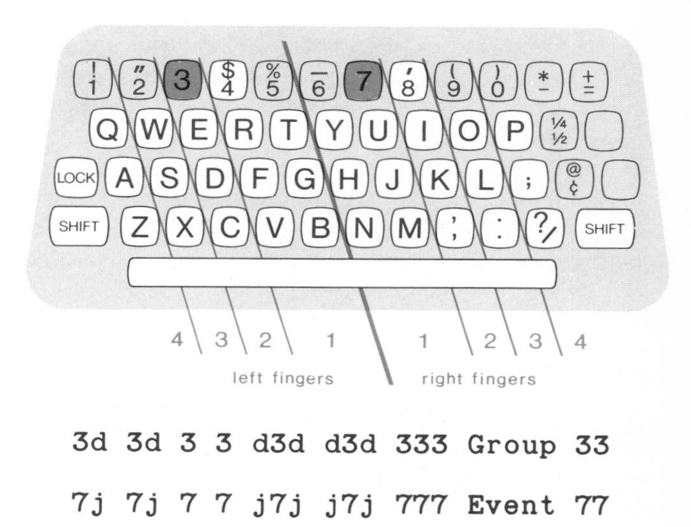

3d 3d 3 3 d3d d3d 333 Group 33

7j 7j 7 7 j7j j7j 777 Event 77

27c ▶8
Improve figure control
once as shown

Goals: Keep your eyes on the copy; keep your hands quiet; let the *fingers* do the typing.

no space

3 On October 31 I typed 33 w.p.m. for 3 minutes with 3 errors.
Sue missed only Problem 33; I missed Problems 3, 13, and 31.

7 Toni and I have read 77 of the 177 pages assigned for May 7.
Tod will be 17 on June 7 and will take Flight 177 to Dallas.

3/7 I based my June 13 report on pages 337 to 377 of Chapter 17.
On November 7, 37 girls and 33 boys sold 377 boxes of cards.

Review John Dixon is now 18 years old; his mother, 37; his dad, 44.
I know 33 of the 378 men worked 37 hours, but 147 worked 48.

27d ▶8
Improve tabulating technique
type once DS:

1. Insert new sheet.

2. Center horizontally and type heading on Line 9; then TS.

3. Clear all tab stops; set new ones according to key.

4. Tab from column to column to type the drill.

TABULATING

came	else	fair	hold	like
body	fine	ways	look	near
late	glad	life	none	plus
fold	mean	tell	what	whom

key | 4 | 10 | 4 | 10 | 4 | 10 | 4 | 10 | 4 |

268b-271b, continued

Job 6
Text of speech
[LM pp. 149, 150]

On 8″ × 5″ cards (or paper cut to 8″ × 5″ size), type the remarks Mr. Cameron will make at the meeting of the Board of Directors. Use ½″ top, side, and bottom margins; DS.

Gemini International continues to grow into a very large multinational company. It is extremely rewarding to note the growth the company has acheived in a very short span of time. During the past fiscal year, we initiated our first branch office in the far east and detailed plans have been developed to extend our operations in that area. These plans will be discussed in detail later in the meeting.

The last fiscal year brought satisfying rewards. Sales reached a new high of $3.9 billion -- up by 21 per cent. Earnings were up too by 46 per cent, despite the change to lifo (last-in, first-out) inventory accounting. Our earnings wouldhave been a great deal more had we not made these changes. These results were acheived under adverse conditions a generally slow economy, higher interest rates, widely fluctuating international rates of current, and exceptional competitive priceing conditions. The acheivements were made show the company's ability to conduce our business uner difficult economic conditions.

The outlook is exceptionally brought as a new fiscal year begins. We plan to enter formerly unexplored markets and to extend our international business. We have been developing and strenghening our human, fiscal, and technological resources to capitolize on future opportunities. We are sure we will be prepared to meet the great challenges that lay ahead, and that Gemini International will set greater sales and records of earnings during the year ahead.

27e ▶20

Goal typing: paragraphs

1. A 1′ *speed* writing on ¶ 1; determine *gwam* for a base rate.

2. Add 4 *gwam* to base rate to determine goal rate.

3. From the goals below, select the one nearest your goal rate.

Goals

	▼	■	●
1′	25	29	33

4. Three 1′ *speed* writings on ¶ 1; try to reach or exceed your goal.

5. Type ¶ 2 in the same way.

6. A 2′ *control* writing on ¶s 1–2 combined; determine *gwam*.

Goal: At least 23 *gwam*.

7. A 3′ *control* writing on ¶s 1–2 combined; determine *gwam*.

Goal: At least 21 *gwam*.

all letters used | LA | 1.4 si | 5.4 awl | 85% hfw |

	gwam 2′	3′
A difference between the expert and a beginning typist	5	4
is that the former has put his act together, but the latter	11	8
is still trying to arrange the props. One works with quiet	17	12
control as the other works in jerks and pauses.	22	15
Like the pieces for a jigsaw puzzle, every movement in	28	18
typing must fit into its specific place. So if you want to	34	22
get your typing act together, study how you type and find a	40	26
quicker way of fitting all the pieces together.	44	30

gwam 2′ | 1 | 2 | 3 | 4 | 5 | 6 |
3′ | 1 | 2 | 3 | 4 |

28

28a ▶7

Conditioning practice

each line 3 times SS (slowly, faster, slowly); DS between 3-line groups

alphabet Berle wants the quartz box for Pam, the jade ring for Vicky.

figures Type these figures: 1, 4, 8, 3, 7, 34, 87, 43, 78, and 137.

fluency The right bid may entitle the girl to the handy ivory forks.

| 1 | 2 | 3 | 4 | 5 | 6 | 7 | 8 | 9 | 10 | 11 | 12 |

28b ▶20

Improve speed/control

Repeat 27e, above; try to type at least 26 *gwam* for 1′, 24 for 2′, 22 for 3′.

28c ▶8

Proofread your copy

1. Note the kinds of errors marked in the sample typed at right.

2. Proofread and mark for correction (using proofreader's marks, page 38) each error you make in a 1′ writing on ¶1 of 27e, above.

Goal: To learn the first step in finding and correcting your errors.

```
    Adifference betwen the expert and a be ginning typist
is that the former put his act together,  but thee latter
is stell tring to arrange the propps.  One works with queit
control as theother works in jekks and pauses.
```

Line 1	Line 2	Line 3	Line 4
① Failure to space	① Omitted word	① Misstroke	① Failure to space
② Omitted letter	② Incorrect spacing	② Omitted letter	② Strikeover, only one error counted per word
③ Faulty spacing	③ Added letter	③ Added letter	
		④ Transposition	

268b-271b, continued

Job 3 [LM pp. 137–144]
Compose and type letters

1. Compose and type a letter for your signature as an Administrative Assistant, dated April 8, 19––, to each manager of the branch offices Mr. Cameron will visit on his trip in June.

2. Tell each manager the date Mr. Cameron will meet with him and the date and time of his arrival and departure.

3. Inform each manager that Mr. Cameron wishes to review the operations of his office during the past year with emphasis on operating costs, to discuss any major problems, and to review plans for future operations.

4. Ask each manager to have someone meet Mr. Cameron at the airport and to arrange for his transportation to the airport on his departure.

Job 4
Agenda for meeting

Center the agenda at the right in reading position on 8½" × 11" paper. Justify the right margin; make 4 cc's.

GEMINI INTERNATIONAL, INC.

Agenda for the Meeting of the Board of Directors

May 14, 19--

1. Call to Order . . . . Mark D. Cameron
2. Reading and Approval of Minutes . . . . Michael P. Dunn
3. Reports of Officers
   President . . . . Mark D. Cameron
   Vice President, Operations . . . . Frank C. Richardson
   Vice President, Finance . . . . Sydney A. Swinford
   Vice President, Development . . . . Susan R. Lipscomb
4. Reports of Special Departments
   Director of Sales . . . . Bryan Q. Vincente
   Director of Purchasing . . . . Allison T. Marcum
   Director of Human Resources . . . . Barry M. Anthony
5. Dividend Declaration . . . . Sydney A. Swinford
6. New Business
   Proposed Expansion in the Far East . . . . Frank C. Richardson

Job 5 [LM pp. 145–148]
Compose and type interoffice memorandums

Compose and type an interoffice memorandum from Mr. Cameron, dated April 12, to each director of the special departments who will speak at the meeting of the Board of Directors. Notify them that the meeting will be held at 10 a.m. on May 14 in the Executive Conference Room. Attach a copy of the agenda. Ask each director to send Mr. Cameron, no later than May 3, a copy of the material he plans to present at the meeting. Make 1 cc of each memorandum.

28d ▶7
Learn new keys: 5 and 9

each tryout drill twice SS

Reach technique for 5 — Reach *up* with *left first* finger.

Reach technique for 9 — Reach *up* with *right third* finger.

left fingers 4 3 2 1 — right fingers 1 2 3 4

```
5f 5f 5 5 f5f f5f 555 Local 55
91 91 9 9 191 191 999 Table 99
```

28e ▶8
Improve figure control

once as shown

Goals: Body erect; wrists low; fingers curved and upright; try to make each reach without moving the hand forward.

no space

5 Does Flight 155 from Los Angeles arrive at 4:55? or at 5:55?
My best golf scores were 85 on August 5 and 75 on August 15.

9 I was 19 on the 9th of May; my sister, 9 on the 9th of June.
See Unit 9, Item 19, page 399, for the answer to Problem 49.

5/9 We sold only 1,195 homes in 1955, but we sold 3,959 in 1975.
Of 959 juniors, 595 take typing but only 159 take shorthand.

Review Reach with your fingers to type 59, 95, 48, 84, 73, and 137.
Linda lives at 837 Laurel Court; Greg, at 1594 Eden Parkway.

29

29a ▶7
Conditioning practice

each line 3 times SS (slowly, faster, slowly); DS between 3-line groups

alphabet Kip, can you have this quaint jug fixed for Ms. Pelz by two?

figures We had a work force of 349 in 1975; we may need 955 by 1985.

fluency Alan may fix the bus panel for the city if the pay is right.

| 1 | 2 | 3 | 4 | 5 | 6 | 7 | 8 | 9 | 10 | 11 | 12 |

29b ▶7
Improve tabulating technique

type once DS:

1. Space up 4 times and center heading; then TS.

2. Clear all tab stops; set new ones according to key.

3. Tab from column to column to type the drill.

TABULATING

bank	eyes	girl	item	knew
play	deal	even	farm	foot
feet	hear	home	live	door
hope	hour	kind	less	note

key | 4 | 10 | 4 | 10 | 4 | 10 | 4 | 10 | 4 |

268b-271b, continued

Job 1, concluded

FRANKFURT OFFICE

20 Kaiserplatz
6 Frankfurt, Germany
Manager: Mr. Horst Bucholtz
Telephone: (0611) 20251

AMSTERDAM OFFICE

30 Dam
Amsterdam, Holland
Manager: Mr. R. L. Brunet
Telephone: 325091

MUNICH OFFICE

4 Karlsplatz
8 Munich, Germany
Manager: Mr. Karl T. Ludwig
Telephone: 5594-237

SAN FRANCISCO OFFICE

835 Market Street
San Francisco, CA 91403
Manager: Mrs. R. T. Akaya
Telephone: (415) 321-2200

Job 2
Travel schedule

In June, Mr. Cameron will visit some of the branch offices in Europe. Type his travel schedule at the right centered on 8½" × 11" paper. Provide an appropriate heading; make 1 cc.

Monday May 31	Leave Kennedy Airport for London, 6:50 p.m. TWA Flight 754
Tuesday June 1	Arrive Heathrow Airport, 7:30 a.m. Confirmed reservations at Grosvenor House
Wednesday June 2	Meet with Mr. D. Charles Higgins, Manager London Office
Thursday June 3	Leave London for Amsterdam, 1:30 p.m. KLM Flight 128
	Arrive Schiphol Airport, 2:25 p.m. Confirmed reservations at the Hotel Amstel
Friday June 4	Meet with Mr. R. L. Brunet, Manager Amsterdam Office
Saturday June 5	Leave Amsterdam for Munich, 10:30 a.m. Lufthansa Flight 755
	Arrive Riem Airport, 11:45 a.m. Confirmed reservations at Hotel Konigshof
Monday June 7	Meet with Mr. Karl T. Ludwig, Manager Munich Office
Tuesday June 8	Leave Munich for Frankfurt, 2:20 p.m. Lufthansa Flight 755
	Arrive Rhein-Main Airport, 3:10 p.m. Confirmed reservations at Hotel Frankfurter Hof
Wednesday June 9	Meet with Mr. Horst Bucholtz, Manager Frankfurt Office
Thursday June 10	Leave Frankfurt for New York City, 12:10 p.m. TWA Flight 741
	Arrive Kennedy Airport, 3:20 p.m.

29c ▶7 Learn new keys: 2 and 0

each tryout drill twice SS

Reach technique for 2

Reach technique for 0

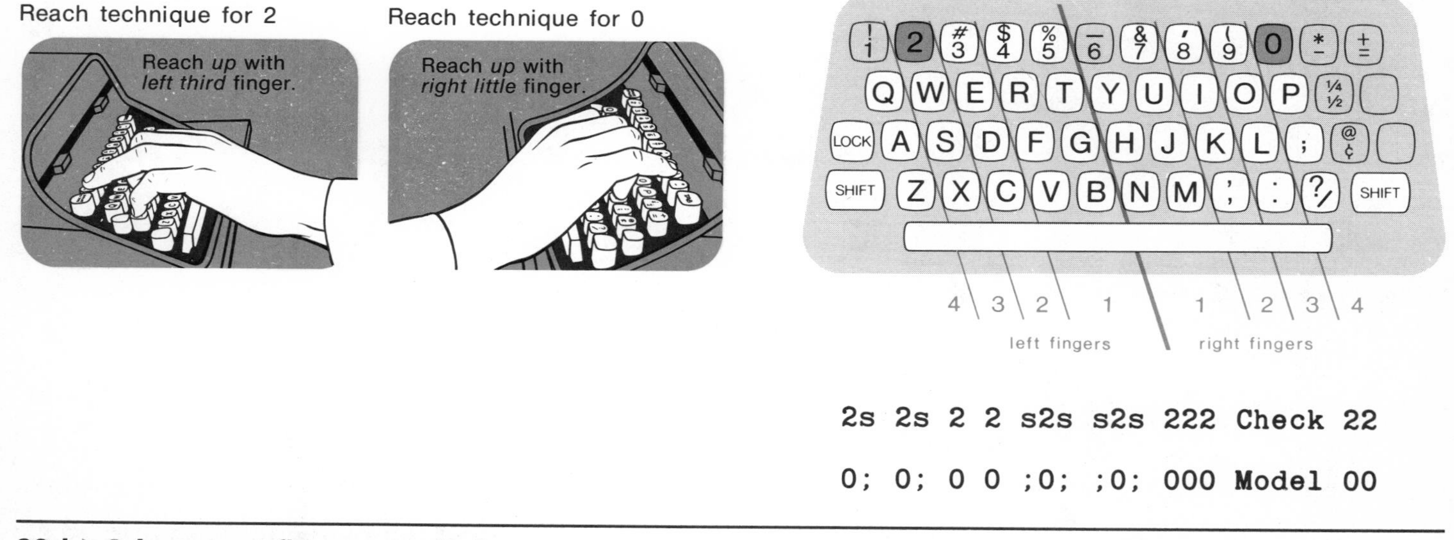

Reach *up* with *left third* finger.
Reach *up* with *right little* finger.
4 3 2 1
left fingers
1 2 3 4
right fingers

2s 2s 2 2 s2s s2s 222 Check 22

0; 0; 0 0 ;0; ;0; 000 Model 00

29d ▶8 Improve figure control

once as shown

Goal: To reach to *2* and *0* without twisting the hands or moving the elbows out.

2	Did 22 of the 42 students type the figure line at 22 w.p.m.? When our firm began on May 22, 1972, we had only 22 workers.
0	Order 40 typing erasers, 80 tablets, and 100 reams of paper. Since Models 300 and 400 are out of stock, ship a Model 500.
2/0	Of the 202 teachers, 200 will visit the 20 firms on June 20. They bought Lot 20 in Block 200 of Subdivision 2002 in 1972.
review	Type these numbers: 20, 59, 37, 48, 12, 93, 85, 72, and 40. Our group sold 950 chili dogs, 487 sandwiches, and 312 pies.

29e ▶21 Improve skill transfer: rough draft

1. Three 1′ writings on ¶ 1; determine *gwam* on best writing.

2. Three 1′ writings on ¶ 2; compare best *gwam* with ¶ 1 *gwam*.

3. Two 2′ writings on ¶ 1, then on ¶ 2. Compare better rate on ¶ 1 with better rate on ¶ 2.

all letters used | LA | 1.4 si | 5.4 awl | 85% hfw |

	gwam 1′	2′	
A vital difference exists between a job done right and	11	5	28
one done just about right. One is given approval while the	23	11	34
other is not. To receive full approval of the work you do,	35	17	40
recognize that just about right is not adequate.	45	22	45
~~Soon~~ *Before long* you will ~~attempt~~ *try* problems inwhich are ap plied	11	5	28
the seemingyl *little* things that are ~~vital~~ *crucial* in learning ~~how~~ to	23	11	34
type. mastery of ~~the~~ little things *now* is ~~sure~~ *certain* to make this	35	17	40
big job ~~considerably~~ easier todo just right *a* little later	44	22	44

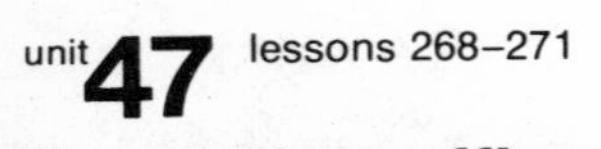

unit **47** lessons 268–271

Executive office typing

Learning goals

1. To enhance production skills by typing typical jobs in an executive office.

2. To improve ability to plan and organize work and to compose correspondence.

268-271

268a-271a ▶5 Conditioning practice

twice SS;
repeat difficult lines

alphabet	The joint executive board will analyze their request for more parking.
figures	I flew 842 miles on May 5, 931 miles on May 6, and 820 miles on May 7.
fig/sym	Multiply $6,570 (the base) times 4 1/2% (the rate) times 3 (the time).
fluency	He says that both of them show a special aptitude for scientific work.

| 1 | 2 | 3 | 4 | 5 | 6 | 7 | 8 | 9 | 10 | 11 | 12 | 13 | 14 |

268b-271b ▶45 Production typing

You have been assigned to be an Administrative Assistant to Mr. Mark D. Cameron, President of Gemini International, Inc., 81 Broadway, New York, NY 10006.

Follow directions carefully. Make carbon copies when directed; address envelopes when appropriate; check all work carefully before presenting it for approval.

Job 1 [LM pp. 133–135]
Address file

1. On 5″ × 3″ cards, prepare an address file of the branch offices of Gemini International, Inc., given at the right and at the top of page 414.

2. Type the branch office on the third line from the top edge; TS; type the company name and the address; DS; type the title and the name of the manager; DS; type the telephone number.

3. Arrange the cards in alphabetic order and keep them for future use.

```
PARIS OFFICE

Gemini International, Inc.
22 Place Vendome
75001 Paris, France

Manager:  Mr. Alex C. Dumaine

Telephone:  063 7750
```

PARIS OFFICE

22 Place Vendome
75001 Paris, France
Manager: Mr. Alex C. Dumaine
Telephone: 063 7750

FAR EAST OFFICE

1102 Pengibu Building
Collyer Quay
Singapore 1, Republic of Singapore
Manager: Ms. Estelle L. Huan
Telephone: 433547

BRUSSELS OFFICE

Avenue de la Ferme Rose 3
1160 Brussels, Belgium
Manager: Miss Cecile A. Baronne
Telephone: 14.07.52

MILAN OFFICE

Corso Italia, 8
Milan 20122, Italy
Manager: Mr. Anthony V. Carsini
Telephone: 977772

MADRID OFFICE

Viajes Melia, S.A.
Princessa, 29
Madrid 15, Spain
Manager: Mr. Petro T. Rafael
Telephone: 3520087

LONDON OFFICE

801 Bond Street
London W1Y 4ED, England
Manager: Mr. D. Charles Higgins
Telephone: 01-499-6363

(continued, page 414)

30

30a ▶7
Conditioning practice
each line 3 times SS (slowly, faster, slowly); DS between 3-line groups

alphabet Did Buzz quickly coax eight avid fans away from Jason Parks?

figures Take Delta 152 at 7:30 p.m.; pick up United 841 at 9:35 p.m.

fluency The signs the eight girls wish to hang may worry their boss.

| 1 | 2 | 3 | 4 | 5 | 6 | 7 | 8 | 9 | 10 | 11 | 12 |

30b ▶7
Learn new keys: 6 and 1
each tryout drill twice SS

Reach technique for 6

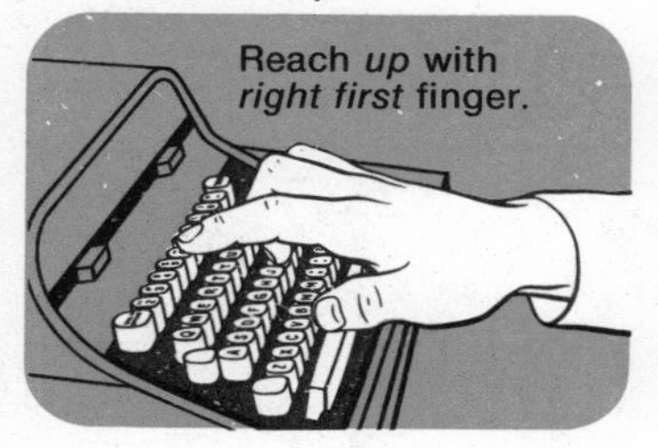

Reach technique for 1

6j 6j 6 6 j6j j6j 666 Route 66

la la l l ala ala lll Agent ll

30c ▶8
Improve figure control
once as shown; repeat selected lines as time permits

Goals: To type *6* and *1* without moving the hands forward.

6 These 66 copies of R66 must be shipped by 6 p.m. on March 6.
I took Route 66 on September 6 and drove 666 miles to Tulsa.

1 We drove Route 101 for 111 miles, then Route 1 to Morro Bay.
On May 11 we took Route 1A1 instead of A1A to Jupiter Inlet.

6/1 I need 16 desks, 16 chairs, and 16 file cabinets by July 16.
He weighed only 6 pounds on May 16, 1961; now he weighs 166.

all figures used On Arbor Day we planted 284 elm, 375 cedar, and 1,690 maple.
Stock those lakes with 628 trout, 759 perch, and 1,340 bass.

30d ▶6
Check tabulating technique
1. Insert plain sheet.
2. Center and type the heading on Line 9; then TS.
3. Clear all tab stops; set new ones according to key.
4. Tab from column to column to type the drill.

TABULATING

unit	fire	idea	late	open
file	pass	past	room	dark
wall	bill	side	blue	thus
film	wait	west	wide	wife

key | 4 | 10 | 4 | 10 | 4 | 10 | 4 | 10 | 4 |

Job 8
Financial statement

Center the statement of income and retained earnings vertically and horizontally. TS between heading and "Income," and between "Net Earnings" and "Retained Earnings."

Ferguson & Henley, Inc.

Statement of income and Retained Earnings

Fiscal Year ended October 31, 19--

Income

lc Net Sales	31 $13,765,000
Less:	
Cost of goods sold	000 26,781,999
Selling, administrative and general expenses . . .	1,709,000
Depreciation	351,000
Income from operations	2,924,000
Other incomes and expense:	
Interest expense	(130,000)
Interest and dividend incomes	35,000
Total	(95,000)
Earnings before taxes on income	29 2,892,000
lc Taxes on Income:	
Federal	1 000 2,316,999
State	70,725
Total	1,386,725
Net earnings	5 $ 1,442,272

Retained Earnings

Retained earnings, beginning of year	0 $ 5,970,000
Net earnings	75 1,442,257
Totals	6,512,275
Dividends ($5 per share)	108,170
Retained earnings, end of year	$ 6,404,105

30e ▶12 Check keystroking speed

1. A 1′ writing on each ¶; record the better *gwam* for later comparison.

Goal: At least 26 *gwam*.

2. Two 3′ writings on ¶s 1–2 combined; record *gwam* on the better writing. Circle errors.

Goal: At least 22 *gwam*.

all letters used

LA	1.4 si	5.4 awl	85% hfw

Text	gwam 1′	3′	
You are now able to type letters and figures by touch,	11	4	33
without gazing at your keyboard. You are also able to type	23	8	37
rapidly from copy containing digits as well as from several	35	12	42
other kinds of copy. You have done quite well.	44	15	44
If you expect to continue to improve, put off the urge	11	18	48
to check the keys as you practice. Keeping the eyes on the	23	22	52
copy material eliminates time lost in trying to locate just	35	26	56
where you quit reading to start your checking.	44	30	59

gwam 1′ | 1 | 2 | 3 | 4 | 5 | 6 | 7 | 8 | 9 | 10 | 11 | 12 |
3′ | 1 | 2 | 3 | 4 |

30f ▶10 Improve skill transfer

1. Two 1′ writings on ¶ 1; determine *gwam* on each.

2. Type ¶ 2, then ¶ 3, in the same way.

3. Determine % of transfer: divide straight–copy *gwam* (Step 1 of 30e, above) into the *gwam* on each of the other types of copy.

Goals
Script: 97%
Rough draft: 90%
Statistical: 94%

all letters/figures used

LA	1.4 si	5.4 awl	85% hfw

Text	gwam 1′
When I read handwritten copy for typing, I fix my eyes	11
carefully on each word. This is essential because a letter	23
that is written improperly can cause me to type a different	35
word. For instance, I may type quite for quiet.	45
Before ^beginning ~~I begin~~ to type from rough^#draft, I ^look ~~glance~~ over	11
the copy to be ^certain ~~sure~~ I under⁀stand ^every ~~all~~ changes that needs	23
to be made. I ~~can~~ improve (hte) speed and accuracy of ^my work ^by	35
not puz⁀zling about the ^corrections when typing. ~~material as I type~~.	45
Numbers vary in difficulty just as words do. A number	11
having only two digits typed by both hands, such as 85, 49,	23
or 27, may be easy. A longer one typed with one hand, such	35
as 176 or 352, often increases the difficulty.	44

gwam 1′ | 1 | 2 | 3 | 4 | 5 | 6 | 7 | 8 | 9 | 10 | 11 | 12 |

Enrichment material for Unit 4 appears on LM p. 15.

264b-267b, continued

Job 7
Financial statement
Center the balance sheet vertically and horizontally. Use this year's date for the heading of Column 2 and last year's date for the heading of Column 3.

WHEELOCK MANUFACTURING COMPANY

Balance Sheet

Years Ended June 30, 19-- and 19--

(000 Omitted)

ASSETS	19--	19--
Current assets:		
Cash	$ 1,494	$ 1,127
Accounts receivable	8,065	6,164
Inventories	10,712	12,060
Prepaid expenses	312	224
Total current assets	20,583	19,575
Property, plant, and equipment, at cost		
Land	479	593
Buildings	3,269	3,027
Machinery and equipment	18,768	16,151
Less: Accumulated depreciation	(8,987)	(6,526)
Net property, plant, and equipment . .	13,529	13,245
Total assets	$34,112	$32,820
LIABILITIES AND SHAREHOLDERS' EQUITY		
Current liabilities:		
Accounts payable	$ 4,093	$ 4,863
Accrued expenses	4,473	4,575
Accrued income tax	1,645	1,012
Total current liabilities	10,211	10,450
Long-term debt	3,431	3,542
Deferred income taxes	1,132	1,150
Shareholders' equity:		
Capital stock of $1 par value:		
Authorized--25,000,000 shares		
Issued--12,653,000 shares	12,653	12,653
Retained earnings	6,685	5,025
Total shareholders' equity	19,338	17,678
Total liabilities and shareholders' equity .	$34,112	$32,820

unit 5 lessons 31–35

Centering memorandums and announcements

Learning goals
1. To type straight copy at higher speeds and with improved control.
2. To type informational memorandums in block style.
3. To center copy vertically as well as horizontally.

Machine adjustments
1. Paper guide at *0*.
2. Ribbon control on *black*.
3. Margin sets: 60-space line.
4. Line-space selector on *1* for drills; on *2* for ¶s; as directed for problems.

31

31a ▶7 Conditioning practice

each line 3 times SS (slowly, faster, slowly); DS between 3-line groups

alphabet Judy Pima took the five new girls to brunch at the Quiz Box.

figures What is the total of 15 and 17 and 28 and 39 and 40 and 156?

fluency If they make such a visit, it may end the fight for a title.

| 1 | 2 | 3 | 4 | 5 | 6 | 7 | 8 | 9 | 10 | 11 | 12 |

31b ▶12 Goal typing: paragraphs

1. From the table below, select the 2′ goal just above your usual 2′ *gwam*.
2. Type two 2′ writings, trying to reach or exceed that speed. Use ▼ ■ ●
3. Select a 3′ goal and type two 3′ writings in the same manner. Use ▽ □ ○

	gwam 2′	3′
Typewriter spacing is uniform; that is, all letters of	5	4
the alphabet take the same amount of space. Most type used	11	8
by printers, though, varies in width; that is, wide letters	17	12
use more space than thin ones. Lines of typed copy line up	23	16
at the left margin but usually not at the right. A printer	29	20
forces lines of various lengths to line up at the right by	35	24
changing the amount of space between words. When you copy	41	28
from print, then, your line endings may not be quite even.	47	31

gwam 2′ | 1 | 2 | 3 | 4 | 5 | 6 |
3′ | 1 | 2 | 3 | 4 |

31c ▶6 Improve technique: margin release and backspacer

each line twice

1. Set right margin stop at center + 30.
2. Return carriage; depress margin release key; backspace 4 times and type number.
3. When carriage locks, depress margin release key and complete the line.

1. Strike all figure keys with the hands quiet, the fingers curved.
2. Of the 33 typists, 9 typed over 40 words while 7 typed under 25.
3. Use figures in dimensions, as in 2 ft. 9 in., 73 cm, and 8.5 km.
4. Flight 94 leaves Boston at 10:30 a.m.; Flight 127, at 12:56 p.m.

31d ▶25 Problem typing: informational memorandums

supplies needed: 2 half sheets
60-space line

1. Study the layout and spacing guides of the memo on page 52.
2. Insert a half sheet with short side against the paper guide.
3. Type a copy of the memo on page 52, following the layout and spacing illustrated there.
4. If time permits, type the memo a second time.

264b-267b, continued

Job 6
Financial report

Type the report at the right as a leftbound manuscript with side headings. Type the side headings in all CAPS; underline the ¶ headings under Note 1.

Notes to Financial Statements of Whitewater Industries

Note 1: Summary of Significant Accounting Policies

Inventories. Inventories at December 31 are valued by the last-in, first-out method (LIFO). Previously, inventories of the Company were valued at cost, not in excess of market, determined generally on an average or standard cost basis.

Depreciation. Depreciation of plant and equipment is provided over the estimated useful lives of the respective assets on the straight-line basis.

Income Taxes. Investment tax credits are recorded as a reduction in the provision for federal income taxes in the year realized.

Note 2: Inventories

Inventories at December 31 were as follows:

Raw materials	$ 6,624,434
Work in process	1,664,844
Finished goods	5,334,340
	$ 13,623,618

Note 3: Pension Plan

The Company has a noncontributory pension plan covering all eligible employees. Effective with this fiscal year, the Company changed its actuarial cost method in computing costs by amortizing the plan's prior service costs at an annual rate of 10%. Total pension costs under this plan aggregated $144,232. As of December 31, the latest actuarial valuation, vested benefits exceeded pension fund assets by approximately $623,000.

Note 4: Earnings per Common Share

Net income per share of common stock has been computed using the weighted average number of shares outstanding during the period (291,483 shares) after making a retroactive adjustment for the 5% stock dividend declared the previous year and giving effect to the convertible preferred stock and stock options as common share equivalents.

Space down 7 times to leave top margin of 1" or 2.54 cm

Shown in pica type 60–space line

```
October 29, 19--
```

Space down 4 times to leave 3 blank line spaces

```
SUBJECT:  Know Your Typewriter
```
TS

```
How many lines can you type per inch on your typewriter?  To
find out, type with single spacing in a column at the left
margin the figures 1 through 6.  Then, measure the vertical
space used.  If your machine has standard spacing, the 6
lines should measure 1 inch or 2.54 centimeters deep.
```
DS

```
Most typewriters made in the U.S.A. are set to type 6 lines
to a vertical inch.  European ones, however, are gauged to
the metric system; thus, they are not made to fit exactly
the vertical spacing of American machines or of the ruled
forms that are currently designed for our typewriters.
```

Informational memorandum: block style

32

32a ▶7
Conditioning practice

each line 3 times SS (slowly, faster, slowly); DS between 3-line groups

alphabet: Jim Verick was quizzed by Mr. Glade on part of his tax form.

figures: Speed up easy pairs of figures: 11, 26, 27, 40, 83, and 95.

fluency: The firms may make a profit if they handle their work right.

| 1 | 2 | 3 | 4 | 5 | 6 | 7 | 8 | 9 | 10 | 11 | 12 |

32b ▶8
Improve technique: shift keys and shift lock

type twice

left shift key:
Linda has an Olympia standard; Harold, an Olivetti portable.
Mr. and Mrs. Picaza sailed to Nassau and Jamaica last month.

right shift key:
Suzanne and Denny Bigner are employed by the Quincy Company.
We drove through Alabama, Georgia, and Florida on that trip.

shift lock:
He uses the CENTURY 21 systems of typewriting and shorthand.
Ms. Evans attended the NABTE and WBEA conventions this year.

| 1 | 2 | 3 | 4 | 5 | 6 | 7 | 8 | 9 | 10 | 11 | 12 |

264b-267b, continued

Job 3 [LM p. 127]
Business letter
block; open

May 26, 19-- Minnesota Department of Revenue Bureau of Corporation Taxes St. Paul, MN 55103 Ladies and Gentlemen (¶ 1) The tax return of the Chatsworth Manufacturing Company, 2620 Columbus Avenue, Minneapolis, Minnesota, submitted for the fiscal year ended December 31, 19--, contained the following errors:

1. Overstatement of fuel inventory through the inclusion of consignment inventory $9,675.90
2. Understatement of depreciation resulting from IRS adjustment--December 31, 19--, return 702.84

These errors result in a decrease of $10,378.74 in taxable income and an overpayment of $965.70 in taxes. (¶ 2) Will you please forward the appropriate forms to us so that the Chatsworth Company can submit a refund claim for the overpayment of taxes. Very truly yours BAKER, SEXTON, AND CAVELL Linda T. Kaminsky, Auditor

---

Job 4 [LM p. 129]
Business letter
block; open

June 14, 19-- Wisconsin Banking Commission State Office Building 4792 Sheboygan Avenue Madison, WI 53705 Ladies and Gentlemen (¶ 1) Your interpretation and clarification of Section 9.18 of Regulation 9 will be appreciated. (¶ 2) We believe that Section 9.18 (c) (3) permits the establishment of a collective investment fund, subject to the 10%/$10,000/$100,000 limitations of this section, for the purpose of investing <u>cash balances received or held by a bank</u> in its capacity as trustee, executor, administrator, or guardian and that Section 9.18 (a) (1) permits the creation of a collective investment fund to be maintained by the bank exclusively for the collective investment and reinvestment of <u>monies contributed thereto by the bank</u> in its capacity as executor, administrator, guardian, or trustee under a will or deed AND that the fund so created is <u>not</u> subject to the $10,000/$100,000 limitations for funds created under the provisions of Section 9.18 (c) (3). (¶ 3) May we have your official comment on our interpretation of Section 9.18 as soon as possible. Very truly yours BAKER, SEXTON, AND CAVELL Joseph T. Baker, President

---

Job 5 [LM p. 131]
Business letter
block; open

July 27, 19-- Mr. Jon C. Stoner, Treasurer Anoka Kiwanis Club 1604 Water Street Anoka, WI 55303 Dear Mr. Stoner (¶ 1) We have examined the transactions relating to the operation of the Anoka Kiwanis Foundation for the fiscal year ended June 30, 19--. The initialed markings in the transaction journal indicate that source documents for each transaction were examined and/or that the transactions were traced to a reconciled record. (¶ 2) The reconciled cash balance in the First National Bank checking account as of June 30 is $864.15. The balance in the First National Bank savings account as of June 30 is $10,528.94. (¶ 3) Please attach this letter to the inside cover of your transaction journal as evidence of the detailed examination. Very truly yours BAKER, SEXTON, AND CAVELL Sara T. VanLant, Auditor

Space down 7 times to leave top margin of 1" or 2.54 cm

Shown in pica type 60-space line

```
October 28, 19--



SUBJECT:  Guides for Typing Memorandums


1.  Insert a half sheet of paper with short side against paper
    guide, long side even with top edge of alignment scale.

2.  Use single spacing and a writing line of 60 spaces.

3.  Space down 7 times and type the date on the 7th line space
    to leave a top margin of 6 blank lines:  1 in. or 2.54 cm.

4.  Space down 4 times to leave 3 blank line spaces between
    date and subject lines.

5.  Space down 3 times to leave 2 blank line spaces between
    subject line and first listed item or paragraph.
```

Space down 4 times to leave 3 blank line spaces

2 spaces

TS

Reset left margin stop 4 spaces to the right

DS

Informational memorandum: numbered list

32c ▶35 Problem typing: informational memorandums

supplies needed: 2 half sheets
60-space line

1. Read the memo shown above, checking each guide against the model.

2. Type the model memo. After typing Line 1 of Item 1, reset left margin stop 4 spaces to the right. Use margin release key and backspace 4 times to position carriage for typing remaining numbers.

3. Type line for line the memo shown in print at the right. If time permits, proofread and correct your copy; then retype the memo from your corrected copy.

October 30, 19—

SUBJECT: Know Your Typing Paper

On typing paper of standard length, you can type 66 lines on a full sheet but only 33 lines on a half sheet.

On paper of standard width, you can type 85 pica or 102 elite spaces on each line. The center point of the paper is 42 for pica type and 51 for elite; however, many teachers and typists prefer to use 50 as the center point for elite type.

If you use a half sheet with the short side up, you can type only 55 pica or 66 elite spaces on each line. In this case, the center point is 27 for pica type and 33 for elite.

264b-267b, continued

Job 2 [LM pp. 119–126]
Form letters
Type the form letter below (block, open) to the addressees indicated. Date the letter August 21, 19—, on Line 12. Obtain the account data from the list of accounts receivable typed in Job 1. Type the confirmation information at the bottom of the letter a triple space below the enclosure notation.

Arnold Wholesale Co.
405 North Central Avenue
Duluth, MN 55807

Chelsea Merchandisers, Inc.
422 East Wisconsin Avenue
Milwaukee, WI 53202

Colfax & Morgan, Inc.
433 E. Locust Street
Des Moines, IA 50309

International Products Co.
220 North LaSalle Street
Chicago, IL 60601

Ladies and Gentlemen

We are examining the financial statements of the Twin Cities Processing Company, 362 North Robert Street, St. Paul, Minnesota, and wish to obtain confirmation of your account with them as of June 30 of this year. The records of the company show the following:

Invoice	Amount

Will you please compare these data with your records, complete the information below, and return the information to us in the envelope enclosed. Your reply within the next ten days will be appreciated.

Very truly yours

BAKER, SEXTON, AND CAVELL

James C. Caulfield, Auditor

xx

Enclosure

__________No exceptions.

Exceptions:

____
Signature

____
Title

33

33a ▶7 Conditioning practice

each line 3 times SS (slowly, faster, slowly); DS between 3-line groups

alphabet JoAnn Vezie quickly won her big chance from DeLuxe Products.

figures Type these numbers with quiet hands: 50, 128, 364, and 957.

fluency The city auditor may handle the penalty for the island firm.

| 1 | 2 | 3 | 4 | 5 | 6 | 7 | 8 | 9 | 10 | 11 | 12 |

33b ▶8 Improve tabulating technique

type twice SS; 60-space line; 8 spaces between columns

27	63	489	577	1,285	10:30
36	80	395	620	2,469	10:45
83	62	784	905	3,593	11:15
66	99	493	488	6,207	11:50
78	89	744	722	7,563	12:40

key | 2 | 8 | 2 | 8 | 3 | 8 | 3 | 8 | 5 | 8 | 5 |

33c ▶15 Learn to center copy vertically

supplies needed: 2 half sheets

1. Determine exact top margin (follow steps below).

2. Type each drill DS, centering each line horizontally.

Vertical centering

1. Count the lines and blank line spaces needed. (Count 2 blank line spaces for triple spacing below main or secondary heading and 1 blank line space between double-spaced lines.)

2. Subtract lines needed from 66 for a full sheet or from 33 for a half sheet.

3. Divide remainder by 2 to get top and bottom margins. If a fraction results, disregard it.

4. Space down from top edge of paper 1 more than number of lines to be left in top margin.

Top margin	11	33
Lines used	10	−10
Bottom margin	12	23 ÷ 2 = 11½

Start on Line 12.

Reading position. For *reading position*, used only for full sheets (or for half sheets with short side up), subtract 2 from lines determined for exact top margin.

PERSONAL INFORMATION

TS

James E. Armstrong

DS

October 18, 1962

3647 Sam Houston Place

San Antonio, TX 78212

PERSONAL INFORMATION

Your Name

Your Birth Date

Your Street Address

Your City, State, and ZIP Code

Did you begin each drill on Line 12?

264b-267b ▶45 Production typing

You have been hired as a clerk–typist by Baker, Sexton, and Cavell, Certified Public Accountants, 526 Marquette Avenue, Minneapolis, MN 55402.

Follow directions carefully. Make carbon copies when directed; address envelopes when appropriate. Proofread your work carefully; accuracy is of vital importance.

Job 1
List of accounts receivable

From the worksheet below, type a list of the accounts receivable for the Twin Cities Processing Company; DS; reading position; 1 cc. Main heading: TWIN CITIES PROCESSING COMPANY; secondary heading: Accounts Receivable as of June 30, 19—. Use the column headings shown in the worksheet; do not type the lines.

ACCOUNTS RECEIVABLE WORKSHEET

Client *Twin Cities Processing Company*

Cutoff date *June 30*

COMPANY	INVOICE	AMOUNT
Arnold Wholesale Co.	793218	$1,245.90
	793415	978.00
	800126	863.25
Barry Distributors, Inc.	792530	2,681.60
	795821	1,009.30
Chelsea Merchandisers, Inc.	789993	3,141.55
	794613	1,873.40
	800436	1,341.70
Colfax & Morgan, Inc.	785321	4,821.60
	794785	2,689.40
	800527	1,732.35
International Products Co.	782463	2,568.22
	797352	2,908.76
	800634	4,563.20
Swensen Wholesale Co.	796732	3,461.80
	800745	956.27

33d ▶20
Problem typing: centering announcements

supplies needed: 2 half sheets

Center each problem vertically, each line horizontally. **To TS when machine is set for DS:** DS, then turn the platen (cylinder) forward one space by hand.

SOPHOMORE CLASS OFFICERS
TS

Carol Shatner, President

Greg Randall, Vice President

Dolores Valdez, Secretary

Evan Jakobs, Treasurer

ANNOUNCING

Metropolitan Typewriting Contest

Tuesday, December 28, 3 p.m.

Convention Center, Room 75

Information: Miss Elise Homan

PRIZES, AWARDS, CERTIFICATES

34

34a ▶7
Conditioning practice

each line 3 times SS (slowly, faster, slowly); DS between 3-line groups

alphabet Janet will quickly explain what Dave Gibson made for prizes.

figures I type 37, 46, and 58 quickly, but I slow up for 23 and 190.

fluency Do rush the worn panels to the auto firm for them to enamel.

| 1 | 2 | 3 | 4 | 5 | 6 | 7 | 8 | 9 | 10 | 11 | 12 |

34b ▶12
Goal typing: paragraphs

1. Select an appropriate 2′ goal; then type two 2′ *speed* writings, trying to reach or exceed that goal.

2. Select a 3′ goal; type two 3′ *speed* writings, trying to reach or exceed that goal.

	gwam 2′	3′
Time is a constant, for all of us have an equal amount	5	4
of it. How we use time determines the extent of our success	12	8
because it is an important ingredient in all our work. Time	18	12
should be prized highly and used wisely if we want to enjoy	24	16
maximum success. Thinking requires time, it is true; but we	30	20
can conserve time by taking time to think before we begin our	36	24
work. The likelihood of having to do work over is increased	42	28
by starting it before thinking through all related problems.	48	32

gwam 2′ | 1 | 2 | 3 | 4 | 5 | 6 |
3′ | 1 | 2 | 3 | 4 |

34c ▶31
Problem typing: review

1. Make a handwritten list of these problems:
page 53, 32c, both problems
page 55, 33d, script problem

2. With your list as a guide, type each problem once as directed. Proofread completed problems, circling each error.

Goal: To improve skill in arranging copy.

263c ▶25 Improve basic skill: statistical copy

1. A 5′ writing on ¶s 1–2 combined. Find *gwam*.
2. Two 3′ writings on each ¶ to increase speed. Find *gwam*.
3. A 5′ writing on ¶s 1–2 combined to measure improvement. Find *gwam*.

all letters/figures used

HA	1.6 si	5.8 awl	75% hfw

	gwam 3′	5′
The demand for bookkeeping workers continues to rise despite the	4	3
growing use of the computer and other complex equipment to process data.	9	6
Between the years 1960 and 1970, for example, the number of bookkeepers	14	8
in the work force rose from 794,000 to 1,290,000, an increase of 496,000	19	11
or more than 62% in a period of 10 years. There were also more than	23	14
58,000 bookkeeping and billing machine operators employed in 1970. The	28	17
median salary for bookkeeping clerks in 1972 ranged from a little less	33	20
than $6,600 annually for a worker new on the job to more than $7,500	38	23
annually for one with some experience. A high school graduate who has	42	26
taken typewriting and bookkeeping can qualify as a bookkeeping clerk.	47	28
A certified public accountant, or CPA, offers financial services	4	31
to the public for a fee. In 1975, more than 720,000 people worked as	9	34
accountants, of whom about 20% were certified public accountants. Any-	14	36
one who serves as a CPA must hold a certificate issued by one of the 50	19	39
states. A survey made in 1975 revealed that the criteria for the CPA	23	42
vary greatly among the 50 states. In 31 states, a person must be 21	28	45
years or older to become a CPA, although 15 states require that the	32	48
individual be only 18 years old. A total of 26 states demand a 4-year	37	50
college degree, whereas the remaining 24 states do not definitely	42	53
specify a college degree. All states administer a written examination.	46	56
Although 40% of the states impose a fee of $50, fees for the examination	51	59
range from $25 to $100. In 37 states, a CPA must be a citizen of the	56	62
United States; in the remaining 13 states, citizenship is not mandatory.	61	65

gwam 3′ | 1 | 2 | 3 | 4 | 5 |
5′ | 1 | 2 | 3 |

264-267

264a-267a ▶5 Conditioning practice

twice SS; repeat difficult lines

A plan to nationalize mining was quickly rejected by the five experts.
Our new Model 38659 has 14 digits, 20 memories, and 578 program steps.
Cut 2″ x 4″ lumber to these lengths: 4′6″, 5′8″, 3′1″, 7′9″, and 10′.
The custodian spends much of his time checking the locks on the doors.

| 1 | 2 | 3 | 4 | 5 | 6 | 7 | 8 | 9 | 10 | 11 | 12 | 13 | 14 |

35

35a ▶7 Conditioning practice

each line 3 times SS (slowly, faster, slowly); DS between 3-line groups

alphabet John Fox left my quiz show and gave back a prize he had won.

figures Long numbers may reduce the speed: 1,579, 2,485, and 5,630.

fluency Keith may amend the six audit forms if it is right to do so.

| 1 | 2 | 3 | 4 | 5 | 6 | 7 | 8 | 9 | 10 | 11 | 12 |

35b ▶8 Improve technique: response patterns

type once untimed; then type a 1′ writing on each of Lines 2, 4, and 6

letter response
1 I agree | you referred | in a million | gets started | at my address
2 At best, I fear only a few union cases were ever acted upon.

word response
3 the bid | turns down | the usual | a visual | with vigor | social work
4 All the social work may end if they turn down the usual aid.

combination response
5 he stated | due regard | usual reserve | the average | their opinion
6 At the start signal, work with great vigor to make the rate.

| 1 | 2 | 3 | 4 | 5 | 6 | 7 | 8 | 9 | 10 | 11 | 12 |

35c ▶10 Check keystroking skill

1. A 1′ writing on each ¶; determine *gwam* and circle your errors.

Goal: At least 28 *gwam*; no more than 2 errors.

2. A 3′ writing on ¶s 1–3 combined; determine *gwam* and circle your errors.

Goal: At least 25 *gwam*; no more than 8 errors.

all letters used | LA | 1.4 si | 5.4 awl | 85% hfw |

Text	gwam 2′	3′
Typing is more fun since I am learning to arrange copy	5	4
in the style of messages. Of course I realize that without	11	8
good basic speed and control, typing a long report or paper	17	12
would become a quite tedious job.	21	14
For that reason I plan to build my basic skill just as	26	18
high as possible even though one vital purpose for practice	32	22
is to learn to apply it. The combination of high skill and	38	26
layout knowledge is needed to produce quality work.	44	29
Even a quick study of the personal papers I compose in	49	33
longhand makes me realize I can expect to type figures plus	55	37
some basic symbols. I am sure both will be used widely for	61	41
office work, too. My preparation must include them.	66	44

gwam 2′ | 1 | 2 | 3 | 4 | 5 | 6 |
3′ | 1 | 2 | 3 | 4 |

unit **46** lessons 263–267

Finance office typing

Learning goals

1. To improve production skill by typing representative jobs found in a finance office.

2. To type straight copy and statistical copy at higher speeds and with improved control.

263

263a ▶5 Conditioning practice

twice SS; repeat difficult lines

alphabet	We have a joint group of experts analyze the bond market each quarter.
figures	Train 137 for Tampa will arrive on Track 6 at 8:45 and depart at 9:20.
fig/sym	The interest due on September 19 is $25.67 ($3,850 for 60 days at 4%).
fluency	It pays to work for both quantity and quality in all that you must do.

| 1 | 2 | 3 | 4 | 5 | 6 | 7 | 8 | 9 | 10 | 11 | 12 | 13 | 14 |

263b ▶20 Increase straight-copy speed: progressive straight copy

1. Three 1′ writings on each ¶; find and compare *gwam*.

2. Three 1′ writings on each of the slower ¶s to increase speed on more difficult copy.

3. A 5′ control writing on ¶s 1–3 combined; find *gwam*; circle errors.

¶				
¶ 1	E	1.3 si	5.2 awl	90% hfw
¶ 2	A	1.5 si	5.6 awl	80% hfw
¶ 3	D	1.7 si	6.0 awl	70% hfw

all letters used

	gwam 1′	5′	
Few of us realize how much we depend on language. When we are	13	3	47
young, we learn to talk very quickly. As we get older, we learn to	26	5	50
read and express our ideas in writing. Rarely, though, do most of us	40	8	52
stop to think that language is an important tool in living. Without	54	11	55
language, our ideas would be of little value and we would make little	68	14	58
or no progress in life.	73	15	59
The effective use of language is based on several vital factors.	13	17	62
Since all communication is based on words, you must develop a rich and	27	20	64
varied vocabulary so that you can use the words that will convey the	41	23	67
exact meaning you wish to express. Words alone, however, are of little	56	26	70
value unless you can link them together properly. This means that you	70	28	73
must be an expert in the mechanics of grammar and style.	81	31	75
Business places a premium on individuals who can utilize language	13	33	78
skillfully. People who are adept in clerical skills can obtain good	27	36	80
jobs, but those who have also developed an ability to express ideas	41	39	83
vividly and concisely receive promotions more quickly. If you excel	54	42	86
in the art of language, you will be rewarded in terms of better jobs.	68	44	89

gwam 1′ | 1 | 2 | 3 | 4 | 5 | 6 | 7 | 8 | 9 | 10 | 11 | 12 | 13 | 14 |
5′ | 1 | 2 | 3 |

35d ▶25
Problem typing: centering memorandums and announcements

supplies needed: 3 half sheets

Problem 1
Beginning on Line 7, type line for line the memo shown at the right. *Remember to reset left margin stop 4 spaces to right after typing Line 1 of Item 2 of the list.*

November 1, 19--

SUBJECT: Spacing with Punctuation Marks

Return without spacing after any punctuation mark that ends a line. Otherwise, follow these guides:

1. Space once after , and ; used as marks of punctuation.
2. Space twice after . ending a sentence. Space once after . following an initial or an abbreviation, but do not space after . within an abbreviation.
3. Space once after ? within a sentence, twice after ? at the end of a sentence.
4. Space twice after : used to introduce a list, an example, or a quotation; do not space after : used to express time.

Problem 2
Center the problem vertically, each line horizontally. TS below heading; DS remaining lines.

THE STREET SINGERS

offer folk music concert

Friday, December 1, 8:30 p.m.

Queen City Playhouse

87 Opera Place

Student Admission: 95 cents

THE STREET SINGERS
offer folk music concert
Friday, December 1, 8:30 p.m.
Queen City Playhouse
87 Opera Place
Student Admission: 95 cents

Problem 3
Center the problem vertically; DS the ¶s. Proofread and mark your errors for correction.

FINDING ERRORS

Typing errors c ost money in an office. They require a lot of time to corect in personal work,too. Since this is so, I must try to prepare an acurate paper now and then.

There is a time to push speed, of course; but their is a time also towork with care or control and I must learn soon to proofread my work and correct earch error that I find in the work.

Enrichment material for Unit 5 appears on LM p. 16.

260b-262b, continued

JOB DESCRIPTION

JOB TITLE: Purchasing clerk | D.O.T. NUMBER: 223.368

ALTERNATE TITLE: Clerk-typist | DEPARTMENT: Purchasing

DATE OF ANALYSIS: July 12, 19-- | NUMBER AUTHORIZED: 15

JOB SUMMARY: Under the direct supervision of the general office manager, performs such clerical duties as typing, filing, compiling and verifying information, and computing costs involved in the purchase of supplies, equipment, and services.

DUTIES OF THE JOB:

1. Maintains up-to-date specification files of supplies and equipment.
2. Maintains file of suppliers and their performance.
3. Types invitations to bid and mails invitations to suppliers.
4. Compiles data to prepare purchase orders.
5. Computes individual and total cost of items purchased.
6. Types purchase orders.
7. Performs other similar and related tasks as required.

MINIMUM JOB REQUIREMENTS:

Education: High school diploma (business course)

Experience: One year of clerical work desirable

Abilities: Type 60 GWAM; operate standard office machines

Personal: Pleasing personality; neat appearance

unit **6** lessons 36–40

The basic symbols

Learning goals

1. To learn to type basic symbols by touch and with good technique.
2. To improve skill in typing statistical copy.
3. To type straight copy at higher speeds and with improved control.

Machine adjustments

1. Paper guide at *0*.
2. Ribbon control on *black*.
3. Margin sets: 60–space line.
4. Line–space selector on *1* for drills; on *2* for ¶s; as directed for problems.

36

36a ▶7 Conditioning practice

each line 3 times SS (slowly, faster, slowly); DS between 3-line groups

alphabet What size desk can Peggy Vixon buy for him at J. L. Squires?

figures Review all figures: 11, 65, 74, 83, 92, 201, 299, 300, 640.

fluency Is the auditor to join us on the panel at the big town hall?

| 1 | 2 | 3 | 4 | 5 | 6 | 7 | 8 | 9 | 10 | 11 | 12 |

36b ▶8 Learn new keys: $ and / (diagonal)

Reach technique for $

Shift; then reach *up* to $ with *left first* finger.

Reach technique for /

Reach *down* to / with *right little* finger.

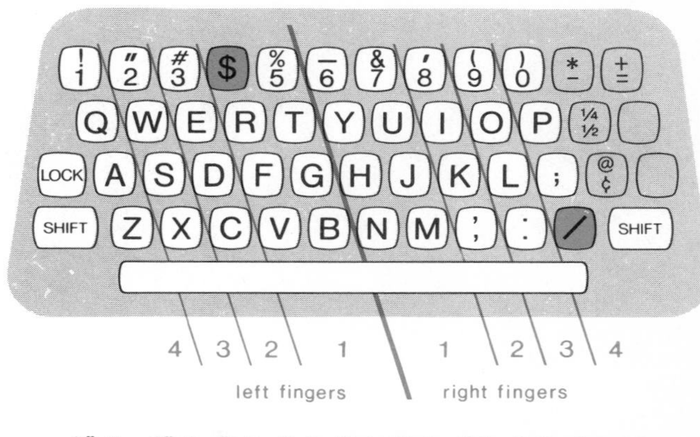

4$f 4$f $f $f $4 $4 $8 $8 $148

?/; ?/; /; /; / 1/3 2/5 and/or

36c ▶10 Improve symbol control

type twice

Use . to type decimal point.

Technique cue: Hands and arms quiet; reach with the fingers.

$ MAY SPECIAL: shoes, $20; slacks, $15; shirts, $6; ties, $4.
The $35 balance includes sales of $8.17, $12.94, and $13.89.

/ Use / to type fractions: 1/4, 1/3, 2/5, 1/2, 3/5, 2/3, 3/4.
Space between a whole number and a fraction: 5 3/4, 16 2/3.

$ / Their new rates are: Kevin, $3.50/hour; Dianne, $3.65/hour.
Jo worked 2 1/2 hours for $6.25; Al, 5 1/2 hours for $14.85.

36d ▶7 Improve tabulating technique

type twice SS; 60-space line; 8 spaces between columns

Each figure is used at least 6 times.

10	638	927	930	$472	5 4/5
20	114	205	916	$658	7 2/3
30	995	288	314	$727	6 5/8
40	637	938	466	$150	4 7/8

key | 2 | 8 | 3 | 8 | 3 | 8 | 3 | 8 | 4 | 8 | 5 |

260b-262b, continued

Job 3 [LM pp. 99–106]
Purchase orders

1. Type the purchase orders at the right with 1 cc to the R. W. Simpson Tool Co., 200 East Market Street, Indianapolis, IN 46204. All terms are 2/10, n/30.

2. Obtain the name and price of each item from the catalog page typed in Job 1, page 398. Compute the cost of each item and the total amount of each purchase order.

Order No.: 58904-P
Date: August 16, 19--
Ship via: Allstate Transfer Co.

Quantity	Catalog No.
25	7M1642
25	8R1297
40	8R6023
50	8T3101

Order No.: 59367-P
Date: November 21, 19--
Ship via: Mack Transportation

Quantity	Catalog No.
100	8M1457
30	8R3922
50	8T3100

Order No.: 59002-P
Date: September 30, 19--
Ship via: Central Motor

Quantity	Catalog No.
30	8T3104
20	8T3353
75	8T6032
15	9T1047

Order No.: 60012-P
Date: December 31, 19--
Ship via: Freidan Van Lines

Quantity	Catalog No.
150	8T3349
45	8T3353
40	8R6022
15	7M1642
15	8R1297

Job 4
Composing a summary of bids

Compose a report, in unbound style, on the bids received in response to invitations to bid dated August 7 for 150,000 molded silvered mica capacitors. Provide an appropriate title. In ¶ 1, point out that seven suppliers submitted bids by the deadline of September 21; then, summarize the bids as shown below. As a final ¶, point out that the lowest bid was $0.76 per unit submitted by the National Electronics Corporation and that this bid represents an increase of approximately 12% in the cost of the item.

Supplier	Bid	Terms
National Electronics Corporation	$114,000	Net
G & L Manufacturing Company	129,500	2/10, n/30
Stellar Electronics, Inc.	130,200	Net
Electroparts Manufacturing Company	133,400	Net
Goodman Electric Supplies Company, Inc.	139,200	3/30, n/60
Ames Electronics Company	141,700	Net
Payne Electronics, Inc.	145,100	Net

Job 5 [LM p. 107]
Job description

Type the job description on page 404. DS between numbered duties. Make a cc on plain paper. If a form is not available, type the form and the information with 1 cc on plain paper. Use 1" top and side margins.

36e ▶18
Goal typing: paragraphs

1. Type ¶ 1 for 1′. If you complete it within the minute, move to ¶ 2 for the next timing, and so on. If you are unable to complete a ¶ within the minute, repeat it until you do. If you complete a ¶ *before* time is called, repeat as much as you can. [10′]

2. Two 3′ writings, beginning with ¶ 1 and typing as far as you can. Determine *gwam*.

Goal: At least 25 *gwam*; not more than 8 errors.

all letters used | LA | 1.4 si | 5.4 awl | 85% hfw

		gwam 1′	3′
¶ 1	I shall soon experience quite effective uses for my new	11	4
	skill. That is one of my major reasons for learning to type.	23	8
¶ 2	During the next few months, I will master the typing of	11	11
	social and business papers. Perhaps, then, they will dub me	23	16
	a real typist.	26	17
¶ 3	Letters, reports, and tables are among the tasks I must	11	20
	master now. According to one recent study, these are simple	23	24
	jobs that I must do very well.	29	26
¶ 4	My speed may indeed drop as I change from straight copy	11	30
	to job typing. Therefore, I must remember to employ my best	23	34
	work habits for every job, whatever its size.	32	37
¶ 5	Skill developed on copy used up to this time will stand	11	41
	me in really good stead. Of particular aid will be my skill	23	46
	in using the return and tabulator, and the backspacer, also.	35	49
¶ 6	Learning to type is hard work; however, the skill built	11	53
	makes my time well spent. If following a better method will	23	57
	speed progress, I will pursue it. I need sufficient ability	35	61
	to do a top job.	38	62

gwam 1′ | 1 | 2 | 3 | 4 | 5 | 6 | 7 | 8 | 9 | 10 | 11 | 12 |
3′ | 1 | 2 | 3 | 4 |

37

37a ▶7
Conditioning practice

each line 3 times SS (slowly, faster, slowly); DS between 3-line groups

alphabet Having pumped in six quick points, Jerry Dow froze the ball.

figure/symbol No space separates $ or / and figures: $49, $320, 5/6, 7/8.

fluency All six of the clerks may work with the auditor of the firm.

| 1 | 2 | 3 | 4 | 5 | 6 | 7 | 8 | 9 | 10 | 11 | 12 |

37b ▶18
Goal typing: paragraphs

Retype 36e, above, beginning with the last ¶ you completed in 1′.

260b-262b, continued

Job 2 [LM pp. 91–98]
Invitation-to-bid letters

1. Type the invitation-to-bid letter below for the signature of Jefferson T. Lincoln, Director of Purchasing, to the suppliers listed below.

2. Date the letters August 7, 19—; provide an appropriate salutation and complimentary close. Insert the information regarding each item, as illustrated at the right, from the cards typed in Job 1.

3. Use modified block style, mixed punctuation with 1" margins; begin the date on Line 12. Make 1 cc of each letter.

```
will be provided upon request.  Bids must be received no later than
September 1, 19--.

ITEM:  CABLE, MULTICONDUCTOR (Type B)

SPECIFICATIONS:

       Govt. specification:  MIL-W-1878D
       Insulation:  .025 mm Polyvinyl
       Temp. range:  -55° C to +105° C
       Voltage rating:  600 volts

QUANTITY:  100,000

DELIVERY:  November 10, 19--

The supplier of this item will be designated as a subcontractor
under U.S. Government Procurement Regulations.  As such, the sup-
```

Supplier:	**G & L Manufacturing Co.** **135 Main Street** **Akron, OH 44308**	Supplier:	**Stellar Electronics, Inc.** **1040 Quarrier Street** **Charleston, WV 25301**
Bids due:	**September 1, 19--**	Bids due:	**September 10, 19--**
Item:	(From Card 1)	Item:	(From Card 5)
Quantity:	**100,000**	Quantity:	**120,000**
Delivery:	**November 10, 19--**	Delivery:	**November 30, 19--**
Supplier:	**Payne Electronics, Inc.** **305 W. Seventh Street** **Fort Worth, TX 76102**	Supplier:	**Ames Electronics Company** **467 Congress Street** **Portland, ME 04111**
Bids due:	**September 10, 19--**	Bids due:	**September 21, 19--**
Item:	(From Card 3)	Item:	(From Card 6)
Quantity:	**50,000**	Quantity:	**150,000**
Delivery:	**November 16, 19--**	Delivery:	**December 14, 19--**

Subject: Invitation to Bid

You are invited to submit a sealed bid for the item listed below with the general specifications indicated. Detailed specifications will be provided upon request. Bids must be received no later than ____________.

ITEM:

SPECIFICATIONS:

QUANTITY:

DELIVERY:

The supplier of this item will be designated as a subcontractor under U.S. Government Procurement Regulations. As such, the supplier must certify that he will abide by all statutory regulations governing the manufacture and supply of goods to the Federal Government, including the provisions of the Walsh-Healey and Davis-Bacon Acts.

Notification of the award of the contract will be made within ten days after the date established for the receipt of bids.

37c ▶8 Learn new keys: - (hyphen) and % (percent)

Reach technique for -

Reach *up* to - with *right little* finger.

Reach technique for %

Shift; then reach *up* to % with *left first* finger.

left fingers 4 3 2 1 — right fingers 1 2 3 4

```
-;- -;- -p -p -- 5-star 4-cent
5%f 5%f %f %f 5% 5% 9% 8 or 8%
```

37d ▶10 Improve symbol control

type twice

Type 2 hyphens to make a -- (dash).

Technique cue: Hands and arms quiet; reach with the fingers.

- and --	I used a 6-inch line--72 elite spaces--for my 2-page letter. I used a 6-inch line--60 pica spaces--for the 5-page report.
%	We offer trade discounts of 10%, 15%, and 20% on all orders. In 1976, 35% of our employees were women; now, over 40% are.
- , --, and %	You expect 12%-15% of our students to place in the upper 5%? A rate change from 9% to 8% will save me 1%--that is $15.25.

37e ▶7 Goal typing: sentences

1. A 1′ *speed* writing on Line 1. Determine *gwam*.

2. Type each of the other sentences in the same way.

Goal: To try to approach your Line 1 *gwam*.

goal line Learn to make the reach to the shift key with proper timing.

Send 135 clipboards, 270 ruled pads, and 68 pens to Room 49.

We borrowed $2,500 last month at an interest rate of 7 1/2%.

They bought 320 sq. yds. of shag carpeting for $8.95/sq. yd.

I found this up-to-date WORD DIVISION MANUAL for just $1.50.

| 1 | 2 | 3 | 4 | 5 | 6 | 7 | 8 | 9 | 10 | 11 | 12 |

Supplemental individualized practice

As time permits during this unit, type a 1′ writing on each line. Compare rates, then type additional writings on slower lines.

balanced-hand	The auditor is to aid the six antique firms with their work.
combination	Pamela saw a car turn into the lane and a young man get out.
third row	Speed is sure to result if you keep typing at a steady pace.
adjacent keys	Were they aware that the union had asked for a new contract?
outside reaches	Quin popped up to our prize pitcher in the top of the sixth.
bottom row	Zane gave a cab card to all men and women at the taxi stand.
direct reaches	Myra found out that curved fingers help her to type numbers.

| 1 | 2 | 3 | 4 | 5 | 6 | 7 | 8 | 9 | 10 | 11 | 12 |

260-262

260a-262a ▶5 Conditioning practice

twice SS;
repeat difficult lines

When will Jack pulverize the sixty bags of defective quinine compound?
Complete Lines 3, 4, 7, 9, and 12 of Form 8560 and return it by May 7.
The local tax is 3%; sales tax, 6%; state tax, 2.5%; and wage tax, 1%.
To avoid a big penalty, the auditor must pay this bill when it is due.

| 1 | 2 | 3 | 4 | 5 | 6 | 7 | 8 | 9 | 10 | 11 | 12 | 13 | 14 |

260b-262b ▶45 Production typing

In these lessons, you will work as a clerk-typist in the Purchasing Department of the Dynalux Manufacturing Co., 331 West Colfax Avenue, Denver, CO 80204.

Read and follow directions carefully; check all work *before* you remove it from the typewriter to insure that it is free of errors.

Job 1 [LM pp. 79, 89]
Index cards for a specification file

1. Type an index card for each of the items listed below.

2. Type the name of the item in all caps on the third line from the top of the card. Type the specifications a triple space below the name of the item, double-spaced.

3. Arrange the cards in alphabetic order and number them from 1 to 6 in the upper right-hand corner.

Note: To type the ± sign, strike the + key, backspace, and strike the underline.

```
CABLE, MULTICONDUCTOR (Type B)                   1

Govt. specification:  MIL-W-1878D

Insulation:  .025 mm Polyvinyl

Temp. range:  -55° C to +105° C

Voltage rating:  600 volts
```

SOLENOID, AC, INTERMITTENT
Govt. specification: MIL-S-9705
Volts: 115
Ohms: 300
Amps: .17
Maximum lift: .255 kg

RESISTOR, SILICON, 1/4 WATT
Govt. specification: MIL-R-16A
Temp. resist. coefficient: .7° C
Tolerance: ± 10%
Dimensions: 6 x 12 mm

CAPACITOR, GLASS
Govt. specification: MIL-C-1127B
Range: 1,000 to 100,000 pf
Voltage rating: 50 VDC
Temp. range: −55° C to +125° C

CABLE, MULTICONDUCTOR (Type B)
Govt. specification: MIL-W-1878D
Insulation: .025 mm Polyvinyl
Temp. range: −55° C to +105° C
Voltage rating: 600 volts

CONVECTION COOLER, FIN DESIGN
Govt. specification: MIL-C-20
Cooling area: 25 cm^2
Convection: 70° C rise at 100 watt power dissipation

CAPACITOR, MOLDED SILVERED MICA
Govt. specification: MIL-C-5
Temp. range: −55° C to +85° C
Tolerance: ± 5%
Dimensions: 6 mm dia. x 12 mm length

38

38a ▶7
Conditioning practice

each line 3 times SS (slowly, faster, slowly); DS between 3-line groups

alphabet — If Cy Zin quits, Ray will pick Vic Fox to judge my big show.

figure/symbol — Shift for $ and %--not for 3/5, 160 ft., 78 yds., or p. 249.

fluency — It is feared they may land on the east end of the wet field.

| 1 | 2 | 3 | 4 | 5 | 6 | 7 | 8 | 9 | 10 | 11 | 12 |

38b ▶8
Learn new keys: left and right parentheses (and)

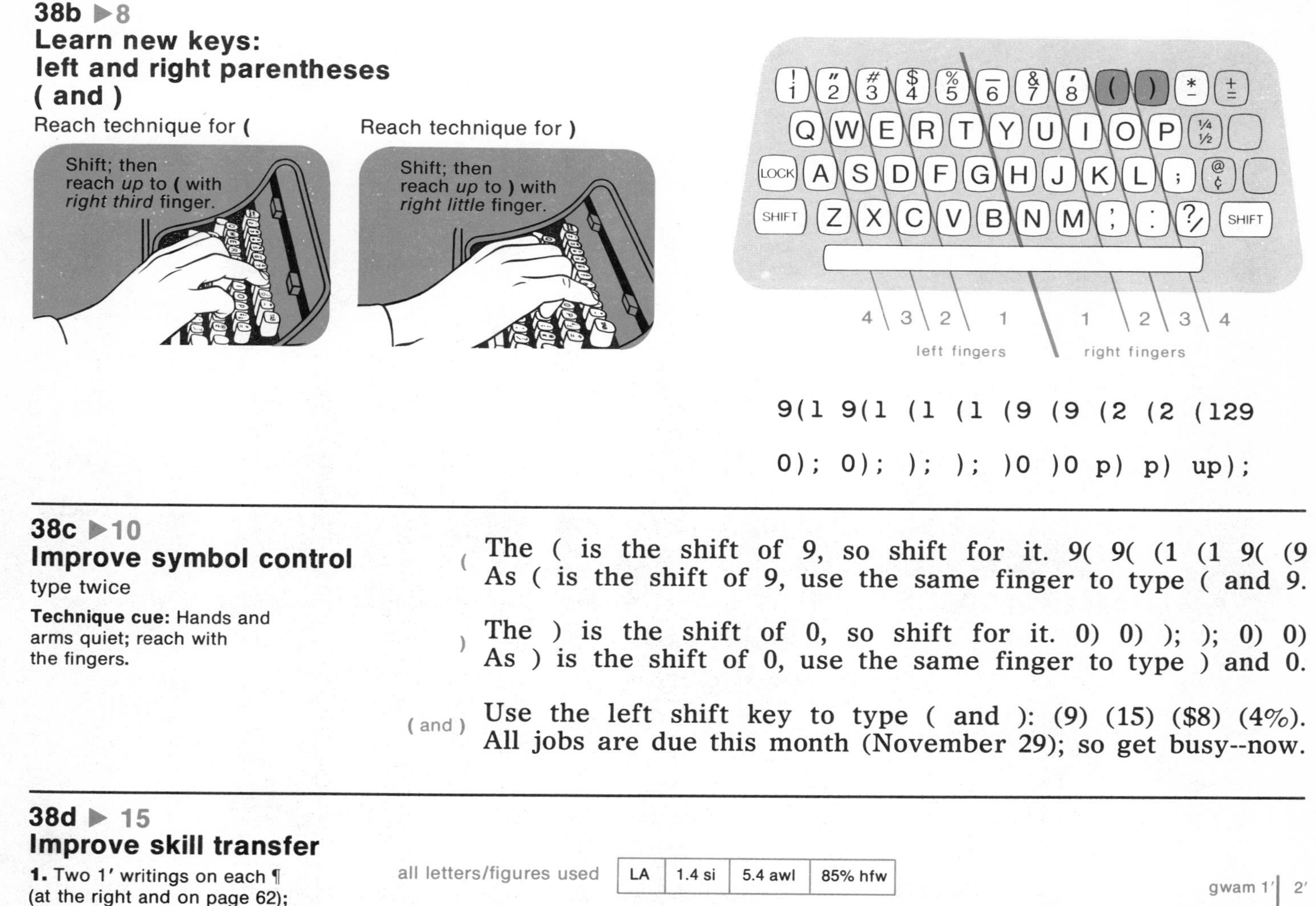

Reach technique for (
Shift; then reach *up* to (with *right third* finger.
Reach technique for)
Shift; then reach *up* to) with *right little* finger.
left fingers
right fingers
4 3 2 1
1 2 3 4

9(1 9(1 (1 (1 (9 (9 (2 (2 (129

0); 0);););)0)0 p) p) up);

38c ▶10
Improve symbol control

type twice

Technique cue: Hands and arms quiet; reach with the fingers.

(— The (is the shift of 9, so shift for it. 9(9((1 (1 9((9
As (is the shift of 9, use the same finger to type (and 9.

) — The) is the shift of 0, so shift for it. 0) 0));); 0) 0)
As) is the shift of 0, use the same finger to type) and 0.

(and) — Use the left shift key to type (and): (9) (15) ($8) (4%).
All jobs are due this month (November 29); so get busy--now.

38d ▶ 15
Improve skill transfer

1. Two 1′ writings on each ¶ (at the right and on page 62); determine better *gwam* on each.

2. Determine % of transfer: straight-copy *gwam* divided into *gwam* on each of the other kinds of copy.

all letters/figures used | LA | 1.4 si | 5.4 awl | 85% hfw |

Text	gwam 1′	2′
It has often been said that everyone should know how to	11	5
type. Although that is stretching the truth a little, no one	24	12
was ever penalized for knowing how. One need not be a clerk	36	18
or secretary to know that typing is a major communication aid	48	24
in private and professional life as well.	56	28

gwam 1′ | 1 | 2 | 3 | 4 | 5 | 6 | 7 | 8 | 9 | 10 | 11 | 12 |
2′ | 1 | 2 | 3 | 4 | 5 | 6 |

(continued, page 62)

257b-259b, continued

Job 4 [LM pp. 77–80]
Order acknowledgment postal cards

1. Prepare order acknowledgment postal cards like the one at the right to Addressees 2, 8, 9, 10, 12, and 13 in the index card file prepared in Job 2.

2. Date the cards August 23, 19––; supply suitable salutations; fill in the appropriate dates from the order register below.

3. Align the fill-ins so that the downstrokes almost touch but do not cut through the underlines.

August 23, 19--

Dear Mr. Lombardo

Thank you for your Order No. S61093.
Shipment will be made on August 30
via Great Lakes Transit.
We appreciate this opportunity to be of service. Whenever you need tools of any kind, remember that we can save you time and money.

R. W. SIMPSON TOOL CO., INC.

ORDER REGISTER				
CUSTOMER	OUR ORDER	CUSTOMER'S ORDER	SHIPPING DATE	SHIPPED VIA (Carrier)
American Allied Mills	719-8	S61093	August 30	Great Lakes Transit
Grinnel Electronics	720-8	AG-30584	September 2	East-West Van Lines
Koenig Appliance Co.	721-8	22401M	August 29	Trailblazer Freight
Peabody Mills	722-8	83257-B	September 3	Thru-Way Express Co.
Standards Instruments Co.	723-8	77-8543	September 6	Coastal Transit Co.
Tenntrex, Inc.	724-8	A 4238	August 29	All-Season Shipping Co.

Job 5 [LM pp. 81–88]
Invoices

1. Type invoices with 1 cc (dated August 29) for Cards 2, 8, 9, and 10 in the index card file prepared in Job 2. The items ordered are shown at the right.

2. Obtain the order numbers, shipping dates, and carriers from the order register above. All terms are net.

3. Obtain the item names and prices from the catalog page typed in Job 1. Compute the cost of each item and the total amount of each invoice.

Addressee 2

Quantity	Catalog No.
10	7M1642
4	8R3922
12	8T3101
100	8T3349

Addressee 9

Quantity	Catalog No.
10	8T3353
15	8T6032
50	8T3349
6	8T3100
20	8M1457

Addressee 8

Quantity	Catalog No.
5	8R1297
20	8R6022
20	8R6023
40	9T1047

Addressee 10

Quantity	Catalog No.
120	8R1297
120	7M1642
200	8R3922

38d, continued

LA	1.4 si	5.4 awl	85% hfw

Read copy carefully.

	gwam 1′	2′
It is known that exact typing skill is often needed for	11	5
getting a job. It can also be an aid in getting promoted.	23	11
Many people often have need for typed documents in private	35	17
life, too. Typing is quite important for all these reasons.	47	23

Study corrections before starting to type.

	gwam 1′	2′
^Good Typists are wokrnig in private a nd public offices	11	5
of every kind. All have a ^wide variety of duties, too. Not	23	12
only do they ^produce ~~type~~ letters of all ^types ~~kinds~~. They also ^compile ~~compose~~	35	18
and type reports, plan and type tables, and fill in forms.	47	23

Keep the hands and arms quiet as you type.

	gwam 1′	2′
In 1973, almost 975 thousand persons in our nation were	11	6
employed as typists at $468 to $594 a month. About 2.9 mil-	23	12
lion people in that same year were in work requiring typing	35	18
as well as shorthand skill, and paid $580 to $758 a month.	47	23

gwam 1′ | 1 | 2 | 3 | 4 | 5 | 6 | 7 | 8 | 9 | 10 | 11 | 12 |
2′ | 1 | 2 | 3 | 4 | 5 | 6 |

38e ▶10
Centering a heading over copy

1. Center the heading TYPEWRITING: A KEY SKILL on Line 13 of a full sheet; then TS.

2. Using the 60-space line for which the margins are set, type DS the ¶s of 38d (pages 61-62).

39

39a ▶7
Conditioning practice

each line 3 times SS (slowly, faster, slowly); DS between 3-line groups

alphabet **Vicki Bold just may win quite a prize for her next pop song.**

figure/symbol **He signed a 36-month note for $1,840 (at 7.5%) on August 29.**

fluency **A key to good form is to sit in a chair of the right height.**

| 1 | 2 | 3 | 4 | 5 | 6 | 7 | 8 | 9 | 10 | 11 | 12 |

39b ▶15
Improve skill transfer

1. Type a 1′ writing on each of the ¶s of 38d, beginning on page 61. Determine *gwam* and compare rates on each kind of copy.

2. Type a 2′ writing on each of the ¶s of 38d, trying to equal your 1′ rate on each of the respective ¶s. Determine % of transfer.

257b-259b, continued

Job 2 [LM pp. 63–67]
Index card file

1. Type an index card for each addressee at the right. On the third line from the top of the card, type the name of the company; space down 4 times and type the complete name and address as shown in the list.

2. Alphabetize the cards by company names; then number the cards from 1 to 14 in the upper right-hand corner.

Dartmouth Corporation
220 West Adams Street
Chicago, IL 60606

Mr. Rex A. Sage, President
Sage-Salem, Inc.
1620 Farnam Street
Omaha, NE 68102

Dr. Sheldon I. Eisen, President
Eisen Scientific Co.
920 South Calhoun Street
Fort Wayne, IN 46802

Mr. Kenneth P. Lombardo
Marketing Vice President
American Allied Mills
12 Lafayette Square
Buffalo, NY 14203

Miss Dora T. McGree, Buyer
Standards Instruments Co.
2950 Quarry Road
St. Paul, MN 55121

Mr. M. W. Eckert, Chief
Purchasing Office
Tenntrex Incorporated
2100 South Division Avenue
Grand Rapids, MI 49507

Mr. Bryan C. Scott
Director of Purchasing
Drake Manufacturing Co.
1002 Marquette Avenue
Green Bay, WI 54304

Miss Helen Goodman, President
Goodman Manufacturing Company
607 Cherry Street
Springfield, MO 65806

Mr. R. E. DeHaven, Chief Buyer
Grinnell Electronics
1102 South Broad Street
Trenton, NJ 08611

Mr. Jacques P. Andre
Purchasing Agent
Peabody Mills
102 West Main Street
Fort Wayne, IN 46802

Mr. Edwin A. Goodrich, President
Goodrich & Sons, Inc.
One 16th Street
Sioux City, IA 51103

Ms. G. T. Gomez, Director
Marketing Division
Ace Fabricators, Inc.
1375 Wisconsin Avenue
Joliet, IL 60432

Koenig Appliance Co.
630 West Market Street
Akron, OH 44303

Mrs. Jan C. Wells, Product Manager
Universal American Appliances, Inc.
2300 Easton Road
Rockford, IL 61107

Job 3 [LM pp. 69–76]
Sales letters

Type the letter at the right on executive-size stationery to Addressees 1, 3, 5, and 14 of the address file typed in Job 2. Use block style with open punctuation. Provide an appropriate salutation and complimentary close.

July 17, 19-- (¶ 1) Although it is only "first down and 9 decimeters to go," the metric revolution has begun. Many businessmen find that they are losing sales because they are unable to provide items with metric dimensions. In a few years, the demand for metric products will increase dramatically. (¶ 2) You can depend on us to supply the tools you need when you convert to metric measurements. We stock a number of general-purpose tools in metric sizes as shown on the enclosed price list. If you need special-purpose tools, we can produce them quickly in our ultramodern factory. (¶ 3) If you are interested in quality, service, and economy in purchasing tools of any kind, call or write to us today. For over 25 years, R. W. Simpson has enjoyed a reputation for outstanding values and service. George T. Albertson Marketing Director

39c ▶8
Learn new keys: ' (apostrophe) and ! (exclamation)

Apostrophe (')

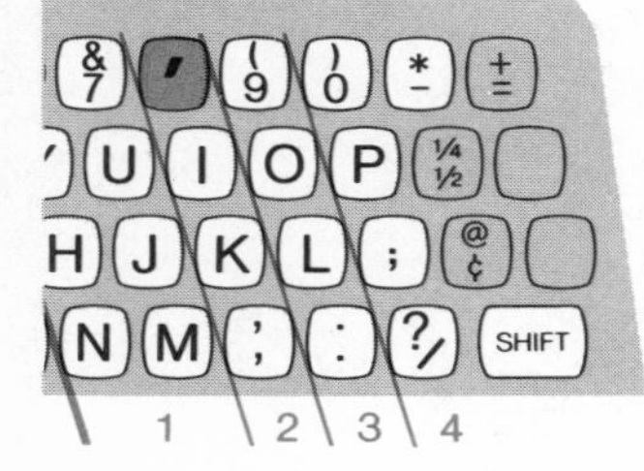

Manual
Type ' (the shift of **8**) with the *right second finger.* Reach with the controlling finger. Try to hold the other fingers over the home keys. Type the following tryout drill:

```
8'k 8'k 'k 'k 8's 8's I'm it's
```

Exclamation (!)

Manual
Type the ' (apostrophe); back-space, and type the period (**!**). *Space twice after* **!** *at the end of a sentence, which may be a single exclamatory word.* Type the following tryout drill:

```
8!1 8!1 8! 8! k! k! Wow!  Wow!
```

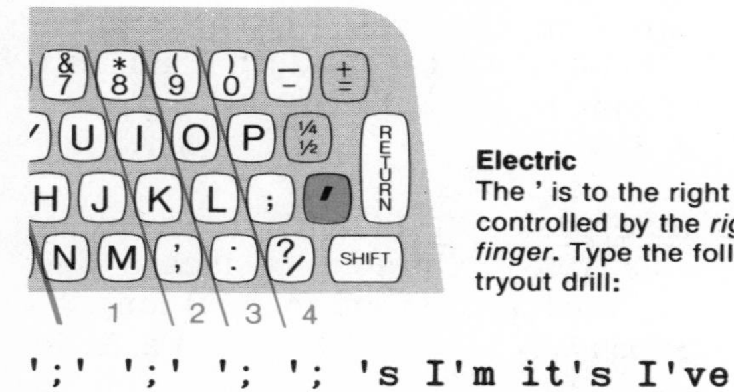

Electric
The ' is to the right of ; and is controlled by the *right fourth finger.* Type the following tryout drill:

```
';' ';' '; '; 's I'm it's I've
```

Electric and some manuals
If your typewriter has a special ! key—often the shift of the special Figure 1—move the finger up to type it.

```
1!a 1!a !a !a 1! 1! Wow!  Wow!
```

39d ▶10
Improve symbol control

type twice

Technique cue: Keep the hands and arms quiet; reach with the fingers.

' it's; I'll; didn't; Is this book Nan's, Kathy's, or Chuck's?
Mrs. O'Fallon can't or won't pay for her son's trip to Troy.

! Oh! Look! Stop! He loudly commanded: Ready! Aim! Fire!
Get set! Begin! You can win if you think you can! Try it!

' and ! Don't stop now! You've only a short way to go! Keep it up!
Hurrah! We've won our eighth straight title! I'm thrilled!

39e ▶10
Improve tabulating technique

type twice SS; 60-space line; 8 spaces between columns

Each figure is used at least 6 times.

50	$92	15%	3's	17-26	(81)
60	$83	23%	4's	18-28	(63)
70	$74	59%	5's	35-40	(72)
80	$65	67%	6's	49-59	(44)
90	$11	89%	7's	60-90	(23)

key | 2 | 8 | 3 | 8 | 3 | 8 | 3 | 8 | 5 | 8 | 4 |

257b-259b ▶45 Production typing

In these lessons, you will work as a clerk–typist in the Sales Department of the R. W. Simpson Tool Co., Inc., 200 East Market Street, Indianapolis, IN 46204.

Follow directions carefully. Make carbon copies when directed to do so; address envelopes when appropriate. Correct errors neatly; strive for attractive, error–free copy.

Job 1
Copy for a sales catalog

Type a model copy of the material at the right for the printer. Arrange the material in 2 columns; SS the items; DS between them. Type the heading on Line 10. Make 1 cc.

TOOLS FOR THE METRIC REVOLUTION

Box-end wrench set. Alloy steel with chrome plating. Six sizes: 6 x 8 mm, 7 x 9 mm, 10 x 11 mm, 12 x 14 mm, 13 x 15 mm, and 17 x 19 mm.
7M1642 Set, $12.60

Combination ignition wrench set. One box-end head and one offset open-end head on each wrench. Nine sizes: 4 x 4.5 mm, 4.5 x 4 mm, 5 x 5.5 mm, 5.5 x 6 mm, 6 x 7 mm, 7 x 8 mm, 8 x 9 mm, 9 x 10 mm, and 10 x 11 mm.
8M1457 Set, $4.99

Combination wrench set. Accurately broached open-end and 12-point box-end openings. Ten sizes: 6, 8, 9, 10, 12, 13, 14, 15, 17, and 19 mm.
8R1297 Set, $17.89

Drive tool set. Vanadium steel chrome-plated with 25 cm handle and reversible ratchet. Socket sizes: 10, 11, 12, 13, 14, 15, 16, 17, 19, 22, and 24 mm.
8R3922 Set, $15.50

Flex-head ratchet. Chrome-plated steel with reversible drive.
8R6022 12 mm drive Ea, $4.25
8R6023 15 mm drive Ea, $5.10

Micrometer. Chrome finish on tempered steel. Direct readings on digital counter to .01 mm, and .001 inch.
8T3100 Ea, $29.70

Micrometer, 0.25 mm. Ground steel surface w/steel frame.
8T3101 Ea, $7.95

Open-end wrench set. Alloy steel with chrome plating. Six sizes: 6 x 8 mm, 7 x 9 mm, 10 x 11 mm, 12 x 14 mm, 13 x 15 mm, and 17 x 19 mm.
8T3104 Set, $8.49

Rule, push-pull. Flexible steel retractable rule calibrated in inches and centimeters, 185 cm (6 feet) long.
8T3349 Ea, $1.10

Socket wrench, 8-way. Chrome-plated forged steel with 12-point sockets. Sizes: 11, 13, 14, 15, 16, 17, 19, and 22 mm.
8T3353 Ea, $5.95

Tap and die set. One inch diameter steel discs. Set includes 17 taps and dies: 3 x 0.6 mm, 4 x 0.75 mm, 5 x 0.9 mm, 6 x 1.0 mm, 7 x 0.75 mm, 7 x 1.0 mm, 8 x 1.25 mm, 10 x 1.5 mm, 12 x 1.75 mm, 3 x .05 mm, 4 x 0.7 mm, 5 x 0.8 mm, 6 x 0.75 mm, 8 x 1.0 mm, 10 x 1.25 mm, 12 x 1.5 mm.
8T6032 Set, $9.95

Torque wrench. Tempered steel with chrome plating. Measures 0 to 500 inch-points in both directions. Calibrated for metric use.
9T1047 Ea, $7.65

40

40a ▶7
Conditioning practice
each line 3 times SS (slowly, faster, slowly); DS between 3-line groups

alphabet Five boys quickly mixed the prizes, baffling one wise judge.
figure/symbol He's sure Questions 36-40 are from Chapter 29 (pp. 481-507).
fluency We may amend the rate if the union agrees to the work rules.

| 1 | 2 | 3 | 4 | 5 | 6 | 7 | 8 | 9 | 10 | 11 | 12 |

40b ▶10
Improve technique: response patterns
type twice; then a 1′ writing on each of Lines 2, 4, and 6

letter response
1 no greater| oil reserves| regards him| was dated| were addressed
2 As oil reserves get scarce, we draw upon a vast pool at sea.

word response
3 turn down| sign them| the theme| formal emblem| the eighth cycle
4 Did the bugle corps toot with the usual vigor for the queen?

combination response
5 all dates | six states | the reader | city streets | is greater than
6 He may also work on the stage sets when the cast is through.

| 1 | 2 | 3 | 4 | 5 | 6 | 7 | 8 | 9 | 10 | 11 | 12 |

40c ▶8
Check keystroking skill
two 3′ writings; determine *gwam* and errors

Goal: At least 25 *gwam*; not more than 8 errors.

all letters used | LA | 1.4 si | 5.4 awl | 85% hfw |

	gwam 2′	3′
A desire to excel is a quality that forces us to try to	6	4
improve our own performance and to surpass that of others.	12	8
All our major achievements have been sparked by a desire to	18	12
improve. The desire, though, had to be turned into a series	24	16
of right actions. Desire alone was not sufficient.	29	19
An excellent performance shows the real concern of the	5	23
performer for the task. It gives one a feeling of personal	12	27
success and causes all as a matter of habit to do our best.	18	31
Really successful men and women take great delight in their	24	35
work and pursue it with a lot of satisfaction.	28	38
A factor common to all who succeed is the need to have	5	42
a good job recognized by others. If good work goes without	12	46
notice, the desire to excel will be reduced. Lucky, indeed,	18	50
are people who can study their own performance, recognize	23	54
its quality, and do what must be done to improve it.	29	57

gwam 2′ | 1 | 2 | 3 | 4 | 5 | 6 |
3′ | 1 | 2 | 3 | 4 |

256c ▶25 Improve basic skill: script

1. A 5′ writing on ¶s 1–3 combined. Find *gwam*.
2. Two 2′ writings on each ¶ to increase speed. Find *gwam*.
3. A 5′ writing on ¶s 1–3 combined to measure improvement. Find *gwam*.

all letters used | HA | 1.6 si | 5.8 awl | 75% hfw

	gwam 2′	5′
Many business firms spend more annually for the machinery, raw ma-	7	3
terials, and supplies they require than they do for salaries, overhead,	14	6
and all the other costs of doing business combined. The task of secur-	21	8
ing these items is usually centralized in one unit which is known as the	28	11
purchasing department. As an overall objective, it is the role of the	35	14
purchasing staff to procure items in the right amount, of the right qual-	43	17
ity, and at the lowest cost.	45	18
The purchasing process is initiated by the submission of a purchase	7	21
request by any unit that requires goods. When the purchasing office gets	14	24
the request, it seeks sources of supply and negotiates with reputable	21	27
vendors to supply the goods at the time they are needed. After a vendor	28	30
has been chosen, a purchase order is typed that gives the description,	36	32
price, and amount desired of each item. After the goods have been re-	43	35
ceived and tallied, payment is made on the basis of an invoice submitted	50	38
by the supplier.	51	39
Sales directors are key executives in almost every business organi-	7	41
zation. It is their job to plan and to organize a program that will	14	44
promote the sale of a company's products and to direct all aspects of	21	47
the company's sales activities. They must be able to compose sales	27	50
letters and creative copy for newspaper, radio, and TV advertisements	34	53
as well as supervise the day-to-day tasks involved in the processing of	42	55
orders for goods. It is also their duty to recruit, train, equip, and	49	58
supervise the sales force.	51	59

257-259

257a-259a ▶5 Conditioning practice

twice SS;
repeat difficult lines

Governor Zumbalt will reject the new tax hike quickly if it is passed.
Public Law 25860, which was passed in 1974, applies in only 36 states.
The single discount equivalent of 33 1/3%, 10%, and 2 1/2% is 58 1/2%.
She must sign and mail this form today if she wants to sell the stock.

| 1 | 2 | 3 | 4 | 5 | 6 | 7 | 8 | 9 | 10 | 11 | 12 | 13 | 14 |

40d ▶7
Check statistical typing skill
a 3′ writing; determine *gwam*

Goal: At least 18 *gwam*.

all figures used

	gwam 1′	3′
The 50 most-used words account for 46% of the total of	11	4
all word uses in a study of 4,100 letters, memorandums, and	23	8
reports. The first 100 account for 53%; the first 500, 71%;	35	12
the first 1,000, 80%; and the first 2,000, just under 88%.	47	16
Of the first 7,027 most-used words (accounting for 97%	11	19
of all word uses), 209 are balanced-hand words (26% of all	23	23
uses) and 284 are one-hand words (14% of all uses). So you	35	27
see, practice on these words can help to improve your rate.	47	31

gwam 1′ | 1 | 2 | 3 | 4 | 5 | 6 | 7 | 8 | 9 | 10 | 11 | 12 |
3′ | 1 | 2 | 3 | 4 |

40e ▶8
Learn new keys: " (quotation) and _ (underline)

Quotation (")

Manual
Type " (the shift of **2**) with the *left third finger*. Reach with the controlling finger. Hold other fingers over home keys.

```
2"s 2"s "s "s "2 I said, "Go."
```

Electric
Type " (the shift of ') with the *right little finger*. Don't forget to shift *before* striking the " key.

```
'"; '"; "; "; '" I said, "Go."
```

Underline (_)

Manual
Type _ (the shift of **6**) with the *right first finger*. Reach with the finger without letting the hand move forward.

6_j 6_j _j _j _6 _6 Type <u>6,246</u>.

Electric
Type _ (the shift of the - key) with the *right little finger*. Reach with the finger without swinging the elbow out.

-_; -_; _; _; _- _- Type <u>stamp</u>.

40f ▶10
Improve symbol control
type twice

Technique cue: Hands and arms quiet; reach with the fingers.

Enrichment material for Unit 6 appears on LM pp. 17, 18.

" "To gain speed," she said, "think the word, not the letter."
Did Carlos type "lose" for "loose" and "chose" for "choose"?

_ <u>Curve</u> your fingers. Keep your wrists <u>low</u>, your hands <u>quiet</u>.
Type a book title in caps, EXODUS; or underlined, <u>The Prize</u>.

" and _ "Staying Thin" is an article from his book, <u>Calory Counters</u>.
"I Am Joe's Heart" is part of the series in <u>Reader's Digest</u>.

unit **45** lessons 256–262

Sales/purchasing office typing

Learning goals

1. To improve production skill by typing typical jobs in a sales department and a purchasing department.

2. To type straight copy and script at higher speeds and with improved control.

256

256a ▶5 Conditioning practice

twice SS; repeat difficult lines

alphabet Jeff organized the complex keyboard and quickly reviewed its function.

figures Note the underlined material on pages 19, 32, 46, 57, 68, 83, and 107.

fig/sym He earned commissions of $35.60, $97.82, and $146--a total of $279.42.

fluency If both of them ask for a loan on the same day, we may have a problem.

| 1 | 2 | 3 | 4 | 5 | 6 | 7 | 8 | 9 | 10 | 11 | 12 | 13 | 14 |

256b ▶20 Guided writing: straight copy

1. A 2′ writing on ¶ 1; find *gwam*.

2. Add 4 *gwam* to set a goal rate.

3. Note ¼′ checkpoints in ¶ 1 for 2′ of typing.

4. Three 2′ writings on ¶ 1 guided by the ¼′ call of the guide.

5. Type ¶ 2 in the same way.

all letters used

HA	1.6 si	5.8 awl	75% hfw

gwam 2′

There is no doubt that the invention of the typewriter completely revolutionized the world of business. In the olden days, the messages, reports, and formal records of a company had to be copied in ink by a large number of clerks. This process took a great deal of time and work, and the writing was so illegible at times that turmoil and even lawsuits resulted. Today, messages, reports, and other vital documents can be produced rapidly and legibly on the typewriter. 7 14 21 28 34 42 47

Before the invention of the typewriter, business was considered to be a man's world. For this reason, almost all of the clerical jobs were held by men. When the typewriter became a reality, schools began to offer courses in typing to supply qualified operators. Many women took these courses and became expert in the use of the machine. Armed with a salable skill, women were admitted to the business office. The typewriter was the key that opened the doors of business to women. 7 14 21 28 35 42 49

gwam 2′ | 1 | 2 | 3 | 4 | 5 | 6 | 7 |

unit **7** lessons 41–48

Personal communications

Learning goals

1. To improve speed and control on straight copy and statistical copy.

2. To learn to divide words properly at line endings.

3. To learn to arrange and type short reports, book reviews, and letters.

Machine adjustments

1. Paper guide at *0*.

2. Ribbon control on black.

3. Margin sets: 60-space line except as directed.

4. Line-space selector on *1* for drills; on *2* for ¶s; as directed for problems.

41

41a ▶7
Conditioning practice

1. Each line twice SS (slowly, faster).

2. Three 1′ writings on Line 3; determine *gwam*.

alphabet	Dixie Jeffington has been quick to try with zeal to improve.
fig/sym	Please see "Think Metric!" in Vol. 47, No. 12 (pp. 598-603).
fluency	Six of the girls may go to the social held by the soap firm.

| 1 | 2 | 3 | 4 | 5 | 6 | 7 | 8 | 9 | 10 | 11 | 12 |

41b ▶13
Improve technique: keystroking

1. Type once untimed.

2. A 1′ writing on Line 3 of 41a, above; determine *gwam*.

3. With your *gwam* as a goal rate, type two 1′ writings on each of Lines 2, 4, and 6 at the right.

Goal: To equal your goal rate.

adjacent keys	1	Fred knew that home row is asdfghjkl; third row, qwertyuiop.
	2	Cass tried various copiers to find one that suits her needs.
direct reaches	3	A great many people must make payment at the central branch.
	4	My group collected a large sum for her musical concert fund.
outside fingers	5	Pat won a quick game of croquet from Zane and amazed us all.
	6	Perhaps the new printing press will require new paper sizes.

| 1 | 2 | 3 | 4 | 5 | 6 | 7 | 8 | 9 | 10 | 11 | 12 |

41c ▶15
Skill-comparison typing: paragraphs

1. Two 2′ writings on ¶ 1; determine *gwam* on each.

2. Using the better *gwam* as a goal rate, type four 2′ writings on ¶ 2.

Goal: To equal your goal rate on each writing.

Copy difficulty

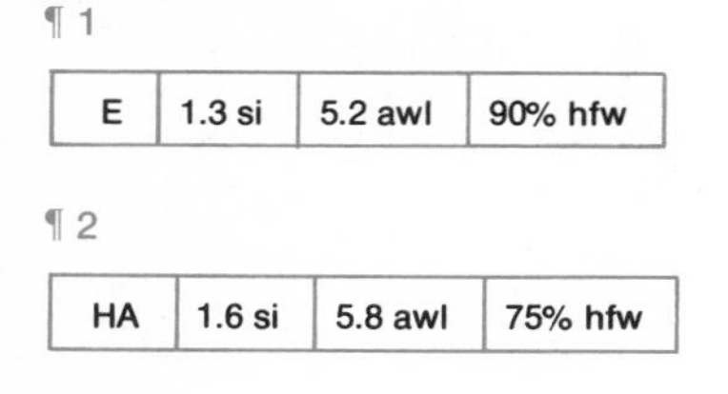

¶ 1

E	1.3 si	5.2 awl	90% hfw

¶ 2

HA	1.6 si	5.8 awl	75% hfw

all letters used

	gwam 2′	
A lot of your effort so far has been on quite easy copy.	6	6
Now you will begin to extend your skill, typing from material	12	12
that is somewhat harder to type. The major words will have a	18	18
higher number of syllables per word, will contain more letters,	25	25
and more of them will be from among the less frequent ones.	30	30
In the days ahead you will have many occasions to select	6	36
words to use as you compose at the typewriter. You will type	12	42
sentences from simple idea starters at first. You will also	18	48
create brief sentences to answer very easy questions. Finally,	24	54
you will organize and compose messages from your own notes.	30	60

gwam 2′ | 1 | 2 | 3 | 4 | 5 | 6 |

252b-255b, continued

Job 7
Bulletin

Type the special bulletin at the right. Center the material attractively on the page.

ADVANCE NEWS OF FUTURE INTERNATIONAL TRAVEL CLUB TOURS

Unusual Tours of Europe, the Middle East, and Africa

THE GRAND TOUR OF EUROPE (22 days)

Travel in the grand style to the major cities in Europe. Enjoy the excitement of the changing of the guard in London, the Lorelei on the Rhine River, the Swiss Mountains, the Austrian Tyrol, the canals of Venice, the Colosseum and St. Peter's Cathedral in Rome, the elegance of Nice and Cannes--and much more. Itinerary includes:

ENGLAND (London)
BELGIUM (Ostend, Brussels, Liege)
WEST GERMANY (Aachen, Bonn, Koblenz, Mainz, Heidelberg)
SWITZERLAND (Zurich, Lucerne)
AUSTRIA (Innsbruck)
ITALY (Venice, Padua, Bologna, Florence, Rome, Pisa, Genoa)
MONTE CARLO
FRANCE (Nice, Cannes, Grenoble, Lyon, Paris, Calais)

CRADLE OF CIVILIZATION (15 days)

Capture the aura of the Middle East--the bazaars, the pyramids, and the temples of Egypt and Lebanon; the Mount of Olives and the Holy Sepulchre in Jerusalem; the Acropolis and the Parthenon in Greece. Major cities include: Cairo, Luxor, Aswan, Beirut, Damascus, Tel Aviv, Jerusalem, Bethlehem, Jericho, Haifa, and Athens.

AFRICAN SAFARI (22 days)

An unusual tour which takes you off the beaten track. Explore the Lagos Islands, typical African villages, the Nairobi National Park, Tanzania's Game Forests, the Blue Nile Gorge, and many other exotic places. Enjoy these major countries and cities:

MOROCCO (Casablanca, Marrakech)
SENEGAL (Dakar)
IVORY COAST (Abidjan, Assinie)
NIGERIA (Lagos)
KENYA (Nairobi)
ETHIOPIA (Addis Ababa)
SUDAN (Khartoum)

WATCH YOUR NEWSLETTER FOR DETAILS ABOUT THESE EXCITING TOURS

Job 8
Alphabetic roster

1. Arrange the cards typed in Job 2 in alphabetic order.

2. Type an alphabetic roster of the new members with the names (in inverse order) and addresses for the Club Newsletter. Use "People Who Joined Us in April" as a heading. Center the material attractively on the page. Make 2 cc's.

41d ▶15

Learn to use the bell cue

1. Set margin stops as directed →

2. Type sentence at right at a slow pace in a single line; stop as soon as typewriter bell rings. Instead of typing remainder of sentence, type figures 1234 and so on until carriage locks.

3. Set margin stop so bell rings as a warning signal 5 spaces before desired line ending: move right stop to the right as many spaces as necessary (usually exact line ending + 3 to 7).

4. Type sentence again to check accuracy of your setting of right margin stop.

5. Using same margin settings, type the ¶ at right. Be guided by bell as signal to return carriage. If carriage locks, depress margin release key and complete the word; then return. Your line endings will not be the same as those shown at the right.

exact 60-space line [center − 30; center + 30]

Set stop for bell to ring 5 spaces before desired line ending.

Typewriters differ greatly in the number of strokes they will permit to be typed between the point where the warning bell rings and where the carriage locks. Soon you will learn to divide words at line endings; but for this drill, you will release the margin, if necessary, and complete the word you are typing when the warning bell rings. A word of one to four letters can be added at the end of the line if the bell rings on the last letter of a word.

42

42a ▶7

Conditioning practice

1. Each line twice SS (slowly, faster).

2. Three 1′ writings on Line 3; determine *gwam*.

alphabet Dave Lanzey was quick to jump for the box but lost his grip.

fig/sym Didn't they say Invoice 9508 was for $476 (plus 3 1/2% tax)?

fluency If they work with the usual vigor, they may make their goal.

| 1 | 2 | 3 | 4 | 5 | 6 | 7 | 8 | 9 | 10 | 11 | 12 |

42b ▶13

Compose as you type

drill sheet; line: 60; DS

Drill 1
Type the sentences at the right, filling in the missing information. X-out and immediately retype words in which you make errors.

Drill 1

1 My full name is (*first, middle, last*).

2 I live in (*names of city and state*).

3 My address is (*house number and street name*).

4 My telephone number is (*area code and telephone number*).

Drill 2
Answer the questions at the right, each with a complete sentence. X-out and retype immediately words in which you make errors.

Drill 2

1 Who is your favorite entertainer?

2 Which is your favorite singing group?

3 Who is your favorite sportsman or sportswoman?

4 What is your favorite holiday?

252b-255b, continued

Job 5 [LM pp. 51–60]
Form letters

1. Type the form letter below on half-sheet stationery (5½" × 8½") with a carbon copy to members whose card numbers are 867, 871, and 873. Use block style with open punctuation.

2. Type the letter to single members 861, 863, and 868. Make these changes in Sentence 3 of ¶ 2: (1) change *married couple* to *single person*; (2) change *couples* to *single people*.

3. Type the letter to senior members 869, 872, and 874. Make these changes in Sentence 3 of ¶ 2: (1) change *a married couple* to *senior citizens*; (2) add the word *mature* between *congenial* and *couples*.

universal travel service
900 Madison Avenue
Memphis, TN 38103
(901) 758 2600

May 5, 19--

Mr. and Mrs. Ray L. Lang
680 Willow Drive
Millington, TN

Dear Mr. and Mrs. Lang

Welcome to the International Travel Club. Your membership will open the door to thrilling and memorable holidays in all parts of the world.

You will find it fun to travel with others who can share the excitement of daily adventures in new places. Our guided tours are limited in size so that we can offer you the personal attention necessary for a pleasant vacation. As a married couple, you will be pleased to meet on our tours other congenial couples of similar tastes and temperament.

Our exciting tours are described in our quarterly newsletter, Adventures in Travel. To avoid disappointment, we urge you to make your reservations early.

Cordially yours

Elsie D. Metcalf

Elsie D. Metcalf, Manager

xx

May 4, 19-- (address and appropriate salutation) (¶ 1) Welcome to the International Travel Club. Your membership will open the door to thrilling and memorable holidays in all parts of the world. (¶ 2) You will find it fun to travel with others who can share the excitement of daily adventures in new places. Our guided tours are limited in size so that we can offer you the personal attention necessary for a pleasant vacation. As a married couple, you will be pleased to meet on our tours other congenial couples of similar tastes and temperament. (¶ 3) Our exciting tours are described in our quarterly newsletter, Adventures in Travel. To avoid disappointment, we urge you to make your reservations early. Cordially yours Elsie D. Metcalf, Manager

Job 6 [LM p. 61]
Itinerary

From the worksheet at the right, type an itinerary with 1 cc. Add under the heading "Additional Information" the following copy: "Accommodations are reserved for you at the CARIBE HILTON HOTEL for 14 nights—May 9 until May 23." Use your name as the confirmation clerk.

universal travel service
900 Madison Avenue
Memphis, TN 38103
(901) 758-2600

ITINERARY FOR Dr. Norma T. Taylor

6840 Poplar Ave., Memphis, TN 38138 -- 758-4632
Address Telephone

CITY	AIRLINE FLIGHT	CLASS	DATE	TIME
Lv Memphis	Delta 241	Y	5/9	9:30 a.m. CDT
Ar Miami			5/9	12:24 p.m. EDT
Lv Miami	PanAm 254	Y	5/9	3:50 p.m. EDT
Ar San Juan			5/9	6:10 p.m. AST
Lv San Juan	Eastern 952	Y	5/23	3:30 p.m. AST
Ar Miami			5/23	5:44 p.m. EDT
Lv Miami	Delta 386	Y	5/23	7:15 p.m. EDT
Ar Memphis			5/23	8:14 p.m. CDT

Shown in pica type
60-space line

Line 10

BASIC GUIDES FOR DIVIDING WORDS AT LINE ENDINGS

TS

You may divide words at line endings to help you maintain a fairly even right margin, but you should avoid excessive word division. These guides will help you.

DS

Reset left margin

1. Divide a word between syllables only (will-ing, pre-fer, em-ploy-ees, fi-nan-cial, pro-gram). To indicate the division of a word, type a hyphen at the end of the line; type the rest of the word on the following line.

DS

2. Do not divide a word of one syllable (toward, reached) or a word of five or fewer letters (into, prior).

3. Do not separate a one-letter syllable at the beginning of a word (across, enough) or a one- or two-letter syllable at the end of a word (steady, highly).

4. You may usually divide a word between double consonants (writ-ten, sum-mer).

5. When adding a syllable to a word that ends in double letters, divide after the double letters of the root word (express, express-ing; process, process-ing).

6. When the final consonant is doubled in adding a suffix, divide between the doubled letters (run, run-ning).

When in doubt about the proper division of a word, consult a dictionary or a word division manual.

42c ▶30 Learn basic guides for dividing words

2 full sheets
60-space line
SS (single spacing)
heading on Line 10

Problem 1

Type a copy of the report shown above which lists the basic guides for dividing words at line endings.

Problem 2

If time permits, type the report as an informational memorandum in block style (as illustrated on page 53). Use current date.

252b-255b ▶45 Production typing

You have been hired by the Universal Travel Agency, 900 Madison Avenue, Memphis, TN 38103 as a clerk-typist for the Universal Travel Club. Follow the directions for each job carefully. Make carbon copies when directed to do so; address envelopes when appropriate. Use your initials in letters and memos (the two x's will no longer be used to indicate reference initials). Correct errors neatly; strive for copy that would be acceptable in a business office.

Job 1
Composing materials for an office procedures manual

Study the material in 251c, page 392, and the illustrations at the right. Then, prepare a list of the steps involved in typing (1) index cards, (2) address or mailing labels, and (3) file folder labels. Number each step. Type the information as page 6 of a leftbound report with side headings.

Index card

```
Benton, Joyce L. (Ms.)                    861

Ms. Joyce L. Benton
1548 Rozelle Street
Memphis, TN 38106
```

File folder label

```
Benton, Joyce L. (Ms.)
Memphis, TN 38106
1548 Rozelle Street
```

Address label

```
Ms. Joyce L. Benton
1548 Rozelle Street
Memphis, TN 38106
```

Job 2 [LM pp. 41–46]
Index cards

Type index cards like the one illustrated at the right for the members listed below who have joined the International Travel Club. Type the membership number in the upper right-hand corner.

Job 3 [LM p. 47]
Folder labels

Type a label (similar to the one illustrated) for the file folder for each new member. Use the cards prepared in Job 2.

Job 4 [LM p. 49]
Address labels

Type an address label (similar to the one illustrated) for each new member. Use the cards prepared in Job 2.

Ms. Joyce L. Benton
1548 Rozelle Street
Memphis, TN 38106
No. 861

Dr. Norma T. Taylor
6840 Poplar Avenue
Memphis, TN 38138
No. 862

Ms. Bernice A. Hill
241 Anderson Avenue
Jonesboro, AR 72401
No. 863

Mr. Paul M. Benton
476 Water Street
Hernando, MS 38632
No. 864

Mr. Wayde O. McIntyre
1518 Lilac Street
Covington, TN 38019
No. 865

Mr. John T. Clifton, Jr.
231 Buntyn Street
Memphis, TN 38111
No. 866

Mr. and Mrs. Ray L. Lang
680 Willow Drive
Millington, TN 38053
No. 867

Mr. Anthony P. DiIorio
R.D. 1
Blytheville, AR 72315
No. 868

Mr. and Mrs. A. F. Klein
922 Lindon Avenue
Memphis, TN 38104
No. 869

Mrs. Juanita C. Ortez
605 Garland Street
Memphis, TN 38107
No. 870

Dr. and Mrs. Joel C. Como
38 Wister Street
Southhaven, MS 38671
No. 871

Mr. and Mrs. Earl M. Kerr
3842 Charleston Road
Memphis, TN 38128
No. 872

Mr. and Mrs. C. L. DePaul
2506 Walnut Road
Memphis, TN 38128
No. 873

Mr. and Mrs. Ken E. Ross
467 Willow Place
Memphis, TN 38107
No. 874

43

43a ▶7 Conditioning practice

1. Each line twice SS (slowly, faster).
2. Three 1′ writings on Line 3; determine *gwam*.

alphabet Joe Bair quickly wrote the zoology exam for advanced pupils.
fig/sym I'm told 18% of them make $649.25 a month; 82% make $637.50.
fluency The auto firm owns the big signs by the downtown civic hall.
| 1 | 2 | 3 | 4 | 5 | 6 | 7 | 8 | 9 | 10 | 11 | 12 |

43b ▶10 Learn to divide words

1. Clear all tab stops; then set new stops as indicated by the key beneath the columns of words.
2. Type the first word in Column 1 as shown; tab; then type the first word in Column 2; and so on.

ACCEPTABLE WORD DIVISION POINTS
TS

toward	ef-forts	agree-ing	sepa-rate
changes	great-est	ap-pears	pos-si-ble
wishes	in-creased	get-ting	av-er-age
boarded	per-sons	ac-tions	be-tween

key | 7 | 8 | 10 | 8 | 9 | 8 | 10 |

43c ▶10 Learn to erase and correct errors

half sheet; line: 60; SS
exact vertical center

GUIDES FOR ERASING ERRORS
TS

1. Use a plastic shield and a typewriter (hard) eraser.
2. Lift the paper bail and turn the paper forward if the error is on the upper two thirds of the page or backward if it is on the lower third.
3. Move the carriage to the left as far as you can (if the error is left of center) or to the right (if the error is right of center).
4. Erase lightly--don't "scrub" the error. Blow eraser particles away as you erase.
5. Return the paper to writing position and type.

43d ▶8 Erase and correct errors

1. Type the sentences as they are shown at the right, but *do not* type the numbers.
2. Study the erasing guides above.
3. Erase and correct each error in your copy.

1 The first step in error corretcion is error detection.
2 Be quick to recongize all errors you maek as you type.
3 Try to corrcet the error so that it is not detectable.
4 Always correct your errors befoer removnig your paper.

251c ▶25 Improve basic skill: rough draft

1. A 5′ writing on ¶s 1–2 combined. Find *gwam*.

2. Two 2′ writings on each ¶ to increase speed. Find *gwam*.

3. A 5′ writing on ¶s 1–2 combined to measure improvement. Find *gwam*.

all letters used | HA | 1.6 si | 5.8 awl | 75% hfw

	gwam 2′	5′
The typing of cards for index files and addresslabels for envelopes	7	3
and file folders in many offices are typical clerical jobs. In this	14	5
case, the names of personnel are typed in reverse order--the last name	21	8
first, given name second, and middel name or initial last. Titles, such	28	11
as ms. or dr., are placed in brackets immediately after the names.	35	14
When typing the cards, The name of the person or the company is usu-	42	17
ally on the third line below the top edge of the card starting about	49	20
three spaces from the left side. Space down 4 times and present the in-	57	23
formation in postal order--name, address, city, state, and zip code.	63	25
Self-stick labels in strips or rolls are used frequently for ad-	7	28
dress lables and file-folder labels since they canbe prepared quickly	14	31
and glued easily. Addresses on lables for envlopes or packages may be	21	34
typed in the normal order. Type the name ofthe individual or company	28	37
on the second line from the top side of the label beginning just 3	35	40
spaces from the left edge. Filefolder labels are completed with the	42	42
spacing, but in different format: after typing the name of the indi-	50	45
vidual, in reverse order, or firm, type the city, state, and zip code	57	48
next with the local address, if essential, on the following line.	63	50

252-255

252a-255a ▶5 Conditioning practice

twice SS; repeat difficult lines

Wallace Quigley emphasized the values of expert analysis to rank jobs.
Published in 1974, this book has 856 pages, 230 pictures, and 72 maps.
Expenses in April were $321.75; in May, $346.89; and in June, $350.21.
He can go with us to the city to see the show if we want him to do so.

| 1 | 2 | 3 | 4 | 5 | 6 | 7 | 8 | 9 | 10 | 11 | 12 | 13 | 14 |

43e ▶15 Improve skill transfer: rough draft

1. A 2′ writing on each ¶.
2. An additional 2′ writing on slower ¶.
3. A 3′ writing on each ¶.

all letters used | A | 1.5 si | 5.6 awl | 80% hfw

	gwam 2′	3′
Letters may be typed in a variety of arrangements. One	6	4
of them is the block style in which you have been typing short	12	8
memorandums. Both personal and business letters may be typed	18	12
in block style, also. In fact, block style has extended its	24	16
popularity quite rapidly in the recent past, being used by just	31	20
under a sixth of the companies in a recent analysis of a large	37	25
collection of letters from a wide variety of business firms.	43	29
# By far the most widely used letter style in use today, however, is the	6	4
modifieed block style you will next learn. In this style format the	12	8
heading (date and return address) and closing lines are started begun	18	12
DS atthe horizontal center of the letterhead paper or, in many some cases, to	24	16
the right of it. This style, either with or without indented	30	20
paragraphs, is adopted by a big majority of firms.	35	23

44

44a ▶7 Conditioning practice

1. Each line twice SS (slowly, faster).
2. Three 1′ writings on Line 3; determine *gwam*.

alphabet Bick can have a jeweler size my antique ring to fit Pam Dix.

fig/sym Car No. 2847-3650 (Track 1) leaves for St. Paul at 9:35 a.m.

fluency The audit by the city signals the end to their profit cycle.

| 1 | 2 | 3 | 4 | 5 | 6 | 7 | 8 | 9 | 10 | 11 | 12 |

44b ▶7 Bell cue and word division

1. Type the ¶ at right with a 70-space line, double-spaced. Listen for bell as signal to return carriage. Divide words as necessary. Erase and correct errors.
2. Type the ¶ again in the same way, but use a 50-space line.

When you compose at the typewriter, X-ing out words is more efficient than erasing them. So when you are asked to compose, X-out and retype words in which you make errors. After your theme, memo, letter, or report is complete, you can type a final copy with errors erased and corrected.

44c ▶15 Improve skill transfer

Retype 43e, above, trying to improve your speed on both straight copy and rough draft.

phase 11 lessons 251–275

Functional office simulations

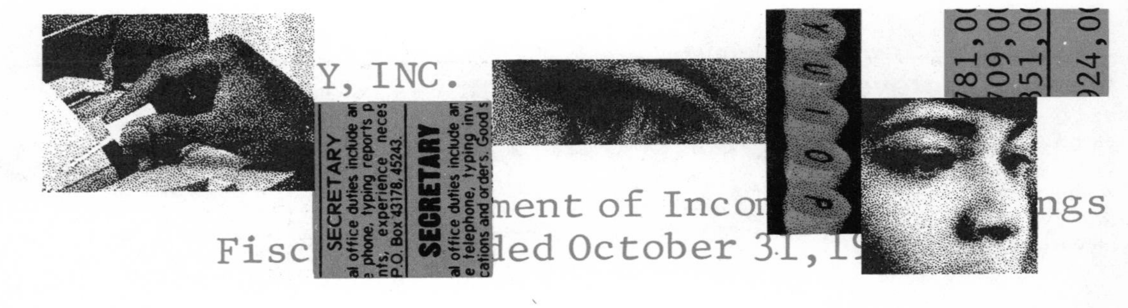

unit 44 lessons 251–255

Administrative office typing

Learning goals

Phase 11 includes a variety of simulated office situations which provide practice on numerous typing jobs found in typical functional offices of a business.

As you type the jobs, strive to:

1. Read and follow directions carefully.

2. Enlarge your knowledge of typical typing tasks found in business.

3. Increase your speed and accuracy in typing production materials.

4. Produce typewritten materials that would be acceptable in a business office.

Machine adjustments

1. Line: 70 for drills and timed writings.

2. Spacing: SS sentence drills; DS ¶s; space problems as directed.

251

251a ▶5 Conditioning practice

twice SS; repeat difficult lines

alphabet Maybe the experts realized we can judge the value of the unique books.

figures Units produced rose from 18,340,528 on May 4 to 25,679,937 on June 16.

fig/sym The monthly premium for $6,000 insurance is $22.85 ($257.52 x .08875).

fluency Did she thank the men for the fine work they did on the special study?

| 1 | 2 | 3 | 4 | 5 | 6 | 7 | 8 | 9 | 10 | 11 | 12 | 13 | 14 |

251b ▶20 Skill-comparison typing

1. Three 1′ writings on each ¶. Compare *gwam*.

2. A 1′ speed writing on slower ¶.

3. A 2′ writing on each ¶; compare *gwa*.

4. Additional 2′ writings on slower ¶ as time permits.

all letters used

¶ 1			
LA	1.4 si	5.4 awl	85% hfw

¶ 2			
D	2.0 si	7.1 awl	70% hfw

Text	gwam 1′	2′	
The jobs done in an administrative office vary from company to	13	6	40
company. A few of the more common jobs a clerk can be expected to do	27	13	47
are to type letters, reports, and forms; file; use the telephone; process	41	20	55
mail; and use office machines of all kinds. A typist can expect to	54	27	61
type a wide range of work from simple labels to long, complex reports.	68	34	68
The administrative office has been called the nerve center of an	13	6	41
organization. The office performs functions that are required for the	27	14	48
smooth, efficient operation of a business. Among the major functions	41	21	55
assigned to an administrative office are accounting, processing oral	55	27	62
and written communications, managing records, and reproducing data.	68	34	68

gwam 1′ | 1 | 2 | 3 | 4 | 5 | 6 | 7 | 8 | 9 | 10 | 11 | 12 | 13 | 14 |
2′ | 1 | 2 | 3 | 4 | 5 | 6 | 7 |

Line 10

BOOK REVIEW

DS

by

DS

Allison Swillinger

TS

WORD DIVISION MANUAL by J. E. Silverthorn and Devern J. Perry (published by South-Western Publishing Co.) is a gold mine of ready-reference assistance to the typist and secre- tary. Into just 160 pages the authors have crammed a wealth of help in easy-to-find sequence.

The "Foreword" describes how three scientifically tabu- lated word lists were analyzed to obtain the 15,659 most use- ful words that are listed in alphabetic order for ease of location. The "Guidelines for Word Division," following the "Foreword," provide a detailed list of rules used to deter- mine the division points identified in the word list itself.

A unique system is used for identifying the points at which words may be divided. A hyphen (-) is used to indicate preferred points of division; a period (.) is used to indi- cate other acceptable points of division. A boldface hyphen indicates that a hyphenated compound word may be acceptably divided only at the point of the existing hyphen.

For any person who is at times unsure about where to di- vide words, this handy little manual is a "must" possession.

44d ▶21 Learn to type a book review

full sheet
60-space line
DS (double-spacing)
heading on Line 10

1. Type a copy of the full-page book review illustrated above. As you type, listen for the bell as signal to return carriage even though you will be typing the copy line for line as shown.

2. If time permits, retype the review. This time, erase and correct any errors you make as you type.

A supplementary book review appears on LM p. 19.

250b ▶45 Measure production skill: forms and tables

1. Type the problems for 30′; correct errors as you type. If you complete the problems before time is called, retype Problem 1 on plain paper as page 2 of an interoffice memo (beginning with ¶ 1).

2. Compute *n–pram*; compare with score you achieved on 240b, page 376.

Problem 1 [LM p. 37]
Interoffice memorandum

words

TO: Juan M. Martinez, Personnel Director FROM: Leslie L. Oliver, Production Manager DATE: September 6, 19-- SUBJECT: Food Bacteriologist (¶ 1) The manufacture of canned dehydrated food items at our Quincy Plant is scheduled to begin on November 3. Before production can begin, however, we must obtain the services of a food bacteriologist. (¶ 2) A food bacteriologist is essential to our operations since he is the one who checks the completed products for bacteria and contamination. In addition, he will investigate activities of bacteria and other microorganisms detected in the manufacture, spoilage, and deterioration of the food products. A more complete description of his duties can be found in the Dictionary of Occupational Titles (Job No. and title: 041.081, Microbiologist). Although previous experience is desirable, it is not absolutely essential in this position. Dr. Jim Longworth of Jefferson University tells me that several of his recent graduates have outstanding records and may fit our needs. (¶ 3) Since the individual who fills this position must be available to begin work on November 1, please give this matter your highest priority. xx

13 23 38 53 67 82 97 112 128 150 165 180 195 210 225 232/241

Problem 2 [LM p. 39]
Purchase order

To: Commercial Products, Inc.
43001 Bluff Park Road
Birmingham, AL 35226

Order No. W-34486 — 7
Date November 23, 19-- — 14
Terms Net — 20
Ship via Seaboard Van Lines — 23

Quantity	Cat. No.	Description	Price	Total	words
10	P8217	Dock plates, aluminum	174.95	1,749.50	34
12	B9398	Dock bumpers, rubber	31.95	383.40	42
20	C7126	Wheel chocks	24.95	499.00	49
4	F7007	Fire extinguishers	59.95	239.80	57
15	C8150	Roller conveyers	76.88	1,153.20	67
				4,024.90	69

Problem 3
Table [reading position; DS items]

SALES RECORD BY DISTRICT — 5

(In Thousands of Dollars) — 10

District	Previous Year	Current Year	Increase	words
				27
Boston	$ 648,161	$ 735,010	$ 86,849	37
Atlanta	518,528	588,007	69,479	43
Indianapolis	466,675	529,207	62,532	50
Dallas	388,896	441,005	52,109	56
Minneapolis	311,117	352,805	41,688	63
Portland	259,265	294,004	34,739	69
Albuquerque	210,347	249,016	38,669	76
Los Angeles	198,573	236,490	37,917	83
Tampa	173,492	195,860	22,368	95
TOTAL	$3,175,054	$3,621,404	$446,350	105

45

45a ▶7 Conditioning practice

1. Each line twice SS (slowly, faster).
2. Three 1′ writings on Line 3; determine *gwam*.

alphabet Cindy Majak was pleased by the old quartz box Fran gave her.

fig/sym Tina asked, "Can't you touch-type 56, 73, $480, and 9 1/2%?"

fluency When did the field auditor sign the audit form for the city?

| 1 | 2 | 3 | 4 | 5 | 6 | 7 | 8 | 9 | 10 | 11 | 12 |

45b ▶10 Learn to divide words

1. Clear all tab stops; then set new stops as indicated by the key beneath the columns of words.
2. Type the first word in Column 1 as shown; tab; then type the first word in Column 2; and so on.

Supplementary word division practice material appears on LM p. 20.

ACCEPTABLE WORD DIVISION POINTS

TS

started	vari-ous	what-ever	per-son-ally
longer	re-turned	pro-vided	be-gin-ning
enough	pre-sented	tele-phone	nec-es-sary
greatly	poli-cies	tech-ni-cal	re-spon-si-ble

key | 7 | 6 | 10 | 6 | 11 | 6 | 14 |

45c ▶10 Type an informational memorandum

half sheet; line: 60; SS

Type the informational memorandum. Be sure to use correct vertical spacing. (Reference: page 52).

Current date

SUBJECT: Finding the Center of Special-Size Paper

Most personal stationery is of special size. It is usually smaller than business stationery. The paper you will use for the personal letters you are to type soon is 7 1/4 inches wide by 10 1/2 inches long.

To determine the horizontal center of a sheet of paper--no matter what its size: (1) read the numbers on the platen or cylinder scale at the left and right edges of the paper; (2) add them; (3) divide the total by 2. The resulting number is the horizontal center at which the return address, date, and closing lines are typed.

45d ▶23 Learn to type personal letters

1. Study Style Letter 1 illustrating the *modified block style, block paragraphs*, and *open punctuation* (page 73). Note the vertical and horizontal placement of letter parts.
2. On special-size paper (7¼″ × 10½″) type a copy of the model letter on page 73. Use LM p. 21.
3. Proofread and mark your copy for correction; then retype it in final form, erasing and correcting errors. Use LM p. 23.

249b, continued

Problem 2
Topbound report with side headings

words

TYPES OF SECURITIES 4

Common Stock (¶ 1) The oldest type of corporation securities, common stock 20
represents ownership in a corporation. The holders of common stock enjoy 35
the basic rights of ownership--the right to vote, to elect directors, to share 51
in dividends, and to share in the distribution of assets. As owners, stock- 66
holders also share the risks of the business. In the event of bankruptcy, 81
holders of common stock receive only that which remains after all debts 95
have been paid and the claims of preferred stockholders have been satisfied. 111

Preferred Stock (¶ 2) As the name implies, preferred stock offers certain 127
preferences to the shareholders. These usually include the right to receive 143
dividends at a specified rate before the common stockholders receive any 157
dividends and preference over the common stockholders in sharing the 171
assets in the event the company is dissolved. 181

Cumulative and Noncumulative Preferred Stock (¶ 3) Although holders of pre- 203
ferred stock have preference over common stockholders, they do not 217
automatically receive dividends. If a company fails to earn a profit, 231
a dividend may still be declared and paid to holders of both classes 245
of stock so long as cash is available. If a preferred stock is cumu- 258
lative, dividends omitted on the preferred stock in previous years 272
must be paid to the preferred stockholders before distribution to 285
the common stockholders. If a preferred stock is noncumulative, divi- 299
dends omitted during previous years need never be made up. 311

Bonds (¶ 4) A bond represents money borrowed by a corporation. In a bond, 325
the company promises to pay the principal (the amount borrowed) at a stated 341
future date and to pay interest at a given rate until the principal is repaid. 357
As creditors, the holders of bonds have priority over the stockholders in 371
the event the company is dissolved. 378

Problem 3
Unbound report

Type the material in 248d, page 387, as an unbound report.
Heading: HISTORICAL HIGHLIGHTS OF THE AUTOMOBILE (8 words)

250

250a ▶5 Conditioning practice

twice SS;
repeat difficult lines

Key executives might quit their jobs if we hold up the reorganization.
Item No. 37595 will be offered in sizes 8, 10, 12, 14, 16, 18, and 20.
Read pages 284-360 in Automation by Boyd & Wray (Third Edition, 1975).
A special sale of the items on this shelf may be held during the week.

| 1 | 2 | 3 | 4 | 5 | 6 | 7 | 8 | 9 | 10 | 11 | 12 | 13 | 14 |

Shown in pica type
50-space line

Tabulate to center to type
return address and date

Return address — Line 14

12648 Benham Road
Florissant, MO 63033
November 15, 19--

Dateline

Operate return 4 times

Letter address

Mr. Evan K. Dunn, Manager
Bel Air West Motor Hotel
4630 Lindell Boulevard
St. Louis, MO 63108

DS

Salutation

Dear Mr. Dunn

DS

Body of letter

Thank you for an interesting summer of work at the Bel Air West. My assignment in the dining room gave me contacts with people under many different conditions. I gained much from my experience.

It is possible that I may apply for a part-time job later in the year, depending on the amount of study time that will be required for my courses at school. If I should apply for a job, may I use your name as a reference?

Your offer of work for next summer is sincerely appreciated. I shall let you know my plans early in the spring. In the meantime, thank you again for a pleasant summer and best wishes to you personally.

DS

Complimentary close — Tab

Cordially yours

Operate return 4 times

Dave

Typed name

David Fielder

In *open* punctuation, no punctuation follows the salutation or the complimentary close.

Style letter 1: personal letter in modified block style

249

249a ▶5 Conditioning practice

twice SS;
repeat difficult lines

Jay Black needs an executive who specializes in quality manufacturing.
My batting average in 1972 was .351; in 1973, .340; and in 1974, .368.
Invoice 47950 from Gos & May for $3,280 (less 6%) was paid on July 21.
The eight men and six women will file their claim at the civic center.

| 1 | 2 | 3 | 4 | 5 | 6 | 7 | 8 | 9 | 10 | 11 | 12 | 13 | 14 |

249b ▶45 Measure production skill: report manuscripts

1. Type the reports for 30′; correct errors as you type. If you complete the reports before time is called, start over.

2. Compute *n–pram*. Compare with score achieved on 233b, page 368.

Problem 1
Leftbound report with footnote

words

PRODUCTIVITY AND PROFIT SHARING 6

(¶ 1) Productivity is a major problem in American industry. Any 18
increase in the cost of production, if not offset by an increase 31
in productivity, must be met with either an increase in the price 44
of goods or a decrease in profits. Increasing productivity in- 57
volves something more, however, than merely stimulating em- 68
ployees to increase production. It includes motivating employees 82
to improve the quality of the product, to reduce operating costs, 95
and to improve work methods. 101

(¶ 2) Industry offers many incentives in an effort to improve 112
productivity. The sharing of profits with employees has been 124
used as a means of encouraging employees to identify with the 137
company and its goals. When employees share in the profits, 149
they are, in a sense, "partners" with a monetary interest in the 162
success of the company. Under these circumstances, it is to their 175
advantage to reduce costs and to increase productivity since they 189
benefit from any increase in profits. 196

(¶ 3) The success of a profit-sharing plan rests almost entirely upon 209
the profit record of the company. If there are no profits to share, 223
it is hardly possible to motivate employees to greater effort. "A 236
company must have a fairly stable history of profits, or the plan 250
is bound to fail."[1] 254

——— 258

[1] Michael J. Jucius, <u>Personnel Management</u> (Homewood, Illinois: 274
Richard D. Irwin, Inc., 1975), p. 319. 282

Problem 2 appears on page 389.

46

46a ▶7 Conditioning practice

1. Each line twice SS (slowly, faster).

2. Three 1′ writings on Line 3; determine *gwam*.

alphabet Pam was quite excited when Jack Fyle bought the bronze vase.

fig/sym My policy (No. G-48956) for $20,000 was paid up May 3, 1977.

fluency They risk a big penalty if they throw a fight for the title.

| 1 | 2 | 3 | 4 | 5 | 6 | 7 | 8 | 9 | 10 | 11 | 12 |

46b ▶20 Learn to address Monarch envelopes and fold letters

Return address. Use block style SS, as shown. Type writer's name, house number and street name (or box number), city, state (followed by 1 space), and ZIP Code in upper left corner (unless envelope with printed return address is being used). Begin on second line space from top edge of envelope and 3 spaces from left edge.

Envelope address: Use block style SS, as shown. Begin about 2¼″ from top and 3½″ from left edge of envelope. Type city name, state name or abbreviation, and ZIP Code on last line of address.

In letter and envelope addresses, direction names (North, South, East, and West) may be abbreviated (N., S., E., and W., respectively) to shorten lines and improve address balance.

Addressing a Monarch envelope (7½″ × 4″)

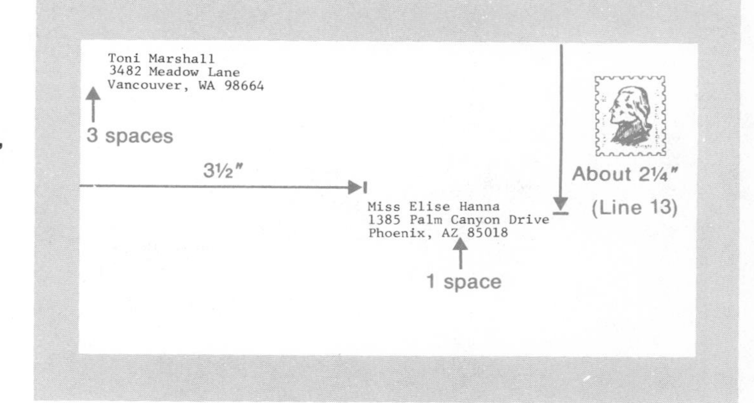

Problems [LM pp. 25, 27]
Address a Monarch envelope to each addressee listed below. Use your own return address.

Mrs. J. Edward Friedman
12399 W. Plainfield Avenue
Milwaukee, WI 53228

Mr. Kevin J. Looby
3308 Park Circle
Baltimore, MD 21215

Ms. Ellen Marie Markham
1764 Seminole Drive
Detroit, MI 48214

If time permits, practice folding 7¼″ by 10½″ paper for insertion into Monarch envelopes.

Folding and inserting letters into Monarch envelopes

Step 1
With the letter face up, fold slightly less than ⅓ of sheet up toward the top.

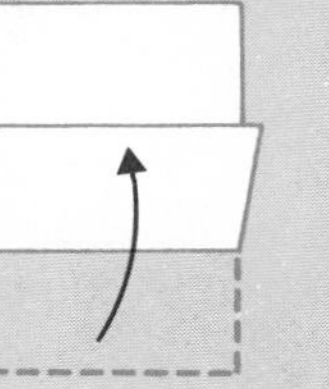

Step 2
Fold down top of sheet to within ½ inch of bottom fold.

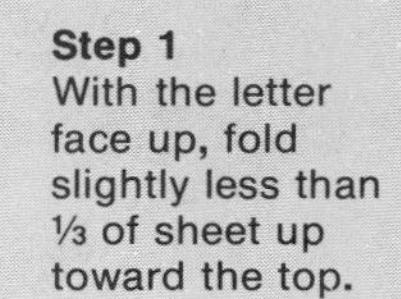

Step 3
Insert letter into envelope with last crease toward bottom of envelope.

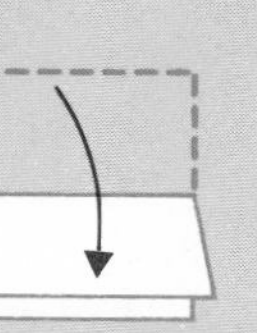

248d ▶17 Measure basic skill: rough draft

1. Two 5′ writings on the ¶s.

2. Record *gwam* and errors on better writing. Compare with scores achieved on 232c, page 367.

3. As time permits, type a 1′ writing on each ¶.

all letters used	A	1.5 si	5.6 awl	80% hfw

	gwam 1′	5′
Following the invention of the steam engene, efforts were made	14	3
to use this means to move a vehicle on land. Successful,but clumsy,	28	6
electric vehicles were made as well cars which could operate on steam.	42	8
It took a long time to get the steam car started andit had limitedfuel	56	11
capacity. The electric car was very bulky and had a relatively short	71	14
span of travel. It was not until the internal-combustoin engine driven	85	17
by gasoline wasdeveloped that the era of the automobile started.	98	20
An automobile was quite costly in the early days and it's use was	13	22
limited to racing. One of the primary problems was that of re-placing	27	25
parts. It wasnot until inter changeable parts were found that it was	41	28
feasible to apply the process of mass production to the fabrication of	55	31
the automobile. Henry ford was the first to sell an automobile at a	70	34
price that was with in the reach of the regular citizen. With in a	83	36
short time, millions of cars were being produced yearly.	96	39
The streets in this country were very bad inthe early days. Prios	13	41
to the end of the last century, turnpikes bilt by private enterprise	28	44
that were much better than the free roads linked most of our largest	41	47
cities. The growing popularity of the automobile forced the state to	56	50
build more and better roads. As a network of roads extended toall parts	70	53
of the country, the use of trucks and busses became popular since they	84	56
were cheap and not restricted to rails more flexible than trians.	98	58

46c ▶23 Type personal letters

2 Monarch letterheads (or 7¼" × 10½" paper); line: 50; SS; in body of letters, listen for bell as signal to return carriage; return address on Line 14; address envelopes

Problem 1 [LM p. 29]

	words
4100 Shore Line Drive	4
Myrtle Beach, SC 29577	9
November 15, 19--	13
Miss Joanne Gibbons	17
10 Hawthorne Park	20
Boston, MA 02138	24
Dear Joanne	26
If you haven't seen the announcement that	34
Dr. Terry, our former teacher of English, has	44
been awarded the Princeton Prize for Distin-	52
guished Teaching, let me be the first to tell	61
you of it.	64
The citation said the award was given for	72
"fruitful teaching, devoted service, and human	82
as well as professional qualities." That fits	91
Dr. Terry to a "T."	95
How is life in Boston? Do you like the new	104
scene? Have you found a congenial group of	113
new friends?	116
Don't be so miserly with your letters. I am	125
now one up on you, so write me soon. Tell me	134
about you, of course, and about life in the	142
"Citadel of Learning."	147
Sincerely	149/**169**

Problem 2 [LM p. 31]

	words
5830 N. Bayshore Drive	5
Miami, FL 33137	8
December 2, 19--	11
Mr. Byron Sherwood	15
Patrician Apartments, 1401E	20
601 Fullerton Parkway	25
Chicago, IL 60614	28
Dear Byron	31
Believe it or not, I survived the regional	39
round in the All-City Tennis Championship.	48
You can't be more surprised than I am or half	57
as happy.	59
Next comes the two-day Finals Tournament.	68
It begins two weeks from today--Friday, De-	76
cember 16. I'd like to have you come down to	85
cheer me on.	88
Can you come? Win or lose, we'll celebrate	97
with a party at our house Saturday after the	106
tournament ends. And if you can stay for sev-	115
eral days, there will be time for some sun	124
and surf!	126
Mother says the guest room will be ready for	135
you. So let us know if we can expect you--	144
and when.	146
Cordially	148/**172**

The final figure in the word count column includes the count for the envelope address.

47

47a ▶7 Conditioning practice

1. Each line twice SS (slowly, faster).
2. Three 1' writings on Line 3; determine *gwam*.

alphabet: Gavin knew Jay and Bix had perfect papers on my weekly quiz.

fig/sym: MUST SELL--objets d'art, antiques--call 841-7596 after 2:30.

fluency: Doris is to handle all title forms for the eight auto firms.

| 1 | 2 | 3 | 4 | 5 | 6 | 7 | 8 | 9 | 10 | 11 | 12 |

47b ▶28 Improve skill in typing letters

2 half sheets
2 Monarch sheets (LM pp. 33, 35)
line: 50; SS

1. On a half sheet (starting on Line 7) type the opening lines (date through salutation) of Problem 1 of 46c, above. Try to complete them within 1'.
2. Type the opening lines of Problem 2 in the same way.
3. On a Monarch sheet (starting on Line 14) type Problem 2 of 46c. Try to complete the letter within 10'.
4. Proofread your copy and prepare a final copy with errors corrected.

Goal: To improve letter typing skill.

248

248a ▶5 Conditioning practice

twice SS; repeat difficult lines

She may jeopardize the next bill which gives equal pay for equal work.
The company's work force rose from 384,347 in 1960 to 528,673 in 1975.
Model 279385 (AC/DC, 60 cycle, 110-120 volts) sells for $450, less 6%.
The judicial panel may discuss the problems of formal civil authority.

| 1 | 2 | 3 | 4 | 5 | 6 | 7 | 8 | 9 | 10 | 11 | 12 | 13 | 14 |

248b ▶11 Build basic skill

Two 1′ writings on each line of 248a.

248c ▶17 Measure basic skill: statistical copy

1. Two 5′ writings on the ¶s.
2. Record *gwam* and errors on better writing. Compare with scores you achieved on 239c, page 375.
3. As time permits, type a 1′ writing on each ¶.

all letters/figures used | A | 1.5 si | 5.6 awl | 80% hfw

Text	gwam 1′	5′
On December 17, 1903, Orville Wright flew a heavier-than-air craft	13	3
a distance of 120 feet. His 12-second flight began another exciting era	28	6
in the history of transportation. By 1905, a plane could remain in the	42	8
air for more than 30 minutes and cover almost 25 miles. The first non-	56	11
stop flight across the Atlantic was made in 1919--a trip of almost 2,500	71	14
miles--in 16 hours, 12 minutes. Domestic air service was started in	85	17
1918, but as late as 1926 only 5,783 people paid to travel by air.	98	20
Amazing progress has been made in air transportation. There were	13	22
2,813 miles of commercial routes in the United States in 1925. This rose	28	25
to 41,915 miles in 1940, to 77,000 miles in 1950, and to 172,000 miles	42	28
in 1970. There was also a remarkable increase in the number of people	56	31
who utilized domestic airlines. In a period of 44 years, the number of	71	34
passengers rose by millions--from 5,728 in 1926 to 169 million in 1970.	85	37
The progress in airliners has also been quite remarkable. In 1930,	14	39
the typical airplane utilized for long distances was a two-engine plane	28	42
carrying 20 passengers at a maximum speed of 300 miles an hour. A plane	43	45
had been developed by 1969 that can carry approximately 500 people at a	57	48
speed of 640 miles an hour--the 747. This jet airliner is 231.3 feet	71	51
long, 63.5 feet high, and has a wingspan of 195.7 feet--75.7 feet longer	86	54
than the first successful flight of 120 feet in 1903.	96	56

gwam 1′ | 1 | 2 | 3 | 4 | 5 | 6 | 7 | 8 | 9 | 10 | 11 | 12 | 13 | 14 |
5′ | 1 | 2 | 3 |

47c ▶15
Improve skill transfer

1. A 2′ writing on each ¶.
2. An additional 2′ writing on slower ¶.
3. A 3′ writing on each ¶.

all letters/figures used | A | 1.5 si | 5.6 awl | 80% hfw

	gwam 2′	3′
Words are the major component of written communication,	6	4
and the typewriter is a very vital tool we use to put those	12	8
words on paper with speed and ease. To exchange information	18	12
effectively, the words we use must be chosen quite carefully	24	16
and typed in a neatly arranged form. We should keep in mind	30	20
that the selection of the precise word is of greater impor-	36	24
tance than the size of the word because clarity is crucial.	42	28
In a recent study of a national sample of 2,061 business	6	4
letters, it was learned that 30.5% of all messages were brief	12	8
(100 words or fewer), 54.5% were medium (101 to 300 words),	18	12
and 15.0% were long (over 300 words). In another vital study--	24	16
this one having to do with letter cost--it was learned that a	30	20
message of medium length cost about $3.79. From all indica-	36	24
tions, message cost will be considerably higher in 1976-1985.	42	28

gwam 2′ | 1 | 2 | 3 | 4 | 5 | 6 |
3′ | 1 | 2 | 3 | 4 |

48

48a ▶7 Conditioning practice

1. Each line twice SS (slowly, faster).
2. Three 1′ writings on Line 3; determine *gwam*.

alphabet Jack Nix hopes to quit my show and give Buzz Rolfe a chance.

fig/sym The 6 deep-pile carpets (15′ × 24 7/8′) were sold at $1,039.

fluency The girl paid a neighbor to fix the turn signal of the auto.

| 1 | 2 | 3 | 4 | 5 | 6 | 7 | 8 | 9 | 10 | 11 | 12 |

48b ▶15 Improve skill transfer: statistical copy

1. A 2′ writing on ¶ 1, then on ¶ 2, of 47c, above. Try to improve speed on both straight copy and statistical copy. Determine % of transfer.

2. Type the two ¶s as a DS report with the heading THE SELECTION AND COST OF WORDS. Begin on Line 10, and use the 60-space line for which your machine is set.

48c ▶10 Compose at the typewriter

drill sheet; line: 60; DS

1. Type the ¶ as given at the right. Proofread your copy; circle errors.
2. Without referring to your copy or the textbook, summarize in three or four lines the idea the paragraph conveys. X-out and retype words in which you make errors.

	words
There is value in work—value to the worker as well as	11
to the one for whom the work is done. The worker who takes	23
pride in a worthwhile job well done rarely has the desire to	35
look for bizarre ways to occupy the mind, the hands, or the	47
leisure time that is available when the work is done.	57

247b ▶45 Measure production skill: letters

Type the letters for 30′, each letter on plain paper; correct errors as you type. If you finish all letters before time is called, start over.

Compute *n–pram*: total acceptable words + ½ unacceptable words ÷ 30. Compare *n–pram* with score achieved on 227b, page 360.

Problem 1
Modified block, mixed

	words
March 26, 19-- Ms. Jeanne LaShelle Director of	9
Training Greenwood Industries, Inc. 110 South	19
Tryon Street Charlotte, NC 28202 Dear Ms.	27
LaShelle (¶ 1) The problems you outlined in	35
your letter of March 10 are typical of those	44
faced by many companies when they begin to	53
use the computer to solve complex managerial	62
problems. A training program for your execu-	70
tives will help solve many of these problems.	80
(¶ 2) We shall be pleased to develop a program	88
to meet your specific needs. This program will	98
cover three major areas: (1) managerial	106
mathematics or the quantitative approach to	115
solving managerial problems; (2) computer	123
technology, with special emphasis on your com-	132
puter system; and (3) business simulations for	141
executives at all levels. (¶ 3) If you will call us	151
immediately, we can complete your training	159
program in approximately 30 days. Sincerely	168
yours EXECUTIVE DEVELOPMENT, INC. C. T.	177
Maynard, President xx (134)	181/203

Problem 2
Modified block, indented ¶s, mixed

	words
February 7, 19-- Mr. Scott D. Wesley, President	10
Junior Chamber of Commerce 705 Congress	18
Avenue Austin, TX 78701 Dear Mr. Wesley	26
(¶ 1) Thank you for inviting me to speak at the	34
meeting of the Junior Chamber of Commerce	43
to be held on March 2 at 6:30 p.m. in the Com-	52
modore Room of the Shorewood Hotel. The	60
topic of my presentation will be "The Decline	69
and Fall of the Free Enterprise System."	77
(¶ 2) I am looking forward with pleasure to	85
meeting you and the members of the Austin	93
Junior Chamber of Commerce on March 2.	101
Sincerely yours Paul N. Black, President xx (77)	110/129

Problem 3
Block, open

	words
April 16, 19-- Mr. Roosevelt C. Jones 573 Taylor	10
Road Wilmington, DE 19804 Dear Mr. Jones	18
(¶ 1) You have been recommended by Mr.	25
Raymond C. Chadwick as a possible replace-	33
ment for the Chief of our Regional Sales Office	42
in Baltimore. Mr. Randolph L. Perkins, who	51
currently occupies this position, will retire on	61
June 30 of this year. (¶ 2) This position calls	70
for an aggressive individual who is capable of	79
supervising and motivating a staff of 35 sales-	88
men whose territories extend from Penn-	96
sylvania to North Carolina. He must also be	105
expert in the fields of marketing and administra-	114
tion. A complete description of the duties and	124
responsibilities of the job is enclosed. The	133
salary is open to negotiation. (¶ 3) If you are	142
interested in applying for this position, please	152
complete the enclosed forms and return them	160
to me before April 30. Sincerely yours Juan	169
M. Martinez Personnel Director xx En-	177
closures (146)	178/190

Problem 4
AMS style

	words
August 3, 19-- Mrs. Eleanor C. Richardson	8
Western Representative Girard & Harrison,	17
Inc. 401 South Main Street Salt Lake City, UT	26
84111 SPECIAL MEETING OF REGIONAL REP-	33
RESENTATIVES (¶ 1) There will be a special	41
meeting of all regional representatives in my	50
office beginning at 9 a.m. on August 20. The	59
major topics for discussion will be the expan-	68
sion and reorganization of our marketing opera-	77
tions and the realignment of our sales districts	87
in the United States and Canada. A copy of the	97
complete agenda is enclosed. (¶ 2) A reserva-	105
tion has been made for you at the Charlton	113
Arms on North Main Street for the evenings of	122
August 19 and 20. If you will notify Eleanor	132
Madsen, my Executive Assistant, of the time	140
of your arrival in Oklahoma City, she will	149
have someone meet you at the airport.	157
DONALD L. MELROSE, DIRECTOR OF MARKET-	164
ING xx Enclosure (120)	167/191

3599 E. Sunrise Drive
Wichita, KS 67217
December 12, 19--

Ms. Rosemary Edens, Manager
Writing Arts Institute, Inc.
214 S. Boulder Avenue
Tulsa, OK 74103

Dear Ms. Edens

For a term project I am to prepare in a course in written communications, I have selected the topic "Rhetoric
Versus Grammar in Writing." I want to evaluate the two
statements "It really doesn't matter how you say something so long as you can be understood" and "To write
effectively, one must know and observe basic rules of grammar."

I want to support my paper with quotations from authori-
ties in general and business communication. As a noted
author in this field, your viewpoint on this topic
would strengthen my report immeasurably.

If you will take the time to give me a brief statement,
I shall be most grateful.

Sincerely yours

Miss Nancy Waterford

48d ▶18 Type a personal letter from script

1 Monarch letterhead (LM p. 37); line: 50; SS; return address on Line 14; address an envelope

1. Review letter layout, placement, and modified block style in Style Letter 1, page 73.

2. Type the letter above, guided by the bell to return carriage. Divide words and correct errors as necessary.

246d ▶17 Measure basic skill: script

1. Two 5′ writings on ¶s 1–3 combined.

2. Record *gwam* and errors on better writing. Compare with scores achieved on 226d, page 359. Note whether you have shown improvement.

3. As time permits, type a 1′ writing on each ¶.

all letters used | A | 1.5 si | 5.6 awl | 80% hfw

	gwam 1′	5′
The next chapter in the history of land and sea trans-	11	2
portation was the development of the steam engine. On sea,	23	5
the transition from the sail to the steam engine as a means	35	7
of propulsion was very slow. In fact, it was not until the	47	9
beginning of this century that steamships were developed that	59	12
could profitably take the place of the fast clipper ship.	71	14
Less than fifty years later, however, liners of great size	83	17
were able to move people and cargo very quickly over the seas.	95	19
A period of rapid change in transportation on land began	11	21
with the development of the steam locomotive. The first rail-	24	24
road was a road made of two tracks for the wheels of wagons.	36	26
These roads were used in mines several hundred years before	48	29
the invention of a steam locomotive early in the nineteenth	60	31
century. By the middle of that century, there were a number	72	33
of trains in operation which ran at very high rates of speed.	84	36
The use of steam in land transportation brought about	11	38
many changes in the social and industrial life of the world,	23	40
especially in the United States. Railroads linked the indus-	35	43
tries of the North with raw materials and markets in the South.	48	45
When the first coast-to-coast line was completed just shortly	60	48
after the end of the Civil War, the way was open to the great	73	50
natural resources of the West. Much of the credit for the	84	53
rapid development of our nation belongs to the railroads.	96	55

247

247a ▶5 Conditioning practice

twice SS; repeat difficult lines

Jeff Zook answered many queries by explaining the vehicle regulations.
The factory produced 301,287 cans in April and 465,839 cans in August.
The Ace Duplicator (Model 96378) is listed at $245, less 10% discount.
Perhaps the author will tell us about the time he spent in the orient.

| 1 | 2 | 3 | 4 | 5 | 6 | 7 | 8 | 9 | 10 | 11 | 12 | 13 | 14 |

unit **8** lessons 49–50

Performance evaluation

Performance goals

Goals (to be supplied by your teacher) include: 1′ straight-copy goal; 3′ straight-copy goal; 3′ statistical-copy goal; time-limit goals for completing problems.

Machine adjustments

1. Paper guide at *0*.

2. Ribbon control on black.

3. Margin sets: 60-space line, except for problems.

4. Line-space selector on *1* for drills; on *2* for ¶s; as directed for problems.

49

49a ▶7 Conditioning practice

1. Each line twice SS (slowly, faster); DS between 2-line groups.

2. Two 1′ writings on Line 3; determine *gwam* on each.

alphabet Zeb Shaw did quick, exceptional engraving work for Jim Raye.

fig/sym File Invoice 9043 and Contract 17-48-562 in my tickler file.

fluency An auditor is apt to visit eight firms to audit their forms.

| 1 | 2 | 3 | 4 | 5 | 6 | 7 | 8 | 9 | 10 | 11 | 12 |

49b ▶12 Check straight-copy skill

1. A 1′ writing on each ¶; determine *gwam* and errors on each. Record better score.

2. Two 3′ writings on ¶s 1–2 combined; determine *gwam* and errors on each. Record better score.

1′ Goal: At least 27 *gwam*.
3′ Goal: At least 25 *gwam*.

all letters used | A | 1.5 si | 5.6 awl | 80% hfw

	gwam 1′	3′	
Words are the building blocks of effective writing. The	11	4	44
better we put our ideas into words, the more likely we are to	24	8	48
persuade the reader to do what we ask. If our letters ramble,	36	12	52
are not clear, or exhibit poor grammar, we increase the like-	48	16	56
lihood of having our ideas rejected and our requests denied.	60	20	60
Any weak letter can be improved by rewriting so that the	11	24	64
final copy quickly conveys its basic ideas in a clear, exact	24	28	68
manner. The reader should not then need to puzzle over its	36	32	72
meaning. All features of style and content should be designed	48	36	76
to enhance the meaning instead of to distract from it.	59	40	80

gwam 1′ | 1 | 2 | 3 | 4 | 5 | 6 | 7 | 8 | 9 | 10 | 11 | 12 |
3′ | 1 | 2 | 3 | 4 |

49c ▶11 Check centering skill

1. Center the lines vertically on a half sheet; center each line horizontally.

2. Proofread and mark errors for correction.

3. Retype problem with errors erased and corrected.

	words
MODERN ART EXHIBIT	4
Original Paintings by Manuel Alvarez	11
Fine Arts Building Portico	17
February 8-10, 10 a.m.-4 p.m.	23
Oils, Watercolors, and Wash Drawings	30
Admission: Student ID Card	35

246c ▶17 Measure basic skill: straight copy

1. Two 5′ writings on ¶s 1–3 combined.

2. Record *gwam* and errors on better writing. Compare with scores achieved on 226c, page 358.

3. As time permits, type a 1′ guided writing on each ¶.

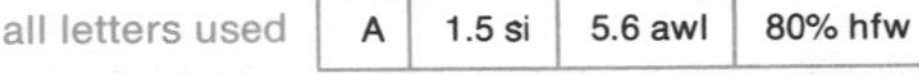

all letters used | A | 1.5 si | 5.6 awl | 80% hfw

gwam 5′

One of the major elements which led to the rise of the civilized world was transportation. Until the means of moving people and goods over long distances were found, little or no progress was possible. As the ability of man to travel improved, trade and commerce began to grow. New markets for goods led to more and better jobs for the people and a higher standard of living. Modern industry, as we know it today, could not exist if it did not have quick and efficient modes of transportation. 20

The first routes of transportation were the rivers. Almost every great city of the world is located on a river or near an ocean and is a major center of trade. The advance from canoes to large ships that were capable of long voyages took place many years before this country was founded. The invention of the sail and exact methods of navigation, such as the compass, opened the way to transportation on the seas. For many centuries, the seas served as the major means of international trade. 40

There is no doubt that one of the greatest events in the history of the world was the invention of the wheel. The wheel led to the use of vehicles which could be used to move people and products over land areas. Land transportation, however, developed at a much slower rate than water transportation. For centuries, carts drawn by animals were the major means of transport over land. Until the invention of the steam engine, the rate of travel on land rarely exceeded ten miles an hour. 59

gwam 5′ | 1 | 2 | 3 |

49d ▶20
Check report typing skill

full sheet; line: 60; heading on Line 10; DS (double-spacing)

Listen for bell as signal to return carriage. Divide words and correct errors as necessary.

Enrichment material for Unit 8 appears on LM pp. 43–46.

	words
THE SECRET OF SKILLED PERFORMANCE	7
Asked to identify the secret of star performance, Coach John	19
Wooden thoughtfully replied, "Speed, poise, and finesse." He was	32
referring to the skill of his legendary basketball teams, but his	45
answer applies to any skilled performance, including typewriting.	58
Speed refers to the rate of motion of an act. Speed is af-	70
fected by reaction time, the time that elapses between perceiving	83
a set of stimuli to act and setting into motion a series of related	97
actions. It includes the speed of the motions themselves. The	110
difficulty of the task influences both the reaction time and the	123
speed of individual motions.	129
Poise is the easy, confident manner of performing. Poise	140
comes from successful repetition of the various actions that make	154
up the total skill. Repetition develops ease, just as success	166
builds confidence in one's ability to perform with skill in similar	180
situations in the future. Poise implies that you do not "lose your	193
cool" under pressure.	198
Finesse means refinement of workmanship. Finesse results from	211
self-analysis in a variety of experiences. The analysis includes	224
the evaluation of what worked well and what did not. It is fol-	237
lowed by refining the successful and eliminating the unsuccessful.	250
Finesse requires speed with control; it typifies the skilled per-	263
former--in both victory and defeat.	270

50

50a ▶7 Conditioning practice

1. Each line twice SS (slowly, faster); DS between 2–line groups.

2. Two 1′ writings on Line 3; determine *gwam* on each.

alphabet Jack Burton said Lyza wove the queer hex signs for Mr. Depp.

fig/sym Issue 3A was rejected by 50,284 (64%) of the voters in 1977.

fluency Signal the chair if their proxy is a key to a big endowment.

| 1 | 2 | 3 | 4 | 5 | 6 | 7 | 8 | 9 | 10 | 11 | 12 |

unit **43** lessons 246–250

Measuring basic/production skills

Learning goals

1. To demonstrate improvement in speed and accuracy in typing straight copy, script, rough draft, and statistical copy.

2. To demonstrate improvement in production rates in typing letters, reports, tables, and business forms.

246

246a ▶5 Conditioning practice

twice SS; repeat difficult lines

alphabet Two biochemical experts have just finished analyzing the black liquid.

figures Of the 1,430 new employees hired in 1976, 852 were production workers.

fig/sym The bill of lading shows that T & W shipped 986# on 3/14/75, not 452#.

fluency Take the black panels from the display window and put them on a shelf.

| 1 | 2 | 3 | 4 | 5 | 6 | 7 | 8 | 9 | 10 | 11 | 12 | 13 | 14 |

246b ▶11 Skill-comparison typing

1. A 1′ writing on ¶ 1. Find *gwam.*

2. Two 1′ writings on ¶ 1 with the 15″ call of the guide.

3. A 1′ writing on ¶ 1. Find *gwam.*

4. Type ¶ 2 in the same manner.

5. Additional 1′ writings on ¶ 2 as time permits in an effort to equal or better your highest speed typed on ¶ 1.

¶ 1				¶ 2			
E	1.3 si	5.2 awl	90% hfw	D	1.7 si	6.0 awl	70% hfw

The most common type of organization in the world of business today [12] is the line and staff. In the line are found those people and units [26] whose work is directly related to the basic goals of the firm. In a [40] retail firm, for example, those involved in sales would be the line. [54] The line also provides a chain of command which flows from the managers [68] at the top to the workers at the lowest level. [78]

The staff consists mostly of specialists whose primary task it is [13] to counsel and assist the line on the numerous complex aspects of an [27] enterprise. Staff executives are experts who formulate policies, but [41] who do not have any authority to give orders to the line. Line execu- [55] tives make all major decisions and issue orders. The purchasing and [68] legal departments are examples of staff divisions in a typical firm. [82]

50b ▶12 Check statistical-copy skill

1. A 1' writing on each ¶; determine *gwam* and errors on each. Record better score.

2. Two 3' writings on ¶s 1–2 combined; determine *gwam* and errors on each. Record better score.

1' Goal: At least 19 *gwam*.
3' Goal: At least 17 *gwam*.

all figures used | A | 1.5 si | 5.6 awl | 80% hfw

	gwam 1'	3'
In 1940, slightly more than 66 2/3% of all males and fe-	11	4
males making up our work force had fewer than 4 years of high	24	8
school education. In 1973, however, only 28.7% of a comparable	36	12
group had fewer than 12 years of formal education.	46	15
Of the 1973 work force, virtually 29% of all participants	12	19
in the 35 to 44 age bracket were not high school graduates.	24	23
Of those workers between 20 and 24 years of age, only 15% had	36	28
not completed a minimum of 12 years of formal schooling.	47	31

gwam 1' | 1 | 2 | 3 | 4 | 5 | 6 | 7 | 8 | 9 | 10 | 11 | 12 |
3' | 1 | 2 | 3 | 4 |

50c ▶31 Check letter typing skill

2 Monarch letterheads;
line: 50; return address:
Line 14; address envelopes

Problem 1 [LM p. 39]

	words
2200 Perdido	3
New Orleans, LA 70119	7
February 10, 19--	11
Mr. William H. Carel	15
Delta High School	18
Biloxi, MS 39530	22
Dear Mr. Carel	25
Because I remember so well the stacks of pa-	33
pers you always checked so thoroughly, I have	43
been hesitant to type this letter even though it	52
is to thank you for all you did for me when I	62
was in your typing class.	67
There were times, I'm sure, when you despaired	76
of my learning anything except the home row,	85
but I learned more than you knew. How you	94
taught as well as what you taught has helped	103
me greatly.	106
My name may not make the Dean's list, but I'm	115
getting along quite well. My classes are often	124
challenging and sometimes even stimulating.	133
For doing well this first year in college, I	142
thank my high school teachers--and I thank you	152
most of all.	155
Cordially yours	158/**180**

Problem 2 [LM p. 41]

	words
304 Aspen Lane	3
Duluth, MN 55804	6
February 10, 19--	10
Miss Betty Good, Director	15
Placement Services, Inc.	20
45 South Seventh Street	25
Minneapolis, MN 55402	29
Dear Miss Good	32
You are quoted in today's Examiner as saying in	44
a recent address, "Research shows that more	52
workers fail as a result of undesirable personal	62
traits than because of weak technical skills."	72
I want to quote this statement in a paper I am	81
writing on "Why Office Workers Fail," and I	90
would like to know the research studies to which	100
you referred so I can list them in my bibliog-	109
raphy.	110
If you will send me the research references upon	120
which you based your statement, I shall be most	130
grateful. I am sure the references will be of	139
great help to me in preparing my paper.	147
Sincerely yours	151
Your typed name	155/**184**

244

244a ▶5 Conditioning practice

twice SS;
repeat difficult lines

Jake Luffy expects the government to subsidize his unique subway plan.
We will meet on May 19, 24, 27, and 30 and on June 3, 5, 6, 8, and 10.
Interest rates ranged from 4 1/2% to 7 1/4% with an average of 5 3/4%.
Is it true that anyone who works hard and does his best, profits most?

| 1 | 2 | 3 | 4 | 5 | 6 | 7 | 8 | 9 | 10 | 11 | 12 | 13 | 14 |

244b ▶45 Improve skill transfer

1. A 5′ writing on each of these copy selections:

Straight copy	226c, p. 358
Script	226d, p. 359
Rough draft	232c, p. 367
Statistical	239c, p. 375

Determine *gwam* on each.

2. Compute % of transfer: Divide straight-copy *gwam* INTO *gwam* on script, on rough draft, and on statistical copy.

Your %-of-transfer goals are shown below.

Script	80–100%
Rough draft	70– 90%
Statistical copy	65– 85%

3. As time permits, type additional 5′ writings on selected copy to increase your % of transfer.

245

245a ▶5 Conditioning practice

twice SS;
repeat difficult lines

Experts will solve the budget dilemma in June if we economize quickly.
Please telephone Mr. Long at 412-386-9756 on September 19 at 2:30 p.m.
Use Voucher 395024 to buy office copies of Time, Fortune, and Redbook.
Didn't the vendor submit a formal bid for the entire quantity of fuel?

| 1 | 2 | 3 | 4 | 5 | 6 | 7 | 8 | 9 | 10 | 11 | 12 | 13 | 14 |

245b ▶45 Sustained production: forms and tabulation

1. Make a list of the problems below:

page 377, 241c
page 378, 242b, Problem 1 [LM p. 25]
page 378, 242b, Problem 2 [LM p. 25]

2. Type the problems for 30′; correct errors as you type. Proofread each problem before you remove it from the typewriter and correct any errors you have missed.

3. If you finish all problems before time is called, type 242c, page 379, as page 2 of an interoffice memorandum on plain paper.

4. Compute *n-pram*.

phase 3 lessons 51–75

Introduction to business typing

Learning goals

In the 25 lessons of Phase 3, you will learn to type letters, tables, and reports in easy-to-type formats—just as they are typed in a business office.

In doing so, you should keep these goals in mind:

1. To improve your basic techniques of typing.

2. To improve efficiency in using special machine parts.

3. To type each problem with care and attention to layout features.

Machine adjustments

1. Paper guide on *0*.

2. Ribbon control on black.

3. Margin sets: 70-space line for drills and ¶s; as directed for problems.

4. Line-space selector on *1* for drills; on *2* for ¶s; as directed for problems.

unit 9 lessons 51–57

Business letters

51

51a ▶7 Conditioning practice

1. Each line twice SS (slowly, faster).

2. A 1′ writing on Line 4, then on Line 1; compare *gwam*.

alphabet	Al criticized my six workers for having such quick tempers on the job.
figures	We have stores at 247 Opera Place, 3805 Avon Court, and 691 Rich Road.
-s / -es	go goes say says eye eyes tax taxes idea ideas your yours radio radios
fluency	It is the wish of all of us to lend a hand to the visitor to the city.

| 1 | 2 | 3 | 4 | 5 | 6 | 7 | 8 | 9 | 10 | 11 | 12 | 13 | 14 |

51b ▶10 Improve skill transfer: statistical copy

1. A 1′ writing on each ¶; compare *gwam*.

2. A 1′ writing on ¶ 2 to increase speed.

3. A 2′ writing on each ¶; compare *gwam*.

A	1.5 si	5.6 awl	80% hfw

	gwam 1′	2′
We are beginning to move to a metric system of measure. Before	13	6
long you will be ordering sugar by the kilogram and milk by the liter.	28	14
Many other familiar items will be ordered differently, also. Making	42	21
the change might be puzzling in the beginning, as most changes are;	55	28
but we will adjust to it by either converting to or thinking metric.	69	35
Changes may occur in typical paper sizes, too. As an example, a	13	6
full sheet of typing paper (once 8 1/2″ x 11″) will likely switch to	27	13
one of 210 x 280 mm (that is 8 1/4″ x 11″). It is also probable that	41	20
a government-size letter (once 8″ x 10 1/2″) will have the standard	54	27
metric dimensions of 210 x 280 mm.	61	31

gwam 1′ | 1 | 2 | 3 | 4 | 5 | 6 | 7 | 8 | 9 | 10 | 11 | 12 | 13 | 14 |
2′ | 1 | 2 | 3 | 4 | 5 | 6 | 7 |

243b, continued

Problem 2 [LM p. 23]
Bill of lading

	words
FROM Minuteman Products, Inc. AT Boston, MA DATE 10/3/-- CONSIGNED	9
TO AND DESTINATION Queens Groceries, Ltd. 30 Charles Street Toronto,	19
Ontario M4Y 1R6 CUST. ORDER NO. 9267 DELIVERING CARRIER CAN-US	24
Van Lines CAR INITIAL AND NO. ICC-18267	28

NO. PACKAGES	DESCRIPTION	WEIGHT	
20	Green beans, 227 gm cans	720#	35
24	Spinach, 220 gm cans	864#	41
36	Stewed tomatoes, 234 gm cans	1,296#	49
12	Kosher dill pickles, .44 l jars	216#	57

SHIPPER Minuteman Products, Inc. PERMANENT POST OFFICE ADDRESS OF	62
SHIPPER 280 Milk Street, Boston, MA 02109 SHIPPER'S NO. 372850	70

243c ▶25 Build production skill: tabulation

Center the table horizontally and vertically in reading position on a full sheet of paper. DS the items. Correct errors as you type. (If necessary, refer to page 324 for spacing.)

Note: Center the 3-digit entries under the columnar headings.

words

MINUTEMAN PRODUCTS, INC. 5

Monthly Sales for Year Ending December 31, 19-- 15

(In Thousands of Dollars) 20

Month	United States	Canada	Iceland	words
				41
				48
				59
January	49.7	34.6	25.2	63
February	48.9	36.4	29.9	68
March	57.6	39.3	34.4	72
April	68.1	45.0	33.8	77
May	59.0	44.9	37.1	80
June	76.4	27.8	41.9	84
July	37.7	27.7	21.9	88
August	46.8	36.0	20.6	93
September	49.0	38.1	25.3	98
October	54.9	39.2	30.1	102
November	57.3	39.1	27.1	107
December	37.6	54.3	21.5	112
				123
Total	643.0	462.4	348.8	127
				149

51c ▶33 Learn to type business letters

1. Study Style Letter 2 (page 83) illustrating *modified block style, block ¶s, open punctuation.* Note the vertical and horizontal placement of letter parts.

2. On plain paper (8½" x 11") type a copy of the letter on page 83.

3. Proofread your copy, mark it for correction, and retype it in final form, correcting all errors.

4. As time permits, type a 2′ writing on opening lines (date through salutation); then a 2′ writing on closing lines (complimentary close through enclosure notation). Push for *speed.*

52

52a ▶7 Conditioning practice

1. Each line twice SS (slowly, faster).

2. A 1′ writing on Line 4, then on Line 2; compare *gwam.*

alphabet Jan very quickly seized the wheel as big cars pulled out from an exit.

fig/sym Ed paid a $92.40 premium on a $5,000 insurance policy (dated 8/13/76).

–ed apply applied carry carried issue issued move moved try tried use used

fluency The city auditor is due by eight and she may lend a hand to the panel.

| 1 | 2 | 3 | 4 | 5 | 6 | 7 | 8 | 9 | 10 | 11 | 12 | 13 | 14 |

52b ▶11 Skill-comparison typing

1. A 2′ writing on each ¶; compare *gwam.*

2. Two 2′ writings on slower ¶.

all letters used

¶ 1			
LA	1.4 si	5.4 awl	85% hfw

¶ 2			
HA	1.6 si	5.8 awl	75% hfw

	gwam 1′	2′
If idle chatter were of value, some office workers would be rich.	14	7
Anyone who hires a worker buys three things: knowledge, skill, and	27	14
time. The first two can grow on the job; time, however, is unvariable.	42	21
If it is wasted or is not put to good purpose, the worker cheats not	56	28
only the company but himself as well--the company, which does not get	70	35
what it pays for; himself, who does not receive the raise or promotion.	85	42
It is an economic axiom that time is money. Time spent in perform-	14	7
ing clerical functions involves a time-equals-money factor that becomes	28	14
a cost of doing business. This cost influences the prices that must	42	21
be charged for items or services supplied by a company in the market-	56	28
place. The concern of a business manager for the efficiency of time	70	35
use by clerical workers is a zealous and legitimate one.	81	41

gwam 1′ | 1 | 2 | 3 | 4 | 5 | 6 | 7 | 8 | 9 | 10 | 11 | 12 | 13 | 14 |
2′ | 1 | 2 | 3 | 4 | 5 | 6 | 7 |

52c ▶12 Build skill in typing business letters

1. A 2′ writing (in letter form) on opening lines of letter on page 83. Push for *speed.*

2. A 2′ writing (in letter form) on closing lines of letter on page 83. Push for *speed.*

3. Type a 5′ writing on the ¶s of letter on page 83.

242c ▶20 Build production skill: interoffice memorandum

Type the memo with 1 cc [LM p. 21]; correct errors as you type.

	words
TO: Brad L. Jeffers, Training Director FROM: Diana M. Martinez, Personnel	13
Director DATE: October 3, 19-- SUBJECT: Personnel Policies and Procedures	25
(¶ 1) Attached is a copy of the final draft of the revised "Manual for Em-	38
ployees" which includes all current personnel policies and procedures.	52
The manual has been reviewed by the Union's legal counsel; and Dominic	67
Minelli, Business Representative of the Union, agrees that the regula-	80
tions do not violate any of the provisions of our current labor agreement.	96
(¶ 2) The courts have ruled that an employee is bound by the provisions of	109
an employee manual only if the specific rules to be followed have been	123
brought to the employee's attention. For this reason, it will be necessary	139
to explain the personnel policies to all employees. (¶ 3) Will you please	152
set up an orientation program to insure that all employees know and under-	167
stand our personnel policies. Although it may be desirable to have each	182
supervisor explain the rules to subordinates, considerable time can be	196
saved if the orientation is given to large groups by members of your staff.	211
(¶ 4) The printer will deliver the new manual on October 17. The orientation	226
program can begin any time after that date. xx Enclosure	237/246

243

243a ▶5 Conditioning practice

twice SS; repeat difficult lines

The shop in Roxburgh Plaza will have quality jackets for men and boys.
The median of 27, 31, 40, 59, 68, 72, 84, 96, 105, 190, and 237 is 72.
Channels 10 (WCAD), 13 (WQMD), and 27 (WJEC) will broadcast the event.
To avoid a big penalty, the editor must pay the bill before it is due.

| 1 | 2 | 3 | 4 | 5 | 6 | 7 | 8 | 9 | 10 | 11 | 12 | 13 | 14 |

243b ▶20 Build production skill: business forms

Type the statement of account at the right and the bill of lading on page 380; correct errors as you type.

Problem 1 [LM p. 23]
Statement of account

Date November 30, 19--

	words
To Conemaugh Wholesale Grocers	9
350 Bedford Street	13
Johnstown, PA 15902	17

Date		Items	Debits	Credits	Balance	words
November	1	Balance due			782.00	23
	4	Invoice GR675456	3,506.50		4,288.50	31
	11	Payment on account		782.00	3,506.50	39
	18	Invoice GR675671	603.80		4,110.30	46
	21	Invoice HI676480	732.60		4,842.90	54
	25	Credit Memorandum 5830		307.40	4,535.50	63
	28	Payment on account		1,500.00	3,035.50	71

Shown in pica type 60-space line

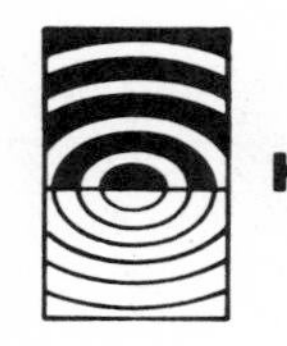

HORIZON PUBLISHERS, INC. 3850 El Camino Real • Palo Alto, CA 94306
(415) 631-2000

		words: parts	words: total
	Tab to center to type date and closing lines		
Dateline	Line 18 December 27, 19--	4	4
	Operate return 4 times		
Letter address	Mrs. Mary Lively, Librarian	9	9
	Washington High School	14	14
	1500 North Fort Myer Drive	19	19
	Arlington, VA 22209	23	23
	DS		
Salutation	Dear Mrs. Lively	26	26
	DS		
Body of letter	After years of research and study by eminent scientists all	12	38
	over the world, we are pleased to announce the publication of	24	51
	our richly illustrated series MYSTERIES OF THE EARTH.	35	62
	DS		
	This series was designed especially for high school students.	48	74
	The text has been written in easy, concise language so that	60	86
	ideas can be grasped quickly. The vivid four-color illus-	72	98
	trations make the series unusually interesting and exciting.	84	111
	We are sure you will want this series for your library. We	96	123
	are therefore sending to you, free of charge, a copy of the	108	135
	first volume. Examine it carefully; then order the series	120	146
	quickly, using the enclosed order form, so you will have the	132	159
	books for the beginning of your next semester.	141	168
	DS		
Complimentary close	Sincerely yours (Operate return 4 times)	3	171
Signature	Brian L. Cole		
Typed name and title	Brian L. Cole, Manager	8	176
Department or division	Marketing Division	12	179
	DS		
Initials of typist	jr	12	180
	DS		
Enclosure notation	Enclosure	14	181

In *open* punctuation, no punctuation follows the salutation or the complimentary close.

Style letter 2: business letter in modified block style, block paragraphs

242

242a ▶5 Conditioning practice

twice SS;
repeat difficult lines

We have begun a check of quarterly expenses itemized in their journal.
Send 3 desks, 16 chairs, 4 tables, and 5 lamps to Room 908 on June 27.
In Lot 5647A, 180 units (25%) were rejected at a total cost of $2,390.
In the future, please send all payments on this loan to the City Bank.

| 1 | 2 | 3 | 4 | 5 | 6 | 7 | 8 | 9 | 10 | 11 | 12 | 13 | 14 |

242b ▶25 Improve production skills: business forms

1. A 10′ writing on each of the forms; correct errors as you type. If you finish a form before time is called, start over.

2. Find *n–pram*.

Problem 1 [LM p. 17]
Purchase order

		words
To: Alliance Equipment Company	Purchase order No. M-8043	7
980 Main Street	Date August 23, 19--	13
Hartford, CT 06103	Terms Net	18
	Ship Via Coastal Freight	21

Quantity	Cat. No.	Description	Price	Total	words
24	D7602	Round barrel dollies, w/rubber wheels	21.95	526.80	34
16	T9683	Platform trucks, steel, 800 lbs.	67.95	1,087.20	45
30	T9710	Hand trucks, w/pneumatic wheels	44.95	1,348.50	56
12	S412A	Barrel stands, w/rubber wheels and swivel casters	21.95	263.40	71
10	T7012	Shelf trucks, steel, 43″ × 20″ × 42″	87.95	879.50	85
				4,105.40	87

Problem 2 [LM p. 19]
Invoice

		words
Sold to Robbins Merchandise Mart	Date September 8, 19--	9
500 North Market Street	Our Order No. HG61603	15
Wilmington, DE 19801	Cust. Order No. 38852-S	21
Terms 2/10, n/30 ROG	Shipped Via Penn Central RR	27

Quantity	Description	Unit Price	Total	words
40	Colander-rinsers, aluminum, 10″ × 4″	3.25	130.00	38
48	Funnel sets, aluminum	.86	41.28	45
60	Jar openers, steel	.67	40.20	52
24	Apple corer-cutters, aluminum, 6″ × 4″	1.10	26.40	62
12	Food mills, steel, 2-qt.	4.90	58.80	71
			296.68	73

52d ▶20

Type a business letter from semiarranged copy

plain sheets; line: 60; date: Line 18; return at line-end indicators in the opening and closing lines; type body line for line

1. Type the letter once to learn to type from semiarranged copy.

2. Evaluate the layout and spacing of your letter by comparing it with the model on page 83.

3. Proofread and mark your copy for correction.

4. If time permits, retype the letter from your marked copy; correct all errors.

Do not type line–end indicators.

	words parts	total
December 28, 19-- | Mr. Edward Gordon, Director | Lovell Tech-	11	11
nical College | 1936 Westlake Avenue | Seattle, WA 98101 |	22	22
Dear Mr. Gordon |	25	25
¶ Just off the press is a new series of six outstanding books	12	37
on OUR EXPANDING UNIVERSE. Although the people who designed	24	49
the enclosed brochure describing the series didn't prepare	36	61
the books, the books are equally beautiful and informative.	48	73
¶ A copy of the first volume is being sent to you today. Put	60	85
it in your library. When your teachers and students get to	72	97
know this interesting and authoritative work, we are sure	84	109
they will want the entire series at the low price of $58.50.	96	121
¶ If you order the series promptly, we will make shipment in	108	133
time for you to use the books next term. But whether you	120	145
order or not, please keep the first volume because we want	131	156
your students to know OUR EXPANDING UNIVERSE.	141	166
Sincerely yours | Brian L. Cole, Manager | Marketing Division |	12	178
xx (use your own initials) | Enclosure	14	180

53

53a ▶7

Conditioning practice

1. Each line twice SS (slowly, faster).

2. A 1′ writing on Line 4, then on Line 1; compare *gwam*.

alphabet: Quite a few very big men like to jump and do exercises on the trapeze.

figures: The letter shows the ZIP Code 45208 and the telephone number 931-6720.

–ing: ask asking come coming get getting give giving have having live living

fluency: He may visit the firm to work with the title forms they handle for me.

| 1 | 2 | 3 | 4 | 5 | 6 | 7 | 8 | 9 | 10 | 11 | 12 | 13 | 14 |

53b ▶10

Improve skill transfer

1. A 1′ writing on each line; compare *gwam*.

2. A 1′ writing on each of the slower lines. Try to equal your best *gwam* in Step 1.

All good workers do their work better than just well enough.

She stated the rate to be paid on the world trade agreement.

Re serve six seats for ~~them~~ him onthe ailse near the center ~~entrance~~ exit.

Ball and Cook long-term bonds (due in 1987) pay 8% interest.

| 1 | 2 | 3 | 4 | 5 | 6 | 7 | 8 | 9 | 10 | 11 | 12 |

53c ▶15

Build skill in typing business letters

1. A 1′ and a 2′ writing (in letter form) on opening lines of letter in 52d, above. Push for *speed*.

2. A 1′ and a 2′ writing (in letter form) on closing lines of letter in 52d, above. Push for *speed*.

3. A 5′ writing on the entire letter in 52d; tab, return, and space forward quickly.

241

241a ▶5 Conditioning practice

twice SS;
repeat difficult lines

We will adjust all prices quickly if we have an embargo on zinc oxide.
Stereo music can be found at 80.2, 93.1, 105.4, and 106.7 on the dial.
The winning pole vault was 17′3″; high jump, 6′9″; triple jump, 54′6″.
It is time for the tour bus to take the women to the park in the city.

| 1 | 2 | 3 | 4 | 5 | 6 | 7 | 8 | 9 | 10 | 11 | 12 | 13 | 14 |

241b ▶17 Improve production skills: interoffice memorandum

1. If necessary, refer to page 311 for style of enumerated items in the memorandum.

2. A 5′ writing on the interoffice memorandum (LM p. 15); correct errors as you type. Determine *n–pram*.

3. A 5′ writing (plain paper) beginning with ¶ 1 as page 2 of a memo. Use vertical form of second-page heading as illustrated on page 376. Correct errors as you type. Determine *n–pram*.

words

TO: Luis Vecchio, President FROM: Robert D. Marks, Controller DATE: 10
August 24, 19-- SUBJECT: Financing for Expansion 19

(¶ 1) If the Board of Directors approves our plans to expand our dehy- 31
drated food processing, it will be necessary to renovate and expand the 46
Quincy Plant. It is estimated that the renovation will cost $2,739,300 60
and the new construction will cost $7,910,900. These figures include 74
the cost of equipment and architect and consultant fees. 86

(¶ 2) To finance the expansion, I recommend that we raise the funds 98
through the use of bonds rather than the issuance of additional stock 112
for these reasons: 1. Our existing debt ratio is relatively low. 2. At this 128
time, the price of common stock in relation to that of bonds is tem- 142
porarily depressed. 3. The interest payment on bonds is deductible as 156
a tax expense. 4. The sale of stock may cause problems of control. 170

(¶ 3) Before the Finance Committee can establish any long-range priori- 183
ties, the manner in which the expansion of the Quincy Plant will be 197
financed must be resolved. xx 203/**210**

241c ▶28 Improve production skills: tables

1. A 10′ writing on the table. Use the mathematical method to determine horizontal placement. Center in reading position; DS the items. Correct errors as you type. Determine *n–pram*.

2. A 10′ writing. Use the backspace-from-center method to determine horizontal placement. Center in reading position; DS the items. Correct errors as you type. Determine *n–pram*.

MINUTEMAN PRODUCTS, INC.

Funds Applied During Previous and Current Fiscal Years

	CURRENT	PREVIOUS	words
			5
			16
			19
Property and equipment acquired	$ 1,094,709	$ 1,342,788	32
Reduction of long-term debt	8,610,720	6,663,509	42
Plant modernization fund	854,672	665,783	51
Redemption of preferred stock	74,260	74,260	60
Cash dividends paid	889,947	885,520	68
Miscellaneous	72,468	58,379	74
Addition to working capital	508,807	1,050,273	88
Total funds applied	$12,105,583	$10,740,512	108

53d ▶18 Learn to address envelopes and fold letters

1. Study the guides and illustrations at the right and below.

Envelope address
Set a tab stop 2½" from left edge of a small envelope, 4" for a large one. Space down 2" from top edge of small envelope, 2½" for a large one. Begin the address at the tab stop position.

Style
Use *block style*, SS, without line-end punctuation unless an abbreviation ends a line. Type city name, 2-letter state name abbreviation, and ZIP Code on last address line. One space precedes the ZIP Code.

Addressing envelopes

Style used above is that recommended by U.S. Postal Service for fastest mechanical mail sorting.

2. Type a small (No. 6¾) and a large (No. 10) envelope for each of the following addresses. (LM pp. 53, 55, 57)

Ms. Vanessa Pate, Editor
Modern Woman Magazine
Market Tower, Suite 9C
Wilmington, DE 19801

Miss Marsha Schoenberg
One Kensington Gate
Great Neck, NY 11021

Mr. Joseph M. Ramirez
Somerset House, Apt. 8G
729 Cooper Landing Road
Cherry Hill, NJ 08034

3. Practice folding and inserting standard-size sheets of paper for both large and small envelopes.

Folding-and-inserting procedure

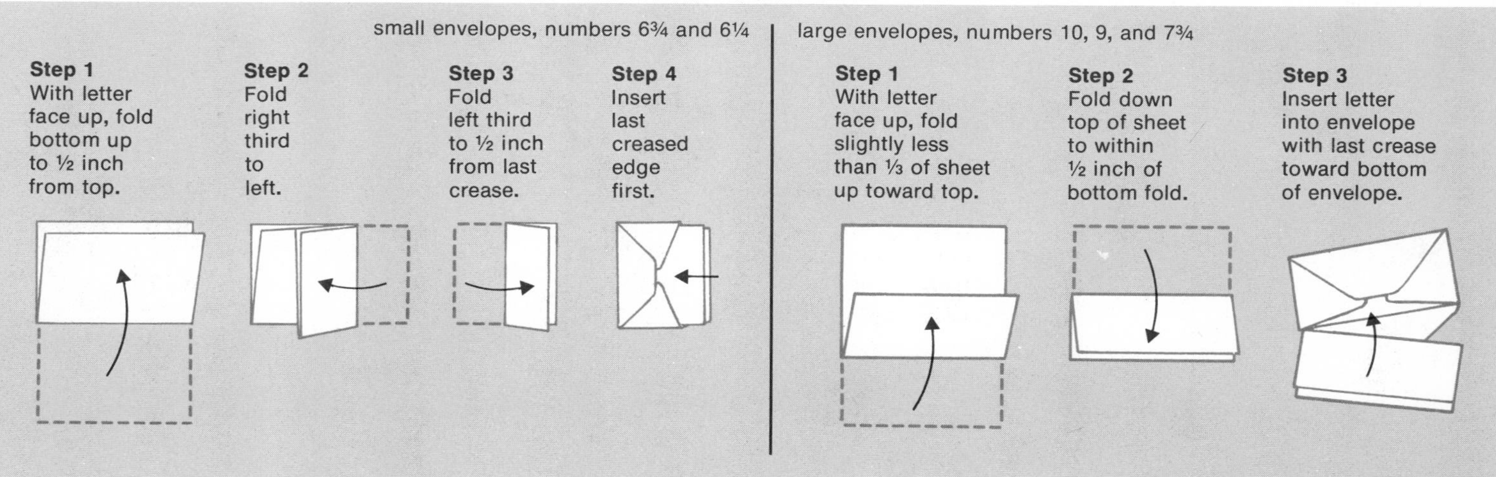

small envelopes, numbers 6¾ and 6¼
Step 1 With letter face up, fold bottom up to ½ inch from top.
Step 2 Fold right third to left.
Step 3 Fold left third to ½ inch from last crease.
Step 4 Insert last creased edge first.
large envelopes, numbers 10, 9, and 7¾
Step 1 With letter face up, fold slightly less than ⅓ of sheet up toward top.
Step 2 Fold down top of sheet to within ½ inch of bottom fold.
Step 3 Insert letter into envelope with last crease toward bottom of envelope.

240b ▶45 Inventory production skill: forms and tables

1. Type the problems for 30′; correct errors as you type.

2. After completing Problems 1, 2, and 3, retype Problem 1 on plain paper as page 2 of an interoffice memorandum. Use the vertical form of a second page heading as shown below.

Second-page heading of an interoffice memorandum:

C. L. Conti
Page 2
July 8, 19--

Begin on Line 7 *at the left margin.* After typing the heading, triple-space and type the ¶s.

3. Compute *n-pram.* Keep a record for comparison with *n-pram* achieved in 250b, page 390.

Problem 1 [LM p. 11]
Interoffice memorandum

words

TO: C. L. Conti, Chief of Labor Relations FROM: P. D. Nash, Vice President 13
DATE: July 8, 19-- SUBJECT: Contract Negotiations (¶ 1) On July 23, we shall 24
begin negotiations with the Lias Food Processing Company to manufacture 39
several canned dehydrated items to be included in a special emergency ration 54
pack for the United States Army. If the negotiations are successful, we will 70
convert our Quincy Plant to food processing. (¶ 2) As a subcontractor under 84
a United States Government contract, we will be subject to the provisions 99
of the Walsh-Healey Public Contracts Act. This means we will be required 113
to compute payments for overtime work in a manner which differs from 127
that set forth in our contract with the Federation of Food Processors. 141
It is vital that these differences be resolved as soon as possible. 155
(¶ 3) Will you please arrange to meet with Dominic Minelli, Business 168
Representative of Local 247 of the Union, to negotiate the necessary 181
changes in the contract. Please tell Mr. Minelli that if we receive the 196
contract with Lias Foods, we will need at least 150 more food processors. 211
(¶ 4) Please keep me informed of the progress of your negotiations. xx 224/232

Problem 2 [LM p. 13]
Purchase requisition

Deliver to:	Frank T. Harris, Foreman	Requisition No.	437	6
Location:	Warehouse A	Date:	August 4, 19--	11
Job No.	Capital Equipment	Date Required:	November 15, 19--	18

Quantity	Description	
12	Barrel trucks, all metal w/rubber wheels	27
4	Manual hoist pulleys, 1/2-ton capacity	35
15	Drum plug wrenches, all-purpose	42
20	Drum de-headers, forged steel	49
18	Hand trucks, 750-lb. load	55

Problem 3
Table [reading position; DS items]

SALES BY MAJOR PRODUCT 5

(In Thousands of Dollars) 10

PRODUCTS	PREVIOUS YEAR	CURRENT YEAR	INCREASE	19
Dairy products	$859,440	$971,242	$111,802	28
Grocery products	838,256	892,296	54,040	36
Meat products	368,804	417,058	48,254	43
Confectionery products	255,782	292,874	37,092	53
Household products	106,854	183,629	76,775	61
Fruits and vegetables	92,146	100,398	8,252	70
Fish products	71,360	82,541	11,181	77
Bakery products	64,529	71,308	6,779	85
Stationery products	49,870	56,213	6,343	94
Gourmet products	36,024	49,875	13,851	102

54

54a ▶7 Conditioning practice

1. Each line twice SS (slowly, faster).

2. A 1′ writing on Line 4, then on Line 2; compare *gwam*.

alphabet With superb form, five or six good ski jumpers whizzed quickly by Van.

fig/sym Does Ms. Chambord's Policy 163045 for $17,500 expire on June 29, 1987?

–er old older send sender high higher large larger long longer form former

fluency When did the widow make the eighty formal gowns for the downtown firm?

| 1 | 2 | 3 | 4 | 5 | 6 | 7 | 8 | 9 | 10 | 11 | 12 | 13 | 14 |

54b ▶8 Improve technique: machine parts

each pair of lines twice SS; DS between 4-line groups

space bar
by my may try way any they duty copy many deny envy party daily really
Any boy who will apply himself fully should be ready for my big relay.

shift keys
Monday or Tuesday | March or April | Dover or Nassau | Oregon and California
A cruise to the Caribbean leaves Port Everglades on Monday, October 9.

shift lock
ZIP and OCR | BBA Degree | UARCO, Inc. | FORTRAN and COBOL | I saw her at NBC.
Did you say that UARCO, Inc., uses FORTRAN or COBOL computer language?

| 1 | 2 | 3 | 4 | 5 | 6 | 7 | 8 | 9 | 10 | 11 | 12 | 13 | 14 |

54c ▶10 Learn to assemble, insert, and correct a carbon pack

full sheets; line: 60; DS

1. Read ¶ 1 at the right; assemble a carbon pack as directed there.

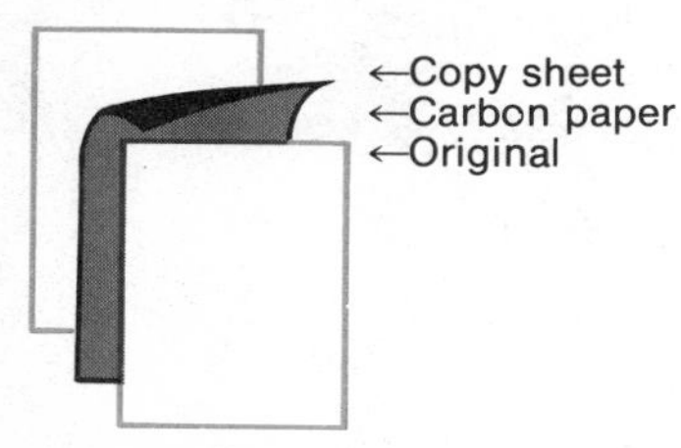

2. Read ¶s 2 and 3, then insert the pack as directed.

3. Type the material as given at the right. Begin on Line 13. Erase and correct your errors.

To correct errors

1. Pull original sheet forward and place a 5″ x 3″ card in front of carbon sheet. Erase error on original with a hard (typewriter) eraser.

2. Remove card; then with a soft (pencil) eraser, erase error on carbon (file) copy.

ASSEMBLE AND INSERT A CARBON PACK
TS

Place on the desk the sheet of paper on which the carbon (file) copy is to be made; then place a sheet of carbon paper, carbon side down, on top of the first sheet. Finally, place the sheet for the original on top of the carbon paper.

Pick up the carbon pack so that the original copy sheet is to the back and the carbon copy sheet is to the front. Tap the bottom edge of the pack lightly on the desk to align the edges. With the carbon copy sheet toward you, place the pack between the platen and the paper table; then twirl the pack into the typewriter.

Position the pack for typing, then check the top left and right corners to see whether they are properly aligned. If they are not, operate the paper-release lever to straighten them; then return the pack to typing position.

239c ▶17 Inventory basic skill: statistical copy

1. Two 5′ writings on the statistical ¶s 1–3 combined.
2. Record *gwam* and errors on better writing. Keep a record for comparison with scores achieved on 248c, page 386, and on 298c, page 456.
3. As time permits, type a 1′ guided speed writing on each ¶.

all letters/figures used | A | 1.5 si | 5.6 awl | 80% hfw

	gwam 5′	
The vision of a means of voice communication over great distances	3	51
was realized with the invention of the telephone in 1876. In 1878, the	6	54
first telephone exchange was opened, and action was taken in 1900 to	8	57
connect the various city exchanges that had been set up. The first	11	60
coast-to-coast telephone call was made in 1915, and by 1950 there were	14	63
39 million phones in the United States with 147 million miles of wire.	17	65
In 1920, the first public radio program started a new era of voice	19	68
communication. By 1922, close to 600 radio stations were on the air,	22	71
and in 1926 the first coast-to-coast service was begun with a network	25	74
of 25 stations. By 1950, just 30 years after the first broadcast, there	28	77
were 2,336 radio stations in the nation serving more than 40 million	31	79
homes and over 90% of all families in America.	32	81
The telephone and radio were combined as early as 1915 to send the	35	84
spoken word over 3,000 miles. It was not until 1927, though, that pub-	38	87
lic service was begun. By 1950, a total of 60 radiotelephone nets were	41	90
in use which linked America with over 90 other nations. Today, a series	44	93
of satellites that hover 22,000 miles over set spots on the equator pro-	47	96
vide verbal contact with most parts of the globe.	49	98

gwam 5′ | 1 | 2 | 3 |

240

240a ▶5 Conditioning practice

twice SS;
repeat difficult lines

Six sizable junks filled with men and cargo went quietly up the river.
Consult all books catalogued under 351.42, 467.80, 591.38, and 687.90.
Model D sells for $34; Model H, $75; Model Q, $129; and Model X, $268.
He may go with them when they cycle to the lake if he is not too busy.

| 1 | 2 | 3 | 4 | 5 | 6 | 7 | 8 | 9 | 10 | 11 | 12 | 13 | 14 |

54d ▶25 Type business letters

2 letterheads (LM pp. 59, 61);
line: 60; date: Line 18; in body, return carriage according to bell;
address an envelope for each letter

Problem 1

	words parts	total
December 29, 19-- | Dr. John B. Wicks | East	8	8
Central College | 1315 Oakwood Avenue |	15	15
Raleigh, NC 27611 | Dear Dr. Wicks |	22	22
¶ Here are two copies of the contract for	30	30
NEW HORIZONS IN MATH. Please sign both	38	38
copies, keep one, and return one to me.	46	46
¶ This contract, which specifies a royalty		54
rate of 5 percent, is for the preparation of the		64
first ten units of manuscript. The remaining		73
units, as you agreed, are to be developed		81
by Dr. Santos.		84
¶ I am pleased to have this opportunity to	8	92
make official your affiliation with us in an	17	101
author-publisher relationship. I am confi-	26	110
dent this relationship will prove both pleas-	34	119
ant and profitable for you and for us.	42	126
Cordially yours | Ms. Kris Kojak | Managing	50	134
Editor | xx | Enclosures 2	54	138
+ Envelope		**153**

Problem 2

	words parts	total
December 29, 19-- | Mr. Kenneth B. Holmes |	8	8
Bookstore Manager | Commonwealth	14	14
Academy | Louisville, KY 40205 | Dear Mr.	22	22
Holmes |	23	23
¶ Here is a copy of our catalog of learning	32	32
materials for the next school year. A number	41	41
of new items have been added; a few have	49	49
been deleted; and some prices have been	57	57
changed to reflect increased production and	66	66
operating costs.	69	69
¶ Of particular interest to you will be the		78
new discount rates to bookstores: 25% off		86
listed prices plus 2% for payment of invoices		96
within 10 days of receipt. As in the past, all		106
invoices are to be paid within 30 days.		113
¶ Please order early so that we can give you	9	122
Horizon's usual good service.	14	127
Sincerely yours | Miss Jaye Fredericks |	22	135
Customer Service | xx | Enclosure	28	141
+ Envelope		**157**

Problem 3 (optional)

Retype Problem 2 on a plain sheet to:
Mrs. Arnola Benson | Bookstore Manager | Southern State College | Charleston, SC 29409.
Be sure to change salutation.

55

55a ▶7 Conditioning practice

1. Each line twice SS (slowly, faster).
2. A 1′ writing on Line 4, then on Line 1; compare *gwam*.

alphabet	James quickly paid a ticket received for a wrong turn by the zoo exit.
figures	I moved my store from 3948 North 56th Street to 1270 West Degas Place.
-ly	day daily easy easily full fully hard hardly high highly simple simply
fluency	I wish to do the work so the girls may go with them to make the signs.

| 1 | 2 | 3 | 4 | 5 | 6 | 7 | 8 | 9 | 10 | 11 | 12 | 13 | 14 |

55b ▶18 Build skill in typing letters

1. Two 2′ writings (in letter form) on opening lines and ¶ 1 of Problem 2 of 54d, above. Try to increase speed in second writing.

2. Two 2′ writings (in letter form) on ¶ 3 and closing lines of Problem 2 of 54d, above. Try to increase speed in second writing.

3. A 5′ writing on the entire letter of Problem 2. Work with speed; reduce waste motion. Determine *gwam*; circle errors.

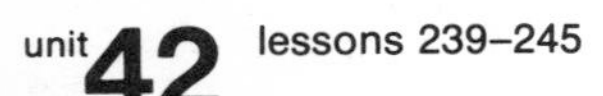

unit **42** lessons 239–245

Basic/forms and tabulation skills

Learning goals

1. To improve skill in typing business forms and tables.

2. To type statistical copy at higher speeds and with improved control.

239

239a ▶5 Conditioning practice

twice SS; repeat difficult lines

alphabet	Maybe we can equalize both groups if we have the tax adjusted quickly.
figures	The arithmetic mean of 19, 24, 38, 55, 64, 79, 83, 102, and 166 is 70.
fig/sym	The balance ($582.39) was paid by Blose & Ray on June 6 by Check 4170.
fluency	If I help them fix the engine, the girls may go with us to the island.

| 1 | 2 | 3 | 4 | 5 | 6 | 7 | 8 | 9 | 10 | 11 | 12 | 13 | 14 |

239b ▶28 Improve skill transfer: straight copy/script/rough draft

1. Three 2′ writings on each ¶. Find *gwam* on best writing.

2. Determine percent of transfer from ¶ 1 to ¶ 2 and from ¶ 1 to ¶ 3.

3. Type additional 2′ writings on ¶s 2 and 3 to increase percent of transfer as time permits.

A	1.6 si	5.8 awl	75% hfw

	gwam 2′	
Competition in a free market system helps to insure that consumers	7	40
will get the kinds of goods they want at fair prices. To attract con-	14	47
sumers away from other sellers, a new company must improve the quality	21	54
of its products, introduce new products, or operate so efficiently it	28	61
can keep its prices lower than those of its competitors.	33	67
Competition assists society as a whole, as well as each	6	37
of us, because it tends to force firms to make more efficient	12	43
use of scarce productive resources. If a company does not	18	49
work efficiently, it will fail, for customers will buy lower-	24	55
priced or higher-quality items from firms that do operate	30	61
more efficiently.	31	63
Price of items is one sort of competitoin. Competition in priace (The; goods; type)	7	47
involves taking sales away from other firms by reducing prices. More (means; rival; lowering the)	14	54
and more, how ever, compeitition takes the pattern of non-price rivalry. (form)	20	60
Customers maybe lured away from a rival Company by a firm that sells (Consumers; attracted)	28	68
goods with excellent qualiteis, by a firm which offers goods with more (items; superior; that; items; better)	35	75
features, or by an enterprise that offers more and better services. (a firm; extra)	40	80

55c ▶25 Type business letters

2 letterheads (LM pp. 63, 65);
1 cc; line: 60; date: Line 18;
address an envelope for each letter

Problem 1

words	parts	total
December 30, 19-- Conrad Hilton Reser-	7	7
vation Service 720 S. Michigan Avenue	15	15
Chicago, IL 60605 Ladies and Gentlemen	23	23
¶ Please reserve a two-room suite for the	31	31
nights of January 10 and 11 in the name of	39	39
Mrs. Alice McGowan. She requests a single	48	48
bedroom with an adjoining sitting room that	57	57
would be suitable for informal conferences of	66	66
three or four people.	70	70
¶ Mrs. McGowan wants to be away from the		78
elevator and heavy traffic patterns. If		86
possible, she would like the sitting room to		95
overlook the lake. If combination facilities		104
are not standard, she prefers tub to shower.		113
¶ Mark the reservation LATE ARRIVAL even	8	121
though Mrs. McGowan expects to arrive	15	129
by 6 p.m. The reservation is guaranteed	24	137
by Horizon Publishers, Inc. Written con-	32	145
firmation will be appreciated.	38	151
Sincerely yours Miss Mischell Frost	45	158
Secretary to Mrs. McGowan xx	50	164
+ Envelope		178

Problem 2

words	parts	total
December 30, 19-- Dr. Sadar Patel Institute	9	9
for Social Studies 850 West Irving Park	17	17
Chicago, IL 60613 Dear Dr. Patel	23	23
¶ Your article entitled "Population Growth	32	32
and the Human Condition" has just arrived. A	41	41
quick reading convinces me that you have	49	49
prepared a paper that will be of great interest	59	59
to our readers.	62	62
¶ I shall give the article a close reading within		71
a day or two after which I may want to talk		80
with you about its specific implications for		89
educators. If so, I shall arrange to meet with		99
you in Chicago.		102
¶ Meanwhile, be assured that we at NEW	7	109
HORIZONS continue to be interested in and	16	118
impressed by your very important work.	23	125
Sincerely yours Mrs. Alice McGowan, Editor	32	134
xx	32	134
+ Envelope		151

Problem 3 (optional)

On a plain sheet, rewrite the letter of Problem 1 in your own words. Compose the letter as you type. Be sure to include all essential data.

56

56a ▶7 Conditioning practice

1. Each line twice SS (slowly, faster).

2. A 1′ writing on Line 4, then on Line 1; compare *gwam*.

alphabet	Janis Partin was quite lax about the zone markings for exact delivery.
fig/sym	Her 9/4/77 wire read: "36 copies Modern Math (Item R2958)--less 10%."
–ble/–cal	able unable usable possible sensible medical musical optical political
fluency	The six girls spent their profit for an ancient memento of the island.

| 1 | 2 | 3 | 4 | 5 | 6 | 7 | 8 | 9 | 10 | 11 | 12 | 13 | 14 |

56b ▶13 Build skill in typing letters

1. A 2′ writing (in letter form) on the opening lines and ¶ 1 of Problem 2 of 55c, above. Push for *speed*.

2. A 2′ writing (in letter form) on ¶ 3 and closing lines of Problem 2 of 55c, above. Push for *speed*.

3. A 5′ writing on the entire letter in Problem 2 of 55c, above. Determine *gwam*; circle errors.

237b ▶45 Timed drills on reports

Type 5′ writings on the report at the right as directed below; correct errors as you type; compute *n–pram*.

1. As an unbound report.
2. Omit title and type as page 2 of unbound report. (Deduct 4 words for title.)
3. As topbound report.
4. Omit title and type as page 2 of topbound report. (Deduct 4 words for title.)
5. As leftbound report.
6. Omit title and type as page 2 of leftbound report. (Deduct 4 words for title.)

	words
Energy for the Future (all caps) (TS)	4
For many years, civilization has relied upon fossel fuels--	16
oil, coal, and natural gas--to provide energy for industrial	28
and home use. Unfortunately, the supply of these fuels is	40
short and other sources of energy must be developed if we are	56
to continue to progress. Among the alternate sources of energy	68
under study are nuclaer, solar, and geo-thermal. It has been	85
estimated that nuclear energy can provide the world with	97
energy for some years. The Sun, which is really a huge nu-	110
clear reactor, is considered by many to offer the greatest	122
potentail as an energy source. Like soler energy, the heat	134
from the earth can also be used to generate power.	146
Many problems remain to be solved be fore we can rely on	158
these new energy sources to meet our needs. Given time, tech-	170
nology can ensure us a continuing flow of energy to meet our	182
needs. Most experts agree, though, that it will be many years--	195
even decades--before it will be feasible to use these alternate	208
sources to provide a significant amount of the energy needed.	220

(Handwritten proofreader's corrections: "all caps" for title; TS; fossel → fossil; short → limited; other → alternate; we are → civilization is; ¶ before "Among"; nuclaer → nuclear energy; solar → solar energy; geo-thermal → geothermal energy; energy → reactors; some → thousands of; Sun → sun; really → actually; potentail → potential; an energy source → a source of energy; soler → solar; power → electricity; be fore → before; rely → depend; DS for last paragraph.)

238

238a ▶5 Conditioning practice

twice SS; repeat difficult lines

Executives may jeopardize a quick merger if they make the news public.
The stock rose today from 39 7/8 to 48 1/2 based on 6,160 shares sold.
The stereo sold for $249 less discounts of 33 1/3% and 25% or $124.50.
Corey is the author of a story about labor problems in the big cities.

| 1 | 2 | 3 | 4 | 5 | 6 | 7 | 8 | 9 | 10 | 11 | 12 | 13 | 14 |

238b ▶45 Sustained production: reports

1. Make a list of the problems below:
page 368, 233b, Problem 1
page 368, 233b, Problem 2
page 370, 234c
page 371, 235c

2. Type the reports for 30′; correct errors as you type. Proofread each page before you remove it from the typewriter and correct any errors you may have missed.

3. If you finish before time is called, start over.

4. Compute *n–pram*: Total acceptable words + ½ unacceptable words ÷ minutes typed (30′).

56c ▶30 Type business letters

2 letterheads (LM pp. 67, 69); 1 cc; line: 60; date: Line 18; type body line for line; erase and correct errors; address an envelope for each letter

Problem 1

Type the letter; proofread and correct your copy before removing it from the typewriter.

	words
January 2, 19-- Mr. Norlin Kominsky Graphic Designs, Inc. P.O.	13
Box 3750 Monterey, CA 93940 Dear Mr. Kominsky	22
¶ After a number of years of the same format, NEW HORIZONS IN	34
EDUCATION has decided to go shopping for a brand new dress!	46
¶ Some of our readers tell us that, although our articles are	58
timely, our format has become a bit dowdy. So we want to	70
"perk the old girl up a bit" and bring some excitement into	82
her life. And that's where you come in.	90
¶ I am told that you are one of the best graphic designers in	102
the area and that magazine layout and illustration are among	114
your specialties. If you would like to tackle NEW HORIZONS,	127
we'd like to talk with you.	132
¶ A copy of the latest issue is being sent to you by separate	144
mail. After you've looked her over and assessed her possi-	156
bilities, may I hear from you about her potential.	166
Sincerely yours Mrs. Alice McGowan, Editor xx	175/**190**

Problem 2

Follow the directions given for Problem 1.

Problem 3 (optional)

Compose a response to the letter of Problem 1. As Mr. Kominsky: convey your thanks to Mrs. McGowan; make some positive comment about the magazine; indicate that you have some ideas to discuss; ask for an appointment.

	words
January 2, 19-- Dr. Sadar Patel Institute for Social Studies	12
850 West Irving Park Chicago, IL 60613 Dear Dr. Patel	23
¶ I am to be in Chicago for several interviews on January 11	35
and 12. While there, I hope to have an opportunity to dis-	47
cuss with you the article you recently sent me.	56
¶ You have presented your topic with great care and depth of	68
thought. It occurs to me, however, that the reader might	80
profit from having some of your data formalized into graphs.	92
It might even be that two or three strategically placed photo-	104
graphs would enhance the urgency of your message.	115
¶ Could you meet me at the Conrad Hilton at 3 p.m. January 11	127
or at 9 a.m. January 12 to discuss these suggestions? I	138
believe an hour would be sufficient time for us to come to	150
a decision about illustrations.	156
Sincerely yours Mrs. Alice McGowan, Editor xx	165/**181**

236c ▶20
Build problem skill: leftbound report with side headings

Type the report as leftbound manuscript; correct errors as you type.

	words
secondary heading / *main heading in all caps*	
Organization for Growth of Coastal Department Stores, Inc.	11
A complete reorganization of the Coastal Department Stores	23
will be ~~finalized~~ *completed* within the next ~~6~~ *six* months. This reorganization	36
~~should~~ *will* add a ~~degree of efficiency~~ *positive new dimension* to our operations and ~~should~~ *will*	49
~~result in greater~~ *lead to increased* efficiency. In ~~broad~~ *general* terms,the reorganization	62
~~should~~ *will* result in *major* changes in ~~these~~ *the following* areas.	73
Regional Organization	82
To facilitate control and communication be tween the home	93
office and our stores, ~~3~~ *three* regional mangers will be ~~established~~ *named to*	106
~~as~~ *open* branch offices in Boston, Philadelphia, and Atlanta. These	119
managers will ~~supply~~ *provide* essentail leader ship and willbe responsi-	131
ble for *all* operations ~~of the~~ store within their respective ~~areas~~ *regions*.	144
Liaison Staff	149
This group will consist of the Regional managers, the direc-	161
tor of Marketing, the Director of Purchaseing, and the Controler.	175
It will be the ~~duty~~ *responsibility* of this group to ~~initiate cooperation~~ *provide liaison* between	189
the home office departments and the stores. They will meet ~~each~~	201
~~week~~ *monthly* to ~~consider~~ *discuss* and recommend solutions to currant and antici-	214
pated problems ~~in~~ operation.	219
Store Organization	226
An Assistant Manager will be selected at each store whose *DS the ¶*	238
primary responsibility will be *to* coordinate and direct the day-ro-	251
day activities of the sales personnel. Thus, the Store Manager	264
will be able to concentrate all efforts on merchandising, bud-	276
geting, security of physical assets, and community relations.	289
Current employees with sales experience and managerial ~~ability~~ *potential*	302
will be ~~designated~~ *appointed* as assistant managers.	310

237

237a ▶5
Conditioning practice

twice SS; repeat difficult lines

They may be required to organize the complex work of the vast project.
Please read the items checked on pages 79, 83, 102, 114, 206, and 375.
Sales in 1975 (based on final reports) rose $284,553 or 20% over 1973.
This manual shows both the cost and the quantity of the items on hand.

| 1 | 2 | 3 | 4 | 5 | 6 | 7 | 8 | 9 | 10 | 11 | 12 | 13 | 14 |

57

57a ▶7 Conditioning practice

1. Each line twice SS (slowly, faster).

2. A 1′ writing on Line 4, then on Line 2; compare *gwam*.

alphabet	Jason Wexford gained amazing typing skill by improving his techniques.
figures	ZIP Codes 45207, 95180, and 60634 must appear on mail to our branches.
–ion/–ous	nation portion section pension union cautious previous serious various
fluency	The panel may then work with the problems of the eight downtown firms.

| 1 | 2 | 3 | 4 | 5 | 6 | 7 | 8 | 9 | 10 | 11 | 12 | 13 | 14 |

57b ▶13 Improve technique: response patterns

1. Each line twice SS (slowly, faster).

2. A 1′ *speed* writing on Line 2; then Line 4; then Line 6.

3. Type additional 1′ writings on slower lines.

letter response	1	as you | you set | as you set | set up | you set up | as you set up | set up rates
	2	Get him a few oil tax cards only after you set up a minimum base rate.
word response	3	of the | the world | of the world | to the | the problem | to handle the problem
	4	It is their wish to name a panel to shape the theme for a town social.
combination response	5	is up | up to | is up to | he was | was to | he was to | if you | you did | if you did
	6	He is quite great when he bases firm opinion on the facts of the case.

| 1 | 2 | 3 | 4 | 5 | 6 | 7 | 8 | 9 | 10 | 11 | 12 | 13 | 14 |

57c ▶15 Check straight-copy skill

two 5′ writings; determine *gwam*; circle errors

Goal: *At least* 25 *gwam* with no more than 10 errors.

all letters used | A | 1.5 si | 5.6 awl | 80% hfw |

Text	gwam 2′	5′
Our society has acquired a desire for instant, effortless living.	7	3
With instant meals and automatic machines, we have moved away from an	14	6
active society to one in which much of our personal and job time is	21	8
spent in a sitting position. We read dials and push buttons while	28	11
things do the work for us. Even our free time is spent in sedentary	35	14
activities such as reading, seeing movies, and just watching TV. Such	42	17
activity makes the body weak and the mind sluggish.	47	19
There is no objection to the fast and easy way of doing essential,	7	21
routine things, of course; but doctors tell us that the increasing time	14	24
spent in sedentary activity is impairing our physical and mental health.	22	27
They tell us to use more of our leisure time for active things. For ex-	29	30
ample, walk more, ride less; take a zestful swim instead of a sunbath;	36	33
take part in athletic activities instead of merely sit and view them.	43	36
They ask us to get a better balance between sitting and acting.	50	39

gwam 2′ | 1 | 2 | 3 | 4 | 5 | 6 | 7 |
5′ | 1 | 2 | 3 |

235c ▶20 Build problem skill: topbound report with table

1. Type the report as a topbound manuscript; correct your errors as you type. DS the columnar items.

2. Use the mathematical method to center the table. (See report in 234c, page 370.)

words

CONSUMERS UNDER THE MICROSCOPE 6

(¶ 1) The American people are under continuous scrutiny as businessmen 19
study the factors which influence the consumption of goods and services. 34
Although income is the most important factor which determines what and 48
how much a consumer will buy, there are many other factors which influence 63
buying. Among the major factors are age, sex, education, and marital status. 79
(¶ 2) Because what people buy is determined to a great extent by their age, 93
the age composition of the population is a matter of great interest to industry. 109
Businessmen keep a close watch on the national birthrate, longevity, and the 125
age distribution of the population. The table below, for example, is typical 140
of the data businessmen use to make decisions regarding future operations. 156
TS

POPULATION OF THE UNITED STATES BY AGE GROUP, 1960-2000 167

(Actual and Estimated by Percents) 174

YEAR	UNDER 20	20-64	65 AND OVER	
				180
1960	38.5	52.3	9.2	184
1970	37.7	52.5	9.9	188
1980	33.1	56.1	10.8	192
1990	31.4	57.0	11.6	196
2000	29.9	58.8	11.3	200

____________ 204

Source: Statistical Abstract of the United States, 1974. 224

236

236a ▶5 Conditioning practice

twice SS; repeat difficult lines

Her quick behavior thwarted six crafty men from seizing the jet plane.
My telephone number was changed on August 6 from 349-1758 to 265-4709.
Reduce Item 378 by 20%; Item 649, 15%; Item 736, 8%; and Item 983, 5%.
He may work with me and the other men to plan the theme for the party.

| 1 | 2 | 3 | 4 | 5 | 6 | 7 | 8 | 9 | 10 | 11 | 12 | 13 | 14 |

236b ▶25 Improve production skills: reports

1. Review leftbound manuscript format. (See RG, page vii.)

2. Type the report in Problem 2, 233b, page 368, as directed, but use leftbound format.

57d ▶15 Check letter typing skill

1 letterhead (LM p. 71); line: 60; date: Line 18; type body line for line; correct errors as you type

Problem 1
Type the letter; proofread it and correct any remaining errors before removing paper from machine.

Goal: At least one copy (neatly arranged, typed, and corrected) within 15′.

	words
January 5, 19-- Mrs. Mary Lively, Librarian Washington High	12
School 1500 North Fort Myer Drive Arlington, VA 22209	24
Dear Mrs. Lively	27
¶ Thank you for your letter with an order for our new series,	39
MYSTERIES OF THE EARTH. I am certain you will be pleased	51
with these exciting books. As you requested, the bill will	63
be sent to your Board of Education.	71
¶ Your name does not appear on our mailing list to receive our	83
monthly publication entitled NEW HORIZONS IN EDUCATION, an	95
informative discussion of trends and problems. I am sending	107
you a copy of this month's issue, as I think it will be of	119
interest to you.	123
¶ If you like NEW HORIZONS as much as I hope you will, I want	135
to add your name to the mailing list to receive the publica-	147
tion free of charge. Just sign and return the enclosed card	159
to receive your copy each month.	166
Sincerely yours Brian L. Cole, Manager Marketing Division xx	179
Enclosure	181/201

Enrichment material for Unit 9 appears on LM pp. 73–76.

Problem 2 (optional)
On plain paper, retype the letter to the address shown at the right.

Mr. Daniel J. Ahrens Geography Department Xavier High School 17205 Douglas Road South Bend, IN 46635

Suggestions for optional compose-as-you-type activities

When directed by your teacher, choose a "Thought Starter" from those listed below. Develop the idea into a 2- or 3-paragraph theme, explaining why.

1. If I had it to do over, I would . . . .
2. If I could have just one wish, I would . . . .
3. If I were President, I would . . . .
4. If I had my choice of career, I would . . . .
5. If I could attend the college or school of my choice, I would . . . .
6. If I had a lot of money, I would . . . .
7. If I were my mother, I would . . . .
8. If I were my father, I would . . . .
9. If I could be the person I want to be, I would . . . .
10. If I could participate in the extracurricular activity of my choice, I would . . . .

When your teacher directs, choose a letter-writing situation from those listed below and prepare a rough draft of a suitable letter.

1. Compose a letter to a friend or relative who lives some distance away to be your houseguest for a weekend. State your plans for the weekend positively so that your friend or relative will be highly motivated to visit you.

2. Compose a letter to a business acquaintance who might help you get a job for the summer. Indicate the kind of work you want to do and what your qualifications are for the job.

3. Compose a letter to your teacher, summarizing what you have learned in typewriting thus far and in what ways you think it will help you in the future.

4. Compose a letter to the U.S. Department of Labor, requesting information in pamphlet or booklet form about job prospects, qualifications, and salary for a career in which you are interested.

234c ▶20 Build problem skill: unbound report

1. Type the report as an unbound manuscript; correct errors as you type.

2. SS and indent the numbered steps 5 spaces from both margins.

	words
CENTERING COLUMNAR MATERIAL MATHEMATICALLY	9
Many typists prefer to use a mathematical method of centering material hori-	23
zontally in columns instead of the backspace-from-center method. To center colum-	40
nar material using the mathematical method, follow these steps:	53
1. Count the strokes in the longest item in each column. (Remember, the	67
heading may be the longest item.) Add these numbers.	78
2. Determine by judgment the number of spaces to be left between columns.	93
Add the total spaces between columns to the total obtained in Step 1.	108
Subtract this sum from the total spaces available (85 pica spaces or 102	122
elite spaces on standard-size paper). Divide the remainder by 2 to find	137
the number of spaces in the left margin (ignore any fraction). OR	150
subtract the total spaces used (Step 1) from the horizontal spaces	164
available and divide the remainder by the <u>number of columns plus one</u>.	183
This figure gives you the position of the left margin stop and also the	197
number of spaces to be left between columns. Leave any extra spaces in	212
the margins.	215
3. To determine the tab stops, add the number of spaces in the left margin to	230
the sum of the spaces required for the first column and the number of	244
spaces between the first and second columns. This figure will be the first	259
tab stop. To this number, add the sum of spaces required for the second	274
column and the spaces between the second and third columns. This figure	289
will be the second tab stop. Continue in this manner for each additional	303
column to be typed.	308
4. If the column heading is the longest item, remember to set the tab stop so	323
that the longest item in the column is centered under the heading.	337
5. Main and secondary headings should be centered by the backspace-	351
from-center method even when the mathematical method is used to cen-	364
ter the columns of material horizontally.	372

235

235a ▶5 Conditioning practice

twice SS;
repeat difficult lines

Working quickly, Juan Sanchez solved the problem by a complex formula.

Items 19, 35, 42, 60, 72, 87, 95, and 104 were tested on September 18.

The price index (base, 1968-1969) rose 42% in 1975--from 130 to 184.6

Did she say the special party for the visitors will be held this week?

| 1 | 2 | 3 | 4 | 5 | 6 | 7 | 8 | 9 | 10 | 11 | 12 | 13 | 14 |

235b ▶25 Improve production skills: reports

1. Review topbound manuscript format. (See RG, page viii.)

2. Type the report in 234b, page 369, as directed, but type it as a topbound manuscript.

unit **10** lessons 58–65

Simple tables

Learning goals

The primary purpose of this unit is to help you learn to center, arrange, and type 2–, 3–, and 4–column tables.

In addition, you will learn to type special symbols, to align figures in columns, and to type a letter including a table.

58

58a ▶7 Conditioning practice

1. Each line twice SS (slowly, faster).
2. A 1′ writing on Line 4, then on Line 1; compare *gwam*.

alphabet	Viva Prinz quickly amazed all of us by her exact knowledge of jujitsu.
figures	I said, "The quiz covering pages 35-149 and 168-270 will be on May 6."
–s/–es	try tries copy copies vary varies area areas study studies wish wishes
fluency	The amendment did signal an end to the rigid social theory of the day.

| 1 | 2 | 3 | 4 | 5 | 6 | 7 | 8 | 9 | 10 | 11 | 12 | 13 | 14 |

58b ▶13 Skill-comparison typing

1. A 1′ writing on each ¶; compare *gwam*.
2. A 1′ *speed* writing on slower ¶.
3. A 2′ writing on each ¶; compare *gwam*.
4. A 2′ *speed* writing on slower ¶.

all letters used

¶ 1: HA | 1.6 si | 5.8 awl | 75% hfw

¶ 2: E | 1.2 si | 4.8 awl | 90% hfw

	gwam 1′	2′
We are becoming increasingly a nation of leisure time. In the past	13	7
quarter century our workweek has become shorter, our workday has become	28	14
shorter, and our paid vacation time has been extended. Of the aggregate	42	21
time available in a week, the typical worker today spends virtually a	56	28
fourth of it riding to and from work and on the job itself. If the typ-	71	35
ical worker averages eight hours of sleep per night, over thirty percent	85	43
of the total time is being utilized for personal and leisure activities.	100	50
Those who study the effect of social and work pressure on people	13	6
say that a desire to make more money and to have more things has put many	28	14
of us under heavy strain. They tell us that we run so hard to catch the	42	21
brass ring or the falling star that the soul has no chance to keep up	56	28
with the body. Although they do not put down hard work, they ask the	70	35
young as well as the old to make time in their daily leisure for a phys-	85	42
ical hour, a social hour, and an hour alone to help the soul catch up.	99	49

gwam 1′ | 1 | 2 | 3 | 4 | 5 | 6 | 7 | 8 | 9 | 10 | 11 | 12 | 13 | 14 |
2′ | 1 | 2 | 3 | 4 | 5 | 6 | 7 |

58c ▶10 Improve technique: tabulating

1. Set margin stops for a 50–space line.
2. Clear all tab stops; set 5 tab stops according to the KEY, starting at left margin.
3. Type drill at least twice.

keep	your	eyes	on	the	copy
2849	5037	3126	56	399	1475
$475	4.5%	it's	8%	$30	4:30

key | 4 | 6 | 4 | 6 | 4 | 6 | 2 | 6 | 3 | 6 | 4 |

234

234a ▶5 Conditioning practice

twice SS; repeat difficult lines

Jerome Waxler apologized quickly for his rude behavior at the meeting.
On June 16, I ordered Item 40972; on August 23, I received Item 58074.
Ad illud means "to that"; ad hoc, "to this"; and adimere, "to remove."
If they spend so much money, they may not make a profit in the future.

| 1 | 2 | 3 | 4 | 5 | 6 | 7 | 8 | 9 | 10 | 11 | 12 | 13 | 14 |

234b ▶25 Improve production skills: reports

1. Review unbound manuscript format. (RG, page vii)
2. Type the ¶s as an unbound manuscript; do not correct your errors.
3. In pencil, correct all typographical errors and errors in style.
4. From your corrected copy, retype the report; correct errors as you type.

words

JOB OUTLOOK FOR CLERICAL WORKERS 7

The number of people employed in ~~who hold~~ clerical jobs 16
has increased rapidly over the years. In 1950, for 26
example ~~instance~~, approximately 7.6 million people held ~~had~~ clerical 38
positions ~~jobs~~. By ~~the year~~ 1975, this number had risen to more 48
than 15 million--an increase ~~a rise~~ of almost ~~approximately~~ 100%. 57
Of that number, more than 25% or 4 million 66
employees ~~workers~~ held jobs ~~positions~~ as typists, stenographers, 75
or secretaries. ¶ The outlook for clerical jobs 84
in the future is bright ~~promising~~. It is anticipated ~~believed~~ 93
that the expansion ~~increase~~ of large and complex organi- 102
zations will result in increased ~~much more~~ paper- 110
work. As a result, the number of jobs ~~clerical~~ 118
available ~~openings~~ is expected to increase rapidly through 128
the mid-1980s. Among the many types of clerical 138
jobs, "Opportunities will be best for secretaries, 148
typists, and other skilled workers whose 156
jobs are not likely to be handled ~~taken over~~ by 163
machines."[1] 166

170

[1]U.S. Department of Labor, Occupational 181
Outlook Handbook (1974-75 ed.; Washington: 193
U.S. Govt. (sp.) Printing Office, 1974), p. 86. 202

58d ▶20

Learn to center a table horizontally and vertically

Steps in horizontal centering of columns

1. Preparatory steps
a. Move margin stops to ends of scale.
b. Clear all tabulator stops.
c. Move carriage (carrier) to center of paper.
d. Decide spacing between columns (if spacing is not specified)—preferably an even number of spaces (4, 6, 8, 10, 12, etc.).

2. Set left margin stop
From center of paper, backspace once for each 2 characters and spaces in longest line of each column, then for each 2 spaces to be left between columns. Set the left margin stop at this point.

If the longest line in one column has an extra letter or number, combine that letter or number with the first letter or number in the next column when backspacing by 2's; as in paper (4) pen.

◀1 1 1 1 1 1
pa pe rp en ## ##

If in backspacing for columnar items 1 stroke is left over, disregard it.

3. Set tabulator stops
From the left margin, space forward once for each letter, figure, symbol, and space in longest line in the first column and for each space to be left between first and second columns. *Set tab stop at this point for second column.* Follow similar procedure for additional columns to be typed.

Center the table vertically and horizontally on a half sheet. If time permits, retype the problem. (See page 54 for a review of vertical centering.)

Center

MEMBERS OF THE BOARD OF DIRECTORS
TS

Daryl Jacobs, Jr.	Chairperson
Pierre F. LaSalle	President
Anthony C. Oliverio	Executive Vice President
Ellen V. Seagoe	General Counsel
M. Joseph Gonzales	Secretary-Treasurer

19 | 12 | 24

233

233a ▶5 Conditioning practice

Type 232a, page 366, as directed there.

233b ▶45 Inventory production skill: report manuscripts

Type the 3 reports for 30′; correct errors as you type. If you complete the reports before time is called, start over. Use page line gauge on LM p. 223. Compute *n-pram*. Record score for comparison with score achieved on 249b, page 388, and on 299b, page 458.

Note: If a page with a footnote is only partially filled, leave extra space between the last text line typed and the footnote divider line so that the bottom margin will be approximately 1″ (6 lines) deep.

Problem 1
Leftbound report with footnote

words

THE IMPORTANCE OF BUSINESS REPORTS (¶ 1) The business report is an essential tool in planning, organizing, directing, and controlling business operations. The success of a business depends almost entirely upon the decisions made by its executives. Decisions, in turn, are based on facts which are usually contained in various kinds of reports. If the reports are inaccurate or obsolete, the decisions may well lead to the failure of a business. (¶ 2) Although many reports are presented orally or informally in writing, most major reports are prepared in manuscript form. It is essential that these reports present an immaculate physical appearance, with no strikeovers or poor erasures. If an executive receives an untidy, poorly typed report, the impression formed of the report and the material contained in it will, in all probability, be negative. (¶ 3) The typist can do a great deal to insure the favorable reception of a report by arranging and typing it so that it is neat and attractive. Special attention should be given to the format of a report, especially the margins and spacing. The impact of appearance is emphasized by Wolf and Aurner when they write, "The appearance of your message is the <u>first</u> stimulus that your reader perceives. And first impressions endure."[1]

7 17 26 35 44 54 63 72 81 90 99 107 117 126 135 143 153 163 172 181 190 200 209 218 227 236 246 254 256

———— 260

[1] Morris Philip Wolf and Robert R. Aurner, <u>Effective Communication in Business</u> (6th ed.; Cincinnati: South-Western Publishing Co., 1974), p. 121.

268 283 293 300

Problem 2
Topbound report with side headings

words

FORMS OF AMERICAN BUSINESS (¶ 1) <u>The Sole Proprietorship</u> A sole proprietorship is a business owned by just one person and operated for personal profit. The owner, aided by only a few workers, conducts a small business that, as a rule, caters to the general public. The capital needed for running the firm is normally supplied by the proprietor from personal wealth but is often augmented by borrowed funds. The responsibility for all decisions rests with the owner, who usually makes them personally rather than delegate them to employees. (¶ 2) <u>The Partnership</u> A partnership is an association of two or more persons who carry on a business for profit. Such a relationship is based on an agreement, written or oral, that is voluntary but legally binding. Even though a typical partnership is bigger than most one-owner firms, most are quite small. A majority of partnerships in the nation consist of two owners who share the responsibility and any profits earned. Upon the death of one of the partners, the partnership is automatically dissolved. (¶ 3) <u>The Corporation</u> The corporation is the dominant form of business ownership in the United States. A corporation is a legal entity, that is, an artificial being endowed with many of the rights, duties, and powers of a person. It does not change its identity, structure, or function with each change in owners, who are known as stockholders. The number of a corporation's owners is seldom less than three, frequently as high as several hundred, and often in excess of many thousands of people.

9 21 30 40 49 59 67 75 84 93 102 110 121 130 139 148 158 167 176 186 195 204 214 225 233 243 253 263 272 281 291 293 308 317 318

Problem 3
Unbound report

Type ¶s of 232c, page 367, as an unbound report. Heading: INNOVATIONS IN TELEPHONIC COMMUNICATION (8 words)

59

59a ▶7 Conditioning practice

1. Each line twice SS (slowly, faster).
2. A 1′ writing on Line 4, then on Line 1; compare *gwam*.

alphabet	Jack Fogarty asked to be given a week to reply to their tax quiz form.
tab	21 6 $46 6 37% 6 $950 6 100% 6 2639 6 4058 6 9462
–ed	ask asked call called hurry hurried ship shipped sign signed ski skied
fluency	The policy of the big auto firm may entitle all of them to make a bid.

| 1 | 2 | 3 | 4 | 5 | 6 | 7 | 8 | 9 | 10 | 11 | 12 | 13 | 14 |

59b ▶13 Improve technique: keystroking

1. Each pair of lines twice SS; DS between 4-line groups.
2. A 1′ writing on Line 2; then Line 4; then Line 6.
3. An additional 1′ writing on each of the slower lines.

combination response
1 for | for him | him to | for him to | to you | you and | to you and | to you and him
2 It is up to you and him to start the polio treatment at my big clinic.

adjacent keys
3 to join | her radio | we hope | upon us | may quit | to equip | post it | per policy
4 We built a radio forum on the premise that expert opinion was popular.

consecutive reaches
5 since then | record it | my bonus | must bring | may serve | any survey | a recent
6 The recent survey is summarized in a brochure she found in my library.

| 1 | 2 | 3 | 4 | 5 | 6 | 7 | 8 | 9 | 10 | 11 | 12 | 13 | 14 |

59c ▶10 Improve skill transfer: script and rough draft

1. A 2′ writing on ¶ 1; determine *gwam*.
2. A 2′ writing on ¶ 2; compare *gwam* with *gwam* in Step 1.
3. Two 2′ *speed* writings on slower ¶.

all letters used | A | 1.5 si | 5.6 awl | 80% hfw |

gwam 2′

A person who has pencils but no erasers cannot afford to make 6
a mistake. Consequently, such a person will rarely attempt any- 13
thing of much importance. No one should be ashamed of making an 19
error occasionally, but everyone should try to avoid making the 26
same one again and again. A person who makes mistakes, corrects 32
them, and learns from them is never afraid to try anything new: a 39
different method of work, a new job, or even a new city or country. 45

As you ~~try~~ attempt to increase your typing power on ~~the~~ skill-building 6
drills, whether ~~it~~ they be on ~~straight~~ regular copy or problems, you ~~should~~ will make 13
quite a ~~few~~ number of errors. Just as in ~~many~~ other skills, however, ~~a few~~ many 20
of the errors will ~~drop~~ fall away ~~sa~~ as you perfect your ~~motions~~ techniques. ~~As soon as~~ After 27
you have ~~built~~ pushed your ~~spede~~ speed to the ~~point~~ level of ~~unacceptable~~ excessive errors, you 33
will often be asked to ~~lower~~ reduce your speed and correct any ~~of the~~ errors you 40
make. Realize that really good typists often use the typing eraser. 47

232c ▶20 Inventory basic skill: rough draft

1. Two 5′ writings on ¶s 1–3 combined. Determine *gwam* and errors.

2. Record *gwam* and errors on the better writing for comparison with scores achieved on 248d, page 387; and on 296c, page 453.

3. As time permits, type a 2′ speed writing on each ¶ to increase skill.

all letters used | A | 1.5 si | 5.6 awl | 80% hfw

	gwam 2′	5′
A telephone network provides us with a greatdeal more than oral	7	3
contact between two parties. The radio and televisoin companies rely	13	5
greatly on telephone service. The use of telephone wires makes it	20	8
possible to transmit radio or television shows from the original point	27	11
to far and distant spots. If we didnot have these wires, many people	34	14
wouldnot be able to see important athletic games such as the super	41	16
bowl or historical events such as a special session of the Congress.	48	19
A unique portable telephone which has been called a Phone Data serves	7	22
many use ful aims. The telephone can be used by a physician to send	14	25
data from the bed side of a person to laboratoreis or specialists for	21	27
instant analysis. This equipment saves not only time but lives as well.	28	30
This telephone canbe used to transmit or get data from established	35	33
data sources of all kinds. When teid in with a computer, this telephone	42	36
can be utilized to process data and answer many complex questions.	48	38
There is a great variety of telephone services in most offices.	7	41
Reports, data, and papers of many typed can be transmitted from point to	14	44
point by using the Picture Phone. Telephone answering systems, which	21	47
record conversations on tape, canbe used to answer phones when no one is	28	50
present. Devices of this kind can be used also by out-of-town sales-	35	53
men to report or record sales. Similer phones may be used by executives	43	55
to dic tate letters directly to a centralized typeing pool.	48	58

59d ▶20 Type 2-column tables

2 half sheets

Problem 1

half sheet, long side up

Center and type the table in exact vertical and horizontal center. DS items in columns. Leave 10 spaces between the two columns.

REGIONAL OFFICE TELEPHONE NUMBERS		words
	TS	7
EASTERN, New York	(212) 475-4320	13
SOUTHERN, Atlanta	(404) 577-1234	20
NORTH-CENTRAL, Chicago	(312) 922-4400	28
MOUNTAIN-PLAINS, Denver	(303) 573-1450	35
WESTERN, San Francisco	(415) 392-8600	43
NORTHERN, Toronto	(416) 924-3361	49

Problem 2

half sheet, long side up

Center and type the table in exact vertical and horizontal center. SS items in columns. Leave 12 spaces between columns.

UNITED FUND COMMITTEE, BY DEPARTMENT		words
	TS	7
Advertising	Alan J. Ash, Chairperson	15
Assembly	Mary Jo Pulaski	20
Data Processing	George M. Trebbi	26
Marketing	Michael Stein	31
Order	Janet Fields	35
Production	Kevin Looby	40
Purchasing	J. Edward Underhill	46
Shipping	Reggie Cochran	50

60

60a ▶7 Conditioning practice

1. Each line twice SS (slowly, faster).

2. A 1′ writing on Line 4, then on Line 2; compare *gwam*.

alphabet Buckner Wilcox puzzled us by endeavoring to qualify for the high jump.

figures The data are given in Figures 26 and 27 of Part 14, Unit 39, page 508.

–ing mail mailing sell selling save saving take taking try trying use using

fluency The auditor found key problems in the rigid audit of eight city firms.

| 1 | 2 | 3 | 4 | 5 | 6 | 7 | 8 | 9 | 10 | 11 | 12 | 13 | 14 |

60b ▶10 Learn to align figures

type twice DS; center according to the KEY on 50-space line

To align figures at right: Set a tab stop for the digit in each column (after Column 1) that requires the least forward and backward spacing. Do not consider fractions as part of the column. To align the figures, space forward > or backward < as necessary.

margin v		tab v		tab v		tab v
604		1483		350		9102
492		>730		314		>627
>65		> 45 2/3		> 90 5/8		>38
109		2037		<2503		1029
key | 3 |	12	| 4 |	12	| 4 |	12	| 4 |

unit **41** lessons 232–238

Basic/report skills

Learning goals

1. To type straight copy and rough-draft copy at higher speeds and with improved control.

2. To improve skill in typing report manuscripts in various styles.

232

232a ▶5 Conditioning practice

twice SS; repeat difficult lines

alphabet	Judge Zane fined me for blocking an exit from the park to Vieques Way.
figures	Paragraphs 190.3, 724.5, and 826.1 of the bylaws apply in these cases.
fig/sym	The tax was 3% in 1946, 5.2% in 1957, 8.6% in 1968, and 10.2% in 1975.
fluency	Judith does hold title to the stock and is entitled to sign the proxy.

| 1 | 2 | 3 | 4 | 5 | 6 | 7 | 8 | 9 | 10 | 11 | 12 | 13 | 14 |

232b ▶25 Improve technique

1. Type the sentences DS at your highest rate.

2. Remove paper from the typewriter and correct your errors in pencil. From your corrected copy, type a 1′ writing on each line.

3. As time permits, type additional 1′ writings on difficult lines.

Group 1—Stroking: Strike each key quickly and sharply; make short, direct reaches.

direct reaches	I doubt she will agree to place any of my funds in the mortgage trust.
double letters	The committee announced the book will be issued to all employees soon.
adjacent keys	The dealer reports that the new trucks received are in poor condition.
home row	Gloria made the fresh salad for all of us; Jack said he made the cake.
third row	We were required to pay for our tour four weeks before the trip began.
bottom row	A maximum of seven cubic inches of zinc can be moved in this size box.

| 1 | 2 | 3 | 4 | 5 | 6 | 7 | 8 | 9 | 10 | 11 | 12 | 13 | 14 |

Group 2—Response patterns: Vary stroking patterns to match difficulty of words.

word	He said it is my job to make plans for the party to be held next week.
stroke	Increasing interest rates adversely affected manufacturing operations.
combination	Construction of a new interchange will facilitate the flow of traffic.
balanced-hand	Now that it is time to pay for the stock, both men may go to the city.
stroke	Capitalization increased $10,482,690--from $67,390,655 to $77,873,345.
balanced-hand	They may name the mayor as the chairman of the special judicial panel.

| 1 | 2 | 3 | 4 | 5 | 6 | 7 | 8 | 9 | 10 | 11 | 12 | 13 | 14 |

60c ▶33 Type 2-column tables

3 half sheets; decide spacing between columns

Problem 1

half sheet, long side up

Center and type the table in exact vertical and horizontal center. SS items in columns.

SOME COMMON BUSINESS ABBREVIATIONS		words
	TS	7
account	acct.	10
balance	bal.	12
bill of lading	b/l	16
catalog	cat.	19
collect on delivery	C.O.D. (c.o.d.)	26
department	dept.	29
free on board	f.o.b.	34
merchandise	mdse.	37
miscellaneous	misc.	41

Problem 2

half sheet, short side up

Center and type the table in reading position (page 54). DS between main and secondary headings; TS between secondary heading and body of table. DS items in columns. *Erase and correct errors.*

Line spaces available: 51
Pica center: 27
Elite center: 33

Main heading: EXPRESSIONS WRITTEN AS TWO WORDS — 7
DS
Secondary heading: According to Most Dictionaries — 13
TS

all right	no one	16
bona fide	parcel post	21
en route	post office	25
high school	postal card	30
inasmuch as	time clock	34
insofar as	vice versa	38

Problem 3 (optional)

half sheet, short side up

Center and type the table in reading position, as directed for Problem 2. Align figures in Column 2 at the decimal (.).

COMMON U.S.-METRIC EQUIVALENTS — 6

Approximate Values — 10

1 inch	25.4 millimeters (mm)	16
1 inch	2.54 centimeters (cm)	22
1 foot	0.305 meters (m)	27
1 yard	0.91 meters (m)	31
1 mile	1.61 kilometers (km)	37
	DS	
1 pint	0.47 liters (l)	41
1 quart	0.95 liters (l)	46
1 gallon	3.91 liters (l)	51
	DS	
1 ounce	28.35 grams (g)	56
1 pound	0.45 kilograms (kg)	62

230c ▶15 Skill-comparison typing

1. Four 1′ writings on ¶ 1; find *gwam* on each. Note highest speed typed.

2. Four 1′ writings on ¶ 2; find *gwam* on each. Note highest speed typed.

Goal: To equal or exceed on ¶ 2 the highest speed typed on ¶ 1.

3. Type additional writings on ¶ 2 as time permits.

¶ 1

E	1.3 si	5.2 awl	90% hfw

¶ 2

D	1.7 si	6.0 awl	70% hfw

gwam 1′

When a product is first put on the market, the initial price may 13
be quite high. If a great many people rush to buy the limited amount 27
produced, you can be sure the price will rise. If the supply of the 41
item increases or the demand decreases, however, the price will drop. 55
In simple language, this is the law of supply and demand at work in a 69
free market. 71

Numerous factors may intervene, however, to modify the effects of 13
the law of supply and demand. Government regulation, not supply and 27
demand, sets the price for some monopolies such as the public utilities. 42
Taxes on producers tend to cause the price of goods to rise whereas a 56
tax on consumers reduces purchasing power which, in turn, reduces the 70
demand for products. 74

gwam 1′ | 1 | 2 | 3 | 4 | 5 | 6 | 7 | 8 | 9 | 10 | 11 | 12 | 13 | 14 |

231

231a ▶5 Conditioning practice

twice SS;
repeat difficult lines

Peg Fisk examined the vivid jacquard weave in the fabric of my blazer.
The index rose 47.8 points on July 29 and 56.1 points on September 30.
Although Room 734 is 20′9″ by 18′6″, Room 1734 is only 15′8″ by 12′6″.
The janitor kept the keys for the auto in the enamel box on the shelf.

| 1 | 2 | 3 | 4 | 5 | 6 | 7 | 8 | 9 | 10 | 11 | 12 | 13 | 14 |

231b ▶45 Sustained production: business letters

1. Make a list of the problems below:
page 360, 227b, Problem 2
page 361, 228b, Problem 2
page 363, 229b, Problem 1
page 363, 229b, Problem 2
page 364, 230b, Problem 2

2. Type the letters for 30′, each letter on plain paper; correct errors as you type. Proofread each letter before you remove it from the typewriter and correct any errors you may have missed. If you finish before time is called, start over.

3. Compute *n–pram*: Total acceptable words + ½ unacceptable words ÷ minutes typed (30′).

61

61a ▶7 Conditioning practice

1. Each line twice SS (slowly, faster).

2. A 1′ writing on Line 4, then on Line 1; compare *gwam*.

alphabet	A quick verdict by that jury amazed everyone except Lewis and Godfrey.
tab	75% 6 $40 6 3's 6 1/2 6 (59) 6 8-26 6 4:30 6 1.50
–er	job jobber late later fine finer dine diner hard harder office officer
fluency	If their cycle turns into the lane, both may be thrown into the rocks.

| 1 | 2 | 3 | 4 | 5 | 6 | 7 | 8 | 9 | 10 | 11 | 12 | 13 | 14 |

61b ▶13 Type a letter including a table

1 letterhead (LM p. 77); line: 60; date: Line 18; center the table horizontally; DS above and below it; SS the table items

Type a copy of the handwritten letter for the **Sales Manager, Lloyd M. Powell.** Use your initials for reference; be sure to note the enclosure. Proofread your copy and correct any errors.

January 8, 19--

Dr. C. J. Stoner, Superintendent
Essex Polytechnic Institute
100 W. Cold Spring Lane
Baltimore, MD 21210

Dear Dr. Stoner

Congratulations on the passage of the bond issue that will permit you to build, equip, and staff a new senior high school. ¶ The following booklets, which you requested, should be of real help in your planning:

6 spaces

Guide to School Plant Planning	Gibbons
Classroom Design and Layout	Marlow
Equipping the Modern School	McHugh

After you have studied the booklets, may we have one of our representatives arrange an appointment to discuss ways in which we may be able to assist you in this new program? Simply fill in and return the enclosed card, and we'll do the rest.

Sincerely yours

230

230a ▶5 Conditioning practice

twice SS;
repeat difficult lines

The unique policy covers six big hazards most workers face on the job.
Local 265 will meet on May 14 to discuss Articles 73, 89, 91, and 103.
Send 75 copies of Destiny, 30 copies of Tyranny, and 20 copies of Spy.
The six fishermen bought fuel for their boats at the dock on the lake.

| 1 | 2 | 3 | 4 | 5 | 6 | 7 | 8 | 9 | 10 | 11 | 12 | 13 | 14 |

230b ▶30 Improve production skills: letters

1. Type the letter in Problem 1 in proper style. Do not correct errors. When you finish, record the number of minutes (to nearest ¼ minute) you typed. Find your appropriate *g–pram* from the table below.

Goal: To complete the letter in 5′ or less.

2. In pencil, correct all typographical errors and errors in style.

3. Retype the letter from your corrected copy; correct errors as you type. When you finish, record the number of minutes (to nearest ¼ minute) you typed. Find your approximate *n–pram* from the table below.

Goal: To complete the letter in 5′ or less.

4. Type the letter in Problem 2 in the same way.

minutes	rate
5	24
4¾	25
4½	27
4¼	28
4	30
3¾	32
3½	34
3¼	37
3	40
2¾	44
2½	48
2¼	53
2	60

Problem 1 [plain paper]
Block, open

	words
June 6, 19-- Yoko Electric Company 600 Broad Street Newark, NJ	13
07102 Ladies and Gentlemen (¶ 1) During the past month, eight of	24
our customers have returned your Model 110 Electric Drill. They	37
complained that the trigger locked in place and they were forced to	51
disconnect the drill in order to turn it off. We checked these drills	65
and found that the customers are correct. (¶ 2) We have removed	77
these drills from our stores, although we have 192 of them in stock.	91
Please let us know as soon as possible what action you wish us to	104
take in this matter. Sincerely yours STAR DEPARTMENT STORES J.	117
L. Rose, Chief Buyer xx (92)	121/**132**

Problem 2 [plain paper]
Modified block, mixed

	words
May 15, 19-- Magree Department Store 650 North State Street	12
Jackson, MS 39201 Ladies and Gentlemen (¶ 1) Thank you very	23
much for the detailed information in your letter of May 10 which	36
helped us trace your order. (¶ 2) We found that your order was	48
ready for shipment except for the men's sweaters, which are no	60
longer available in beige. To avoid further delay, we have	72
substituted light tan sweaters to replace the beige ones. If these	86
sweaters do not meet your needs, please return them at our	98
expense. (¶ 3) Your order was shipped today by RIO Express, and	110
you should receive it within the next week. Sincerely yours Norma	123
C. Brown Sales Manager xx (94)	128/**141**

61c ▶30 Type 3-column tables

3 half sheets

Problem 1

half sheet, long side up

Center and type the table in exact vertical and horizontal center. SS items in columns. Leave 10 spaces between columns.

words

MAJOR U.S. CITIES 4

DS

ZIP Code Prefixes and Area Codes 10

TS

			words
New York	100	212	14
Chicago	606	312	17
Los Angeles	900	213	21
Philadelphia	191	215	25
Detroit	482	313	28
Houston	770	713	31
Baltimore	212	301	35
Dallas	752	214	38
Washington, D.C.	200	202	43
Indianapolis	462	317	47

Problem 2

half sheet, long side up

Center and type the table in exact vertical and horizontal center. DS items in columns. Leave 8 spaces between columns. Align figures at the right.

RESULTS OF CLERICAL APTITUDE TEST 7

DS

Scores and Ratings 11

TS

			words
Childs, Raymond E.	68	Poor	16
Dawson, Marilyn	115	Excellent	22
Gregory, David L.	92	Fair	27
Marshall, Cecil B.	103	Good	33
Porter, Donna Sue	74	Poor	38
Tolliver, James S.	87	Fair	43
Updyck, Keith L.	98	Good	48
Wallace, Zelda	109	Excellent	54

Problem 3 (optional)

half sheet, short side up

Center and type the table in reading position. DS items in columns. Decide spacing between columns.

Line spaces available: 51
Pica center: 27
Elite center: 33

SAMPLE CONVERSION OF CLOTHING SIZES 7

U.S. to Metric 10

			words
Shoes	6	38	12
Hosiery	9	2	15
Blouses	36	44	18
Dresses	12	40	20

229b ▶30 Improve production skills: letters

1. Type a 5′ writing on each letter, using plain paper. Find *gwam*; check correctness of letter style. If you finish a letter before time is called, start over.

2. Type another 5′ writing on each letter. Find *gwam*.

Goal: Higher *gwam* on second writing on each letter.

Problem 1
Modified block, indented ¶s, mixed

	gwam 5′
May 5, 19-- Mr. Frank C. Adams 5748 Davis	2
Street SW Atlanta, GA 30313 Dear Mr. Adams	4
(¶ 1) At the request of Mr. C. R. Gates, Person-	5
nel Director for the Maze Company, we are en-	7
closing a listing of the condominiums available	9
in the Monroeville area. (¶ 2) There are a	10
number of excellent values on the market at this	12
time. We recommend either the Murray Towers	14
or the Elwyn Center. Both of these complexes	16
offer a wide variety of floor plans; both are lo-	18
cated within minutes of the Maze Plant. (¶ 3)	20
Please let us know when you plan to be in this	21
area. If it will be more convenient for you to	23
inspect properties in the evening, we can make	25
special arrangements for you to do so. Sin-	27
cerely yours EASTWOOD REALTORS, INC. J. A.	29
Levin, President xx Enclosure (116)	30

Problem 2
AMS style

	gwam 5′
November 1, 19-- Ms. Lenore M. Sievers Direc-	2
tor of Advertising Redick Department Store	3
1600 Farnam Street Omaha, NE 68102 NEW	5
ADVERTISING RATES (¶ 1) It has been two	6
years since we were last forced to raise our	8
advertising rates. Since then, the cost of	10
newsprint and other items has risen steadily.	12
Reluctantly, therefore, we must raise our rates	14
again the first of next year. (¶ 2) As the en-	15
closed rate schedule shows, rates will increase	17
little more than ten percent. So that you may	19
plan your advertising budget, these rates will	21
remain in effect for at least a year. (¶ 3) If you	23
need any assistance in planning your advertis-	25
ing campaign for next year, one of our experts	27
will be happy to help you. E. J. DUNLAP, AD-	28
VERTISING MANAGER xx Enclosure (108)	30

229c ▶15 Timed drills on business letters

1. A 5′ writing on the letter in straight-copy form, beginning with the date. Find *gwam*.

2. A 5′ writing in letter form: modified block, open punctuation. Do not correct errors. Find *gwam*.

3. Compare *gwam* on the 2 writings.

	gwam 5′
June 8, 19-- Marcus Stores, Inc. 2402 Canal Street New Orleans, LA	3
70119 Attention Mr. M. C. Rosen, Purchasing Officer Ladies and Gentlemen	6
Thank you for your order for 5,000 of our Model C7256 transistor radios	8
to be marketed under your brand name, "MARCO." We know you will find our	11
transistor radio a quality item that will please your customers.	14
Our chief of production assures me we can deliver the radios on the	17
dates requested in your delivery schedule. We must, however, have the design	20
of the crest to be embossed on the radio no later than July 6.	22
It has been a real pleasure working with you on your first order. We	25
hope that it marks the beginning of a mutually satisfactory and profitable	28
association.	29
Sincerely yours John C. Wray Director of Marketing xx (114)	31

gwam 5′ | 1 | 2 | 3 |

62

62a ▶7 Conditioning practice

1. Each line twice SS (slowly, faster).

2. A 1′ writing on Line 4, then on Line 2; compare *gwam*.

alphabet	Vera Wykle quizzed the top men about the next golf match set for June.
figures	My Social Security number is 938-27-5026; my work permit number, R415.
–ly	kind kindly like likely near nearly real really sure surely true truly
fluency	It is essential for him to sign the form if she is to handle the case.

| 1 | 2 | 3 | 4 | 5 | 6 | 7 | 8 | 9 | 10 | 11 | 12 | 13 | 14 |

62b ▶10 Guided writing: sentences

1. Each line once for orientation.

2. A 1′ writing on each line, guided by the 15″ call of the line ending.

Goal: To reach the end of the line *exactly* when "Return" is called.

		gwam 15″
1	Just relax and let your fingers do this work.	36
2	Our audit of the books proves their work is right.	40
3	Curve your fingers and hold them lightly over the keys.	44
4	Drop back in speed to gain the skill of typing with control.	48
5	Poise is the ability to do things well while others just look on.	52
6	The real problem of your leisure time is to keep others from using it.	56

| 1 | 2 | 3 | 4 | 5 | 6 | 7 | 8 | 9 | 10 | 11 | 12 | 13 | 14 |

62c ▶13 Guided writing: paragraphs

1. A 1′ writing on ¶ 1; determine *gwam*.

2. Add 4 *gwam* to your *gwam* in Step 1 for a goal rate. Note ¼′ checkpoints in ¶ 1.

3. Two 1′ *speed* writings on ¶ 1. Try to equal your goal rate as ¼′ guides are called.

4. Type ¶ 2 in the same way.

5. A 3′ writing on ¶s 1–2 combined. Erase and correct any errors you make as you type. Determine your *corrected words a minute*: words typed ÷ 3.

all letters used | A | 1.5 si | 5.6 awl | 80% hfw |

gwam 3′

Office typists are expected to correct their errors. Making cor- (4)
rections takes time and skill. The greater the skill, the less time a (9)
correction requires and the lower the cost of the error. Accordingly, (14)
you are often being told now in your daily work to erase and correct (18)
the errors you make as you type a letter, a table, or a report. (23)

It certainly pays to be skillful in correcting errors; however, it (27)
will pay better when you learn to pace the typing at just the level you (32)
can control with accuracy and remove the need to correct so many errors. (37)
About thirty seconds are required to erase and correct an error. If you (42)
make five errors in five minutes and must stop to correct them, you cut (46)
your speed fifty percent. Realize this now and begin pacing yourself. (51)

gwam 3′ | 1 | 2 | 3 | 4 | 5 |

228c ▶15 Timed drills on business letters

1. A 5′ writing on the letter in straight-copy form, beginning with the date. Find *gwam*.

2. A 5′ writing in letter form: modified block style, indented ¶s, mixed punctuation. Do not correct errors. Find *gwam*.

3. Compare *gwam* on the 2 writings.

	gwam 5′	
September 16, 19-- Mr. Leonard C. Fillmore 548 Old	2	38
Point Road Charleston, SC 29412 Dear Mr. Fillmore	4	40
In view of the experience you have had with your new	6	42
Norlee Electric Razor, we can understand your concern and	8	45
dissatisfaction. The conditions you describe in your let-	11	47
ter of August 28 obviously require the close attention of	13	49
our expert repairmen.	14	50
As soon as you receive this letter, please return the	16	52
razor to us in the enclosed shipping container. The con-	18	55
tainer will assure that your razor will receive priority	21	57
handling. We have enclosed the correct postage for the re-	23	59
turn of the razor, but you may wish to add more postage in	25	62
order to insure the package at the local post office. We	28	64
urge you to do so since we have encountered some losses in	30	66
the mail.	31	67
When we receive your razor, we will repair and return	33	69
it promptly.	33	69
Sincerely yours R. R. Cominsky Director of Cus-	35	71
tomer Service xx Enclosures (146)	36	72

229

229a ▶5 Conditioning practice

twice SS;
repeat difficult lines

My objective was to standardize our freight and express rates quickly.
Jim bowled 198, 235, and 246, but Joe's scores were 197, 209, and 237.
The minimum for Job 79381 (Technician) is $6,750; the maximum, $8,420.
They plan to take a special inventory today of certain items in stock.

| 1 | 2 | 3 | 4 | 5 | 6 | 7 | 8 | 9 | 10 | 11 | 12 | 13 | 14 |

62d ▶20 Type 3-column tables

1 half sheet; 1 full sheet; decide spacing between columns

Problem 1

half sheet, long side up

Center and type the table in exact vertical and horizontal center. DS items in columns.

			words
PRICE COMPARISON OF SELECTED ART SUPPLIES			8
DS			
(Comparing Last Year with This Year)			16
TS			
Photographic paper, per set	$28.35	$32.20	25
Mylar-base film, per set	45.25	50.50	32
Film activator, per cubitainer	14.00	15.60	41
Film fixer, per cubitainer	15.40	17.20	49
Red sable art brushes, each	1.85	2.95	57
Waterproof drawing ink, per ounce	.75	1.05	66

Problem 2

full sheet; line spaces available: 66

Center and type the table in reading position. DS items in columns; DS between the total line and the total figure. *Erase and correct errors.*

To type totals

1. Type an underline the length of the longest item in the column.

2. DS and type the total figure.

JANUARY SALES REPORT			4
(Comparing Estimated and Actual Sales)			12
Alexander, John C.	$ 5,000	$ 5,200	20
Brumfield, Arthur D.	4,500	4,370	27
DeMarco, Emily J.	5,500	5,640	33
Gilchrist, Jane M.	6,000	5,950	39
Jarlinski, Marvin B.	3,500	3,675	45
McCormick, Elaine P.	4,000	4,125	52
O'Toole, William H.	5,000	5,250	58
Ramundo, Marjorie J.	4,500	5,050	65
St. Clair, Gerald R.	6,500	6,750	72
Tomlinson, Richard A.	7,000	6,840	78
Underwood, Jay D.	10,000	9,575	85
Weismann, Norma Jean	3,500	3,620	94
	$65,000	$66,045	97

228

228a ▶5 Conditioning practice

twice SS;
repeat difficult lines

Peggy Bixby was amazed at the quantity of junk mail we received daily.
Movies will be shown at 2:30 p.m. and 6:45 p.m. on May 17, 18, and 19.
Item 3952 rose $11.39 (6.7%) while Item 87484 decreased $26.90 (5.1%).
If the light is not visible on the display panel, check both switches.

| 1 | 2 | 3 | 4 | 5 | 6 | 7 | 8 | 9 | 10 | 11 | 12 | 13 | 14 |

228b ▶30 Improve production skills: letters

1. Study appropriate letter styles in Reference Guide, page v.

2. Determine margins and dateline positions for letter lengths indicated. (If necessary, see RG, page iv.)

3. Type a 5′ writing on each letter, using plain paper. Find *g–pram*; check correctness of letter style.

4. Type another 5′ writing on each letter. Find *g–pram*.

Goal: Higher *g–pram* on second writing on each letter.

Problem 1
Block, open

words

April 3, 19-- Mr. T. C. Peters, President Lee Enterprises, Inc. 1200 Con- 14
cord Road Chester, PA 19013 Dear Mr. Peters (¶ 1) Enclosed are the 27
revised plans for the new plant you plan to construct in Darby. All 40
changes you requested in your letter of March 14 have been incorporated 55
into the plans. (¶ 2) The addition of the office wing on the north side of 69
the building poses a problem. This places the building within 15 feet of 83
Ridley Road. The local code provides that all structures must be at least 98
20 feet from the highway, and it is unlikely we can obtain a variance. 113
The best solution to this problem is to construct the office wing on the 127
east side of the building. This can be done with but minor changes in the 142
plans. (¶ 3) After you have had an opportunity to study this matter, I 156
suggest we meet again for a comprehensive review of your building 169
plans. Sincerely yours SINGER ASSOCIATES John T. Braun, Architect 182
xx Enclosure (147) 185/**202**

Problem 2
Modified block, mixed

May 17, 19-- Mr. Itaru Suzuki, Purchasing Officer Ashley Industries, 14
Inc. 47 Church Street Paterson, NJ 07505 Dear Mr. Suzuki Subject: 28
Model LV-2000 Calculator (¶ 1) Thank you for your recent inquiry about 41
our Model LV-2000 Calculator. (¶ 2) The Model LV-2000 is a fully au- 53
tomatic calculator which offers amazing shortcuts in payroll calcula- 66
tions, percentages, invoicing, and discounts. It speeds the computation of 81
taxes, interest, inventory, and engineering and statistical problems of 96
every kind. Negative and cumulative multiplication are added features 110
on the LV-2000. (¶ 3) Enclosed is our catalog describing the Model LV- 123
2000 Calculator and other quality office machines and equipment we 136
carry. If there is any other information you would like, please call me 151
collect. (¶ 4) We hope that you will join the ranks of our many satisfied 165
customers in the very near future. Sincerely yours Patricia L. Parks 179
Sales Representative xx Enclosure (137) 185/**205**

63

63a ▶7 Conditioning practice

1. Each line twice SS (slowly, faster).

2. A 1′ writing on Line 4, then on Line 1; compare *gwam.*

alphabet	Four complex keyboard reviews were quickly organized by Patrick Johns.
tab	3/4 6 95% 6 $82 6 4's 6 2-16 6 7:45 6 0.5% 6 (36)
–ble/–cal	liable capable visible credible local vocal typical vertical practical
fluency	Lana is to inform them within six days if she is to chair their panel.

| 1 | 2 | 3 | 4 | 5 | 6 | 7 | 8 | 9 | 10 | 11 | 12 | 13 | 14 |

63b ▶10 Learn to type special symbols

half sheet, long side up

Center problem vertically DS; center columns horizontally with 6 spaces between them. Type the symbols in Column 3 as directed in Column 2. *Erase and correct errors.*

Before typing the last 2 lines, study the directions in the block below.

SPECIAL SYMBOLS

		last my/day
Insert	Diagonal (/); roll platen back one line	last my/day
Minus	Hyphen (-) with space before and after	8 - 4
Plus	Diagonal; backspace; hyphen	6 ≁ 9
Division	Colon (:); backspace; hyphen	10 ÷ 5
Times	x with space before and after	7 x 3
English pound	Capital L; backspace; lowercase f	£
Superscript	Letter; platen backward slightly; figure	$Knox^1$
Subscript	Letter; platen forward slightly; figure	H_2O

Typing superscripts and subscripts

Superscript
To type a figure or symbol above the line:

1. Operate *ratchet release* or *automatic line finder* (6);

2. Turn platen *backward* (toward you);

3. Type the figure or symbol, then return automatic line finder and platen to normal position.

Subscript
To type a figure or symbol below the line, follow the same procedure *except* turn the platen *forward* (away from you).

63c ▶8 Guided writing: sentences

a 1′ writing on each line, guided by the 15″ call of the line ending

Goal: To reach the end of the line *exactly* when "Return" is called.

		gwam 15″
1	Hold the hands and arms as quiet as possible.	36
2	A lot of good will come from just a little praise.	40
3	Build a skill to prize, then prize the skill you build.	44
4	Learn to make the reach to the shift key with proper timing.	48
5	He will slow down for figures and symbols but speed up for words.	52
6	All workers can do a lot more through push than they can through pull.	56

| 1 | 2 | 3 | 4 | 5 | 6 | 7 | 8 | 9 | 10 | 11 | 12 | 13 | 14 |

227b ▶45 Inventory production skill: letters

Type the letters for 30′, each letter on plain paper; correct errors as you type. If you finish all letters before time is called, start over.

Compute *n–pram*: total acceptable words + ½ unacceptable words ÷ 30. Record *n–pram* for future comparison with score achieved on 247b, page 385.

Problem 1
Modified block, indented ¶s, mixed

	words
April 14, 19-- Mr. Elton C. Warrington, President	10
Warrington Enterprises, Inc. 731 Marquette	19
Avenue, Minneapolis, MN 55402 Dear Mr.	26
Warrington (¶ 1) Enclosed are two copies of	34
the proof of the program for the data processing	44
colloquium to be held at the Drake Hotel on	53
May 15. (¶ 2) Will you please make any neces-	61
sary corrections on the program and return	69
one corrected copy to me before April 19. I	78
would like to send the final proof to the printer	88
no later than April 20. (¶ 3) We are looking	96
forward with pleasure to your presentation at	106
the colloquium. Sincerely yours Bruno Santos	115
Program Chairman xx Enclosures (80)	121/142

Problem 2
Block, open

May 13, 19-- Ms. Jeanne Maurois 32 Colony	8
Drive Providence, RI 02919 Dear Ms. Maurois	17
(¶ 1) Thank you for calling our attention to the	26
problems you have experienced with your sub-	34
scription to MANAGEMENT MONTHLY. (¶ 2)	41
Several months ago, we found it necessary to	50
convert our subscription processing procedures	60
to a new high-speed computer system. Unfor-	68
tunately, unforeseen problems arose which	77
severely hampered our ability to process sub-	85
scriptions. It was for this reason that your	95
subscription was not renewed. (¶ 3) Your sub-	102
scription to MANAGEMENT MONTHLY has been	111
reinstated and will remain in effect for two	120
years effective this month. (¶ 4) We surely	127
appreciate your continued interest in MANAGE-	136
MENT MONTHLY and are very sorry for any	144
inconvenience you may have been caused.	152
Sincerely yours Charles W. Hartman Circulation	162
Manager xx (134)	164/175

Problem 3
Modified block, mixed

	words
November 17, 19-- Quincy Office Supply Com-	8
pany 450 Main Street Hartford, CT 06103 At-	17
tention Mr. W. R. Polk, Sales Manager Ladies	26
and Gentlemen (¶ 1) Thank you for your	33
prompt attention to our order of October 30.	42
The entire shipment was received yesterday.	51
(¶ 2) Unfortunately, there was an error on the	59
printed letterheads and envelopes we ordered.	69
Our corporate name is BEAUFERD BOUTIQUES,	77
INC. On the letterheads and envelopes it ap-	86
pears as BEAUFORD BOUTIQUES, INC. (¶ 3) Will	94
you please send us letterheads and envelopes	103
with the correct spelling as soon as possible.	113
We shall hold the incorrect letterheads and en-	122
velopes in our warehouse until we hear from	131
you. Sincerely yours Frances L. Alberts Pur-	140
chasing Director xx (108)	144/156

Problem 4
AMS style

April 2, 19-- Mr. Roosevelt C. Green Placement	9
Officer Jefferson King College 215 North 20th	19
Street Birmingham, AL 35203 CAREERS IN	26
INSURANCE FOR YOUR STUDENTS (¶ 1) The	33
Columbia Insurance Company has many career	41
opportunities for college graduates in major	50
cities throughout the United States. Our busi-	60
ness is so varied and complex that openings	68
exist for people with a great variety of qualifi-	78
cations. (¶ 2) Can you arrange for us to talk	86
with your students who may be interested in	95
the field of insurance? Although we are par-	104
ticularly interested in business administration	113
students, we invite students in the humanities, as	123
well as scientific and technical fields, to apply	133
for our trainee program. (¶ 3) Please write	141
or call us collect so that we may send our	150
representative to your campus at a time con-	158
venient for you and the students. CHARLENE	167
E. ROBBINS, DIRECTOR OF EMPLOYMENT xx	175/196
(133)	

63d ▶25 Type 4-column tables

2 full sheets; 4 spaces between columns; DS items in columns

Problem 1
Center and type the table in reading position.

Problem 2
As time permits, type a 3′ writing on planning, making machine adjustments, and typing the headings and the first few lines of the table. *Use 6 spaces between columns.*

words

SUMMARY OF PROMOTION COSTS — 5
DS
Department, Item, Amount Budgeted, and Amount Spent — 16
TS

Department	Item	Amount Budgeted	Amount Spent	words
Advertising	Circulars, brochures	$ 60,000	$ 58,285	27
"	Magazine advertising	7,000	7,150	35
"	Mailing costs	45,000	46,100	41
Graphic Arts	Layout, design	12,000	12,560	49
Customer Service	Special communications	13,000	12,950	60
Marketing	Catalogs	19,000	18,490	66
"	Computer expense	15,000	14,750	73
"	Product exhibits	18,000	17,585	83
		$189,000	$187,870	86

64

64a ▶7 Conditioning practice

1. Each line twice SS (slowly, faster).
2. A 1′ writing on Line 4, then on Line 2; compare *gwam*.

alphabet The audience was quite amazed by the report Felix Kline gave the jury.
figures The decorator chairs we back-ordered are Nos. C2175, K4038, and Z6395.
–ion/–ous option caption station famous generous anxious tedious devious dubious
fluency Both neighboring towns paid a penalty for removing coal from the land.

| 1 | 2 | 3 | 4 | 5 | 6 | 7 | 8 | 9 | 10 | 11 | 12 | 13 | 14 |

64b ▶8 Improve technique: machine parts

each pair of lines twice SS; DS between 4-line groups

space bar
if my | do my work | if any go | so they are | to buy it | so many men | go by the
If you want to buy the pony for the boy, you may come for him any day.

shift keys
Gulf of Mexico | Lake of the Woods | Oakland Bay | Missouri River | Lake Tahoe
Marsha and Alton left with Janet and Appley on a South Pacific cruise.

automatic line finder
In the words of Fred M. Vinson:[1] "What man has made, man can change."
Use $NaHCO_3$ as the formula for baking soda; $KHC_4H_4O_6$ for baking powder.

64c ▶35 Improve table typing skill

1. Make a list of the problems identified at the right.

page 95, 59d, Problem 2
page 98, 61c, Problem 3
page 102, 63d, Problem 1

2. Type as many of the problems listed as you can in 30′.

226d ▶17 Inventory basic skill: script

1. Two 5′ writings on ¶s 1–3 combined.

2. Record *gwam* and errors on better writing. Keep a record for comparison with scores achieved on 246d, page 384, and on 296d, page 454.

3. As time permits, type a 1′ goal writing on each ¶.

all letters used	A	1.5 si	5.6 awl	80% hfw

	gwam 1′	5′	
The telephone is the most widely used instrument for	11	2	51
communication in a business office. As an employee in an	22	4	54
office, you will be asked to make and answer many kinds of	34	7	56
phone calls daily. How effective you are in using the phone	46	9	59
depends to a large extent upon how well your callers react	58	12	61
to you and comprehend you. It is vital, therefore, that you	70	14	63
master the proper techniques for using the telephone.	81	16	66
Using the telephone is not a very difficult task. Talk	11	18	68
directly into the receiver in your normal tone; it is not	23	21	70
necessary to shout. Speak naturally, but emphasize your ideas	35	23	73
by the use of inflection, by stressing key words and phrases,	48	26	75
and by varying the rate at which you talk. Speak simply; do	60	28	78
not confuse the other person with technical jargon. Since	72	31	80
you cannot be seen, you must make the best use of your voice.	84	33	82
Your telephone manner is just as important as your voice.	12	35	85
If you wish to impress your callers, you should be pleasant,	24	38	87
courteous, and helpful. You must show a sincere interest in	36	40	90
the inquiries and ideas of your callers. You must be a good	48	43	92
listener as well as a good conversationalist. Using the phone	61	45	94
is not just a routine task. You can help build valuable good-	73	48	97
will for your company if you use it properly.	82	49	99

227

227a ▶5 Conditioning practice

twice SS; repeat difficult lines

Wise executives will analyze the facts before passing quick judgments.
Correct pages 3, 6, 7, 8, and 9; retype pages 46, 48, 73, 91, and 205.
The trade discount was increased from 15%, 10%, and 3% to 20% and 10%.
Sign the special report of audit and airmail it to the four attorneys.

| 1 | 2 | 3 | 4 | 5 | 6 | 7 | 8 | 9 | 10 | 11 | 12 | 13 | 14 |

65

65a ▶7 Conditioning practice

1. Each line twice SS (slowly, faster).

2. A 1′ writing on Line 4, then on Line 2; compare *gwam*.

alphabet	Jack Foxe now sells bronze jars and handmade bisque pottery in Geneva.
tab	20% 6 $75 6 1/3 6 8's 6 9:30 6 6.25 6 4-12 6 (83)
–ful/–ment	use useful help helpful state statement ship shipment agree agreements
fluency	A formal audit of eight divisions may be made by the end of the month.

| 1 | 2 | 3 | 4 | 5 | 6 | 7 | 8 | 9 | 10 | 11 | 12 | 13 | 14 |

65b ▶8 Check keystroking skill

a 5′ writing; determine *gwam*; circle errors

all letters used | A | 1.5 si | 5.6 awl | 80% hfw |

	gwam 5′
If success is vital to you, you have a distinct advantage over many	3
people who have no particular feeling one way or the other. The desire	6
to succeed is helpful, for it causes us to establish goals without which	9
our actions have little or no meaning. Success may not necessarily mean	11
winning the big prize, but it does mean approaching a goal.	14
The pages of our history books are alive with stories of famous	16
men and women who had harsh strikes against them in mental capacity, in	19
education, and in health. But one asset they did have: They wanted to	22
learn; they wanted to succeed; they expected to reach their goals. So	25
they put together the qualities of desire and action.	27
It is foolish, of course, to believe that we can all be whatever	30
we wish to become. It is just as foolish, though, to wait around hop-	32
ing for success to overtake us. We should analyze our aspirations, our	35
abilities, and our limitations. We can then decide from various choices	38
what we are best fitted with effort to become.	40

gwam 5′ | 1 | 2 | 3 |

65c ▶10 Build basic skill

1. A 1′ writing on ¶ 1, above; determine *gwam*.

2. Add 4 *gwam* to this base rate.

3. Note ¼′ checkpoints in ¶ 1.

4. Two 1′ guided *speed* writings on ¶ 1.

5. Type ¶ 2 in the same way. Use good techniques to increase your speed.

226c ▶17 Inventory basic skill: straight copy

1. Two 5′ writings on the 3 ¶s combined.
2. Record *gwam* and errors on better writing. Keep a record for comparison with scores achieved on 246c, page 383, and on 298d, page 457.
3. As time permits, type a 1′ goal writing on each ¶.

all letters used | A | 1.5 si | 5.6 awl | 80% hfw |

gwam 5′

The use of the telephone in the office of today is so routine that it is difficult to imagine that the first telephone exchange was opened less than a hundred years ago. At the turn of the century, the letter was the primary medium of communication, although the telegraph was used for quick contact over long distances. At first, the telephone was used chiefly as a burglar alarm. It did not take too long, though, for business firms to recognize the merits of a network of telephones. 20

Initially, the telephone system was a private rather than a public one. Business firms set up direct lines between their offices and major clients and with sources of data, such as a stock market. As the use of the telephone grew, however, the telephones within many cities were tied together by a central exchange manned by operators. The network grew as many cities were linked by cable, but it was not until just before the first world war that the first coast-to-coast call was made. 39

Great progress in technology was needed to meet the great demand for telephone service. The dial phone eliminated the need for an operator on many calls. The coaxial cable, which can carry a large number of circuits, took the place of single lines. To meet the demand for even more service, a series of radio relays was used for calls. By mating radio waves with earth satellites, a global network was set up. We can now talk with others all over the world by merely pushing buttons. 59

gwam 5′ | 1 | 2 | 3 |

65d ▶25 Check table typing skill

2 half sheets; decide spacing between columns

Problem 1

half sheet, short side up

Center and type the table in reading position. DS items in columns. *Erase and correct errors.*

words

MAIL DISTRIBUTION SCHEDULE 5

For the Week Ending January 9 11

		words
Monday, January 5	Mary Ann Groza	18
Tuesday, January 6	Denny Kirby	24
Wednesday, January 7	Olamae Printner	31
Thursday, January 8	Jerry Herzog	38
Friday, January 9	Harvey Johnston	45

Problem 2

half sheet, long side up

Center and type the table in exact vertical and horizontal center, making the changes indicated. *Erase and correct your errors.*

SS the a.m. appointments; DS; then SS the p.m. appointments

MS. WEXLER'S ^TUESDAY INTERVIEW SCHEDULE 8

Time, Applicant, and Position 14

			words
Mary Ann Simms	8:30	Senior Stenographer	22
Michael J. Conti	9:15	~~Order~~ File Clerk	29
Han Song Ki	10:00	Clerk-typist	36
Juan D. Perez	10:45	Key Punch Operator	44
Catherine Quinn	11:30	Clerk-Typist	50
Marie Tallcheif	1:30	~~Executive~~ Secretary	56
Debra Kirkland	2:15	Order Clerk	63
Stephen B. DeMar	3:00	Accounting Clerk	70
Susie Yamaguchi	3:~~30~~ 45	MT/ST operator	78
Joy Condorodis	4:30	~~Administrative Assistant~~ Secretary	84

Enrichment material for Unit 10 appears on LM pp. 79, 80.

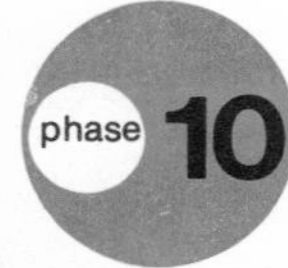

lessons 226–250

Improving basic/production skills

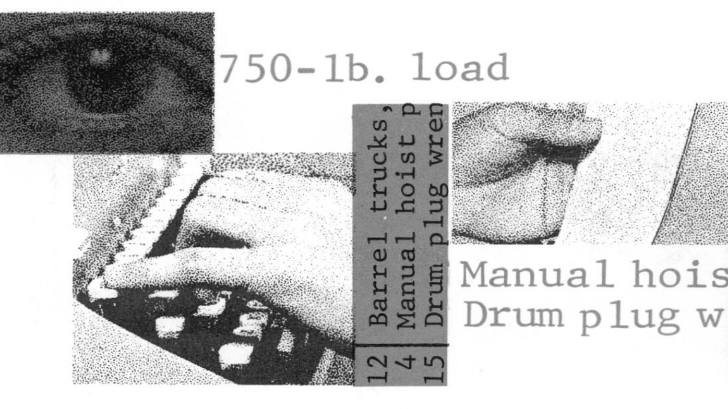

unit **40** lessons 226–231

Basic/letter skills

Learning goals

1. To increase your production rate in typing business letters, business reports, tabulated reports, and business forms.

2. To increase your speed and accuracy on straight copy, script, rough draft, and statistical copy.

To help you reach these goals, Units 40–42 contain inventory lessons to measure your present level of basic and production skill, followed by intensive drills to improve your speed and accuracy. Unit 43 includes a series of measurement activities to check your improvement.

Machine adjustments

1. Line: 70 for drills and timed writings.

2. Spacing: SS sentence drills; DS ¶s; space problems as directed.

226

226a ▶5 Conditioning practice

twice SS;
repeat difficult lines

alphabet	They will be expected to provide quality flight jackets in many sizes.
figures	A4 paper is 210 mm x 297 mm; A5, 148 mm x 210 mm; A6, 105 mm x 148 mm.
fig/sym	We received checks for $1,279, $28, $50.61, $9.25, $36.14, and $78.94.
fluency	The fight for the world title will be held at the downtown civic hall.

| 1 | 2 | 3 | 4 | 5 | 6 | 7 | 8 | 9 | 10 | 11 | 12 | 13 | 14 |

226b ▶11 Improve skill transfer

1. A 1′ writing on each sentence; find *gwam*.

2. Additional 1′ writings on more difficult lines as time permits.

			words
straight copy	1	If they do not make their payments on time, they must pay the penalty.	14
statistical copy	2	One portion of Item 37901 equals 285 calories and 46 grams of protein.	14
script	3	The panel may vote on the eight amendments when it meets here tonight.	14
rough draft	4	Do not (Please don't) send the rental receip to us; Send it (them) to the bank in the city.	14
statistical copy	5	On Job 7905, 16,865 transistors were accepted and 2,743 were rejected.	14
script	6	Did she say the special party for the visitors will be held this week?	14
rough draft	7	The officials of the company wouldnot consent (agree) to rearrange (a major change in) the agenda.	14

unit **11** lessons 66–72

Outlines and short reports

Learning goals
The basic purpose of this unit is to help you learn to type topic outlines and unbound reports (some with and some without footnotes).

In addition, you will improve your basic skills, further refine your techniques, and learn to reinsert paper, align the typed copy, and correct errors.

66

66a ▶7 Conditioning practice

1. Each line twice SS (slowly, faster).
2. A 1′ writing on Line 4, then on Line 2; compare *gwam*.

alphabet Keifka was just amazed that everyone expected a large quarterly bonus.
figures Our group read 45 plays, 186 books, and 203 articles during 1975-1976.
trigraphs the their either another you your bayou yourself and land handle stand
fluency I may go with them to see if the boys or girls will do the job for me.

| 1 | 2 | 3 | 4 | 5 | 6 | 7 | 8 | 9 | 10 | 11 | 12 | 13 | 14 |

66b ▶18 Guided writing: paragraphs

1. A 2′ writing on ¶ 1; determine *gwam*.
2. Add 4 *gwam* to set a goal rate.
3. Note ¼′ checkpoints in ¶ 1 for 2′ of typing.
4. Two 2′ writings on ¶ 1, guided by the ¼′ call of the guide.
5. Type ¶ 2 in the same way.

all letters used | A | 1.5 si | 5.6 awl | 80% hfw |

gwam 5′

Three steps should be taken in planning a report. Selecting the topic is not merely the first but also the most important one. It is vital that you choose a topic in which you are sufficiently interested to do the required research. Next, it is essential that you limit the topic so that you can treat the subject adequately within the space and time limitations that have been set. Finally, you should decide upon and list in outline format the major ideas that you wish to convey. 3 5 8 11 14 17 19

Three steps should be followed in preparing the report, also. The first of these is to look for data and authoritative statements to support the ideas you want to convey. The next step is to type a rough draft of the report, organizing the material into a series of related paragraphs, each with a topic sentence to announce its major idea. The final step is to read the rough draft carefully for thought, clarity, and grammar and to type the final copy. 22 25 28 31 33 36 38

gwam 5′ | 1 | 2 | 3 |

225b, continued

Problem 3
Invoice

	words
Broward Broward Office Supplies, 7028 Miramar Blvd., Hollywood, FL 33023 (305) 271-4397 — Invoice 32786	1
Babcock & St. Clair, Inc. / 427 Ocean Ave., East / Boynton Beach, FL 33435 — Date April 24, 19--	9
Our Order No. 69472-J	15
Cust. Order No. BSS-0319	22
Terms 2/10, n/30 — Shipped Via McLean Trucking	27

Quantity	Description	Unit Price	Total	words
50 lbs.	Puccini rubber bands	7.04	352.00	35
35 doz.	Thinwrite pencils, orange ochre	1.44	50.40	46
7	#310 legal-size, single-drawer file bases, gray	13.10	91.70	52, 58
4	4-drawer file cabinets with lock	125.50	502.00	64, 69
			996.10	70

Problem 4
Voucher check

Problem 5
If time permits, retype the Problem 1 purchase order.

Babcock & St. Clair, Inc.
427 Ocean Ave., East
Boynton Beach, FL 33435

63-891/670

May 1 19-- No. 427 — words 3

PAY to the order of Broward Office Supplies $ 976.18 — 9

Nine hundred seventy-six 18/100------------------------------------ Dollars — 23

Second Bank & Trust
Boynton Beach, FL 33435

⑆0670⑈0891⑆ 143⑈062⑈46⑈

Detach this stub before cashing this check.

TO
Broward Office Supplies — 28
7028 Miramar Blvd. — 32
Hollywood, FL 33023 — 36

IN PAYMENT OF THE FOLLOWING INVOICES:

Date	Invoice	Amount	words
4/24/--	32786	$996.10	40
	Less 2%	19.92	44
		$976.18	45

Babcock & St. Clair, Inc.
427 Ocean Ave., East
Boynton Beach, FL 33435

66c ▶10 Learn to align Roman numerals

1. Set left margin stop for a 50-space line.

2. Clear all tab stops; set new tab stops as indicated by the KEY and the guides above the table.

3. Align the columns of Roman numerals at the right. Tabs should be set to require the least forward and backward spacing.

margin	tab	tab	tab
I	VI	XV	XL
II	VII	XX	L
III	VIII	XXV	LXXV
IV	IX	XXX	XC
V	X	XXXV	C

key | 3 | 12 | 4 | 12 | 4 | 12 | 4 |

66d ▶15 Learn to type a topic outline

full sheet; line: 65; begin on Line 20; space as directed

First-order subheadings preceded by **A.**, **B.**, etc.

Second-order subheadings preceded by **1.**, **2.**, etc.

words

```
                    TOPIC OUTLINES                                   3
                                 TS
I.  CAPITALIZING HEADINGS IN TOPIC OUTLINES                         12
                                 DS
    A.  Title of Outline in ALL CAPS (May Be Underlined)            26
    B.  Major Headings in ALL CAPS (Not Underlined)                 35
    C.  Important Words of First-Order Subheadings Capitalized      47
    D.  Only First Word of Second-Order Subheadings Capitalized     59
                                 DS
II. SPACING TOPIC OUTLINES                                          66
                                 DS
    A.  Horizontal Spacing                                          70
        1.  Title of outline centered over the writing line         91
        2.  Identifying numerals for major headings typed at the    93
            left margin (periods aligned), followed by 2 spaces    103
        3.  Identifying letters and numerals for each subsequent   115
            level of subheading aligned beneath the first word of  126
            the preceding heading, followed by 2 spaces            135
    B.  Vertical Spacing                                           140
        1.  Title of outline followed by 2 blank line spaces       151
        2.  Major headings (except the first) preceded by 1 blank  162
            line space; all followed by 1 blank line space         172
        3.  All subheadings single-spaced                          179
```

Annotations: Space forward once from margin (before I.); 2 spaces (after I. and after A.); Reset margin (at A.); Backspace 5 times (before II.); Set 2 tab stops 4 spaces apart: 1st tab (at 1.), 2d tab (at "left margin"). "May Be Underlined" is underlined in the title line.

225b ▶45 Measure production skill: common business forms

Follow the time schedule given for 222b, page 350. [LM pp. 215–224]

Problem 1
Purchase order

Babcock & St. Clair, Inc.
427 Ocean Ave., East Boynton Beach, FL 33435 (305) 321-7272

PURCHASE ORDER

Broward Office Supplies
7028 Miramar Blvd.
Hollywood, FL 33023

Purchase order No. BSS-0319 (words: 2)
Date March 31, 19-- (10)
Terms 2/10, n/30 (16)
Ship Via McLean Trucking (23)

Quantity	Cat. No.	Description	Price	Total	words
35 doz.	736-R	Thinwrite pencils, orange ochre	1.44 doz.	50.40	31, 35
50 lbs.	19-BT	Puccini rubber bands, 3½ x 1/32 x 1/16 (1,750 per lb.)	7.04 lb.	352.00	44, 53
4	314-G	4-drawer file cabinet with lock	125.50 ea.	502.00	59, 64
7	FB-3000	#310 legal-size, single drawer file base, gray	13.10 ea.	91.70	72, 80
				996.10	81

By______________________ Purchasing Agent

Problem 2
Bill of lading

STRAIGHT BILL OF LADING—SHORT FORM—Original—Not Negotiable

RECEIVED, subject to the classifications and tariffs in effect on the date of issue of this Original Bill of Lading.

AGENT'S NO.______

FROM Broward Office Supplies AT Hollywood, FL DATE 4/6/-- (words: 9)

CONSIGNED TO AND DESTINATION:
Babcock + St. Clair, Inc. (14)
427 Ocean Ave., East (18)
Boynton Beach, FL 33435 (23)

CUST. ORDER NO. BSS-0319 (25)
DELIVERING CARRIER McLean Trucking Co. CAR INITIAL AND NO. EHF28215 (31)

the property described below, in apparent good order, except as noted (contents and condition of contents of packages unknown) marked, consigned, and destined as indicated below, which said carrier (the word carrier being understood throughout this contract as meaning any person or corporation in possession of the property under the contract) agrees to carry to its usual place of delivery at said destination, if on its route, otherwise to deliver to another carrier on the route to said destination. It is mutually agreed, as to each carrier of all or any of said property over all or any portion of said route to destination, and as to each party at any time interested in all or any of said property, that every service to be performed hereunder shall be subject to all the terms and conditions of the Uniform Domestic Straight Bill of Lading set forth (1) in Official, Southern, Western and Illinois Freight Classifications in effect on the date hereof, if this is a rail or a rail-water shipment, or (2) in the applicable motor carrier classification or tariff if this is a motor carrier shipment. **Shipper hereby certifies that he is familiar with all the terms and conditions of the said bill of lading, including those on the back thereof, set forth in the classification or tariff which governs the transportation of this shipment, and the said terms and conditions are hereby agreed to by the shipper and accepted for himself and his assigns.**

NO. PACKAGES	DESCRIPTION OF ARTICLES	WEIGHT	RATE	CHK.	words
4	4-drawer file cabinets	480#			37
7	1-drawer file bases	49#			42
2	Puccini rubber bands	50#			47
1	Thinwrite colored pencils	13#			58

*If the shipment moves between two ports by a carrier by water, the law requires that the bill of lading shall state whether it is "carrier's or shipper's weight." Note—Where the rate is dependent on value, shippers are required to state specifically in writing the agreed or declared value of the property. **The agreed or declared value of the property is hereby specifically stated by the shipper to be not exceeding** ______ per ______

Subject to Section 7 of conditions of applicable bill of lading, if this shipment is to be delivered to the consignee without recourse on the consignor, the consignor shall sign the following statement:
The carrier shall not make delivery of this shipment without payment of freight and all other lawful charges.

(Signature of Consignor)

If charges are to be prepaid, write or stamp here, "To be Prepaid."

Received $______ to apply in prepayment of the charges on the property described hereon.

Agent or Cashier

Per______
(The signature here acknowledges only the amount prepaid.)

Charges Advanced: $______

†Shipper's imprint in lieu of stamp; not a part of Bill of Lading approved by the Interstate Commerce Commission.

Broward Office Supplies SHIPPER (63)
Per______ Agent, Per______

PERMANENT POST-OFFICE ADDRESS OF SHIPPER: 7028 Miramar Blvd., Hollywood, FL 33023 (71)

†"The fibre boxes used for this shipment conform to the specifications set forth in the box maker's certificate thereon, and all other requirements of Uniform Freight Classification."

SHIPPER'S NO. 2 741956 (72)

67

67a ▶7 Conditioning practice

1. Each line twice SS (slowly, faster).
2. A 1′ writing on Line 4, then on Line 1; compare *gwam*.

alphabet My sizable rebate check was given to adjust for a parish tax inequity.
fig/sym Hendrick-Smith's Order P2859-6 (dated 10/23) amounts to $746.59 C.O.D.
trigraphs for form before effort ate date rate water ill will willed with within
fluency Did the six men sign the land title forms with a pen or with a pencil?

| 1 | 2 | 3 | 4 | 5 | 6 | 7 | 8 | 9 | 10 | 11 | 12 | 13 | 14 |

67b ▶8 Improve technique: machine parts

type drill twice
exact 60-space line
6 spaces between columns

tabulator and return

am	aid	and	also	auto	body	born
an	air	apt	both	busy	city	down

shift keys and lock
Epworth took TWA Flight 69 at 3:15; Hahn, AA Flight 72 at 4.
Mark read the book, DESTINY, but not the review in Newsweek.

margin release and backspacer
I have now learned to apply my typing skill to prepare useful papers.
A. She must release the margin and backspace four times to type A.

67c ▶15 Type an outline

full sheet; line: 65; center in reading position

1. Space forward once from margin to type Roman numeral **I.** Reset margin 2 spaces to right of period in **I.** for subheadings **A.** and **B.**

2. Set 3 tab stops 4 spaces apart, beginning at left margin, for typing subheadings; use margin release and backspace to type **II.**

Note: Space once after closing parenthesis

words

UNBOUND MANUSCRIPTS 4

I. MARGINS AND SPACING 9

A. Margins 11
1. Side and bottom margins: approximately 1″ 21
2. Top margin, first page: elite, 2″; pica, 1 1/2″ 32
3. Top margin, additional pages: 1″ 40

B. Spacing 42
1. Body of manuscript: double 49
2. Paragraph indentions: 5 or 10 spaces uniformly 59
3. Quoted paragraph 64
a. Four or more lines 69
(1) Single-spaced 73
(2) Indented 5 spaces from each margin 81
(3) Quotation marks not required--may be used 91
b. Fewer than 4 lines 96
(1) Quotation marks used 102
(2) Not separated from text 108
(3) Not indented from text margins 116

II. PAGE NUMBERING 121

A. First Page: Number Centered 1/2″ from Bottom Edge 132
B. Other Pages: Number Typed Even with Right Margin, 1/2″ from Top Edge of Paper 143 148

224b, continued

Problem 3
Boxed table from handwritten copy

full sheet; DS; center vertically; 4 spaces between columns; type horizontal rules and draw vertical rules

Problem 4

If time permits, retype Problem 1 as a boxed table.

words

EAT-A-WAY CHOCOLATE SHOPPE 5

Comparative Statement of Cost 11

Confection	Cost per Box This Year	Cost per Box 5 Years Ago	words
			39
			44
			50
			64
Imperial Almonds	$1.45	$ .90	70
Peanut Butter Crunch	.85	.56	75
Milk Chocolate with Almonds	1.00	.77	83
Chocolate Covered Pecan Patties	1.70	1.25	91
Krisp Nuggets	.98	.73	96
Chocolate Covered Cordial Cherries	.65	.49	104
Continental Almonds	1.35	.99	110
Mint Melt-A-Ways	.59	.30	115
Cashew Butter Crunch	.95	.72	121
Chocolate Nut Mels	.84	.55	126
Huff-N-Puff	.30	.16	130
Toasted Almond Chocolate Bar	.62	.38	138
			151

225

225a ▶5 Conditioning practice

each line twice SS; repeat selected lines as time permits

First prize went to Rex Joby, who quickly mastered three group events.
Report to 9678 Elm Street at 12:45 p.m. on September 30 for a checkup.
Interest on a $15,000 note at 8% was $1,200 annually and $100 monthly.
If you always work diligently, you may not have that last-minute rush.

| 1 | 2 | 3 | 4 | 5 | 6 | 7 | 8 | 9 | 10 | 11 | 12 | 13 | 14 |

67d ▶20 Type page 1 of an unbound manuscript

Margins

top: 2″ elite
1½″ pica
side: 1″
bottom: approx. 1″

1. Type the copy as an unbound report DS.

2. As this is page 1 of a 2-page report (to be completed in Lesson 68), center and type the figure 1 a half inch above the bottom edge of the sheet: on 4th line space (pica) or 3d line space (elite) below last line of the last ¶.

elite

pica

words

ELECTRONIC MAIL SORTING 5
TS

The ZIP Code system of sorting mail was begun in 1963. ZIP 17
(Zoning Improvement Plan) divides the country into delivery units, 30
each given a 5-digit number. The first digit represents one of ten 44
geographic areas; the second, a certain part of a geographic area; 57
the third, one of the sectional center areas for sorting mail; the last 72
two, a zone number for internally zoned cities or the delivery station 86
for smaller ones. 90

ZIP Coding was only one step in a massive program designed to 102
bring efficiency to the chaotic condition of mail handling. This 115
coding system foresaw the eventual use of the Optical Character 128
Reader (an electronic mail sorter) that depends upon a numeric 141
language (the ZIP Code) for maximum efficiency in handling mail. 154

The marriage of ZIP and OCR occurred in 1967 when the Optical 166
Character Reader began full-time operation in the Detroit Post 179
Office. Since then, the OCR has been installed in about twenty major 193
cities, including New York, Los Angeles, and Chicago. 204

The OCR has peculiar reading habits. For example, it first 216
scans from right to left to find the beginning of the address lines 232
on the envelope; then it reads from left to right, starting with the 249
bottom line and reading toward the top. Thus, addresses on en- 261
velopes must appear within a specified "read zone"; otherwise, the 274
envelopes will be rejected and will have to be manually sorted. 287

Addressing guides supplied by the U.S. Postal Service are 299
recommended for both personal and business mail. 309

1

224

224a ▶5 Conditioning practice

each line twice SS; repeat selected lines as time permits

The big, quaint plaza in Jamaica provides a folk dancer ways to relax.
In Chapter 7, Section 6, read the following pages: 198, 205, and 234.
The rate on Tom's $4,350 note went up from 7% to 8.5% on May 12, 1976.
The big brown canine with many spots remained motionless on the porch.

| 1 | 2 | 3 | 4 | 5 | 6 | 7 | 8 | 9 | 10 | 11 | 12 | 13 | 14 |

224b ▶45 Measure production skill: tables

Follow the time schedule for 222b, page 350. Center by longest item in each column, whether a heading or an entry.

Problem 1
Four-column table

full sheet; DS; center vertically; 4 spaces between columns

words

BUSINESS MACHINES INVENTORY 6

For the Year Ended December 31, 19-- 13

Equipment	Manufacturer	Model	Serial No.	words
				29
Electronic calculator	Texas Instruments	1310A	17253	39
Card programmer	Wang	CP-2-M	485988	46
Offset duplicator	Gestetner	1000	12841	54
Mimeograph	A. B. Dick	MP418	315845A	61
Adding machine	Friden	ACY 10	927093	68
Electric typewriter	Royal	590	14-3746314	77
Electric typewriter	IBM	Standard D	6914432	85
Posting machine	Burroughs	91053	B0091138	93

Problem 2
Ruled table with 2-line headings

full sheet; SS; reading position; 8 spaces between columns

words

DATA ON THE FIRST THIRTEEN STATES 7
TO JOIN THE UNION 10

37

State	Capital City	Entered Union	Population 1970 Census	words
				43
				48
				62
Delaware	Dover	1787	548,104	67
Pennsylvania	Harrisburg	1787	11,793,090	75
New Jersey	Trenton	1787	7,168,164	82
Georgia	Atlanta	1788	4,589,575	88
Connecticut	Hartford	1788	3,032,217	96
Massachusetts	Boston	1788	5,689,170	103
Maryland	Annapolis	1788	3,992,399	110
South Carolina	Columbia	1788	2,590,516	117
New Hampshire	Concord	1788	737,681	124
Virginia	Richmond	1788	4,648,494	131
New York	Albany	1788	18,241,266	137
North Carolina	Raleigh	1789	5,082,059	145
Rhode Island	Providence	1790	949,723	152

165

68

68a ▶7 Conditioning practice

1. Each line twice SS (slowly, faster).
2. A 1′ writing on Line 4, then on Line 2; compare *gwam*.

alphabet We requested twelve cans of zone marking paint expressly for that job.
figures They purchased 205 pines, 167 firs, and 83 blue and 49 silver spruces.
trigraphs mat matter format automate store restore storage cause because caustic
fluency They must work with vigor to stay within it when they submit a budget.
| 1 | 2 | 3 | 4 | 5 | 6 | 7 | 8 | 9 | 10 | 11 | 12 | 13 | 14 |

68b ▶13 Learn to align and type over words

1. Type the sentence as shown below.

I can align this copy.

2. Study and follow the numbered steps given at the right.

Your typed line should look like this:

I can align this copy.

Not like this:

I can align this copy.

I can align this copy.

3. As time permits, repeat the drill to develop skill in aligning and typing over to make corrections in copy.

Aligning and typing over words

It is sometimes necessary to reinsert the paper to correct an error. The following steps will help you learn to do so correctly.

1. Type a line of copy in which one or more *i's* appear (such as *I can align this copy* which you have just typed). Leave the paper in your typewriter.

2. Locate **aligning scale (21)** and **variable line spacer (3)** on your typewriter.

3. Move carriage (carrier) so that a word containing an *i* (such as *align*) is above the aligning scale. Note that a vertical line points to the center of *i*.

4. Study the relation between top of aligning scale and bottoms of letters with downstems (*g, p, y*).
Get an exact eye picture of the relation of typed line to top of scale so you will be able to adjust the paper correctly to type over a word with exactness.

5. Remove the paper; reinsert it. Gauge the line so bottoms of letters are in correct relation to top of aligning scale. Operate the *variable line spacer,* if necessary, to move the paper up or down.

Operate the *paper release lever* to move paper left or right, if necessary, when centering the letter *i* over one of the lines on the aligning scale.

6. Check accuracy of alignment by setting the *ribbon control* in stencil position and typing over one of the letters. If necessary, make further alignment adjustments.

7. Return ribbon control to normal position (to type on black).

8. Type over the words in the sentence, moving paper up or down, to left or right, as necessary for correct alignment.

223b, continued

Problem 2
Unbound report with side headings

	words	Prob. 2	Prob. 3

NORTHWEST POWER AND LIGHT COMPANY 7
Dividends Report 10 20

(¶ 1) The Board of Directors of the Northwest Power and Light Company declared the regular cash dividend of $1.20 per share of common stock and $2.75 per share of preferred stock for the first quarter. These dividends are payable May 20, 19--, to shareholders of record March 21, 19--. 23 33 / 38 48 / 54 63 / 67 76

Change in Dividend Payment Dates 80

(¶ 2) A change in quarterly dividend payment dates from the present schedule of the first day of February, May, August, and November to the 20th day of each of these months was approved by the Board at its last meeting. This change will become effective with the May, 19--, dividend payment. 93 90 / 108 105 / 124 120 / 137 134

(¶ 3) The recently adopted Securities and Exchange Commission regulations make it desirable for a company's independent auditors to review interim financial statements prior to their release. Therefore, the dividend payment dates have been changed to allow additional time for preparing quarterly interim financial reports to shareholders. 151 148 / 165 162 / 181 178 / 196 192 / 204 201

Tax Status of Dividends 214

(¶ 4) All Company dividends paid on common and preferred stocks during the past year will be taxable in full. According to present estimates, this will be true for the current year as well. This information will be helpful in preparing Federal income tax returns. 227 / 244 / 260 / 265

Problem 3
Interoffice memorandum
[LM pp. 213, 214]
Address envelope.

Type ¶s 1, 2, and 3 of the Problem 2 report as an interoffice memorandum.

1. Omit the main, secondary, and side headings.

2. Use the memo headings shown below.

TO: Your teacher's full name FROM: Your name, **Secretary-Treasurer**
DATE: Current SUBJECT: **Dividends**

Problem 4
Page 2 of interoffice memorandum

Prepare 1 cc. Address the second page to Albert Hyde and use the current date.

words
Heading 8

checking service exists. Monthly statements provide accurate tax records. Customers who average 30 checks a month save $46 a year. (¶) Regular savings offer the convenience of the old-fashioned passbook where the current balance is always available. Interest is computed daily and paid quarterly. The schedule is as follows: 20 / 32 / 44 / 55 / 67 / 73

Minimum Deposit	Interest Earned	Minimum Time	words
			78 / 87
$ 1	5%	none	89
$ 100	6 %	1 year	92
$ 500	6½ %	2½ years	97
$ 1,000	7¼ %	4 years	102

(¶) Many other banking services--foreign and domestic--are available. A memo about some of them will be circulated next week. Please file these memos in your policy manual. 113 / 124 / 136

68c ▶30 Type page 2 of an unbound report

Problem 1

Type the copy at the right (the second page of the report begun in Lesson 67) in unbound report form. Type the page number at the right margin on the 4th line space from the top edge of the paper; TS below page number. SS the table with 8 spaces between columns.

Problem 2

Proofread your copy, using proofreader's marks to indicate needed corrections; then retype the copy, erasing and correcting errors as necessary.

elite

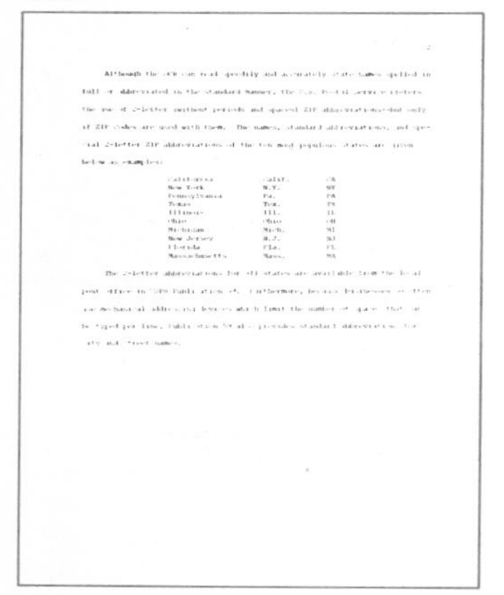

pica

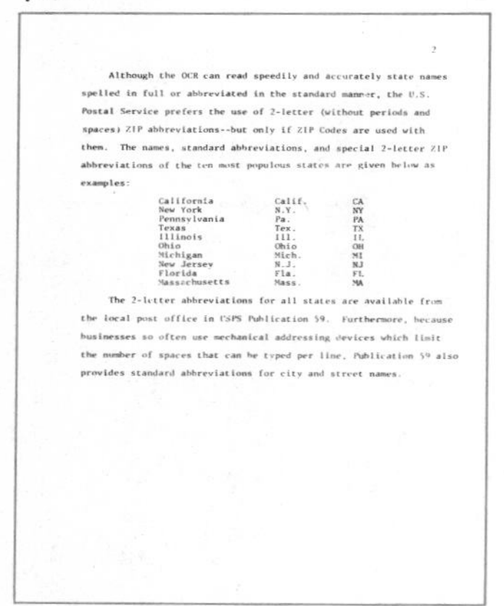

2

Although the OCR can read speedily and accurately state names spelled in full or abbreviated in the standard manner, the U.S. Postal Service prefers the use of 2-letter (without periods and spaces) ZIP abbreviations--but only if ZIP Codes are used with them. The names, standard abbreviations, and special 2-letter ZIP abbreviations of the ten most populous states are given below as examples:

California	Calif.	CA
New York	N.Y.	NY
Pennsylvania	Pa.	PA
Texas	Tex.	TX
Illinois	Ill.	IL
Ohio	Ohio	OH
Michigan	Mich.	MI
New Jersey	N.J.	NJ
Florida	Fla.	FL
Massachusetts	Mass.	MA

The 2-letter abbreviations for all states are available from the local post office in USPS Publication 59. Furthermore, because businesses so often use mechanical addressing devices which limit the number of spaces that can be typed per line, Publication 59 also provides standard abbreviations for city and street names.

	words
Although the OCR can read speedily and accurately	10
state names spelled in full or abbreviated in the	20
standard manner, the U.S. Postal Service prefers	30
the use of 2-letter (without periods and spaces) ZIP	40
abbreviations--but only if ZIP Codes are used	50
with them. The names, standard abbreviations, and	60
special 2-letter ZIP abbreviations of the ten most	70
populous states are given below as examples:	79

California	Calif.	CA	83
New York	N.Y.	NY	87
Pennsylvania	Pa.	PA	91
Texas	Tex.	TX	94
Illinois	Ill.	IL	97
Ohio	Ohio	OH	100
Michigan	Mich.	MI	103
New Jersey	N.J.	NJ	107
Florida	Fla.	FL	110
Massachusetts	Mass.	MA	115

The 2-letter abbreviations for all states are	124
available from the local post office in USPS Publi-	134
cation 59. Furthermore, because businesses so	143
often use mechanical addressing devices which	152
limit the number of spaces that can be typed	161
per line, Publication 59 also provides standard	171
abbreviations for city and street names.	179

222b, continued

Problem 3
Letter with subject line and listed enclosures

executive size, modified block, mixed

	words
Current date Mrs. Fred V. Bluberg 114 Padre Island Drive Corpus Christi,	15
TX 78410 Dear Mrs. Bluberg Subject: Bank Services (¶ 1) The many omi-	28
nous news stories about dwindling bank profits and foreclosed real estate loans	44
do not apply to Peoples National Bank. According to the enclosed Statement of	60
Condition, we can feel justifiably proud of our progress in loans, deposits,	75
and earnings. (¶ 2) Our philosophy has always been to minimize expenses.	89
Rather than investing in a high-cost, hard-to-maintain facility, we operate in	105
a leased building in a convenient shopping mall--and we plan to continue this	120
practice. (¶ 3) Thank you for your support in the past, particularly through	135
your loan and deposit relationship with us. You will be interested in the addi-	150
tional services we offer, which are described in the enclosed brochure. Sin-	166
cerely yours Ray M. Kline President xx Enclosures Statement of Condition	180
Bank Services Brochure (139)	185/**198**

Problem 4
AMS letter

1. Type the Problem 3 letter in the AMS style on full-size stationery.

2. Substitute the ¶ at the right for ¶ 3.

	words
We hope you will continue our pleasant financial	10
relationship. Please read the enclosed brochure.	20
It describes some additional services we offer	29
that may be new to you. (Total letter count: 190 words)	34

223

223a ▶5 Conditioning practice

each line twice SS; repeat selected lines as time permits

As experts may have zero proof, both keen judges will acquit the lady.
The meeting was held at 9376 East Street on Monday, June 28, at 10:45.
Furnace OTT/85 weighs 365#, uses 16″ by 20″ filters, and costs $1,293.
Walk down the aisle to the front if the balcony lights are turned off.

| 1 | 2 | 3 | 4 | 5 | 6 | 7 | 8 | 9 | 10 | 11 | 12 | 13 | 14 |

223b ▶45 Measure production skill: interoffice memorandums and reports

Follow the procedures and time schedule given for 222b, page 350.

Problem 1
Interoffice memorandum
[LM pp. 211, 212]
Address COMPANY MAIL envelope.

	words
TO: Rebecca W. Lang FROM: Lytle C. Estes, Manager DATE: February 15,	11
19-- SUBJECT: Monthly Service Rate Increase (¶ 1) The cost of materials,	22
labor, and associated services have increased considerably during the past 18	38
months. We have preferred to absorb these rising costs rather than pass them	53
on to our customers. However, we now find it necessary to make a modest	68
adjustment in our monthly service rate. (¶ 2) Effective March 1, 19--, the	82
monthly service charge for a primary outlet will be $15. Charges for connec-	97
tion and additional outlets will remain unchanged. The coupon book now being	113
prepared will reflect the new rate. (¶ 3) Please make all necessary prelimi-	127
nary arrangements for distribution of these coupon books when they are	141
delivered. xx	144/**151**

69

69a ▶7 Conditioning practice

1. Each line twice SS (slowly, faster).

2. Remove the paper; reinsert it; gauge the line and letter and type over Line 1.

alphabet	Jo climaxed her talk by awarding the prized silver plaque for service.
fig/sym	Check 48 (dated 6/1) for $93 covers Invoice 572 less the 10% discount.
trigraphs	use used uses write writing written since sincere grade graded upgrade
fluency	If their theory is right, they may be able to get it approved quickly.

| 1 | 2 | 3 | 4 | 5 | 6 | 7 | 8 | 9 | 10 | 11 | 12 | 13 | 14 |

69b ▶5 Improve technique: superscripts/subscripts

each line twice SS (slowly, faster); DS between 2-line groups

super	The exponent of x is 4 in the monomial $10x^4$ (10x to the fourth power).
sub	Heavy doses of vitamins B_1, B_6, and B_{12} were prescribed by Dr. Gorham.
both	A discussion of vitamin B_6 is given on page 8 of Vol. 23, Britannica.[1]

69c ▶15 Goal typing: paragraphs

1. A 1′ writing on ¶ 1; determine *gwam*.

2. Add 4 *gwam* to set a new goal rate.

Goals

	▼	■	●
1′	31	37	43

▼ acceptable
■ good
● excellent

3. Select from goals in ¶ 1 the one nearest your goal rate.

4. Two 1′ writings on ¶ 1, trying to reach or exceed your goal.

5. Type ¶ 2 in the same way.

6. A 5′ writing on ¶s 1–3 combined; determine *gwam*; circle errors.

all letters used | LA | 1.4 si | 5.4 awl | 85% hfw |

gwam 5′

People who study the problems of nutrition and the human body say 3
that many of us are overfed but undernourished. They mean that we use 5
too much of the wrong types of food. They quip that if we are what we 8
eat, many people are little more than cola, cheeseburger, and potatoes. 11

Students of nutrition tell us that variety in our food may be even 14
more important than how much we take in. They call for balance in daily 17
diets. For example, they ask us to include more fruit and green vege- 20
tables each day and to lower the quantity of sweets, starches, and fats. 22

Just as balance is wanted in what we eat, so it is with when we 25
eat. Nutritionists suggest that everyone have at least a light break- 28
fast. Further, they say we should have a sizable meal at midday. Fi- 31
nally, they think we should take only a limited amount of food at night. 33

gwam 5′ | 1 | 2 | 3 |

222

222a ▶5 Conditioning practice

each line twice SS; repeat selected lines as time permits

The vain jester quickly seized the glowing report from the box office.
The serial number of the RDL-106 electronic calculator is 283-00-5974.
Jackson & Fryer's invoice #63958, dated November 4, totaled $7,182.20.
When you have finished the eight problems, just signal the instructor.

| 1 | 2 | 3 | 4 | 5 | 6 | 7 | 8 | 9 | 10 | 11 | 12 | 13 | 14 |

222b ▶45 Measure production skill: business letters

Time schedule
Preparation .... 5′
Timed production ... 30′
Final check; compute *n–pram* .. 10′

1 cc; envelope for each letter; correct errors

Arrange letterheads [LM pp. 203–210], carbon paper, second sheets, and eraser for easy handling.

1. For 30′, type Problems 1–4. If you complete the letters before time is called, start again with Problem 1 on plain paper.

2. Proofread, circle any uncorrected errors. Compute *n–pram*.

Problem 1
Block style, open

words

Current date Mr. Samuel W. Privette, Jr. 99 Laramie Drive Reno, NV 89502 15

Dear Mr. Privette 19

(¶ 1) Now is the time for us to ask our members to pledge their commitment 33
to animal welfare by renewing their memberships in the Humane Society. For 48
your convenience, a membership card and envelope are enclosed for your 62
contribution or pledge. (¶ 2) Your Society last year answered more than 75
20,000 calls and traveled over 30,000 miles in the interest of animals, pro- 90
viding medical treatment and care. It was your generous gift last year that 106
enabled our volunteers to relieve the suffering of many helpless animals and 121
to bring the message of respect for all living things to thousands of citizens. 137
With your financial backing and interest, the Society will continue its dedica- 153
tion to the "welfare of the helpless" and its service to animals and people. 169
(¶ 3) Please mail your membership card and contribution or pledge in the 182
preaddressed envelope. 187

Sincerely yours CHURCHILL COUNTY HUMANE SOCIETY 196

Mrs. Ann M. Suarez, President xx Enclosures (168) 205/**217**

Type the Problem 1 letter, but substitute ¶s 2 and 3 at the right.

Problem 2
Modified block, mixed

words

(¶2) Numerous members of the Society gave lectures, seminars, and 12
programs on "the welfare of the helpless" to schools, churches, and 26
civic groups in the country. We estimate that over 15,000 children 39
and adults attended these presentations. (¶3) May we receive your 52
financial support or pledge within the next ten days? To know 64
your concern for animal welfare will help our efficiency in the year 78
ahead. (Total letter count: 176 words) 79

69d ▶23 Learn to type footnotes

1. Adjust your machine for typing an unbound report.
2. Study the guides and illustrations for typing report footnotes.
3. From the appropriate model (pica or elite), type the final line of the report and the footnotes beneath it.
4. Check the spacing of your completed work.
5. From the appropriate model, type all lines of the report as shown.

Guides for typing footnotes

1. Type a superior figure (superscript) in the text to indicate each footnote reference.
2. In planning a manuscript page, save 2 lines for a divider line and the spaces before and after it. Save 3 or 4 lines for each footnote to be typed on the page and 6 lines for the bottom margin.
3. Type a footnote on the same page with its corresponding superior figure.
4. After typing last line of text on a page, SS and type a 1½" divider line; then DS and type the footnote SS with a 5-space ¶ indention.
5. If two or more footnotes are to be typed on same page, DS between them.
6. A *page line gauge* will help in planning footnotes. (See LM p. 81). Place it back of a full sheet with the line numbers extending to the right; insert the two sheets; note the number of lines to be left for the divider line and footnotes; make a light pencil mark at that point on your copy sheet.

pica

22 According to one source, "Today it is estimated that job changes
21
20 are expected several times in each worker's life."[1] Moreover, as
19
18 Aurner and Burtness have said, "Your personal skill in telling
17
16 what you can do is your best insurance for job security."[2]
15
14 ________________
13
12 [1]W. L. Blackledge, E. H. Blackledge, and H. J. Keily, The Job You Want--How to Get It (2d ed.; Cincinnati: South-Western Publishing Co., 1975), p. ii.
11
10
9 [2]R. R. Aurner and P. S. Burtness, Effective English for Business Communication (6th ed.; Cincinnati: South-Western Publishing Co., 1970), p. 501.
8
7
6
5
4
3
2
1

elite

20 According to one source, "Today it is estimated that job changes are expected
19
18 several times in each worker's life."[1] Moreover, as Aurner and Burtness have
17
16 said, "Your personal skill in telling what you can do is your best insurance
15
14 for job security."[2]
13
12 ________________
11 [1]W. L. Blackledge, E. H. Blackledge, and H. J. Keily, The Job You Want--How to Get It (2d ed.; Cincinnati: South-Western Publishing Co., 1975), p. ii.
10
9
8 [2]R. R. Aurner and P. S. Burtness, Effective English for Business Communication (6th ed.; Cincinnati: South-Western Publishing Co., 1970), p. 501.
7
6
5
4
3
2
1

221c ▶15 Measure basic skill: statistical copy

1. A 2′ writing on each ¶; determine *gwam*; circle errors.
2. A 5′ writing on ¶s 1–3 combined; determine *gwam*; circle errors.

all figures used | A | 1.5 si | 5.6 awl | 80% hfw

	gwam 2′	5′
A recent study of about 3,000 students at the end of the first year	7	3
of high school typewriting determined the percent of transfer of straight-	14	6
copy rate to various types of copy. It was found that the straight-copy	22	9
rate percent of transfer had a range from 90% to 91% on statistical copy,	29	12
80% to 82% on letter copy, 73% to 77% on rough-draft copy, and 48.5% to	36	14
57% on 3-column tabulation copy. Timings of 5 minutes in length and	43	17
gross words a minute were used.	46	18
When production timings of 20 minutes and gross words a minute were	7	21
used, the percent of transfer was somewhat lower than on the 5-minute	14	24
timings. The percent of transfer of straight-copy rate to letter pro-	21	27
duction was from 67% to 70%; rough-draft production, 61% to 70%; 3-column	29	30
tabulation production, 51% to 54%; and 5-column tabulation production,	36	33
27% to 29%. Net production rate a minute was also used on letter produc-	43	36
tion; the percent of transfer was from 50% to 52%.	48	38
Another study found after 18 weeks of typewriting that the percent	7	40
of transfer of straight-copy rate of the top 25% of the students was	14	43
from 54% to 89% on statistical copy, 69% to 93% on rough-draft copy, and	21	46
77% to 100% on script copy. At the end of four semesters, the percent	28	49
of transfer was from 70% to 82% on statistical copy, 80% to 90% on rough-	36	52
draft copy, and 95% to 100% on script copy.	40	53

gwam 2′ | 1 | 2 | 3 | 4 | 5 | 6 | 7
5′ | 1 | 2 | 3

221d ▶10 Improve tabulating technique

70-space line; DS

1. Clear tab stops. Set stops 10 and 25 spaces to the right of the center of the paper.
2. Align columns of figures at the right.

Investments	418,365.20	
Cash	170,913.00	
Common stock		500,000.00
Accounts receivable	225,875.48	
Notes payable		138,926.47
Accounts payable		97,531.50
Accrued interest receivable	2,783.45	
Income tax payable		10,475.00
Retained earnings		71,004.16
Total	817,939.13	817,937.13

70

70a ▶7 Conditioning practice

1. Each line twice SS (slowly, faster).
2. A 1′ writing on Line 4, then on Line 1; compare *gwam*.

alphabet	Joel found that good executives were able to analyze problems quickly.
figures	FOR URGENT CALLS: Fire, 561-7232; Police, 461-7000; Doctor, 841-5839.
trigraphs	are aware careful men mentioned amend women able table unable valuable
fluency	If they do not sign the agreement, all work will stop within six days.

| 1 | 2 | 3 | 4 | 5 | 6 | 7 | 8 | 9 | 10 | 11 | 12 | 13 | 14 |

70b ▶8 Align, erase, and correct an error

1. Type the ¶ once; proofread.
2. Remove the paper; reinsert it.
3. Gauge the line and letter. Select a word (in which there is an error, preferably).
4. Erase a letter and retype it correctly aligned with the other letters in the line.

Even though 4 years of college education are not required for many good jobs, 1 or 2 years of specialized training beyond high school often are. Furthermore, recent salary data indicate that workers with just 1 to 3 years of education beyond high school earn from $1,700 to $2,800 more per year than those with 3 or 4 years of high school education. It is possible, of course, to add to your earning power by attending evening school after starting a full-time job.

70c ▶10 Improve statistical typing skill

1. A 2′ writing on each ¶.
2. A 3′ writing on ¶s 1–2 combined; determine *gwam*; circle errors.

all figures used

	gwam 2′	3′
The day of the 1-cent postal card and the 3-cent first-class stamp	7	4
seems like a fond memory. In all likelihood, the 9-cent postal card,	14	9
the 13-cent first-class stamp, and the 18-cent overseas stamp will soon	21	14
pass into memory, also. Such has been the history of the U.S. Post	28	18
Office Department and its successor since 1971, the U.S. Postal Service.	35	23
Only 25 years ago, when 9 of 10 letters were sorted by hand and a	7	28
first-class stamp cost 3 cents, the postal worker earned $2,600 a year.	14	32
In 1976, with increased automation of mail handling and a first-class	21	37
stamp costing 13 cents, the average postal worker earned $13,921 a year.	28	42
It is little wonder, therefore, that postal officials are predicting a	35	47
postage increase to 14, 15, or even 16 cents for a first-class stamp.	42	51

gwam 2′ | 1 | 2 | 3 | 4 | 5 | 6 | 7 |
3′ | 1 | 2 | 3 | 4 | 5 |

unit **39** lessons 221–225

Measuring typewriting competence

Measurement goals

In the 5 lessons of Unit 39 you will demonstrate your ability to:

1. Type 5′ writings on straight copy and statistical copy of average difficulty at acceptable levels of speed and accuracy.

2. Arrange and type business letters, interoffice memos and reports, tables, and business forms at reasonable levels of quality (acceptability) and quantity (*n–pram* or number of problems).

Machine adjustments

1. Paper guide at *0*.

2. Ribbon control on black.

3. Margin stops: 70–space line for drills and ¶s; as directed for problems.

4. Line–space selector on *1* for drills; on 2 for ¶s; as directed for problems.

221

221a ▶5 Conditioning practice

each line twice SS; repeat selected lines as time permits

alphabet The exquisite black evening gown was fashioned by designer Joy Zampel.

figures Kurt met with 370 to 425 men from 7:45 to 8:30 p.m. on April 12, 1976.

fig/sym A set of 4 luggage tags (#132607) costs $8.50, plus $.95 for handling.

fluency The element of understanding the goals of men helps us in tight spots.

| 1 | 2 | 3 | 4 | 5 | 6 | 7 | 8 | 9 | 10 | 11 | 12 | 13 | 14 |

221b ▶20 Measure basic skill: straight copy

1. A 1′ writing on each ¶; determine *gwam*.

2. Two 5′ writings on ¶s 1–3 combined; determine *gwam* and circle errors on each writing.

all letters used

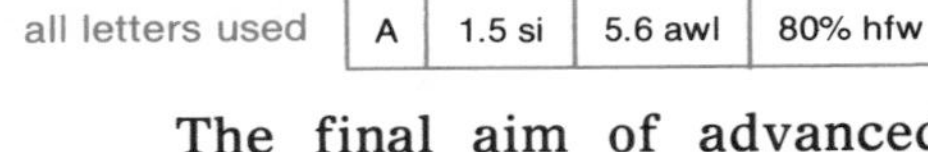

A	1.5 si	5.6 awl	80% hfw

	gwam 1′	5′
The final aim of advanced typewriting is to develop skills at the	13	3
production level necessary in the business world. It is recognized that	28	6
now less stress need be put on the development of straight-copy speed.	42	8
Basic skills such as control and accuracy must have been mastered if	56	11
production levels are to be achieved. A few other factors, too, must be	71	14
learned if efficient use is to be made of the basic skills.	82	16
In production typing, a number of jobs are assigned for a set period	14	19
of time. These jobs are concerned not only with basic skills but also	28	22
with the ability of the typist to read and to follow directions, to plan	43	25
how to type each problem, to make decisions before and during the typing	57	28
of each problem, to handle paper and supplies, to prepare carbon copies,	72	31
to check and correct errors carefully and neatly, to work under pressure,	87	34
and to produce work of an acceptable amount and quality.	98	36
As production jobs gain in complexity, it is noticeable that as the	14	39
amount of time spent in nontyping work increases, the rate of production	28	42
gets lower. In the area of production skills, the student should be	42	44
given goals to work toward; and both quality and quantity standards need	57	47
to be set up. These will enable the student to transfer skill mastery to	71	50
the actual tasks to be done in an office.	80	52

gwam 1′ | 1 | 2 | 3 | 4 | 5 | 6 | 7 | 8 | 9 | 10 | 11 | 12 | 13 | 14 |
5′ | 1 | 2 | 3 |

Enrichment material for Unit 39 appears on LM pp. 197–200.

70d ▶25 Type an unbound report with footnotes

1. Adjust your machine for typing an unbound report.

2. Before typing the report, type the footnotes to be certain of the number of lines each will take.

3. Use a *page line gauge* to plan vertical spacing and footnotes. (LM p. 81)

4. SS and indent the listed items from the left margin; DS above and below the list.

words

EMPLOYMENT COMMUNICATION 5

A good job is a major goal of most people. According to one source, 19
"Today it is estimated that job changes are expected several times in 33
each worker's life."[1] Employment involves three phases: (1) locating a 47
job, (2) getting it, and (3) keeping it. 56

A variety of sources may be used in obtaining full- or part-time 69
or summer employment. The following ones may be helpful. 81

1. Relatives and friends can provide job leads. 91
2. Teachers and counselors have employment contacts. 102
3. Local newspapers carry help-wanted advertisements. 113
4. Local employment agencies have many job listings. 124
5. Local companies have employment offices. 133

Once a job contact is made, both oral and written communication be- 146
come important. As Aurner and Burtness have said, "Your personal skill 161
in telling what you can do is your best insurance for job security."[2] 175
Their statement implies that communication is vital in both securing and 189
keeping a job. A personal interview is an essential step in getting a 203
job, and it requires primarily oral communication. Often an application 218
letter is required, and a data sheet is generally requested, also. Each 233
of these is a test of your skill in writing effectively. 244

Keeping the job once you have been hired is as much a matter of per- 258
sonal attitude and behavior as it is of performance skill. 269

______________ 273

[1] W. L. Blackledge, E. H. Blackledge, and H. J. Keily, <u>The Job You Want--How to Get It</u> (2d ed.; Cincinnati: South-Western Publishing Co., 1975), p. ii. 289 307 309

[2] R. R. Aurner and P. S. Burtness, <u>Effective English for Business Communication</u> (6th ed.; Cincinnati: South-Western Publishing Co., 1970), p. 501. 328 346 347

220b, continued

Problem 2
Bill of lading

words

FROM Antrim Wholesale Jewelers, Inc. AT Dallas, TX DATE 2/15/-- (10)
CONSIGNED TO AND DESTINATION Mongo Jewelry Company 1845 Fairmount (18)
Street Wichita, KS 67208 CUST. ORDER NO. CK-057269 DELIVERING CARRIER (25)
Griffith Express CAR INITIAL AND NO. ZP-39820 (30)

NO. PACKAGES	DESCRIPTION	WEIGHT	words
8	5-piece coffee and tea service	190#	38
10	Food warmer, 2 qt. capacity	87#	44
24	Covered vegetable dish w/glass liner	105#	53
24	Relish dish, 15" diameter w/glass insert	175#	63

SHIPPER Antrim Wholesale Jewelers, Inc. PERMANENT POST OFFICE ADDRESS (70)
OF SHIPPER 1321 Commerce Street, Dallas, TX 75202 SHIPPER'S NO. H-205684-J (80)

Problem 3
Invoice

SOLD TO: Mongo Jewelry Company — DATE February 20, 19-- (8)
1845 Fairmount Street — OUR ORDER NO. KE-1905627 (15)
Wichita, KS 67208 — CUST. ORDER NO. CK-057269 (20)
TERMS: Net 10 days — SHIPPED VIA Griffith Express (26)

QUANTITY	DESCRIPTION	UNIT PRICE	TOTAL	words
8	5-piece coffee and tea service;			36
	covered sugar bowl; tray	153.00	1224.00	44
10	Food warmer, 2 qt. capacity	39.00	390.00	52
24	Covered vegetable dish with glass liner	31.00	744.00	64
24	Relish dish, 15" diameter, 5-compartment			72
	glass insert	42.50	1020.00	79
			3378.00	81
	Tax		202.68	85
			3580.68	86

Problem 4
Bridal registry

words

Mongo Jewelry Company (4)
Bridal Registry (8)

Name	Address	Wedding Date	Silver Pattern	China Pattern	words
					12
					19
Myra Abrams	4019 Westlake	5/20/--	Mystique	Nocturnal	29
Dianne Baker	3687 Auburn	5/23/--	Lancelot	Bouquet	39
Nancy Caputo	1025 Larimer	5/27/--	Romanesque	Dawn	49
Maria Chavez	6934 Pacific	6/1/--	Tropicana	Sunburst	60
Marilyn Davis	7801 Rosewood	6/3/--	Louis VI	Normandy	70
Doris Rubin	2639 Bigelow	6/8/--	Regal	Enchant	80
Rose Sanchez	4758 Escuela	6/10/--	Barcelona	Floral	90
Carole Snell	3046 Winslow	6/15/--	Baroness	Tudor	100
Martha Street	1928 Emerald	6/20/--	Princely	Encore	110
Paula Zimmer	5701 Wilkins	6/27/--	Transcend	Embassy	120

71

71a ▶7 Conditioning practice

1. Each line twice SS (slowly, faster).
2. Remove the paper; reinsert it; gauge the line and letter and type over Line 4.

alphabet	Wise judges of the market expect a big zoom in our quarterly dividend.
fig/sym	He said, "Check Sections 4-5, pages 230-259, of Volume XVI (6/18/77)."
trigraphs	her here otherwise per permit proper time sometime very every everyone
fluency	It is the height of idiocy to fight change, as change is sure to come.

| 1 | 2 | 3 | 4 | 5 | 6 | 7 | 8 | 9 | 10 | 11 | 12 | 13 | 14 |

71b ▶8 Improve rough-draft typing skill

70-space line; be guided by the bell to return

two 3′ writings on ¶s 1–2 combined; determine *gwam*; circle errors

all letters used

	gwam 3′
What type of careeer do you hope to enter after you have com-	4
pleted school?The selection available to you is almost endless.	8
Name your choice and it is available. However, each choice comes	13
with its ownset of education, training and skill requirements.	17
Moreover, every career choice has an amazingly large assortment of	21
specific job categories; yet each of thees has a different require-	25
ments.	28
In the last twenty-five years, the work picture has been changed	32
quite rapidly and sometimes quite drastically. As new types of	36
jobs was created, other job categories disappeared completely	41
or were severly reduced in numbers of people needed to man	45
them. Even though the growth in office jobs is expected to con-	49
tinue unabated, the characteristics of those jobs will change--	53
in location, in type of service or industry, and in requirements.	57

71c ▶35 Review outline and report style

1. Make a list of the problems identified at the right for quick reference.

page 107, 67c
page 112, 69d, Step 5
page 114, 70d

2. Type as many of the problems as you can as you are timed for 30′. Correct errors.

220

220a ▶5
Conditioning practice

each line twice SS; repeat selected lines as time permits

Kim Zajac gave exquisite flowers for their beauty pageant decorations.
They bought 209 locks, 178 keys, 63 chains, and 54 tires for bicycles.
Wise & Cook signed a note for $13,375 ($12,500 + $875 interest at 7%).
It is essential that all invoices be verified for accuracy when typed.

| 1 | 2 | 3 | 4 | 5 | 6 | 7 | 8 | 9 | 10 | 11 | 12 | 13 | 14 |

220b ▶45
Measure production: purchase orders, bills of lading, invoices

Time schedule

Preparation .... 6′
Timed production ... 30′
Final check;
compute *n–pram* .. 9′

1. Arrange supplies [LM pp. 179–186], second sheets, carbon paper, eraser.

2. Make 2 cc's of each problem typed (1 on plain paper).

3. When directed to begin, type for 30′ from the following problems, correcting all errors neatly. Proofread before removing problems from the typewriter.

4. If you finish all problems in less than 30′, retype Problem 4 on plain paper; then compute *n–pram* for the 30′ period.

5. Turn in all problems in the order listed.

Problem 1
Purchase order

words

MONGO JEWELRY COMPANY
1845 FAIRMOUNT STREET WICHITA, KS 67208
PHONE: (316)662-0589

PURCHASE ORDER

Purchase order No. CK-057269 — 2

Antrim Wholesale Jewelers, Inc. — 6
1321 Commerce Street — 12
Dallas, TX 75202

Date February 11, 19-- — 12
Terms Net 10 days — 19
Ship Via Griffith Express — 25

Quantity	Cat. No.	Description	Price	Total	words
8	Z-57-8923	5-piece coffee and tea service; covered sugar bowl; tray	153.00	1224.00	34 / 42
10	J-03-6411	Food warmer, 2 qt. capacity	39.00	390.00	53
24	L-36-4905	Covered vegetable dish with glass liner	31.00	744.00	61 / 66
24	P-20-3159	Relish dish, 15" diameter, 5-compartment glass insert	42.50	1020.00	74 / 84
				3378.00	85

By ______________________ Purchasing Agent

72

72a ▶7 Conditioning practice

1. Each line twice SS (slowly, faster).
2. A 1′ writing on Line 4, then on Line 2; compare *gwam*.

alphabet	Margie expertly sewed five square white buttons on a jet black blazer.
figures	These stock numbers need to be replenished: X2938, B10562, and J4702.
trigraphs	any many company end ends extend year yearly midyear cent cents recent
fluency	Shelby has the right data, but he obviously drew the wrong conclusion.

| 1 | 2 | 3 | 4 | 5 | 6 | 7 | 8 | 9 | 10 | 11 | 12 | 13 | 14 |

72b ▶8 Check keystroking skill

a 5′ writing; determine *gwam*; circle errors

all letters used | A | 1.5 si | 5.6 awl | 80% hfw |

	gwam 1′	5′
You are on your way now to becoming a real typist. You have built	13	3
your basic skill to at least a minimum level with acceptable technique.	28	6
You have demonstrated that you can type from handwritten and corrected	42	8
copy with a fair degree of skill. You can type copy that contains num-	56	11
bers and common symbols without often looking at the keys. Finally, you	71	14
have learned to arrange and type copy in the most common forms.	84	17
If your basic skill level is just barely thirty words a minute, you	14	19
should by all means take another term of typewriting to add another ten	28	22
words to your rate. If you are pushing forty words a minute, one more	42	25
term should help you reach fifty--the minimum level for really effective	57	28
usability. And if you want to become a vocational typist, you will want	71	31
the advantages of a vocational course offered in a second year.	84	34
You are on the brink of discovering that typewriting is not only	13	36
faster but also easier than writing with pen or pencil. As you become	27	39
more expert, you will realize that your fingers can keep up with your	41	42
thoughts as you begin to develop, compose, and type your letters, re-	55	45
ports, or other papers for personal and school use. So don't stop with	69	48
the first success. Persist and develop a very vital skill.	81	50

gwam 1′ | 1 | 2 | 3 | 4 | 5 | 6 | 7 | 8 | 9 | 10 | 11 | 12 | 13 | 14 |
5′ | 1 | 2 | 3 |

218c, continued

Problem 2
Invoice

				words
SOLD TO:	United Metals, Inc.	DATE	January 30, 19--	7
	110 South State Street	OUR ORDER NO.	PW-30751-B	14
	Chicago, IL 60604	CUST. ORDER NO.	N-75042	19
TERMS:	2/10, n/30	SHIPPED VIA	Ace Trucking	24

QUANTITY	DESCRIPTION	UNIT PRICE	TOTAL	words
100 reams	Bond paper, 25% rag, 8 1/2″ × 11″ water-			34
	marked, printed letterhead	5.25	525.00	42
250 reams	Offset paper, white, 60#, 8 1/2″ × 11″,			52
	printed masthead	3.80	950.00	58
10,000	Envelopes, #10 white, 24# base, printed			67
	return address	10.60	106.00	73
10,000	Envelopes, #9 white, 24# base, printed			82
	return address	10.00	100.00	89
			1681.00	91

Problem 3
Invoice

				words
SOLD TO:	United Metals, Inc.	DATE	January 30, 19--	7
	110 South State Street	OUR ORDER NO.	GJ-095627	14
	Chicago, IL 60604	CUST. ORDER NO.	N-75043	19
TERMS:	2/10, n/30	SHIPPED VIA	Badger Freight	25

QUANTITY	DESCRIPTION	UNIT PRICE	TOTAL	words
32	Steel file, full suspension, 26″ deep			33
	w/lock. Beige	129.65	4148.80	39
10	25-drawer, Slim Form cabinets,			46
	45″ × 34″ × 1 1/8″ high	790.00	7900.00	53
1	Light table w/shelf	345.00	345.00	61
2	Paper cutter, automatic	217.00	434.00	70
			12827.80	72

219

219a ▶5 Conditioning practice

each line twice SS; repeat selected lines as time permits

Lew Zaretsky sold adjustable hiking equipment to five expert climbers.
He shipped 173 cars, 209 light trucks, 64 buses, and 85 vans overseas.
Cox & May will receive $9,510.46 ($8,765.40 cash + $745.06 in checks).
If you save time in handling materials, your production will increase.
| 1 | 2 | 3 | 4 | 5 | 6 | 7 | 8 | 9 | 10 | 11 | 12 | 13 | 14 |

219b ▶45 Build sustained production: purchase orders, bills of lading, invoices

Time schedule

Preparation .... 6′
Timed production ... 30′
Final check;
compute *n–pram* .. 9′

1. Make a list of problems to be typed:

page 342, 216c, Problem 2
page 343, 217c, Problem 2
page 345, 218c, Problem 2
page 342, 217b

2. Arrange supplies [LM pp. 173–178] second sheets, carbon paper, eraser.

3. Make 2 cc's for each problem typed (1 on plain paper).

4. When directed to begin, type for 30′ from the list of prob–lems, correcting all errors neatly. Proofread before removing the problems from the machine.

Determine *n–pram* for the 30′ period.

5. Turn in problems in the order listed.

72c ▶35 Type a 2-page unbound report with footnotes

1. Adjust your machine for typing an unbound report.

2. Use a *page line gauge* to plan vertical spacing, page number location, and footnotes [LM p. 81]. Type the footnotes on the same page as their reference figures.

3. Indent listed items 5 spaces from both margins; SS individual items; DS between items.

Note: With the footnote placed to leave a 6-line (1") bottom margin, there will be on page 1 one additional space in the pica solution and three additional spaces in the elite solution above the footnote divider line.

words

ADDRESSING FOR EFFICIENT MAIL HANDLING 8
TS

All who depend upon the U.S. Postal Service to process, sort, and deliver their mail to proper destinations seek two benefits: speed and low cost. From Pony Express to rail service through piston planes to jets, the speed of transporting mail from "here" to "there" has been drastically increased. But so has postage cost to the mailer--individual and business alike. 82

Major attempts have been made recently to match the internal speed and efficiency of processing and sorting mail with the external speed of moving mail from place to place once it has been processed and sorted. These efforts include the use of ZIP Codes, OCR's, bar coding devices, and a variety of sorting machines. 146

It is difficult to tell, however, just how efficient these new systems are because of the steadily increasing volume of mail that must be handled. According to a report of the Postmaster General, the total number of pieces of first-class mail processed in fiscal year 1970-71 was 48,640,276,000,[1] less than 4 percent of which were processable by OCR. Both the volume of first-class mail and the percent processable by OCR have increased since 1971. Nevertheless, it is reliably estimated that probably 95 percent of first-class mail must be sorted by less sophisticated, less efficient sorting equipment or sorted by hand.[2] 271

______________ 275

[1] Annual Report of the Postmaster General, 1971. 285

[2] Letter from Program Director, Preferential Mail Processing Department, U.S. Postal Service, 1976. 305

words

2 305

To increase the percentage of mail processable by OCR and other mechanical equipment, and thus reduce the cost, the U.S. Postal Service suggests the following addressing practices: 341
DS

1. Use block-style format, all lines having a uniform left margin. 355
DS
2. Use uppercase letters without punctuation. 365
3. Type account numbers, attention lines, and so forth, above the second line from the bottom. 385
4. Type the street address or box number on the second line from the bottom. 401
5. Type apartment numbers (when used) immediately after the street address and on the same line. 421
6. Type the city name, the two-letter state abbreviation, and the ZIP Code on the last line. (The ZIP Code should not be typed on a line by itself.) 452
DS

OCR equipment can read ALL-CAP, unpunctuated addresses more efficiently than those typed in cap-and-lowercase letters with punctuation. Human sorters, however, read the latter more efficiently when hand sorting or precoding for subsequent mechanical processing. It is likely, therefore, that cap-and-lowercase addresses will be acceptable by the U.S. Postal Service for at least several years. 531

Enrichment material for Unit 11 appears on LM pp. 83, 84.

218

218a ▶5 Conditioning practice

each line twice SS; repeat selected lines as time permits

Val Mazurek acquired major wax pieces early in the firm's big auction.
She lectured to four classes having 203, 178, 59, and 46 new students.
Ray & Park's new machine (Model GO-5701) cost $3,785.50 last December.
You will improve your figure-typing skill on invoices and other forms.

| 1 | 2 | 3 | 4 | 5 | 6 | 7 | 8 | 9 | 10 | 11 | 12 | 13 | 14 |

218b ▶10 Improve tabulating technique

1. Clear all tab stops.
2. Set stops to leave 8 spaces between columns given at the right.
3. Three 2′ writings. DO NOT TYPE HEADINGS.

Year	Net Sales	Profits Earned	Profits as % of Sales	words
This year	$168,000	$14,600	8.7	6
1 year ago	167,000	13,650	8.2	12
2 years ago	163,000	12,900	7.9	18
3 years ago	159,000	11,050	6.9	25
4 years ago	140,000	10,750	7.7	31

218c ▶35 Learn to type invoices

[LM pp. 167–172]

Problem 1
Invoice

CRAVER FURNITURE CO. 1709 Piedmont Avenue High Point, NC 27263 (919) 653-9042

Invoice

words

United Metals, Inc.
110 South State Street
Chicago, IL 60604

Date January 30, 19-- (3)

(7)

Our Order No. XP-570932 (14)

(18)

Cust. Order No. N-75041 (19)

Terms 2/10, n/30

Shipped Via N. C. Transport (22)

Quantity	Description	Unit Price	Total	words
8	Double-pedestal walnut executive desk, 72" x 36" x 29"	289.50	2316.00	31 / 37
4	Contour executive chair, swivel and tilt, 32" high	115.00	460.00	44 / 50
4	Executive chair, black, wood armrests, 17" high	90.00	360.00	58 / 62
8	Armchair, black, vinyl upholstery, 22 1/2" x 22 1/2" x 32"	70.00	560.00	70 / 79
			3696.00	81

unit **12** lessons 73–75

Performance evaluation

Measurement goals

In the 3 lessons of Unit 12 you will demonstrate your ability to type:

1. A series of average-difficulty 5′ writings on straight copy, rough draft, and statistical copy—each at levels of speed/control specified by your teacher.

2. Letters, announcements, tables, and unbound reports in proper format from semi-arranged copy according to specific directions.

73

73a ▶7 Conditioning practice

1. Each line twice SS (slowly, faster).

2. A 1′ writing on Line 4, then on Line 2; compare *gwam*.

alphabet Jack Zales will bring five exotic plants to display at the old mosque.

fig/sym A contract (No. 149370) signed May 28 raised the hourly rate to $8.56.

trigraphs act acted facts contact out outline south about rest arrest interested

fluency The six workers kept a log of the time spent on each phase of the job.

| 1 | 2 | 3 | 4 | 5 | 6 | 7 | 8 | 9 | 10 | 11 | 12 | 13 | 14 |

73b ▶8 Measurement: 5′ rough draft

70-space line; listen for bell

a 5′ writing; determine *gwam*; circle errors

all letters used | A | 1.5 si | 5.6 awl | 80% hfw |

	gwam 5′
Experts tells us that when we have something [a plan] that we wa nt	2
others to accept, the more expertly [skillfully] we put [convert] our plan into written	5
form the more likeyl we are to convince [persuade] the reeder [a] to adopt it.	8
If in our letters we ramble, use obscure [vague] references, make weak [poor]	10
choice of words, or use bad [poor] grammar, weincrease the likelihood of	13
having [our] ideas rejected. The receivers [recipients] of such letters will form [have]	16
a quite low opion [ni] of us, of our purposes [intentions,] and certainly of the	18
organization we represent in [through] our messages.	20
Like a good speech, our final copy should represent [reflect] our very best	23
effort. It should express [convey] what it has to say in a clear and con-	25
cise way [manner]. There should be no distracting features, such as smudges,	28
unattractive form [style], poor placement, or uneven [unequal] margins. In other	31
word, [s] if we are tobecome truly adept in the art of written com-	33
munication, we must avoid calling [drawing] attemtion [n] to how we present	36
something instead of [to] what we way [s]. Then only can we be certain	38
that our letters [messages] will result in [produce] the response or [the] action we want.	41

words

STRAIGHT BILL OF LADING—SHORT FORM—Original—Not Negotiable

RECEIVED, subject to the classifications and tariffs in effect on the date of issue of this Original Bill of Lading,

AGENT'S NO. ______

FROM Craver Furniture, Inc. AT High Point, NC DATE 1/24/-- 9

CONSIGNED TO AND DESTINATION

United Metals, Inc. 13
110 South State Street 18
Chicago, IL 60604 21

Subject to Section 7 of conditions of applicable bill of lading, if this shipment is to be delivered to the consignee without recourse on the consignor, the consignor shall sign the following statement:
The carrier shall not make delivery of this shipment without payment of freight and all other lawful charges.

(Signature of Consignor)

CUST. ORDER NO. N-75041 23
DELIVERING CARRIER North Carolina Transport CAR INITIAL AND NO. Y-9562 29

If charges are to be prepaid, write or stamp here, "To be Prepaid."

the property described below, in apparent good order, except as noted (contents and condition of contents of packages unknown) marked, consigned, and destined as indicated below which said carrier (the word carrier being understood throughout this contract as meaning any person or corporation in possession of the property under the contract) agrees to carry to its usual place of delivery at said destination, if on its route, otherwise to deliver to another carrier on the route to said destination. It is mutually agreed, as to each carrier of all or any of said property over all or any portion of said route to destination, and as to each party at any time interested in all or any of said property, that every service to be performed hereunder shall be subject to all the terms and conditions of the Uniform Domestic Straight Bill of Lading set forth (1) in Official, Southern, Western and Illinois Freight Classifications in effect on the date hereof, if this is a rail or a rail-water shipment, or (2) in the applicable motor carrier classification or tariff if this is a motor carrier shipment. **Shipper hereby certifies that he is familiar with all the terms and conditions of the said bill of lading, including those on the back thereof, set forth in the classification or tariff which governs the transportation of this shipment, and the said terms and conditions are hereby agreed to by the shipper and accepted for himself and his assigns.**

Received $ ______ to apply in prepayment of the charges on the property described hereon.

Agent or Cashier

NO. PACKAGES	DESCRIPTION OF ARTICLES	WEIGHT	RATE	CHK.	words
8	Double-pedestal executive desks	1925#			37
4	Contour shaped executive chairs	135#			45
4	Executive chairs, wood armrests	150#			53
8	Armchairs, black, vinyl upholstery	201#			61

Per ______ (The signature here acknowledges only the amount prepaid.)

Charges Advanced: $ ______

*If the shipment moves between two ports by a carrier by water, the law requires that the bill of lading shall state whether it is "carrier's or shipper's weight." Note—Where the rate is dependent on value, shippers are required to state specifically in writing the agreed or declared value of the property. **The agreed or declared value of the property is hereby specifically stated by the shipper to be not exceeding** ______ per ______

†Shipper's imprint in lieu of stamp; not a part of Bill of Lading approved by the Interstate Commerce Commission.

Craver Furniture, Inc. SHIPPER 66

Per ______ Agent, Per ______

†"The fibre boxes used for this shipment conform to the specifications set forth in the box maker's certificate thereon, and all other requirements of Uniform Freight Classification."

PERMANENT POST-OFFICE ADDRESS OF SHIPPER: 1709 Piedmont Avenue, High Point, NC 27263 75

SHIPPER'S NO.

2 Z-31074 76

217c ▶35 Learn to type bills of lading

[LM pp. 161–166]

Problem 1

Type bill of lading shown above.

Problem 2

Type bill of lading shown at right.

words

FROM **Lammey Printing & Paper Supply Co.** AT **Chicago, IL** DATE **1/24/--** 11
CONSIGNED TO AND DESTINATION **United Metals, Inc. 110 South State Street** 20
Chicago, IL 60604 CUST. ORDER NO. **N-75042** DELIVERING CARRIER **Ace** 26
Trucking CAR INITIAL AND NO. **J-9027** 29

NO. PACKAGES	DESCRIPTION	WEIGHT	words
10	Watermarked bond paper	530#	35
25	Offset paper, white	1424#	41
4	Envelopes, #10 white	125#	46
4	Envelopes, #9 white	125#	52

SHIPPER **Lammey Printing & Paper Supply Co.** PERMANENT POST OFFICE 59
ADDRESS OF SHIPPER **603 West Walnut Street, Chicago, IL 60606** SHIPPER'S 67
NO. **Q-10578** 69

Problem 3

Type bill of lading shown at right.

FROM **Schurtz Office Equipment Co.** AT **Milwaukee, WI** DATE **1/24/--** 10
CONSIGNED TO AND DESTINATION **United Metals, Inc. 110 South State Street** 19
Chicago, IL 60604 CUST. ORDER NO. **N-75043** DELIVERING CARRIER **Badger** 25
Freight CAR INITIAL AND NO. **P-8056** | **32 Steel files, full suspension** 35
4320# | **10 25-drawer, Slim Form cabinets 2200#** | **1 Light table, with shelf** 49
175# | **2 Paper cutters, automatic 80#** | SHIPPER **Schurtz Office Equipment Co.** 62
PERMANENT POST OFFICE ADDRESS OF SHIPPER **507 W. Wisconsin Ave.,** 67
Milwaukee, WI 53203 SHIPPER'S NO. **K-9856** 72

73c ▶35 Measurement: personal/business letters

3 letterheads (LM pp. 85, 87, 89)

In body of letter, listen for bell as signal to return carriage (or carrier); proofread and correct your work before removing it from the typewriter; address an envelope for each letter you type.

Problem 1

Monarch letterhead; line: 50; return address: Line 14; use the current date

	words
P.O. Box 1275 Kenton, OH 43326 Ms. Denise L. Ryan, Registrar	16
Lima Vocational/Technical School 1744 Shawnee Road Lima, OH 45806	29
Dear Ms. Ryan	32
¶ Thank you for sending to me the literature telling about course	45
offerings at Lima Vocational/Technical School. The information will	59
be quite helpful.	62
¶ Next month I shall be visiting friends in the Lima area. While	75
I am there, I would like very much to inquire about housing accom-	88
modations in the city. Does your office maintain a listing of	101
families who desire to rent rooms to students?	110
¶ Any assistance you can give me will be appreciated, since I do	123
not wish to wait until the last minute to locate housing for the	136
summer term. Sincerely yours Your name	146/**165**

Problem 2

Standard-size letterhead; line: 60; current date: Line 18

Mr. Stephen R. Gates Audiovision, Inc. One West Genesee Buffalo,	16
NY 14202 Dear Mr. Gates	21
¶ Thank you very much for submitting the outline and one unit of	33
manuscript for Think Metric.	42
¶ Your material has been studied carefully by several members of	55
our manuscript committee. Everyone believes you have an idea that	68
will be popular in the schools.	75
¶ We should like you to come to Palo Alto at our expense to dis-	87
cuss a number of development and production details with selected	100
members of our staff. Will you please let me know when it would	113
be most convenient for you to come.	120
Sincerely yours Stanford DeMille, Editor xx	129/**143**

Problem 3

Follow the directions given for Problem 2.

Dr. Edna Greenstreet Reading Laboratories, Inc. 535 Gravier New	16
Orleans, LA 70130 Dear Dr. Greenstreet	24
¶ Thank you for inquiring about the readability scale we apply to	36
the articles and features published in NEW HORIZONS.	47
¶ Because we have found that a single reading difficulty index is	60
inadequate, we actually use three: the Dale-Chall formula, the	73
Gunning Fog Index, and the Flesch formula. As you are aware, the	86
three formulas measure somewhat different factors.	96
¶ Our readership is somewhat above the norm in educational back-	108
ground. We therefore try to gear our articles at a readability	121
level of 12 to 14. Technical terminology, however, that is an in-	134
trinsic part of the language of any specialized field tends to	147
raise somewhat the readability level according to the formulas	159
we use.	161
¶ I hope these comments will be of some help to you.	172
Sincerely yours Mrs. Alice McGowan, Editor xx Enclosure	183/**199**

216c, continued

Problem 2
Purchase order

			words
TO: Lammey Printing & Paper Supply Co.	Order No.	N-75042	9
603 West Walnut Street	Date	January 11, 19--	17
Chicago, IL 60606	Terms	2/10, n/30	22
	Ship Via	Ace Trucking	25

QUANTITY	CAT. NO.	DESCRIPTION	PRICE	TOTAL	
100 reams	X-9506	Bond paper, 25% rag, 8 1/2″ × 11″,			35
		watermarked, printed letterhead	5.25	525.00	44
250 reams	X-3074	Offset paper, white, 60#,			53
		8 1/2″ × 11″, printed masthead	3.80	950.00	61
10,000	T-0987	Envelopes, #10 white, 24# base,			70
		printed return address	10.60	106.00	77
10,000	T-1735	Envelopes, #9 white, 24# base,			86
		printed return address	10.00	100.00	95
				1681.00	97

Problem 3
Purchase order

TO: Schurtz Office Equipment Co.	Order No.	N-75043	7
507 West Wisconsin Avenue	Date	January 11, 19--	16
Milwaukee, WI 53203	Terms	2/10, n/30	22
	Ship Via	Badger Freight	25

QUANTITY	CAT. NO.	DESCRIPTION	PRICE	TOTAL	
32	T-627-4208	Steel file, full suspension,			34
		26″ deep, w/lock. Beige	129.65	4148.80	42
10	T-402-3679	25-drawer, Slim Form cabinets,			51
		45″ × 34″ × 1 1/8″ high	790.00	7900.00	58
1	T-162-5403	Light table w/shelf	345.00	345.00	68
2	T-084-6129	Paper cutter, automatic	217.00	434.00	80
				12827.80	81

217

217a ▶5 Conditioning practice

each line twice SS; repeat selected lines as time permits

Jim Zilkowski acquired expert skill in playing ball for Victoria High.
He flew on trips of 34, 87, 195, and 260 miles during spring vacation.
West & Lee paid $12,309.85 ($7,634.85 + $4,675) for the extra acreage.
The purchase order is a basic business form used by many corporations.
| 1 | 2 | 3 | 4 | 5 | 6 | 7 | 8 | 9 | 10 | 11 | 12 | 13 | 14 |

217b ▶10 Alignment drill

1. With a pencil and ruler draw 3 horizontal lines about 4″ long.

2. Insert the paper and gauge the line of writing by using the variable line spacer.

3. Type the names and flight numbers given at the right, each on a separate ruled line. Check line alignment before typing.

	10 spaces	words
Ann Easton	Flight 706	4
Samuel Kim	Flight 458	9
David Stein	Flight 312	13

74

74a ▶7 Conditioning practice

1. Each line twice SS (slowly, faster).
2. A 1′ writing on Line 4, then on Line 1; compare *gwam*.

alphabet	The key project was proved adequate to give the magazines flexibility.
figures	On May 8 she ordered 750 sets of 6-ply NCR paper--No. 294731--for you.
trigraphs	par parts separate red reduce offered art articles each reach teachers
fluency	Our firm civic policy came as a mandate from the citizens of the city.

| 1 | 2 | 3 | 4 | 5 | 6 | 7 | 8 | 9 | 10 | 11 | 12 | 13 | 14 |

74b ▶8 Measurement: 5′ statistical copy

a 5′ writing; determine *gwam*; circle errors

all figures used | A | 1.5 si | 5.6 awl | 80% hfw |

	gwam 1′	5′
"The average cost of a business letter rose from $1.83 in 1960 to	13	3
$3.79 in 1975," says a recent report of Bergman-Carter, a well-known firm	28	6
of business consultants. This letter-cost increase of $1.96 per letter	42	8
(107.1%) is a crucial factor in the rising cost of doing business	56	11
today. If a firm produces 1,400 letters a week (at $3.79 a message),	70	14
cutting message-production cost by 10% would result in a saving in ex-	84	17
cess of $530.	86	17
To bring about this saving, special machines are being used in of-	13	20
fices all over the country. For example, an automatic typewriter which is	28	23
run by either punched or magnetic tape can type letters at a rate of 150	43	26
to 175 words a minute. A skilled operator can run 4 of these machines	57	29
at a time with each machine producing as many as 100 average-length	71	32
letters a day. Finally, a program can be run through a computer to print	85	34
letters at 600-700 lines a minute. Still, typists are needed to prepare	100	37
the original masters to operate these machines and to type in personalized	115	40
information at strategic points.	121	42

gwam 1′ | 1 | 2 | 3 | 4 | 5 | 6 | 7 | 8 | 9 | 10 | 11 | 12 | 13 | 14 |
5′ | 1 | 2 | 3 |

216b ▶10 Learn to arrange common business forms

Study the tips at the right and the illustration below for pointers on typing business forms.

Purchase order

A form used to order merchandise.

Bill of lading

A form issued by a common carrier to acknowledge receipt of goods to be shipped.

Invoice

A form for billing a customer for merchandise purchased.

Tips for typing purchase orders, bills of lading, and invoices

1. Set margin stop for address and first column; set tab stops for other "columnar" items, using the same stop more than once if possible.

2. SS the items in the description column unless there are 3 or fewer lines. With 2 or 3 single-line items, DS.

3. With an item of more than 1 line, indent the second and succeeding lines 3 spaces.

4. In the *total* column, underline the amount for the last item; then DS and type total.

5. Begin the items in the description column about 2 spaces from the ruled line.

6. Business papers like these are often mailed in window envelopes. (See RG p. vi.)

Note: The total amounts in the forms in this unit are shown without commas separating thousands and hundreds. The use of commas is equally correct.

216c ▶35 Learn to type purchase orders

Procedures for business forms in Lessons 216–218

Time schedule

Preparation .... 5′
Timed production ... 25′
Final check;
compute *n–pram* .. 5′

1. Arrange supplies [LM pp. 155–160]; carbon paper; eraser.

2. When directed to begin, assemble a carbon pack, insert it into the machine, and complete the forms according to the appropriate illustration provided.

3. Correct errors.

4. At signal to stop, make a final check of your work; circle any uncorrected errors.

Problem 1
Purchase order

UMI
UNITED METALS, INC.
110 SOUTH STATE ST.
CHICAGO, IL 60604 (312) 332-0574

Tab **PURCHASE ORDER**

		words
Purchase order No.	N-75041	2
Date	January 11, 19--	5
Terms	2/10, n/30	16
Ship Via	N. C. Transport	23

Craver Furniture, Inc. (10)
1709 Piedmont Avenue (16)
High Point, NC 27263 (20)

Quantity	Tab Cat. No.	Tab 2 spaces from rule — Description	Tab Price	Tab Total	words
DS					
8	S715-643	Double-pedestal walnut execu- tive desk, 72" x 36" x 29"	289.50	2316.00	31 40
4	S401-689	Contour executive chair, swivel and tilt, 32" high	115.00	460.00	47 55
4	S358-160	Executive chair, black, wood armrests, 17" high	90.00	360.00	63 69

8	S201-976	Armchair, black, vinyl uphol-
		   stery, 22 1/2" x 22 1/2" x
		   32"
			70.00	560.00	77
					83
					88

Approximate center	Approximate center	Indent 3 spaces	Approximate center	DS 3696.00	89

By ______________________ Purchasing Agent

74c ▶35 Measurement: announcements and tables

2 half sheets; 1 full sheet

Problem 1

half sheet, short side up

Center and type (DS) the announcement in reading position; erase and correct errors.

	words
YOU--ARE INVITED	3
TS	
to become a member of the	9
Business Education Club	13
February 8, 3:30 p.m.	18
Room 112, Conant Auditorium	23
Membership Fee, $3.00	28

Problem 2

half sheet, long side up

Center and type (DS) the table in exact vertical and horizontal center; decide spacing between columns; erase and correct errors.

BASE UNITS OF METRIC MEASURE 6

Units and Names 9

TS

		words
Unit of length	meter (m)	14
Unit of mass (weight)	kilogram (kg)	21
Unit of temperature	kelvin (K)	27
Unit of time	second (s)	32
Unit of electrical current	ampere (A)	39
Unit of luminous intensity	candela (cd)	47
Unit of substance	mole (mol)	53

Problem 3 (full sheet)

Center and type (DS) the table in reading position; decide spacing between columns; erase and correct errors.

SCHOOL ENROLLMENTS 4

Comparing Last Year with This Year 11

			words
Central Vocational School	1,088	1,157	18
James B. Conant High School	2,405	2,371	26
Amelia Earhart High School	946	1,148	34
Thomas A. Edison High School	1,583	1,620	42
Lincoln High School	3,039	2,942	49
Metropolitan Trade-Technical	850	993	57
Northwest Technical Institute	475	820	65
Mark Twain High School	1,827	1,813	72
Washington High School	2,064	1,946	79
John Greenleaf Whittier High School	2,634	2,589	92
	16,911	17,399	94

215c ▶30
Learn to type business cards

5″ × 3″ cards or paper cut to size [LM pp. 151–154]

Type a card for each customer listed below. On one side, type the name and address as shown in the first illustration; on the reverse side, type the data as shown in the second illustration.
Align the information with the headings as shown. Erase and correct all errors neatly.

```
TS
McNiff, Robert E. (Mr.)
                        TS
Mr. Robert E. McNiff
1057 East Main Street
Greenwood, IN 46142
↑
4 spaces
```

```
        ELECTRIC APPLIANCE REPAIR, INC.

Customer's Name:    Mr. Robert E. McNiff
Telephone Number:   337-1056
Date Received:      May 8, 19--
Appliance:          Electric toaster
Serial Number:      GE-562084
Repairs:            Replace heating unit
```

Mr. Robert E. McNiff
1057 East Main Street
Greenwood, IN 46142
(Insert name)
337-1056
May 8, 19--
Electric toaster
GE-562084
Replace heating unit

Ms. Alberta Miller
2048 Scenic Drive
Beech Grove, IN 46107
(Insert name)
632-4806
May 8, 19--
Food mixer
KM-159738
Adjust speed control

Mrs. Peggy Saylors
1562 Walnut Street
Westfield, IN 46074
(Insert name)
663-8742
May 8, 19--
Upright sweeper
HO-150928
Overhaul motor

Mr. Lexie Mills
7093 Western Avenue
Carmel, IN 46032
(Insert name)
361-5802
May 8, 19--
Coffee mill
KA-479128
Replace grinders

Mrs. Barbara Haynes
3007 Logan Avenue
Whiteland, IN 46184
(Insert name)
721-4083
May 8, 19--
Broiler/oven
TM-569102
Replace timer

Miss Diana Kutzer
1205 Spring Street
Speedway, IN 46224
(Insert name)
281-7032
May 8, 19--
Blender
ZE-36219
Replace switch

Mrs. Betty Treisback
107 East Oak Street
Noblesville, IN 46060
(Insert name)
621-7359
May 8, 19--
Steam/dry iron
JC-408592
Replace thermostat

Miss Patricia Goins
8056 Maple Avenue
Southport, IN 46217
(Insert name)
563-0138
May 8, 19--
Clock-radio
JW-091528
Replace tubes

Ms. Betty Mercer
5603 Baxter Street
Fishers, IN 46038
(Insert name)
921-5648
May 8, 19--
Hair dryer
LH-037165
Rewire blower

216

216a ▶5
Conditioning practice

each line 3 times (slowly, rapidly, in-between rate)

Extra crews reported quickly to Jim Bizal for hints on vigorous games.
She auctioned 395 records, 164 vases, 80 paintings, and 72 sculptures.
Bill's check for $6,578 (due on May 19) was sent to Graham & Sullivan.
It takes very little extra effort to gain real skill in office typing.
| 1 | 2 | 3 | 4 | 5 | 6 | 7 | 8 | 9 | 10 | 11 | 12 | 13 | 14 |

75

75a ▶7 Conditioning practice

1. Each line twice SS (slowly, faster).
2. A 1′ writing on Line 4, then on Line 1; compare *gwam*.

alphabet	Zero winds may exhaust Faye Jeffrey, but she will not give up quickly.
fig/sym	APARTMENTS FOR RENT: two 5-room at $187.40 ea.; three 6-room at $239.
trigraphs	can cancel cannot has purchased man manner demand thin within thinking
fluency	Both of the girls may go with the busy auditor to visit the auto firm.

| 1 | 2 | 3 | 4 | 5 | 6 | 7 | 8 | 9 | 10 | 11 | 12 | 13 | 14 |

75b ▶8 Measurement: 5′ straight copy

a 5′ writing; determine *gwam*; circle errors

all letters used | A | 1.5 si | 5.6 awl | 80% hfw |

	gwam 1′	5′
Someone has said that the hardest thing about holding a job is the	13	3
work it requires. That may be clever; however, as an expression of the	28	6
attitudes some people have regarding their work, it points up the tragic	42	8
plight of people who fail to match interest and ability with available	57	11
jobs when they place themselves on the job market.	67	13
Almost everyone has to work at one time or another in life. Over	13	16
fifty percent of us must work during all of our eligible working years.	28	19
Many people work with joy in what they do, whereas others consider their	42	22
jobs boring regardless of the work they are assigned. Bored workers let	57	25
their work master them instead of mastering their work.	68	27
Whether your work is a chore or a satisfaction depends more upon	13	30
you than upon the work itself. Most days have both a routine and an ex-	27	32
citing period. The fortunate worker gets enough pleasure from the excit-	42	35
ing elements to be able to accept the routine ones. If that should not	56	38
turn out to be the case, the worker should consider changing jobs in	70	41
order to realize job satisfaction.	77	42

gwam 1′ | 1 | 2 | 3 | 4 | 5 | 6 | 7 | 8 | 9 | 10 | 11 | 12 | 13 | 14 |
5′ | 1 | 2 | 3 |

unit **38** lessons 215–220

Processing business forms

Learning goals

1. To improve straight-copy speed and accuracy.

2. To learn how to type common business forms (purchase orders, bills of lading, invoices).

3. To improve skill in handling materials.

4. To improve proofreading and correcting skills.

5. To improve skill in typing figures.

Machine adjustments

1. Line: 70 for drills and timed writings.

2. Spacing: SS sentence drills; DS and indent ¶s; as directed for problems.

215

215a ▶5 Conditioning practice

each line 3 times (slowly, rapidly, in-between rate)

alphabet Jinx Quilvey bought dazzling gifts from workers at exceptional prices.

figures The test scores for the five new students were 90, 81, 73, 62, and 54.

fig/sym Hill & Cox today paid $8,419.13 ($7,850 principle + $569.13 interest).

fluency Office typists must learn how to handle many different business forms.

| 1 | 2 | 3 | 4 | 5 | 6 | 7 | 8 | 9 | 10 | 11 | 12 | 13 | 14 |

215b ▶15 Improve speed/control

1. Two 1′ *speed* writings on each ¶; determine *gwam*.

2. A 5′ *control* writing on ¶s 1–3 combined; circle errors; determine *gwam*.

all letters used | A | 1.5 si | 5.6 awl | 80% hfw |

Text	gwam 1′	5′
Management as a profession is a relative newcomer in the world of	13	3
business. There are many who assume that management is a science, but	27	5
it is much more than that. Management is a skill, an art, a process, a	42	8
practice, and an occupation. Management is an essential element of any	56	11
concerted endeavor be it politics, religion, or business. Management is	71	14
the activity that sets the objectives, plans what work is to be done,	85	17
how and when it is to be done, and who will do it. It also establishes	99	20
the essential controls to insure that the work is done correctly.	113	23
Most colleges offer courses in management, and some of them offer	13	25
it as a major field. A special area of interest in the field of man-	27	28
agement is office management which deals with the flow of data, usually	41	31
in the form of paperwork, in an office. So that executives can acquire	55	34
timely and accurate data when it is needed, there must be those who	69	36
collect, process, record, and transmit data in a proper manner. It is	83	39
the duty of an office manager to oversee these workers and tasks so	97	42
that busy executives can focus their minds on more specialized matters.	112	45
As the systems and the technology used in the office grow more	13	47
complex, business is insisting that only those with formal training can	27	50
qualify as an office manager. Despite this trend, there are many office	42	53
managers who began a career as a clerk or as a typist and who worked	55	56
their way up through the ranks. By extensive experience and, in many	69	59
cases, by taking a special management program on the college level, they	84	62
qualified for the job. As time goes by, though, this road to the top	98	64
may be closed and only those with the college degree may be acceptable.	112	67

gwam 1′ | 1 | 2 | 3 | 4 | 5 | 6 | 7 | 8 | 9 | 10 | 11 | 12 | 13 | 14 |
5′ | 1 | 2 | 3 |

75c ▶35 Measurement: unbound reports

2 full sheets

Margins
top: 2″ elite
1½″ pica
side: 1″
bottom: approx. 1″

Problem 1

Type the copy as an unbound report (DS). Use a *page line gauge* (LM p. 81) to plan vertical spacing and footnotes. Erase and correct errors.

	words
LEVELS OF PRACTICE IN TYPEWRITING	7
How you practice is just as important as what you produce in learn-	22
ing to typewrite. How you practice is determined largely by the level	36
(speed) of your practice effort. There are three practice levels in type-	51
writing: (1) exploration (high-speed) level, (2) control level, and (3) optimum	67
(speed-with-control) level.[1]	72
When the purpose of practice is to break through the ceiling of	85
control and discover new and faster patterns of stroking, type on the	99
exploration level. On this level you should try to make faster motions	117
even at the temporary expense of accuracy.	126
When the purpose of practice is to type with acceptable accuracy,	139
drop back in speed to type with ease and confidence on the control level.	157
"Control" means more than mere accuracy of copy produced, however; it	171
means control over the precise movements of fingers that result in accu-	185
rate typescript.	189
The optimum level of practice is somewhere between the exploration	205
(high-speed) level and the control (drop-back) level. It is a level of per-	220
formance that is easy to maintain without tension.	230
According to a research study by Weise,[2] it is the wise use of levels	240
of practice (rather than the use or nonuse of repetition) that enhances	258
typewriting skill.	263
______________	266
[1] Jerry W. Robinson (ed.), Strategies of Instruction in Typewriting	288
(Cincinnati: South-Western Publishing Co., 1972), pp. 13-14.	300
[2] Barbara S. Weise, "The Effects of Repetition and Alternating Levels	314
of Practice on Learning to Typewrite" (Doctoral dissertation, University	329
of California, Los Angeles, 1975), pp. 62-63.	338

Problem 2 appears on page 124.

214b, continued

Problem 3
Unbound 2-page report with quotation, listed items, and footnotes

Margins
top: 1½" pica, 2" elite
side: 1"
bottom: 1"

words

WORD PROCESSING 3

TS

Word processing is simply the transformation of ideas into typewritten or printed form. The function of word processing is not new to business or other organizations because typists and stenographic workers have been processing words in offices since the turn of the century. What is new about word processing are current attempts to make the function operate more systematically and efficiently by using electronic equipment, specialized personnel, and centralized word processing stations. 17 33 47 63 77 92 103

DS

A big impetus to the electronic word processing movement is the cost of communication. Getting words onto paper is becoming more and more expensive.[1] 117 131 133

DS

> Average annual cost of one typing station, for example, is estimated at over $20,000 (this includes salary, benefits, equipment, etc.). And the cost of producing just one business letter is approaching $4. 145 158 172 175

SS

DS

Each type of electronic equipment used for word processing serves a distinct function. Sound-recording machines receive and store sounds (voice); playback machines recreate those sounds as words for typists to encode on a typewriter. The encoding typewriters are of two basic types: "magnetic-media machines such as the MT/ST, MC/ST, and CRT and the paper-tape-media machines such as the Edityper, Flexowriter, and the Quin-Typer."[2] 189 205 220 234 248 263

end of page 1

Although electronic word processing centers are quite expensive to install and equip, "power" typing equipment such as that just mentioned increases typing productivity in important ways. 276 290 300

DS

SS with DS between items

1. It greatly speeds up the correction of typing errors. 312
2. It eliminates the manual retyping of an entire message or page when editorial changes are necessary. 325 333
3. It minimizes the reduction in typing speed caused by the "fear of making an error." 346 351
4. It permits the high-speed duplication of messages, each with personalized inserts such as names, addresses, and amounts. 364 375 377

SS

______________ 381

DS

[1] "Update on Word Processing," Research Institute Personal Report for the Professional Secretary (July 10, 1975), p. 1. 402 417

DS

[2] J Marshall Hanna, Estelle L. Popham, and Rita Sloan Tilton, Secretarial Procedures and Administration (6th ed.; Cincinnati: South-Western Publishing Co., 1973), p. 62. 432 453 459

75c, continued

Problem 2

Using the machine adjustments given for Problem 1, type the 1-page report.

1. Use a *page line gauge* to plan vertical spacing and footnotes (LM p. 81). Extra space must be left between the table and the footnote divider line so that the bottom margin will be 6 lines (1″) deep.

2. DS above the table; SS the items; leave 8 spaces between columns. Erase and correct errors.

words

INTERNATIONAL TYPEWRITING CONTESTS 7

The first practical typewriter in this country was patented by 20
Sholes, Glidden, and Soule in 1868.[1] Thereafter, many changes were made 34
in the machine--in everything except the keyboard which soon became 48
universal in its arrangement of letter keys. 57

Early in the twentieth century, competition among makers of type- 70
writers became intense. To display the superiority of their machines, 84
manufacturers set up what became known as international contests, 97
each company sponsoring high-speed typists who had been trained on 111
its own make of machine. The typewriter on which a contest was won 124
became the "machine of the year" until the next competition was held 138
and a new winner was declared. 144

From early in the century to the onset of World War II, the war 157
between typewriter manufacturers raged. After World War II, however, 171
the international contests were not resumed; but innovations in typewriters 186
have continued unabated. 191

Here are the results of three international contests, showing the year 206
of competition, winner, and net speed of the typist.[2] 217

1917	George Hossfield	145	222
1923	Albert Tangora	147	227
1941	Margaret Hamma	149	231

________________ 235

[1] A. R. Russon and S. J. Wanous, Philosophy and Psychology of 253
Teaching Typewriting (2d ed.; Cincinnati: South-Western Publishing Co., 272
1973), p. 2. 275

[2] D. D. Lessenberry and S. J. Wanous, College Typewriting (5th ed.; 292
Cincinnati: South-Western Publishing Co., 1955), p. 116. 303

214

214a ▶5
Conditioning practice

1. Each line twice SS.
2. Repeat difficult lines.

My new optician puzzled both Jack and Gavin Quixote for a few minutes.
Get No. 2159 in a 3.6 m x 4.5 m, a 2.8 m x 3.7 m, and a 2.5 m x 3.0 m.
The note for $6,250 at 7% interest requires a monthly payment of $200.
When the union amendment passes, more than eighty workers will profit.

| 1 | 2 | 3 | 4 | 5 | 6 | 7 | 8 | 9 | 10 | 11 | 12 | 13 | 14 |

214b ▶45
Measure production skill: alpha-numeric memos, letters, and reports

1. Arrange needed supplies, including memo form and letterhead [LM pp. 143–146], carbon paper, second sheets, and eraser. Prepare 1 cc and an envelope for the memo and the letter.
2. When directed, type for 30′ on the problems given here and on p. 338. Correct any errors you make as you type. If you finish before time is called, retype Problem 3.
3. When time is called, proofread and circle any uncorrected errors.
4. Compute *n–pram*; then arrange all problems in textbook order and turn them in.

Time schedule
Preparation .... 5′
Timed production ..... 30′
Final check; compute *n–pram* .... 10′

Problem 1
Memo with table

Problem 2
Letter with table
Use modified block style, mixed punctuation, and the line length used for the memo. Type the memo copy as a letter to:

Ms. Tina Moravia
10504 Royal Drive, Apt. 3
St. Louis, MO 63136

Supply an appropriate salutation and needed closing lines.

words

TO: Tina Moravia, Regional Representative 8
FROM: Juan C. Martinez, Promotion Director 15
DATE: January 12, 19-- 18
SUBJECT: Demonstration Schedule 23

(¶ 1) Your reports of comments on the new Paragon line of office calculators 37
are most gratifying. The Dayton and the Louisville branches have reported 52
similar reactions. It would seem that we can go ahead with plans pre- 66
pared in October by the Promotion Department. 76
(¶ 2) As an opening step, we have arranged the following demonstration- 87
display schedule for you the week of February 2. 99

				words
2/3	Quincy	Rayco, Inc.	8:30-10:30 a.m.	106
	Hannibal	Mark Twain College	2:30- 3:30 p.m.	115
2/5	St. Charles	Marshall's, Inc.	9:30-11:15 a.m.	125
	St. Louis	Regional IRS Office	2:30- 4:00 p.m.	134
2/7	Sikeston	Office Services, Inc.	10:00-11:15 a.m.	144
	Poplar Bluff	MBEA Conference	3:30- 5:00 p.m.	153

(¶ 3) This schedule should allow you to do one or two demonstrations on the 167
4th and the 6th. With this in mind, I'm enclosing a list of requests that we 183
have received from your area. I've checked those that I believe should be 198
given priority, but you will have to set up your own appointments. 211
(¶ 4) I know you will do your usual competent job. Please let me have a 225
report on the reactions both to the new models and the displays and pro- 239
grams. Lou Phelps would like a copy, too. xx Enclosure 251/263

The lessons of Cycle 2 represent a *Planned Program* to improve your typing skills

step 1 Position

Maintain good typing posture and hand-and-finger position; wrists low and relaxed (base of hand just above front edge of typewriter).

Typing posture

Finger position

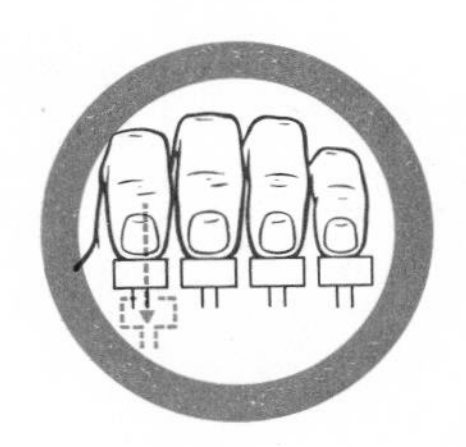

step 2 Purpose

Give a purpose to all typing practice.

A. Improve techniques
keystroking
spacing
shift-key reaches
return

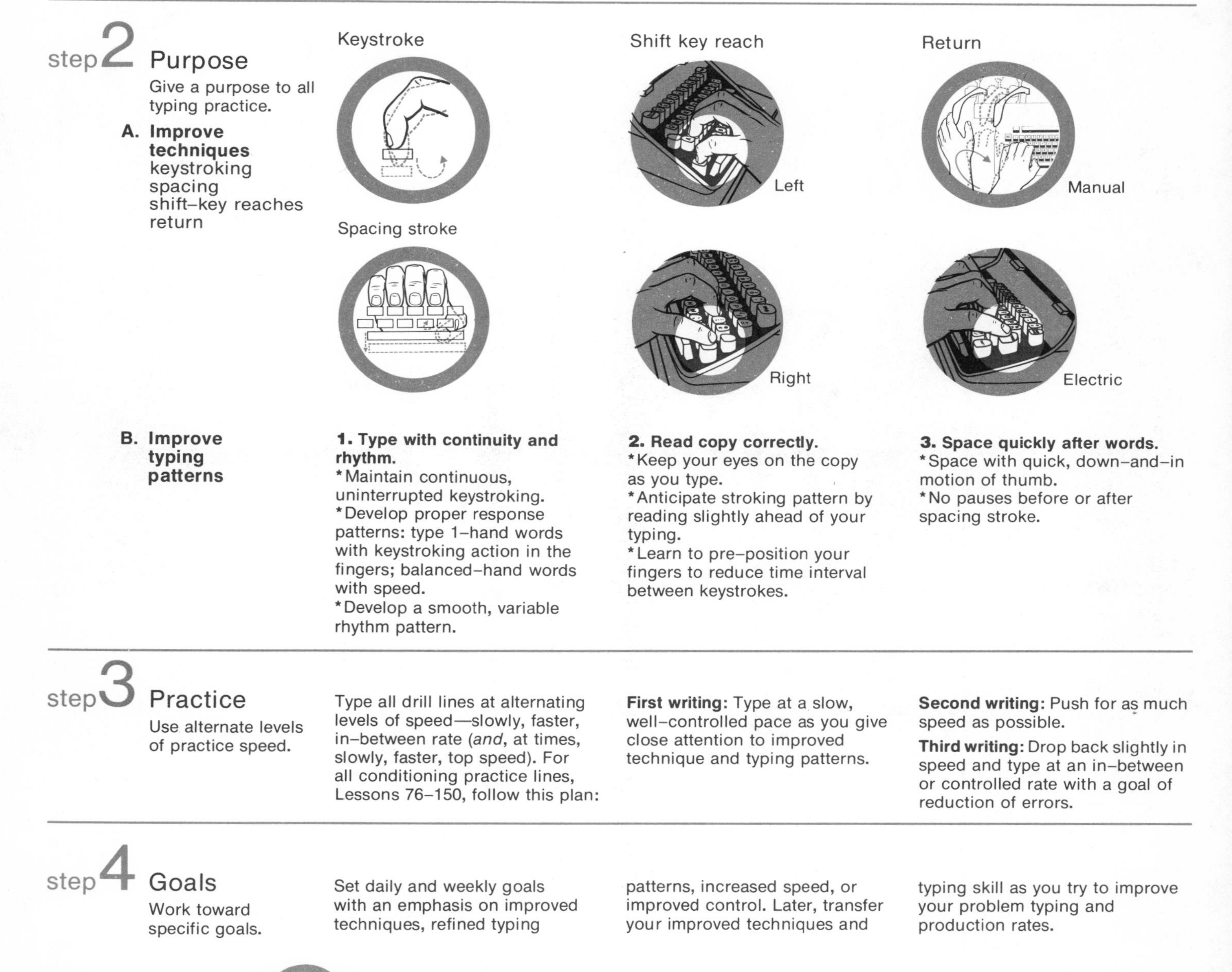

Keystroke

Spacing stroke

Shift key reach

Left

Right

Return

Manual

Electric

B. Improve typing patterns

1. Type with continuity and rhythm.
*Maintain continuous, uninterrupted keystroking.
*Develop proper response patterns: type 1-hand words with keystroking action in the fingers; balanced-hand words with speed.
*Develop a smooth, variable rhythm pattern.

2. Read copy correctly.
*Keep your eyes on the copy as you type.
*Anticipate stroking pattern by reading slightly ahead of your typing.
*Learn to pre-position your fingers to reduce time interval between keystrokes.

3. Space quickly after words.
*Space with quick, down-and-in motion of thumb.
*No pauses before or after spacing stroke.

step 3 Practice

Use alternate levels of practice speed.

Type all drill lines at alternating levels of speed—slowly, faster, in-between rate (*and*, at times, slowly, faster, top speed). For all conditioning practice lines, Lessons 76–150, follow this plan:

First writing: Type at a slow, well-controlled pace as you give close attention to improved technique and typing patterns.

Second writing: Push for as much speed as possible.

Third writing: Drop back slightly in speed and type at an in-between or controlled rate with a goal of reduction of errors.

step 4 Goals

Work toward specific goals.

Set daily and weekly goals with an emphasis on improved techniques, refined typing patterns, increased speed, or improved control. Later, transfer your improved techniques and typing skill as you try to improve your problem typing and production rates.

212c ▶35
Letters with tables

On plain paper type the letter to each of the following addressees. Use modified block; mixed punctuation; 1 cc of each letter; correct errors. Because of the address length and the table, 1" margins should be used.

Mr. Robert R. Kocher
Director, Office Services
Kocher & Sons, Inc.
809 South Calhoun
Fort Wayne, IN 46802

Ms. Jean Hanna, Office Manager
Edwards Manufacturing Company
1200 Niagara Street
Buffalo, NY 14213

Mr. William R. Strang
Purchasing Department
Dynamics Industries, Ltd.
10 King Boulevard
WINDSOR, Ontario, Canada
N8C 1R2

words

Date, address, and salutation 27

(¶ 1) Thank you for asking about prices on the new Paragon series of 39
Teletron Electronic Printing Calculators. Your comments on my recent 53
demonstration are generous and much appreciated. 63
(¶ 2) I am enclosing a brochure that gives information about all models 76
of the Paragon series of Teletron Office Machines. The data on the 90
calculators in which you are interested begin on page 4 and continue 104
through page 7. The prices listed in the brochure are, of course, retail 119
prices. Wholesale prices are given below for the quantities you 132
customarily order. 136

	6-50	51-100	
			140
Model PS-100	$165	$150	145
Model T-1500	270	250	149
Model PT-250	325	300	153

(¶ 3) You have seen these machines demonstrated and are aware of 165
the dramatic improvements they exhibit over their predecessors. Our 179
engineers scored a major triumph in designing the Paragon series to 193
permit us to offer such sophisticated models at these low prices. I know 207
you will agree. 211
(¶ 4) May I have one of our representatives call on you soon to discuss 224
your electronic calculator requirements? An order placed now can be 238
delivered within 30 days. 243

Sincerely yours Alan C. Bunker Assistant Sales Manager xx 255
Enclosure (234) 257

213

213a ▶5
Conditioning practice

1. Each line twice SS.
2. Repeat difficult lines.

Kyle Bixby will adjust the size of this antique ring to fit Pam Vance.
Her July 15 memo indicates she is low on items J2937, M4068, and R647.
Grayson & Sons ordered 175# of A-394 and 205# of F-860 on February 18.
Their audit statement shows that the penalty for default was not paid.

| 1 | 2 | 3 | 4 | 5 | 6 | 7 | 8 | 9 | 10 | 11 | 12 | 13 | 14 |

213b ▶45
Sustained production: alpha-numeric memos, reports, and letters

1. Make a list of problems to be typed:
   page 331, Problem 2, 209c
   page 333, Problem 2, 210c
   page 335, Problem 2, 211c
2. When directed to begin, type for 30′ from the list, using plain paper.
3. Prepare a carbon copy of each problem; erase and correct errors.
4. Compute *n-pram*. Turn in all problems in the order listed.

Time schedule
Preparation .... 5′
Timed production ..... 30′
Final check; compute *n-pram* .... 10′

phase 4 lessons 76–100

Developing word processing power

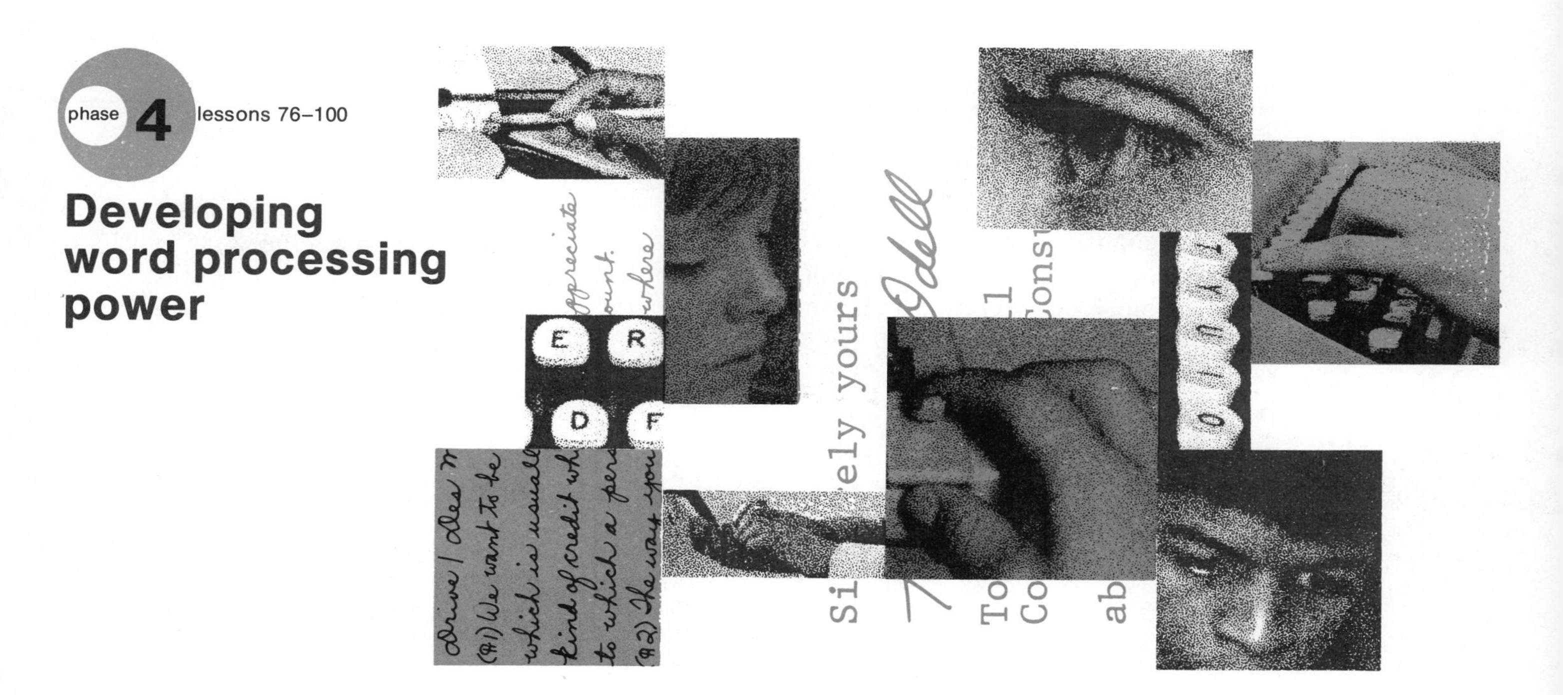

unit 13 lessons 76–85

Improving typing techniques and basic skills

The 25 lessons of Phase 4 reflect a *Planned Program* (see page 125) to achieve the following learning goals:

1. Improved technique and practice patterns.

2. Increased basic skill on straight, statistical, rough-draft, and script copy.

3. Improved learning and composing skills.

4. Increased application skill on personal/business letters.

Machine adjustments

(for each lesson of Cycle 2)

1. Set paper guide at *0* on most typewriters.

2. Set paper-bail rolls to divide paper into thirds.

3. Set ribbon control to type on upper portion of the ribbon (on black).

Use:

- 70-space line and single spacing for drills
- 5-space ¶ indention
- double spacing (DS) for all timed writings of more than 1 minute (1′)
- double spacing (DS) after each single-spaced (SS) group of drill lines
- triple spacing (TS) after drills and lesson parts

76

76a ▶5 Conditioning practice

each line 3 times; as time permits, retype selected lines

Use Step 3 of *Planned Program* (page 125) for Lessons 76–150.

alphabet	Just work for improved basic techniques to maximize your typing skill.
figures	The shipment included 132 divans, 156 lamps, 48 desks, and 790 chairs.
quiet hands	Purposeful repetition leads to rapid improvement of stroking patterns.
fluency	The map of the ancient land forms may aid them when they work with us.

| 1 | 2 | 3 | 4 | 5 | 6 | 7 | 8 | 9 | 10 | 11 | 12 | 13 | 14 |

76b ▶5 Improve speed/control

two 1′ writings on Line 1, then on Line 4, of 76a, above

Goals: Writing 1, control
Writing 2, speed

Compare rates. Did you make fewer errors when you typed for control? In these lessons make a lesson-by-lesson evaluation of your typing skill, then try to improve those aspects of your skill in which you are weak.

211c, continued

Problem 2

Type the copy at the right, beginning with the second ¶, as page 2 of the 2-page letter. Begin the second-page heading on Line 7 (see RG page iv).

Problem 3

If time permits, retype the table in the letter.

words

It used to be said that anyone who could be replaced by a machine should be. It is now being said frequently that any machine that can be replaced by a person should be. There is room for both in our society, of course, but finding the right mix of people and machines is a problem that will be with us for a long time. As far as education is concerned, it is our judgment in view of the mixed results of experiments with "teaching machines" that all such devices should be used as aids to good teaching, not substitutes for effective instruction. 13 27 41 55 69 82 96 110

The following table summarizes the basic findings of four research studies which compared multimedia and traditional instruction in the area of typewriting. 124 138 142

DS

153

Researcher	Area of Significant Difference*		
	Speed	Accuracy	Production
Jones, 1974	0	0	0
Schellstede, 1964	+	0	0
Thoreson, 1971	+	+	+
Wiper, 1969	0	0	0

159 167 174 185 189 194 198 201 212

*0 indicates an insignificant difference; + indicates a significant difference favoring multimedia. 223 233

TS

We hope these comments with supporting data will be of interest to you. If we can be of further assistance, please let us know. 247 259

Sincerely yours Armondo Linea, Research Director xx 269

212

212a ▶5 Conditioning practice

1. Each line twice SS.
2. Repeat difficult lines.

Vic Goff quizzed all workers about the six jobs that were open in May.
Our March statement covers unpaid invoices A-4138, C-2076, and G-5936.
Use * for a single footnote: *See Table 3 of Appendix C, pages 57-60.
The six maps may come in very handy when she takes her big motor trip.

| 1 | 2 | 3 | 4 | 5 | 6 | 7 | 8 | 9 | 10 | 11 | 12 | 13 | 14 |

212b ▶10 Compose as you type

1. On a plain sheet, center on Line 10 the heading CHANGES IN THE OFFICE

2. Compose a short report in which you mention some of the changes in equipment and procedures that have recently occured.

If necessary, refer to the ¶s in 209b, page 330; 210b, page 332; and 211b, page 334.

76c ▶12 Improve technique: keystroking

each line 3 times (slowly, faster, top speed); as time permits, repeat selected lines

Keystroking: manual or electric

- Strike each key with a quick, snappy stroke.
- Use a quick, down-and-in motion of the finger.
- Release key quickly.
- Keep wrists low and relaxed; hands quiet.
- Use finger-reach action.

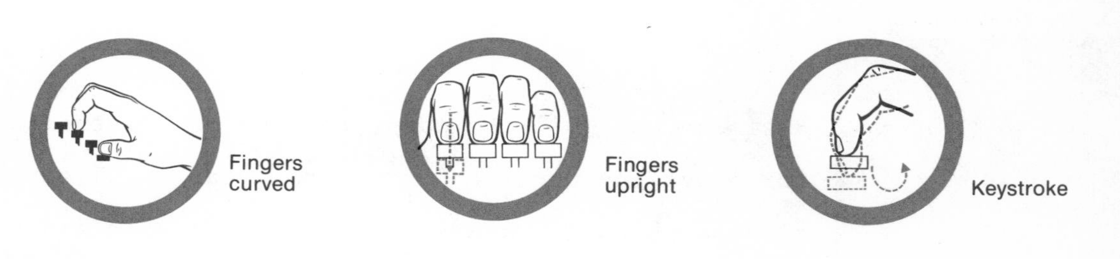

Home row

1 ff jj dd kk ss ll aa ;; gg hh asdf jkl; fjfj dkdk slsl a;a; a;sldkfjgh
2 a jag; add gas; a fall fad; all had a flag; a lad has had half a glass
3 J. J. Hall has had half a glass. Jad asked dad to add a dash of hash.

Third row

4 u uj r rf y yj t tf i ik e ed o ol w ws p p; q qa try quote typewriter
5 we wrote it; your typewriter; you were to try to quote it; your quips;
6 Are you trying to type on the upper row by reaching with your fingers?

Bottom row

7 m mj v vf n nj b bf , ,k c cd . .l x xs / /; z za men cab van fix many
8 five or six names, many men can mix the zinc, a number of men can fix,
9 Aza C. Bonham calmed an excited lynx as the men carried it to the van.

A Technique Check Sheet is provided on LM pp. 1, 2.

76d ▶13 Apply improved technique: guided writing

1. A 2′ writing (at a controlled pace with good keystroking techniques).

2. Determine *gwam*. Add 8 to your *gwam* rate. Determine ¼′ goals for 1′ writing at new rate. (Example: *48* = 12, 24, 36, 48).

3. Three 1′ writings at your goal rate as your teacher calls the ¼′ guides.

4. Two 2′ writings for speed. Try to reach your goal rate.

all letters used (home-, third-, and bottom-row reaches)

Would you like to become an expert typist? The drills in the ten lessons of this unit are designed to start you on your way. The overall goal is to increase your typing speed a minimum of six words a minute. To achieve this goal, give a purpose to all your practice and type the drill lines at alternating levels of speed. In each lesson, just try to improve your typing techniques and to eliminate all waste motion. You will be amazed at your skill gain.

211b ▶10 Improve speed/control

1. A 1′ *speed* writing on each ¶; determine *gwam*.

2. A 5′ *control* writing on ¶s 1–3 combined; determine *gwam*; circle errors.

	gwam 1′	5′
Business was quick to adapt the use of electronic systems	15	3
for procesing words. For several years, colleges and school	31	6
also haveused computers to schedule classes and process en-	43	9
rollment information. Hospitals have found electronic devices	61	12
useful in there work, too. In fact, the area of word processing	75	15
is one that offers a great possibility for thsoe interested in	88	18
careers in the area of word and data processing.	92	18
Schools are now usig some of these maazing electronic	11	21
devises to deliver instruction that oncewas presented by	23	23
"live" teachers. One ofthe best examples with which you may be	36	26
familiar is the recored lesson. Others include pacing machine	49	28
that gear the rate of practice to student goals, TV presentations	64	31
that permitt students to learn in large groups in "class" or	76	34
individualy at home, and machines with which the student can	88	36
"talk" and can "talk back" to the student.	98	38
The history of the media movement hasbeen viewed with mixed	12	40
emotions. Machines have replaced many workers in business and	25	43
industry while reducing the monotonous routine of many others.	37	45
The have become usful aids to hurried and harried teachers while	51	48
making other virtually usless. They have "turned on" some stu-	64	51
dents for whom teacher's are anathema, but have turned off others	77	53
who prefer the warmth of an inetrested human being to a machine	90	56
that can do only what it it told.	97	57

211c ▶35 Letter with table

Problem 1 [plain paper]
Modified block, mixed punctuation

Type the ¶s of 211b, above, and the first ¶ on p. 335 as page 1 of a 2-page letter. Prepare 1 cc; correct errors.

Address the letter to: Mrs. Alvina Roth, Director
Brookwood Vocational Institute
802 North Meridian
Indianapolis, IN 46204

Enrichment material for Unit 37 appears on LM pp. 147–150.

76e ▶15 Measure basic skill: straight copy

two 5′ writings; determine *gwam*; proofread and circle errors; record *gwam* of better writing on the charts, LM pp. 3, 4.

all letters used | A | 1.5 si | 5.6 awl | 80% hfw

	gwam 1′	5′
As you type, just be very sure to give consideration to those steps,	14	3
or factors, given at the start of this cycle. These factors include such	28	6
important aspects of typing skill as proper hand-and-finger position,	42	8
fast keystroking, correct operation of the space bar after each word,	56	11
and a prompt return at the end of a line with an immediate start of the	71	14
new line. The proper operation of the shift keys is very important, too.	86	17
How you type and what you type are fundamental to the rapidity of skill	100	20
growth. You can make rapid skill growth by consistently typing drill	114	23
lines at alternating levels of speed.	121	24
Students who have a desire to become excellent typists set daily	13	27
and weekly goals for all their activities. For example, a long-range	27	30
goal for the ten lessons of this unit should be to try to increase your	41	33
present speed a minimum of six words a minute. Your daily goal should	56	35
be to try to develop your typing technique patterns according to the	69	38
specific techniques emphasized in every lesson. Students in a high-	83	41
speed research program made amazing skill gains using drill copy of the	97	44
kind given in these ten lessons, and so can you.	107	46

gwam 1′ | 1 | 2 | 3 | 4 | 5 | 6 | 7 | 8 | 9 | 10 | 11 | 12 | 13 | 14 |
5′ | 1 | 2 | 3 |

77

77a ▶5 Conditioning practice

each line 3 times (slowly, faster, in-between rate)

alphabet	Freshly squeezed grape juice was served at breakfast the next morning.
figures	I ordered 720 pencils, 36 pens, 49 erasers, and 185 cardboard folders.
adjacent keys	Rewards received for services rendered are related to effort expended.
fluency	She may make the goal if she works with vigor and with the right form.

| 1 | 2 | 3 | 4 | 5 | 6 | 7 | 8 | 9 | 10 | 11 | 12 | 13 | 14 |

77b ▶15 Improve basic skill: straight copy

1. Add 4 words to your *gwam* rate on 76e above.

2. Three 1′ writings on each ¶ of 76e trying to equal or exceed your new goal rate.

3. A 5′ writing on 76e.

Goal: To maintain new goal rate for 5′. Type with good techniques to do this. Determine *gwam*; proofread for errors.

210c ▶35 Report with alpha-numeric table

Problem 1
Page 1 of topbound report

Margins
top: 2" pica, 2½" elite
side: 1"
bottom: 1"

Type the ¶s of 210b, page 332, as page 1 of a topbound report. Use MODES OF BUSINESS DICTATION as a heading. Correct any errors you make as you type.

Problem 2
Page 2 of topbound report

Type the copy at the right as page 2 of the report. Leave a 1½" top margin (type the page number ½" from the bottom). Correct errors.

Note: If a page with a footnote is only partially filled, leave extra space between the last text line typed and the footnote divider line so that the bottom margin will be approximately 1" (6 lines) deep.

words

Relative merits of the two basic dictation modes aside, dictation systems which connect many remote dictators to a recording and transcribing center are destined to enjoy substantial growth in the years ahead. According to Kreitler of Dictaphone: "Word processing has accelerated the overall dictation idea, which up until now hasn't experienced the growth rate of other sectors of the business equipment industry."[1] 10 19 30 40 50 60 70 80 84

Voice recording equipment is not expensive, however, as summarized below from a recent tabulation:[2] 93 101 104

Type	Unit Cost Range	average cost	words
			120
			126
			142
Direct wire systems	$440-1,750	$ 1,204	150
Telephone dictation systems	180-2,400	1,293	159
Desktop dictation/transcription units	160-593	400	169
			184

188

[1] "Tec-Pak: Dictation," _Modern Office Procedures_ (April, 1974), p. 56. 203 207

[2] _Ibid._, pp. 54, 56, 58. 212

211

211a ▶5 Conditioning practice

1. Each line twice SS.
2. Repeat difficult lines.

Extra technique emphasis will help Jeffrey Gavitz boost speed quickly.
Have her strip the following files: 24-37-16, 30-75-20, and 38-29-36.
I use Monarch stationery (7 1/4" x 10 1/2") for all executive letters.
He was elected to chair the union meeting and did so with great vigor.

| 1 | 2 | 3 | 4 | 5 | 6 | 7 | 8 | 9 | 10 | 11 | 12 | 13 | 14 |

77c ▶15 Improve technique: keystroking

each line 3 times (slowly, faster, top speed)

Practice goal: curved, upright fingers; finger action, hands quiet

3d and 4th fingers
1 At the school sale, Paul and Aza sold the sample paper press to Quinn.
2 Six zebra were seen eating wet, waxy poppy pods at that old world zoo.
3 Wally was appalled by the zealous opinion expressed by the simple man.

Practice goal: fingers in typing position, hands quiet

adjacent keys
4 Are you aware that my new report may be returned after it is reviewed?
5 With reduced oil reserves, every conservation effort must be stressed.
6 We were quite pleased that the popular opinion was to buy the company.

Practice goal: quick, finger-reach action; fingers curved

long reaches
7 A number of union members may be at the unveiling of the unique mural.
8 An eccentric man bought bright, unique bronze statues at the ceremony.
9 A musical ceremony will have precedence over the unique presentations.

Practice goal: curved, upright fingers; quick, snappy keystroking

fingers
1st 10 Five hungry men helped James save a battered boat from further damage.
2d 11 Dick decided to dedicate his new musical work to an educational group.
3d 12 An old wax sample was used by Wally Olds to wax those new wood floors.
4th 13 Aza Quinn quizzed a popular polo player about scaling the Alpine peak.

| 1 | 2 | 3 | 4 | 5 | 6 | 7 | 8 | 9 | 10 | 11 | 12 | 13 | 14 |

77d ▶15 Apply improved technique: guided writing

1. A 2′ writing at a controlled pace with good keystroking techniques.

2. Determine *gwam*. Add 8 to your *gwam* rate. Set ¼′ goals for 1′ and 2′ writings at your new rate.

3. Three 1′ writings at your goal rate as your teacher calls the ¼′ guides.

4. A 2′ guided writing; try to maintain your goal rate for 2′.

5. A 2′ writing for speed. Try to exceed your goal rate.

all letters used (outside keys, adjacent keys, and direct reaches)

The concept of repetition as it applies to learning to typewrite frequently is misunderstood by many people who may not have had much experience in teaching typewriting. Just remember that rather amazing skill growth can take place through concentrated, intensive practice with purposeful repetition of copy. Repetition may be used for improving typing techniques, for improving continuity through concentration, and for building speed or improving accuracy.

210b ▶10 Improve speed/control

1. A 1′ *speed* writing on each ¶; determine *gwam*.
2. A 5′ *control* writing on ¶s 1–3 combined; determine *gwam*; circle errors.

	gwam 1′	5′
Do electronic dictating devices spell the doom of short-	11	2
hand in the near future? No, according to predictors	22	4
of change in the business scene. Both dictating equip-	33	7
ment and shorthand have been used in business offices	44	9
in this country for more than a century. Although	54	11
machine dictation has enjoyed much growth in the	64	13
past decade, so has the number of office workers	74	15
classified as stenographers and secretaries. As	83	17
many business managers say, each has too many	93	19
unique advantages for either to replace the other.	103	21
The secretary has long been eulogized as a most	10	22
valuable asset in the business office--a human	19	24
asset who thinks as well as does, who anticipates	29	26
as well as follows, who plans and organizes as	38	28
well as implements, who suggests as well as accepts,	49	30
who feels as well as endures. Old or young, the	59	32
business executive or administrator learns from	68	34
as well as teaches the office secretary. What	78	36
dictating machine can perform more than half	87	38
these functions? None!	91	39
On the other hand, a dictating machine offers	9	41
conveniences of its own. It can and will	18	42
travel wherever the "boss" must go. It permits	27	44
business executives to dictate at their own con-	37	46
venience, during or after hours. It requires the	47	48
time of just one person at a time--the execu-	56	50
tive's when dictating, the transcriber's when	65	52
transcribing. It also permits any transcriber	74	54
to transcribe its message. But its electric cur-	84	56
rent or its batteries sometimes "go dead" at	93	57
critical times.	96	58

78

78a ▶5 Conditioning practice

each line 3 times (slowly, faster, in-between rate)

alphabet	After a wild jump ball, the guards very quickly executed a zone press.
learning*	one, 1; forty, 40; one, twenty-seven, 127; twelve, seventy-three, 1273
third row	Type upper-row keys properly by making quick reaches with the fingers.
fluency	They may make the six men pay for the ancient ornament or do the work.

| 1 | 2 | 3 | 4 | 5 | 6 | 7 | 8 | 9 | 10 | 11 | 12 | 13 | 14 |

* Read, think, and type figures in 2-digit sequences, whenever possible.

78b ▶12 Improve techniques: space bar; shift key; return

each line 3 times (slowly, faster, top speed); type Lines 9-18 as directed below; stress speed

Practice goal: quick, down-and-in motion (toward palm) of right thumb

space bar

1 and and and, the the the, they they they, then then then, pay them for
2 if it is, and the, they may pay, when they try, to help you, the drain
3 pay them when they, pay them when they work, pay them when and if they
4 Jim may question many men and women as they try to leave the map room.

Learning cue
Release shift lock before typing the – in Line 6.

Practice goal: little-finger reach; other fingers in typing position

shift keys
5 Ja Ja Ja Jack Jack Jack; F; F; F; Floyd Flynn; Paul McNaulty; Al Dyane
shift lock
6 Sol Quinn, Paul McNeil, and Jack Bunne attended the ABC-TV Convention.
7 R. J. Zule, E. H. Black, A. P. Byrd, and Jan Zinke made A's in typing.
8 Halle V. McGil, President of McGil and McDuff, left for New York, N.Y.

Manual: Use a quick, flick-of-hand motion to return carriage.

Electric: Make a quick, little-finger reach to the return key.

Practice goal: quick return and start of new line

tab: center + 10

tab and return
9 tab ——→ and the
10 lake —— tab ——→ and the
11 work —— tab ——→ repeat 3 times

12 tab ——→ A quick return
13 of the carriage or element —— tab ——→ with an immediate
14 start of the new line —— tab ——→ will result in an
15 increased speed rate. —— tab ——→ Be sure to
16 keep your eyes —— tab ——→ on this copy
17 as you make the —— tab ——→ quick return
18 and start the new line. —— tab ——→ repeat 3 times

209c ▶35 Interoffice memo with alpha-numeric table

Problem 1 [LM pp. 137, 138]
Page 1 of memo

Type ¶s 1–3 of 209b, p. 330, as a memo. Use following headings:

TO: Ms. Olga Werner, Regional Manager
FROM: H. J. McKay, Systems Director
DATE: Current
SUBJECT: Magnetic-Unit Typewriters

Do not erase errors; instead, backspace and type the correction over the error as suggested in the ¶s.

Problem 2 [plain paper]
Page 2 of memo

Type the copy at the right as page 2 of a memo. Erase and correct any errors you make as you type.

Problem 3 [LM pp. 139, 140]

If time permits, retype Problem 1. Erase and correct your errors.

words

Ms. Olga Werner 3
Page 2 5
Current date 8

The advantages of magnetic-tape typewriters (such as the MT/ST) 21 that have been discussed here can be summarized as follows: Let- 33 ters, tables, and reports--all types of communications, in fact-- 46 can go from first or "rough" draft to finished form in a single 59 operation on the keyboard. Corrections, revisions, and insertions 73 can be made at any time during the typing process. The typist can 86 work with ease and assurance and can edit and improve the copy 99 without appreciably slowing the work flow. 107

In addition to two models of MT/ST units, IBM produces a model 120 that uses magnetic cards. The cards offer advantages similar to 133 those of the tape. Some features of three models of magnetic- 145 unit typewriters are given below. 152

	Model II MT/ST	Model IV MT/ST	Model 975 Mag Card	words
				158 / 162
15.5″ paper capacity	+	+	+	168
13″ writing line	+	+	+	172
Operating speed (characters per second), 15.5	+	+	+	178 / 183
Two tape stations	0	+	0	187
Automatic switchover between stations during retyping	0	+	0	193 / 199
Active keyboard and transfer (optional item)	0	+	0	205 / 210

xx 210

210

210a ▶5 Conditioning practice

1. Each line twice SS.
2. Repeat difficult lines.

Jack Yantz said unique exotic drugs will solve future health problems.
Please repair the following typewriters: 3, 5, 9, 31, 38, 47, and 60.
The rule reads: "Don't use don't for doesn't with singular subjects."
He set the dial of the visual pacer eight words above his usual speed.

| 1 | 2 | 3 | 4 | 5 | 6 | 7 | 8 | 9 | 10 | 11 | 12 | 13 | 14 |

78c ▶13 Improve speed/control: statistical copy

1. Two 1′ writings. Start second writing at ending point of first writing. Try to maintain same, or better, rate.
2. Two 2′ writings for speed. Compute your average *gwam* rate.
3. Subtract 4 words from your average rate; then type two 2′ *guided writings* at this new rate for control (not over 2 errors in each writing).

all figures used

How do you say "A miss is as good as a mile" in the metric system? It doesn't sound quite right to say, "A miss is as good as 1.6 kilometers." "Twenty-eight grams of prevention are worth 0.45 kilograms of cure" isn't at all like "An ounce of prevention is worth a pound of cure"; or, "Give him an inch and he'll take a mile" becomes "Give him 2.5 centimeters and he'll take 1.6 kilometers." Texans may be wearing a 38-liter hat instead of the traditional 10-gallon hat. Normal body temperature becomes 37 degrees Celsius instead of 98.6 degrees Fahrenheit.

78d ▶20 Measure basic skill: statistical copy

1. Two 5′ writings; determine *gwam*; circle errors.
2. Compute % of transfer: statistical-copy rate divided by straight-copy rate on 76e, page 128. Record better rate and % of transfer. *Expected* transfer: 70%.
3. In the time that remains, type additional 1′ writings on ¶ 1; then on ¶ 2. Work for speed or control, according to your needs.

all figures/letters used | A | 1.5 si | 5.6 awl | 80% hfw |

Text	gwam 1′	5′
Recently you requested some estimates of costs to produce a letter.	14	3
Research findings reveal that some typists take as long as 10 minutes,	28	6
or even more, to type a typical letter of, say, 125, 167, or 190 words.	43	9
If the typist is paid from $2.40 to $3.60 an hour, this indicates that	57	11
the letter costs from 40 to 60 cents to produce in terms of the typist's	71	14
time alone. When other factors are evaluated, the ordinary letter may	86	17
cost from $2.42 to $5.19 to produce. This finding is a somewhat amazing	100	20
statistic, isn't it?	104	21
Information storage costs, too, should be examined. On the average,	14	24
it costs 7 cents to retain one copy of a business letter in the files	28	26
for one year. Just to file the copy costs a cent. It costs $8.25 annu-	42	29
ally to maintain one cubic foot of documents in the ordinary office,	56	32
exclusive of employee costs. It costs $215 a year to maintain a 4-drawer	71	35
file, including personnel. It has been estimated that it costs $6,820	85	38
just to create and file the contents of a 4-drawer file. Add these cost	100	41
factors to the letter production expenses, and the ordinary business	113	44
letter may really cost as much as $2.57 to $6.49 to produce and retain.	128	46

gwam 1′ | 1 | 2 | 3 | 4 | 5 | 6 | 7 | 8 | 9 | 10 | 11 | 12 | 13 | 14 |
5′ | 1 | 2 | 3 |

unit **37** lessons 209–214

Processing alpha-numeric communications

Learning goals

1. To build skill on copy of above-average difficulty.
2. To improve skill on script and rough-draft copy.
3. To build skill on memos, letters, and reports that include alpha-numeric data.
4. To learn about machines used in word/data processing.

209

209a ▶5 Conditioning practice

1. Each line twice SS.
2. Repeat difficult lines.

alphabet Vicki James will display exquisite fabrics in a shop in the big plaza.
figures She gave the 6 tests to 198 women, 157 men, and 104 youths on June 23.
fig/sym Rayco offers a worker 50 shares ($36/share) at 23% below market value.
fluency The penalty will not be assessed if we get your payment by the eighth.

| 1 | 2 | 3 | 4 | 5 | 6 | 7 | 8 | 9 | 10 | 11 | 12 | 13 | 14 |

209b ▶10 Improve speed/control

1. A 1′ *speed* writing on each ¶; determine *gwam*.
2. A 5′ *control* writing on ¶s 1–3 combined; determine *gwam*; circle errors.

all letters used

HA	1.6 si	5.8 awl	75% hfw

	gwam 1′	5′
The work scene of the typist in a modern office is quickly being	13	3
changed. Manual machines have largely been replaced by electric ones.	27	5
Repetitive typing of the same letter or report to a large mailing list	42	8
of people is now being done automatically. In addition, the inputting	56	11
of original messages and data is now possible at rough-draft speeds be-	70	14
cause of the growing use of magnetic-tape machines that permit a typist	84	17
to make corrections just by striking over any error made.	96	19
Most of the major typewriter companies now have a single-element	13	22
machine that uses magnetic storage units. Operating one of these ma-	27	25
chines, a typist types the message or data in unarranged form but with	41	27
special signals to determine style or arrangement of the printout that	55	30
results when the tape is played back at speeds far in excess of a hun-	69	33
dred words a minute. A variety of letters, tables, reports, and other	83	36
documents can be produced error free at an amazing speed in this manner.	98	39
Typists in school have long "corrected" errors by backspacing and	13	41
typing over. Of course that does not correct errors on a typical ma-	27	44
chine, but it is exactly how a typist corrects the errors if using one	41	47
with a magnetic unit. It is now being recommended that students in	55	50
training be given occasional practice in using the rough-draft speed,	69	52
backspace-and-strikeover technique to prepare them for some of the new	83	55
equipment now being used in the new word and data processing center.	96	58

gwam 1′ | 1 | 2 | 3 | 4 | 5 | 6 | 7 | 8 | 9 | 10 | 11 | 12 | 13 | 14 |
5′ | 1 | 2 | 3 |

79

79a ▶5 Conditioning practice

each line 3 times (slowly, faster, in-between rate)

alphabet Forty big jets climbed into a hazy sky at exactly quarter past twelve.

figures They sold 40 watches, 129 rings, 35 clips, 56 tie pins, and 27 clocks.

shift keys Kimberly A. Patterson spoke on "A Formula for Success in Typewriting."

fluency He may sign the usual form by proxy if they make an audit of the firm.

| 1 | 2 | 3 | 4 | 5 | 6 | 7 | 8 | 9 | 10 | 11 | 12 | 13 | 14 |

79b ▶15 Improve techniques: response patterns

1. Each line 3 times (slowly, faster, top speed).

2. As time permits, type from dictation the lines preceded by the arrow (▶).

Color bars (___) under words indicate *word* response. Read and type these words or word groups for speed.

Color dots (. . .) under words indicate *letter* response. Read and type these words letter by letter. Type with continuity.

Practice goal: finger-action keystroking; fingers curved and upright

letter response one-hand words

1 was you saw pin far him are ill few pop get ink bad joy cab hum tax ply
2 dear pull were lump data look test jump gate hook best link rate only
3 union draft imply aware pupil staff nylon weave plump great jumpy react

Practice goal: high-speed word response—think word, type word

word response balanced-hand words

▶ 4 own men did box big end six she fit got aid via bid map key bit cut oak
▶ 5 with paid name held city both hand sign busy firm kept half risk rush
▶ 6 right world forms title eight firms spent usual spend corps civic visit

Practice goal: variable rhythm; uniform keystroking

combination response

7 to the pin | for him | she saw | they were | their date | right union | hand weave
8 their union | sight draft | right pupil | busy staff | firms react | usual weave
▶ 9 and the date | for the staff | if the pupil | is he aware | they may visit him
10 They gave the statement to the union at the address shown on the card.

79c ▶10 Improve speed/control: statistical copy

Repeat 78c, page 131, Steps 2 and 3 only.

In Step 3, add 4 words to average *gwam* rate for the guided writings.

Goal: Increased speed.

79d ▶20 Improve basic skill: statistical copy

Repeat 78d, page 131.

Goal: Increased speed.

208b, continued

Problem 2
Ruled table with leaders
center vertically; SS body; DS between groups; 16 spaces between Columns 1 and 2; 6 spaces between Columns 2 and 3; insert leaders and rulings

words

FINANCIAL SUMMARY 4
PORTER AND O'NEIL CHEMICAL PRODUCTS, INC. 12

(In Thousands of Dollars) 17

	This Year	Last Year	words
			42
			44
			46
			59
Net sales	$160,828	$151,884	70
Net income	7,705	8,215	80
Shareholders' equity			84
Common	70,616	66,849	94
Return	10.9%	12.3%	103
Common stock dividends	3,548	3,520	113
Earnings per share	3.91	4.21	122
Working capital	39,940	38,651	133
Current assets	60,311	57,610	142
Current liabilities	20,371	18,959	152
Number of shareholders	6,269	6,350	162
			175

Problem 3
Boxed table
center vertically in reading position; determine spacing between columns; box the table by inserting proper rulings

words

PATTERSON MANUFACTURING COMPANY 6
COMPARATIVE STATEMENT OF RETAINED INCOME FOR TWO-YEAR PERIOD 19

	This Year	Last Year	words
			46
			48
			50
			63
Net income retained			67
at beginning of year	$8,230,389,290	$7,738,848,793	78
Net income for the year	1,710,695,164	1,731,914,777	94
Total	9,941,084,454	9,470,763,570	100
Common stock dividends			105
March 15 (Share $0.85)	242,778,174	242,738,530	114
June 15 (Share $1.10)	314,178,898	314,169,870	123
Sept. 15 (Share $0.85)	242,617,382	242,641,266	133
Dec. 15 (Share $1.50)	427,854,719	427,896,341	142
Total dividends	1,227,429,173	1,227,446,007	151
Net income retained			155
at end of year	$8,713,655,281	$8,243,317,563	165
			178

80

80a ▶5 Conditioning practice

each line 3 times (slowly, faster, in-between rate)

alphabet Seven quiet boys extracted juicy chunks from the sizzling pot of stew.

figures Today we typed 40 letters, 15 reports, 369 orders, and 278 statements.

shift keys R. H. Smith, of McNeil, Paine and Winn Company, is visiting in Newark.

fluency She may pay the firm for the work when they sign the right audit form.

| 1 | 2 | 3 | 4 | 5 | 6 | 7 | 8 | 9 | 10 | 11 | 12 | 13 | 14 |

80b ▶15 Improve techniques: response patterns

each line twice (slowly, top speed); as time permits, a 1′ writing on each combination-response sentence

Return quickly

Manual

Electric

Space quickly

Practice goal: finger–action keystroking with fingers curved and upright

letter response

1 as my | are you | no date | you read | save him | act upon | we were | my area taxes
2 we are in | extra jump | oil reserves | only water rates | exaggerated opinion
3 only after you were | minimum facts | great pupil | greatest link | estate tax

4 Please be sure to state the minimum facts of the monopoly case for me.
5 Jim said that the extra increase in oil reserves was very exaggerated.
6 Only after you were aware of the water rates was it possible to start.

Practice goal: high–speed word response; space quickly

word response

7 and the | and then | and if they | and if they go | go to the | pay for | the work
8 the key city | spend the day | sign the form | the busy firm | the right title
9 and sign | pay the men | pay the men for the work | sign their form for them

10 Jan may spend the day with them when they pay the men of the key city.
11 Is it right to make me sign the name of the firm when I make an audit?
12 They may spend the profit of the firm and then visit the ancient city.

Practice goal: variable rhythm; uniform keystroking

combination response

13 Please send us a quantity of the forms and refer the statement to him.
14 Through use of a computer, the busy staff has decreased its work time.
15 Send the statements and the sight drafts to them at the union address.

| 1 | 2 | 3 | 4 | 5 | 6 | 7 | 8 | 9 | 10 | 11 | 12 | 13 | 14 |

207

207a ▶5 Conditioning practice

each line 3 times (slowly, rapidly, in-between rate)

A dairy executive bought new equipment for some amazing lake projects.
Recorded temperatures for one day were 87, 90, 62, 31, and 54 degrees.
On May 9, Coe & May paid $1,905.78 for 485# of seed (for shady areas).
A good office typist can arrange and type tables at impressive speeds.

| 1 | 2 | 3 | 4 | 5 | 6 | 7 | 8 | 9 | 10 | 11 | 12 | 13 | 14 |

207b ▶45 Build sustained production: tables with rulings and leaders

Time schedule

Preparation .... 6′
Timed production ... 30′
Final check;
compute *n–pram* .. 9′

1. Make a list of problems to be typed:
page 323, 203d, Problem 1
page 324, 204d, Problem 2
page 326, 205d, Problem 1
page 327, 206c, Problem 2

2. Arrange supplies (full sheets, second sheets, carbon, eraser, etc.)

3. Make 1 cc for each problem typed.

4. When directed to begin, type for 30′ from the list of problems, correcting all errors neatly. Proofread before removing the problems from the typewriter; if you finish all problems in less than 30′, start over and type until time is called.

5. When time is called, compute *n–pram* for the 30′ period.

6. Turn in problems in the order listed.

208

208a ▶5 Conditioning practice

Repeat 207a, above.

208b ▶45 Measure production: tables with rulings and leaders

Use Time Schedule in 207b, above.

full sheets; carbon paper; second sheets; 1 cc; erase and correct errors

Problem 1
Table with horizontal rulings

center vertically in reading position; DS body; 4 spaces between columns; insert rulings.

words

FUTURE CAREERS IN COMPUTER FIELDS 7

(Projections for a 10-year Period) 14

Occupation	1976 Employment	1985 Requirements	Percent of Change	
				40
				44
				52
				65
Machine repairers	57,960	120,500	+108.0%	74
Systems analysts	140,080	224,200	+ 60.1%	82
Programmers	220,600	270,000	+ 22.4%	89
Equipment operators	225,000	420,000	+ 86.7%	98
Keypunch operators	265,000	200,000	− 24.5%	106
				119

Source: Lecture by economist at conference on "Business Careers." 132

80c ▶20 Measure basic skill: rough draft

1. Two 5′ writings; determine *gwam*; circle errors.

Goal: At least 70% of rate on 76e, page 128.

2. Compute % of transfer: rough-draft rate divided by straight-copy rate on 76e, page 128. Record better rate and % of transfer on LM pp. 3, 4.

3. As time permits, two 1′ writings for speed on ¶ 1; then two 1′ writings for speed on ¶ 2.

all letters used | A | 1.5 si | 5.6 awl | 80% hfw |

	gwam 1′	5′
Some matereail from which you type in the business office may be	13	3
in rough draft form. the copy will con tain various kinds of cor-	30	6
rections which usually will be handwritten. The corrections may be	46	9
difficult to read as they may have been hurriedly written by a	58	12
business person who changed the copy. Often, to your employer may	73	15
ask you to type a letter in rough-copy from. Your employer may be	89	18
in a hurry for therough copy and, therefore, may tell you to strike-	103	21
over any typewriting errors you make. If readable, such rough copy is satisfactory for use by your employer.	118	24
The employer then uses the rough draft as a way to eval uate	127	25
the content of the letter, often making many changes and other cor-	12	28
rections before returning the copy to you. You will then be expected	25	30
to amke the corrections indicated. You will need to read it care-	49	35
fully to be certain you understand all corrections and that the	68	39
copy makes good sense. As a final step you will proofread carefully	84	42
the final copy that you prepared before submitting it to your employer.	99	45
When the rough draft is returned to you.	116	49

80d ▶10 Improve composing and self-evaluation skills

line: 60; DS; 5-space indention for ¶s

Drill 1: Compose and type in ¶ form your response to the self-evaluation question. As you type, x-out and retype words on which you make errors. Save copy for Lesson 81.

Drill 2: Compose and type, in enumerated form, complete sentence answers to the special questions. X-out and retype words on which you make errors. Save copy for use in Lesson 81.

Self-evaluation question (separate sheet)

What are some of the things you think you need to work on now so as to improve your typewriting skill?

Special questions (separate sheet)

1. Are you learning to make an evaluation of your typing performance as you type? What are some of the things you try to evaluate?

2. Do you now type with a minimum of waste motion? (with quiet hands and arms? with your fingers curved and upright? with the keystroking action in your fingers? without breaks or pauses? with your right thumb curved and on or close to the space bar? with your wrists low and relaxed? with your eyes on the textbook copy?)

3. Are you able to type balanced-hand words at a word level, or as rapidly as you can pronounce each word?

206b ▶15 Learn to type boxed tables

Boxed tables

1. Type table in usual manner, inserting horizontal rulings as you type. (Extend rulings one space beyond each margin.)

2. Remove the page and, using a ball-point pen, (preferably black ink), draw vertical lines at the midpoint between columns.

Drill: After studying the illustration to the right, type the problem with 10 spaces between columns. Insert the horizontal lines, spaced as shown, as you type. Remove the page and insert the vertical lines midway between columns with a ball-point pen.

WESNER DEVELOPMENT CORPORATION

DS

(Analysis of Costs)

DS

DS

Distribution Costs	Budget at Standard Cost	Actual Cost of Operations
Selling	$12,000	$14,328
Shipping Salaries	7,000	9,456

SS DS SS DS

Source: Annual Report.

206c ▶30 Type boxed tables

full sheets; carbon paper; second sheets; 1 cc; erase and correct errors

Problem 1

center vertically in reading position; DS body; 6 spaces between columns; insert rulings

words

SALES INCOME OF 3
ALLEGHENY COMMODITIES EXCHANGE 9

(Reported by Midwest Industrial Agents) 17

Agent	Total Sales in First Quarter	Total Sales in Second Quarter	Change in Sales Income	words
				43 / 49 / 52 / 61 / 74
Bernstein	$30,156	$36,651	+$6,495	81
Colazzi	25,131	28,225	3,094	86
Mehaffey	19,875	22,084	2,209	92
O'Neil	17,465	21,175	3,710	97
Ortiz	16,800	20,750	3,950	103
Stevenson	15,075	19,005	3,930	109
Zeleznik	12,775	17,250	4,475	114
				127

Problem 2

center vertically in reading position; DS body; 6 spaces between columns; insert rulings

GRIFFITH TRUCKING CORPORATION 6

Converted Depreciation Charges 12

Cost	Amount of Depreciation at 5%	Current Conversion Ratio *	Amount of Adjusted Depreciation	words
				37 / 42 / 49 / 55 / 67
$20,000	$1,000	150/100	$1,500.00	74
8,000	400	150/120	500.00	79
9,000	450	150/125	540.00	84
6,000	300	150/130	346.15	88
7,000	350	150/145	362.07	93
				106
$50,000	$2,500		$3,248.22	111
				123

* Depreciation computed for a year in which the index number is 150. 133 / 136

81

81a ▶5 Conditioning practice

each line 3 times (slowly, faster, in-between rate)

alphabet Hugh was quietly drizzling extra syrup and butter over warm flapjacks.

figures Type 1 and 2 and 3 and 4 and 5 and 6 and 7 and 8 and 9 and 10 and 213.

third row Jerry Pettie won't quote you a good price on any of those typewriters.

fluency They may use eight or more of the angle forms in order to do the work.

| 1 | 2 | 3 | 4 | 5 | 6 | 7 | 8 | 9 | 10 | 11 | 12 | 13 | 14 |

81b ▶15 Improve technique: keystroking

each line 3 times (slowly, faster, top speed)

Practice goal: quick, finger-reach keystroking; quiet hands

long, direct reaches

1 ce ce ec ec br br un un nu nu mu mu ny ny my my num num rv rv ym ym ym

2 ecce eccentric ny many num number br brief rv curve my myth ym symptom

3 My uncle will receive a bright uniform from the eccentric game umpire.

Practice goal: curved, upright fingers; quick, snappy keystroking

3d and 4th fingers

4 A poll of six zealous politicians was looked upon as a quick solution.

5 Paul was opposed to the use of lollipops to placate the quizzical lad.

6 Cool-as-a-breeze cottons, in the popular new azure color, are on sale.

Practice goal: continuity of typing; concentration on copy

long words

7 Fan the spark of possibility within you into the flame of achievement.

8 Free men protect freedom by accepting the responsibilities of freedom.

9 The science of electroencephalography probes the mystery of the brain.

Practice goal: curved, upright fingers; finger-reach action; quiet hands

difficult reaches z 10 Zestful, quizzical quiz kids dizzily zigzagged round a buzzing bazaar.

y 11 Today you may improve yesterday's typing rate if you just keep trying.

b 12 The bright baby boys babbled with joy as the abbey cobbler hurried by.

x 13 The extra exercise provided by mixing the wax in a box may tax Xerxes.

81c ▶20 Improve basic skill: rough draft

Repeat 80c, page 134. **Goal:** Increased speed or improved accuracy.

81d ▶10 Improve composing skill: rough draft

1. Make in longhand whatever corrections (spacing, spelling, mistyped words, or other corrections you wish to make that may be necessary in the composition you prepared as Drill 1, 80d, page 134; then retype the material in good form. Erase errors. (See Reference Guide, p. xii.)

2. Follow a similar plan for your composition of Drill 2.

205d ▶30 Type ruled tables with leaders

full sheets; carbon paper; second sheets; 1 cc; erase and correct errors

Problem 1

center vertically in reading position; DS body; 14 spaces between Columns 1 and 2; 6 spaces between Columns 2 and 3; insert rulings and leaders

words

NORTHCLIFF ENGINEERING CORPORATION 7

(Analysis of Balances) 12

Liabilities and Fund Balances*	This Year	Last Year	words
			36
			42, 47
			59
Accounts payable	$ 9,000	$ 7,000	71
Accrued expenses	3,000	4,000	82
Advance from convention fund	11,000	12,000	93
Dues collected in advance	26,000	23,000	104
Fund balance on December 31	81,000	76,000	116
			128

*Figures taken from annual report. 137

Problem 2

center vertically in reading position; DS body; 10 spaces between Columns 1 and 2; 4 spaces between Columns 2 and 3, and 4 spaces between Columns 3 and 4; insert leaders and rulings

words

PRODUCTION PERFORMANCE REPORT 6

(December, 19--) 9

Variable Manufacturing Costs*	Budgeted Costs	Actual Costs	Over or (Under)	words
				35
				44, 50
				63
Direct materials	$30,000	$32,000	$2,300	74
Direct labor	48,000	51,000	3,000	84
Indirect labor	15,000	14,500	(500)	95
Indirect materials	9,000	8,700	(300)	105
Supplies, etc.	4,000	4,560	560	114
Idle time	3,000	2,900	(100)	124
Material handling	10,000	11,000	1,000	135
Overtime premium	2,500	2,400	(100)	145
				158

*Based on normal activity of 10,000 hours. 166

206

206a ▶5 Conditioning practice

each line 3 times (slowly, rapidly, in-between rate)

Major Rizzo worked extra hours to acquire cash for buying vinyl lamps.
They sent 582 sheets, 140 pillows, 73 chairs, and 69 lanterns to camp.
Lee & Chin paid $1,884.50 for fowl (678# at $3.27), less 15% discount.
It takes a little effort and practice to build skill in typing tables.

| 1 | 2 | 3 | 4 | 5 | 6 | 7 | 8 | 9 | 10 | 11 | 12 | 13 | 14 |

82

82a ▶5 Conditioning practice

each line 3 times (slowly; faster; in-between rate)

alphabet The voluble judge quizzes expert witnesses before making any decision.
figures We received 129 chairs, 30 typewriters, and 75 desks on order No. 648.
long reaches The unusual aluminum bridge is decorated with many bright nylon flags.
fluency They lent the ancient ornament to their neighbor by the big city dock.

| 1 | 2 | 3 | 4 | 5 | 6 | 7 | 8 | 9 | 10 | 11 | 12 | 13 | 14 |

82b ▶15 Improve techniques: space bar; shift keys; shift lock

each line 3 times (slowly, faster, top speed); then application ¶ twice

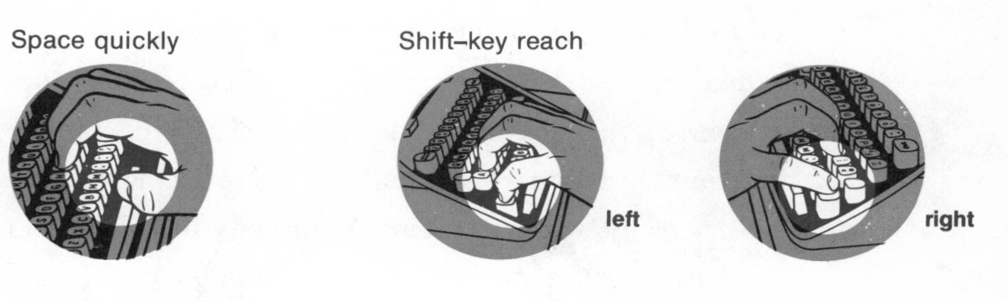

Practice goal: quick, down–and–in spacing stroke; hands quiet

space bar 1 and the and the (repeat for full line; space quickly without pauses)
2 If it is so, then he may do the work for us and the men from the city.
3 Please pay them when they have the plan for the map room for John May.

Practice goal: quick, little finger reach; other fingers in typing position

shift keys 4 Order the Damp Proof Red Primer from Barton P. Delaney, New York, N.Y.
shift lock 5 Jack, Frank, Paul, and Quinn read the book HOW TO SUCCEED IN BUSINESS.
underline 6 Kate Sutton and Jane McNeil wrote the book How to Succeed in Business.

Book titles may be typed in all caps or with the underline.

Practice goal: quick use of space bar, shift lock, shift keys, backspacer, and underline

application ¶

UNDERLINE the next three words: Type with Speed. Did you use the backspacer to move the carriage (or element) back for the underline? It may be quicker to push the carriage back with the left hand (or to use the Express Backspace Key, if you are using a Selectric), and then use the space bar to position the words to be underlined. Use the backspacer, however, when it is necessary to backspace ONLY A FEW SPACES.

205

205a ▶5 Conditioning practice

each line 3 times (slowly, rapidly, in-between rate)

May was given exquisite prizes by the judge for clever makeup schemes.
She reported camp attendance for three days to be 368, 297, and 1,540.
Interest rose from 7 1/2% to 8 1/2% on Smith & Baker's long-term note.
Jobs requiring considerable table typing are quite common in business.

| 1 | 2 | 3 | 4 | 5 | 6 | 7 | 8 | 9 | 10 | 11 | 12 | 13 | 14 |

205b ▶7 Improve speed/control

1. A 1′ speed writing on each ¶; determine *gwam.*

2. A 3′ control writing on both ¶s combined; circle errors; determine *gwam.*

all letters used | A | 1.5 si | 5.6 awl | 80% hfw

Text	gwam 1′	3′
Rules regulate most of our actions in life. Rules affect our daily	14	5
activities and behavior. In our individual relations with others, we are	28	9
guided by the rules of etiquette. Local, state, and federal laws direct	43	14
or control the actions of people and groups in our society. These laws	57	19
limit our freedom of action, but it would not be easy to live or to work	72	24
in any group without them. With no rules, confusion and strife can lead	87	29
to chaos. Regulations must be made and obeyed.	96	32
You will find many rules and regulations when you enter the industrial	14	37
scene. There may be rules about the hours of work, wages, absences,	28	41
safety, and many other phases of the job arrangement. Most employers	42	46
take the time and effort to explain the rules to new employees during	56	51
the first day or period of employment. Since rules are as essential to	70	56
the efficiency of business as they are to society as a whole, top firms	85	60
reward individuals who obey the rules that have been laid down for them.	99	65

gwam 1′ | 1 | 2 | 3 | 4 | 5 | 6 | 7 | 8 | 9 | 10 | 11 | 12 | 13 | 14 |
3′ | 1 | 2 | 3 | 4 | 5 |

205c ▶8 Learn to type ruled tables with leaders

To align leaders

1. Type the first line of the first column; space twice: note the position of the printing point indicator (13) (on an odd or even number); type a period, then a space alternately across the line; stop 2 or 3 spaces before the second column.

2. On lines that follow, align the periods with those in Line 1, typing on odd or even numbers.

Drill: Type the illustration to the right, inserting rulings and leaders as shown. Remove the paper and check your work.

STEVENSON CORPORATION

DS

Sales by product groups	Current year
Chemicals	$1,224
Industrial gases	781
Plastics	1,015
Metals	975

DS DS SS DS SS

82c ▶15 Apply improved techniques: progressive difficulty paragraphs

1. One 1′ writing on ¶ 1 using your best typing techniques. Divide rate by 4 for ¼′ goals.

2. Two 1′ guided writings on ¶ 2 at Step 1 rate. Repeat step for ¶ 3.

Goal: To maintain Step 1 rate on ¶s 2 and 3.

3. Two 1′ writings on ¶ 1 for speed. Repeat step for ¶s 2 and 3; try to maintain ¶ 1 rate.

¶ 1
Balanced–hand words = 60%

¶ 2
Balanced–hand words = 26%
One–hand words = 14%
Combination words = 60%

¶ 3
One–hand words = 60%

In typing, all of us should make as our first goal typing with the right form. When we use the right form at the typewriter, the work is much easier. Also, the right form pattern may help us solve the problem of typing with speed and accuracy which is an end goal of typewriting.

One of the first ways by which you are usually judged is on your appearance. It seems safe to say that a well-groomed person makes a much better impression on others than a person who is not and, in addition, causes an impression of a person who is competent and sure of himself.

Were you aware that after that date only a minimum number of the area abstracts can be saved? In my opinion, you should reserve these extra area abstracts for the trade union. You may recall that the trade union group saw this request after we were able to reverse the tax rate.

82d ▶15 Measure basic skill: script

1. Two 5′ writings; determine *gwam*; circle errors.

Goal: At least 80% of straight–copy rate of 76e, page 128.

2. Compute % of transfer: script–copy rate divided by straight–copy rate of 76e, page 128. Record better rate and % of transfer.

all letters used | A | 1.5 si | 5.6 awl | 80% hfw

	gwam 1′	5′
The beginning worker has to cope with many exacting prob-	11	2
lems in the business office. Not the least of these enigmas is	24	5
the art of getting along with others. A significant solution to	37	7
the puzzle of human relations is to do your own tasks in	48	10
the right way. This precise mode of working is one identi-	60	12
fication of the mature person. A mature person does not	71	14
commit the same mistakes again and again and will reason	83	17
with other employees rather than punching them in the nose.	95	19
Just practicing good manners at home or in school, with	11	21
your family or with others, will help you gain poise and	23	24
quiet confidence. Being well mannered means following the	34	26
accepted rules of behavior which aid in making your con-	45	28
tacts more genial. A basis of good manners is kindness	57	30
and a real concern for every person. You must like or	68	33
tolerate everyone, and then be sure to make an extra	78	35
effort to relate to them.	83	36

204c ▶8 Learn to type horizontal rules

Horizontal rulings

1. Single rulings: depress the shift lock and use the underline key.

2. Double rulings: type the first line; then use the variable line spacer (3) to move the paper forward slightly. Type the second horizontal line. Extend rulings one space beyond each margin.

Drill: Study the illustration at the right, observing the spacing between typewritten lines and the single and double rulings.

Type the problem, inserting rulings at the points indicated. Decide number of spaces between columns. Check your completed work to learn how well you made the rulings.

AREA BUSINESS ACTIVITY

DS

(Seasonally Adjusted)

DS

	March	September
Production	125.6	121.7
Trade and services	120.3	124.0
Transportation	150.9	150.5

Source: Area Chamber of Commerce.

(Spacing marks at right: DS, DS, DS, SS, DS, SS, DS)

204d ▶30 Type tables with horizontal rulings

full sheets; carbon paper; second sheets; 1 cc; erase and correct errors

Problem 1

center vertically; DS body and footnotes; 4 spaces between columns; insert rulings

	words
JOB FUTURE IN TRANSPORTATION CAREERS*	8
(Annual Report)	11
(double ruling)	37

Job Position	Employment This Year	Employment* in Ten Years	Percent of Change	words
				43 / 53 / 66
Flight engineers	7,500	12,000	59.3	73
Airline dispatchers	1,200	1,600	33.3	80
Locomotive engineers	3,500	3,300	−5.7	88
Pilots and copilots	52,000	114,000	116.9	96
Intercity bus drivers	24,000	28,000	17.5	104
Truck drivers-over-				108
the-road	640,000	800,000	24.7	114
				127

* Estimated. 129

Source: Bureau of Labor Statistics. 136

Problem 2

center vertically in reading position; SS body; DS between groups; 4 spaces between columns; insert rulings

	words
COMMONWEALTH SUPPLY COMPANY	6
(Direct Labor Budget)	10
(double ruling)	37

Division	Labor Cost Last Year*	Dollar Sales Last Year*	Labor-Sales Ratio	Projected Ratio	words
					46 / 55 / 68
1	$18,500	$300,000	6.17	6	73
2	16,900	205,000	8.24	7	78
3	14,800	195,000	7.59	7	83
4	11,600	170,000	6.82	6	88
5	8,400	90,000	9.33	8	92
6	4,500	80,000	5.63	5	96
					110

* Rounded to nearest hundred. 115

83

83a ▶5 Conditioning practice

each line 3 times (slowly; faster; in-between rate)

alphabet Fine cooks brought piquant flavor to exotic foods with zesty marjoram.

figures I have read 127 books, 364 magazines, 50 newspapers, and 89 pamphlets.

quiet hands The major exercise for many people comes from jumping to a conclusion.

fluency I may work with them or their friends in the ancient city by the lake.

| 1 | 2 | 3 | 4 | 5 | 6 | 7 | 8 | 9 | 10 | 11 | 12 | 13 | 14 |

83b ▶15 Correct common errors

each line twice (slowly; faster)

Goal: Not over 1 error in each line. As time permits, retype any line on which you made more than 1 error.

Practice goal: quiet hands; fingers in typing position

adjacent-key and long-reach errors

1 In my opinion, few errors of a covert type were made by the policeman.
2 The new colonel quickly assumed responsibility in all new quasi-areas.
3 A number of economic reports predict a bright outlook for the economy.

Practice goal: fingers curved and upright; finger-reach action

uneven stroking errors

4 Paul saw a plump polo pony near the old wax owl in that ancient plaza.
5 Zaza quickly saw and pointed out a loophole in the archaic quota laws.
6 An old wagon lost an axle as it was pulled from a cold swamp by Sally.

Practice goal: continuity; concentration on copy

vowel confusion errors (ie; ei)

7 A thief stole a pie from my neighbor during the weird and quiet storm.
8 I tried to seize the foreign piece before it was weighed by the chief.
9 Neither he nor I will receive a science degree because of our beliefs.

Practice goal: right thumb curved on space bar; down-and-in spacing motion

spacing errors

10 If he is to do the work for us, she may not be able to work with them.
11 Many men and women may share my interest in this work of pop artisans.
12 If Leon does not return soon, Jan may go to the swamp to look for him.

83c ▶15 Apply improved techniques

Repeat 82c, page 137. **Goal:** Increased speed.

83d ▶15 Improve basic skill: script copy

Repeat 82d, page 137. **Goal:** Increased speed or improved accuracy, according to your needs.

203d ▶30 Four-column tables with column headings

Type the following problems with 1 cc. Correct errors.

Problem 1

full sheet; center vertically in reading position; DS body; 6 spaces between columns

CONSOLIDATED PLUMBING CORPORATION

Breakdown of Total Expenses

Expense	January	February	Variation	words in cols.	words total
					7
					12
					26
Payroll & Benefits	$53,903	$42,100	−11,803	9	35
Printing--Conventions	25,651	15,020	−10,631	17	44
Travel--Conventions	6,088	14,320	+ 8,232	25	52
Distribution	5,244	3,210	− 2,034	32	58
Public Relations	7,777	4,029	− 3,748	39	66
All Other	26,753	32,678	+ 5,925	46	72

Problem 2

half sheet; center vertically; SS body; 8 spaces between columns

REPORT OF SALES AND BONUSES

Week of June 14, 19--

Salesperson	Sales	Bonus Rate	Bonus Earned	words
				6
				10
				26
Anderson, Sara	$3,105	4 1/2%	$139.73	34
Bulger, Richard	2,460	4	98.40	40
Cornetto, Joseph	1,800	3 1/2	63.00	47
Starman, Mildred	4,675	5	233.75	53
Steinberg, David	5,015	6	300.90	60
Woodruff, Paula	1,300	3 1/2	45.50	66
Yingling, Ruth	2,185	4	87.40	72

204

204a ▶5 Conditioning practice

each line 3 times (slowly, rapidly, in-between rate)

Mary Jane ate the extra pizza quickly before leaving with the dancers.
The four bowlers rolled 207, 163, 95, and 84 in the first league game.
Joe's check for $1,416.59 covered purchases and an 18% finance charge.
Most tables are not difficult to type if you take time to plan wisely.

| 1 | 2 | 3 | 4 | 5 | 6 | 7 | 8 | 9 | 10 | 11 | 12 | 13 | 14 |

204b ▶7 Table typing drills

1. Arrange and type the headings and the first line in the body of Problem 1 of 203d, above.

2. If time permits, type a 1′ writing on the columnar items in the body of the table. Omit the headings.

84

84a ▶5 Conditioning practice

each line 3 times (slowly, faster, in-between rate)

alphabet The winning team just broke every existing record for playing bezique.
figures Jack typed 15 letters, 48 envelopes, 73 tags, 29 labels, and 60 cards.
long reaches She executed many zany swan dives at the aquacade dedication ceremony.
fluency When he paid for the land, he also signed the audit form for the firm.

| 1 | 2 | 3 | 4 | 5 | 6 | 7 | 8 | 9 | 10 | 11 | 12 | 13 | 14 |

84b ▶15 Improve technique: keystroking

each line twice (slowly, top speed); as time permits, repeat selected lines for speed

Practice goal: uniform keystroking; variable rhythm

double letters
1 Full summers for swimming, tennis, and football seem too good to miss.
2 A teenager ate Swiss cheese and apples on a grassy hill in the valley.
3 A book of well-written essays on freedom was appreciated by the class.

Practice goal: continuity; no pauses as you type—concentrate on copy

long words
4 A living language is a changing, diversified, and creative phenomenon.
5 Double negatives are grammatically improper but semantically harmless.
6 Technically, hypersonic speed may revolutionize aeronautical concepts.

Practice goal: fingers curved and upright; quick, snap keystrokes

letter response
7 rare link debt pink edge pulp ease kiln aware nylon eager union faster
8 we are | my data | you were | get him | oil tax | at best | saw no cards | at my age
9 As you are aware, we read union data based on defect tests in my area.

Practice goal: think word or phrase, then type it with speed

word response
10 also body dual fork hang iris lens turn goals risks shape vigor height
11 if it is | to do so | and the | with them | their work | such form | both men wish
12 If it is so, then I may go with them and make them do the work for us.

Practice goal: variable rhythm; uniform keystroking; finger action

combination response
13 the date | they were | to the pin | for the case | and the address | the opinion
14 sign the agreement | held the statement | join the union | state the problem
15 If your address is correct, they may sign the agreement for the union.

Practice goal: finger reaches; fingers well-curved; quiet hands

long reaches
16 Order 75 pencils, 36 pens, 12 desk pads, 48 desk sets, and 90 erasers.

unit **36** lessons 203–208

Processing tabular reports

Learning goals

1. To improve speed and accuracy on straight copy.

2. To plan and type tables having multiple columns and two- and three-line columnar headings.

3. To learn how to type tables with rulings and with leaders.

4. To learn procedures for boxing tables.

Machine adjustments

1. Line: 70 for drills and timed writings.

2. Spacing: SS sentence drills; DS ¶s with 5-space indentions; as directed for problems.

203

203a ▶5 Conditioning practice

each line 3 times (slowly, rapidly, in-between rate)

alphabet Major Saxby was amazed to find the elegant antique kept in a big cave.

figures The caterers served groups of 189, 207, 56, and 34 out-of-town guests.

fig/sym Invoice 4096 (terms 2/10, n/30) listed 835# of Hygrade flour at $2.37.

fluency The ability to plan and type tables is a skill that is much in demand.

| 1 | 2 | 3 | 4 | 5 | 6 | 7 | 8 | 9 | 10 | 11 | 12 | 13 | 14 |

203b ▶7 Tabulating drill

type twice SS; DS between groups

Leave 10 spaces between columns.

				words
2,036	$1,489	1785#	29%	5
3,147	1,500	1325#	15%	9
4,295	2,850	400#	90%	13
5,362	3,947	965#	50%	17
6,574	4,628	829#	33%	22
7,380	5,534	637#	72%	26
8,926	6,419	2318#	68%	30
9,305	7,768	756#	49%	34

203c ▶8 Arranging column headings

Review centering and tabulating in Reference Guide, pages ix and x. Then type the drills shown at the right as directed below.

Drill 1: Center by column entries.

Drill 2: Center by column headings.

Drill 3: Center by longest item in each column, whether a heading or an entry.

Note: This procedure should be used in future problems unless otherwise specified.

Drill 1

Inventory	Cost	Retail
Purchases during January	$98,000	$1,002,638

Drill 2

Stockholders' Equity	Current Year	Prior Year
Capital Stock	87,320	64,511

Drill 3

Liabilities	Amount	Percent of Change
Current liabilities	$4,205,600	8.2%

Enrichment material for Unit 36 appears on LM p. 135.

84c ▶15 Beat-the-clock speed spurts

line: 70; tabs: each 15 spaces apart

1. Four 15″, 12″, or 10″ speed spurt writings on each line, as directed by your teacher.

Goal: To beat the clock by trying to get to end of line before time is called. Tab quickly across line.

Word-response phrases

					gwam 15″	12″	10″
and the	and the	and the	and the	and the	32	40	48
and they go	and they go	and they go	and they go	and they go	48	60	72

Letter-response phrases

					15″	12″	10″
are you	are you	are you	are you	are you	32	40	48
saw him get	saw him get	saw him get	saw him get	saw him get	48	60	72

Combination-response phrases

					15″	12″	10″
if the case	if the case	if the case	if the case	if the case	48	60	72
and the date	and the date	and the date	and the date	and the date	52	65	78

2. One 1′ writing on each sentence.

Goal: To maintain speed as sentences become more difficult.

Progressive-difficulty sentences

	15″	12″	10″
I may sign an amendment form if they do the work for the city auditor.	56	70	84
You will deliver the statement and the contract to them for signature.	56	70	84
Were you aware that the first draft of the union case was exaggerated?	56	70	84

| 1 | 2 | 3 | 4 | 5 | 6 | 7 | 8 | 9 | 10 | 11 | 12 | 13 | 14 |

84d ▶15 Measure basic skill: straight copy

two 5′ writings; determine *gwam*; circle errors; compare rate with rate of 76e, page 128; record better rate and speed gain on LM pp. 3, 4

all letters used | A | 1.5 si | 5.6 awl | 80% hfw

	gwam 1′	5′
It often is so easy to take many things for granted. Consider for	13	3
a moment what amazing equipment our hands really are. Just think of the	28	6
many difficult things, often without conscious thought, our hands do for	43	9
us every day. We utilize our hands for clapping approval, for waving	57	11
goodbye, for tugging at zippers, buttoning buttons, fumbling for door	71	14
keys, or for the quick and skillful operation of the keys of a typewriter.	86	17
Our hands and fingers do all these things for us and we hardly ever give	101	20
a thought to their wonder and adaptability. It is so easy to do this.	115	23
Yet there is more to hands than mere utility. Our hands and fingers	14	26
are used to express the deepest of human emotions. Our fingers touch	28	28
the strings of a guitar or the keys of a piano to express our mood and	42	31
feeling. Our hands are used in communicating with another individual,	56	34
whether orally or in writing. We use our hands to draw and to paint,	70	37
and we have developed beautiful and individual works of art with our	84	40
hands. Combined with our mind, our hands are one of the principal meth-	99	43
ods we use in learning. A youngster touches and feels everything to	113	45
gain knowledge about it, and the process is continued for a lifetime.	126	48

gwam 1′ | 1 | 2 | 3 | 4 | 5 | 6 | 7 | 8 | 9 | 10 | 11 | 12 | 13 | 14 |
5′ | 1 | 2 | 3 |

202b ▶15
Improve technique: shift keys and shift lock

1. Type each line twice; first, to improve skill in shift controls; second, to increase speed in controlling shift keys and the shift lock.

2. Select lines causing difficulty for additional writings.

left shift
Mary, Janet, Nancy, and Karen will go to New Orleans late in November.
Paul, Harry, Michael, and Oscar drove to New Mexico on a camping trip.

right shift
Carl, Frank, David, and Albert will go to South Bend late in February.
Betty, Dianne, Grace, and Angela wrote to school friends in Vera Cruz.

left and right
Frank and Jim joined Betty and Leonard in Hot Springs to review plays.
The group will travel to Des Moines, St. Paul, De Kalb, and St. Louis.

shift lock
The books, MONEY PROBLEMS and INCOME AVERAGING, will be released soon.
We gave two books, INFLATION and CONSUMERISM, as prizes for fine work.

202c ▶30
Improve speed/control

1. Two 3′ writings on each ¶; determine *gwam* for each writing.

2. Two 5′ writings on the combined ¶s; circle errors and determine *gwam.*

all letters used | A | 1.5 si | 5.6 awl | 80% hfw

Text	gwam 3′	5′
When a family has a specific amount of money that they want to	4	3
invest, they often give first consideration to getting a house. They	9	5
would be wise first, however, to be sure of a proper amount of life	13	8
insurance on the head of the family. Once the family insurance needs	18	11
are met and a home obtained, if one is desired, the family's aims can	23	14
be switched to investing in stocks and bonds. Many programs are offered.	28	17
Of those designed around negotiable securities, the two most used are	32	19
the mutual fund and the personal portfolio of securities planned by a	37	22
broker. The mutual fund enables one to buy shares in the fund, whereas	42	25
the portfolio is made up of shares of specific securities. The investor	47	28
must decide which plan is better for him. Brokers are happy to advise	51	31
investors, and any public library has a number of books on the subject	56	34
to assist the new investor.	58	35
The two types of corporation stock are the common and the preferred.	5	38
If only one type is to be issued, it is the common stock; for it is this	10	41
type that controls the way the business is executed. Holders of common	14	43
stock are most often the only owners with voting rights, which means that	19	46
they elect the board of directors, who in turn select corporate officers	24	49
and determine the firm's policies as well. Common stock has no guarantee	29	52
of return; it shares equally any profit or loss; and in case of a liqui-	34	55
dation, it is the last to be paid. While it is generally nonvoting, the	39	58
preferred stock is pledged a set amount of the annual earnings; on cumu-	43	61
lative preferred stock, any unpaid dividends of preceding years must be	48	64
paid in full prior to any disbursal on common stock. Participating stock	53	67
is that on which more than a set annual dividend is permitted.	57	69

gwam 3′ | 1 | 2 | 3 | 4 | 5
5′ | 1 | 2 | 3

85

85a ▶5 Conditioning practice

each line 3 times (slowly, faster, in-between rate)

alphabet	Brave mice make journeys through perplexing mazes in quest of rewards.
figures	I may buy 15 jackets, 289 blankets, 74 kits, 360 lamps, and 110 tires.
long words	Democracy is based upon the extraordinary possibilities in each of us.
fluency	The eight girls wish to go with me when I pay the firm for their work.

| 1 | 2 | 3 | 4 | 5 | 6 | 7 | 8 | 9 | 10 | 11 | 12 | 13 | 14 |

85b ▶15 Improve techniques: shift keys; space bar; keystroking

each line twice (slowly, top speed); as time permits, retype selected lines

Practice goal: quick shift-key reach with little finger

shift keys

1 Refer the papers to Miss Jan Q. O'Brien, secretary to McCrae and McGill.
2 Jack LeConte and Mary McLaird accepted jobs with S. Bobb Wooland, Inc.
3 J. C. McNeil, Vice-President of Roxy's, Inc., is now in New York City.

Practice goal: quick, down-and-in spacing motion; no pauses

space bar

4 If it is so that I am to do the work, then I may need to go with them.
5 If the men and women do all the work for us, Jay will pay them for it.
6 Many of us do plan to go with you on that excursion flight to England.

Practice goal: curved, upright fingers; quiet hands

3d and 4th fingers

7 The zealous politician was appalled by the losses in the wool markets.
8 Paula quizzed Wally about the use of that old wax on a new wood floor.
9 Opal and Zaza saw a buzzard hovering over the zebras down by the quay.

Practice goal: fingers in typing position; hands quiet

adjacent keys

10 Were you going to trade the seesaw in the recreation area for a swing?
11 Robert tired quickly as he tried to remove the five turrethead rivets.
12 As we drew near, a weaverbird wasted little time in vacating her nest.

Practice goal: quick, finger-reach action keystroking; quiet hands

long reaches

13 Cecil threw a minimum number of curve balls to many eccentric batters.
14 Myrna became concerned over a bad decision by the brazen young umpire.
15 Manny gave my uncle many bright nylon flags at an economic conference.

85c ▶15 Increase speed

Repeat 84c, page 140.

85d ▶15 Improve basic skill: straight copy

Repeat 84d, page 140. **Goal:** Increased speed.

Enrichment material for Unit 13 appears on LM pp. 5, 6.

201c ▶20 Improve speed/control

1. A 2′ writing on each ¶.
2. Two 5′ writings on the combined ¶s; circle errors; determine *gwam* for each 5′ writing.

all letters used | A | 1.5 si | 5.6 awl | 80% hfw

	gwam 2′	5′
Life is filled with risks. Each day we face the risk of losing	7	3
our property, our health, and even our lives. Our homes may be damaged	14	5
or ruined by fire, water, or wind. Our automobiles may be damaged by	21	8
collision or vandals. It is also possible we may, by accident, injure	28	11
others or effect damage to their property. Although we do not like to	35	14
think about these affairs, there is always a possibility they may occur.	42	17
Unless we take specific action to eliminate or to minimize the effect	49	20
of these risks, we can expect to face a financial loss. A reliable	56	22
way of guarding against these losses is through insurance.	62	25
Insurance is a means of providing protection against the risk of	7	27
financial loss. Not all risks, however, are insurable. Since insur-	14	30
ance is based on the consideration that the losses of a few are paid for	21	33
by the contributions of many, a large number of people must take part	28	36
in an insurance program. The annual loss caused by a risk or event must	35	39
also be predictable. The number of houses that will burn each year or	42	41
the number of highway accidents that will occur can be predicted with	49	44
great accuracy. The risk must also be spread over a large geographical	56	47
area to offset a loss that may be caused by a disaster in any one area.	64	50
Among the common types of risks for which insurance may be purchased are	71	53
fire, accident, theft, lawsuits, illness, and death.	76	55

gwam 2′ | 1 | 2 | 3 | 4 | 5 | 6 | 7
5′ | 1 | 2 | 3

201d ▶15 Composing at the typewriter

1. Use a plain sheet of paper for making notes.
2. Read the ¶s of 201c above, listing the main ideas contained therein.
3. Using your list as a guide, compose in your own words a summary of the thoughts presented in the paragraphs.
4. Proofread and mark your copy for correction; if time permits, type it in final form, correcting all errors made.

202

202a ▶5 Conditioning practice

1. Each line twice SS.
2. A 1′ writing on Line 4; determine *gwam*.

Jack Bigelow amazed friends by inquiring about a very expensive hotel.
Flight 485 will leave at 6:37 a.m. and arrive in Chicago at 10:29 p.m.
They charged Ray & Ash 6 1/2% on the $5,000 note (dated June 1, 1977).
She said they hoped to pay the bill before the next accounting period.

| 1 | 2 | 3 | 4 | 5 | 6 | 7 | 8 | 9 | 10 | 11 | 12 | 13 | 14 |

unit **14** lessons 86–88

Using the typewriter for special learnings

Learning goals

1. To improve skill in grammar, spelling, composing, and word division.

2. To develop skill in arranging material from unarranged copy.

3. To develop skill in centering on lines of varying length and paper of various sizes.

4. To develop skill in arranging column headings and column entries.

Machine adjustments

1. Paper guide at *0*.

2. 70–space line and single spacing (SS) unless otherwise directed.

3. Line space selector on *1*, or as directed for problems.

86

86a ▶5 Conditioning practice

each line 3 times (slowly, faster, in-between rate)

alphabet The qualified expert analyzed water from seventy cracked jugs by noon.

figures Today Vi sold 34 dresses, 56 hats, 78 ties, 90 shirts, and 12 jackets.

long words Work for typing perfection through thoughtful and purposeful practice.

fluency The proper keystroke is made with your fingers held close to the keys.

| 1 | 2 | 3 | 4 | 5 | 6 | 7 | 8 | 9 | 10 | 11 | 12 | 13 | 14 |

86b ▶15 Improve grammar skill: related learning

Margins
top: page 1, 1½″
other, 1″
side: 1″
bottom: 1″ (approx.)
vertical spacing: as shown in the copy

1. Reset left margin for blocked items; use margin release and backspace into the left margin for line identifications.

2. Type underlines as shown in illustrative sentences and note grammar applications.

3. If your teacher so directs, correct errors.

These guides are continued in Lessons 87 and 88. Retain paper for use there.

SERIES 1: GRAMMAR GUIDES
DS
(Some Common Errors)
TS

1. Verbs and subjects: The form of the verb must agree with the subject of the sentence. SS DS

a. A singular subject requires a singular verb. DS

A line of students is waiting to see the counselor.
One of the applicants is here for an interview.

b. Compound subjects (usually joined by and) require plural verbs.

My mother and my father are away this week.
BUT: My mother, as well as my father, is away this week.

c. Indefinite pronouns (each, every, any, everyone, either, and neither) when used as subjects are singular and require singular verbs.

Everyone in the class is typing well.
Each of the students is ready to go on the field trip.

d. Singular subjects linked by or or nor require a singular verb; however, if one subject is singular and the other plural, the verb agrees with the one that is closer.

Either my sister or my brother is going.
Neither the teacher nor the students are here.

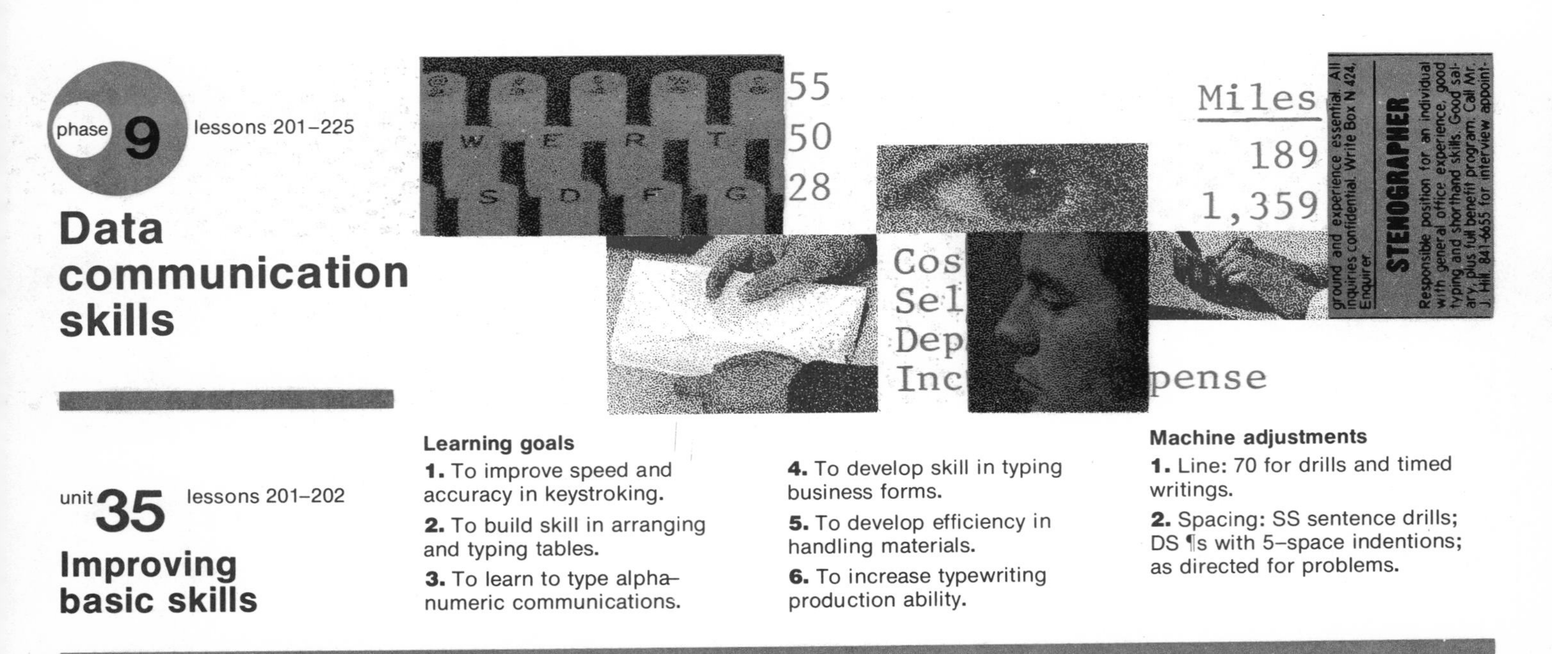

phase **9** lessons 201–225

Data communication skills

unit **35** lessons 201–202

Improving basic skills

Learning goals

1. To improve speed and accuracy in keystroking.
2. To build skill in arranging and typing tables.
3. To learn to type alpha-numeric communications.
4. To develop skill in typing business forms.
5. To develop efficiency in handling materials.
6. To increase typewriting production ability.

Machine adjustments

1. Line: 70 for drills and timed writings.
2. Spacing: SS sentence drills; DS ¶s with 5-space indentions; as directed for problems.

201

201a ▶5 Conditioning practice

each line 3 times (slowly, rapidly, in-between rate)

alphabet	Jack Boswell said the earthquake paralyzed six fine game reservations.
figures	A group was asked to add the following numbers: 106, 94, 275, and 83.
fig/sym	Ten percent, sometimes written .10 (or 10%), is equal to 1/10 of 100%.
fluency	You can improve your production rate by adding to your stroking skill.

| 1 | 2 | 3 | 4 | 5 | 6 | 7 | 8 | 9 | 10 | 11 | 12 | 13 | 14 |

201b ▶10 Improve stroking skill on script and rough draft

1. A 1′ writing on ¶ 1.
2. Practice those parts of ¶ causing difficulty.
3. A 1′ writing on ¶ 1; determine *gwam.*
4. Repeat steps 1–3 for ¶ 2.
5. A 2′ writing on the combined ¶s; determine *gwam.*

all letters used | HA | 1.6 si | 5.8 awl | 75% hfw |

	gwam 1′	2′
At some time or other, most alert folks find that unless and	12	6
until they lay aside funds to fall back upon in time of crisis	25	13
or to use in seizing rare chances for personal advancement,	37	19
business venture, or investment dividend, advance in economic	49	25
status comes very slowly. One way to distinguish a developed	62	31
country from an underdeveloped one is in the reservoir of	73	37
usable capital owned by the people in those countries.	84	42
~~Personal~~ Capital ~~may be~~ [can be] in the form of savings of many types and canbe	13	49
held and used ~~discriminatively~~ [in a lot of ways]. [Ranging] From simple to complex the ~~chief~~ [major] types in-	29	57
clude [creating cash balances in] bank demand deposits; holding savings [deposits] or ~~checking~~ accounts in cerdit	50	67
unions; enclarging equitys in pension funds, annuties, or [life] insurance; buying	66	75
~~long range convertible~~ [capital] assets such as a home, a personal ~~company~~ [chattel], or stocks	78	81
and bonds; [and buying other top securities.]	87	86

86c ▶10
Learn to center on lines, align, type over

half sheet, short side up
top margin: 1"

1. Read the directions at the right.

2. Type a 26-space underline starting 1" from the left edge of your paper.

3. Center and type your full name on the underline typed in Step 1. Determine center of underline according to formula given at the right.

```
______Philip V. Bailey______
```

Center of paper

```
_______Sally Phelps_|_______
```

↑ Elite line-of-writing scale

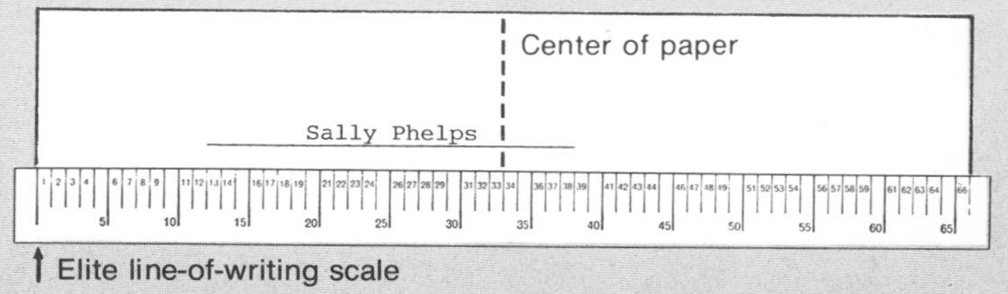

Find center of paper:	
Read scale at left edge of paper	0
Read scale at right edge of paper	+ 66
Total	66
Total ÷ 2 = Center point (66 ÷ 2 = 33)	

Find center of line or column:	
Read scale at first letter or item	12
Read scale at last letter or item	+ 38
Total	50
Total ÷ 2 = Center point (50 ÷ 2 = 25)	

4. Study the relationship of typed letters to underline. Note that only a slight space separates the letters of your name from the underline. As shown in the illustration, downstem letters (p, y, q, j, g) may touch the line. Now note on your typewriter the relationship of the typed letters and underline to the **aligning scale (21).**

5. Space down about 2" and type a 30-space underline starting 1½" from the left edge of your paper.

Center and type your name on the underline. Remove the paper.

6. Reinsert the paper. Align the paper and type over your name typed in Step 5.

Note: One way to check alignment is to set the ribbon control in stencil position and strike a letter key; then make any needed adjustments in the position of the paper.

86d ▶20
Learn to type on postal cards

1. Type the message side of 3 postal cards [LM p. 7] (or use paper cut to 5½" by 3¼") as illustrated at the right.

2. Type the following names and addresses on the blank lines of the postal cards typed in Step 1.

Ms. Barbara Weise
Star Route, Box 612
Carson City, NV 89701

Dr. Venay Gupta
514 Frankfurt Avenue
W. Covina, CA 91792

Mrs. Violet Kendall
567 Barcelona Road
Denver, CO 80229

3. Address each card: type appropriate return address, then the organization address shown below.

American Education Association
9066 Wilshire Boulevard
Los Angeles, CA 90136

```
4 → February 10, 19--   ↓ 1 2 3

2DS

Gentlemen:
DS
Please send me the free copy of "Skills That
Build Teaching Success," and enter my subscrip-
tion to the Teacher's Review for two years.
DS
Name_________________________________________
DS
Address______________________________________
DS
City__________________State______ZIP Code_____
```

```
↓ 1 2
Ms. Barbara Weise
Star Route, Box 612
Carson City, NV 89701
↑
2 or 3 spaces                    About 2"

——about 2"——→ American Education Association
              9066 Wilshire Boulevard
              Los Angeles, CA 90136
```

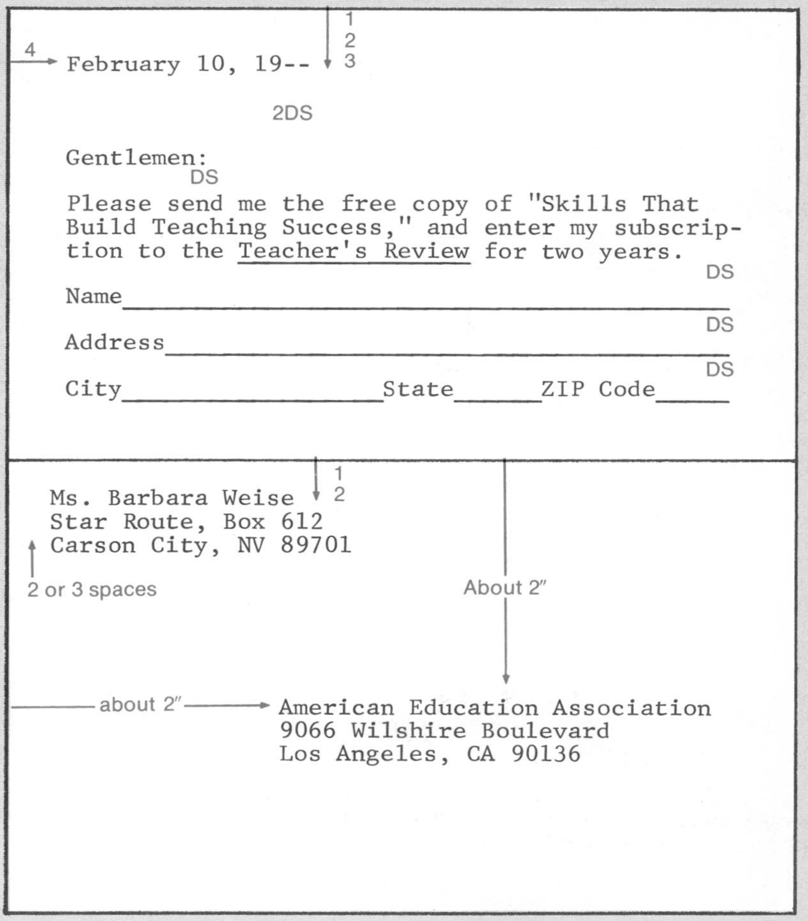

200

200a ▶5 Conditioning practice

Repeat 199b, page 316.

200b ▶10 Measure basic skill: straight copy

Repeat 199b, page 316.

200c ▶35 Measure production skill: special letters and communications

[LM pp. 117–124]

Follow the time schedule and procedures outlined in 199c, page 317.

Problem 1
Letter with subject line and listed enclosures
executive-size stationery; modified block, mixed

	words
December 28, 19-- Mr. Donald S. Chaney 1850	9
Columbia Pike Arlington, VA 22204 Dear Mr.	17
Chaney: Subject: Tax Savings Plans (¶ 1) This	26
is a request for you to read the enclosed	34
booklets dealing with tax problems faced by	43
successful executives. We want you to stay	52
abreast of changing tax laws and to benefit	61
from expanding opportunities in investment	69
programs and retirement plans. The enclosed	78
booklets should prove useful in helping you	87
plan new investments. (¶ 2) Please take a few	95
minutes to examine the materials we are en-	104
closing; then let us help you work out some	112
investment plans that should prove highly	121
profitable. Very sincerely yours, Milton E.	130
Shaw Tax Department xx Enclosures Tax	137
Breaks in Real Estate Build Retirement In-	145
come Use Insurance Dividends	151/163

Problem 2
AMS letter

	words
December 28, 19-- Mrs. Judy McClain Man-	8
ager, Office Services National Food Proces-	16
sors 620 Delaware Avenue Buffalo, NY 14202	25
SEMINAR ON OFFICE SERVICES (¶ 1) We are	32
offering an unusual management seminar to	40
a select group of executives who are con-	48
cerned about increasing office efficiency. The	58
following meetings have been organized with	66
you in mind: 1. Utilizing office space effec-	76
tively 2. Managing time wisely 3. Stream-	85
lining records management 4. Modernizing	94
through telecommunications (¶ 2) The en-	101
closed brochure gives complete program details	110
and costs. Please read it carefully and plan	119
to join us for these important sessions. A	128
reservation form is enclosed for your con-	136
venience. CHESTER J. ELSON, VICE PRESIDENT	145
xx Enclosures	148/169

Problem 3
Informal government letter

	words
DATE: December 28, 19-- REPLY TO ATTN. OF:	4
BPJR SUBJECT: Reclassification of Office	10
Positions TO: Ms. Linda Lucas, Supervisor	18
Secretarial and Clerical Staff U.S. Department	27
of State Washington, DC 20520 (¶ 1) In a recent	35
directive from the Chief of Personnel, we were	45
asked to review all secretarial and clerical	54
positions in our division. It is hoped that we	63
may be able to reclassify or eliminate some of	73
the positions now under our control. Thus, I	82
should like to have you: a. Prepare an accurate	92
list of all jobs under your supervision. b. Make	102
a detailed list of all activities assigned to each	112
of the jobs on your list. c. Indicate positions	122
for which changes in job specifications should	132
be made. d. Identify which, if any, positions	141
are no longer needed. (¶ 2) Please proceed with	150
this assignment at once and report to me	158
periodically on your progress. Enclosed is a	167
copy of official guidelines for your use. MRS.	177
SHIRLEY BARTLEY Division Director xx	184
Enclosure	186

Problem 4
Retype Problem 1, using the address below; supply an appropriate salutation.

Mr. Max Fleetwood
3301 Gallows Road
Falls Church, VA 22046

87

87a ▶5 Conditioning practice

each line 3 times (slowly, faster, in-between rate)

alphabet Zak requested extra guava jelly for making his peanut butter sandwich.

figures In 1976, we had 83 office chairs, 40 office desks, and 52 work tables.

fingers 3, 4 A plump yellowtail swallowed the squid as I attempted to set the hook.

fluency If you do all your work in the right way, the work will be easy to do.

| 1 | 2 | 3 | 4 | 5 | 6 | 7 | 8 | 9 | 10 | 11 | 12 | 13 | 14 |

87b ▶15 Improve grammar skill: related learning

1. Reinsert sheet used for typing grammar guides of 86b, page 142.

2. Align copy properly and continue with Guide **e.** The copy is set in semiproblem form, so you will need to space it properly. Use your typed copy as the guide to spacing.

Recall

1. Margins: 1″ side; 1″ (approx.) bottom on all pages that are full.

2. Reset left margin for blocked items; use margin release to backspace into the left margin for line identifications.

3. Type underlines as shown in illustrative sentences and note grammar applications.

e. Collective nouns (committee, team, class, jury, etc.) when used as subjects are usually singular and require a singular verb.

The team has gone to the locker room.
The jury has returned its verdict.

f. Subjects such as all and some, as well as fractions and percentages, are plural if their modifiers are plural and singular if their modifiers are singular.

All the students have been working diligently.
All the food has been frozen.
Two thirds of the work is completed.
Two thirds of the workers are here.

g. Some subjects are confusing; you must know if they are singular or plural.

Some of the data in your report are erroneous.
In my opinion, the national news is good today.

h. Don't (do not) and doesn't (does not), as verbs, are often confused.

The scale doesn't work properly.
BUT: The scales don't work properly.
She doesn't want to order new letterheads now.
They don't want to order new letterheads now.
It doesn't matter; use either style for the letter.

i. A number as the subject is usually plural and requires a plural verb; the number is usually singular and requires a singular verb.

A number of students are here for the tour.
The number of students is smaller this year.

2. Pronouns and their antecedents: A pronoun (he, she, it, they, their) should agree with its antecedent in person, gender, and number (singular or plural).

a. Person

Marla, who goes to college, finds that she has to study.
Students who go to college find that they have to study.

199c ▶35 Measure production skill: special letters and communications

Time schedule

Preparation .... 5′
Timed production ... 25′
Final check;
compute *n–pram* .. 5′

1. Follow time schedule shown at the left.

2. Arrange supplies (forms, plain sheets, erasers). [LM pp. 113–116]

3. Make 1 cc and correct errors neatly.

4. Address envelopes.

5. When directed to begin, type for 25′ from the problems given below. If you finish all problems in less than 25′, retype Problem 3 on a plain half sheet.

6. Proofread and circle uncorrected errors found in final check. Compute *n–pram* for the 25′ period.

7. Arrange and turn in all problems in the order in which they are numbered.

Problem 1
Message side for a message/reply memo

words

TO: Mr. Lloyd J. Grubb Director of Mainte- 7
nance 104 Services Building DATE: December 15
20, 19-- (¶ 1) I have received a number of 22
complaints about the air-control systems in the 32
third-floor word processing area. Specifically, 42
the supervisors have reported extreme changes 51
in room temperatures, ranging from too hot to 60
too cold, in relatively short periods of time. 70
(¶ 2) Please investigate these complaints, 77
arrange with our engineers to inspect the 85
equipment, and report your findings to me. 94
Thank you. BY: David Smith, Personnel 101
Relations 102/**115**

Problem 2
Interoffice memo

TO: Frank E. Liguori, Office Manager FROM: 7
Hobart Adams, Vice President DATE: Decem- 13
ber 20, 19-- SUBJECT: Equipment Reports 20
(¶ 1) Within a few weeks, it will be necessary 28
for us to submit a detailed report on equip- 36
ment. For that report, we have been asked to 46
designate by type, brand name, serial number, 55
and acquisition date all equipment used in 63
our administrative offices. (¶ 2) Accom- 70
panying our equipment report must be a com- 79
pilation of future needs. This statement must 88
identify those needs considered to be imme- 96
diate (within the next six months) and those 105
considered to be long range. Replacement 114
and new equipment items must be shown 121
separately. (¶ 3) Please begin now to assemble 130
data essential to the preparation of these re- 139
ports. xx 141/**147**

Problem 3
Letter on half-size stationery
Modified block, mixed

words

December 21, 19-- Mr. John Hyde 3527 7
Leesburg Pike Alexandria, VA 22302 Dear 15
Mr. Hyde: (¶ 1) You are a prominent business 23
leader; you spend much of your life planning. 33
But have you planned for your family as 41
carefully as you plan for the affairs of your 50
business? Family estates often suffer from 59
inadequate planning. (¶ 2) The value of any 67
estate can fluctuate considerably, depending 76
upon economic conditions and the cost of liv- 84
ing. Good estate planning must consider these 94
eventualities. (¶ 3) Please read the enclosed 102
booklet; then give me the pleasure of talking 111
with you about our estate planning service. 120
Sincerely yours, Mrs. Mary Jane Trinkle 128
Investment Counselor xx Enclosure 135/**145**

Problem 4
Reply to message of Problem 1

DATE: December 22, 19-- (¶ 1) The word 5
processing area on the third floor was having 15
air-control problems because of a faulty 23
thermostat in the air-conditioning system and 32
a broken fan in a blower unit in the ventilating 42
system. (¶ 2) Our engineers have replaced the 50
thermostat, and the air-conditioning system is 59
working well again. (¶ 3) We have had to order a 68
part for the fan, however. When it arrives, we 78
shall repair the blower unit. In the meantime, 87
I'm sure the work area will have comfortable 96
temperatures. SIGNED: Lloyd J. Grubb 102/**109**

87c ▶15 Learn skill applications

Drill 1

Column headings shorter than column entries

Problem-solving steps

1. Recall: Center column entries horizontally. Leave 4 spaces between columns.

2. Tryout: Center, type, and underline the headings on the second and third line spaces above the column entries.

3. Check: Check your work with the suggested procedure given at the right.

4. Redo: Repeat drill following steps of forward-space, backspace method.

Study Each Word	Pronounce by Syllables	Capitalize Trouble Spots
superintendent	su-per-in-tend-ent	superinTENDent

Forward-space, backspace method

From first letter of column (or column heading, if it is used for horizontal centering), space forward (→) 1 space for each 2 spaces in column entry (or heading, when it is used for centering), ignoring any odd or leftover letter. This point will be the center of the column (or heading).

Forward space

→

1 2 3 4 5 6 7 spaces

su /pe /ri /nt /en /de /nt

From this point, backspace (←) once for each 2 spaces in heading to be centered (or longest column entry if it is to be centered under a column heading), ignoring any odd or leftover letter.

Backspace

←

1 2 3 4 spaces

Ea /ch /#W /or

From this point, type and underline second heading line (Drill 1). It will be centered over the column. Next, center and type the first heading line and it, too, will be centered over the column as shown above.

Drill 2

Column headings longer than column entries

1. When column headings are longer than column entries, center the column headings horizontally first (in this drill leave 4 spaces between headings).

2. DS and center the longest column entry under the heading. Use forward-space, backspace method. Check your solution by the mathematical method. (See 86c, page 143.)

Study Each Word	Pronounce by Syllables	Capitalize Trouble Spots
superintendent	su-per-in-tend-ent	superinTENDent

87d ▶15 Apply skill

full sheet; center table vertically; TS after centered heading; DS after column headings; DS column entries; 6 spaces between columns

Recall

Use procedures suggested in 87c, above, for centering headings over longest column entry. When a heading is only slightly longer than an entry, center it over the longest column entry. (See Column 3.)

The table suggests a study procedure, using the typewriter, for words that are often misspelled. The procedure is recommended for any words you may have trouble spelling.

WORDS OFTEN MISSPELLED — words 5

Study Each Word	Pronounce by Syllables	Capitalize Trouble Spots	words
			24
appearance	ap-pear-ance	apPearANCE	31
athlete	ath-lete	atHletE	36
business	busi-ness	busIness	42
chief	chief	chIEf	45
February	Feb-ru-ar-y	FebRUary	51
friend	friend	frIEnd	56
necessary	nec-es-sar-y	neCESSary	62
omitted	o-mit-ted	omitTED	67
passed	passed	passED	72
quantity	quan-ti-ty	quanTity	77
receive	re-ceive	recEIve	82
separate	sep-a-rate	sepArate	88

unit **34** lessons 199–200

Measuring office communication skills

Measurement goals

In the next two measurement lessons, you will demonstrate your ability to type:

1. For 5′ on copy of average difficulty at levels of speed and control indicated by your teacher.

2. Business letters containing special features, an informal government letter, an interoffice memo, and a message/reply memo, all in correct style from semiarranged copy according to specific directions.

Machine adjustments

1. Line: 70 for drills and timed writings.

2. Spacing: SS sentence drills; DS and indent ¶s; as directed for problems.

199

199a ▶5 Conditioning practice

each line 3 times (slowly, top speed, in-between rate)

alphabet Jack Bizal may acquaint the vigorous pupils with ideas for excellence.

figures Hays sold 495 tires, 83 doors, 172 wheels, and 60 panels for the vans.

fig/sym A 4% sales tax of $9.42 (on $235.60) was added to Sims & Baker's bill.

fluency If you will organize your work well, you will produce at higher rates.

| 1 | 2 | 3 | 4 | 5 | 6 | 7 | 8 | 9 | 10 | 11 | 12 | 13 | 14 |

199b ▶10 Measure basic skill: straight copy

a 5′ writing; circle errors; determine gwam

all letters used | A | 1.5 si | 5.6 awl | 80% hfw |

Text	gwam 1′	5′
There are very few people who do not need to utilize some of the	13	3
many services provided by banks. Banks are so common that we often	27	5
forget what a vital role they play in our daily lives. Under the capi-	41	8
talistic system, money is a prime requisite; and a bank is actually a	54	11
business which deals in the deposit, custody, remittance, and issue of	69	14
money. Without banks, it would not be possible for us to conduct our	83	17
monetary affairs. Without banks, no modern system of business would	96	19
be able to function.	101	20
Inasmuch as a bank may obtain its charter from either a state or	13	23
the federal government, a dual banking system exists in this country.	27	26
A state bank is one that is set up as a corporation under a charter that	42	29
is issued by the state in which it operates. A national bank obtains	56	31
its charter to operate under federal banking laws. Banks also differ in	70	34
the types of services they provide for their customers. Among the many	85	37
banks are the commercial bank, the savings bank, and the trust company.	99	40
The most popular of all banks, however, is the commercial bank.	112	43
The commercial bank performs numerous services for its patrons.	13	45
One of the most significant is the famed checking account, which is	27	48
based on demand deposits. A demand deposit is one that the depositor	41	51
can withdraw at any time without advance notice to the bank. The demand	55	54
is in the form of checks or written orders by which the depositor directs	70	57
the bank to disburse a given sum of money to a stated payee.	82	59

gwam 1′ | 1 | 2 | 3 | 4 | 5 | 6 | 7 | 8 | 9 | 10 | 11 | 12 | 13 | 14 |
5′ | 1 | 2 | 3 |

88

88a ▶5 Conditioning practice

each line 3 times (slowly, faster, in-between rate)

alphabet Remarks of the zealous junior executive were quashed by game partners.

figures The zoo ordered 785 birds, 4 bears, 20 bison, 9 lions, and 163 snakes.

fingers 3, 4 The plump squaw was coloring wax apples as the zany tourists appeared.

fluency If they do the work, they may go to the lake to fish and to dig clams.

| 1 | 2 | 3 | 4 | 5 | 6 | 7 | 8 | 9 | 10 | 11 | 12 | 13 | 14 |

88b ▶15 Improve grammar skill: related learning

End of Series 1

1. Reinsert sheet used for typing grammar guides of 87b, page 144 (or use new sheet, if sheet is full).

2. As you type, arrange and space copy properly.

After completing series

1. Arrange sheets in order.

2. Number all pages (except first) on Line 4 at the right margin.

3. Save sheets for later use in a special *Type-writing Manual* that you will be directed to prepare.

b. Gender

Everyone in this class has finished his or her work. (mixed group)
BUT: The class has finished its work. (class as a unit)
Each sorority member named her favorite sport.
Each fraternity member named his favorite sport.

c. Number (singular or plural)

All of us have completed our work.
Neither Jane nor Mary has her book.
Janet and Ken have lost their workbooks.
The committee has completed its report. (committee as a group)
The committee did not complete their reports. (committee as individuals)

3. Other errors: Take steps to reduce other grammatical errors.

a. Don't confuse fewer (meaning number) with less (meaning quantity).

We have had fewer typewriter service calls this year.
We have had less typewriter maintenance cost this year.

b. Don't confuse bad (describing health and quality) with badly (describing behavior or other action).

He said that he felt bad. (state of health)
He handled the situation badly. (behavior)

c. It is not incorrect to end a sentence with a preposition, but it is incorrect to add a preposition unnecessarily.

WRONG: Where is the office at?
RIGHT: Where is the office?

WRONG: They went there to rest up.
RIGHT: They went there to rest.

RIGHT: Where is the new employee from?
RIGHT: This is the house I live in.

d. Avoid faulty pronoun references in sentences you write.

WRONG: Maria collected many scraps of fabric and saved it for a quilt.
RIGHT: Maria collected many scraps of fabric and saved them for a quilt.

198b, continued

Problem 2
Message/Reply Memo

	words
TO: Miss Mary Stuart Parke Director of Personnel 1032	10
Administration Building DATE: December 14, 19-- (¶) Mary,	20
how are you acquainting our administrative support personnel	32
with recent changes in company policy regarding increased	43
employee fringe benefits? As you know, the enacted policy	55
changes provide unusual opportunities for greater financial	67
security for our employees. (¶) Please update me on your	78
steps to implement executive releases directing us to	89
publicize these new financial opportunities.	98
BY: Donald Hobbs, Vice President	104/**121**

Problem 3
Reply to message

	words
DATE: December 15, 19-- (¶1) I have circulated to all personnel	11
copies of material dealing with (1) possibilities for indi-	22
vidual contributions to the company retirement plan,	33
(2) procedures for authorizing payroll deductions for the	44
purchase of savings bonds, and (3) opportunities for par-	56
ticipation in company stock option plans. (¶2) I have	66
scheduled follow-up seminars in the offices of each of	77
the corporate divisions for employees indicating an interest	89
in our programs. (¶3) Upon completion of the seminar pro-	99
grams, I shall report to you on the success of our efforts.	111
SIGNED: Mary Stuart Parke	115/**123**

Problem 4
Telegraphic message on plain paper

	words
PHONED TELEGRAM Night Letter December	8
14, 19--, 4:50 p.m. Mr. Carl Routt, Traffic	16
Manager Central States Railroad 901 S.	24
Michigan Avenue Chicago, IL 60605 (¶ 1) Need	32
three freight cars for special shipments from	41
our siding in Indianapolis to the Norwood Sta-	50
tion in Cincinnati, Ohio, from December 27	59
to 29. Anticipate 7 1/2-hour loading time at our	69
warehouse and 6-hour unloading time at desti-	78
nation. Please inform on your ability to supply,	88
types of cars available, approximate arrival	97
time of cars to be furnished, and when cars	105
must be unloaded and released. Request	113
prompt reply with statement of estimated costs.	123
Donald Brummett, Vice President Schurtter	132
Steel Products, Inc. xx	136

Problem 5
Letter of confirmation

modified block; open

	words
December 15, 19-- Mr. Maurice Lindborg,	8
President Central States Railroad 901 S.	16
Michigan Avenue Chicago, IL 60605 Dear Mr.	25
Lindborg (¶ 1) We must make an unanticipated	33
shipment to one of our special customers at a	42
time when no empty freight cars are on our	51
siding. As a matter of fact, we can expect no	60
cars until January 24. Late yesterday I tele-	69
graphed your traffic manager as follows:	77
(Insert message of Problem 4)	170
(¶ 2) It is critical that these shipments leave our	179
premises on schedule. I ask your help in	187
processing this request and in making the	196
required cars available on the dates specified.	205
Thank you for your cooperation. Sincerely	214
yours Donald Brummett, Vice President xx	222/**241**

88c ▶30 Apply skill

Problem 1
Word-division checkup

half sheet; long side up; center table vertically; DS columnar data; leave 6 spaces between column headings; center longest column entry under each heading; set tabs at these points

As you type the table, show in the second column the correct division of each word in Column 1. The first 2 words are shown correctly divided.

Note: If a word should not be divided, type it without hyphens.

WORD DIVISION REVIEW

Syllables of Word	Acceptable Division Points
knowl-edge	knowl-edge
stud-y-ing	study-ing
op-er-ate	
math-e-mat-ics	
im-me-di-ate-ly	
a-re-a	
planned	
com-mit-tee	
will-ing	
re-fer-ring	

Problem 2
Composing

1. Check your division of the words in Problem 1 by referring to the basic word-division guides on page 68. In longhand, show any needed corrections.

2. In complete sentence form, compose the rule guide that applies to each word in the table. Refer to guides on page 68, if necessary.

Problem 3
Typing from dictation

drill sheet; 1″ top and 1″ left margin; DS

1. From your teacher's dictation of the words in Column 1, 87d, page 145, type the words in a single vertical column (book closed).

2. Check your spelling by referring to 87d, page 145. Circle any spelling error.

3. Reinsert drill sheet; align copy; reset left margin 10 spaces to left of center; start at this point and type 3 times each word you mis-spelled, capitalizing the letters that caused you trouble.

Problem 4
Special table

half sheet, long side up; 70-space line; 1″ top margin; elite tabs: 34, 63; pica tabs: 26, 55; block column headings as shown

1. Type copy line for line and space it vertically as shown.

2. Study copy suggestions as time permits.

Practice cues

Eyes on textbook copy; return and type or tab quickly.

COMMON TYPING ERRORS
TS

Type of Error	Probable Cause	Correction Steps DS
Adjacent-key; long reach	Fingers out of typing position; bouncing hands and arms	Check hand-and-finger position; type with fin-ger keystroking action. DS
Uneven keystroking	Failure to strike each key with uniform force	Concentrate on uniform keystroking, especially with third and fourth fingers. DS
Spacing	Incorrect thumb position; failure to strike space bar with quick, down-and-in motion	Keep right thumb curved and on or near space bar; strike and release space bar quickly. DS
Transposition; vowel confusion	Inattention to letter sequences in copy	Concentrate on copy to be typed.

Enrichment material for Unit 14 appears on LM pp. 9, 10.

197

197a ▶5
Conditioning practice

each line 3 times SS (slowly, top speed, in-between rate)

Major Jack Sterling watched five zealous boys build aquatic expertise.
They will ship 109 locks, 248 keys, 65 bolts, and 73 electric buzzers.
Check 8157 covering 695# of seed at $3.78 was sent to Jackson & Kelly.
There are times when typists handle the inner secrets of big business.

| 1 | 2 | 3 | 4 | 5 | 6 | 7 | 8 | 9 | 10 | 11 | 12 | 13 | 14 |

197b ▶45
Build sustained production: special business communications

Time schedule
Preparation .... 6′
Timed production ... 30′
Final check:
compute *n–pram* .. 9′

1. Make a list of problems to be typed:

page 310, 194c, Problem 1
page 311, 195d, Problem 2
page 313, 196c, Problem 1
page 309, 193c

2. Arrange supplies (forms and plain sheets) [LM pp. 101–104] for rapid handling. Prepare 1 cc of each problem.

3. Type for 30′ when directed to begin; follow directions given for each problem; correct all errors neatly. Proofread carefully before removing a problem from the typewriter.

4. Compute *n–pram*: Total acceptable words + ½ of your unacceptable words ÷ minutes typed.

5. After computing *n–pram*, turn in all problems arranged as listed in Step 1.

198

198a ▶5
Conditioning practice

Repeat 197a, above.

198b ▶45
Measure production skill: special business communications

[LM pp. 105–110]

1. Use 197b time schedule.

2. Arrange supplies (forms and plain sheets).

3. Make 2 cc and address appropriate envelopes.

4. Type for 30′ from the problems provided; correct errors as you type.

5. Circle uncorrected errors found in final check; compute *n–pram* for the 30′ timing.

Problem 1
Interoffice memo

words

TO: Tim Denny, Traffic Control 5
FROM: James Campbell, Vice President 12
DATE: December 14, 19-- 15
SUBJECT: Unloading Delays at Warehouses 21

During the past few weeks, a number of complaints have been filed by 35
hostile truckers over the amount of time required to unload incoming 49
trucks at our St. Louis warehouses. 56

Of particular concern to the truckers involved has been our alleged prac- 71
tice of permitting small pickup trucks to occupy dock spaces previously 85
assigned to larger rigs, thus denying the larger vehicles access to docks 100
where cargos are to be unloaded. It has been claimed by some truckers 114
that they have encountered delays of 10-12 hours after reaching our ware- 129
house area. 131

I want you to investigate traffic control and unloading schedules at the 146
warehouses involved and give me a detailed report of your findings. 160

xx 160

cc Daniel Hays, Receiving Clerk 166/174

unit **15** lessons 89–98

Personal/business letters

Learning goals

1. To improve basic skill on straight, statistical, and rough-draft copy.

2. To transfer good typing technique patterns to problem copy.

3. To develop and improve skill in arranging and typing letters in modified block (indented paragraphs) and block styles.

4. To do all work with a minimum of waste time and motion.

Machine adjustments

1. Paper guide at *0*.

2. 70-space line and SS, unless otherwise directed.

3. Line space selector on *1*, or as directed for various activities.

4. Ribbon indicator on black (on *R* for Selectric).

Special letter placement points

Stationery

Most business letters are typed on standard-size letterheads (8½" × 11"), at the top of which are printed a name, address, and other desired information about a company.

For letters longer than 1 page, plain paper of the same size, color, and quality is used after the first page.

For short letters, smaller letterheads, usually 5½" × 8½" (half-size), may be used.

Margins/vertical placement

Some offices use standard margins (a set line length) for all letters. Other offices vary the margins according to letter length. A placement table is given here to help you place letters properly. With time, you *must* be able to estimate letter length and place letters properly without using a placement aid.

Letter placement table

Letter Classification		5-Stroke Words in Letter Body	Side Margins	Margin Settings Elite	Margin Settings Pica	Dateline Position (From Top Edge of Paper)
Short		Up to 100	2"	24 – 83	20 – 70	Line 20
Average	1	101 – 150	1 1/2"	18 – 89	15 – 75	18
	2	151 – 200	1 1/2"	18 – 89	15 – 75	16
	3	201 – 250	1 1/2"	18 – 89	15 – 75	14
	4	251 – 300	1 1/2"	18 – 89	15 – 75	12
Long		301 – 350	1"	12 – 95	10 – 80	12
Two-page		More than 350	1"	12 – 95	10 – 80	12
Standard 6" line for all letters*		As above for all letters	1 1/4"	15 – 92	12 – 77	As above for all letters

* Use only when so directed. Some business firms use the standard 6" line for all letters.

Placement table pointers

1. Vertical placement of the dateline varies with the letter length. The address is *always typed on the fourth line* (3 blank line spaces) below the date.

2. *Special* lines (attention, subject, etc.) or features like tables, lists, extra opening or closing lines will require adjusting dateline placement.

If a deep letterhead prevents typing the date on the designated line, type it on the second line below the last letterhead line.

89

89a ▶5 Conditioning practice

each line 3 times (slowly, faster, in-between rate)

alphabet Perky zither quintets climax enjoyable evenings of wild, earthy music.

figures Please ship Order 7421750 for 36 typewriters, 49 desks, and 128 lamps.

double letters The difference between success and luck may well be a matter of pluck.

fluency The efficient way to gain speed is to type with continuity and rhythm.

| 1 | 2 | 3 | 4 | 5 | 6 | 7 | 8 | 9 | 10 | 11 | 12 | 13 | 14 |

196b ▶25 Learn to type a memo about telegraphic messages

1. Type this memo on a full-size interoffice memo form [LM pp. 99, 100].
2. Proofread and indicate corrections needed.
3. As time permits, study content and discuss procedures with your teacher.
4. Retain your copy for reference in 196c.

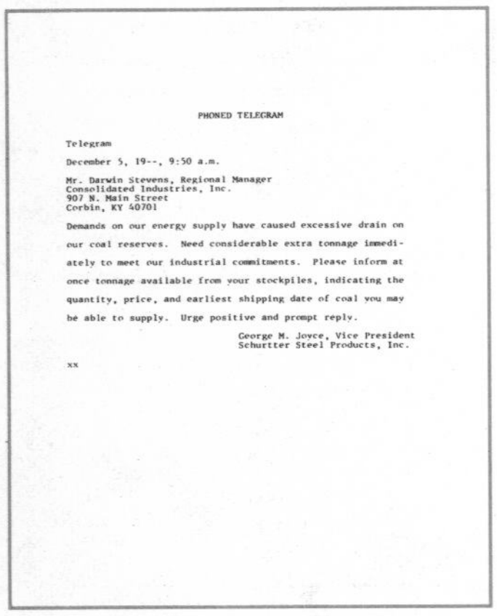
PHONED TELEGRAM

Telegram

December 5, 19--, 9:50 a.m.

Mr. Darwin Stevens, Regional Manager
Consolidated Industries, Inc.
907 N. Main Street
Corbin, KY 40701

Demands on our energy supply have caused excessive drain on our coal reserves. Need considerable extra tonnage immedi- ately to meet our industrial commitments. Please inform at once tonnage available from your stockpiles, indicating the quantity, price, and earliest shipping date of coal you may be able to supply. Urge positive and prompt reply.

George M. Joyce, Vice President
Schurtter Steel Products, Inc.

xx

words

TO: All Word Processors 4
FROM: Janet Rutherford, Director 9
DATE: December 5, 19-- 13
SUBJECT: Telegraphic Messages 17

Telegraphic messages are frequently transmitted to Western Union 30
by telephone. Messages to be sent by telephone are typed on plain 43
paper in a 60-space line. Follow these guides when typing 55
telegraphic messages to be phoned: 62

1. Center the heading (Phoned Telegram) 2 inches from top of page. 75
2. Type class of service (Telegram or Night Letter) at left margin 89
   on third line below heading. 95
3. Type name of account to be charged (only if not that of the 108
   sender) at left margin on third line below class of service. 120
   (omitted in illustration)
4. On a single line, type the date and the time the message was filed. 135
5. Type complete address of addressee (including phone number if 148
   known) single-spaced and blocked at left margin. 158
6. Double-space the message. 164
7. Double-space after message and type name and title of sender, 178
   followed by company name. 183
8. Type your initials for reference. If company name is used as 196
   signature, include initials of person sending message. 207

Prepare at least one carbon copy (for Accounting Department 219
records). Prepare additional copies if required for other uses. 233
xx 233

196c ▶20 Learn to type telegraphic messages

Problem 1

Type the message on a plain sheet; proofread and circle errors.

Problem 2

Type the same message as a night letter, using the same day and 4:20 p.m. Send to the following addressee:

Mr. Alfred J. Pedron, President
Commonwealth Coal Company
295 Allegheny Street
Russellton, PA 15076

PHONED TELEGRAM words 3
TS

Telegram 5
DS
December 5, 19--, 9:50 a.m. 11
DS
Mr. Darwin Stevens, Regional Manager 18
Consolidated Industries, Inc. 24
907 N. Main Street 28
Corbin, KY 40701 31
DS

Demands on our energy supply have caused excessive drain on 43
our coal reserves. Need considerable extra tonnage immedi- 55
ately to meet our industrial commitments. Please inform at 67
once tonnage available from your stockpiles, indicating the 79
quantity, price, and earliest shipping date of coal you may 91
be able to supply. Urge positive and prompt reply. 101
DS

George M. Joyce, Vice President 108
Schurtter Steel Products, Inc. 114

xx 114

89b ▶15 Improve speed/control: straight copy

1. Two 1′ writings. Start second writing at ending point of first writing. Try to maintain same, or better, rate.

2. Two 2′ writings for speed. Compute average *gwam*.

3. Subtract 4 words from your average rate; then type two 2′ *guided writings* at this new rate for control (not over 2 errors in each writing).

4. As time permits, type 1′ writings for speed or control, according to your needs.

Practice goal

Continuity with quick spacing; fingers curved and upright.

all letters used (adjacent keys; outside keys; long reaches)

Every second we live is a new and unique moment in our lives, a moment that never was before and never will be again. We should recognize that time is probably our most precious asset. What we do with time and how we manage it can and does have a significant effect on our lives. If we manage time properly, we can become whatever we would like to become. So just remember that in all the world, there is no other person exactly like you. And for that special person, time is important; with it you can do almost anything you want to do.

89c ▶30 Learn skill applications

plain sheets, 8½″ × 11″

Problem 1
Learn letter style

Type Style Letter 3, page 150, in modified block style with 5-space ¶ indentions as shown (215 words).

In typing the letter in correct form, be guided by the placement and spacing notations given in color.

Type the letter at rough-draft speed (top speed); x-out or strike over any typing errors.

Problem 2
Proofread and make rough-draft corrections

Proofread the letter you typed as Problem 1. Show by handwritten corrections any changes that you need to make in the copy.

Where you x'd-out or struck over any words or letters, write such words correctly. Use the standard proofreader's marks you learned (Reference Guide page ix) to make the needed handwritten corrections.

Problem 3
Build skill

Using your corrected rough-draft copy, retype the letter. As you type, make the corrections you have indicated in your copy.

Type on the control level; erase and correct neatly any errors you make as you retype the letter. Compare your letter with Style Letter 3.

90

90a ▶5 Conditioning practice

each line 3 times (slowly, faster, in-between rate)

alphabet Just strive for maximum progress by quickly organizing the daily work.

figures Jack and Lee labeled 12,967 illustrations, 450 tables, and 38 figures.

adjacent keys It will help to remember that anger is but one letter short of danger.

fluency To type rapidly, hold your arms quiet and let the fingers do the work.

| 1 | 2 | 3 | 4 | 5 | 6 | 7 | 8 | 9 | 10 | 11 | 12 | 13 | 14 |

195d, continued

REPLY-O-GRAM

SCHURTTER STEEL PRODUCTS INC.
301 N. MERIDIAN STREET INDIANAPOLIS, IN 46204

MESSAGE	REPLY
TO Miss Mary Jane Crawford Director, Personnel Development 1036 Administration Building DATE November 21, 19-- In determining and allocating operating costs for administrative divisions, we have found we need to upgrade the performance of many office workers. The Board feels that we can thereby achieve greater productivity in all office functions and prevent excessive costs. Will you initiate at once a program with all office supervisors to develop an "increased productivity" program. BY Ronald Thompson, Controller *R. T.*	DATE November 24, 19-- I have requested a day-long meeting with all office supervisors to discuss the problems you raised. The meeting is scheduled for 8:30 a.m. Monday in the Conference Room. We'll try to develop criteria for evaluating performance and to compile meaningful guidelines for use later in work measurement activities. I intend to develop programs to improve the performance of experienced workers as well as the productivity of our new employees. I shall report the results of our meetings to you. SIGNED Mary Jane Crawford *MJC.*

Problem 2
Type a message/reply memo

(Message for Problem 2) — words

TO: Ms. Dorinda Clippinger Director of Publications 305 Services Building (8, 14)
DATE: November 25, 19-- (¶ 1) Can you furnish 75 copies of our new Procedures Manual to be distributed to our office supervisors? (¶ 2) Since we plan to use the manuals in our in-service training programs, their cost should be charged to the Division of Personnel Development. (21, 30, 38, 47, 56, 64, 67)
BY Maureen Millar, Office Services (73/87)

(Reply for Problem 2) — words

DATE: November 26, 19-- (¶ 1) I have only 55 new manuals at the present time. Others have been ordered and should reach us at least by December 1. (¶ 2) To avoid exhausting our present stock, I am sending you now only 40 copies. As soon as the new shipment is received, I shall send the remaining 35 manuals to you. (¶ 3) I'm sorry our stock is so depleted that I cannot send all copies ordered. (7, 16, 25, 32, 41, 49, 59, 67, 75)
SIGNED Dorinda Clippinger (79/88)

196

196a ▶5
Conditioning practice

each line 3 times SS (slowly, top speed, in-between rate)

Kevin and Jim ate big pizzas with six recently acquired opera friends.
We fixed 35 globes, 287 maps, 104 books, and 69 old coins for exhibit.
On May 12, Baker & Thompson paid $2,187 to avoid a penalty of 18 1/2%.
It is generally true that capable typists enjoy their work activities.
| 1 | 2 | 3 | 4 | 5 | 6 | 7 | 8 | 9 | 10 | 11 | 12 | 13 | 14 |

75 EAST WACKER DRIVE, CHICAGO, IL. 60601
(312) 747-2121

		words parts	total
	Start at center point of paper		
Dateline	Line 14 March 29, 19--	3	3
	4 line spaces (3 blank lines)		
Letter address	Mr. Greg Taylor	6	6
	517 Randwich Road	10	10
	Dothan, AL 36301	13	13
Salutation	Dear Greg:	16	16
Body of letter	Decisions! Decisions! Life is full of decisions.	11	27
	Some decisions you can make with little thought or plan-	22	38
	ning; other decisions require much thought and careful	33	49
	planning, as they can have a profound effect on your life.	45	61
	One such decision is that of career choice. Every deci-	56	72
	sion you make about a career leads to still other ques-	67	83
	tions to be answered.	72	88
	What are the answers? Don't drown in a sea of inde-	82	98
	cision. Take steps now that will help you make wiser	93	109
	career decisions. One of these steps is to read our	103	119
	monthly magazine, <u>Careers</u>. This magazine is designed	116	131
	especially for students. It will help you evaluate career	127	143
	options and choose that career which is best for you.	138	154
	A copy of the latest issue of <u>Careers</u> is enclosed.	150	166
	Examine it; read it; study it. Discuss it with your par-	162	177
	ents, your teachers, and your classmates. After you do	172	187
	these things, we know you will want to subscribe to it.	183	199
	The student rate is only $5 a year. Make a wise decision	195	210
	now by returning the enclosed subscription card. We'll	206	222
	bill you after you receive your first issue.	215	230
Complimentary close	Sincerely yours,	3	234
Signature	*Susan Drexel*		
Typed name and official title	Ms. Susan Drexel, Editor	8	239
Reference initials	xx	9	240
Enclosure notation	Enclosures	12	242

Shown in pica type
1½" side margins

Style letter 3: modified block with indented paragraphs and mixed punctuation.

195

195a ▶5 Conditioning practice

each line 3 times SS (slowly, top speed, in-between rate)

Lex and Jack won the favored prizes early in the big aquatic jamboree.
Janet gave 93 dolls, 80 pillows, 146 jumpers, and 275 rings to a club.
On June 6, 1977, the rate on Ed's $6,000 note rose from 7% to 10 1/2%.
You will now learn to apply your skill in new business communications.

| 1 | 2 | 3 | 4 | 5 | 6 | 7 | 8 | 9 | 10 | 11 | 12 | 13 | 14 |

195b ▶5 Improve speed/control

Two 1′ writings on Line 1 of 195a, then on Line 4. Compare rates.

195c ▶20 Type a memo about the message/reply form

1. On a full-size interoffice form [LM pp. 93, 94], type the memo.

2. Proofread and indicate any corrections needed.

3. As time permits, study the content and discuss procedures with your teacher.

4. Keep your copy for reference in 195d.

		words
TO:	All Word Processors	4
FROM:	Janet Rutherford, Director	9
DATE:	November 15, 19--	13
SUBJECT:	Message/Reply Memos	17

A message/reply memo is a two-way, within-company communication in (30) which both the message and the reply are typed on the original copy of (45) multiple-copy forms. These forms are used when very brief messages are (59) exchanged among staff members. The following procedure should be (72) followed in their use: (77)

1. Sender types message in left-hand column, keeps the second copy (91) (yellow), and forwards others (white and pink) to addressee. (103)
2. Addressee types reply in right-hand column, keeps third copy (pink), (117) and returns original copy (white) to sender. (128)
3. The type of envelope and form of address to be used depend upon (140) whether the message travels through U.S. Postal channels or through (154) COMPANY MAIL. (157)
4. To insert into envelope, fold from bottom to top, creasing horizontally at (173) center of page. (176)
5. Signatures of both parties may be handwritten, or typed and then (190) initialed. (192)

xx (193)

195d ▶20 Learn to type two-way communications

Problem 1

On a message/reply form (LM pp. 95, 96), type the message and reply shown at the top of page 312. Circle errors and address an envelope marked COMPANY MAIL.

Note: Although most message/reply forms come in sets of three to provide the necessary two carbon copies, the Laboratory Materials provide for only one carbon.

Problem 2

On a message/reply form (LM pp. 97, 98), type the message and the reply given below the model on page 312. Circle errors and address an envelope marked COMPANY MAIL.

90b ▶15 Build basic skill: letter parts

plain paper; margins, 1½″

1. Four 1′ writings on the opening parts (dateline through salutation) of Style Letter 3, page 150. When you have typed through the salutation, DS, tab for the date, and repeat the drill. Type these parts as many times as you can during the 1′ timings. Leave proper spacing between parts. Determine *gwam*.

2. Using Style Letter 3, type four 1′ writings on the closing parts (complimentary close through enclosure notation). When you have typed through the enclosure notation, DS, tab for the complimentary close, and repeat the drill. Type for speed. Determine *gwam*.

3. On another sheet of paper, type a 3′ writing on the body of the letter. Determine *gwam* by dividing the total words typed by 3.

Note: On which of the timed writings did you make the highest speed: opening lines? closing lines? body of the letter? Why?

90c ▶30 Build production skill: letters

plain paper, 8½″ × 11″

Type the two letter problems as directed below.

Style

Use modified block, 5-space ¶ indention, mixed punctuation (colon after salutation, comma after complimentary close); date and closing lines started at center. Use your initials as the reference initials for the letters.

Placement

Use the Letter Placement Table, page 148. The number of words in the letter body is indicated by the number in parentheses at the end of each letter.

Problem 1
Skill building

	words
April 10, 19-- | Mr. Joseph N. Feinstein | 5042 Stern Avenue | Sherman Oaks,	14
CA 91423 | Dear Mr. Feinstein:	20
(¶ 1) If you sometimes feel like just another number at your present bank,	34
Heritage National Bank now offers college students a unique alternative.	49
(¶ 2) The enclosed folder describes in detail various aspects of our Student	63
Banking Program. We think you'll agree that this program, with the special	78
banking benefits it offers college students, is truly a new dimension in bank-	94
ing service. (¶ 3) Please pay us a visit soon. You'll like our friendly approach.	109
Sincerely yours, | Yutako Masago | Vice President | xx | Enclosure (89)	121

Problem 2
Skill building

May 5, 19-- | Miss Margaret O'Connor | 241 Moreno Drive | Beverly Hills,	13
CA 90212 | Dear Miss O'Connor:	19
(¶ 1) A few weeks ago we sent you information about our new Student	32
Banking Program. Mrs. Roberts, our Student Services Officer, tells me that	47
you haven't responded to our invitation to pay us a visit. (¶ 2) Our new	61
Student Banking Program means that you will be able to save money when	75
you use our flexible student checking account, which is especially designed	90
to meet your needs. We also have a credit plan for students. Why not	104
enjoy this new credit convenience when making purchases on campus or in	119
town. A proven credit record now will put you a step ahead of the crowd	133
when you want to establish a credit rating after graduation. (¶ 3) The	146
enclosed brochure describes the various aspects of our Student Banking	161
Program. Please take a moment to review it. We think you'll agree that	175
our Student Banking Program with the special benefits it offers is indeed	190
a new dimension in banking services for students. If you have any ques-	204
tions about any aspect of this program, just call Mrs. Roberts at 871-2341.	220
You'll like her. (¶ 4) We hope to see you soon. Sincerely yours, | Yutako	233
Masago | Vice President | xx | Enclosure (209)	240

194c ▶25 Learn to type interoffice communications

1″ side margins; proofread; circle errors; address envelopes marked COMPANY MAIL [LM pp. 91, 92]

Problem 1
Half-size interoffice memo

Type the memo from the model shown at right.

words

SCHURTTER STEEL PRODUCTS INC.
301 N. MERIDIAN STREET INDIANAPOLIS, IN 46204 (317) 421-1212

INTEROFFICE COMMUNICATION

TO: Juan M. Garcia 3

FROM: Jack Ellis, Executive Vice President 10

DATE: November 10, 19-- 14

SUBJECT: Warehouse Inventories 18

At its last meeting, the Board of Directors spent considerable 31
time discussing the flow of products from our production and 43
distribution points. Corporate officials are concerned about 56
the growing trend throughout our organization to warehouse goods 69
for prolonged periods of time. Figures cited by the Inventory 81
Control Division show excessive capital tied up in products 93
stored interminably in our warehouses. The Board feels that 105
tying up valuable space with items that can and should be moved 118
is completely indefensible. 124

You know that storage space is at a premium. Please take steps 137
immediately to alleviate our serious warehousing problem. 149

xx 149
154

A one-page memorandum

Problem 2
Page 2 of a memo
plain half sheet

1. Type the heading SS, beginning on Line 7.
2. TS, then type the body with SS.
3. DS above and below the tabulation.
4. Allow 8 spaces between columns of table.

words

Juan M. Garcia 3
Page 2 4
November 10, 19-- 8

The Controller, responding to a request by the Board of Directors for 22
information concerning the approximate dollar value of items now stored in 37
our company warehouses, supplied the following figures for each of our 51
distribution centers: 56

		words
Atlanta, GA	$3,869,247.50	61
Boston, MA	782,964.50	65
Denver, CO	2,976,438.50	70
St. Louis, MO	4,023,816.75	76
Philadelphia, PA	3,869,247.50	82

I should like to have you study the enclosed inventory data and report to 96
me within 10 days on possible steps that you think may be taken to attack 111
and solve our warehousing problems. 119

xx 119

Enclosure 121
126

91

91a ▶5 Conditioning practice

each line 3 times (slowly, faster, in-between rate)

alphabet	Liza picked several exquisite flowers which grew by the jungle swamps.
figures	The fishermen caught 84 albacore, 3,215 barracuda, and 7,690 mackerel.
fingers 3, 4	A plucky polo player amazed us as he zigzagged crazily down the field.
fluency	She may go with them to the town by the lake to do work for the widow.
	| 1 | 2 | 3 | 4 | 5 | 6 | 7 | 8 | 9 | 10 | 11 | 12 | 13 | 14 |

91b ▶15 Build basic skill: letter parts

plain paper; 1" margins

1. Three 1' writings on the opening lines of Problem 2 below. Leave proper spacing between letter parts. Determine *gwam*.

2. Three 1' writings on the closing lines of Problem 2. Determine *gwam*.

3. A 1' writing on each of the ¶s of the letter of Problem 2. Type with as much speed as possible. Type with good techniques. Determine *gwam*.

91c ▶30 Build production skill: letters

Problem 1
Personal business letter on executive-size stationery (7¼" × 10½") [LM pp. 13, 14]

modified block style, block ¶s (see page 73);

1" side margins; mixed punctuation; start return address on Line 14

Note: Titles of magazines or newspapers need not be underlined in letter addresses.

	words
Randolph School |2611 Pontchartrain Blvd. |New Orleans, LA 70124 |April	14
10, 19-- |Ms. Susan Drexel, Editor |Careers Magazine |75 East Wacker	27
Drive |Chicago, IL 60601 |Dear Ms. Drexel:	36
(¶ 1) Here at Randolph School, a number of us are studying career oppor-	48
tunities. We have found your magazine, <u>Careers</u>, most helpful. I have been	65
designated by our class to write to you about some of our career concerns.	80
(¶ 2) Do you have any information about growth trends in business and	93
industry that may affect career opportunities? What are some of the fields	108
in which there will be continuing or increasing employment opportunities?	123
Some of us would like to enter the teaching field, but we have learned that	138
there may be decreasing demands for teachers in the future. Our teacher	153
tells us that there always will be employment opportunities in the service	168
fields. What are the future trends in the service area? (¶ 3) We know	181
there are no easy answers to the questions our class has raised about career	196
opportunities, but we shall appreciate any help you may be able to give us.	212
Sincerely, |Scott Lightfoot (176)	217

Problem 2
Skill building
[LM pp. 15, 16]

modified block style; indented paragraphs; mixed punctuation

Use Letter Placement Table, page 148, to determine margins and dateline placement.

	words parts	total
April 21, 19-- |Mr. Scott Lightfoot |Randolph School |2611 Pontchartrain	14	14
Blvd. |New Orleans, LA 70124 |Dear Scott:	22	22
(¶ 1) You have raised good questions about career opportunities for young	14	36
people in school today. Let me review briefly some points that may help	28	50
you and your classmates assess future career prospects.	39	61
(¶ 2) As in the past, there will always be career opportunities for the per-	14	75
son who is creative and imaginative, who has learned some salable skills,	29	90
and who is willing to work. A need will continue for good teachers, doctors,	44	105
lawyers, farmers, and office workers--to name just a few of the present	59	120
career fields.	62	123

(¶ 3--*Please turn to page 153*)

193c ▶25 Type a report on interoffice communications

Margins
top: 1½"
side: 1"

DS ¶s; SS enumerated items; DS above, between, and below them

1. Type the report.

2. Proofread and indicate corrections needed.

3. As time permits, study content and discuss procedures with your teacher.

4. Keep your copy for reference in 194c.

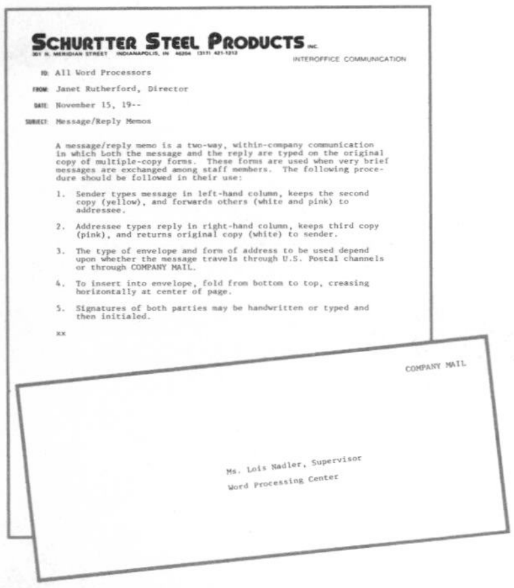

SCHURTTER STEEL PRODUCTS INC.
301 N. MERIDIAN STREET INDIANAPOLIS, IN 46204 (317) 421-1212
INTEROFFICE COMMUNICATION

TO: All Word Processors

FROM: Janet Rutherford, Director

DATE: November 15, 19--

SUBJECT: Message/Reply Memos

A message/reply memo is a two-way, within-company communication in which both the message and the reply are typed on the original copy of multiple-copy forms. These forms are used when very brief messages are exchanged among staff members. The following procedure should be followed in their use:

1. Sender types message in left-hand column, keeps the second copy (yellow), and forwards others (white and pink) to addressee.

2. Addressee types reply in right-hand column, keeps third copy (pink), and returns original copy (white) to sender.

3. The type of envelope and form of address to be used depend upon whether the message travels through U.S. Postal channels or through COMPANY MAIL.

4. To insert into envelope, fold from bottom to top, creasing horizontally at center of page.

5. Signatures of both parties may be handwritten or typed and then initialed.

xx

COMPANY MAIL

Ms. Lois Nadler, Supervisor
Word Processing Center

words

INTEROFFICE COMMUNICATIONS 5

Interoffice memos are used frequently to communicate with 17
others within a business firm. The following guides highlight the 30
features of memo style: 35

1. Memos may be typed on either half sheets or full 46
sheets, depending on message length. 54

2. A special letterhead is used for within-company mess- 65
ages. 66

3. Space twice after printed headings to set left margin 78
for typing heading items. 83

4. Personal titles (Mr., Miss, Ms., Mrs., Dr., etc.) usually 96
are omitted from the heading. They are included, how- 107
ever, on the envelope. 111

5. No salutation or complimentary close is used. 122

6. TS between headings and message; SS the para- 131
graphs; DS between paragraphs; DS above and below a 142
tabulation. 144

7. Side margins are usually 1 inch, printed headings 155
being aligned at the right so that the left margin stop 166
guides the typing of the heading data and the body. 177

8. Reference initials are included. 185

Special colored envelopes are usually used for interoffice 196
communications. When plain, unmarked envelopes are used, how- 209
ever, type COMPANY MAIL (in all capitals) in the postage location. 222
The address includes the addressee's name, personal title, and busi- 236
ness title or name of department. 242

194

194a ▶5 Conditioning practice

each line 3 times SS (slowly, top speed, in-between rate)

Lexie departed vehemently before taking a quick journey to Switz City.

They found 692 stamps, 174 records, 50 puzzles, and 83 decks of cards.

Invoice 695-240, due on February 1, showed a discount for cash at 15%.

Many typists are required to send messages to persons within the firm.

| 1 | 2 | 3 | 4 | 5 | 6 | 7 | 8 | 9 | 10 | 11 | 12 | 13 | 14 |

194b ▶20 Improve speed and control

Repeat 193b, page 308. **Goal:** Improved *gwam*; reduced errors.

91c, continued

	words parts	total
(¶ 3) Future industrial growth will most likely occur in the chemical and	14	137
allied fields, in rubber and plastic products, and in electric utilities and	29	152
machinery. The discovery of new sources of energy is certain to develop	44	167
a demand for employees. As more and more persons are covered by some	58	181
type of health insurance, opportunities in the health care field will increase.	74	197
(¶ 4) In the service industries, people who can fix things--mechanics, electri-	14	212
cians, television repair persons--will be in demand. As leisure time continues	30	228
to increase, industries that serve leisure-time needs will provide many	45	242
employment opportunities. Then, too, basic-need industries--food, clothing,	60	257
shelter, and transportation--will continue to provide career opportunities.	76	273
(¶ 5) People in school today will likely have a serial career pattern; they will	92	289
enter various career fields during their lifetimes. The best advice, then,	107	304
for most students would be to get both a specialized education that permits	122	319
flexibility and a broad education that provides for adaptability.	136	333
Sincerely yours, | Ms. Susan Drexel, Editor | xx (311)	9	342

92

92a ▶5 Conditioning practice

each line 3 times (slowly, faster, in-between rate)

alphabet	These children were amazed by the quick, lively jumps of the gray fox.
figures	Please notice Rule 36 on page 210 as well as Rule 85 on pages 479-482.
first row	Six brave men helped Aza C. Bonman carry an excited lynx to a zoo van.
fluency	She may go with them down the lane to the shale rocks by the big lake.

| 1 | 2 | 3 | 4 | 5 | 6 | 7 | 8 | 9 | 10 | 11 | 12 | 13 | 14 |

92b ▶15 Improve speed/control: statistical copy

1. Two 1′ writings. Start second writing at ending point of first writing.

2. Two 2′ writings for speed. Compute your average *gwam*.

3. Subtract 4 words from your average rate; then type two 2′ guided writings at this new rate for control (not over 2 errors in each writing).

Practice goal
Finger reaches; quiet hands.

all figures used

How does the average family allocate its income to such categories [4, 8, 12] as food, clothing, and shelter. The national averages for all income levels [16, 20, 24, 28] are approximately as follows: 27 to 30 percent of income goes for housing [32, 36, 40] and household operation; 19 to 25 percent is used for food; transportation [44, 48, 52, 56] expenses take another 14 to 17 percent; clothing absorbs from 9 to 13 [60, 64, 68, 72] percent of the family budget; another 6 to 8 percent is expended for [76, 80, 84] medical care; and 13 to 21 percent is used in other ways. [88, 92, 96]

unit **33** lessons 193–198

Special business communications

Learning goals

1. To improve speed and control on straight copy.
2. To develop skill in typing inter- and intra-office communications.
3. To develop power in typing message/reply memos.
4. To develop skill in typing telegraphic messages.

Machine adjustments

1. Line: 70 for drills and timed writings.
2. Spacing: SS sentence drills; DS and indent ¶s; as directed for problems.

193

193a ▶5 Conditioning practice

each line 3 times SS (slowly, top speed, in-between rate)

alphabet	The six judges made amazingly quick verdicts about fine points of law.
figures	The shop record was 98,536 units above the 740,215 units of last year.
fig/sym	Belth & Wise bought 1,825# of finished fiber for $6,743.90 last month.
fluency	Those typists having high production skill usually do well in offices.

| 1 | 2 | 3 | 4 | 5 | 6 | 7 | 8 | 9 | 10 | 11 | 12 | 13 | 14 |

193b ▶20 Improve speed and control

1. A 5′ writing; determine *gwam*; circle errors.
2. Two 1′ writings on ¶ 1, then on ¶ 2, then on ¶ 3.
3. A 5′ control writing; determine *gwam*; circle errors.

all letters used | A | 1.5 si | 5.6 awl | 80% hfw |

	gwam 1′	5′
In a recent meeting of top business executives, questions were	13	3
raised about the type of skill young people need in order to get to	26	5
the top in business. Those to whom the queries were directed were quick	41	8
to assert that, even more than the type or amount of education a worker	55	11
may have, the basic powers of solving problems in an orderly manner and	70	14
thinking analytically are the skills most commonly sought.	81	16
All executives stressed the fact that too many persons seeking a	13	19
career in business place too much emphasis on the little job tasks at	27	22
the expense of learning how to work out solutions to their problems in a	42	25
systematic and logical way. The executives emphasized, too, the need	56	27
for workers of all types to be able to complete acceptably the work they	70	30
are assigned and, in addition, to be able to analyze the elements of the	85	33
work being done with a view to understanding and improving their status.	99	36
Of particular interest to advisors assisting persons preparing for	13	39
a job in business is the fact that the worlds of business and school are	28	42
not far apart in terms of the demands and expectations set for young	42	44
people. Amazingly, the qualities coveted in all workers by most astute	56	47
executives are the same traits sought in students by top teachers who	70	50
try to get their students ready for a world of work. It is a pity,	84	53
then, when so many young people do not cultivate their career potential.	98	56

gwam 1′ | 1 | 2 | 3 | 4 | 5 | 6 | 7 | 8 | 9 | 10 | 11 | 12 | 13 | 14 |
5′ | 1 | 2 | 3 |

92c ▶30 Build sustained production skill: letters

Time Schedule

Planning and preparing .. 4′
Production timing .... 20′
Proofreading; computing *g-pram* .... 6′

Type a 20′ sustained production writing on the problems listed here (make pencil notations of the problems and pages): page 151, Problems 1, 2 pages 152, 153, Problem 2 [LM pp. 17-22]

If you complete the letter problems before time is called, start over. Type on the control level; do not correct errors. When time is called, proofread each letter. Compute *g-pram* (gross production rate a minute). *G-pram* = total words ÷ minutes typed.

93

93a ▶5 Conditioning practice

each line 3 times (slowly, faster, in-between rate)

alphabet	Most companies emphasize extra valuable jobs for good quality workers.
figures	The inventory includes 96 pamphlets, 1,827 books, and 3,450 magazines.
adjacent keys	John asked Fred to cover the boxes for the six men before you came in.
fluency	Pay the man for the form and ask the auditor to make the usual checks.

| 1 | 2 | 3 | 4 | 5 | 6 | 7 | 8 | 9 | 10 | 11 | 12 | 13 | 14 |

93b ▶15 Improve speed/control: rough draft

1. Two 2′ writings for speed. Compute your average *gwam*.

2. Subtract 4 words from your average rate; then type three 2′ writings for control (not over 2 errors in each writing).

3. As time permits, type 1′ writings for speed or control, according to your needs.

Practice goal
Type with continuity.

	gwam 1′	2′
The explorat<u>oi</u>ns in (outer) space have been trul<u>l</u>y exciting, but	12	6
perhaps even more excit ing <u>aer</u> the explorations of so called	25	13
"inner space," Our brains (have been) ~~are~~ termed the most highly orga-	46	23
nized (3) pounds of matter in the Universe. The brain (is believed to) contains	62	31
something on the order of 100 billion sells. (of this number,) About 10 billion	77	33
nerve cells, or neurons, forme the substance of a thini ing	89	45
and feeling instrument. (by which we learn and become aware of our existence.)	104	51

(or that space which is called the brain.) (spell out)

93c ▶30 Measure production skill: letters

Time Schedule

Planning and preparing .. 4′
Production timing .... 20′
Proofreading; computing *n-pram* .... 6′

Type each letter on page 155 on a separate letterhead or plain sheet [LM pp. 23-26]. Determine placement: See table, page 148. Make notes of needed directions. Erase and correct all errors. If you complete the letters before time is called, start over on plain paper. Proofread your work. Deduct 15 words from total words for each uncorrected error; divide remainder by 20 to determine *n-pram* (net production rate a minute).

Compare your *n-pram* with your *g-pram* of 92c. If your *n-pram* is much lower, you may need to try to improve your accuracy, give attention to your error correction skill, or try to reduce your nontyping time.

Problem 2
modified block; mixed;
subject line; listed enclosures

	words
October 12, 19-- Mrs. Eileen B. Gentry,	8
Director Administrative Support Systems Plas-	17
tics Manufacturing Company 110 North Divi-	25
sion Avenue Grand Rapids, MI 49502 Dear	33
Mrs. Gentry: Subject: Office Landscaping	42
Conference (¶ 1) Landscaping offices through	49
total environmental planning is a concept that	59
is revolutionizing the interior of modern offices;	69
it is increasingly influencing the design of new	79
office buildings. The concept appeals to ex-	88
ecutives. (¶ 2) To provide for an exchange of	96
information on this innovative concept, we	104
are sponsoring a two-day conference devoted	113
entirely to "Office Landscaping." This con-	122
ference is one designed to be especially ap-	130
pealing to you and your staff; it will enroll	140
top managers from all parts of the country.	149
(¶ 3) I am enclosing materials relating to the	157
conference which I should like to have you	165
examine carefully; then return the registra-	174
tion form as quickly as possible to assure	183
your inclusion in these worthwhile sessions.	192
Sincerely yours, Mrs. Shirley McReynolds	200
Director, Conference Bureau xx Enclosures	208
Brochure on Office Landscaping Conference	217
Program Registration Form (147)	222/**250**

Problem 3
AMS Simplified letter
with enumerated items

	words
October 12, 19-- Mrs. Rebecca Van Matre	8
Executive Vice President Missouri Chemical	17
Corporation 1327 Baltimore Avenue Kansas	25
City, MO 64105 REPORT OF RECORDS FACILI-	33
TIES (¶ 1) We are now in the process of pre-	40
paring our preliminary report on your records	49
system. To make this report as thorough as	58
possible, however, we need some additional	67
information concerning your company opera-	75
tions in the Independence, Missouri, location.	84
Specifically, we need data on the following:	94
1. Facilities now in use for records process-	103
ing 2. The types and number of offices served	112
by the records division of the Independence	121
branch 3. The numbers and kinds of equipment	130
now in operation 4. The amount of space now	139
committed to records storage and processing;	148
and the amount of space, if any, available	156
for expanding records facilities. (¶ 2) I am	164
enclosing an Inventory of Records Facili-	172
ties form which I should like you to use in	181
reporting these data; please return it promptly.	191
The information you supply will contribute	200
greatly to our analysis and to the completion	209
of our final report. MRS. WILLIE CRITTENDON,	218
SYSTEMS ANALYST xx Enclosure (179)	223/**248**

Problem 4
Informal government letter
with lettered items

Date: October 12, 19-- Reply to Attn. of:	3
NMYP Subject: Inquiry on Training Programs	10
To: Dr. Jessie M. Colson, Coordinator Com-	18
munications and Clerical Skills Programs U.S.	27
Department of State Washington, DC 20520	35
(¶ 1) I have just learned that you conduct in-	43
service training programs for clerical workers	53
in the State Department and that employees	61
benefit greatly therefrom. To help me learn	70
more about the work you do, will you please	79
answer the following questions: a. Are em-	88
ployees in other departments eligible to enroll	97
in your programs? b. Do you conduct programs	107
for other departments? c. What costs are in-	116
volved? (¶ 2) Your responses will be useful	124
in helping me decide the feasibility of provid-	133
ing training for workers in our organization.	143
Thank you. ALICE M. GONZALES Director of	151
Personnel NMYP: AMGonzales: xx 10-12---	159
(No envelope)	

93c, continued

Problem 1
Modified block, indented ¶s,
mixed punctuation [LM pp. 23, 24]

	words
April 26, 19-- | Miss Catherine Swinski | 2170	9
South Goebbert Road | Arlington Heights, IL	17
60005 | Dear Miss Swinski: (¶ 1) In response to	25
the question raised in your letter, I can assure	35
you that a good vocabulary is important, regard-	44
less of your career choice. Although you can	54
learn the specialized vocabulary of a particular	63
field as you study for that career, it also is	73
important to develop a broad general vocabu-	81
lary that will help you communicate more	90
effectively with people in other fields.	98
(¶ 2) Here are one or two suggestions for in-	106
creasing your general vocabulary. Nearly	114
every day new words and new terms, such as	123
petrochemicals, recycled pollutants, and psy-	131
chochemistry, are popping into our vocabu-	140
laries. When you hear or see a word for the	149
first time, look it up in a dictionary. Study its	159
pronunciation and meaning, and then add it to	168
your vocabulary. Vocabulary building can be	177
an exciting adventure. (¶ 3) Still another way to	186
add words to your vocabulary is to read widely.	196
Not only will you increase your vocabulary by	205
reading, but also you will increase your general	215
knowledge. A good vocabulary and broad gen-	223
eral knowledge are marks of the educated per-	232
son. (¶ 4) I enjoyed having this opportunity to	241
respond to your letter. We plan to publish your	250
letter and my response in the "Letters to the	260
Editor" section of the June issue of Careers.	270
Sincerely yours, | Ms. Susan Drexel, Editor | xx	279
(248)	

Problem 2
Modified block, indented ¶s,
mixed punctuation [LM pp. 25, 26]

	words
May 13, 19-- | Mr. Warren Sikora, Executive	8
Secretary | Ball, Hunt, Hart, Brown, and	16
Baerwitz | 450 North Roxbury Drive | Beverly	24
Hills, CA 90210 | Dear Mr. Sikora: (¶ 1) Careful	33
planning is the first step in increasing your	42
letter production rate. Quickly note the length	52
of the letter so that you can place it properly	61
on the letterhead. Next, assemble all materials	71
(eraser, correction tape or fluid, reference	80
books) that you may need as you type the letter.	90
Keep these items within easy reach so that you	99
can use them without waste time or motion.	108
(¶ 2) As you type the letter, remember the im-	116
portance of good typing techniques. Try to keep	126
your eyes on the copy you are typing; concen-	136
trate on it. In this way, you can avoid breaks	146
in your typing rhythm. Type with your fingers	156
well curved and close to the keys; space quickly	166
after each word. When the bell rings, either	175
finish the word you are typing, if this can be	184
done in a few keystrokes, or divide it with a	193
hyphen at a proper division point. Then make	202
the return and start the new line immediately.	212
Your overall emphasis should be on continuity	221
and rhythm as you type. (¶ 3) These suggestions	230
will help you increase your letter production	239
rate. Try them and see. Sincerely yours, | Mrs.	249
Kay Seibert | Communications Consultant | xx	257
(213)	

94

94a ▶5 Conditioning practice

each line 3 times
(slowly, faster,
in-between rate)

alphabet	This bright jacket has an amazing weave and is of exceptional quality.
figures	In 1976, 583 new employees were added. Read pages 14, 20, 63, and 98.
space bar	If what you say is so, then they should find the work very easy to do.
fluency	They plan to see the ancient ornaments when they visit the old museum.

\| 1 \| 2 \| 3 \| 4 \| 5 \| 6 \| 7 \| 8 \| 9 \| 10 \| 11 \| 12 \| 13 \| 14 \|

191

191a ▶5 Conditioning practice

each line 3 times (slowly, rapidly, in-between rate)

Judge Tommy Newman quickly awarded seven prizes for the best exhibits.
Evelyn's new address is 10867 Colerain Avenue, Cincinnati, Ohio 45239.
They bought 26 of #50870 at a total cost of $36.14 (26 at $1.39 each).
In the business world there are many different forms of communication.

| 1 | 2 | 3 | 4 | 5 | 6 | 7 | 8 | 9 | 10 | 11 | 12 | 13 | 14 |

191b ▶45 Build sustained production: letters with special features

Time schedule
Preparation .... 7′
Timed production ..... 30′
Final check; compute *n-pram* .... 8′

1. Make a list of problems to be typed:
page 299, 187c, Prob. 2
page 303, AMS letter
page 305, informal government letter [LM pp. 77–82]

2. Arrange supplies (plain sheets or letterheads) for rapid handling. Make 1 cc.

3. When directed to begin, type for 30′; follow directions given for each problem; correct all errors neatly. Proofread carefully before removing a problem from the typewriter. If you finish all problems before time is called, type 188d, Prob. 2, page 301, on plain paper.

4. Compute *n-pram*:
total acceptable words
+ ½ unacceptable words
÷ number of minutes typed

5. After computing *n-pram*, arrange all problems in the order listed in Step 1 and turn them in.

192

192a ▶5 Conditioning practice

Retype 191a, above.
Goal: Improved continuity.

192b ▶45 Measure production skill: letters with special features

4 letterheads [LM pp. 83-90]
Use time schedule for 191b, above.

1. Arrange supplies.

2. Make 1 cc and address an envelope for each letter.

3. Correct errors; circle any uncorrected errors found in final check; compute *n-pram*.

Problem 1
modified block, mixed; mailing notation; attention line; company name in closing lines; enclosure; postscript

	words
October 12, 19-- REGISTERED MAIL National Advertising Corp. 800 West	14
Erie Avenue Chicago, IL 60622 Attention Mr. James R. Anglin Ladies and	28
Gentlemen: (¶ 1) Thank you for preparing and sending the legal documents	42
authorizing you to publicize our many services. We have examined the papers	57
and find them in good order. (¶ 2) Enclosed are signed contracts covering all	71
advertising services you are to furnish for the twelve-month period extending	87
from January 1 through December 31. It is our understanding that you are	102
agreeable, too, to submitting a monthly report indicating the media used, the	117
type of advertising released, and costs incurred. (¶ 3) We appreciate your send-	132
ing the contracts so promptly, and we look forward to pleasant associations	147
with you. Sincerely yours, GURNICK & HERSHEY ENTERPRISES Gerald L.	161
Hershey, Treasurer xx Enclosures 2 Postscript In your monthly report,	173
please show comparative cost figures for radio-television compared with	187
magazines-journals. (119)	191/213

Continue with Problem 2, page 307.

94b ▶15 Measure basic skill: straight copy

two 5′ writings; determine *gwam*; proofread; circle errors; record better rate

all letters used | A | 1.5 si | 5.6 awl | 80% hfw

	gwam 1′	5′
When typing letters, or in other typing activities, typists often	13	3
make many waste motions of which they may not be aware. Do you recall	27	5
the necessity for typing with proper techniques? For example, do you	41	8
realize that much time is lost every time you look away from the copy	55	11
you are typing? Many typists make the return slowly, or they fail to	69	14
get the next line started quickly. They may type with bouncing hands	83	17
and arms rather than with most of the action in the fingers. Avoid	97	19
these and other waste motions and your problem-typing rates will benefit.	112	22
Research studies indicate that many typists spend about one third	13	25
of their total time in actual typing, and two thirds of their time in	27	28
nontyping activities such as assembling carbon packs, making error cor-	41	31
rections, determining format for the copy to be typed, and many other	55	33
activities which reduce typing production speeds. A very good goal for	70	36
you to set now would be to try to type every letter at a rate which is	84	39
at least fifty percent of your straight-copy rate. As has often been	98	42
said, just plan your work and work your plan and your typing rates will	112	45
increase.	114	45

gwam 1′ | 1 | 2 | 3 | 4 | 5 | 6 | 7 | 8 | 9 | 10 | 11 | 12 | 13 | 14 |
5′ | 1 | 2 | 3

94c ▶30 Learn skill applications: block style letter

Problem 1
Learn letter style
plain paper

Type Style Letter 4, page 157, in the block style with open punctuation as shown (words in body: 221).

Use standard 6″ line (see Placement Table, page 148). Type the letter at rough-draft speed; x-out or strike over any errors you make.

Problem 2
Proofread and make rough-draft corrections

Proofread the letter you typed as Problem 1. Indicate by handwritten corrections any changes that you need to make in the copy. Use standard proofreader's marks to indicate the needed corrections.

Problem 3
Build skill [LM pp. 27, 28]

Using your corrected rough-draft copy, retype the letter in block style. As you type, make the corrections indicated in your copy.

Erase any errors you make as you retype the letter. Compare your copy with the style letter.

Block style: placements of official titles in closing lines

Cordially yours

Ms. Nicole Jackson, Director

lwe

Enclosures

Sincerely yours

Torrance C. Odell
Communications Consultant

lwe

PUBLIC SERVICE AGENCY

Washington, D.C. 20406

words

		words
Date:	October 27, 19-- (DS)	3
Reply to Attn of:	NMRW (DS)	4
Subject:	Format for the Informal Letter (TS)	11

To: Director, Administrative Services Division (AFAS) 21
Federal Supply Agency 25
1889 Inverson Street 29
San Francisco, CA 94102 34

1" side margins

start body on 6th line below *To:*

This letter shows the format for preparing letters for agencies of the United States Government. This format expedites the preparation of correspondence and saves effort, time, and materials. 46 58 70 73

The following features of this format should please typists. 85

a. All elements except the first line of lettered items are blocked at the left margin. This block style minimizes the use of the space bar, the tabulator set, and the tabulator bar or key. 97 109 120 124

b. Salutations and complimentary closes are omitted in most letters. They may be used in letters to any individual on a personal or private matter (notices of serious illness, letters of condolence, where a warm and personal feeling is paramount, etc.), or where protocol or tradition dictates. 135 147 160 172 184

c. The address is positioned to be visible after insertion into a window envelope, eliminating the need for typing an envelope. 195 207 210

(3 blank lines)

JOHN B. SMITH 213
Administrator of Correspondence 219

NMRW:JBSmith:xx 10-27--- on carbon only 224

To type on carbon only:
1. Position carriage to point where note is to be started.
2. Insert slip of paper between the ribbon and the original copy.
3. Type notation and remove slip.

Style letter 6: informal government letter

Office Services, Inc.

129 Commonwealth Avenue ■
Boston, Mass. 02116 ■
617-891-2296 ■

Experts in Research

		words parts	total
Dateline started at left margin	November 12, 19-- (Line 16; 4 line spaces (3 blank lines))	4	4
Letter address	Dr. VierlieAnn Malina, President	10	10
	Transcontinental Corporation	16	16
	1005 Ala Lilikoi Street	21	21
	Honolulu, HI 96818	25	25
Salutation	Dear Dr. Malina	28	28
Body of letter	Today many business firms use the block style letter for their	13	40
	correspondence. This letter is an example of that style. You	25	53
	will note that all lines start at the left margin. The advan-	38	65
	tage of this style is that the mechanical process of indenting	50	78
	opening and closing lines, or paragraphs, is eliminated. This	63	91
	practice saves typing time as well as space.	72	99
	Open punctuation is used with this letter. Punctuation is	83	111
	omitted after the salutation and the complimentary close, thus	96	124
	helping to increase letter production rates. Another time-	108	135
	saving feature we recommend is to type only the initials of	120	147
	the typist for reference when the dictator's name is typed in	132	160
	the closing lines.	136	163
	As you can see, the block style letter gives good placement	148	175
	appearance. Because many extra typing strokes and motions are	160	188
	eliminated, the use of this style does help to increase letter	173	201
	production rates. It is the letter style I recommend for use	185	213
	in the business office.	190	218
Complimentary close	Sincerely yours	3	221
Signature	*Torrance C. Odell*		
Typed name and official title	Torrance C. Odell	7	224
	Communications Consultant	12	230
Reference initials	ab	12	230

Style letter 4: block style with open punctuation and standard 6″ line

190

190a ▶5
Conditioning practice

1. Each line twice, SS.

2. A 1′ writing on Line 1; determine *gwam*.

Joe Biznick made plans with Rex Marquette for visiting Oakwood Valley.
They need 120 quarts of J53679 liquid masking compound and 48 brushes.
Hayes & Fishel paid Invoice 58936 totaling $740.25, less 10% discount.
Their company will initiate a new policy regarding risks on shipments.

| 1 | 2 | 3 | 4 | 5 | 6 | 7 | 8 | 9 | 10 | 11 | 12 | 13 | 14 |

190b ▶15
Measure speed and control

1. Two 5′ writings; proofread and circle errors.

2. Determine *gwam* for each writing.

all letters used | A | 1.5 si | 5.6 awl | 80% hfw

Text	gwam 1′	5′
The day in which we live is often referred to as the age of the	13	3
computer. Most of us have been or soon will be influenced in some way	27	5
by this marvel of modern technology. There are some workers who state	41	8
that the computer represents the greatest application of inventive genius	56	11
known to our civilized world, a claim hard to deny. While some persons	71	14
think the computer performs in some magic way, those who understand the	85	17
way in which it operates know it functions in a very logical, orderly	99	20
manner, responding very reliably to established controls. All of us	113	23
must be prepared to live and work in a world influenced by computers.	126	25
Actually, a computer is just a machine--one made to utilize raw data	14	28
with amazing speed. Most computers are so quick in doing their assigned	28	31
work that they can go through millions of arithmetic problems in a matter	43	34
of seconds; and because of this exceptional ability, computers have been	58	37
called electronic brains. But a computer cannot think; it can do only	72	40
those things it is told to do. A human operator must put all facts and	86	43
figures into the machine and then tell it, in a precise way, what to do	101	45
with the information. It is true that computers work only as programmed.	116	48
The way in which they are programmed determines the quality of responses	130	51
they are able to give.	135	52

gwam 1′ | 1 | 2 | 3 | 4 | 5 | 6 | 7 | 8 | 9 | 10 | 11 | 12 | 13 | 14 |
5′ | 1 | 2 | 3 |

190c ▶30
Learn to type the informal government letter

1. Study Style Letter 6 shown on page 305.

2. Type the letter [LM pp. 71–74], observing the placement features shown in the illustration.

3. Proofread and circle errors.

4. Retype the letter, addressing it to:

Ms. Gail Stautamoyer
Supervisor, Office Services
Department of Commerce
Washington, DC 20520

5. Proofread and circle errors.

Note: Letters typed on the government agency form shown are mailed in window envelopes. The folding procedure for such letters is described and illustrated on RG p. vi.

Enrichment material for Unit 32 appears on LM p. 70.

95

95a ▶5 Conditioning practice

each line 3 times (slowly, faster, in-between rate)

alphabet	Will Jim realize that excellent skill develops by refining techniques?
figures	Will you enter machine Nos. 12-93-45 and 10-87-36 on the repair cards.
shift keys	They read the articles "Fatigue," "How to Relax," and "Saving Energy."
fluency	The six men may go down to the rifle field to fix the eight-day dials.

| 1 | 2 | 3 | 4 | 5 | 6 | 7 | 8 | 9 | 10 | 11 | 12 | 13 | 14 |

95b ▶45 Build production skill: letters

plain sheets, 8½" × 11"
1" margins; date on Line 12

Problem 1
Block style; open punctuation

	words
Current date | Mrs. Rita Beck, Chairperson |	9
Town Hall Program Committee | 701 South Hope	17
Street | Los Angeles, CA 90030 | Dear Mrs.	25
Beck | (¶ 1) The title for my presentation at	33
your National Convention is "Education and the	42
Human Condition." In preparing my material,	51
I plan to draw heavily from a recent article,	60
"Signals from the Butterfly," by Paul Showers.	70
Mr. Showers emphasizes that moths and butter-	79
flies are barometers of our industrial civiliza-	88
tion and that their elimination from our human	97
habitat is a danger signal we must heed. (¶ 2)	106
In the United States today, because of the	114
depredations inflicted upon the environment by	124
human-created waste and pollution, over 100	132
kinds of animals and birds are under Federal	141
protection as endangered species. Many per-	150
sons wonder when the human race will be	158
added to the list of endangered creatures that	167
now includes the grizzly, alligator, peregrine	177
falcon, whooping crane, and other less pub-	185
licized birds and animals such as Kirtland's	194
warbler, the saltmarsh harvest mouse, and the	203
Houston toad. (¶ 3) I strongly believe that if all	213
of us are made aware of the fact that our earth	222
is being irrevocably transformed under the con-	231
tinuing pollution of air and water and other	240
by-products of humankind's assault upon the	249
land, we shall begin to recognize our respon-	258
sibilities to preserve and conserve our environ-	267
ment and resources for the benefit of future	276
generations. (¶ 4) Here, then, in a nutshell,	285
you have a brief overview of the material I	293
plan to cover in my speech. If you have any	302
questions or suggestions, I shall welcome	311
them. Cordially yours | Nikita V. Podrutsky |	319
Consulting Engineer | xx (298)	324

Problem 2
Proofread; make rough-draft corrections

Often, in the business office, extensive changes are made in the original draft of materials. You are to make such changes in the letter that you typed as Problem 1. (You will need to show most of your longhand corrections in the margins; however, indicate clearly by lines-and-arrows where the changes are to be made or inserted in your original letter.)

¶ 1:

Sentence 1
Add of Town Hall after the words National Convention

Sentence 2
Change from a recent article to from an article

As Sentence 3
Add (immediately following *Paul Showers*) This article appeared recently in the New York Times Magazine.

End of last sentence
Change heed to be aware of and heed

¶ 2:

Sentence 2
Change Many persons to Many concerned persons

¶ 3:

Sentence 1
Change made aware of the fact to made aware, through education, of the fact

End of last sentence
Add of humans, animals, birds, and insects.

¶ 4:

After Sentence 1
Add I hope these comments will give you the information you need.

Problem 3
Type from rough-draft copy [LM pp. 29, 30]

Type the corrected rough-draft copy of Problem 1 in block style with open punctuation. Erase and correct neatly any errors you make as you retype the letter.

ADMINISTRATIVE SYSTEMS, INC.

511 WEST WISCONSIN AVENUE
MILWAUKEE, WI 53203
(414) 782-4047

Margin note	Letter	words in parts	total words
Begin all major lines at left margin	October 10, 19--	3	3
Begin address 3 blank line spaces below date	Mrs. Ann C. Wenstrup	8	8
	Universal Fabrics Company	13	13
	9105 Hurstbourne Lane	17	17
	Louisville, KY 40220	22	22
Omit salutation			
Subject line in all capital letters Triple-space above and below it	AMS SIMPLIFIED STYLE LETTER	27	27
	The Administrative Management Society recommends using a	39	39
	simplified arrangement for all letters, typed as follows:	50	50
Begin enumerated items at left margin; indent unnumbered items 5 spaces	1. Use block format.	5	55
	2. Type the address four lines below the date.	14	65
	3. Omit the salutation and complimentary close.	24	75
	4. Always use a subject line, typed in ALL CAPS, on the	36	86
	third line below the address; triple-space from the	46	97
	SUBJECT line to start the body of the letter.	56	106
	5. Start enumerated items at the left margin; indent	66	117
	unnumbered items five spaces.	72	123
	6. Type the writer's name and title in ALL CAPS at least	84	135
	four lines below the body of the letter.	92	143
	7. Type reference initials (typist's only) in lowercase	104	154
	a double space below the writer's name. Separate en-	114	165
	closure notations, carbon copy references, and post-	124	175
	scripts (if used) by one blank line.	132	183
	Adopt a new letter format. The enclosed report shows the	12	195
	savings that result from using this style.	20	203
Omit complimentary close			
Writer's name and title in all caps at least 3 blank line spaces below letter body	WALTER A. GREENWOOD, PRESIDENT	27	209
	xx	27	210
	Enclosure	29	212
			230

Style letter 5: AMS Simplified

96

96a ▶5 Conditioning practice

each line 3 times (slowly, faster, in-between rate)

alphabet	The unique weave of the blue-gray jacket pleased many zealous experts.
figures	Did he order the 16-, 20-, and 24-foot beams (5 7/8″ × 9 3/4″) for us?
uniform stroking	Don't wonder about your ability; wonder if you are using your ability.
fluency	If they work to cut the lawn for the widow, she will pay them in cash.

| 1 | 2 | 3 | 4 | 5 | 6 | 7 | 8 | 9 | 10 | 11 | 12 | 13 | 14 |

96b ▶15 Build basic skill: letters

1. Type a 10′ writing on Style Letter 4, page 157. If you complete the letter before time is called, start over on a new sheet. Determine *gwam*.

2. Proofread your copy and circle all errors; determine *gwam* (total words typed ÷ minutes typed). Record your letter-copy rate.

96c ▶30 Build application skill

plain paper, 8½″ × 11″; block style; 1½″ margins; date on Line 20

1. Type a 3′ writing on the letter to establish a base rate. If you finish before time is called, start over.

2. Determine *gwam*; to this rate add 8 *gwam* to set a new goal. Divide the goal rate by 4 and note the ¼′ checkpoints for guided writings.

3. Type the dateline near the top of the sheet; leave proper spacing between letter parts. Starting with the date, type three 1′ guided writings on the opening parts of the letter and ¶ 1 at your goal rate. DS after each of the 3 writings.

4. Repeat Step 3, using ¶ 2 and the closing lines of the letter.

5. Type another 3′ writing on the complete letter. Try to maintain, or exceed, your new goal rate for this writing. Determine *gwam* and compare it with the rate you attained in Step 1 and in 96b.

6. Type the letter from your teacher's dictation. Type the date on Line 20.

	words in parts	gwam 3′
September 30, 19--/ Mr. David Barton/ 1199 Riverview	10	3
Drive/ Des Moines, Iowa 50313/ Dear Mr. Barton:	20	7
(¶1) We want to be sure to give you credit, but not the kind of credit	13	11
which is usually given by a credit manager. We mean the	24	15
kind of credit which is defined by Webster as "praise or approval	38	19
to which a person is entitled."	44	21
(¶2) The way you have handled your account with us during	11	25
the past year certainly merits our praise. We appreciate	22	29
the promptness with which you pay your account. So	33	32
we want to say thank you and "give credit where	42	35
credit is due." It is a pleasure to be of service to you.	54	39
Sincerely yours,/ Robert Burns, Credit Manager/ lwe	10	43

(98)

189

189a ▶5 Conditioning practice

each line 3 times (slowly, rapidly, in-between rate)

Six major coal firms gave equipment prizes for helping backward youth.
The company planned for 74,632 new road workers between 1985 and 1990.
On March 31, they reported earnings of $12,536,147, up 5.8% this year.
They will make a new effort to have the old mansion closed for winter.

| 1 | 2 | 3 | 4 | 5 | 6 | 7 | 8 | 9 | 10 | 11 | 12 | 13 | 14 |

189b ▶10 Improve speed/control: rough draft

1. A 1′ writing for speed on ¶ 1, then on ¶ 2, determine *gwam* for each.

2. A 5′ writing for control on ¶s 1 and 2 combined; proofread and circle errors; compute *gwam*.

all letters used | HA | 1.6 si | 5.8 awl | 75% hfw

	gwam 1′	5′
The business world is a place concerned about evaluating work	12	2
frequently and precisely conscientious managers are curious	24	5
about the quantity as well as quality produced by their office	37	7
employees;and the appraisal of behavior is an atcivity now	50	10
claiming a great share of executive time. one of the practices	63	13
emerging in top management today is is the realm of	75	15
work measurement Office workers are amazed to find that	87	17
able bosses want employees who are efficient in their jobs.	100	20
Managers involved in determining the actual output of	12	22
workers tell us that job production is lowered many times bythe	25	25
failure of lax typists to handle directions. they tell us too	38	28
that some persons hired to be productive have not leraned how to	51	30
organize themselves or their work and quite a point is made of	65	33
the fact that many workers have shown only very meager talent	77	35
in processing materials. Work evaluation in offices now is	88	38
causing some staff to examin their own output records.	99	40

189c ▶35 Learn to type the AMS Simplified letter

1. Study Style Letter 5 shown on page 303.

2. Type the letter, on plain paper, observing the placement directions shown in color on the illustration.

3. Proofread and circle errors; check copy for correct style.

4. Type two 1′ writings on the opening lines and ¶ 1; determine *gwam*.

5. Type two 1′ writings on ¶ 2 and the closing lines; determine *gwam*.

6. Type a 5′ writing on the entire letter; determine *gwam*.

97

97a ▶5 Conditioning practice

each line 3 times (slowly, faster, in-between rate)

alphabet Six skaters jumped grotesquely in a veritable frenzy of wacky rhythms.

fig/sym After May 5, Jenny's new address will be 4782 Polk Avenue (ZIP 93106).

adjacent keys Opportunity comes to a person as a result of dedication and hard work.

fluency If they are to go with us to the big city, we shall be there at eight.

| 1 | 2 | 3 | 4 | 5 | 6 | 7 | 8 | 9 | 10 | 11 | 12 | 13 | 14 |

97b ▶15 Measure basic skill: statistical copy

two 5′ writings; determine *gwam*; proofread and circle errors

Compute % of transfer: statistical copy rate divided by straight-copy rate of 94b, page 156. Record better rate and % of transfer. *Expected* transfer: 75–80%.

all figures used

A	1.5 si	5.6 awl	80% hfw

Text	gwam 1′	5′
Why does it take the ordinary typist, who types about 40 words a	13	3
minute, so long to type an average letter of approximately 176 words?	27	5
Standard time studies show that it takes such a typist approximately	41	8
18.3 seconds just to pick up, insert, and align a sheet of paper in the	55	11
typewriter. At the rate of 40 words a minute, the typist makes about	69	14
3.3 keystrokes a second, so another 4.4 minutes are needed in typing	83	17
a letter of 176 words, assuming that no errors are made.	94	19
What other things consume time? Every error that has to be cor-	13	22
rected may take from 30 to 98 seconds to correct, depending on the number	28	25
of carbon copies that are made of the letter. Do you realize that the	43	27
average typist uses 1.32 seconds just to make the return? To proofread a	57	30
letter of 176 words takes 1.87 minutes of time. Waste time (pauses,	71	33
looking up, finding place in the copy, checking typing) as the letter	85	36
is typed consumes yet another 1.05 minutes. The average typist, then,	99	39
uses 8.17 minutes, or even more, just to type a letter of 176 words.	112	41

gwam 1′ | 1 | 2 | 3 | 4 | 5 | 6 | 7 | 8 | 9 | 10 | 11 | 12 | 13 | 14 |
5′ | 1 | 2 | 3 |

97c ▶30 Build sustained production skill: letters

block style; open punctuation; don't correct errors

Time schedule

Planning and preparing .. 4′
Production timing .... 20′
Proofreading;
computing *g–pram* ..... 6′

Type each letter on page 161 on a separate letterhead [LM pp. 31–36] or plain sheet. Standard 6″ line (see table, page 148). Make notes of needed directions. If you complete all letters before time is called, start over.

When time is called, proofread your letters; determine *g–pram* (total words ÷ 20). Is your *g–pram* at least 60% of your straight–copy rate of 94b, page 156?

Proofreading steps

1. Check placement.

2. Check accuracy of all figures and correctness of word division.

3. Proofread entire letter with care; read for meaning.

188d ▶25 Learn to type letters with special features

1. Study comments at the right and illustrations below.

2. On plain paper type Problems 1 and 2 below in modified block style as directed there, mixed punctuation; 1 cc; date on Line 12.

3. Proofread finished copy; circle errors.

Subject line: Type a DS below salutation at left margin, at paragraph point, or centered. Type SUBJECT in all caps or cap only the S; follow *Subject* with a colon and 2 spaces.

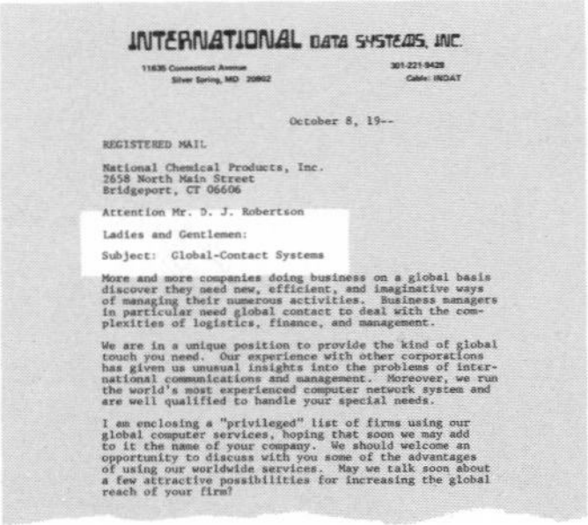

INTERNATIONAL DATA SYSTEMS, INC.
11635 Connecticut Avenue
Silver Spring, MD 20902
301-221-9428
Cable: INDAT

October 8, 19--

REGISTERED MAIL

National Chemical Products, Inc.
2658 North Main Street
Bridgeport, CT 06606

Attention Mr. D. J. Robertson

Ladies and Gentlemen:

Subject: Global-Contact Systems

More and more companies doing business on a global basis discover they need new, efficient, and imaginative ways of managing their numerous activities. Business managers in particular need global contact to deal with the complexities of logistics, finance, and management.

We are in a unique position to provide the kind of global touch you need. Our experience with other corporations has given us unusual insights into the problems of international communications and management. Moreover, we run the world's most experienced computer network system and are well qualified to handle your special needs.

I am enclosing a "privileged" list of firms using our global computer services, hoping that soon we may add to it the name of your company. We should welcome an opportunity to discuss with you some of the advantages of using our worldwide services. May we talk soon about a few attractive possibilities for increasing the global reach of your firm?

Company name in closing lines: Type in ALL CAPS a DS below complimentary close. Type writer's name on 4th line space below company name.

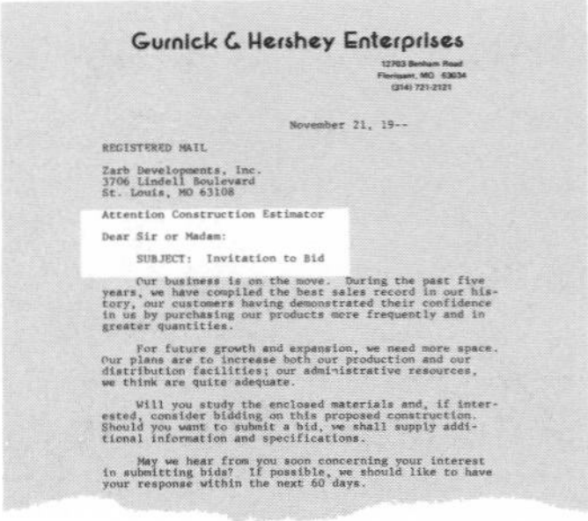

Gurnick & Hershey Enterprises
12703 Benham Road
Florissant, MO 63034
(314) 721-2121

November 21, 19--

REGISTERED MAIL

Zarb Developments, Inc.
3706 Lindell Boulevard
St. Louis, MO 63108

Attention Construction Estimator

Dear Sir or Madam:

SUBJECT: Invitation to Bid

Our business is on the move. During the past five years, we have compiled the best sales record in our history, our customers having demonstrated their confidence in us by purchasing our products more frequently and in greater quantities.

For future growth and expansion, we need more space. Our plans are to increase both our production and our distribution facilities; our administrative resources, we think are quite adequate.

Will you study the enclosed materials and, if interested, consider bidding on this proposed construction. Should you want to submit a bid, we shall supply additional information and specifications.

May we hear from you soon concerning your interest in submitting bids? If possible, we should like to have your response within the next 60 days.

Listed enclosures: Type *Enclosure* at left margin a DS below reference initials. Type listed items on succeeding lines, indented 3 spaces from left margin.

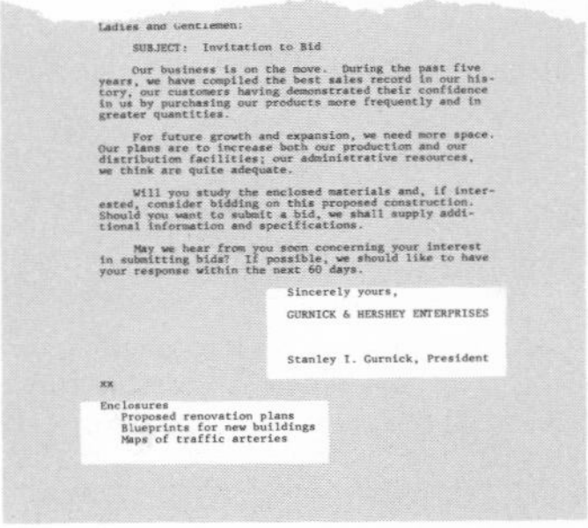

Ladies and Gentlemen:

SUBJECT: Invitation to Bid

Our business is on the move. During the past five years, we have compiled the best sales record in our history, our customers having demonstrated their confidence in us by purchasing our products more frequently and in greater quantities.

For future growth and expansion, we need more space. Our plans are to increase both our production and our distribution facilities; our administrative resources, we think are quite adequate.

Will you study the enclosed materials and, if interested, consider bidding on this proposed construction. Should you want to submit a bid, we shall supply additional information and specifications.

May we hear from you soon concerning your interest in submitting bids? If possible, we should like to have your response within the next 60 days.

Sincerely yours,

GURNICK & HERSHEY ENTERPRISES

Stanley I. Gurnick, President

xx

Enclosures
   Proposed renovation plans
   Blueprints for new buildings
   Maps of traffic arteries

Problem 1
Letter with mailing notation, attention line, and subject line

block ¶s — words

October 8, 19-- REGISTERED MAIL National 8
Chemical Products, Inc. 2658 North Main 16
Street Bridgeport, CT 06606 Attention Mr. 25
D. J. Robertson Ladies and Gentlemen: Subject: 34
Global-Contact Systems (¶ 1) More and more 42
companies doing business on a global basis 50
discover they need new, efficient, and imagi- 59
native ways of managing their numerous 67
activities. Business managers in particular 76
need global contact to deal with the com- 84
plexities of logistics, finance, and manage- 92
ment. (¶ 2) We are in a unique position to 100
provide the kind of global touch you need. 109
Our experience with other corporations has 117
given us unusual insights into the problems 126
of international communications and manage- 135
ment. Moreover, we run the world's most ex- 143
perienced computer network system and are 152
well qualified to handle your special needs. 161
(¶ 3) I am enclosing a "privileged" list of firms 170
using our global computer services, hoping 178
that soon we may add to it the name of your 187
company. We should welcome an opportunity 196
to discuss with you some of the advantages 204
of using our worldwide services. May we talk 213
soon about a few attractive possibilities for in- 223
creasing the global reach of your firm? Sin- 231
cerely yours, Mrs. Judy Richardson, Director 241
International Data Systems xx Enclosure Post- 249
script Many new European, Latin American, 256
and Far Eastern cities have been added to our 265
network of computer installations. (192) 272

Problem 2
Letter with subject line, company name in closing lines, and listed enclosures

indent ¶s — words

October 8, 19-- REGISTERED MAIL Zarb 7
Developments, Inc. 3706 Lindell Boulevard 16
St. Louis, MO 63108 Attention Construc- 23
tion Estimator Dear Sir or Madam: SUBJECT: 32
Invitation to Bid (¶ 1) Our business is on the 41
move. During the past five years, we have 49
compiled the best sales record in our his- 57
tory, our customers having demonstrated their 67
confidence in us by purchasing our products 75
more frequently and in greater quantities. 84
(¶ 2) For future growth and expansion, we 91
need more space. Our plans are to increase 100
both our production and our distribution facili- 110
ties; our administrative resources, we think, 119
are quite adequate. (¶ 3) Will you study the 127
enclosed materials and, if interested, con- 135
sider bidding on this proposed construction. 144
Should you want to submit a bid, we shall 153
supply additional information and specifica- 161
tions. (¶ 4) May we hear from you soon 168
concerning your interest in submitting bids? 177
If possible, we should like to have your re- 186
sponse within the next 60 days. Sincerely 195
yours, GURNICK & HERSHEY ENTERPRISES 202
Stanley I. Gurnick, President xx Enclosures 211
Proposed renovation plans Blueprints for new 220
buildings Maps of traffic arteries (156) 227

97c, continued

Problem 1 [LM pp. 31, 32]

	words
September 10, 19-- | Mrs. Jean H. Nicklaus | 6300	9
Evergreen Road | Detroit, MI 48228 | Dear Mrs.	18
Nicklaus | (¶ 1) The profile of skills that sets the	27
successful teacher apart does not stem from in-	36
tuition or talent alone. Teaching skills are ac-	46
quired by practice, honed by experience, and	54
tempered by responsibility. (¶ 2) It is this pro-	63
file that the editors of the TEACHER'S REVIEW	72
examine in depth in a new 140-page manual,	81
<u>Skills That Build Teaching Success</u>. A copy	95
has been reserved for you with the renewal of	104
your subscription to the TEACHER'S REVIEW.	113
(¶ 3) To get your free copy, just mail the	120
enclosed reply envelope today. You'll be glad	130
you did. Sincerely yours | Miss Karen Perkins,	139
Editor | xx | Enclosure (119)	143

Problem 2 [LM pp. 33, 34]

	words
December 13, 19-- | Ms. Henrietta A. Smith |	8
13316 South Wilton Place | Gardena, CA 90249 |	17
Dear Ms. Smith | (¶ 1) Your Music Center cap-	24
tures the hearts and minds of people from all	33
walks of life. But what of those deprived in our	43
community--young or old--whose lives remain	52
untouched by the performing arts? What of	61
those students who have never enjoyed the	69
Music Center's unique cultural and educational	78
activities such as Philharmonic and Chorale	87
concerts for youth? (¶ 2) Every day, every ex-	95
perience is a process that shapes and molds	104
tomorrow's adult--love, care, concern, and in-	113
volvement are important. You can help bring	122
the world of music and drama to all our people.	132
You can help expand the capabilities of the	141
Music Center in this its tenth year. (¶ 3) Won't	149
you please make a tax-deductible gift today to	159
the Music Center Arts and Education Fund.	167
Your check will help you and your neighbors to	177
a better future. Sincerely yours | Mrs. Brian	186
Billington | Fund Chairperson | xx (161)	192

Problem 3 [LM pp. 35, 36]

	words
June 10, 19-- | Mr. and Mrs. Charles Riley | 23110	9
Blossom Hill Road | San Jose, CA 95154 | Dear	18
Mr. and Mrs. Riley | (¶ 1) Lightning W Ranch	25
Estates nestle against the backdrop of the High	35
Sierras. There is the smell of pine trees in the	45
crisp mountain air. The view across the valley	54
is superb. (¶ 2) At Lightning W Ranch Estates	62
you can fish, swim, hike, go boating or horse-	72
back riding; or you can just relax and enjoy	81
nature's wonderland. (¶ 3) Why not pay us a	89
visit soon. Just call 783-8418 for a reservation.	98
You'll enjoy a stay with us. Cordially yours |	108
Grant Weise, President | xx (85)	114

98

98a ▶5 Conditioning practice

each line 3 times (slowly, faster, in-between rate)

alphabet	Five quick-fingered women played jazz rhythms and blues on saxophones.
figures	Is American Flight 738 scheduled to arrive at 9:25 a.m. or 10:46 a.m.?
shift keys	Mrs. Gregory B. McCrary, Jr. lives on Madison Avenue in New York City.
fluency	If they do the work for us, she may spend a day with the busy auditor.

| 1 | 2 | 3 | 4 | 5 | 6 | 7 | 8 | 9 | 10 | 11 | 12 | 13 | 14 |

98b ▶15 Improve basic skill: statistical copy

Repeat 97b, page 160.

98c ▶30 Measure production skill: letters

Time schedule
Planning and preparing ... 4′
Production timing .... 20′
Proofreading; computing
n-pram .... 6′

Repeat problems of 97c, above (block style, open). In this timing, however, erase and correct all errors. Proofread your completed copy with care. [LM pp. 37–42]

Deduct 15 words from total words typed for each uncorrected error; divide remainder by 20 to determine *n-pram* (net production rate a minute).

Enrichment material for Unit 15 appears on LM pp. 43–48.

188

188a ▶5 Conditioning practice

each line 3 times (slowly, rapidly, in-between rate)

Jo quoted on providing the new black and bronze fixtures for my house.
In 1976, Baxter polled 2,093 votes; Vance, 4,568; and Lawrence, 1,732.
Boyd & Kelly were billed for 650# of meat at $1.95, less 12% for cash.
They will make a special effort to attract special groups of tourists.

| 1 | 2 | 3 | 4 | 5 | 6 | 7 | 8 | 9 | 10 | 11 | 12 | 13 | 14 |

188b ▶10 Improve keystroking technique

1. Type drill once to improve keystroking patterns.

2. A 1′ writing on Line 3, then on Line 6, then on Line 9; determine *gwam* on each; compare rates.

balanced-hand 1 Helen is to pay the girls for all the work they did for the lake firm.
one-hand 2 In our opinion fastest car racers are at ease in minimum garage areas.
combination 3 They may regard the award to the winner as an excess in terms of cost.

common phrases
4 we may be | to go | and this | will be | if we are able | this should be | to them
5 with them | by the time | before this | is advertised | for a period | into that
6 We may be able to go with them by the time the new play is advertised.

long words
7 attitude exceptional remember attractive ambitious frequently personal
8 fine attitude frequently ambitious may remember is attractive may show
9 One who is attractive frequently shows exceptional personal qualities.

188c ▶10 Improve statistical typing

three 3′ writings; determine *gwam*

Goal: To improve speed on copy containing figures.

all letters/figures used | HA | 1.6 si | 5.8 awl | 75% hfw |

gwam 3′

Young people are now talking more urgently about extending their 5
education beyond the secondary era. For one year, 1973-1974, it was 9
quoted that almost 1,313,200 new degrees were granted to able graduates 14
of programs in our colleges and universities; and the numbers are said 18
to be rising. It is evident that those wishing to excel in a country 23
emphasizing ability should plan to add to their normal time for study. 28

It has been estimated that, in the years ahead, pupil enrollments 32
in higher education will rise rapidly. While in 1970 there were only 37
8,649,000 persons actually enrolled in courses in higher education, it 42
is projected that by 1980, there may be 11,402,000 enrollees; by 1990, 46
roughly 11,670,000 pupils may be enrolled; and by the year 2000, such 50
enrollments may expand to a big new assembly of 14,295,000 students. 56

gwam 3′ | 1 | 2 | 3 | 4 | 5 |

unit **16** lessons 99–100

Performance evaluation

Evaluation goals

1. To measure and help you evaluate your overall typing skill.

2. To help you identify areas of needed improvement.

Machine adjustments

1. Paper guide at *0*.

2. 70–space line, SS, unless otherwise directed.

3. Line space selector on *1* or as directed.

4. Ribbon indicator on black (on *R* on Selectric).

99

99a ▶5 Conditioning practice

each line 3 times (slowly, faster, in-between rate)

alphabet New key equipment will be purchased for the junior magazine executive.

figures His life insurance was under Group Policies 11-7542-65 and 90-4831-56.

long words Systems engineers had complete responsibility in space communications.

fluency Both of them will help the city auditor with the work that is pending.

| 1 | 2 | 3 | 4 | 5 | 6 | 7 | 8 | 9 | 10 | 11 | 12 | 13 | 14 |

99b ▶15 Check grammar skill

full sheet, DS; 1″ top margin; 1″ left margin

1. Type each sentence in enumerated form, choosing the correct word in the parentheses as you type the line. Revise Sentences 24–25 to make the meaning clear.

2. As your teacher reads the correct words for each sentence, circle the number of any sentence in which you made a grammatical error.

3. Reinsert your paper, align it, then retype any sentence in which you made a grammatical error in the blank space below that sentence.

Awareness cue
Remember to reset margin for figure *10*.

1. One of the men (is, are) here.
2. My favorite snack (is, are) french fries.
3. Jason and David (is, are) going.
4. Jason, as well as David, (is, are) going.
5. Neither of my friends (is, are) with me.
6. Each of the girls (is, are) typing.
7. The committee (is, are) in the meeting room.
8. Some of the students (is, are) here.
9. Half of the students (has, have) gone.
10. Half of the winter (is, are) gone.
11. He (don't, doesn't) like this food.
12. It (don't, doesn't) seem right.
13. Neither John nor Robert (has, have) done (his, their) work.
14. (Fewer, Less) students will be going to the game.
15. Everyone is expected to do (his or her, their, your) own work.
16. I feel (bad, badly) today.
17. The committee has completed (its, their) work.
18. The class behaved (bad, badly).
19. The team won (its, their) last game.
20. A group of visitors (is, are) in the hall.
21. Either of the letter styles (is, are) satisfactory.
22. Neither the leader nor the musicians (is, are) here.
23. Fifty percent of the work (is, are) completed.
24. When he stepped on the dog's tail, it barked.
25. Bob's friend moved to Europe when he was 15.

187c ▶25 Learn to type letters with special features

1. Study the information and the illustrations at the right and below.
2. On plain paper type Problems 1 and 2 below in modified block style with mixed punctuation. Proofread and circle errors.
3. Check correct placement of special features.

Mailing notation: When used (AIRMAIL with foreign mail, REGISTERED, CERTIFIED, etc.) type at the left margin of the letter address in all capitals a double space below the dateline.

Note: In letter and envelope addresses, type the name of a foreign country in all capitals.

Postscript: Type a double space below the last item at the end of the letter. Block or indent to agree with letter style.

Note: Omit the letters *P.S.* at the beginning of a postscript.

Attention line: Type a double space below city/state line, preferably at left margin.

Note: The salutation must agree with the letter address, not with the attention line.

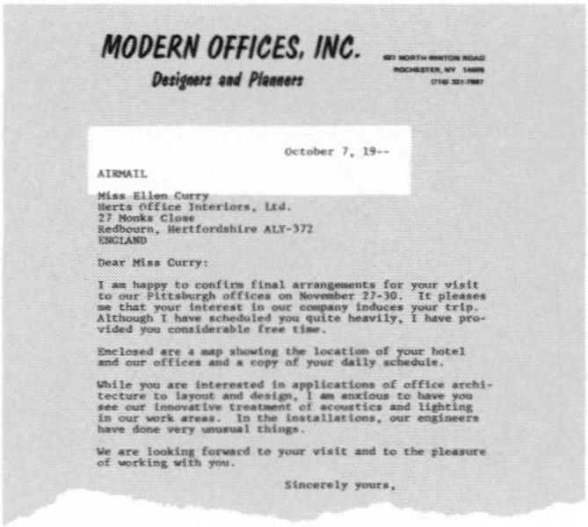

MODERN OFFICES, INC.
Designers and Planners

October 7, 19--

AIRMAIL

Miss Ellen Curry
Herts Office Interiors, Ltd.
27 Monks Close
Redbourn, Hertfordshire ALY-372
ENGLAND

Dear Miss Curry:

I am happy to confirm final arrangements for your visit to our Pittsburgh offices on November 27-30. It pleases me that your interest in our company induces your trip. Although I have scheduled you quite heavily, I have provided you considerable free time.

Enclosed are a map showing the location of your hotel and our offices and a copy of your daily schedule.

While you are interested in applications of office architecture to layout and design, I am anxious to have you see our innovative treatment of acoustics and lighting in our work areas. In the installations, our engineers have done very unusual things.

We are looking forward to your visit and to the pleasure of working with you.

Sincerely yours,

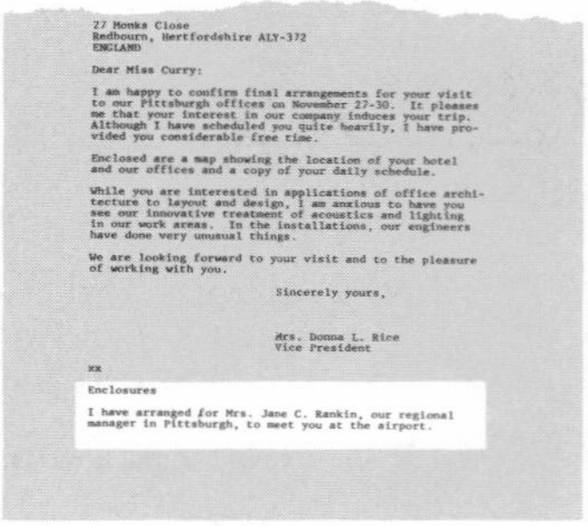

27 Monks Close
Redbourn, Hertfordshire ALY-372
ENGLAND

Dear Miss Curry:

I am happy to confirm final arrangements for your visit to our Pittsburgh offices on November 27-30. It pleases me that your interest in our company induces your trip. Although I have scheduled you quite heavily, I have provided you considerable free time.

Enclosed are a map showing the location of your hotel and our offices and a copy of your daily schedule.

While you are interested in applications of office architecture to layout and design, I am anxious to have you see our innovative treatment of acoustics and lighting in our work areas. In the installations, our engineers have done very unusual things.

We are looking forward to your visit and to the pleasure of working with you.

Sincerely yours,

Mrs. Donna L. Rice
Vice President

xx

Enclosures

I have arranged for Mrs. Jane C. Rankin, our regional manager in Pittsburgh, to meet you at the airport.

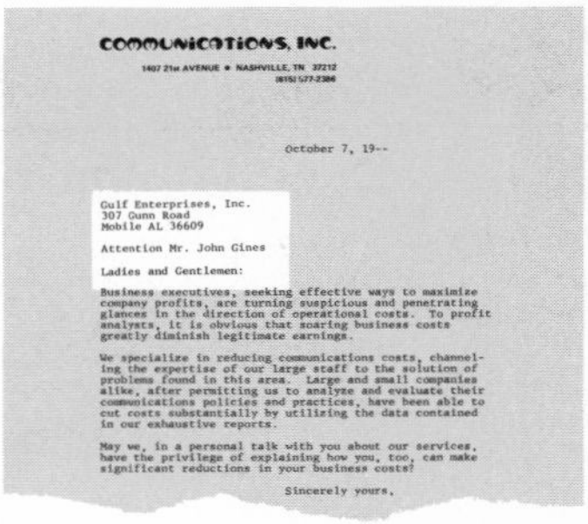

COMMUNICATIONS, INC.
1407 21st AVENUE • NASHVILLE, TN 37212
(615) 577-2386

October 7, 19--

Gulf Enterprises, Inc.
307 Gunn Road
Mobile AL 36609

Attention Mr. John Gines

Ladies and Gentlemen:

Business executives, seeking effective ways to maximize company profits, are turning suspicious and penetrating glances in the direction of operational costs. To profit analysts, it is obvious that soaring business costs greatly diminish legitimate earnings.

We specialize in reducing communications costs, channeling the expertise of our large staff to the solution of problems found in this area. Large and small companies alike, after permitting us to analyze and evaluate their communications policies and practices, have been able to cut costs substantially by utilizing the data contained in our exhaustive reports.

May we, in a personal talk with you about our services, have the privilege of explaining how you, too, can make significant reductions in your business costs?

Sincerely yours,

Problem 1
Letter with mailing notation and postscript

plain paper; 1 cc; date: Line 14 — words

October 7, 19-- | AIRMAIL | Miss Ellen Curry | 8
Herts Office Interiors, Ltd. | 27 Monks Close | 17
Redbourn, Hertfordshire ALY-372 | ENGLAND | 25
Dear Miss Curry: (¶ 1) I am happy to confirm 33
final arrangements for your visit to our Pitts- 42
burgh offices on November 27-30. It pleases 51
me that your interest in our company induces 60
your trip. Although I have scheduled you quite 70
heavily, I have provided you considerable free 79
time. (¶ 2) Enclosed are a map showing the loca- 88
tion of your hotel and our offices and a copy of 97
your daily schedule. (¶ 3) While you are in- 105
terested in applications of office architecture to 115
layout and design, I am anxious to have you see 125
our innovative treatment of acoustics and light- 134
ing in our work areas. In the installations, our 144
engineers have done very unusual things. (¶ 4) 153
We are looking forward to your visit and to the 162
pleasure of working with you. Sincerely yours, 172
Mrs. Donna L. Rice Vice President xx Enclo- 180
sures, Postscript I have arranged for Mrs. Jane 187
C. Rankin, our regional manager in Pittsburgh, 197
to meet you at the airport. (139) 202

Problem 2
Letter with attention line

plain paper; 3 cc; date: Line 14 — words

October 7, 19-- Gulf Enterprises, Inc. 307 Gunn 10
Road Mobile, AL 36609 Attention Mr. John 18
Gines Ladies and Gentlemen: (¶ 1) Business 26
executives, seeking effective ways to maximize 35
company profits, are turning suspicious and 43
penetrating glances in the direction of opera- 52
tional costs. To profit analysts, it is obvious 62
that soaring business costs greatly diminish 71
legitimate earnings. (¶ 2) We specialize in 79
reducing communications costs, channeling the 88
expertise of our large staff to the solution of 98
problems found in this area. Large and small 107
companies alike, after permitting us to ana- 116
lyze and evaluate their communications policies 125
and practices, have been able to cut costs sub- 134
stantially by utilizing the data contained in 144
our exhaustive reports. (¶ 3) May we, in a per- 152
sonal talk with you about our services, have 161
the privilege of explaining how you, too, can 170
make significant reductions in your business 179
costs? Sincerely yours, Miss Myra C. Gold- 187
berg Consultant Services xx cc Mr. Carl 195
Zimmer Ms. Yvonne Zetko (157) 200/**211**

Note: When two persons receive carbon copies, block the second name below the first.

99c ▶15 Measure basic skill: rough-draft copy

two 5′ writings; determine *gwam*; proofread and circle errors

Compute % of transfer: rough-draft copy rate divided by straight-copy rate of 94b, page 156.

Record better rate and % of transfer.
Expected transfer: 70–75%

all letters used	A	1.5 si	5.6 awl	80% hfw

	gwam 1′	5′
It is rather interesting just how much work efficiency can be	9	2
increased by carefully planning all work tasks. This is as treu for	28	6
class room work as it is for work in the o ffice area. In the office,	42	8
there is a trend toward simplification of work andthe utilization of	55	11
time principles in all work. Office employees learn to increase there	71	14
efficiency by grouping tasks. They change their work pace to the diffi-	87	17
culty of the tasks. They try to reduce waste motions by getting	101	20
materials needed for the job they are to do.	119	24
In the ty pewriting class room, you should plan all work and then	13	26
work in the right way. This right way of operating means that you type	33	30
with proper form, that you work for a good keystroking pattern with the	49	33
action limited to the fingers only, that you eliminate all unnecessary	79	40
motions, and that you type with an increasing sense of relaxation.	97	43
Then, too, boys and girls must make a real effort to improve. A real	125	49
effort to improve is an essential element of success.	135	51

99d ▶15 Evaluate techniques

each line twice; repeat as time permits

Make a self-evaluation of your techniques (see page 125); compare with your teacher's evaluation of you as you type.

keystroking 1 I may wish to make the usual audit and then bid for title to the firm.
Send these forms and the statement to them at the address on the card.

space bar 2 If they do the work for us, then I may pay them if they sign the form.
If they sign the form, he may make them handle the profit for the man.

shift keys 3 James H. Forgie and Emmett Jones will visit Salt Lake City and Newark.
Jan McNeil and Amy Presley will meet Lisa Roberts in Sioux City, Iowa.

tab and return 4 ——tab to center——→ (tab set) Make a quick return without looking up
and start the new line. ——tab——→ (repeat twice)

continuity 5 With my eyes on this copy, I can type a line without a break or pause.
I can avoid pausing if I try to concentrate on this copy as I type it.

186d ▶20
Improve typing from script

1. Two 2′ writings on each ¶; determine *gwam*.

2. A 5′ writing on the combined ¶s; determine *gwam*; circle errors.

all letters used | HA | 1.6 si | 5.8 awl | 75% hfw

	gwam 2′	5′
Many fine persons get perplexed over their inability to	6	2
move ahead in their chosen area of work. They are usually	12	5
quite puzzled and often upset because promotions they want	18	7
do not come as quickly as hoped, and salary increases based	24	9
on past performance tend to be awarded all too sparingly.	30	12
Experts who have made studies of issues relating to job be-	35	14
havior and promotion practices inform us that many	40	16
able workers, while doing their jobs well, do not always merit	47	19
the maximum rewards because of too much wasted time.	52	21
An amazing yet crucial fact about the area of business	6	23
is that highly regarded workers have had to learn the vital	12	25
skill of managing company time wisely. While it is essen-	18	28
tial for all assigned jobs to be completed in minimum	23	30
time, it is equally important for the entire workday	28	32
to proceed with few costly interruptions. Astute observers	34	34
say that time wasted each day costs business organizations	40	37
untold sums of money and that as much as one extra	45	39
hour a day can be saved by each worker adopting and	50	41
personally using helpful time-management ideas.	55	43

187

187a ▶5
Conditioning practice

1. Each line twice SS.

2. A 1′ writing on Line 4; compute *gwam*.

Twenty Mexican pilots made a quick jet flight over the blazing valley.
The index for all items increased from 134.8 in 1976 to 205.9 in 1977.
Item No. 42389 was sold to Coe & Long for $475.60 (less 10% for cash).
There are many fine books that will help you increase your job skills.

| 1 | 2 | 3 | 4 | 5 | 6 | 7 | 8 | 9 | 10 | 11 | 12 | 13 | 14 |

187b ▶20
Compose as you type

1. Read the ¶s of 186d above, noting the main points or ideas.

2. On a plain sheet, center on Line 10 the heading

TIME MANAGEMENT

3. Compose paragraphs showing the relationship between time management in school and on the job.

100

100a ▶5 Conditioning practice

each line 3 times (slowly, faster, in-between rate)

alphabet	The travel expert frequently amazed us with talks about jungle dances.
fig/sym	What is the sum of 16 7/8 and 23 3/4 and 45 1/2 and 10 8/9 and 90 1/4?
adjacent keys	To permit emotions to control actions seriously hampers use of reason.
fluency	I can type with my fingers curved and upright and with my hands quiet.

| 1 | 2 | 3 | 4 | 5 | 6 | 7 | 8 | 9 | 10 | 11 | 12 | 13 | 14 |

100b ▶15 Measure basic skill: straight copy

two 5′ writings; determine *gwam*; proofread and circle errors; record better rate

all letters used | A | 1.5 si | 5.6 awl | 80% hfw |

	gwam 1′	5′
The business letter is, in a significant way, the personal envoy	13	3
of the business office that produces it. All business firms give careful	28	6
attention to the content of the letter so that it will be as effective	42	8
as possible; however, if the letter is carelessly typed or poorly placed	57	11
on the page, much of its effect may be lost. Depending upon the first	71	14
impression a letter makes, it tends to give a good or a poor image of the	86	17
company that sends it. Every typist should recognize that good placement	100	20
of the letter on the letterhead page is, then, of primary importance.	114	23
A letter must be carefully proofread before it is removed from the	13	26
typewriter. Just be sure that you acquire this necessary proofreading	28	28
habit. Given here is an idea of some of the basic steps to follow:	41	31
First, observe the placement and the format of the letter. It should	55	34
be well placed on the page, and it should look much like a picture in a	70	37
frame. Every keystroke should be even or uniform. Second, be sure that	84	40
every figure and amount are exact. Check to be sure that the address is	99	43
correct. Lastly, verify the content of the letter; also, the grammar	113	45
and spelling. Be certain that every typing error has been neatly cor-	127	48
rected, and that there are no errors of word division.	138	50

gwam 1′ | 1 | 2 | 3 | 4 | 5 | 6 | 7 | 8 | 9 | 10 | 11 | 12 | 13 | 14 |
5′ | 1 | 2 | 3 |

100c ▶30 Measure production skill: letters

Time schedule

Planning and preparing .. 4′
Production timing .... 20′
Proofreading; computing *n–pram* .... 6′

Type a 20′ production writing on the problems listed here (make notations of problems and pages):

page 150, Style Letter 3
page 152, 91c, Problem 1
page 157, Style Letter 4
[LM pp. 49–54]

Type each letter with a standard 6″ line (see Placement Table). Erase and correct errors. Proofread your completed work; circle errors; then deduct 15 words from total words for each uncorrected error. Compute *n–pram*.

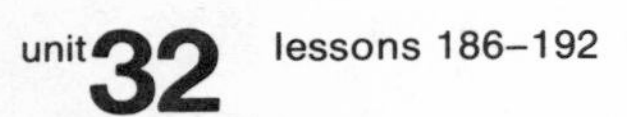

unit **32** lessons 186–192

Letters with special features

Learning goals

1. To improve keystroking skill on straight copy, script, statistical copy, and rough draft.

2. To transfer basic skill to problem material.

3. To develop skill in typing business letters containing special features.

4. To improve skill in handling materials and in proofreading.

Machine adjustments

1. Line: 70 for drills and timed writings.

2. Spacing: SS sentence drills; DS ¶s with 5-space indentions; as directed for problems.

186

186a ▶5 Conditioning practice

1. Each line twice SS.

2. A 1′ writing on Line 4; compute *gwam*.

alphabet Bob excitedly gave prizes of aquatic masks to the two junior swimmers.

figures The five groups added new members as follows: 19, 26, 37, 40, and 58.

fig/sym Invoice No. 47209 for 360 lbs. of meat at $1.85 per lb. has been paid.

fluency It is quite true that most workers seek a chance to prove their worth.

| 1 | 2 | 3 | 4 | 5 | 6 | 7 | 8 | 9 | 10 | 11 | 12 | 13 | 14 |

186b ▶15 Skill-comparison typing

1. Three 1′ writings on each ¶; compute *average gwam* for each ¶. Compare average gwam for ¶ 1 with average gwam for ¶ 2.

2. A 1′ writing for speed on slower ¶.

3. A 1′ writing on each ¶; compare gwam rates with previous writings.

4. Additional writings as time permits.

all letters used

¶ 1			
A	1.5 si	5.6 awl	80% hfw

¶ 2			
D	1.7 si	6.0 awl	70% hfw

gwam 1′

This is an age in which young people are encouraged to do their own (14) thing, to minimize inhibitions, and to be as independent as they judge (28) necessary. In some areas, there are those who hold that a person must (42) be allowed to function as an individual; yet, there are few occasions (56) for persons entering the business world to operate solely as loners. (70)

Able managers seldom ask their staff of office workers to operate (13) singly; more typically, an expert manager organizes an office force (27) into units or work groups. Employers tend to expect, then, that chosen (41) workers will possess initially, or acquire soon after being hired, a (55) sense of group, as well as personal, duty and loyalty to the company. (69)

gwam 1′ | 1 | 2 | 3 | 4 | 5 | 6 | 7 | 8 | 9 | 10 | 11 | 12 | 13 | 14 |

186c ▶10 Improve tabulating technique

half sheets

1. Type drill twice.

2. Do NOT type headings.

3. DS body. Leave 6 spaces between columns.

CITY	STATE	POPULATION	ZIP CODE	RADIO	TV	words
Akron	Ohio	275,425	44309	WAKR	WCOT	7
Ames	Iowa	39,505	50010	KASI	WOI	14
Ogden	Utah	69,478	48801	KQPD	KOET	21
Orono	Maine	9,989	04473	WMEB	WMEM	28
Waco	Texas	95,326	76703	KWTZ	KWTX	34

phase 5 lessons 101–125

Developing personal/ professional typing skills

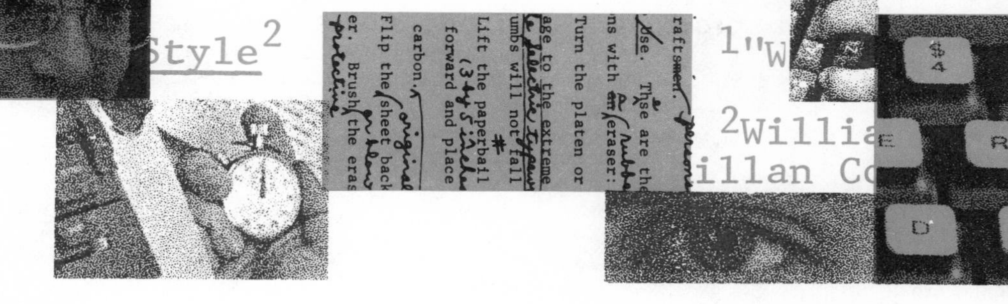

Learning goals

The 25 lessons of Phase 5 continue the emphasis given in the 4 steps of the *Planned Program* to improve your typing skills (see page 125). In addition, you will:

1. Improve your manuscript- and report-typing skill.
2. Learn basic guides for:
a. typing numbers
b. capitalization
3. Increase your speed and improve your accuracy.
4. Improve your proofreading skills (as directed).
5. Improve and extend your tabulation skills.
6. Continue to refine your basic typing techniques.

Machine adjustments

1. Paper guide at *0*.
2. 70-space line and SS or as directed.
3. Line space selector on *1* or as directed.
4. Ribbon control on black (*R* on Selectric).

unit 17 lessons 101–108

Manuscripts/ reports

101

101a ▶5 Conditioning practice

each line 3 times (slowly, faster, in-between rate)

alphabet The explorer quickly adjusted the beams as the freezing wave hit them.
fig/sym Is the total charge on order No. 2378, dated June 10, $45.69 or $4.56?
adjacent keys Being merely a knocker requires neither cerebral powers nor education.
fluency The eight men handled the historical ornament with the utmost caution.

| 1 | 2 | 3 | 4 | 5 | 6 | 7 | 8 | 9 | 10 | 11 | 12 | 13 | 14 |

101b ▶8 Learn symbol reaches: & *

each drill line 3 times (slowly, faster, slowly); application ¶ once

When used in company names, the **&** is typed without spacing with initials, as in J&B Products; but it is preceded and followed by a space when the name is spelled, as in Jones & Company. The **#**, when used, is typed next to the figure with which it is used, as #10 or as 10#.

Reach technique for &
The & is the shift of the *7* key.

7&j 7&j &j &j J&B Products

Reach technique for #
The # is the shift of the *3* key.

3#d 3#d #d #d #10; 14,783#

Reach technique for *
Manual: The * is the shift of the – (hyphen) key.

–*; –*; *; *; Jones & Co.*

Electric: The * is the shift of the *8* key.

8*k 8*k *k *k Jones & Co.*

application ¶

The & (ampersand) is used only in company names: C&NW Railway; Swift & Company; Brown & Jordon, Inc. The * (asterisk) may be used to refer to a footnote. The # is used mostly as a written symbol for <u>number</u> (No.) or <u>pound</u> (lb.), as #10 nylon thread or 10# sugar. It is used infrequently in typewritten business communications.

185c ▶40 Measure production skill: letters on special-size stationery

Time schedule

Assembling materials ... 3′
Timed production ...... 30′
Final check; compute *n–pram* .... 7′

1. Arrange stationery [LM pp. 61–68] and supplies for easy handling.
2. Make 1 cc and address an envelope for each letter.
3. Correct errors; circle uncorrected errors found in final check.
4. Compute *n–pram*.

Problem 1 (half–size)
Block style; open

words

October 25, 19-- Ms. Naomi R. Goldberg 473 9
Snowden Road Alexandria, VA 22308 Dear Ms. 17
Goldberg (¶ 1) Thousands of persons interested 25
in wise and profitable investments have bene- 34
fited from our unbiased advice. Hundreds have 44
amassed sizable fortunes by following the ad- 52
vice of our staff. (¶ 2) To help small investors 61
with some of the problems they have encoun- 70
tered in their investment programs in our 78
changing economy, we've planned a series of 87
seminars, to be held in 25 cities, to deal with 96
crucial problems and to offer practical solu- 105
tions. The seminar schedule is enclosed. (¶ 3) I 114
invite you to attend one or more meetings to 123
learn about our exceptional services in the in- 132
vestment field. Sincerely yours Mrs. Marlene 142
Stout, President xx Enclosure 147/**159**

Problem 2 (government–size)
Block style; mixed

October 25, 19-- Mr. David E. Faris 369 N. 9
Overview Drive Spencer, IN 47460 Dear Mr. 17
Faris: (¶ 1) Thank you for advising me of your 25
views with respect to H. R. 636, the Tax 34
Policy Review Act, which would eliminate tax 43
deductions for charitable contributions to 51
churches, educational institutions, and non- 60
profit organizations. (¶ 2) This bill was intro- 68
duced in the 93d Congress and was referred to 77
the House Committee on Ways and Means. The 86
committee did not act on this bill, and it died 96
when the 93d Congress adjourned. Not only did 105
the committee refuse to act on the bill, but the 115
primary sponsor of the bill notified the commit- 124
tee that he wished to withdraw his support for 134
the measure and that he would not encourage 143
the committee to hold hearings or to report the 152
bill to the House floor for a vote. (¶ 3) This bill 162
has not been reintroduced in the 94th Con- 170
gress. However, if a bill which would prohibit 179

words

tax deductions for charitable contributions is 189
ever presented to the House for a vote, you 198
may rest assured that it would not have my 206
support. I firmly believe these deductions 215
should remain a part of our federal income tax 224
structure. 226
Sincerely, John Myers xx 231/**243**

Problem 3 (executive–size)
Modified block style; open

October 25, 19-- Dr. Frank E. Busch 4527 Col- 9
lins Avenue Miami, FL 33140 Dear Dr. Busch 17
(¶ 1) The Executive Board of the Foundation 25
has decided to expand its activities in the area 35
of international business. In the past, we have 45
worked with business firms operating in the 53
European market; now we should like to become 63
involved with companies doing business in 71
Africa and Southeast Asia. (¶ 2) We have com- 79
piled a list of 12 projects in which we have 88
special interest; a copy of that list is enclosed. 98
We should like to have you rank these sug- 106
gested projects in terms of their importance 115
to the international business community, plac- 124
ing a "1" next to the project you consider 133
MOST important, a "2" next to the SECOND 141
MOST important, etc. With each rating, we 150
should like to have your comments supporting 159
the ratings you assign. (¶ 3) For your help, 167
we shall pay you $250 upon receipt of your com- 176
pleted rating sheet. Will you let me know by 185
return mail whether or not you will accept this 195
invitation? Sincerely yours Ms. Lee Rutkowski, 204
Manager International Programs xx Enclosure 213/**224**

Problem 4 (executive–size)
Retype Problem 3. Address it to:

Mr. Howard Green
805 Broadway
Nashville, TN 37203

Supply an appropriate salutation.

101c ▶15 Improve number expression: related learning

Certain basic rules or guides must be followed if your writing is to meet acceptable writing standards. Type the number-usage and capitalization guides given in this unit on separate sheets of paper for later use in a special *Typewriting Manual* that you are to prepare and assemble later. When complete, this manual will be stapled in the upper left corner and will include a title page, a table of contents (to be typed last), and a variety of typed copy. After completing the manual, you will number the pages as directed; temporarily number each page lightly in pencil in the upper left corner as you complete it.

Note: The *content* of some of the material you will type contains important directions and information that you will need to use in preparing the *Typewriting Manual.* Be sure to follow these directions so that the completed project will represent your best work.

1. For all *Related Learnings* in Cycle 2, use:

Margins

- top, page 1: 1½″
- top, all other pages: 1″
- side: 1″
- bottom (approx.): 1″

2. Reset left margin for blocked items, and use margin release to backspace into the left margin for item numbers.

3. Type underlines where shown in illustrative sentences and note the guide application each time.

4. Correct errors.

center ——▶ SERIES 2: NUMBER GUIDES

2 spaces ↓ TS

1. Spell numbers from one to ten except when used with numbers above ten.*

   DS

   He ordered _8_ typewriting books and _15_ English books.

   DS

2. Always spell a number beginning a sentence even though figures are used later in the sentence.

   Eight persons accepted our invitation; _15_ declined.

3. As a general rule, spell the shorter of two numbers used together.

   Please send _ten_ 50-gallon drums and _350_ six-gallon cans.

4. Spell isolated fractions in a sentence, but type a series of fractions in figures. Use the diagonal (/) for "made" fractions.

   Nearly _one third_ of the work is completed.
   Type _1/8_, _1/2_, _3/4_, _5/6_, and _7 9/10_.

Retain paper for use in next lesson.

101d ▶22 Learn to type an unbound manuscript without footnotes

full sheets; DS the ¶s
5-space ¶ indention

Margins

- top, page 1:
  - pica 1½″
  - elite 2″
- bottom (approx.): 1″
- top, page 2: 1″
- side: 1″

Type page numbers in proper position; correct errors.

1. Study the illustration and the paragraphs on manuscript or report form on pages 167, 168.

2. Type the unbound manuscript as directed. Indent the enumerated items 5 spaces from the left and right margins; space them as illustrated in the copy.

Note: Make a light pencil mark at the right edge of the page about 1″ from the bottom edge (and again at 1½″) or use a backing sheet to alert you to leave a 1″ bottom margin and at least 2 lines of a paragraph on the page.

A page line gauge (backing sheet) is provided on LM p. 65. This sheet will indicate the number of line spaces above or below your line of typing.

2

Side headings. Side headings are typed even with the left margin and underlined; main words are started with a capital letter. These headings are preceded by 2 blank line spaces and followed by 1 blank line space. Side headings serve as guideposts to the reader of a report.

Paragraph headings. You have just typed a paragraph heading. It is indented and underlined. Usually, only the first word is capitalized. Paragraph headings, also, are an aid to the reader.

Page Numbers

The first page may or may not be numbered. The number, if used, is centered and typed a half inch from the bottom edge. As a general rule, other page numbers are typed on the fourth line in the upper right corner approximately even with the right margin; however, if the manuscript or report is to be bound at the top, the page numbers are typed in first-page position (centered and typed a half inch from the bottom edge).

Other General Guides

Avoid ending a page with 1 line of a new paragraph or carrying 1 line of a paragraph to a new page. This general rule, however, is no longer strictly observed, even in formal writing.

184b ▶5 Carbon-pack assembly and erasing tips

Desk-top method

1. Turn the noncarboned side of the carbon paper toward you as you assemble the carbon pack.

2. Insert the pack into the type-writer with the heading down and facing the back of the machine.

Machine method

1. Insert the letterhead and second sheets until they are barely gripped by the feed rolls.

2. Insert the carbon paper between the gripped sheets, being sure that the carboned side of each carbon sheet is facing you. Then roll the pack into typing position.

Notes

1. To straighten the pack in the typewriter, hold the pack firmly, operate the paper–release lever, move the pack until it is aligned properly, then reset the paper–release lever.

2. Both methods of assembling a carbon pack are fully illustrated on RG page xi.

Erasing

Before erasing on the original sheet, place a 5″ × 3″ card *in front of* the first carbon sheet. To erase the first carbon copy, move the card to the same position in front of the second carbon sheet, etc. (See page RG page xii.)

184c ▶40 Build sustained production skill: letters on special-size stationery

Time schedule

Preparation .... 3′
Timed production . . 30′
Final check; com–
pute *n–pram* .... 7′

1. Make a list of problems to be typed:

page 291, 181c, Problem 1
page 292, 182c, Problem 1
page 294, 183c, Problem 1

2. Arrange supplies (letterheads [LM pp. 57–62] or plain sheets) for rapid handling. Make 1 cc; address envelopes.

3. When directed to begin, type for 30′. Follow directions given for each problem; cor–rect all errors neatly. Proofread carefully before removing paper from the machine. If you finish all problems before time is called, retype the first problem on a standard plain sheet.

4. After computing *n–pram*, turn in all problems arranged in the order in which they are given in Step 1.

n–pram = Total acceptable words + ½ unacceptable words ÷ minutes typed.

185

185a ▶5 Conditioning practice

each line 3 times (slowly, top speed, in-between rate)

Joyce Clarke won six clubs and other golf equipment at Hazelwood Cove.
Dick issued 302 wristbands, 67 nets, 94 rackets, and 185 tennis balls.
Invoice 8520-J for $3,467.19 was mailed to Webber & Payne for payment.
You will find a real challenge in trying to improve your basic skills.

| 1 | 2 | 3 | 4 | 5 | 6 | 7 | 8 | 9 | 10 | 11 | 12 | 13 | 14 |

185b ▶5 Arrange completed work

1. As you complete each letter/envelope in 185c, page 296, place the letter under the envelope flap.

2. Lay the letter face down on the desk.

3. If work is to be turned in or evaluated, turn the stack of completed work face up so that your work will be in correct sequence.

Step 1
Remove letter from typewriter; address an envelope; place letter under envelope flap.

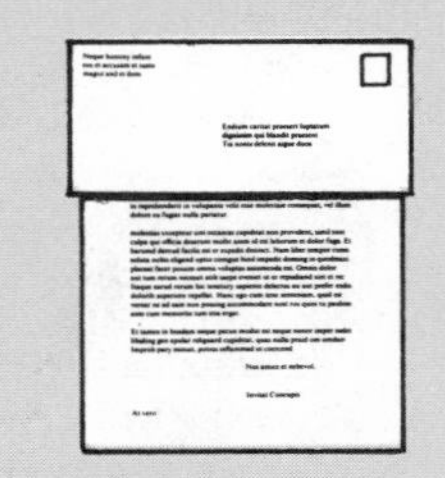

Step 2
Place letter and envelope face down on desk.

Step 3
When work is to be turned in, turn stack face up and your work will be in correct sequence.

1½" top margin (pica type)

Main heading

MANUSCRIPT OR REPORT FORM Line 10

TS

The guides presented here represent one acceptable form of typing manuscripts or reports.

TS

Side heading

Spacing and Margins

DS

Manuscripts or reports may be either single- or double-spaced. The form that is followed is dependent upon the type of report that is prepared. School reports, formal reports, and manuscripts to be submitted for publication should be typed in double-spaced form. Reports that are prepared for use in the business office often are typed in single-spaced form.

1" 1"

Maintain an approximate 1-inch bottom margin. Leave 1-inch top and side margins on all pages with these exceptions:

DS

1. Leave a 1 1/2-inch (pica) or 2-inch (elite) top margin on the first page of an unbound or leftbound manuscript; a 2- or 2 1/2-inch top margin on the first page of a topbound manuscript.

DS

2. Leave a 1 1/2-inch top margin on the second and succeeding pages of a topbound manuscript.

3. Leave a 1 1/2-inch left margin on all pages of a leftbound manuscript.

2 spaces

Indent numbered items 5 spaces from left and right margins

The first line of a paragraph may be indented either 5, 7, or 10 spaces. Quoted material of 4 lines or more is single-spaced and indented 5 spaces from the left and right margins. It is preceded and followed by 1 blank line space.

Headings and Subheadings

¶ heading

Main heading. A main heading is centered over the line of writing in all capitals and is followed by 2 blank line spaces.

Approximately 1"

1

½"

183c ▶35 Learn to type letters/tables on half-size stationery

2 letterheads, 2 plain sheets (half-size) [LM pp. 55, 56]
1 carbon, 2 second sheets

Type for 25′ from Problems 1–4. Proofread; circle errors. If time permits, start over.

Goals: Correct format; improved procedure; good output.

Problem 1

block style, open; 1 cc; ¾″ side margins; date on Line 8; address envelope

	words
October 23, 19-- Mr. John S. Portella 6061 Arlington Blvd. Falls Church, VA	15
22044 Dear Mr. Portella (¶ 1) Are you interested in good financial invest-	29
ments? If so, you and we should get together . . . soon!	40
(¶ 2) Our specialty is helping people make money; our business is designed to	55
alert clients like you to good investment opportunities. Last year we counseled	71
scores of people in building their initial investment portfolios; we helped	86
others revise their existing investment programs. Now we should like the	101
privilege of working with you on some attractive investment possibilities.	116
(¶ 3) Enclosed is a list of our investment staff, all well qualified in a wide	131
range of investment areas. Why not call one of these experts soon to dis-	145
cuss your investments. Sincerely yours Mrs. Marlene Stout, President xx	159
Enclosure	161/174

Problem 2
Table enclosure for Problem 1

1 cc; reading position; short side up; DS body; SS indented items; 2 spaces between columns

Problems 3 and 4

Retype Problems 1 and 2, no carbons. Address letter to:

Mr. Gaza A. Katona
1368 Homewood Drive
Lynchburg, VA 24502

Supply salutation.

DIRECTORY OF INVESTMENT COUNSELORS (7)

Located in Home Office (12)

Counseling Area	Name	Telephone	words
			23
Bond funds	Mrs. Hammer	466-3598	30
Common stocks	Mr. Fritz	467-1259	36
Government securities	Mr. Mabone	466-3708	45
Mutual funds	Ms. McVay	467-1072	51
Real estate	Mrs. Dunlap	466-1059	57
Retirement plans			61
Indent 3→ Keogh	Mr. Wyllie	465-2057	66
Independent	Ms. Kuiper	465-1389	72

184

184a ▶5 Conditioning practice

each line 3 times (slowly, top speed, in-between rate)

Pat Dowby gave Judge Traxler some quaint sketches of a sunset horizon.
The House Committee reported on H.R. 958 and H.R. 7063 on December 14.
Profits (after taxes) were $835,240 in 1977--an increase of almost 8%.
If you learn to push yourself without tension, you will gain in skill.

| 1 | 2 | 3 | 4 | 5 | 6 | 7 | 8 | 9 | 10 | 11 | 12 | 13 | 14 |

101d, continued

Side headings. Side headings are typed even with the left margin and underlined; main words are started with a capital letter. These headings are preceded by 2 blank line spaces and followed by 1 blank line space. Side headings serve as guideposts to the reader of a report.

Paragraph headings. You have just typed a paragraph heading. It is indented and underlined. Usually, only the first word is capitalized. Paragraph headings, also, are an aid to the reader.

Page Numbers

The first page may or may not be numbered. The number, if used, is centered and typed a half inch from the bottom edge. As a general rule, other page numbers are typed on the fourth line in the upper right corner approximately even with the right margin; however, if the manuscript or report is to be bound at the top, the page numbers are typed in first-page position (centered and typed a half inch from the bottom edge).

Other General Guides

Avoid ending a page with 1 line of a new paragraph or carrying 1 line of a paragraph to a new page. This general rule, however, is no longer strictly observed, even in formal writing.

The general word division rules govern the division of words at the ends of lines. Avoid dividing words at the ends of more than 2 consecutive lines or at the end of a page.

102

102a ▶5 Conditioning practice

each line 3 times (slowly, faster, in-between rate)

alphabet	Maxine was puzzled by the lack of interest in the five good quay jobs.
fig/sym	Order the 38#, 56#, and 79# packages (untaped) from J. C. Carl & Sons.
fig/sym	Special sale items are identified by the *; as 101*, 631*, 792*, 845*.
fluency	The authenticity of the six amendments may torment the skeptical boys.

| 1 | 2 | 3 | 4 | 5 | 6 | 7 | 8 | 9 | 10 | 11 | 12 | 13 | 14 |

102b ▶10 Improve number expression: related learning

End of Series 2

In these concise guides, not every acceptable alternative is included—to do so would merely lead to confusion. The guides given, however, can be used with confidence; they represent basic guides to good usage.

1. Reinsert sheet used for typing guides of 101c, page 166.

2. Align copy properly and continue with Guide 5. Space copy properly as you type it.

3. Number the pages (see page 166) and retain for your *Typewriting Manual*.

5. Numbers preceded by nouns are usually expressed in figures.

   Type Rule 6 on page 136 in Monograph 110.

6. Express measures, weights, and dimensions in figures without commas.

   Lee Beatty is 6 ft. 9 in. tall. The package weighs 4 lbs. 7 oz.

7. Use the percent sign (%) with definite numbers typed in figures. Use percent (spelled) with approximations and in formal writing.

   The interest rate is 8 1/2%. About 50 percent of the wood is here.

8. Spell names of small-numbered avenues and streets (ten and under). Type house numbers in figures except for house number One.

   My office is at 901 Fifth Avenue; my store, at 13 W. 42d Street. They plan to move from One Polk Avenue to 1915 Sixth Street.

type 1½" underline

______________ SS
DS

*A common practice in business is to use figures for all numbers except those which begin a sentence.

182c, continued

Problem 2
Table enclosure for Problem 1

1 cc; reading position;
6 spaces between columns;
DS body, SS 2-line items

Problems 3 and 4

Retype Problems 1 and 2 (no cc).
Address letter and envelope to:

Mrs. Peggy Bender
4408 Baywood Drive
Bloomington, IN 47401

Supply an appropriate salutation.

IMPORTANT RIVERS IN THE UNITED STATES

(By Length)

Name	Source	Miles	words
			8
			10
Name	Source	Miles	17
Mississippi	Lake Itasca, Minnesota	2,348	25
Missouri	Junction of Jefferson, Madison,		33
	and Gallatin Rivers, Montana	2,315	39
Rio Grande	San Juan County, Colorado	1,885	48
Yukon	Junction of Lewes and Pelly		55
	Rivers, Yukon	1,770	59
Arkansas	Lake County, Colorado	1,459	66
Red	Curry County, New Mexico	1,270	73
Snake	Teton County, Wyoming	1,038	80

183

183a ▶5 Conditioning practice

each line 3 times (slowly, top speed, in-between rate)

Amazing beds of mixed flowers cover the park along the Jet d'Eau quay.
The sports store had 95 gloves, 174 bats, 362 shoes, and 80 pup tents.
Bell & King's Order 48962 for 370# of seed at $3.35 totaled $1,239.50.
If you would like to add to your production rate, plan your work well.

| 1 | 2 | 3 | 4 | 5 | 6 | 7 | 8 | 9 | 10 | 11 | 12 | 13 | 14 |

183b ▶10 Improve skill in typing from rough draft

1. A 1′ writing on each ¶; determine *gwam*.
2. A 3′ writing on both ¶s; determine *gwam*.
Goal: To learn to type from rough draft.

all letters used | D | 1.6 si | 5.8 awl | 75% hfw |

Text	gwam 1′	3′
~~We are living in a~~ The day in which we live has been characterized	10	3
by many ~~persons~~ folks as the age of knowledge. We are said to	21	7
be witnessingan # immense ~~information~~ intellectual explosion, with new	32	11
knowledge accumulating at a pace so ~~rapid~~ incredible that humans kind	45	15
just cannot ~~hope~~ expect to absorb it all.	52	17
but today's ambitious young people ~~are~~ trying to learn as much	11	21
as ~~possible~~ they can while they are able to do so; they ~~are~~ using	21	24
libraries, enrolling in unusual courses, attending lec-	31	28
tures and programs, and are active in many ~~out-of-school~~ extra-curricular	43	32
projects designed to ~~inform~~ acquaint them ~~of~~ with new and exiting ideas.	56	36

102c ▶35 Type an unbound manuscript from rough draft and straight copy

full sheets; carbon pack;
DS the ¶s; 5-space ¶ indention

Margins

top, page 1:	pica	1½"
	elite	2"
additional pages:		1"
side:		1"
bottom (approx.):		1"

Number all pages in proper position.

Note: You are not expected to complete the manuscript in this lesson; additional time is provided in Lesson 103.

1. Study copy on correcting errors (this page and page 170). Note that enumerated items are sometimes indented and double-spaced, as illustrated in the copy on this page.

2. Assemble a carbon pack (copy sheet on desk; then carbon paper, carbon side down; then original sheet); insert pack with carbon side facing you.

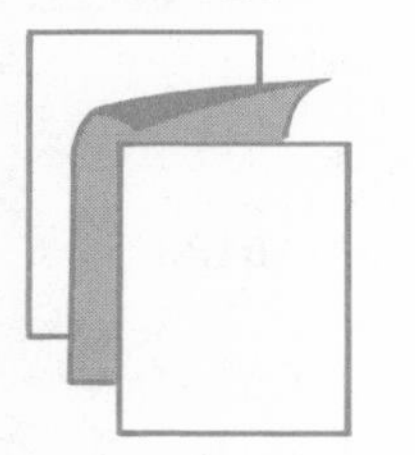

3. Type material in unbound manuscript form. Make corrections indicated in the copy. Erase and correct errors.

CORRECTING TYPING ERRORS

In most typewritten work, errors should be corrected. several methods that may be used for error correction are given in breif form in this report.

Rubber Typeriter eraser

Process. The rubber eraser actually removes the error from the paper.

Types of rubber erasers. Rubber erasers are available in several types: (1) wheet type, with or without a brush; (2) pencil types--one type has a rub ber eraser on one end with a brush on hte other; another type has a regular eraser on one end with a rubber eraser on the other end; and, (3) electric erasers similiar to those used by draftsmen.

Method to Use. Thse are the steps to fol low in making corrections with an eraser:

1. Turn the platen or cylinder forward; then move the carriage to the extreme ri-ght or left so that the eraser crumbs will not fall into the machine.

2. Lift the paperbail out of the way. pull the original sheet forward and place a card in front of, not behind, the first carbon.

3. Flip the sheet back and make the erasuer with a hard eraser. Brush the eraser crumbs off the paper.

4. Move the card to a positoin in front of the second carbon if more than one copy is being made. Erase the error on the first carbon

(continued, page 170)

182

182a ▶5 Conditioning practice

each line 3 times (slowly, top speed, in-between rate)

Carl Heinz gave Phyllis Boyd an exquisite jacket from Grandview Lodge.
Use Social Security Records 187-01-8959, 279-26-4863, and 306-94-4586.
Bill's check for $1,876.45 was written on May 29 and mailed on May 30.
Most office typists are required to handle a variety of letter styles.

| 1 | 2 | 3 | 4 | 5 | 6 | 7 | 8 | 9 | 10 | 11 | 12 | 13 | 14 |

182b ▶10 Improve speed/control

1. One 1′ writing on each of ¶s 1, 2, and 3 of 180d, page 289; determine *gwam*.

2. One 5′ control writing on all ¶s combined. Determine *gwam*; circle errors.

Enrichment material for Unit 31 appears on LM p. 69.

182c ▶35 Learn to type letters/tables on government-size stationery

2 letterheads, 2 plain sheets (government-size) [LM pp. 47-54] 1 carbon sheet, 2 second sheets

Type for 25′ from Problems 1–4. Proofread; circle errors. If time permits, start over.

Goals: Correct format; efficient materials handling; good output.

Problem 1
Block style, mixed

1 cc; 1″ side margins; date: DS below letterhead; address envelope

	words
October 22, 19-- Mr. Ronald L. Hardman 760 Highridge Greencastle, IN 46135	15
Dear Mr. Hardman:	19
(¶ 1) Thank you for your letter regarding the proposal by the Army Corps	32
of Engineers which would redefine the concept of "navigable waters" for	46
purposes of determining the scope of authority of the Corps over the waters	62
of the United States.	66
(¶ 2) I am well aware of this proposal and directed many questions about	80
it to the Chief of the Corps of Engineers when he testified before the House	95
Appropriations Subcommittee on Public Works last February. I am the rank-	110
ing minority member on this subcommittee. A copy of my remarks, along	124
with the response by the Chief of the Corps of Engineers, is enclosed.	138
(¶ 3) Since then, the Corps has issued several alternative proposals. I do not	153
know when final action will be taken in this matter or what the ultimate	168
rules or new definitions, if any, will be. However, I can assure you it is	183
something in which I am vitally interested and that I am closely follow-	197
ing all developments. States, as well as individuals, are concerned that	212
any new definition not infringe on their rights or smother them under more	227
bureaucratic rule. I agree and intend to do all I can to assure this does	242
not happen.	244
(¶ 4) I hope this information will be useful to you, and I am glad you have	258
taken the time to let me know your views.	267
Sincerely, John Myers xx Enclosures	274/285

copy and on all other copies in a like manner.

5. Remove the card and type the correction.

When erasing, be careful that your fingers do not smudge the copy as you hold the paper. Some typists use an eraser shield to protect the surrounding typing. To erase on the upper two thirds of the paper, turn the cylinder forward; on the lower third, turn the cylinder backward so that the paper will not slip out of the typewriter as you erase the error.

Disadvantages. A rubber eraser must be used with care, as it is possible to rub a hole in the paper. Also, eraser crumbs must be brushed away from the typewriter because if they fall into the type basket they can cause sticky key action.

Correction Paper

Process. Correction paper covers (masks) the error with a powderlike substance. Correction paper comes in colors to match the colors of paper commonly used in the business office--white, blue, pink, yellow, etc.

Types of correction paper. Correction paper is available in several types, among which are the following: (1) correction tape (reel-type dispensers) and (2) correction paper strips. A slightly different type of correction paper is available for making corrections on carbon copies. The latter type of correction paper also is available in a variety of colors.

Method to use. Follow the steps outlined below:

1. Backspace to the beginning of the error.

2. Insert the correction tape or paper strip behind the typewriter ribbon and in front of the error.

3. Retype the error exactly as you made it. In this step, powder from the correction paper is pressed by force of the keystroke into the form of the error, thus masking it.

4. Remove the correction paper; backspace to the point where the correction begins and type the correction.

Disadvantages. The powder correction can rub off and expose the original error. Also, at the present time, correction-paper corrections may not be satisfactory for copying an original by certain photocopying processes because the original error may appear on the copies.

Correction Fluid

Process. Correction fluid covers or masks the error with a penetrating liquid which leaves an opaque substance on the paper. Correction fluid is available in colors to match paper commonly used in the business office.

Type. Correction fluid is packaged in a small bottle with an applicator brush attached to the inside of the cap. A liquid thinner can be used for thinning the correction fluid if necessary.

Method. Here are the steps to follow when using correction fluid:

1. Turn the cylinder up a few spaces.

2. Shake the bottle; remove the applicator from the bottle; daub excess fluid on inside of bottle opening.

3. Apply fluid sparingly to error by a touching action over entire error.

4. Return applicator to bottle and tighten cap; blow on error to speed drying process.

5. When fluid is dry, type the correction.

Disadvantages. With the passage of time, the dried mask may crack or peel, exposing the error or, even more serious, making the correction unreadable. For this reason, this error-correction method is not acceptable for copy that is to be stored for long periods of time, such as in the archives of a library. Correction fluid must be dry before the correction is typed, or the correction will not be sharp and clear.

Lift-off Tape

Process. An adhesive substance on the tape lifts the incorrect character off the paper.

Type. Presently, a special lift-off tape is available for use only with the IBM Correcting Selectric Typewriter although new devices may be marketed at any time.

Procedure. The procedure to follow is relatively simple: When an error is made, a special key is used to backspace to the error; the incorrect character is lifted off the paper by again striking the incorrect character. The typing element stays in place, and the correct character is typed.

Disadvantages. The lift-off tape can be used only with typewriters with this special device or equipment.

181c ▶35 Learn to type letters/tables on executive-size stationery

2 letterheads, 2 plain sheets (executive-size) [LM pp. 39-46], 1 carbon sheet, 2 second sheets

Type for 25′ from Problems 1–4. Proofread; circle errors. If time permits, start over.

Goals: Correct format; improved procedure; good output.

Problem 1
1 cc; modified block style, open; margins: 1″; address envelope

	words
October 21, 19-- Mr. Richard Huybers, President Bluegrass Industrial Cor-	14
poration 3167 Taylorsville Road Louisville, KY 40205 Dear Mr. Huybers	28
(¶ 1) Five years ago, we launched an idea which we thought would benefit	42
business and industrial organizations operating in the Southeast. At that	57
time, we created a Resources Development Fund for the purpose of under-	71
writing research, for developing innovative management programs, and	85
for promoting imaginative ideas relating to business and/or management	99
practices. Today that idea emerges as both a sound and a profitable one.	114
(¶ 2) Our first attempts to solicit support for the Resources Development Fund	128
resulted in only modest contributions; however, since our first efforts five	144
years ago, we have seen remarkable increases in the number of contributors	159
to the Fund and in the total amount of money received. The enclosed table	174
shows very dramatically the support given during the five-year period.	188
(¶ 3) I know you are interested in good investments; here's an opportunity for	203
you, now, to make an investment with high yield possibilities. Why not take	218
a few minutes to complete the enclosed card and join the impressive list of	233
investors contributing so generously to the advancement of business through	248
our Resources Development Fund. Very sincerely yours Ms. Mary Campbell,	263
Director Fund and Project Development xx Enclosures 2	273/**295**

Problem 2
Table enclosure for Problem 1
1 cc; reading position; DS body; 4 spaces between columns

Problem 3
Retype Problem 1 in modified block style, no carbon copy. Address letter and envelope to:

Mr. Harold Utley, Manager
Volunteer Finance Corp.
151 Union Avenue
Memphis, TN 38103

Supply appropriate salutation.

Problem 4
Retype the table shown at right, no carbon copy.

FOUNDATION FOR BUSINESS DEVELOPMENT (words 7)

Personal and Corporate Gifts (words 13)

Year	No. of Gifts Received	Annual Gift Receipts	Endowment Gift Receipts	words
1973	497	$17,950	$213,268	41
1974	458	29,805	74,717	46
1975	840	42,786	117,273	51
1976	985	64,025	165,805	56
1977	1136	85,200	221,409	61

Header row words: 36

103

103a ▶5 Conditioning practice

each line 3 times (slowly, faster, in-between rate)

alphabet	This quick quiz will cover exceedingly important factors of job skill.
fig/sym	Use finger-reach action (hands quiet) to type 103#, $4,628, and 97.5%.
shift key	The salesmen are from Brown & Co., J&J Products, Inc., and Lynn & Son.
fluency	If they give him a key to the office, he might finish the work for us.

| 1 | 2 | 3 | 4 | 5 | 6 | 7 | 8 | 9 | 10 | 11 | 12 | 13 | 14 |

103b ▶10 Check number expression

The sentences are in problem form. To type them correctly, you must recall the number guides.

Check your work with the guides (the code 1–2:166 means Guides 1–2, page 166).

Number and type the sentences in correct form.

1–2:166	1. 8 persons were invited; only 4 came.
1:166	2. Please get 15 books, three pads, and twelve pencils.
3:166	3. Did you order 10 100-gallon drums or one hundred ten-gallon cans?
4:166	4. Only 1/2 of the work is completed.
4:166	5. Please add one half, three fourths, and seven eighths.
5:168	6. Check Guide five on page one hundred sixty-eight.
6:168	7. Nancy, who is five feet 4 in. in height, weighs ninety-eight pounds.
7:168	8. Nearly 40% of the homes carry a 7 percent mortgage interest rate.
8:168	9. He lives at 264 3d Street, not 1 Dakota Avenue.

103c ▶25 Learn to type an unbound manuscript

Complete 102c, pages 169, 170.

103d ▶10 Footnote review

full sheet; 1½″ left margin; 1″ right margin; DS ¶ and start it on Line 42; indent ¶ 5 spaces

When footnotes are used in a report, they should be typed so that the last line of the last footnote ends about one inch from the bottom edge of the paper. One style that may be used in typing footnotes is illustrated below.

____

footnote reference to a book

[1] John Lolley, Your Library: What's in It for You (New York: John Wiley & Sons, Inc., 1974), p. 15.

footnote reference to a magazine article

[2] D. M. Glixon, "Gift Books for the Graduate's Reference Shelf," Saturday Review (May 17, 1975), pp. 27-28.

footnote reference to a source cited earlier in the report

[3] Lolley, p. 28.

footnote reference to a magazine article—no author cited

[4] "Look Up Your Friends at the Library," Writer's Digest (June, 1975), pp. 10-13.

unit **31** lessons 181–185

Letters using special-size stationery

Learning goals

1. To develop skill in typing letters on special-size stationery.

2. To improve skill in organizing work and materials.

Machine adjustments

1. Line: 70 for drills and timed writings.

2. Spacing: SS sentence drills; DS ¶s and indent 5 spaces; as directed for problems.

181

181a ▶5 Conditioning practice

each line 3 times (slowly, top speed, in-between rate)

alphabet Jim and Gaza Key won five trophies in six matches at the racquet club.

figures Of the votes cast, Mercer received 1,586; Snell, 724; and Street, 390.

fig/sym Al's commission on Order 9463 will be just $157.25 (8 1/2% of $1,850).

fluency Many leaders in business use special-size stationery in their offices.

| 1 | 2 | 3 | 4 | 5 | 6 | 7 | 8 | 9 | 10 | 11 | 12 | 13 | 14 |

181b ▶10 Letters on special-size stationery

Study the model letters shown at the right; use the placement table to arrange the letters on these special sizes of stationery.

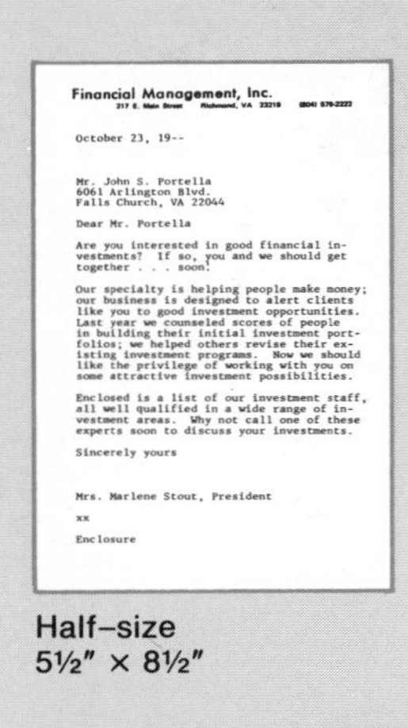

Financial Management, Inc.
217 E. Main Street Richmond, VA 23219 (804) 579-2222

October 23, 19--

Mr. John S. Portella
6061 Arlington Blvd.
Falls Church, VA 22044

Dear Mr. Portella

Are you interested in good financial investments? If so, you and we should get together . . . soon!

Our specialty is helping people make money; our business is designed to alert clients like you to good investment opportunities. Last year we counseled scores of people in building their initial investment portfolios; we helped others revise their existing investment programs. Now we should like the privilege of working with you on some attractive investment possibilities.

Enclosed is a list of our investment staff, all well qualified in a wide range of investment areas. Why not call one of these experts soon to discuss your investments.

Sincerely yours

Mrs. Marlene Stout, President

xx

Enclosure

Half-size
5½" × 8½"

Foundation For Business Development
(404) 721-7493 263 Peachtree Street Atlanta, GA 30303

October 21, 19--

Mr. Richard Huybers, President
Bluegrass Industrial Corporation
3167 Taylorsville Road
Louisville, KY 40205

Dear Mr. Huybers

Five years ago, we launched an idea which we thought would benefit business and industrial organizations operating in the Southeast. At that time, we created a Resources Development Fund for the purpose of underwriting research, for developing innovative management programs, and for promoting imaginative ideas relating to business and/or management practices. Today that idea emerges as both a sound and a profitable one.

Our first attempts to solicit support for the Resources Development Fund resulted in only modest contributions; however, since our first efforts five years ago, we have seen remarkable increases in the number of contributors to the Fund and in the total amount of money received. The enclosed table shows very dramatically the support given during the five-year period.

I know you are interested in good investments; here's an opportunity for you, now, to make an investment with high yield possibilities. Why not take a few minutes to complete the enclosed card and join the impressive list of investors contributing so generously to the advancement of business through our Resources Development Fund.

Very sincerely yours

Ms. Mary Campbell, Director
Fund and Project Development

xx

Enclosures 2

Executive-size
7¼" × 10½"

JOHN T. MYERS

APPROPRIATIONS

Congress of the United States
House of Representatives
Washington, D.C. 20515

October 22, 19--

Mr. Ronald L. Hardman
760 Highridge
Greencastle, IN 46135

Dear Mr. Hardman:

Thank you for your letter regarding the proposal by the Army Corps of Engineers which would redefine the concept of "navigable waters" for purposes of determining the scope of authority of the Corps over the waters of the United States.

I am well aware of this proposal and directed many questions about it to the Chief of the Corps of Engineers when he testified before the House Appropriations Subcommittee on Public Works last February. I am the ranking minority member on this subcommittee. A copy of my remarks, along with the response by the Chief of the Corps of Engineers, is enclosed.

Since then, the Corps has issued several alternative proposals. I do not know when final action will be taken in this matter or what the ultimate rules or new definitions, if any, will be. However, I can assure you it is something in which I am vitally interested and that I am closely following all developments. States, as well as individuals, are concerned that any new definition not infringe on their rights or smother them under more bureaucratic rule. I agree and intend to do all I can to assure this does not happen.

I hope this information will be useful to you, and I am glad you have taken the time to let me know your views.

Sincerely,

John Myers

xx

Enclosures

Government-size
8" × 10½"

Letter placement on special-size stationery

Kind of stationery	Size	Margins*	Date Placement*	Special Tips
Half-size	5½" × 8½"	1" or ¾"	Line 8–10	This size is suitable for short letters (130 words or fewer). Date may vary from Line 8 to Line 10.
Executive-size	7¼" × 10½"	1" or ¾"	Line 10–16	Side margins may be decreased from 1" to ¾" for longer letters. Date may vary from Line 10 to Line 16.
Government-size	8" × 10½"	1½" or 1"	DS below letterhead at the left margin	Side margins may be decreased from 1½" to 1" for longer letters; date to begin at the left margin, DS below letterhead; reference initials in lowercase and on file copy only, a DS from last notation.

*Margin width and date placement depend upon the letter length; the shorter the letter, the wider the margins, the lower the date. Always leave 3 blank line spaces below the dateline.

104

104a ▶5 Conditioning practice

each line 3 times (slowly, faster, in-between rate)

alphabet The proud man quickly won five prizes in the high jumping exhibitions.

fig/sym McNeil, Jones & Sons refused to pay Invoice 34/05 ($268.70) on June 1.

fingers 3, 4 Aza Quando said that Wally saw a plump polo pony down by the aqueduct.

fluency The authenticity of the ancient amendment may help them gain clemency.

| 1 | 2 | 3 | 4 | 5 | 6 | 7 | 8 | 9 | 10 | 11 | 12 | 13 | 14 |

104b ▶10 Improve capitalization skill: related learning

as directed in 101c, page 166

1. Space copy properly as you type it; erase and correct errors.

2. Save sheet for use in next lesson.

SERIES 3: CAPITALIZATION GUIDES

1. Capitalize the first word of every sentence and the first word of every complete direct quotation.

   She said, "Hard work is necessary for success."

2. Do not capitalize fragments of quotations.

   He stressed the importance of "a sense of values."

3. Do not capitalize a quotation resumed within a sentence. Type the comma or period before the ending quotation mark.

   "When all else fails," he said, "try following directions."

4. Capitalize the first word after a colon if that word begins a complete sentence. Space twice after the colon.

   Here is a daily reminder: Be sure to type with good techniques.

5. Capitalize first and last words and all other words in titles of books, articles, periodicals, headings, and plays, except words of four letters or fewer used as articles, conjunctions, or prepositions.

   Please read the article "Wonders of the Space Age."

104c ▶35 Learn to type leftbound manuscripts with footnotes

full sheet; center heading over line of writing; DS the ¶s; 5-space ¶ indention

Margins

top, page 1:
pica 1½"
elite 2"
top, page 2: 1"
left margin: 1½"
right margin: 1"
bottom (approx.): 1"

Type page numbers in proper position; correct errors as directed by your teacher.

Note: You are not expected to complete the manuscript in this lesson; additional time is provided in Lessons 105–108.

The first page of the manuscript (in pica type) is shown in arranged form on page 173; other pages are typeset.

Number the footnotes as shown in the report. Type each footnote on the same page as its reference number.

Guide: To leave space for the footnotes and a 1" bottom margin, *do this*:

Make a light pencil mark at the right edge of the sheet 1" from the bottom. As you type each footnote *reference number*, add another pencil mark ½" above the previous one. In this way you will reserve about 3 line spaces for typing each footnote. Erase these marks when you have completed the page.

Also use the page line gauge provided on LM p. 65.

180c ▶10 Improve technique: response patterns

1. Each line at least twice SS.

2. A 1′ writing on Line 2, then on Line 4, then Line 6.

3. Determine *gwam* on each writing; compare speed scores.

word response	If it is to be done, they will find a way to solve the energy problem. The work form is to be mailed to the truck firm having a world agency.
letter response	Several important inventions came from the unique nylon-sampling data. In its written announcement, the board declared payment of a dividend.
combination response	They mailed the financial statement to the firm for prompt settlement. A formal report detailing all expenditures was prepared by the member.

| 1 | 2 | 3 | 4 | 5 | 6 | 7 | 8 | 9 | 10 | 11 | 12 | 13 | 14 |

180d ▶15 Measure basic skill: straight copy

two 5′ writings; determine *gwam*; circle errors

all letters used | A | 1.5 si | 5.6 awl | 80% hfw |

	gwam 1′	5′
In our complex business world, we now hear loud voices being raised	14	3
steadily in the interest of the consumer. Many marketing students feel	28	6
that various ways remain untried in the field of helping the consumer,	42	8
the man on the street, to buy more wisely. Among the practices that seem	57	11
to raise the majority of questions are the differing ways of packaging an	72	14
item, the validity with which an item is labeled, and the methods used	86	17
to fix a selling price for an item.	93	19
The first step for anyone hoping to make buying a less costly pro-	13	21
cess is to learn more about the sellers with whom one deals--whether	27	24
they be owner-operated shops or large firms. Do the names of those with	42	27
whom you plan to do business connote reliability? It is a commonly	55	30
accepted fact that a well-known, reputable business may be far more	69	32
likely to protect the consumer's interest than will a small, newly estab-	83	35
lished firm.	86	36
Also essential to wise buying is the determination of the real need	14	39
of an item to the buyer. If the need is actually a real one, is the item	29	41
being contemplated the one that will best satisfy this need? Too fre-	43	44
quently we buy objects about which we know very little and then discover	57	47
belatedly that they are unsuited for the uses we had in mind. We did not	72	50
take time to consider the features, price, or quantity of our purchase in	87	53
terms of our original goal. We must also ask ourselves if each purchase	101	56
is justified. Today's consumers are realizing that they must be alert,	116	59
inquisitive, and wary. It's just good sense to spend each dollar wisely.	130	62

gwam 1′ | 1 | 2 | 3 | 4 | 5 | 6 | 7 | 8 | 9 | 10 | 11 | 12 | 13 | 14 |
5′ | 1 | 2 | 3 |

1½" top margin (pica type)
(1" on all other pages)

CHOOSING A CAREER

1½" → 1"

One of life's greatest satisfactions is a career that "fits." In choosing your career goal, therefore, you should "be honest with yourself." Munschauer supports this statement when he says, "Of all the things that comprise a career choice, the <u>human</u> factors and attitudes shouldn't be overlooked."[1] It is important that you choose a career you like.

You cannot expect to drift into a career that fits. You must choose it deliberately. You will need to match your aptitudes, interests, and personal qualifications with a career that requires your abilities and interests. Feingold and Swerdloff emphasize this point in the following statement:

Indent 5 spaces from left and right margins; SS

> Before you can choose anything intelligently, you must have some basis for your choice. Choosing without knowing is merely taking a chance, as you do when you reach into a grab bag for a prize. Given several opportunities, you must know enough about each to select the one that suits your needs better than the others, stimulates your interest, and tests your sense of values. Otherwise, you will choose blindly.[2]

They suggest, also, that choosing a career "may be the first really complex adult decision you will be called upon to face."[3] This decision will determine the pattern of your life, the type of friends you have, where you will live, and

---

[1]John L. Munschauer, "The Anatomy of a Career," <u>Journal of College Placement</u> (February-March, 1970), p. 35.

[2]S. Norman Feingold and Sol Swerdloff, <u>Occupations and Careers</u> (New York: McGraw-Hill Book Co., Inc., 1969), p. 2.

[3]Feingold and Swerdloff, p. 2.

Approximately 1"

1

179c ▶25
Skill comparison: progressive rough-draft copy

1. A 2′ writing on each ¶; compare *gwam.*
2. Two 2′ writings on each of the slower ¶s; determine *gwam.*
3. A 5′ control writing on the 3 ¶s combined; determine *gwam*; circle errors.

all letters used | A | 1.5 si | 5.6 awl | 80% hfw

	gwam 2′	5′
On entering the business world, one faces many new ~~things~~ *ideas*.	6	2
There are vital policies with which to become familiar, new	12	5
rules to ~~memorize~~ *identify*, new facts to absorb, and newprocedures to	18	7
adopt. At first, it may seem that adjusting to ~~a~~ *the* work ~~en-~~	24	9
~~vironment~~ *scene* is too demanding; but ~~we need~~ *with* an all-out effort and	29	12
a positive attitude. *we soon find areas that were strange now seem quite comfortable.*	38	15
When you show your employer that you ~~can do your~~ *are able to* work	6	17
capably, you willfind without a doubt exciting chances *to move ahead*.	13	20
Actually, you will be amazed at how ~~fast~~ *quickly* your talents will be	20	23
~~seen~~ *detected* and rewarded. It is not *un*usual for ~~some employers~~ *an executive* to give	26	25
~~added~~ *more* responsibility to ~~a typist~~ *an improved worker* who has shown keen interest *and vigor on the job*.	35	29
It is not ~~smart~~ *wise*, however, for ~~young~~ *new* office ~~employees~~ *workers* to ~~want~~ *expect*	6	31
to be given *more* advanced work or high*er* salaries until they learn	13	34
tobe productvie. Many employers rergет that a ~~sizeable amount~~ *great deal*	19	36
of time is taken by new ~~workers~~ *employees* to learn thier ~~given~~ assign-	24	39
ments ~~sufficiently~~ well *enough* to perform *profitably. Truly then,*	30	41
patience as well as skill is needed to get ahead	34	42
in the business world.	36	43

180

180a ▶5
Conditioning practice

1. Each line twice SS.
2. A 1′ writing on Line 3; determine *gwam.*

She quickly organized a complex keyboard review for Jim Baker to type.
The class sold 79 locks, 250 pictures, 84 records, and 163 date books.
Caplan & Millar will order 758# at $3.60 for delivery to their market.
In a few months, there will be extra lanes added to the aging highway.

| 1 | 2 | 3 | 4 | 5 | 6 | 7 | 8 | 9 | 10 | 11 | 12 | 13 | 14 |

180b ▶20
Skill comparison: progressive rough-draft copy

Retype 179c, above, as directed there.

Goal: Improved speed on corrected copy.

Note: The ellipsis, indicating omission of words from a quotation, is typed by alternating 3 periods and spaces (. . .) or 4 (. . . .) if the end of a sentence is included in the quotation.

the circumstances under which you will live. There are three prime requisites for a career decision. The first is self-understanding; the second is knowing the requirements of the career in which you have an interest; and the third is taking the steps to achieve your career goal.[4]

Understanding Yourself

If you could see yourself as others see you, the task of self-understanding would not be so difficult. Writing down facts and opinions about yourself will make your task easier. This listing will enable you to compare your characteristics and abilities objectively with the requirements of a career. Tennyson suggests that it may help you clarify your self-concept if you try to identify your needs, interests, attitudes, values, work role perceptions, and competencies.[5] Other questions to ask yourself include those of physical fitness, mental qualifications, educational qualifications, and personality. Your teachers or your guidance counselor should be able to help you with some of the specific questions to ask yourself. Most libraries have "choosing-a-career" books, often containing questionnaires to guide you in self-analysis. These books are listed in the card catalog under such headings as "Careers" or "Occupations."

Aptitude tests have been designed to help you look within yourself for career clues. Such tests can provide valuable information about such things as your aptitudes, abilities, skills, and interests. All test results, however, should be evaluated with caution. Feingold and Swerdloff indicate that "No tests, by themselves, will tell you what you should do . . . . Tests can, however, provide clues to narrow down the possible fields."[6] In other words, tests are tools for guidance, not answers. Your teachers or counselor may utilize these tools in assisting you with your self-appraisal. In addition, testing services are available to you; however, they usually charge a fee for their service. In making your self-analysis, be sure (1) to consider actual work experiences you may have had and (2) to talk, if possible, with persons doing work in which you are interested.

When you have completed your self-inventory, you are ready to compare your personal characteristics, interests, and aptitudes with occupational or career requirements.

Career Requirements

Your next step in choosing a career is to investigate the careers which seem to match your self-inventory. A good place to start may be the Dictionary of Occupational Titles. This government publication describes more than 35,000 jobs and lists their titles. When you have identified those careers which interest you and which seem to match your qualifications, consult the Occupational Outlook Handbook. This handbook is revised and reissued every two years. Copies are available in most libraries. The handbook gives the qualifications and education required for entry into a particular career as well as the opportunities and trends for that career. Presently, one of the major occupational trends is toward the service occupations, which include many opportunities in the clerical and office work area.

After completing these steps, you should try to narrow your selection to a few career choices--those that most nearly match your abilities and interests. Now you are ready to compile detailed information on the specific careers you have selected. Look in the library card catalog and the indexes under the titles of your proposed careers or career. You can find information also under such headings as "Careers," "Professions," "Occupations," and "Vocational Information." Many trade

---

[4] Don Dillion, "Toward Matching Personal and Job Characteristics," Occupational Outlook Quarterly (Spring, 1975), pp. 3-18.

[5] W. Wesley Tennyson, "Career Exploration," Career Education, Third Yearbook, ed. by Joel H. Magisos (Washington: American Vocational Association, 1973), p. 104.

[6] Feingold and Swerdloff, p. 15.

178c ▶20
Skill comparison: progressive script copy

1. A 2′ writing on each ¶; compare *gwam*.

2. A 2′ writing on each of the slower ¶s; determine *gwam*.

Goal: To equal your highest speed in Step 1.

3. A 5′ control writing on the 3 ¶s combined; determine *gwam*; circle errors.

all letters used | A | 1.5 si | 5.6 awl | 80% hfw

Text	gwam 2′	5′
It is essential for all students to give serious thought	6	2
to the need for developing word power. To be able to use a	12	5
variety of words effectively—to express ideas clearly—is a	18	7
trait worth possessing. But word power is not a sure outcome	24	10
of just living; it is acquired only through diligent effort. We	32	12
can learn to make words accrue to our benefit and stature	36	14
by zealous involvement in word-building programs.	41	16
There is much to be said for attempting to build power with	6	19
words to improve our personal magnetism. In social circles,	12	21
a person who is able to speak fluently usually gains much	18	24
attention; and in our daily affairs with friends and neigh-	24	26
bors, good word usage is a sign of achievement. Real power in	30	28
using words effectively can be built by devoting a little time	36	31
each day learning how to select and use words properly.	42	33
In the area of business, an easy command of words is a	6	35
skill to be prized. Employees who are able to express their ideas	12	38
clearly in written and oral communications are now much in	18	40
demand. Many firms are looking for some capable and reliable	25	43
workers for promotion to higher job levels; and those persons	31	45
who know, through useful word power, how to please an em-	36	48
ployer are likely to get the best promotions.	42	49

179

179a ▶5
Conditioning practice

1. Each line twice SS.

2. A 1′ writing on Line 4; determine *gwam*.

Major Rex Quigley was amazed at the five canopies held just by bricks.
Yvonne sent 582 stamps, 469 labels, 73 cards, and 10 pens to the camp.
Bill's check for $250 was sent to the Bricci & Hall Company on May 12.
There are many fine programs for young persons wanting to learn music.

| 1 | 2 | 3 | 4 | 5 | 6 | 7 | 8 | 9 | 10 | 11 | 12 | 13 | 14 |

179b ▶20
Skill comparison: progressive script copy

Retype 178c, above, as directed there.

Goal: Improved speed on script copy.

and professional associations have published career materials helpful in matching your self-inventory to occupational requirements. Magazines are another source of up-to-date career information. Some magazine articles provide information on those occupational areas that have increasing opportunities for young people. Two such articles describe young people in challenging jobs that do not require a college degree.[7,8]

Means to Achieve Your Career Goal

In his discussion of career planning, Munschauer notes that "when goals have been set, and ends determined, there is the matter of means."[9] The major means to achieving your career goal will be getting the education required for it. In your study of careers and the matching of your abilities and interests to career requirements, you should have determined the kind of education you will need. You should have asked yourself these very important questions: What am I willing to do in preparation for a career? Am I willing to make the sacrifices that a good education requires?

Once you have narrowed your career choices, you should plan your educational program in relation to this career choice. If your career goal requires a college education, you must be sure to include in your high school program those courses necessary to meet the admission requirements of the college or university of your choice. Consider at least three colleges or universities which are accredited in your special career program, for as Patton and Steiner have noted, "You may not be accepted by your first choice."[10]

---

[7] "Jobs: Where Are They?" Senior Scholastic (April, 1974), pp. 8-11.

[8] "Who Doesn't Need a College Degree," Money (September, 1975), pp. 23-26.

[9] Munschauer, p. 38.

[10] Evelyn D. Patton and Dora W. Steiner, Let's Look at Your Future (Metuchen, N.J.: The Scarecrow Press, Inc., 1966), p. 243.

Lack of needed funds should not discourage you from seeking the education or training necessary to a career. Available student aid is an important part of career planning for many young people. Millions of dollars in scholarship money are unused each year because young people do not know about the funds. Academic scholarships are widely available, as are some government scholarships. Many industrial and fraternal organizations award scholarships. Also, student loans are an aid to young people in getting the necessary education. Lederer highlights the availability of loan funds:

> If for some reason you don't get a scholarship or grant, don't give up the idea of school. Nearly every college and vocational school has loan funds at its disposal. Most loans provide for repayment plans following graduation.[11]

One magazine article describes the Work-Study Program; and another, the Co-operative Education Program, in which thousands of students can earn while they learn.[12,13]

Summary

Successful career planning includes three important steps. The first is to understand and appraise yourself, the second is to investigate careers and compare requirements with your abilities, and the third is to organize the means to achieve your goal. Plan and prepare; only you can decide what your life will be. And your choices are vital when they involve your career and your future. Be honest with yourself, follow the steps given in this report, and you will increase your chances for a rewarding career that "fits."

---

[11] Muriel Lederer, The Guide to Career Education (New York: The New York Times Book Company, 1974), p. 19.

[12] "All in a Day's Work-Study," American Education (January-February, 1970), p. 13.

[13] "Catching on at Colleges: Earning While Learning," U.S. News and World Report (February 19, 1973), pp. 72-73.

177c ▶20
Skill comparison: progressive statistical copy

1. A 2′ writing on each ¶; compare *gwam*.

2. A 2′ writing on each of the slower ¶s; determine *gwam*.

Goal: To increase speed on more difficult copy.

3. A 5′ control writing on the 3 ¶s combined; determine *gwam*; circle errors.

all letters/figures used | A | 1.5 si | 5.6 awl | 80% hfw |

	gwam 2′	5′
We have been called a nation of people who like and demand things	7	3
that are both unusual and unexpected. Our efforts in space travel have	14	5
proved the idea quite impressively. A major event of national and world	21	8
curiosity was the launching on July 28, 1965, of the lunar spaceship	28	11
Ranger VII, which explored the moon and prepared the way for others who	35	14
followed later. Three days after being launched, an able space crew sent	43	17
4,316 pictures of the moon to the earth, then a modern record.	49	19
People all over the world were amazed at the activities in space	7	22
of American astronauts and Soviet cosmonauts. On July 15, 1975, space-	14	25
ships of the two nations were put in orbit, planning to rendezvous and	21	28
link up over Germany at 12:15 p.m. on Thursday, July 17. The big project	28	31
was estimated to have cost each nation about $250 million and was said	35	33
to be the end of 18 long years of space rivalry. It was felt that good	42	36
communications between the nations would result from this event.	49	39
Prior to the unique space trip of July, 1975, there were other space	7	42
missions of major significance. A 28-day trip running from May 25 to	14	44
June 22, 1973, ended in a three-member space agency unit doing 80 percent	22	47
of its proposed work, taking 30,000 pictures of the sun, and getting data	29	50
on 182 research sites for earth in numerous areas. Later a similar group	36	53
spent 59 days 11 hours in space and provided 37,000 photographs with data	44	56
included on 17 miles of tape.	47	57

gwam 2′ | 1 | 2 | 3 | 4 | 5 | 6 | 7 |
5′ | 1 | 2 | 3 |

178

178a ▶5
Conditioning practice

1. Each line twice SS.

2. A 1′ writing on Line 4; determine *gwam*.

Jenny said that six quiz prizes will be given by the Franklin Company.
We have 570 pads, 164 books, 93 crayons, and 82 stencil maps on order.
Kay's 5 1/2% commission on Order 719 and Order 248 will be about $630.
One or two men should plan to spend a few days working on the program.

| 1 | 2 | 3 | 4 | 5 | 6 | 7 | 8 | 9 | 10 | 11 | 12 | 13 | 14 |

178b ▶25
Skill comparison: progressive statistical copy

Retype 177c, above, as directed there.

Goal: Improved control of figures and symbols.

105

105a ▶5 Conditioning practice

each line 3 times (slowly, faster, in-between rate)

alphabet Visitors did enjoy the amazing water tricks of six quaint polar bears.

fig/sym A special "J&B" rug (981-012**) sells for $1,346.79 less 15% discount.

shift lock A sample was printed in four colors on BEST Papers PKG 34*20# BRISTOL.

fluency The clansmen got into the dory by the shale rock and circled the lake.

| 1 | 2 | 3 | 4 | 5 | 6 | 7 | 8 | 9 | 10 | 11 | 12 | 13 | 14 |

105b ▶10 Improve capitalization skill: related learning

1. Reinsert paper used for typing 104b, page 172.

2. Align and space copy properly.

3. Save sheet for use in next lesson.

6. Capitalize an official title when it immediately precedes a name. When used elsewhere, type the title without the capital unless it is a title of high distinction.

   He will see President Johns on Friday.
   Brian Zahl is the vice president of the club.

7. Do not capitalize business or professional titles used without the name of the person.

   The dean will see you soon.
   The doctor will not be in today.

8. Capitalize all proper nouns and their derivatives.

   We attended the Canadian Shakespearean Festival.

9. Capitalize the names of the days of the week, months of the year, holidays, periods of history, and historic events.

   Capitalize these words: Monday, June, Labor Day, and Ice Age.

10. Capitalize the seasons of the year only when they are personified.

   I like all seasons--fall, winter, spring, and summer.
   The icy fingers of Winter are still with us.

105c ▶35 Learn to type leftbound manuscripts with footnotes

Continue 104c, pages 172-175.

106

106a ▶5 Conditioning practice

each line 3 times (slowly, faster, in-between rate)

alphabet By his frequent adjustments, an amazing executive kept their goodwill.

fig/sym Is Check 01576 for $48.90, dated May 23, made out to McNeil & O'Brien?

double letters Three letters will go to Bill and Betty Ott about the Tennessee deeds.

fluency They may make them do the work for the city auditor by the end of May.

| 1 | 2 | 3 | 4 | 5 | 6 | 7 | 8 | 9 | 10 | 11 | 12 | 13 | 14 |

176c ▶25
Skill comparison: progressive straight copy

1. A 2′ writing on each ¶; compare *gwam*.

2. Two 2′ writings on each of the slower ¶s; determine *gwam*.

Goal: To increase speed on more difficult copy.

3. A 5′ control writing on the 3 ¶s combined; determine *gwam*; circle errors.

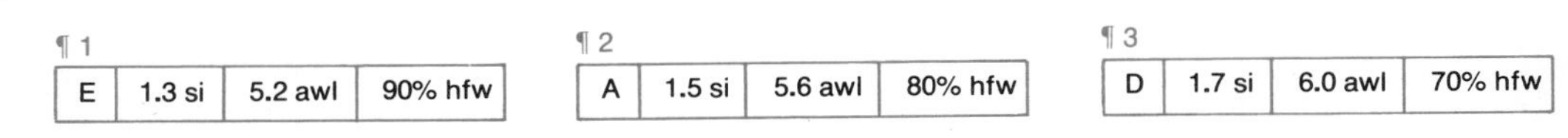

¶				
¶ 1	E	1.3 si	5.2 awl	90% hfw
¶ 2	A	1.5 si	5.6 awl	80% hfw
¶ 3	D	1.7 si	6.0 awl	70% hfw

all letters used

	gwam 2′	5′
For the person looking for work as a typist in a business office,	7	3
it is important to get a sound idea of what is to be expected on the	14	5
job. Most employers assume a typist will be able to type well, making	21	8
fine copy at top rates and with few errors. This demand should not be	28	11
viewed as either a difficult or a simple one; it does suggest, though,	35	14
that the person looking for a job in a good office should be willing to	42	17
prove the acquisition of outstanding skills.	47	19
To be ready for the kind of office job requiring typing, then, you	7	21
must prepare to do a variety of typewriting activities well. You need	14	24
the best stroking skill possible; and you must develop power to put that	21	27
skill to work on a number of different typing tasks. There is no place	29	30
in business for modest skill or limited ability to complete work in	35	33
minimum time periods. Now is the time to prepare yourself for the kind	43	36
of office position you really desire upon finishing school.	48	38
To realize your ambition to work as a typist in a modern office,	7	40
you must direct serious attention to many crucial factors influencing	14	43
your typing power. High stroking skill is the result of many hours of	21	46
vigorous practice on basic elements called techniques, and ability in	28	49
typing office problems is the product of learning how to utilize your	35	52
stroking skill in typical job situations. The abilities sought by an	42	55
employer are the same as those emphasized by a capable teacher.	48	57

gwam 2′ | 1 | 2 | 3 | 4 | 5 | 6 | 7 |
5′ | 1 | 2 | 3 |

177

177a ▶5
Conditioning practice

1. Each line twice SS.

2. A 1′ writing on Line 4; determine *gwam*.

If Dan Paxom adjusts it, I believe we can energize the rocket quickly.
Golf team players reported scores of 85, 93, 72, and 64, totaling 314.
On April 20 they reported earnings up 8.5%, for a total of $1,936,724.
The new field manager talked with our staff about office productivity.

| 1 | 2 | 3 | 4 | 5 | 6 | 7 | 8 | 9 | 10 | 11 | 12 | 13 | 14 |

177b ▶25
Skill comparison: progressive straight copy

Retype 176c, above, as directed there.

Goal: Improved keystroking.

106b ▶10 Improve capitalization skill: related learning

End of Series 3
Save work for use in *Typewriting Manual.*

11. Capitalize geographic regions, localities, and names. Do not capitalize points of the compass when used to indicate directions or in a descriptive sense.

    I live in the South, but I plan to move north next year.

12. Capitalize such words as street, avenue, company, etc., when used with a proper noun.

    Is 123 Tenth Street the address of the Voit Company?

13. Capitalize names of organizations, clubs, and buildings.

    The Boy Scouts met at the Commercial Club of the Fairmont Hotel.

14. Capitalize a noun preceding a figure, except for common words such as line, page, and sentence, which may be typed with or without a capital.

    Use Style 34 as shown on page 110 of Catalog 5.

106c ▶35 Learn to type leftbound manuscripts with footnotes

Continue 104c, pages 172-175.

107

107a ▶5 Conditioning practice

each line 3 times (slowly, faster, in-between rate)

alphabet	Six big juicy steaks sizzled in a pan as five workmen left the quarry.
fig/sym	Pay Lee & Co.'s bill for $137.56 before you pay Al & Ed's for $248.90.
adjacent keys	A source of wisdom which is denied none is experience and observation.
fluency	It is by our daily work that we make our future what we want it to be.

| 1 | 2 | 3 | 4 | 5 | 6 | 7 | 8 | 9 | 10 | 11 | 12 | 13 | 14 |

107b ▶15 Check capitalization skills

Correct as you type; use guide codes to check your work.

1:172	1. heed well his advice, "what is easy is seldom excellent."
2:172	2. her basic theme concerned "our dedication to quality work."
3:172	3. "success comes," he said, "From attempting the difficult."
4:172	4. follow this procedure: type with good techniques.
5:172	5. i read the article by james lee, "you and your career."
6:176	6. they asked ambassador kirkland to speak at the meeting.
7, 8:176	7. the secretary gave a report on grecian myths.
9, 10:176	8. school will start on wednesday, september 10, next fall.
11, 12, 13:177	9. the century club is on fifth street, east of the civic plaza.
14:177	10. check lines 14-20 on page 37 in volume IX.

107c ▶30 Learn to type leftbound manuscripts with footnotes

Continue 104c, pages 172-175.

phase **8** lessons 176–200

Office communication skills

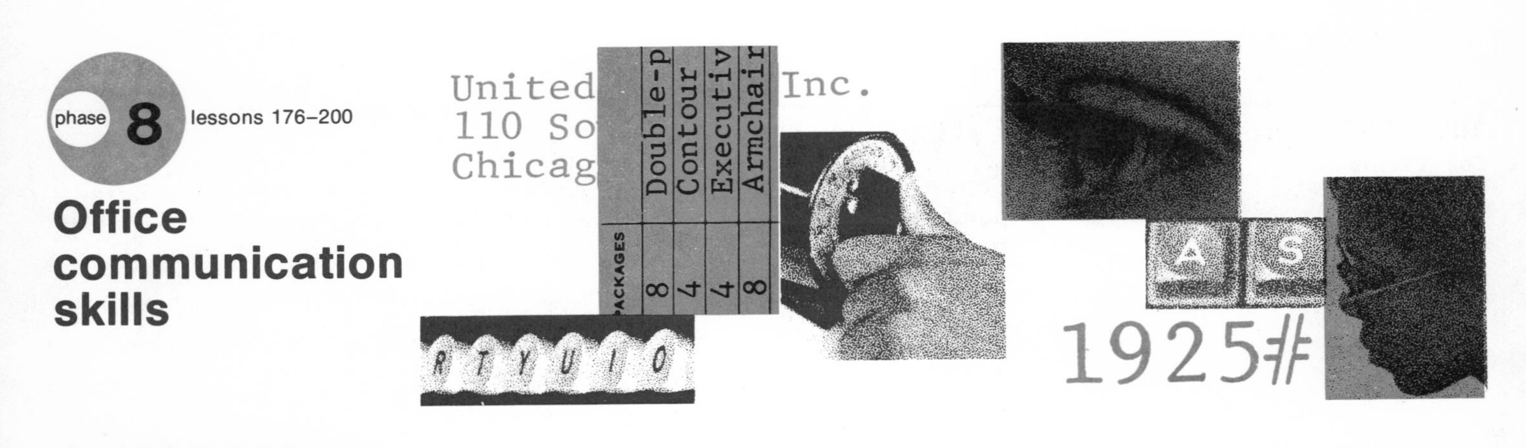

unit **30** lessons 176–180

Improving basic skills

Learning goals

In the lessons of phase 8, you will add impressively to your already-acquired abilities and achieve these goals:

1. Increased keystroking and manipulative skill.

2. Ability to type business letters on special-size stationery.

3. Skill in typing letters with special features, and other communications.

4. Increased ability to handle directions and materials.

Machine adjustments

1. Paper guide at *0.*

2. Ribbon lever on black.

3. Margin stops: 70-space line for drills and ¶s; as directed for problems.

4. SS drills; in timed writings, DS ¶s, indent 5 spaces.

176

176a ▶5 Conditioning practice

1. Each line twice SS.

2. A 1′ writing on Line 4; determine *gwam.*

alphabet Bad weather in July kept Zoe from viewing Niagara's exquisite scenery.

figures Our new bowlers rolled games of 168, 172, 197, 205, 206, 239, and 243.

fig/sym Fox & Hart 6 1/2% bonds (due May 25, 1997) sold at 108 to 113 on May 4.

fluency They expect to finish the work on the office by the end of this month.

| 1 | 2 | 3 | 4 | 5 | 6 | 7 | 8 | 9 | 10 | 11 | 12 | 13 | 14 |

176b ▶20 Improve machine parts operation

each set of lines twice SS; then 1′ writings on selected lines as time permits

Goals, line by line

1-2. Quick tab-and-return motions.

3-5. Down-and-in motion on space bar.

6-8. Shift, type; then release shift key quickly.

9-11. Use shift lock for ALL CAPS and underline.

12-14. Use margin release and backspacer quickly.

↓ Set tab (left margin + 35)

1 A more rapid use of the tab control
2 and carriage or element return will help boost your performance rates.

3 It is up to us to plan the work of this camp for the next week or two.
4 If it is the right thing for all of us to do, he and I will do it now.
5 She and her new office friends will go to the next meeting in a group.

6 Les and Sue will go with Jane and Bob to the new camp at River Forest.
7 David James and Nancy Jeanne played tennis on the courts at Pine Wood.
8 Cynthia Ann swam with Mary Jane in the new company pool at Hill Crest.

9 Book titles may be underlined or typed in ALL CAPS: Family or FAMILY.
10 Agnes Sabino typed the book title, THE ECONOMIC STRUGGLE, in all caps.
11 In his paper, Jim Hudek underlined the book title, Marketing Channels.

12 By quickly flicking the margin-release key, I can type outside the margins.
13 A good office worker knows how to use the various machine parts skillfully.
14 You will be much more productive as you learn how to operate machine parts.

108

108a ▶5 Conditioning practice

each line 3 times (slowly, faster, in-between rate)

alphabet The kind queen received extra jewels from a dozen brave young pirates.

fig/sym Write checks for these amounts: $41.44, $53.26, $178.90, and $414.45.

long words These laboratories specialize in solid-state space propulsion systems.

fluency It is a good plan to do your very best on each typing job that you do.

| 1 | 2 | 3 | 4 | 5 | 6 | 7 | 8 | 9 | 10 | 11 | 12 | 13 | 14 |

108b ▶45 Learn to type leftbound manuscripts with footnotes

Complete the manuscript report, 104c, pages 172-175.

Problem 1 Bibliography

top margin: same as p. 1; other margins as in report; center heading over line of writing, then TS; start first line of each entry at left margin; indent additional lines 5 spaces; SS each entry; DS between entries

BIBLIOGRAPHY

TS

"All in a Day's Work-Study." American Education (January-February, 1970), p. 13. (Indent 5 →)

"Catching on at Colleges: Earning While Learning." U.S. News and World Report (February 19, 1973), pp. 72-73.

Dillion, Don. "Toward Matching Personal and Job Characteristics." Occupational Outlook Quarterly (Spring, 1975), pp. 3-18.

Feingold, S. Norman, and Sol Swerdloff. Occupations and Careers. New York: McGraw-Hill Book Co., Inc., 1969.

"Jobs: Where Are They?" Senior Scholastic (April, 1974), pp. 8-11.

Lederer, Muriel. The Guide to Career Education. New York: The New York Times Book Company, 1974.

Munschauer, John L. "The Anatomy of a Career." Journal of College Placement (February-March, 1970), pp. 35-38.

Patton, Evelyn D., and Dora W. Steiner. Let's Look at Your Future. Metuchen, N.J.: The Scarecrow Press, Inc., 1966.

Tennyson, W. Wesley. "Career Exploration." Career Education, Third Yearbook, edited by Joel H. Magisos. Washington: American Vocational Association, 1973, p. 104.

"Who Doesn't Need a College Degree." Money (September, 1975), pp. 23-26.

Problem 2 Title page

1. Center title over line of writing used in report, 2½" from top edge.

2. Center and type your name 2½" below title; DS; center and type name of school.

3. Center and type current date 2½" below name of school.

2½"

CHOOSING A CAREER

2½"

Name of Student

Name of School

2½"

Current Date

2½"

Enrichment material for Unit 17 appears on LM pp. 67, 68.

175c ▶35 Measure production skill: reports/tables

plain sheets; erase and correct errors; number the pages 10 and 11

Problem 1
Leftbound report

	words
Section 3	2
OFFICE ETIQUETTE	5
"Etiquette" includes dressing, grooming,	14
and acting in such a manner as not to call un-	23
favorable attention to oneself. The following	32
suggestions should prove helpful.	39
Proper Attire and Grooming	50
All employees should report for work	57
dressed and groomed in a manner that will be	66
acceptable to other employees and to visitors.	76
Although the company does not prescribe a	84
dress code, employees are expected to be	92
dressed suitably for any business office.	101
"Good taste" should be the rule in both cloth-	110
ing and hair styles.	114
To avoid offending, employees are ex-	121
pected to be clean and to wear clothing that is	131
in good condition.	135
Smoking	138
Smoking is permitted in the general office	147
areas during regular working hours. To prevent	156
fires and to avoid offending other employees,	165
discretion should be used when smoking.	174
Because of insurance and fire regulations,	182
smoking is not permitted in specified areas of	192
the warehouse and shipping department. All	200
employees shall observe this rule.	208
Personal Use of Telephones	218
Because a large percentage of our cus-	226
tomer and supplier contact is by telephone,	234
company telephones should be used only for	243
company business. Only personal calls of an	252
emergency nature may be made or received by	261
employees on company telephones. Pay tele-	269
phones are located on each floor of the build-	278
ing for personal use in making outside calls.	288
Such calls should be made during coffee and	296
lunch breaks.	299
Use of Personal Radios	308
All departments are equipped with a	316
piped-in music system. Personal radios, there-	325
fore, are not permitted in the office areas,	334
except for special broadcasts that are an-	342
nounced well in advance of air time.	349

Problem 2 [half sheet]
Two-column table with main and secondary headings

SCHEDULE OF CHRISTMAS BONUSES		words
(By Duration of Employment)		6 / 12
1 month or over but less than 2	$ 5.00	20
2 months or over but less than 6	10.00	27
6 months or over but less than 12	15.00	35
1 year or over but less than 5	35.00	43
5 years or over but less than 10	50.00	51
10 years or over but less than 20	75.00	59
20 years or over	100.00	63

Problem 3 [full sheet]
Three-column table with columnar headings

CHANGES IN SIZE OF WORK FORCE — 6

Department	Last Year	This Year	words
Accounting	11	10	19
Advertising/Art	8	7	24
Assembly	48	63	27
Credit	8	9	29
Data Processing	15	13	34
Filing	8	9	36
Marketing	135	140	40
Order	24	25	42
Personnel	4	5	45
Production	300	325	49
Purchasing	5	5	52
Receiving/Shipping	63	66	59
Total	629	677	61

(Header row words: 16)

If you finish before time is called, retype Problem 1.

unit **18** lessons 109–113

Speed/accuracy emphasis

Learning goals

1. To improve and refine your typing techniques.
2. To increase your speed and improve your accuracy.
3. To increase your skill on straight, statistical, and rough-draft copy.

Machine adjustments

1. Paper guide at *0.*
2. 70-space line and single spacing (SS) unless otherwise directed.
3. Line space selector on *2* (DS) for all timed writings of more than 1′.

109

109a ▶5 Conditioning practice

each line 3 times (slowly, faster, in-between rate)

alphabet The quick, ambiguous quiz on job pay vexed all who had studied for it.

fig/sym The purchase price is $14,673.89 plus 5% sales tax and 20% excise tax.

home row J. Kagal asked a lad if he had added a dash of salt to a dish of hash.

fluency The auditor will send a statement to the firm by the end of the month.

| 1 | 2 | 3 | 4 | 5 | 6 | 7 | 8 | 9 | 10 | 11 | 12 | 13 | 14 |

109b ▶15 Measure basic skill: straight copy

two 5′ writings; determine *gwam*; proofread and circle errors; record better rate

all letters used | A | 1.5 si | 5.6 awl | 80% hfw |

	gwam 1′	5′
Have you ever wondered how a timed writing is developed to measure	13	3
and to help you improve your typing skills? The paragraph you are typing	28	6
is designed with care to include just the right proportions of the three	43	9
elements involved in the control of copy difficulty. The first element	57	11
is syllabic intensity, or the ratio of all the syllables to all the words	72	14
in the copy. The second element is concerned with the average size of	86	17
the words. It is determined by dividing the total number of strokes by	101	20
the total number of words in the paragraph.	109	22
The third element involved in the control of copy difficulty is the	14	25
percent of high-frequency words used in the copy. To compute this fac-	28	27
tor, the sum of all such words is divided by all the words in the para-	42	30
graph. The copy you are now typing meets these exact standards for the	56	33
control of copy difficulty. So you can see that this copy is carefully	71	36
designed to help you improve and to measure your basic typing skills.	85	39
The control of copy difficulty in a timed writing is important for the	99	42
reason that it is directly related to vocabulary studies of all the words	114	45
used in business communications.	120	46

gwam 1′ | 1 | 2 | 3 | 4 | 5 | 6 | 7 | 8 | 9 | 10 | 11 | 12 | 13 | 14 |
5′ | 1 | 2 | 3 |

174c, continued

Problem 3
Block style, open

	words
Current date Mr. Roger C. Dromboski The	8
Johnson-Hardin Company 1285 Main Street	16
Waco, TX 76704 Dear Mr. Dromboski Subject:	25
Impact! (¶ 1) Surely you agree that few things	33
are more personal than the letters you write.	43
They convey your thoughts, your wishes, and	52
your ideals. They are you--on paper. But are	61
the letters that bear your signature giving you	71
fair representation? (¶ 2) Study this message	79
for a moment and decide for yourself. Notice	88
how it is centered on the page. Then observe	97
that the margins are balanced and clearly de-	106
fined. (¶ 3) Note also that every type character	115
is clean-cut, uniform in impression, and evenly	124
spaced. The capitals, which in so many cases	134
show a tendency to jump above the line, are in	143
perfect alignment. (¶ 4) Compare and see! Let	151
us deliver a new IMPACT ELECTRIC TYPE-	159
WRITER to your office where you can see for	168
yourself how the performance of an IMPACT	176
will give you better-looking letters for better	186
representation. Your signature on the enclosed	195
card is all it takes to arrange an appointment.	205
Sincerely yours CENTURY SUPPLY COMPANY	213
Dennis R. Knox, Regional Manager xx En-	221
closure cc LeRoy J. Michaels (178)	226/**242**

If you finish before time is called, retype Problem 1 on plain paper.

175

175a ▶5 Conditioning practice

each line 3 times SS (slowly, faster, slowly); DS between 3-line groups

Evelyn explained that the quilted warm-up jacket was Bob Graft's size.
They replaced at cost 50 plates, 194 forks, 362 spoons, and 78 knives.
Both start today (9/17): Jay Maze at $98.50/wk.; Jo Robb at $2.75/hr.
These social problems may be as long in the solution as in the making.

| 1 | 2 | 3 | 4 | 5 | 6 | 7 | 8 | 9 | 10 | 11 | 12 | 13 | 14 |

175b ▶10 Check word-division skill

half sheet; DS; begin on Line 8

1. Set left margin stop and tab stops according to KEY.

2. Type first line as shown.

3. Type other lines in a similar manner, indicating in Columns 2 and 4 all acceptable division points in the words typed in Columns 1 and 3.

above-mentioned	above-mentioned	marketable	mar-ket-able
accepted		mechanical	
beneficial		needlessly	
bookkeeping		oppressive	
cancellation		parallel	
determining		realistic	
dominant		reinforced	
gradually		successful	
itemization		transcribe	
legitimate		within	

key | 15 | 4 | 15 | 8 | 10 | 4 | 12 |

109c ▶20 Improve speed/technique

1. Two 1′ writings on each sentence. Try to maintain rate set on Sentence 1 of each group.

2. As time permits, practice those sentences on which you made your lowest rates.

Practice goal: fingers curved and upright; quick, snap keystrokes

easy	She may pay the men for the eight forms and then send six forms to me.
average	It is the opinion of their busy staff that the statement is incorrect.
difficult	You were to get his opinion only after the estate taxes had been paid.

| 1 | 2 | 3 | 4 | 5 | 6 | 7 | 8 | 9 | 10 | 11 | 12 | 13 | 14 |

Practice goal: quick, down-and-in spacing strokes; finger reaches to top row; quiet hands; little-finger reaches to shift keys

space bar	Jim may help the men pump the oil when they work today for many of us.
figures	Type 1 and 9 and 2 and 8 and 3 and 6 and 5 and 7 and 4 and 10 for her.
shift keys	Jack A. MacDuff, President of MacDuff & O'Brien, lives in Walla Walla.

| 1 | 2 | 3 | 4 | 5 | 6 | 7 | 8 | 9 | 10 | 11 | 12 | 13 | 14 |

109d ▶10 Improve accuracy/technique: weak fingers

each line 3 times (slowly, faster, top speed)

Goal: As many lines as possible without error.

Practice goal: curved, upright fingers in home position; quick keystroking

q	1	Quinton expressed qualms about the quantity and quality of the quartz.
p	2	A popular polo player ate apples and pears as he mopped the pop stand.
w	3	Watson wowed wharf workers with his wit and wisdom about the wildwood.
l	4	Lilly fell asleep listening to Bill tell tall tales about leprechauns.
z	5	After quizzing Zeus about zircons, Zizka realized that Zeus was dizzy.
x	6	X. Xerxes fixed six wax candles on xyloid boxes for X-ray examination.
s	7	Successful speed hints suggest snappy, sharp strokes with the fingers.

110

110a ▶5 Conditioning practice

each line 3 times (slowly, faster, in-between rate)

alphabet	Flo Peck answered the very last exam question just as the buzzer rang.
fig/sym	Order No. 8475 for 6 chairs ($39.75 ea.) will be shipped May 19 or 20.
3d row	You were to quote your best prices on those typewriters, were you not?
fluency	Keep your eyes on the copy and type with continuity to increase speed.

| 1 | 2 | 3 | 4 | 5 | 6 | 7 | 8 | 9 | 10 | 11 | 12 | 13 | 14 |

110b ▶5 Improve speed/technique

each line of 109c, above, twice (slowly, top speed)

Goal: Try to maintain good techniques as you type each line with increased speed.

unit **29** lessons 174–175

Measuring typing competence

Measurement goals

1. To type a straight-copy writing with speed and control.

2. To produce mailable letters at an acceptable rate.

3. To arrange and type a report and tables quickly and accurately.

Machine adjustments

1. Paper guide at *0*.

2. Ribbon control on black.

3. Margin stops: 70-space line for drills and ¶s; as directed for problems.

4. Line-space selector on *1* for drills; on *2* for ¶s; as directed for problems.

174

174a ▶5 Conditioning practice

each line 3 times SS (slowly, faster, slowly); DS between 3-line groups

alphabet	Dr. Mei Bach did exceptionally good work for the Java quartz industry.
figures	We ordered 209 keys, 148 locks, 73 doors, and 65 files for a building.
fig/sym	Terms on Arnold & Dodson's order dated 4/6 for $587.90 are 2/10, n/30.
fluency	It is a part of the work of a proficient typist to proofread the work.

| 1 | 2 | 3 | 4 | 5 | 6 | 7 | 8 | 9 | 10 | 11 | 12 | 13 | 14 |

174b ▶10 Measure basic skill: straight copy

a 5′ writing on 173b, page 279

174c ▶35 Measure production skill: letters

3 letterheads [LM pp. 29-34];
place letters according to RG table, p. iv;
1 or 2 cc's as needed and an envelope for each letter; type for 30′; proofread and correct each letter before removing it from the machine;
compute *n-pram*

Problem 1
Modified block, mixed

	words
Current date Ms. Estelle Van Horn 3446 Happy	9
Valley Road Santa Rosa, CA 95404 Dear Ms.	18
Van Horn: (¶ 1) Thank you for your letter tell-	26
ing me that you can meet me in San Francisco	35
for an interview for the position of sales rep-	44
resentative in the Northern California area.	53
(¶ 2) Since I shall be staying at the St. Francis	62
Hotel during my trip, I shall be glad to meet you	72
there for lunch at 11:30 on Thursday of next	81
week. If either the suggested time or the place	91
is inconvenient for you, we can make other	100
arrangements for the interview appointment.	109
A copy of my interview schedule is enclosed.	118
(¶ 3) As soon as I arrive in San Francisco, I	126
shall telephone you to confirm the interview	135
appointment. Sincerely yours, Jack V. Story,	144
Manager xx Enclosure (117)	148/**161**

Problem 2
Modified block, indented ¶s, mixed

	words
Current date Mr. John B. Phillips, President	9
Phillips Secretarial College 509 South Boston	19
Avenue Tulsa, OK 74103 Dear Mr. Phillips:	27
Subject: Caroline Dempsey (¶ 1) Several weeks	35
ago you recommended for a position in our	44
office a young woman by the name of Caroline	53
Dempsey. We employed her to work as admin-	61
istrative assistant to our advertising depart-	70
ment manager, Mr. Veloz. In this position she	79
has been highly successful, and we want to	88
thank you for suggesting her to us. She has	97
demonstrated not only high skill in secretarial	107
duties but also unusual ability to work with	116
others throughout the company. (¶ 2) Mr. Veloz	124
and I both congratulate you on the excellent	133
program you have developed at your institution.	143
Believe me, when another vacancy occurs, you	152
will be hearing from us again; and I hope you	161
will have another Caroline to send to us. Cor-	170
dially yours, Mrs. Madge Baransy Personnel	179
Director xx cc Miss Caroline Dempsey	186/**206**
(157)	

Problem 3 appears on page 282.

110c ▶25 Improve speed/accuracy

Step 1—Speed
Type three 1′ writings on each ¶.

Goal: To reach your top speed on the ¶.

Step 2—Accuracy
Type three 1′ guided writings on each ¶ at 8 *gwam* below your Step 1 rate on the ¶.

Goal: Not over 1 error on each writing.

Note: If you complete a ¶ before time is called, start again at the beginning of that ¶.

all letters

Often typists just do not realize how important good typewriting techniques are when it comes to building speed and accuracy. Observe the expert typists. They make it a habit to type with good form.

all figures

The average man in a lifetime spends 19 to 20 years working. He spends another 18 to 20 years sleeping, 16 to 17 years playing, 4 years shaving and dressing, 5 years eating, and 3 years just waiting.

rough draft

California is a unique state. It the is sunniest and foggiest state. It has no snow in some parts; yet tam arack in the high sierras may have record snow falls. *It has the biggest trees and the oldest trees.*

110d ▶15 Measure basic skill: statistical copy

two 5′ writings; determine *gwam*; proofread and circle errors

Record better rate and % of transfer (better rate ÷ better rate of 109b, page 179).

all letters/figures used | A | 1.5 si | 5.6 awl | 80% hfw |

	gwam 1′	5′
During the decade of the 1980's, the size of the aggregate work force	14	3
will expand from 102 million in 1980 to 113 million in 1990; albeit the	28	6
growth factor will be only 11 percent as compared with almost 20 percent	43	9
in the 1970's. The rate of expansion for workers in the 25 to 34 age	57	11
category will drop quite dramatically from 51 percent to 14 percent.	71	14
Conversely, workers in the 35 to 44 age category will jump notably from	85	17
18.7 million to 27.6 million, an increment of 48 percent. The median age	100	20
of the work force will rise from 35 years in 1980 to 37 years in 1990.	114	23
Collectively, the tally of workers 16 to 24 years old will drop from	14	26
23.8 million in 1980 to 20.3 million in 1990, a decline of 15 percent.	28	28
The collection of males in this young work force will exceed that of	42	31
females by only 2 percent, in comparison with 4.2 percent in 1970 and	56	34
3.2 percent in 1980. The declining trend in employment of young men is	70	37
based on the anticipated intensified enrollment of this group in high	84	40
school and in college in the decade of the 1980's. At the same time,	98	43
an upward trend in both employment and school enrollment is projected	112	45
for young women until 1990.	118	46

gwam 1′ | 1 | 2 | 3 | 4 | 5 | 6 | 7 | 8 | 9 | 10 | 11 | 12 | 13 | 14 |
5′ | 1 | 2 | 3 |

173c ▶ 35 Measure production skill: report

1. Type the copy at the right as a new section of the office manual. Start with a new sheet.
2. Type the next page number appropriate for your manual, centered at the bottom as on page 1.
3. Insert appropriate page numbers on the Contents page.
4. After all pages of the manual (Contents and Sections 1 and 2) have been typed, proofread, and corrected, assemble the pages in page sequence, staple them together along the left side (about 1/2" from the left edge), and submit them to your teacher for evaluation.

words

Section 2 2
EMPLOYEE TIME-OFF BENEFITS 7

Military Service 14

If an employee is a member of one of the military reserve pro- 26
grams or the national guard and is required to attend camp period- 40
ically, arrangements can be made thru the appropriate department 53
head. An employee is not compensated during such training periods 68
but he may use vacation time with during this period if he desires. 81

Maternity Leave 87

A reasonable time will be allowed for a leave due to preg- 101
nancy. Absence because of pregnancy will be paid on the same basis 115
as regular sickness. (See next section.) The company may request 124
a doctors note confirming the advisability of the employee continu- 137
ation if we feel the condition is affecting one's work. 151

Jury Duty 155

Any employee who is called for jury duty and performs this 168
service will be granted a leave of absence if notice of such call 180
for jury duty is submitted to the company. The employee will re- 194
ceive regular straight-time salary during jury service less the 207
amount received for jury duty. Employees will be expected to be 221
on the job when presence is not required in court. 231

Illness 234

In the event of illness, a full-time employee will be paid 246
as follows: 249

1. During the first 3 months of employment, no pay- 259
ment will be made for absence do to illness. 268
2. After 3 months of employment and up to one year, pay- 279
ment will be made for as much as 5 days due to illness. 291
3. After one year of service, payment will be made for 302
up to 5 days of absence due to illness in each 6-month 313
period between January-June and July-December. 323

Unused sick days not used can be accumulated up to a total of 333
50 days and used in case of serious illness or accident. 346

Funerals 349

Any permanent full-time employee will be granted three day's 361
leave for absence due to attendance at a relative's funeral. 374

111

111a ▶5 Conditioning practice

each line 3 times (slowly, faster, in-between rate)

alphabet	Jack found seven quaint game boxes at the new little bazaar in Waypol.
fig/sym	He paid $1,830.45 in 1976 for an oriental rug (8′ x 12′) for his home.
fingers 3, 4	The happy porpoise easily leaped through the loop and caught the ball.
fluency	He may hand me the clay and then go to the shelf for the die and form.

| 1 | 2 | 3 | 4 | 5 | 6 | 7 | 8 | 9 | 10 | 11 | 12 | 13 | 14 |

111b ▶25 Select-a-goal practice: progressive difficulty sentences

1. Beat-the-clock speed spurt. Try to type Sentence 1 as you are timed for 20″; 15″; and 12″.
Repeat for other sentences.

2. Accuracy emphasis. Repeat Step 1, but with emphasis on reducing errors.

3. Check rates. Type a 1′ writing on each sentence.

Figures give 1′ rate in terms of guide call.

guide	gwam													
20″	3	6	9	12	15	18	21	24	27	30	33	36	39	42
15″	4	8	12	16	20	24	28	32	36	40	44	48	52	56
12″	5	10	15	20	25	30	35	40	45	50	55	60	65	70

balanced hand	She may make the form and then go to the city to do the work for them.
combination	Please send all these statements to their office staff for processing.
long words	The psychiatrist acted as ombudsman and counselor for the specialists.
shift keys	Jay Smith, Jack Dunn, and Robie Quinn play for the Cincinnati Bengals.
figures	We received 123 balls, 57 bats, and 62 gloves on Order 9041 of May 28.
one hand	We are aware, as you imply, of decreasing monopoly action in Honolulu.

| 1 | 2 | 3 | 4 | 5 | 6 | 7 | 8 | 9 | 10 | 11 | 12 | 13 | 14 |

111c ▶15 Improve speed/accuracy: statistical rough draft

1. Two 1′ writings for speed; then two 1′ writings for accuracy (not over 1 error in each writing).

2. A 2′ writing for speed; then a 2′ writing for accuracy (not over 2 errors).

all figures used

	gwam 1′	2′
¶ Surveys ~~give evidence~~ indicate that 64% (spell out) of all house holds own the housing unit	14	7
~~in which~~ they ~~live~~ occupy. Home ownership ~~varies~~ may vary from about 50% (spell out) for house-	28	14
holds with # incomes under $3,000 to nearly 85% (sp.) with incomes ~~above~~ of $15,000 or over.	46	23
About 42% (sp.) of all households with a head under 39 years ~~old~~ of age own their	61	31
own homes. Ownership rate for the above-39 age group is	73	37
70% (sp.) or over.	76	38

111d ▶5 Improve accuracy: vowel keys

each line twice (slowly, faster)

Goal: As many lines as possible without error.

a	Again and again, an agitated armadillo attacked the arena area guards.
e	Helene decided to strive for excellence in every educational endeavor.
i	Irol may visit Hawaii, Tahiti, Fiji, and other islands in the Pacific.
o	Okumo's good work may open new doors for our products in Rangoon.
u	Did you and Urey use the unusual vacuum tube as you cleaned our house?

173

173a ▶5 Conditioning practice

each line 3 times SS (slowly, faster, slowly); DS between 3-line groups

Oxygen from the liquid gas jets kept oozing over into the wet cubicle.
His Sony 4310S and Dual 1059 arrived in the mail on December 28, 1976.
The "no-fault"* policy carried a $150 deductible (42% of the premium).
We canvassed the city in the afternoon either individually or by twos.

| 1 | 2 | 3 | 4 | 5 | 6 | 7 | 8 | 9 | 10 | 11 | 12 | 13 | 14 |

173b ▶10 Measure basic skill: straight copy

a 5′ writing; determine *gwam*; circle errors

all letters used | A | 1.5 si | 5.6 awl | 80% hfw

	gwam 1′	5′
A good vocabulary is vital to every business person. And the larger	14	3
the vocabulary, the greater is the benefit attained. Words are but	27	5
symbols for ideas. If you do not have enough command of these symbols,	42	8
it is very difficult for you to form complex thoughts or to reveal them	56	11
to someone else. How do words help you think? According to one expert,	71	14
our brains think with words.	76	15
We all have the power of recognition. We all use a vocabulary.	13	18
The greater our recognition, the greater the usefulness of our vocabu-	27	21
lary. Most of us can recognize about ten times the number of words we	41	24
actually use in speaking and writing. We can use a word only when we	55	26
know it exists, and we must know its exact definition to convey just	69	29
the shade of meaning needed to communicate our thoughts.	80	31
Does all this mean that a large vocabulary is important to you?	13	34
Yes, indeed it does. There is a high correlation between intelligence	27	37
quotient and vocabulary as well as between vocabulary and one's rank in	42	40
a firm. Top managers who got where they are by hard work are usually	56	42
facile in their use of language. They read, speak, listen, and write	70	45
well. They know the power of words.	77	47
You can enhance your word power in numerous ways. First, join a	13	49
book club. An avid reader is invariably an avid word lover. Second,	27	52
become a student of words. Develop a real interest in words, in their	41	55
meanings, in their origins. Most importantly, acquire the dictionary	55	58
habit. It's one you will never want to break. Words are like people--	70	61
once you get to know them, they can give you a lot of pleasure.	82	63

gwam 1′ | 1 | 2 | 3 | 4 | 5 | 6 | 7 | 8 | 9 | 10 | 11 | 12 | 13 | 14 |
5′ | 1 | 2 | 3 |

112

112a ▶5 Conditioning practice

each line 3 times (slowly, faster, in-between rate)

alphabet	Sixteen pretty ladies served flawless jam cakes in the quaint gazebos.
fig/sym	The new pool (15′ wide x 60′ long x 7′ deep) will cost but $13,248.90.
double letters	A committee will meet the bookkeeping class to discuss current assets.
fluency	Learn to space quickly between words in order to type with continuity.

| 1 | 2 | 3 | 4 | 5 | 6 | 7 | 8 | 9 | 10 | 11 | 12 | 13 | 14 |

112b ▶15 Measure basic skill: rough draft

two 5′ writings; determine *gwam*; proofread and circle errors

Record better rate and % of transfer (rough-draft rate ÷ straight-copy rate of 109b, page 179).

all letters used | A | 1.5 si | 5.6 awl | 80% hfw

Text	gwam 1′	5′
Clerical jobs make up the largest occupational group in our ~~economy~~ nation.	14	3
Their number ~~will continue~~ is certain to grow at a ~~rapid rate~~ fast pace during the next ten or so	28	6
years due to the increase in paperwork and changes in technology. The rapid increase in paper-	47	9
work is a result of ~~the~~ a continuing expansion of business and a growing need for a variety of reports. The use of	70	14
computers and other devices to do routine work may reduce the need for	84	17
payroll, stock, bank, and file clerks; but it will increase the need	97	19
for office machine operators and others who are required to	109	22
prepare input material for computers.	117	23
On the other hand, many clerical jobs will not be highly affected by the	15	26
changes in technology. Among such jobs are typists and secretaries, as well as other	32	30
office workers who possess the needed office skills and who can meet and deal with the public. Persons with such	55	34
skills will find a rising demand for their skills. The biggest demand	69	37
will be ~~in banking, insurance, and manufacturing firms, and in govern-~~	87	41
~~mental as well as other service groups~~. It is recognized that The growing demand for skilled	97	43
office workers by these firms will account for about half of the total	112	46
growth in the clerical area in the next ten or so years.	123	48

in the industries and service firms that employ large numbers of office workers.

172c, continued

Breaks

In all departments of the office, coffee breaks and rest periods[1] should be arranged by the department head so that no more than half the people in a particular department will be away from their desks at the same time. When all employees are gone at once, a bad impression is often made on office visitors. Also, the normal work flow is needlessly interrupted.

A total of not more than 30 minutes daily should be taken for coffee breaks, rest periods, and other time away from a work station. Studies have shown that periodic breaks from routine work result in increased efficiency. Remember, however, that 30 minutes a day is 150 minutes a week or over 3 full workweeks of 37 1/2 hours in one year.

Exigencies

There will be times when an employee must be away from the desk or from the office. Generally, only emergencies shall excuse workers from being where they should be. We feel that all employees should be engaged in productive work at least 7 hours of the 7 1/2-hour workday.

Tardiness. All employees hired for regular employment are expected to be at work on time when the office and plant are open for business. Deductions for tardiness will be made as follows:

Time	Deduction
5-15 minutes	1/4 hour
16-30 minutes	1/2 hour
31-45 minutes	3/4 hour
46-60 minutes[2]	1 hour

When deductions are made for tardiness and when overtime is worked that day, the employee must make up the time (15, 30, 45, 60 minutes) at the regular rate before being entitled to the overtime rate for the day.

[1] See Section 4 of this manual for the policy statement regarding lunch schedules.

[2] Anything over 60 minutes late without notice will result in an individual conference with one's supervisor.

Absences. When an employee cannot report for work, the employee's immediate supervisor must be notified by 9 a.m. so that arrangements can be made to carry on the work scheduled in the employee's absence. If there is a likelihood that an employee might be out for more than one day, this too should be reported.

Leaving the premises. Employees are not allowed to leave the company premises during working hours (except for lunch periods) unless prior approval is obtained in writing from the department head or unless the nature of the work being performed requires that an employee leave the premises. When it is necessary to leave during working hours, the department head should be informed of your destination and expected time of return.

Hiring Policies

Probationary period. All employees are hired for a probationary period of 30 workdays, and they may be terminated in 30 workdays without recourse.

Temporary help. Temporary employees are hired with the understanding that their employment is temporary, either for a specific or for an indefinite length of time, with no assurance of permanent employment. Their employment can be terminated when they are no longer needed.

Full-time employees who work the 7 1/2 hours per day for a full year are entitled to all the benefits provided by the company as they fulfill the requirements. Temporary employees are not entitled to these benefits until they become full-time employees.

Relatives. Spouses and relatives of full-time employees may be considered for full-time employment. Where a question of confidentiality exists or where employment would result in a supervisor-and-supervised relationship, spouses and relatives will not be hired.

Retired workers. An employment condition is that all employees must retire at age 65. A retired employee in good health may be considered for temporary work by the personnel manager after consultation with the appropriate department head.

112c ▶22 Improve speed/accuracy

1. Speed emphasis—Set 1. Starting with Sentence 1, Set 1, gradually increase your speed as you type each new sentence as the 15″, 12″, *or* 10″ guide is called by your teacher.

Move from one sentence to the next when the "return" is called. Push your speed to its highest possible level.

2. Accuracy emphasis—Set 2. Starting with Sentence 1, Set 2, repeat Step 1 except that your goal is errorless writing on each sentence; if you make an error, stay on that sentence until you can type it without error.

3. Speed/accuracy emphasis—Set 3. Type each sentence of Set 3 as a 1′ writing.

Goal: To type with not more than 1 error on each writing.

Set 1: high-frequency, balanced-hand words emphasized

		gwam 15″	12″	10″
1	He may also make me go with them to do their work.	40	50	60
2	They may sign the city amendment forms for the auditor.	44	55	66
3	The firm may make a profit if the men do a quantity of work.	48	60	72
4	Eight of the firms may make a bid for half of the rich land.	52	65	78
5	It is their wish to sign the forms and then pay the firm for the work.	56	70	84

| 1 | 2 | 3 | 4 | 5 | 6 | 7 | 8 | 9 | 10 | 11 | 12 | 13 | 14 |

Set 2: high-frequency, one-hand words emphasized

		gwam 15″	12″	10″
1	After you rate him, read only a few reserve cases.	40	50	60
2	John can get you only a minimum tax rate on the estate.	44	55	66
3	We regret that you were referred to him for the tax opinion.	48	60	72
4	The average reserve tax rate is greater than the minimum you set.	52	65	78
5	Were you to refer all or only a few area tax cases to him for opinion?	56	70	84

| 1 | 2 | 3 | 4 | 5 | 6 | 7 | 8 | 9 | 10 | 11 | 12 | 13 | 14 |

Set 3: high-frequency, two- and three-letter combinations emphasized

		gwam 15″	12″	10″
1	When are you and she going to the station for her?	40	50	60
2	During this testing session, you will be on your honor.	44	55	66
3	Either you or they can bring action in a regional court for the rents.	48	60	72
4	When they leave at the end of this hour, are you going with them?	52	65	78
5	You and I were to go there to do the work before the end of this week.	56	70	84

| 1 | 2 | 3 | 4 | 5 | 6 | 7 | 8 | 9 | 10 | 11 | 12 | 13 | 14 |

112d ▶8 Improve basic skill: statistical copy

a 5′ writing on ¶s of 110d, page 181

Goal: Increased speed *or* improved accuracy.

113

113a ▶5 Conditioning practice

each line 3 times (slowly, faster, in-between rate)

alphabet	Patient quarriers uncovered famous Greek bronzes with onyx-jewel eyes.
fig/sym	The #5346 item will cost Oakley & Company $921.78 (less 10% for cash).
long words	A habit may be an outgrowth of physiological or psychological motives.
fluency	The successful typewriting student is one who has formed right habits.

| 1 | 2 | 3 | 4 | 5 | 6 | 7 | 8 | 9 | 10 | 11 | 12 | 13 | 14 |

Overtime hours. At certain times during the year, various departments find it necessary to work overtime. During these periods a condition of employment is that employees work overtime if at all possible when requested to do so. Department heads will notify those who are qualified or who are expected to perform overtime work. Employees should try to arrange their personal affairs so that they can work overtime when necessary. No employee should remain at work after regular hours or report to work on weekends unless requested to do so by a department head.

Overtime rate of pay. Employees who work more than 7 1/2 hours in any one day will receive one and one-half times the straight-time rate of pay for hours worked beyond 7 1/2 hours in any one workday.

An employee required to work overtime on Saturday will receive one and one-half times the straight-time rate if he or she has worked 37 1/2 hours from Monday through Friday (30 hours if a paid holiday falls in the regular workweek) with the following exceptions:

1. One day of approved vacation (7 1/2 hours) may be included in the hours stated above. For Saturday overtime purposes, an absence on a Friday will be allowed where otherwise proper except during the months of August and September.

2. If an employee is absent due to illness, jury duty, military duty, funeral of a relative, or some other approved absence, the hours absent will be considered as hours worked.

An employee required to work overtime on Sunday will receive twice the straight-time rate of pay, provided he or she has met the requirements stated above and has worked at least 7 1/2 hours on Saturday.

An employee required to work on a holiday will receive double rate of pay, in addition to pay to which he or she may be entitled for the holiday.

NOTE: To be eligible for a double pay rate on a holiday, an employee shall have worked both the scheduled workday before and the scheduled workday following the holiday unless he or she is on vacation or is absent with approval.

Employees hired on a part-time or temporary basis must actually work 37 1/2 hours per week before being eligible for overtime pay on Saturday or six days of at least 7 1/2 hours per day before being eligible for double time on Sunday.

Separation pay. Separation pay is defined as remuneration to which an employee may be entitled when severing employment with the company after having completed one full year of full-time employment. When termination is made after a full year of service, an employee entitled to a two-week vacation will be given separation pay in lieu of the earned vacation.

If separation is requested by the company and an employee is released during the first year of employment, no separation pay can be received. If an employee is released after one year, two weeks' notice is given the employee. On termination of employment, the employee will receive separation pay equal to the earned vacation for persons leaving voluntarily as stated in the preceding paragraph. If, however, an employee is released because of misconduct or dishonesty in connection with company employment, separation pay will not be given.

Promotions

Our policy is to employ the best people available to fill any openings for which new personnel are needed. Another policy of the company is to make promotions from within the organization if persons are properly qualified for available positions. For initial employment opportunities, we seek the best available talent and hire strictly on the basis of merit and personal qualifications. Whenever a position opens up that involves an opportunity for one of the present staff, every qualified person is considered for the opening before any attempt is made to recruit a new person from the outside.

113b ▶20 Improve speed/accuracy technique

1. Long reaches—Set 1. Type each line 3 times (slowly, faster, top speed).

Goal: Increased speed.

2. Concentration drills—Set 2. Type each line 3 times (slowly, faster, in-between rate).

Goal: Improved accuracy.

Set 1 practice goal: fingers curved, upright; quiet hands; snappy keystroking

1 Abelle Babar had to abandon the abacus that was made of abalone shell.
2 The baby boy was baffled as he batted the balloons off the abbey wall.
3 Did you or Yasuda see the yak eat the yucca that grew down by the bay?
4 Agatha may take the mortgage payment to Bart Naylor today or tomorrow.
5 Check their branch in Irvine for carbon paper in volume at low prices.

| 1 | 2 | 3 | 4 | 5 | 6 | 7 | 8 | 9 | 10 | 11 | 12 | 13 | 14 |

Set 2 practice goal: eyes on copy; continuity of typing

1 The kind king may make them keep their word about the work to be done.
2 Drew drove the horse into the house without thinking a thing about it.
3 As they work in "think tanks," former farmers practice practical arts.
4 Imai Imrie applauded as Rie Young received an award for her good work.
5 I saw six swans swimming in the azure-blue water of the bay by Bagaba.

| 1 | 2 | 3 | 4 | 5 | 6 | 7 | 8 | 9 | 10 | 11 | 12 | 13 | 14 |

113c ▶15 Measure basic skill: straight copy

two 5′ writings; determine *gwam*; proofread and circle errors; record better rate

all letters used | A | 1.5 si | 5.6 awl | 80% hfw |

Text	gwam 1′	5′
Just what does it mean to be young and when is a person young? To	13	3
be young is perhaps a feeling or disposition, a particular manner of	27	5
looking at things and responding to them. To be young is never a chrono-	42	8
logical period or time of life, although it might be a young person	55	11
examining some material with fascination and pleasure or the composer	69	14
Verdi in his eighties writing his best opera. To be young might be a	83	17
person "hanging ten" on a surfboard or swinging to a musical composi-	97	19
tion. To be young might be Einstein in his seventies still working with	112	22
his field theory, sailing his boat, or playing his cherished fiddle.	125	25
To be young is never the monopoly of youth. It flourishes every-	13	28
where visionaries have stimulated our thinking or amazed us. To be young	28	31
in nature is quite desirable whether you are a young person, a middle-	42	33
aged person, or a chronologically old person. To be young should be	56	36
respected whether the beard is soft and curly or firm and gray. To be	70	39
young has no color; it seems always translucent with its own imaginative	84	42
light. There is no generation space between the young of any age because	99	45
they see things as they ought to be.	106	46

gwam 1′ | 1 | 2 | 3 | 4 | 5 | 6 | 7 | 8 | 9 | 10 | 11 | 12 | 13 | 14 |
5′ | 1 | 2 | 3 |

113d ▶10 Improve accuracy

Type six 1′ writings of 113c, above; start second and succeeding writings at ending point of previous writing.

Goal: Not over 1 error in each writing.

Section 1

EMPLOYMENT CONDITIONS

The following statement of policy in this manual does not mean that policies are fixed rules. Policies are major guides to help us all to follow the same procedures under similar conditions. Individual decisionwill be made and many of these are not covered by p olicies if we follow these practices, there will be less misunderstanding and our customers and employees will be hapier.

Compensation

Payday Schedule. Employees who arenot exempt from the overtime provisions of the Labor Standards Act (clerical shipping and assembly room personel) are paid by check each Friday for all time worked during the week ending the previous Saturday. Employees exempt from the overtime provisions of the Fir Labor Standards Act (supervisors, managers, and executives are paid semimonthly on the 15thand the last day of the month unless they fall on a Saturday or Sunday, in which case payment is made on the preceding friday. Compensation for clerical employees is quoted on a monthly basis and each weeks pay will be approximately 4 and a third divided into the monthly rate. Exempt employees recieve half of the monthly rate each payday. Compensation for shipping and assembly personnell is quoted and computed on an hourly rate. Payday schedules may vary depending upon whether you are a part-time or a full-time employee.

, or if Friday is a holiday, on the last workday of the pay period.

unit **19** lessons 114–123

Tabulation

Learning goals

1. To improve skill in arranging material in table (tabulated) form.
2. To improve spelling skills.
3. To improve word–use skills.
4. To learn basic guides for use of punctuation.

Machine adjustments

Make the usual machine adjustments as required for the various activities.

114

114a ▶5 Conditioning practice

each line 3 times (slowly, faster, in-between rate)

alphabet Jerome quickly realized that six lively polliwogs would soon be frogs.

fig/sym The terms of discount on Order 47#28-96 dated June 15 were 2/10, n/30.

1st row Can Van Bonn mix the zinc? Nan coaxed a nimble zebra back to the zoo.

fluency Try to let the fingers do the typing and your skill will grow rapidly.

| 1 | 2 | 3 | 4 | 5 | 6 | 7 | 8 | 9 | 10 | 11 | 12 | 13 | 14 |

114b ▶5 Improve figure- and tab-key control

four 1′ writings; line: 74; tab stops at 10-space intervals; last 2 digits of each group give word count

Practice goal: finger–reach action; quick tab spacing

3701	7302	4603	6404	5805	8506	9507	5908
3409	7410	6311	8912	6713	9514	8315	7416
6517	7218	3819	4920	8921	5622	6823	7924
4025	4926	5627	4728	5829	9430	8631	3732

114c ▶25 Learn table placement

full sheets

Margins
side and bottom: 1″
top, page 1: 1½″
top, page 2: 1″

Vertical spacing

Space copy properly as you type it.

As a page–end reminder, use a line gauge backing sheet [LM p. 65]; or make a light pencil mark at the right edge of sheet 1″ from the bottom and another mark about ½″ above the 1″ mark to alert you to be ready to end the page. Erase marks when page is completed.

TABLE PLACEMENT SUMMARY
TS

I. VERTICAL PLACEMENT OF MATERIAL
DS

A. Mathematical Placement Review
  1. Count all lines to be used for table (including all blank line spaces).
  2. Subtract this figure from total lines available on sheet.
     Note: Because most typewriters have six line spaces to the vertical inch, paper 8 1/2 x 11 inches has 66 line spaces (11 x 6 = 66).
  3. Divide the remainder by 2. This figure will indicate the number of blank lines to be left in the top margin.

B. Spacing After Heading Lines
  1. Leave 1 blank line space (DS) between MAIN HEADING and the Secondary Heading (when used).
  2. Leave 2 blank line spaces (TS) after a main heading if a secondary heading is not used--or after the secondary heading when both a main heading and a secondary heading are used.
  3. Leave 1 blank line space (DS) after column headings (when used).

C. Reading Position
  1. Reading position (visual center) is a point approximately 2 line spaces above actual vertical center.

(continued on page 187)

171

171a ▶5
Conditioning practice
each line 3 times SS (slowly, faster, slowly); DS between 3-line groups

Income tax itemizing is a vexing job and requires plenty of hard work.
Continental has a flight at 8:26; Delta, at 9:37; and Ozark, at 10:54.
Poe & Co. is one of 75 top-rated firms in Fortune magazine this month.
In the fall, this field is full of giant weeds that give me hay fever.

| 1 | 2 | 3 | 4 | 5 | 6 | 7 | 8 | 9 | 10 | 11 | 12 | 13 | 14 |

171b ▶10
Improve capitalization skills
1. Read and type the sentence, supplying correct capitalization.
2. Check the accuracy of your work.
3. Retype the drill at increased speed.

1 this quote morley found in volume 9: "thank god for tea and england."
2 all seniors take speech 110, but not history, for a bachelor's degree.
3 The salvation army aided all victims of the tornado in east st. louis.
4 he asked to see president Damon, who used to be treasurer of the club.
5 "On saturday," Dorothy said, "old man winter will greet us in boston."
6 my dear ms. samos, here's what I'd do: see the counselor immediately.

171c ▶35
Type an office manual

Continue typing the office manual where you stopped in Lesson 170.

172

172a ▶5
Conditioning practice
each line 3 times SS (slowly, faster, slowly); DS between 3-line groups

High expenses led them to centralize equipment for every woodwork job.
Their teams won some close games: 97 to 96, 84 to 83, and 105 to 102.
They said, "Our current $2,716 tax is only 3% off last year's $2,800."
The giant firm spent millions to enrich the city in which it operated.

| 1 | 2 | 3 | 4 | 5 | 6 | 7 | 8 | 9 | 10 | 11 | 12 | 13 | 14 |

172b ▶10
Review number-expression skills
1. Read and type the sentences, using words or figures to express numbers correctly.
2. Check your work.
3. Retype the drill.

1 I once lived at 1 Park Drive; I now live at 18 W. Lincoln Boulevard.
2 The interest rate was 7 1/2 percent, but fewer than 50% of us knew it.
3 15 boys went on the twelve-mile hike; only 11 took less than 4 hours.
4 A million-dollar fire spread to 4 eight-story buildings on 15th Street.
5 About seventy-five people attended the 4 meetings at eight o'clock.

172c ▶35
Type an office manual

Continue typing the office manual where you stopped in Lesson 171.

114c, continued

Note: Remainder of copy is in unarranged form. Indent and space copy properly as you type it. Stay alert!

2. To center copy in reading position, determine the top margin as usual; then subtract 2 from the number of lines to be left in the top margin.

II. HORIZONTAL PLACEMENT OF COLUMNS IN TABLES

A. Backspace-from-Center Method

1. Move margin stops to ends of scale and clear all tab stops.
2. From the horizontal center of the sheet, backspace once for each 2 strokes in the longest line in each column and for each 2 spaces to be left between columns (ignore any extra space at the end of the last column).

Note: The usual center point for pica-type machines is 42 or 43; for elite-type, 50 or 51.

3. Set the left margin stop at point where backspacing ends.
4. From the left margin stop, space forward once for each stroke in the longest line in the first column and for each space to be left between the first and second columns. Set a tab stop at this point for the start of the second column. Continue procedure for any additional columns.

B. Spacing Between Columns

1. As a general rule, leave an even number of spaces between columns (4, 6, 8, 10, or more).
2. The number of spaces to be left between columns is governed by the space available, the number of columns used, and the requirement of ease of reading.

C. Column Headings

1. Column headings (if used) usually are centered over the columns.
2. If a table contains single-line column headings and also some headings of 2 or more lines, type the bottom line of each heading on the same line as the single-line headings.

Save sheets for *Typewriting Manual*.

114d ▶15
Apply learning

Problem 1
3-column table
half sheet, long side up; center vertically; DS data; 6 spaces between columns; check your solution with placement cues at the bottom of this page

Problem 2
Build skill
Retype Problem 1; half sheet, short side up; DS; 4 spaces between columns.

lines used			
1	WORDS FREQUENTLY MISSPELLED		
2			
3			
4	accessible	beginning	decision
5			
6	advisable	brochure	embarrass
7			
8	all right	casualty	excel
9			
10	analyze	committee	forty
11			
12	attorneys	conferred	fourth

key | 10 | 6 | 9 | 6 | 9 |

Placement cues for Problem 1

Vertical placement

Formula: $\frac{\text{lines available} - \text{lines used}}{2}$ = top margin

$\frac{33 - 12}{2}$ = 10 blank line spaces in top margin (extra line space left at bottom)

Proof: 10 + 12 + 11 = 33 (lines available for use)

Horizontal placement

Backspace from center of paper 1 space for each 2 spaces in longest columnar lines and for spaces between columns:

ac|ce|ss|ib|le|12|34|56|be|gi|nn|in|g1|23|45|6e|mb|ar|ra|ss

Set left margin; then space forward to determine tab stops for Columns 2 and 3.

169b ▶10 Improve punctuation skill

1. Read the sentence to determine correct punctuation.
2. Type the sentence, supplying needed punctuation.
3. Check the accuracy of your work.
4. Retype the drill at increased speed.

1 These first_class schools were involved_ Lancaster_ Gray_ and Pierce_
2 Mr_ E_ Fox_ an oil magnate_ gave Raleigh_ N_C__ the sum of _97_475_00_
3 In May_ 1976_ Law & Son_ Inc__ which was badly managed_ went bankrupt_
4 This article_ _Classrooms in Process__ was written by Rob_s assistant_
5 _Oh__ shouted Sam_ _if Joe makes this basket_ the score will be tied__
6 Joan Starling_ Ph_D__ was a good professor_ and I enjoyed her classes_
7 If you can_t make the six o_clock_ take the early_morning bus to Nice_
8 Mr. Samuelson_ here is my suggestion_ Study Chapter 6 very carefully_
9 A one_ or a two_year contract is available_ take the longer one_ Mary_
10 Martinez_ after striking out two men_ allowed a hit_ we lost the game_

169c ▶35 Type an office manual

1. Begin typing the office manual, pages 276–278, 280. Use leftbound format (See p. 272 and RG pp. vii, viii).
2. Proofread each completed page and correct each error *before* removing the paper from the typewriter.
3. At the end of the class period, complete any line you have begun. Begin the next production period where you ended the last one.

170

170a ▶5 Conditioning practice

each line 3 times SS (slowly, faster, slowly); DS between 3-line groups

The judge kept quizzing Mr. Voyles, executor of the will, about dates.
Gymnasium lockers 48 and 27 have the same combination: R39, L16, R50.
On 5/8/76 (May 8, 1976) the first invoice--terms 4/12, n/30--was sent.
The fact is, only a dear friend can make you see and accept the truth.
| 1 | 2 | 3 | 4 | 5 | 6 | 7 | 8 | 9 | 10 | 11 | 12 | 13 | 14 |

170b ▶10 Improve punctuation skill, continued

Follow the directions given with 169b, above.

1 The Small Claims Court allowed Lily Foster seventy_five dollars _$75__
2 Boris Pasternak_ who was born on March 19_ 1890_ wrote Doctor Zhivago_
3 The Sun Times quoted Dr_ Walsh as saying__ Today_s Johnny can_t read__
4 The speech__ to use the word loosely_ was badly prepared and delivered_
5 Wasn_t he in Dover_ Delaware_ on May 3_ 1976_ to buy_ sell_ and trade_

170c ▶35 Type an office manual

Continue typing the office manual where you stopped in Lesson 169.

115

115a ▶5 Conditioning practice

each line 3 times (slowly, faster, in-between rate)

alphabet	The quiet king came forth to extend prizes to very bewildered jesters.
fig/sym	A 100% hardwood 3-shelf bookcase (38" x 23" x 7 3/4") sells for $9.65.
adjacent keys	A very popular aquanaut tried a new sort of wet suit for water sports.
fluency	Keep the stroking action in the fingers to increase your typing skill.
	| 1 | 2 | 3 | 4 | 5 | 6 | 7 | 8 | 9 | 10 | 11 | 12 | 13 | 14 |

115b ▶20 Improve punctuation skill: related learning

These punctuation guides are to be added to the *Typewriting Manual* you are preparing. The guides and illustrative sentences should be typed according to the directions given in 101c, page 166.

Margins
top: 1½", page 1
side: 1"
bottom: 1" (approx.)

Arrange copy properly as you type it.

SERIES 4: PUNCTUATION GUIDES

Comma

1. Use the comma after (a) introductory words, phrases, or clauses and (b) words in a series with a final conjunction.

   If you can go, we shall visit Chicago, St. Louis, and Dallas.

2. Do not use commas to separate two items treated as a single unit within a series.

   He ordered bacon and eggs, toast, and coffee.

3. Use the comma to set off short direct quotations.

   Thoreau once said, "Be not simply good: Be good for something."

4. Use the comma before and after (a) words in apposition (words which come together and refer to the same person, thing, or idea) and (b) words of direct address.

   Dr. Case, the new committee member, will give the report.
   You realize, Larry, that your manuscript is late.

5. Use the comma to set off nonrestrictive clauses (not necessary to meaning of sentence). Do not use commas to set off restrictive clauses (necessary to meaning).

   Unit 17, which relates to the problem, is well written.
   Typists who practice with a purpose will be successful.

6. Use the comma to separate the day from the year and the city from the state.

   She was born May 15, 1960, in San Diego, California.

7. Use the comma to separate two or more parallel adjectives (adjectives that could be separated by the word "and" instead of the comma).

   The happy, excited crowd cheered when our team tied the score.

8. Do not use commas to separate adjectives so closely related that they appear to form a single element with the noun they modify. Note: If "and" cannot replace the comma without creating a meaningless effect, the comma should not be used.

   A dozen large red roses were delivered to this address.

Save sheet for *Typewriting Manual*.

168d ▶26
Type a contents page of an office manual

Type the contents page in leftbound manuscript style. Insert page numbers after you complete the report in Lessons 169–173.

Leaders are made by alternating periods and spaces.

CONTENTS

Section 1: Employment Conditions

Page

Section 2: Employee Time-Off Benefits

169

169a ▶5 Conditioning practice

each line 3 times SS (slowly, faster, slowly); DS between 3-line groups

The executive queried citizens of Jacksburg on why the market toppled.
Of 1,089 pages, 764 were textual pages and 325 were appendix material.
The bimonthly statement read, "Your total payment will now be $50.73."
In the future, please send your monthly payment to the downtown store.

| 1 | 2 | 3 | 4 | 5 | 6 | 7 | 8 | 9 | 10 | 11 | 12 | 13 | 14 |

115c ▶25 Improve tabulating skill: applications

Problem 1
4-column table

half sheet, long side up; SS data; center vertically; 6 spaces between columns; note spelling of each word as you type it

Problem 2
Build skill

Retype Problem 1; full sheet; reading position; DS data; 8 spaces between columns.

SPELLING DEMONS

				words in cols.	total
					3
argue	argument	postpone	postponement	7	11
confer	conferred	employ	employed	14	17
copying	copied	trying	tried	19	23
desire	desirable	notice	noticeable	26	30
stop	stopping	gain	gaining	32	35
gully	gullies	valley	valleys	38	41
brief	chief	either	neither	43	46
seize	leisure	weird	height	48	52
neighbor	weigh	true	truly	54	57

Problem 3
5-column table

half sheet, long side up; DS data; center vertically; 6 spaces between columns

VARIATIONS IN SPELLING
OF LONG VOWEL SOUNDS SS

					words in cols.	total
						5
						9
a	name	grain	play	break	5	14
e	see	cream	shield	region	10	19
i	smile	light	died	style	15	24
o	float	doe	plateau	elbow	20	29
u	mule	few	continue	juice	25	34
oo	stoop	route	true	suit	30	39

Problem 4
Table with column headings

full sheet; space data as shown; reading position; 8 spaces between columns

COMMON METRIC UNITS

Measure	Name	Symbol	words in cols.	total
				4
				12
area	hectare	ha	3	15
electric current	ampere	A	8	20
length	millimeter	mm	13	24
	centimeter	cm	15	27
	meter	m	17	29
	kilometer	km	20	31
mass	gram	g	22	34
	kilogram	kg	24	36
	tonne	t	26	38
temperature	Celsius	°C	31	42
time	second	s	33	45
volume	milliliter	ml	38	49
	liter	l	39	51

unit **28** lessons 168–173

Building report typing competence

Learning goals

In this unit your major goals are to:

1. Increase your basic typewriting skill.

2. Demonstrate your mastery of related English skills.

3. Learn to arrange and type leftbound reports.

4. Develop report typing skill by preparing a portion of an office policy manual.

Machine adjustments

1. Paper guide on *0*.

2. Ribbon control on black.

3. Margin stops: 70-space line for drills and ¶s; as directed for problems.

4. Line-space selector on *1* for drills; on *2* for ¶s; as directed for problems.

168

168a ▶5 Conditioning practice

each line 3 times SS (slowly, faster, slowly); DS between 3-line groups

alphabet	Ask Jim Glaze if our quarterly dividend was influenced by the proxies.
figures	Over 4,850 people attended the 236 exhibits at the 1976 New Arts Fair.
fig/sym	Total cost is $36.04: $34.00 plus $2.04 tax on 2 items at $17.00 each.
fluency	The average and median rates on the production writing differ greatly.

| 1 | 2 | 3 | 4 | 5 | 6 | 7 | 8 | 9 | 10 | 11 | 12 | 13 | 14 |

168b ▶7 Center a heading over the line of writing

1. Set left margin stop 1½″ from left edge of paper; right stop, 1″ from right edge of paper.

2. Add platen scale readings at left and right margin stops; divide total by 2 to find center of line.

3. Center and type the heading of the report shown below; then type the first 3 lines of ¶ 1.

168c ▶12 Type a leftbound report

Margins
top: 1½″ pica, 2″ elite
side: 1½″ left, 1″ right
bottom: 1″ (approx.)
Headings
centered over line of writing
Spacing
DS ¶s; SS numbered items, DS between them

words

TYPING LEFTBOUND REPORTS 5

Many business reports are bound at the left. Such reports are typed slightly "off center" to the right to allow space at the left for binding. These guides will help you prepare them properly: 44

1. Set the left margin stop 1 1/2″ from the left edge of the paper; the right stop, 1″ from the right. 65
2. Determine the center of the writing line: scale reading at left margin stop plus scale reading at right margin stop divided by 2. Use this adjusted center point for centering main headings. 105
3. Begin the first page 1 1/2″ or 2″ from the top edge of the paper; all other pages, 1″ from the top. Maintain a bottom margin of <u>approximately</u> 1″ on all pages. 140
4. Number each page: first page, 1/2″ above the bottom edge, centered; all other pages, on Line 4 from the top edge and even with the right margin. 170

116

116a ▶5 Conditioning practice

each line 3 times (slowly, faster, in-between rate)

alphabet The maze box puzzle was quickly solved by the good students from Fiji.
fig/sym He sent $234.98 for the camera and $16.75 for the case (plus 20% tax).
shift key H. A. McLain and P. T. Hall are employed by the Adams & Brown Company.
fluency Send a draft of the statement to the union at the address on the card.

| 1 | 2 | 3 | 4 | 5 | 6 | 7 | 8 | 9 | 10 | 11 | 12 | 13 | 14 |

116b ▶15 Improve punctuation skill: related learning

Follow standard directions.

9. Use the comma to separate (a) unrelated groups of figures which come together and (b) whole numbers into groups of three digits each (however, policy, year, page, room, telephone, and most serial numbers are typed without commas).

   During 1976, 1,750 cars were insured under Policy 806423.

Exclamation Mark

10. Use an exclamation mark after emphatic interjections and after phrases or sentences that are clearly exclamatory.

    What a beautiful view!
    "Hey there man!" he shouted. (**Note:** space only once after closing quotation mark.)

Question Mark

11. Use a question mark at the end of a sentence that is a direct question; however, use a period after a request in the form of a question.

    When are you leaving for work?
    Will you type this letter before you leave.

Dash

12. Use a dash (a) for emphasis; (b) to indicate change of thought; (c) to introduce the name of an author or a reference when it follows a direct quotation; and (d) for other special purposes. Note: For the dash, type two hyphens without space before or after.

    The icy road--slippery as a fish--made driving hazardous.
    "Hitting the wrong key is like hitting me."--Armour.

Colon

13. Use a colon to introduce an enumeration or a listing.

    He named his three favorite song writers: Dylan, Denver, and Collins.

14. Use a colon to introduce a question or a long direct quotation.

    The question is this: Are you typing with good techniques?

15. Use a colon between hours and minutes expressed in figures.

    When it is 1:30 p.m. in New York, it is 10:30 a.m. in Oregon.

Save sheet for *Typewriting Manual.*

167b, continued

Problem 3
4-column table
Decide spacing between columns.

Problem 4
3-column table
Retype Problem 3 omitting Column 4. Use the following 2–line headings for the 3 columns:
Col. 1
Newspaper
Morning and Evening
Col. 2
Average Daily
Circulation
Col. 3
Sunday
Circulation

words

SELECTED U.S. DAILY NEWSPAPERS' CIRCULATION 9

(Based on Average Paid Circulation) 16

Newspaper	Daily	Sunday	Weekly	words
Akron Beacon Journal	172,971	211,833	1,249,659	37
Buffalo Courier-Express	129,897	284,737	1,064,119	47
Cincinnati Enquirer	193,972	302,462	1,466,294	56
Cleveland Plain Dealer	412,444	511,679	2,986,343	66
Dallas News	263,175	308,664	1,887,714	73
Fort Worth Press	44,401	49,088	135,494	82
Los Angeles Times	1,036,666	1,226,233	7,446,229	92
Santa Ana Register	200,899	216,741	1,422,135	101
South Bend Tribune	117,453	123,712	828,430	109

(Header line: 27 words)

167c ▶10 Measure basic skill: straight copy

a 5′ writing; determine *gwam*; circle errors

all letters used | A | 1.5 si | 5.6 awl | 80% hfw

Text	gwam 1′	5′
All of us are aware of individuals who we feel should have been	13	3
successful in life. We speak in glowing terms of their warm personali-	27	5
ties and their natural abilities, and yet they have not been able to	41	8
climb the ladder of success. On the other hand, there are individuals	55	11
who, while not so charming or so talented, have gone further and achieved	70	14
more, even though no one expected them to succeed with such flying colors.	85	17
This leads us to a vital and frequently discussed topic. Why do	13	20
so many people who are judged most likely to succeed become such failures	28	23
to their friends and to themselves while others who appear to be ordinary	43	25
individuals more than make the grade? In most cases the answer is easy:	57	28
Success in life is measured not merely by our abilities but by our	72	31
attitude toward life as well.	77	32
Ability in itself is meaningless; it must be utilized before it	13	35
develops any value. We all have potential regardless of who we are or	27	38
what we do. Granted some of us possess greater potential than others,	41	41
but the important thing is how well we use the talents we have. Take	55	43
the time to analyze your recent achievements and to determine your future	70	46
goals; your potential for success can be as infinite as you make it.	84	49

gwam 1′ | 1 | 2 | 3 | 4 | 5 | 6 | 7 | 8 | 9 | 10 | 11 | 12 | 13 | 14
5′ | 1 | 2 | 3

116c ▶30
Improve tabulating skill: applications

Problem 1
Table with column headings

full sheet; DS data; center vertically in reading position; leave 8 spaces between columns

COMMON BUSINESS TERMS

Accounting	Business Law	Insurance	words in cols.	total
				4
				17
capital	acceptance	beneficiary	6	23
depreciation	collateral	cash value	13	30
distribution	consideration	clause	20	37
equity	contract	coverage	25	42
inventory	foreclosure	face value	31	49
ledger	lien	insured	35	53
operations	offer	rider	40	57
proprietorship	performance	risk	46	64
revenue	revoke	underwriter	52	69

Problem 2
Table with secondary and column headings

full sheet; DS data; center vertically in reading position; leave 8 spaces between columns

WORD STUDY

Synonyms and Antonyms

Word	Synonym	Antonym	words in cols.	total
				2
				7
				14
agreement	assent	dissent	5	19
concern	care	neglect	9	23
cause	origin	effect	13	27
change	variation	stability	18	33
courage	valor	cowardice	23	38
economy	thriftiness	waste	28	43
hinder	impede	assist	33	47
inquiry	question	answer	37	52
meaning	significance	absurdity	44	58
opposition	resistance	cooperation	50	65
permission	freedom	restraint	56	71
pleasure	enjoyment	pain	61	75
sale	disposal	purchase	66	80
success	accomplishment	failure	72	86

Problem 3
Table with secondary and column headings

half sheet, long side up; DS data; center vertically; leave 4 spaces between column headings; center data under headings.

Note: In Column 1, plan ahead for aligning the last number, *100*.

SCORES ON 5-MINUTE STRAIGHT-COPY TIMED WRITINGS

(End of First-Year Typewriting)

Percent of Students	Speed (gwam)	Errors (total)	words in cols.	total
				10
				16
				34
0 - 25	38 or less	13 or more	6	40
26 - 50	39 - 44	8 - 12	12	46
51 - 75	45 - 50	5 - 7	18	52
76 - 100	51 - up	0 - 4	24	56

167

167a ▶5 Conditioning practice

each line 3 times SS (slowly, faster, slowly); DS between 3-line groups

A wild squabble jeopardized the outcome of the next five hockey games.
The 8,752 full-time and 90 part-time workers recorded 1,634 sick days.
Key indicators: cost index 249.5 (up 27.7%), profits 187.2 (up 8.3%).
The two checks paid both firms for the bodywork they did on the autos.
| 1 | 2 | 3 | 4 | 5 | 6 | 7 | 8 | 9 | 10 | 11 | 12 | 13 | 14 |

167b ▶35 Measure production skill: tables

full sheets; reading position; DS body of tables; type the following 4 tables for 30′. Compute *n–pram*.

Problem 1
2-column table
12 spaces between columns

CAR, TRUCK, AND BUS DRIVERS IN THE NORTH-CENTRAL REGION

(Estimated Total Licenses in Force)

		words
CAR, TRUCK, AND BUS DRIVERS IN THE NORTH-CENTRAL REGION		11
(Estimated Total Licenses in Force)		18
Missouri	2,874,676	22
Minnesota	2,384,410	26
Iowa	1,780,781	29
Kansas	1,593,442	33
Nebraska	1,086,797	36
South Dakota	417,071	41
North Dakota	353,574	48
	10,490,751	50

Problem 2
3-column table
Decide spacing between columns; proofread and circle errors.

ANALYSIS OF THE USES OF WORKING CAPITAL

(Rate Based on Percentage of Total Working Capital)

Account	Amount	Rate	words
ANALYSIS OF THE USES OF WORKING CAPITAL			8
(Rate Based on Percentage of Total Working Capital)			18
Account	Amount	Rate	26
Capital Expenditures	$730,000	80.7	33
Cash Dividend Payments	73,651	8.1	40
Increase in Investments	28,210	3.1	47
Intangible Assets Acquired	7,129	0.8	54
Net Increase in Long Term Receivables	3,780	0.4	64
Other Uses	10,700	1.2	68
Prepayment of Pension Costs	8,410	0.9	76
Purchase of Company's Own Stock	2,212	0.2	85
Reduction of Prior Borrowings	40,482	4.5	95
	$904,574	99.9	98

117

117a ▶5
Conditioning practice
each line 3 times (slowly, faster, in-between rate)

alphabet — Jack's brevity always complements his quietly expressed zeal for good.

fig/sym — The Persian rug (3758*--9′ x 12′) lists for $640.75 less 15% for cash.

long reaches — Cecil will bring a number of bright lights to a civic center ceremony.

fluency — The right techniques coupled with the right attitudes aid your typing.

| 1 | 2 | 3 | 4 | 5 | 6 | 7 | 8 | 9 | 10 | 11 | 12 | 13 | 14 |

117b ▶15
Improve punctuation skill: related learning
Follow standard directions.

Hyphen

16. Use the hyphen to join compound numbers from twenty-one to ninety-nine.

    Spell these numbers: forty-five, sixty-six, and ninety-three.

17. Use the hyphen to join compound adjectives preceding a noun that the adjectives modify as a unit.

    In the last five-year period, our business has increased.

18. Use the hyphen after each word or figure in a series of words or figures that modify the same noun (suspended hyphenation).

    Please check the rates on first-, second-, and third-class mail.

Parentheses

19. Use parentheses to enclose parenthetical or explanatory matter and added information. (Commas or dashes may also be used.) Note: When parentheses apply to the entire sentence, the closing parenthesis is placed outside the closing punctuation, as above.

    We are enclosing the contracts (Exhibit A).

20. Use parentheses to enclose identifying letters or figures in lists.

    He stressed two factors: (1) speed and (2) accuracy.

21. Use parentheses to enclose figures that follow spelled-out amounts for added clarity or emphasis. Enclose the appropriate item:

    I agreed to pay the sum of three hundred (300) dollars.
    I agreed to pay the sum of three hundred dollars ($300).

Underline

22. Use the underline with titles of complete works such as books, magazines, and newspapers. (Such titles may be typed in ALL CAPS without the underline.)

    The new book Learning How to Learn was reviewed in Harper's.

23. Use the underline (or you may use quotation marks) to call attention to special words or phrases. Note: Use a continuous underline unless each word is to be considered separately.

    Type fast and accurately.
    Please do not start typing until the signal is given.

Save sheet for *Typewriting Manual.*

165d ▶30 Type 4-column tables

full sheets; reading position; DS body of tables

Problem 1
Arrange and center the table at the right; center by column headings.

Problem 2
Retype the table; center according to longest entry in each column.

EXAMPLES OF SECURITIES WITH HIGH RETURNS (8)

(Based on Latest Dividends Reported) (16)

Common and Preferred Stocks	Dividend	Price	Yield	words
American Can	$2.40	$28.88	8.3%	38
American Electric Power	2.00	18.88	10.6	46
Beneficial Corporation	2.50	24.00	10.4	54
Borg-Warner	1.35	17.00	7.9	60
Commonwealth Edison	2.00	21.25	9.4	67
General Motors	5.00	62.75	8.0	73
Gulf Oil	1.70	20.50	8.3	79
Kaiser Aluminum & Chemical	2.38	39.50	6.0	87
Liggett & Meyers	2.50	29.25	8.5	94
Norfolk & Western Railway	5.00	63.25	7.9	102

(Column headings line: 32 words)

166

166a ▶5 Conditioning practice

each line 3 times SS (slowly, faster, slowly); DS between 3-line groups

Peggy and Franz will back the council vote on the major tax questions.
Net sales from July 1, 1975, to June 30, 1976, increased 28.4 percent.
Over <u>any</u> 3-to-6-year period between now and 1980, we expect a <u>7% gain</u>.
Henry laid eight bushels of corn on the sod by the dock for the ducks.

| 1 | 2 | 3 | 4 | 5 | 6 | 7 | 8 | 9 | 10 | 11 | 12 | 13 | 14 |

166b ▶10 Improve skill transfer

1. A 1′ writing on each line; determine *gwam*.

2. Type additional writings on slower lines.

		words
straight copy	Probe to find and to analyze the cause of any typing errors.	12
script	*Sellers should be able to display their individual products.*	12
statistical	Today's indexes: volume 19,206, utilities 35.7, bonds 48.2.	12
rough-draft	failureto deleagate power is the caause of amny problems. (corrections: capitalize F, insert space #, delete a, delete a, insert "our" for "amny")	12

166c ▶35 Sustained production: tables

1. Make a list of the problems identified at the right.

page 266, 162d, Problem 2
page 267, 163d, Problem 2
page 269, 165d, Problem 2

2. As you are timed for 30′, type as many of the problems as you can. Compute *n–pram*.

117c ▶30 Build sustained production skill: tabulation

Time schedule
Planning and preparing .. 6′
Production timing .... 20′
Proofreading; computing *g-pram* .... 4′

Type a 20′ sustained production writing on the problems given below. If you complete the problems before time is called, start over. Plan and prepare for each problem with a minimum of waste time. Have needed materials ready so you can move quickly from one problem to the next.

Problem 1
full sheet; DS data; center vertically, reading position; 16 spaces between columns

Alertness cue: Reset tab stop for Column 2 as needed.

Problem 2
Retype Problem 1, but center vertically in exact center.

Problem 3
Retype Problem 1 with these changes: half sheet, short side up; DS data; center vertically; 8 spaces between columns.

DECIBEL SCALE* (words total: 3)

Type of Sound	Decibels	words in cols.	words total
			12
Thunder, jet planes	120	5	17
Nearby riveter	110	9	21
Loud street noise	100	13	25
Unmuffled truck	90	17	29
Police whistle	80	20	33
Average street noise	70	25	37
Noisy home	60	28	40
Average conversation	50	33	45
Quiet home	40	36	48
Private office	30	39	51
Quiet conversation	20	44	56
Whisper	10	46	58
Threshold of audibility	0	51	63

_____________ 67

Type the footnote the width of the table.

*A decibel is a measure of noise level. 75
Each increase of 6 decibels corresponds to 84
a doubling of the noise-pressure level. 91

Problem 4
half sheet, short side up; DS data; center vertically; 10 spaces between columns

Note: The dollar sign may be placed one space to the left of the horizontal beginning point of the longest line in the column, or it may be placed next to the first digit of the top figure in the column, whether or not this is the longest line in the column.

PORTRAITS ON U.S. CURRENCY (words total: 5)

Amount	Portrait on Face	words in cols.	words total
			15
$1	Washington	3	18
2	Jefferson	5	20
5	Lincoln	7	22
10	Hamilton	10	24
20	Jackson	12	27
50	Grant	14	28
100	Franklin	16	31
500	McKinley	19	34
1,000	Cleveland	22	37
5,000	Madison	25	40
10,000	Chase	27	42
100,000*	Wilson	31	45

_____________ 49

*Used only in transactions be- 55
tween Federal Reserve System 61
and Treasury Department. 66

164c ▶35
Type 3-column tables with column headings

Problem 1
full sheet; DS
Center by longest item in each column; 14 spaces between Columns 1 and 2; 10 spaces between Columns 2 and 3.

Problem 2
Retype Table 2 of 163d, page 267, adding the following headings:
Col. 1: **State**
Col. 2: **Low**
Col. 3: **High**

APPROXIMATE DISTANCES BETWEEN NEW YORK AND SELECTED CITIES

(0.6 Conversion Factor Used from Kilometer to Mile)

City	Kilometers	Miles	words
			8
			12
			22
			30
Boston	315	189	34
Detroit	782	469	38
Houston	2 265	1,359	42
Los Angeles	3 925	2,355	47
Miami	1 750	1,050	51
New Orleans	1 880	1,128	55
St. Louis	1 410	846	60
San Francisco	4 118	2,471	65
Seattle	3 850	2,310	69

style for metric measurement omits the comma and substitutes space

165

165a ▶5
Conditioning practice

each line 3 times SS (slowly, faster, slowly); DS between 3-line groups

Gloria and Fritz quietly enjoyed the massive sculpture work exhibited.
These 96 buildings house 1,420 offices, 387 apartments, and 51 stores.
F & D Brokers, Inc., quoted the Krugerrand at $171.75 (as of 8-17-75).
The firm may risk title to the lake and to the dock with a proxy vote.
| 1 | 2 | 3 | 4 | 5 | 6 | 7 | 8 | 9 | 10 | 11 | 12 | 13 | 14 |

165b ▶8
Drill on column headings

Review centering and tabulating in Reference Guide, page x. Then type the drills shown at the right as directed below.
Drill 1
Center by column entries.
Drill 2
Center by column headings.
Drill 3
Center by longest item in each column, whether a heading or an entry. **Note:** This procedure should be used in future problems unless otherwise specified.

Drill 1

Licenses	Revenue	City
120,586	$27,506,325	Philadelphia

Drill 2

Table Reference	Average Charge per Year	Median Value
614	29.6%	$24,210

Drill 3

Period	Total Kilometers	Average Cost per Kilometer
May 1-May 31	185	$1.72

165c ▶7
Improve centering/tabulating

1. Arrange and type the headings and the first two lines of Problem 1, 164c.

2. A 2′ writing on headings and first two or more lines of the problem.

118

118a ▶5 Conditioning practice

each line 3 times (slowly, faster, in-between rate)

alphabet We've frequently seen big jets zoom past exactly like birds in flight.
fig/sym Was the total of Hartley & Mann's bill $1,586.73, or was it $2,490.75?
space bar Please pay the men for all this work and then send me the bill for it.
fluency Education discloses to the wise not how much they know but how little.

| 1 | 2 | 3 | 4 | 5 | 6 | 7 | 8 | 9 | 10 | 11 | 12 | 13 | 14 |

118b ▶15 Improve punctuation skill: related learning

Follow standard directions.

Quotation Marks

24. Use quotation marks to enclose direct quotations. Note: When a question mark applies to the entire sentence, it is typed outside the quotation mark.

    She asked, "When did the shipment arrive?"
    Was it Emerson who said, "To have a friend is to be one"?

25. Use quotation marks to enclose titles of articles and other parts of complete publications, short poems, song titles, television programs, and unpublished works like theses and dissertations.

    I read the article "The Next Twenty Years."
    Children enjoy watching "Sesame Street."

26. Use quotation marks to enclose special words or phrases for emphasis or coined words (words not in dictionary usage).

    I have "limited resources" and "unlimited wants."
    His mother "chicken-souped" him whenever he had a cold.

27. Use single quotation marks (the apostrophe) to indicate a quotation within a quotation.

    He said, "We must have, as Tillich said, 'the courage to be.'"

Semicolon

28. Use a semicolon to separate two or more independent clauses in a compound sentence when the conjunction is omitted.

    To be critical is easy; to be constructive is not so easy.

29. Use a semicolon to separate independent clauses when they are joined by a conjunctive adverb (however, consequently, etc.).

    They did not follow directions; consequently, they got lost.

30. Use a semicolon to separate a series of phrases or clauses (especially if they contain commas) that are introduced by a colon.

    Our sales were: 1976, $1,250,984; 1977, $2,302,850.

31. Place the semicolon outside a closing quotation mark; the period, inside the quotation mark.

    Mr. Carr spoke on "Building Speed"; Mr. Bronski, on "Accuracy."

Apostrophe

32. Use the apostrophe as a symbol for feet in billings or tabulations or as a symbol for minutes. (The quotation mark may be used as a symbol for inches or seconds.)

    The room was listed as 12'6" x 16'. He ran the mile in 3'54".

Save sheet for *Typewriting Manual.*

163d ▶25
Type 3-column tables

Problem 1

half sheet, long side up; exact vertical center; SS body of table; 6 spaces between columns

words

CURRENT CROP FORECAST 4

(Based on Conditions as of August 1) 12

			words
Corn	5.85 billion bushels	26% increase	20
Cotton	9.40 million bales	18% decrease	28
Soybeans	1.46 billion bushels	18% increase	36
Tobacco	2.22 billion pounds	12% increase	44
Wheat	2.14 billion bushels	19% increase	52

Problem 2

half sheet, short side up; reading position; DS body of table; decide spacing between columns

Problem 3

retype Problem 1 on a full sheet; DS body of table; decide spacing between columns

words

LOW AND HIGH TEMPERATURE RECORDS 7
SELECTED THROUGH 1972 11

(National Weather Service) 16

			words
Alabama	−27	112	20
California	−45	134	23
Hawaii	18	100	26
Montana	−70	117	29
Texas	−23	120	32
Washington	−48	118	36

164

164a ▶5
Conditioning practice

each line 3 times SS (slowly, faster, slowly); DS between 3-line groups

An oversized lady quickly jumped from her box seat to watch the fight.
The index slipped 0.79 point to 86.34, as sales hit 13,725,000 shares.
A shipment of 13,648# of peanuts (totaling $10,368) was not delivered.
Both of the firms may fight with vigor an amendment to the audit rule.

| 1 | 2 | 3 | 4 | 5 | 6 | 7 | 8 | 9 | 10 | 11 | 12 | 13 | 14 |

164b ▶10
Learn to proofread figures

1. Type a copy of the ¶ at the right.

2. Proofread your copy as directed in the ¶.

If possible, verify statistical copy by reading aloud to a co-worker. Read each punctuation mark and special symbol individually. Read figures, however, in groups: read 4719 as _forty-seven-nineteen_; read 1,562 as _one-comma-five-sixty-two_. Read 0 (the number) as _oh_ and the decimal point as _point_. Read .00068 as _point-oh-oh-oh-sixty-eight._ Type and then proofread the following series of figures: 1705; 25,834; .0069; 42.79; 6.08.

118c ▶30 Measure production skill: tabulation

Time schedule
Planning and preparing .. 6′
Production timing .... 20′
Proofreading; computing *n-pram* .... 4′

Erase and correct all errors. If you complete the problem before time is called, start over on a new sheet.

Proofread your work. Determine *n-pram*. (Deduct 15 words from total words for each uncorrected error; divide remainder by 20.)

full sheet; DS data; center vertically; 4 spaces between columns

Note: Longest entry in each column is color underlined for easy identification.

NEW CLIENTS

Name	Street	City, State, ZIP Code	words in cols.	total
				2
Name	Street	City, State, ZIP Code		15
Mr. James Allen	5416 Fairview Ave.	Boise, ID 83704	10	26
Mrs. Colette Berman	248 E. Capital	Jackson, MS 39201	21	36
Dr. Lyn Clark	515 Marquette Ave.	Minneapolis, MN 55402	32	47
Dr. James E. Deitz	220 Ward Parkway	Kansas City, MO 64112	43	59
Mrs. Mercedes Henderson	3902 Dodge Ave.	Omaha, NE 68131	55	70
Mr. Steven Husted, Jr.	1033 Madeira Drive	Albuquerque, NM 87108	67	83
Ms. Shirley Jones	3525 Tates Creek Road	Lexington, KY 40502	79	95
Mrs. Rosalyn Kalmar	636 S. Michigan Ave.	Chicago, IL 60605	91	107
Ms. Barbara Locke	600 Fremont Ave.	Las Vegas, NV 89101	102	118
Mr. Claude Martinez	1911 House Ave.	Durham, NC 27707	113	128
Mr. Thomas McDonnell	14041 East Light St.	Whittier, CA 90605	125	140
Mr. Ronald Minske	323 Franklin	Manchester, NH 03101	135	151
Mrs. Vivian Neches	1500 Pine Valley	Ann Arbor, MI 48104	147	162
Mrs. Carol O'Brien	659 Peachtree, N.E.	Atlanta, GA 30383	158	173
Miss Wilma Oksendahl	509 University Ave.	Honolulu, HI 96814	170	185
Miss Janice Quon	319 W. 48th St.	New York, NY 10036	180	196
Dr. James Stiehl	485 Cumberland Ave.	Portland, ME 04101	192	207
Mr. S. Edward Tomaso	11 Ashburton Place	Boston, MA 02108	203	218
Miss Cristy Young	7301 Park Heights Ave.	Baltimore, MD 21208	215	230
Mrs. Zelda Zinke	1150 Boyd Ave.	Baton Rouge, LA 70802	226	241

119

119a ▶5 Conditioning practice

each line 3 times (slowly, faster, in-between rate)

alphabet Fools won't likely adopt the unique economizing objectives of experts.
fig/sym He thought $37.96 too much for a 150# bag of sugar and offered $32.84.
even stroking Please make the address corrections on all the old computer printouts.
fluency The more that is left to chance, the less chance there is for success.

| 1 | 2 | 3 | 4 | 5 | 6 | 7 | 8 | 9 | 10 | 11 | 12 | 13 | 14 |

162d ▶20 Type 2-column tables

half sheets, long side up; exact center;
DS body of tables; 12 spaces between columns

Problem 1

SPACING MEASUREMENTS FOR TYPEWRITING

(Vertical and Horizontal Summary)

Pica spaces to a horizontal inch	10
Elite spaces to a horizontal inch	12
Pica spaces to an 8 1/2″ line	85
Elite spaces to an 8 1/2″ line	102
Vertical lines to an 11″ sheet (pica/elite)	66
Vertical lines to a 5 1/2″ (half) sheet	33

Problem 2

		words
DISTINGUISHED BLACK AMERICANS		6
(Selected for Outstanding Achievement)		14
Mary McLeod Bethune	Educator	19
Ralph Bunche	Diplomat	24
George Washington Carver	Scientist	31
Matthew Henson	Explorer	36
Henry Johnson	Soldier	40
Martin Luther King, Jr.	Civil Rights Leader	49
Thurgood Marshall	Supreme Court Justice	57
Willard Townsend	Labor Leader	63

163

163a ▶5 Conditioning practice

each line 3 times SS
(slowly, faster, slowly);
DS between 3-line groups

A few citizens jokingly explained the circumstances verified in Quebec.
A review of 19,287 shares traded indicated 635 stocks down and 504 up.
Weekly retail sales (seasonally adjusted) grew 0.5% to $1,148 million.
Their theory is to handle key problems and to form sound social goals.

| 1 | 2 | 3 | 4 | 5 | 6 | 7 | 8 | 9 | 10 | 11 | 12 | 13 | 14 |

163b ▶10 Improve skill transfer

1. A 1′ writing on each line; determine *gwam*.
2. Additional typings on the slower lines.

Enrichment material for Unit 27 appears on LM p. 25.

		words
straight copy	All the original problems in their theory have been handled.	12
script	Learn to observe the needs and wants of your fellow workers.	12
statistical	The map indicated 5,043 cities, 1,297 lakes, and 186 rivers.	12
rough-draft	an air of alretness is patr of the immage your must project. (handwritten corrections: should)	12

163c ▶10 Improve technique: centering/tabulating

1. Set left margin and a tab stop to type Problem 2 of 162d, above.

2. Center horizontally on a half sheet the headings of Problem 2 in 162d, above.

3. A 2′ writing on the headings and first two or more lines of Problem 2 of 162d, above.

119b ▶15 Improve punctuation skill: related learning

Follow standard directions.

33. Use the apostrophe as a symbol to indicate the omission of letters or figures (as in contractions).

    The "Spirit of '76" pervaded the Bicentennial Celebration.
    She won't be in class today.

34. Use the apostrophe and s to form the plural of most figures, letters, and words (6's, A's, five's). In market quotations, form the plural of figures by the addition of s only.

    Your f's look like 7's.
    Boston Fund 4s are due in 1990.

35. To show possession, add the apostrophe and s to (a) a singular noun and (b) a plural noun which does not end in s.

    A boy's bicycle was found, but the men's shoes are missing.

36. To show possession, add the apostrophe and s to a proper name of one syllable which ends in s.

    Please pay Jones's bill for $230 today.

37. To show possession, add only the apostrophe after (a) plural nouns ending in s and (b) a proper name of more than one syllable which ends in s or z.

    The girls' camp counselor will visit the Adams' home soon.
    Mrs. Fritts's secretary dialed Mrs. Perez' number.

38. To show possession, add the apostrophe after the last noun in a series to indicate joint or common possession by two or more persons. Note: Separate possession by two or more persons is indicated by adding the possessive to each of the nouns; as, the manager's and the treasurer's reports.

    I read about Lewis and Clark's expedition.

End of Series 4. Save sheets for *Typewriting Manual*.

119c ▶30 Improve tabulating skill: applications

Problem 1

half sheet, long side up; SS data; center vertically; 10 spaces between Column 1 and the Column 2 heading, 6 spaces between headings for Columns 2 and 3; center columnar data below the Column 2 and 3 headings.

Note: When 2 or more columns of a table are closely related, leave fewer spaces between them than you leave between other columns. This spacing emphasizes the relationship.

Problems 2, 3 appear on page 197.

CENTS–PER–MILE CAR COST*

(Annual Mileage of 10,000 Miles)

Size of Car	Low-Cost Range	High-Cost Range	words in col.	words total
				5
				12
				28
Subcompact	10.6	15.5	4	32
Compact	12.1	17.9	8	36
Intermediate	15.2	21.0	12	41
Standard	16.4	23.2	16	44
				48

*Includes both variable and fixed costs. (57)

Source: American Automobile Association. (65)

unit **27** lessons 162–167

Building table typing competence

Learning goals
In this unit you will review the procedure for planning and typing tables, develop skill in centering main, secondary, and column headings, and build competence in table production.

Machine adjustments

1. Paper guide on *0*.

2. Ribbon control on black.

3. Margin stops: 70-space line for drills and ¶s; as required for problems.

4. Line-space selector on *1* for drills; on *2* for ¶s; as directed for problems.

162

162a ▶5 Conditioning practice

each line 3 times SS (slowly, faster, slowly); DS between 3-line groups

alphabet Ray Pizlo became quite sick Friday from jogging over to the next town.

figures The 405 members voted 267 to 138 to delay the tax increase until 1982.

fig/sym Our new dealership (T & T Agency) sold 157 new cars and 246 used cars.

fluency The duty of the auditor is to sign the final audit forms for the city.

| 1 | 2 | 3 | 4 | 5 | 6 | 7 | 8 | 9 | 10 | 11 | 12 | 13 | 14 |

162b ▶13 Compose as you type

1. Read the ¶s of 160b, page 263; noting the main points or ideas.

2. On a plain sheet, center on Line 10 the heading
FIRST IMPRESSIONS

3. Compose a 2-paragraph statement about the relationship between appearance and quality of work.

162c ▶12 Report on typing tables

Margins
top: 2″
sides: 1″

5-space indentions; DS ¶s; SS enumerated items, DS between them

Neatly arranged table

EXAMPLES OF SECURITIES WITH HIGH RETURNS
(Based on Latest Dividends Reported)

Common and Preferred Stocks	Dividend	Price	Yield
American Can	$2.40	$28.88	8.3%
American Electric Power	2.00	18.88	10.6
Beneficial Corporation	2.50	24.00	10.4
Borg-Warner	1.35	17.00	7.9
Commonwealth Edison	2.00	21.25	9.4
General Motors	5.00	62.75	8.0
Gulf Oil	1.70	20.50	8.3
Kaiser Aluminum & Chemical	2.38	39.50	6.0
Liggett & Meyers	2.50	29.25	8.5
Norfolk & Western Railway	5.00	63.25	7.9

words

CENTERING SUMMARY 4

Centering involves the orderly arrangement of data. Information must be presented conveniently and clearly to the reader. Apply the following basic guides to vertical centering and spacing: 18 32 42

1. Exact center--count total lines used, including blank lines; subtract from total lines available; divide remainder by 2. 57 67

2. Reading position--subtract 2 from exact center. (See 1, above.) 81

3. Double-space between main and secondary headings; triple-space between last line of heading and first line of columns. 95 106

Horizontal spacing and alignment contributes to the usefulness of a table. To avoid retyping, plan a table before starting to type. As you plan your work, follow these procedures: 120 135 143

1. Clear all margin and tab stops. 150

2. Backspace from center once for each 2 strokes in longest line of each column, then for each 2 spaces between columns. Set left margin. 165 178

3. Space forward once for each stroke in the first column and once for each space between Columns 1 and 2--set tab. Follow this procedure to set tab stops for the remaining columns. 193 206 215

119c, continued

Problem 2

half sheet, long side up; SS data; center vertically; 4 spaces between columns

Use line finder (ratchet release) to position the paper for typing the second of the double underlines.

Alertness cue: Reset tab stops for Columns 2, 3, and 4 for most frequently occurring items; then forward space or backspace as required.

AVERAGE ANNUAL LIVING COST
IN URBAN UNITED STATES*

(Family of Four)

Item	Low	Average	High	words in cols.	total
					5
					10
					14
Item	Low	Average	High		22
Food and beverages	$2,058	$ 2,673	$ 3,370	8	30
Housing	1,554	2,810	4,234	13	35
Transportation	546	979	1,270	19	41
Clothing and personal care	864	1,217	1,770	28	49
Medical care	629	632	659	33	54
Other goods and services	378	702	1,159	41	62
Taxes	992	1,857	3,129	45	67
Misc. (life insurance, etc.)	365	576	967	57	79
Indent 5 → Total	$7,386	$11,446	$16,558	70	96
______________					99
* Estimate of dollar amount required at each level of living.					112

Problem 3

Retype Problem 2 with these changes: full sheet, reading position. DS data—substituting the data at the right for Columns 2, 3, 4, and the footnote.

Use Problem 2 for copy for headings and Column 1. Leave 6 spaces between columns.

Be alert as you retype table with new data.

(The word count includes all copy typed to that point.)

Low	Average	High	words in cols.	total
Low	Average	High		22
27.9	23.4	20.3	7	28
21.0	24.6	25.6	11	33
7.4	8.6	7.7	17	39
11.7	10.6	10.7	26	47
8.5	5.5	4.0	31	53
5.1	6.1	7.0	39	61
5.0	5.0	5.8	44	65
13.4	16.2	18.9	55	77
100.0	100.0	100.0	65	87

Footnote:
* Estimate of percent of budget required at each level of living.
(17 words, including the divider line)

120

120a ▶5 Conditioning practice

each line 3 times (slowly, faster, in-between rate)

alphabet James saw a big gray fox move quickly along a building near the plaza.
fig/sym This rug (12′ x 13′6″) was $417.90, but it is now on sale for $381.50.
shift key Jack Flood, Mary E. Langs, and C. O. Quaile work for Black & Williams.
fluency It is easier to make the figure-key reaches if the fingers are curved.

| 1 | 2 | 3 | 4 | 5 | 6 | 7 | 8 | 9 | 10 | 11 | 12 | 13 | 14 |

120b ▶7 Improve accuracy

Type a 1′ writing on each sentence of 120a.

Goal: Not over 1 error in each writing.

120c ▶8 Build tabulating skill

full sheet

1. Quickly determine left margin stop and tab stops for column data only of Problem 2 above (10 spaces between columns).

2. Type four 1′ writings on data of columns only. Start about 1″ from top edge of sheet. If you complete columns, start over.

Goal: To increase speed with each writing.

161

161a ▶5 Conditioning practice

Repeat 160a, page 263.

161b ▶10 Measure basic skill

Repeat 160b, page 263.

161c ▶35 Measure production skill: letters

3 letterheads [LM pp. 17-22];
1 cc and envelope for each letter;
proofread; correct errors; 30′ timing;
compute *n-pram* (see page 263)

Problem 1
Block style, open punctuation

	words
Current date Mrs. Marie Oldham, Office Man-	9
ager Kosho Oshiro & Company, Inc. 1320 S.W.	18
Broadway Portland, OR 97201 Dear Mrs. Old-	26
ham Subject: The Way to Get Ahead (¶ 1) The	34
way to get ahead is to work with the company,	44
not against it. This should be obvious, but it	53
often isn't. In almost every firm there are	62
people who don't understand why they weren't	71
promoted, or why they didn't receive a raise.	81
They think they have worked hard--yet the	89
truth is that they have played against the team,	100
not with it. (¶ 2) If you tell them this, they are	110
apt to deny it hotly. That's why we created the	120
enclosed booklet, The Way to Get Ahead--so all	133
workers can examine their own conduct in the	142
privacy of their own thoughts. (¶ 3) All who go	151
to work for your company should receive a copy	160
of this booklet. It will help them get started on	171
the right track. Those who are truly interested	180
in getting ahead should reread it now and	189
then--just to be sure they are still on the	198
beam. (¶ 4) To order copies, just check how	205
many on the enclosed card and drop it in the	214
mail. Your booklets will be shipped immedi-	223
ately. Sincerely yours WORD PROCESSING	231
SYSTEMS, INC. Jack V. Story, Manager Educa-	239
tional Services xx Enclosures (184)	*245/**265**

***Note:** The first figure is the count for the letter; the second includes the count for the envelope.

Problem 2
Modified block, mixed punctuation

	words
Current date Creighton Loan Company Fifth	9
and Main Streets Roswell, NM 88201 Attention	18
Ms. Effie Jackson Ladies and Gentlemen: (¶ 1)	26
Your order for CENTURY file guides, cards,	35
folders, and labels is being sent to you today by	45
Intercity Delivery Service. (¶ 2) We believe	53
that you will be as well pleased with the	61
efficiency and economy of these top-quality	70
materials as we are to welcome you to our	78
ever-growing family of CENTURY users. Cus-	87
tomer satisfaction is our greatest asset, and you	97
can be sure that through our products and our	106
service we shall try with each order to increase	116
your confidence in us. (¶ 3) Thank you for order-	124
ing CENTURY filing supplies. Your next order	133
will assure us that this "test run" pleased you.	143
We hope it will be soon. Sincerely yours, CEN-	153
TURY SUPPLY COMPANY Gene E. Studer	160
Assistant Sales Manager xx (122)	165/**183**

Problem 3
Modified block, indented ¶s, mixed punctuation

	words
Current date Miss Margaret Wilson Route #1,	9
Box 295 Joplin, MO 64801 Dear Miss Wilson:	18
(¶ 1) You will be glad to know that you have	26
been awarded advanced placement in both	34
typewriting and shorthand. The results of your	43
performance tests place you in our advanced	52
typewriting program and in the intermediate	60
course in shorthand. With advanced standing in	70
these basic skills courses, you will have the	79
opportunity to take courses in office proce-	88
dures, secretarial administration, and personal	97
development and to participate in our work-	106
experience program in local offices. (¶ 2) Your	114
performance score on the accounting test, un-	123
fortunately, does not qualify you for advanced	133
standing. Nevertheless, we have a special re-	142
fresher course in accounting principles that	151
will hasten your completion of our accounting	160
requirement. (¶ 3) We are looking forward to	168
having you with us when the new term begins	177
soon. Cordially yours, Ms. Gwen McNeely	185
Director of Admissions xx cc Mr. John B.	193
Phillips (160)	195/**206**

120d ▶30 Improve tabulating skill: applications

Problem 1
Table with leaders*

full sheet; reading position; space data as shown; 20 spaces between columns; leave 2 spaces after last leader

Problem 2
Build skill

Retype Problem 1 with these changes: half sheet, short side up; exact center; 10 spaces between columns; omit leaders.

EDUCATION AND LIFETIME EARNINGS (DS)

(Full-time Male Workers, 18 Years and Over) (TS)

Grade Completed	Earnings	words in cols.	total
			6
			15
			25
Elementary School:		4	29
Less than 8 years . . . . (Indent 3)	$297,997	13	38
8 years	343,730	22	47
High School:		25	50
1 to 3 years	389,208	34	59
4 years	478,873	44	68
College:		46	70
1 to 3 years	543,435	55	79
4 years	710,569	64	89
5 years or more	823,759	73	98
All Education Groups	$470,795	83	108
________________			111
Source: Bureau of the Census.			117

* Leaders (made by alternating the period and the space) are sometimes used to connect typed material. When typing leaders, note on line-of-writing scale whether you strike the first period on an odd or an even number; then strike all periods for additional lines on either odd or even numbers to align them vertically. Use left first finger on space bar.

121

121a ▶5 Conditioning practice

each line 3 times (slowly, faster, in-between rate)

alphabet: Six big rocket ships unlawfully zoomed over the new project equipment.

fig/sym: The 5 reams of 8 1/2" x 11" paper (24#) on Order 179 will cost $16.30.

shift key: Order the Damp Proof Red Primer from Bartons & Delaney, New York, N.Y.

fluency: They may do the problems for us when the city auditor signs the forms.

| 1 | 2 | 3 | 4 | 5 | 6 | 7 | 8 | 9 | 10 | 11 | 12 | 13 | 14 |

121b ▶7 Improve accuracy

Type a 1' writing on each sentence of 121a.

Goal: Not over 1 error in each writing.

121c ▶8 Build tabulating skill

Type two 3' writings on data in columns only, plus leaders, in 120d, Problem 1, above.

1. Determine quickly left margin stop and tab stops for columns. Start typing about 1" from top of sheet (do not center vertically).

2. If you complete columns, start over.

160

160a ▶5 Conditioning practice

each line 3 times SS (slowly, faster, slowly); DS between 3-line groups

Dave Bell quickly jumped for joy when the A's won the zany sixth game.
Our warehouse stored 205 tables, 183 chairs, 69 lamps, and 47 mirrors.
Shipment 21467 of 158 cartons of books (7300#) left Pier 18 on 9/3/76.
You did tell us that a big majority of the members like the amendment.

| 1 | 2 | 3 | 4 | 5 | 6 | 7 | 8 | 9 | 10 | 11 | 12 | 13 | 14 |

160b ▶10 Measure basic skill: straight copy

a 5′ writing; determine *gwam*; circle errors

all letters used | A | 1.5 si | 5.6 awl | 80% hfw |

	gwam 5′
First impressions are quite important. When a person is introduced	3
to you, you are apt to form a judgment about him instantly. The decision	6
may not stay with you, for a later action may modify your opinion. The	9
first reaction, though, may lead you to consent to or refuse an offer	11
involving the person to whom you were just introduced.	14
First impressions are vital in the appearance of a letter, too. If	16
someone were to get from you an application letter with messy erasures,	19
misspelled words, or bad placement, the impression might lose a job for	22
you. Perhaps you know better, but your copy may not show it. A letter	25
may also represent a company for which you work, so have it make a very	28
favorable impression.	29
To develop more effective images in the minds of the recipients of	31
your work, do every job well. No assignment is small enough for you to	34
complete it sloppily. The impressions made by small tasks may be just as	37
important as are those made by much larger ones. Demonstrate daily your	40
zeal for doing both small and large jobs exceptionally well.	42

gwam 5′ | 1 | 2 | 3 |

160c ▶35 Build sustained production skill: letters

4 letterheads [LM pp. 9-16]
1 cc and an envelope for each letter; proofread; correct errors

Begin with Problem 1, 159c, page 262. Type as many letters as you can in 30′. Compute *n-pram*.

$$\text{N-PRAM (net production rate a minute)} = \frac{\textbf{gross (total) words} - \textbf{penalty}^*}{\textbf{length (in minutes) of writing}}$$

* Penalty:
Deduct 15 words
for each uncorrected error

121d ▶30 Improve tabulating skill: applications

Tryout drill

Read the directions for typing a boxed table. As a tryout drill on a separate sheet, use the table below and follow Steps 2–7; then type horizontal rulings as directed in Step 8.

Repeat, if necessary, until you understand the procedure.

Follow these steps:

1. Determine vertical placement disregarding horizontal rulings. Your count of lines used for table, including blank lines, should be 36.

2. Center main and secondary headings; then space down 4 line spaces which will position the paper for typing the year headings.

3. Determine and set left margin and tab stops in usual way.

4. Move carriage or element to first tab stop and type year headings as shown—be sure you are on 4th line space below the secondary heading.

5. Center and type the primary headings (Male, Female) 1 space above the year headings.

6. Space down to year heading position. Starting at left margin stop, type first column heading ½ space above year heading horizontal position. Use ratchet release and roll paper back (down) the extra ½ space. When you have typed first–column heading, return ratchet release to normal position.

7. Space down even with year headings, then DS, and type first three entries of table as shown.

8. Type the horizontal rulings, using the underline key. Start the horizontal ruling between the primary and secondary column headings 1 space to left of first tab stop.

Problem 1
Boxed table

full sheet; reading position; type data as shown in table; leave 2 spaces between *column headings*

1. Repeat Steps 1–7, this time typing the entire table.

2. Type horizontal rulings as directed in Step 8.

3. Rule vertical lines with a ball-point pen (see Reference Guide, page x).

Problem 2

As time permits, retype the Problem 1 table in exact vertical center.

words

PROJECTED DISTRIBUTION OF LABOR FORCE 8

DS

BY EDUCATION AND SEX 12

DS

(In Percent) 14

TS

Years of School Completed	Male			Female			words
	1980	1985	1990	1980	1985	1990	28
Elementary							30
Less than 5 years	1.6	1.1	0.7	0.9	0.6	0.4	39
5 to 7 years	3.8	2.8	2.0	2.6	1.9	1.3	48
8 years	6.1	4.7	3.7	4.4	3.3	2.5	56
High School							58
1 to 3 years	17.0	14.9	13.4	17.8	16.4	15.4	67
4 years	37.2	37.9	38.0	45.3	45.0	44.2	74
College							76
1 to 3 years	16.3	17.8	18.8	15.2	16.2	16.8	85
4 years	9.8	10.8	11.6	9.6	11.3	12.7	92
5 years or more	8.2	10.0	11.7	4.4	5.4	6.6	101

(Spacing marks: DS after heading row; DS, DS, DS within Elementary; TS before High School; DS, DS; TS before College; DS, DS, DS; SS before bottom rule; DS before source.)

Source: Bureau of Labor Statistics. 108

159c ▶35 Type business letters in various styles

plain sheets; use the Margin and Date Placement Guide (Reference Guide, p. iv); proofread and circle errors

Problem 1
Letter in block style, open punctuation

	words
Current date Mr. Carlos G. Vega Buckeye In-	9
surance Company 1501 Euclid Avenue Cleve-	17
land, OH 44115 Dear Mr. Vega Subject: Word	26
Processing Study (¶ 1) Thank you very much	33
for the courtesies extended to our Ms. Edwards	43
when she called on you last week. (¶ 2) It is	51
gratifying to know that we shall be working to-	60
gether during the next few months. I am certain	70
that the results of our efforts to reduce the cost	80
of producing memos, letters, and reports will	89
please you. (¶ 3) Ms. Edwards will give us her	97
detailed analysis of your current word process-	107
ing system and procedures. As soon as she	115
does, our staff of consultants will proceed with	125
the work of planning a word processing system	134
that will save you time, effort, and money. (¶ 4)	143
You will hear from me again within the next	152
two or three weeks. At that time, we shall have	162
some recommendations to discuss with you.	170
Sincerely yours WORD PROCESSING SYSTEMS,	179
INC. Anthony J. Romero, Assistant Manager	187
xx cc Ms. Elise Edwards (141)	*192/**209**

Problem 2
Letter in modified block style, mixed punctuation

Current date Bardach & Gerson, Inc. 1551	9
Fourth Avenue San Diego, CA 92101 Attention	17
Mrs. Phyllis Jacoby Ladies and Gentlemen:	26
(¶ 1) The enclosed brochure announces the	33
highly efficient, small-scale version of the	42
widely used INSTAMATIC Word Processing	50
System. Called the MINIMATIC, this system	59
was designed for use by small to medium-size	68
firms and for decentralized word processing	76
centers of larger ones. (¶ 2) Because the	84
full-color illustrated brochure speaks for itself,	94
you will want to study it carefully in terms of	104
your own communication needs. Then you'll	112
want to call our representative in your area	121
to discuss its potential for you. His name is	131
Gregory Tyler; his telephone number in San	139
Diego is 231-4028. Sincerely yours, Ms. Shirley	149
Simpson Advertising Manager xx Enclosure	157
(117)	***169**

Problem 3
Letter in modified block style, indented ¶s, mixed punctuation

	words
Current date Mrs. Patricia Perin Gibson-Perin	10
Associates 5619 Fannin Houston, TX 77004	18
Dear Mrs. Perin: Subject: Century Advertising	27
Campaign (¶ 1) I have studied with intense	35
interest the advertising campaign you propose	44
for CENTURY filing systems and supplies. Your	53
report is well prepared, and it shows a good	62
understanding of our products and markets.	71
(¶ 2) The sample layouts for promotion bro-	78
chures and magazine ads are cleverly devel-	87
oped. I particularly like the diagrammatic	96
drawings to show the essential features of	104
subject, geographic, and numeric files. You	113
may wish to consider, also, the use of draw-	122
ings of this type to show how these three	130
filing methods may be made an integral part of	140
a basically alphabetic system. (¶ 3) As soon as	148
we have developed some copy reflecting your	157
advertising concept, we shall want you to come	166
to Fort Worth to discuss this whole program	175
with us. It is highly important that layouts,	185
copy, and major and minor headlines be	192
carefully coordinated. (¶ 4) Will your schedule	201
permit you to make a two-day trip to Fort	209
Worth during the first week of next month? If	219
this time is not convenient, we could sched-	227
ule a conference either the week before or	236
the following week. Sincerely yours, CENTURY	245
SUPPLY COMPANY LeRoy J. Michaels, Manager	253
xx (211)	*254/**269**

***Note:** The first figure is the count for the letter; the second includes the count for the envelope.

Problem 4 (optional)
Retype Problem 1 in the style of Problem 2. Address the letter to:

Mr. Donald A. Lusk, Jr.
Luria Brothers & Co.
55 Public Square
Cleveland, OH 44113

Supply appropriate salutation.

122

122a ▶5 Conditioning practice

each line 3 times (slowly, faster, in-between rate)

alphabet	Jay will make executive organizational plans for the old Quebec firms.
fig/sym	Send Order 12801 ($4,936.70 less 15%) for 4 1/2 C&B pine via C&NW R.R.
double letters	Lesson by lesson, the necessary effort will help you boost your speed.
fluency	True merit is like a river--the deeper it is, the less noise it makes.

| 1 | 2 | 3 | 4 | 5 | 6 | 7 | 8 | 9 | 10 | 11 | 12 | 13 | 14 |

122b ▶15 Measure basic skill: straight copy

two 5′ writings; proofread, circle errors; record better rate

Technique goals

Fingers curved and upright

Snappy keystroking

Quick spacing

all letters used | A | 1.5 si | 5.6 awl | 80% hfw |

	gwam 1′	5′
There are two kinds of typists who rarely achieve in the business	13	3
office--those who cannot do what they are directed to do and those who	27	5
can do little else. One of the important things every student must learn	42	8
to do is to proofread quickly and accurately every piece of work produced	57	11
on the typewriter. The letter, report, or memorandum with every error	71	14
neatly corrected represents a pride in work that reflects to the credit	86	17
of the typist who produced it. Nearly all of us need to be reminded that	100	20
the work we produce is our personal representative in the eyes of others.	115	23
Often, it is the primary basis on which quality judgments are made.	129	26
It is important to find and correct neatly all errors before the	13	28
finished copy is given either to the teacher to check or to the execu-	27	31
tive in the business office to use. Some typists fail to find their	41	34
errors because they are careless. They often do not realize the impact	55	37
an error may have on those who evaluate the finished copy. In proof-	69	40
reading your copy, be very careful to verify the accuracy of each date,	83	42
figure, and amount. Check, too, to determine that all words are divided	98	45
correctly at the ends of lines. Then read the copy carefully to be	112	48
certain that each word is spelled correctly and that each typing error	126	51
is corrected.	128	51

gwam 1′ | 1 | 2 | 3 | 4 | 5 | 6 | 7 | 8 | 9 | 10 | 11 | 12 | 13 | 14 |
5′ | 1 | 2 | 3 |

158d ▶23
Type a letter in modified block style with indented paragraphs

plain sheets; 1½" margins; date on Line 14; ¶ indention: 5; proofread and circle errors

Problem 1
Review modified block style with indented ¶s.
Type the letter to review layout and placement.

Problem 2
Skill building on modified block style
1. Two 1' writings on opening lines (date through salutation); determine *gwam*.
2. Two 1' writings on closing lines (complimentary close through cc notation); determine *gwam*.
3. A 5' writing on entire letter; determine *gwam*; circle errors.

	words parts	5' gwam
Current date Miss Ida Mae Mathis 859 West Eighth Street Ponca	13	3
City, OK 74601 Dear Miss Mathis:	20	4
(¶ 1) Thank you for requesting information about our shorthand pro-		6
gram. I am pleased to send you the information you wanted about		9
advanced placement.		10
(¶ 2) We hope you are one of those students who can be given		12
advanced placement, for it is our policy to take each student where		15
she is and move her along as quickly as possible. On the other hand,		18
we never like to place any student in our program at a level that is		20
beyond her current level of ability. That is why we have a placement		23
testing service.		24
(¶ 3) I am enclosing a brochure that describes our placement testing		26
service and lists all the requirements for advanced standing in our		29
accounting, shorthand, and typing courses.		31
(¶ 4) If you have any questions after you have studied the brochure,		33
please give me the opportunity to answer them for you. We should		36
like to see you here at Phillips when the new term opens.		38
Cordially yours, Ms. Gwen McNeely Director of Admissions xx	12	41
Enclosure cc Mr. John B. Phillips	19	42

159

159a ▶5
Conditioning practice

each line 3 times SS (slowly, faster, slowly); DS between 3-line groups

Frank Lowe gave a quick report on rockets that just amazed Boyd Nixon.
He will print 173 calendars, 850 cards, 96 leaflets, and 24 circulars.
Order 21846 (File 957-20) must be shipped to Day & O'Dell by March 31.
Many of their problems need to be thought through to a final solution.
| 1 | 2 | 3 | 4 | 5 | 6 | 7 | 8 | 9 | 10 | 11 | 12 | 13 | 14 |

159b ▶10
Letter and address placement

1. Study Special Letter Placement Points, page iv of the Reference Guide, prior to typing the letters in 159c.
2. Study Addressing Envelopes, page vi of the Reference Guide, prior to typing the letters of 159c.
3. Study the tips for arranging completed work as illustrated at the right.

Step 1
Remove letter from typewriter; address an envelope; place letter under envelope flap.

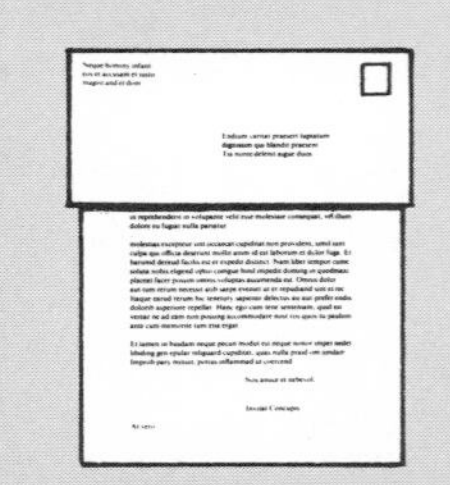

Step 2
Place letter and envelope face down on desk.

Step 3
When work is to be turned in, turn stack face up and your work will be in correct sequence.

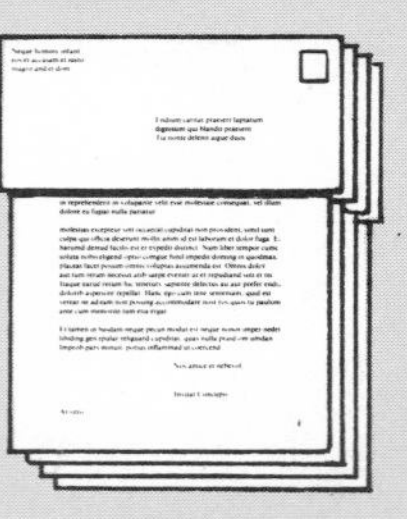

122c ▶30 Build sustained production skill: tabulation

Time schedule

Planning and preparing .. 6′
Production timing .... 20′
Proofreading; computing *g–pram* .... 4′

Type a 20′ sustained production writing on the problems given below. If you complete the problems before time is called, start over. Plan, prepare, and have needed materials ready for typing each problem. When time is called, proofread your work, circle errors, and compute *g–pram*.

Problem 1

full sheet, DS data; reading position; spaces between columns: 6–4–6–4

Alertness cue

Set tab stops for most frequently occurring items; remember to backspace or space forward as necessary.

STATE POPULATION CHANGES, 1940-1973 (words 6)

(000 Omitted) (9)

State	1973	Rank	1940	Rank	words
California	20,601	1	6,907	5	25
New York	18,265	2	13,479	1	30
Pennsylvania	11,902	3	9,900	2	36
Texas	11,794	4	6,415	6	41
Illinois	11,236	5	7,897	3	46
Ohio	10,731	6	6,908	4	51
Michigan	9,044	7	5,256	7	56
Florida	7,678	8	1,897	24	61
New Jersey	7,361	9	4,160	9	67
Massachusetts	5,818	10	4,317	8	73

(Header row: 19 words)

Problem 2

full sheet, long side up; SS data; 8 spaces between Columns 1, 2, and 3 and Column 4 *heading*

Note: Full sheets long side up provide the following spaces.

51 vertical lines
110 horizontal pica spaces
132 horizontal elite spaces

Alertness cue

Use the figures shown above in determining center points for this problem.

SELECTED MAJOR UNIVERSITIES (words 6)

Name	Location	School Colors	Enrollment	words
Arizona State	Tempe	Maroon and Gold	28,724	29
Brigham Young	Provo	Blue and White	26,515	37
California	Berkeley	Blue and Gold	26,650	45
Florida	Gainesville	Orange and Blue	28,332	54
Illinois	Champaign	Orange and Blue	35,045	62
Indiana	Bloomington	Cream and Crimson	30,623	71
Iowa	Iowa City	Old Gold and Black	23,271	80
Louisiana State	Baton Rouge	Purple and Gold	24,440	90
Michigan	Ann Arbor	Maize and Blue	35,149	98
Missouri	Columbia	Old Gold and Black	22,101	107
Nebraska	Lincoln	Scarlet and Cream	21,581	115
Ohio State	Columbus	Scarlet and Grey	49,275	124
Penn State	University Park	Blue and White	31,235	134
Tennessee	Knoxville	Orange and White	28,011	143
Texas	Austin	Orange and White	44,936	150
UCLA	Los Angeles	Blue and Gold	31,960	158
Wisconsin	Madison	Cardinal and White	36,915	166

(Header row: 20 words)

________________ 170

Source: College Blue Book, 1975. 180

158

158a ▶5 Conditioning practice

each line 3 times SS (slowly, faster, slowly); DS between 3-line groups

Jackie Darvel did type the next history quiz for Mrs. Biggs last week.
The 16 girls typed 203 letters, 45 reports, and 87 invoices on July 9.
Will she receive a discount of 2% when she pays Invoice 8470 for $935?
Did both of the lake towns face a severe fuel problem again this year?

| 1 | 2 | 3 | 4 | 5 | 6 | 7 | 8 | 9 | 10 | 11 | 12 | 13 | 14 |

158b ▶10 Proofreading: correct-it-as-you-type

1. Read the ¶, mentally noting the points where corrections are needed.

2. Type the ¶, making the noted corrections. Correct any errors you make as you type, also.

One of the many beenfits that comes from learning to typewell is the ability to compose at the type writer. Have you notice how much faster it is to put your thoughts down on paper now that you know how to type than too write everything out in long hand? being able to record your thoughts rapidly should improve your reports as well as the letters your write.

158c ▶12 Type a report on modified block style with indented paragraphs

Margins
top: 2″
side: 1″
DS the ¶s

Modified block, indented ¶s

Phillips Secretarial College
509 South Boston Avenue   Tulsa, OK 74103   (918) 251-3020

Current date

Miss Ida Mae Mathis
859 West Eighth Street
Ponca City, OK 74601

Dear Miss Mathis:

Thank you for requesting information about our shorthand program. I am pleased to send you the information you wanted about advanced placement.

We hope you are one of those students who can be given advanced placement, for it is our policy to take each student where she is and move her along as quickly as possible. On the other hand, we never like to place any student in our program at a level that is beyond her current level of ability. That is why we have a placement testing service.

I am enclosing a brochure that describes our placement testing service and lists all the requirements for advanced standing in our accounting, shorthand, and typing courses.

If you have any questions after you have studied the brochure, please give me the opportunity to answer them for you. We should like to see you here at Phillips when the new term opens.

Cordially yours,

Ms. Gwen McNeely
Director of Admissions

xx,

Enclosure

cc Mr. John B. Phillips

OTHER FEATURES OF MODIFIED BLOCK STYLE

In modified block style with indented paragraphs, the usual indention is 5 spaces; however, some companies prefer 10 spaces. When paragraphs are indented, the subject line (if any) may be indented to the same point as the paragraphs or it may be centered. All other placement points are the same as for the modified block style with block paragraphs.

Either <u>open</u> or <u>mixed</u> punctuation may be used with modified block style. With block style, however, it is customary to use open punctuation, which is in keeping with the simplicity and efficiency of the block style letter.

In <u>open</u> punctuation, no punctuation follows the salutation or the complimentary close. In <u>mixed</u> punctuation, though, a colon follows the salutation and a comma follows the complimentary close.

123

123a ▶5 Conditioning practice

each line 3 times (slowly, faster, in-between rate)

alphabet	Liquid oxygen fuel was used to give this big jet rocket amazing speed.
fig/sym	Sell Item 394* (nylon) to Browne Company at list--120 gross at $68.75.
adjacent key	Remember that courtesy is to human relations what oil is to machinery.
fluency	In life, your position is not nearly so important as your disposition.

| 1 | 2 | 3 | 4 | 5 | 6 | 7 | 8 | 9 | 10 | 11 | 12 | 13 | 14 |

123b ▶15 Measure basic skill: statistical copy

two 5′ writings; proofread and circle errors

Record better rate and % of transfer (better rate ÷ better rate of 122b, page 200).

Technique goals

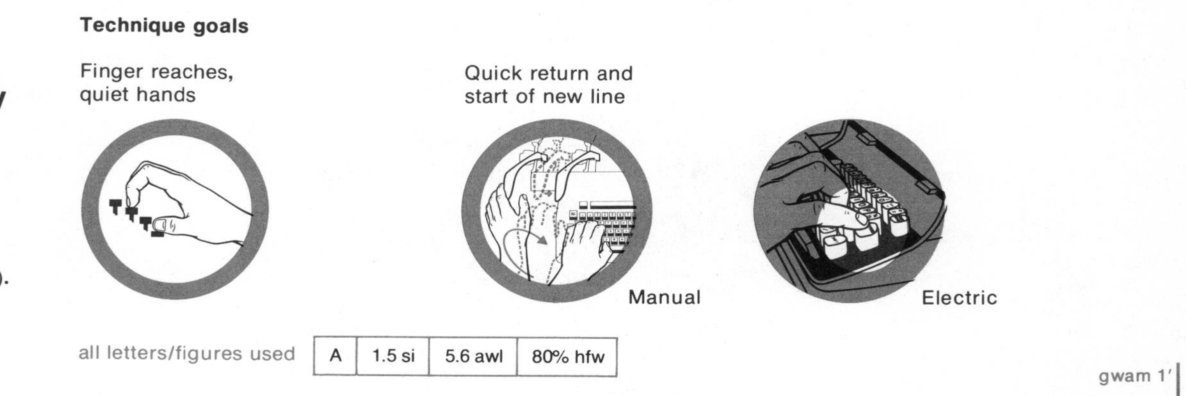

all letters/figures used | A | 1.5 si | 5.6 awl | 80% hfw |

	gwam 1′	5′
The earth has only one natural satellite, the moon. Approximately	13	3
238,850 miles separate one body from the other. The earth's diameter	27	5
is 7,926.4 miles while that of the moon is just 2,159.9 miles. It would	42	8
take 81.3 moons to equal the mass of the earth. Traveling at a speed	56	11
of 2,287 miles per hour, the moon orbits the earth entirely in 27.32	70	14
days. However, the process of change from one new moon to another re-	84	17
quires 2.21 additional days because the earth is going around the sun	98	20
during the same period. Approximately 365.25 days are needed for that	112	22
body to travel around the sun.	118	24
Only 59 percent of the moon's surface can be seen directly from the	14	26
earth. The other 41 percent was first seen in photographs taken during	28	29
a space probe in 1959. An ancient desire was finally realized when a	42	32
man walked on the moon on July 21, 1969. Sample materials taken then	56	35
and on later missions have been soil dated from 4,700 million to 4,720	70	38
million years. Without water, there is no sea level on the moon, so it	85	41
is difficult to measure mountain elevations; but some are considered to	99	43
be over 20,000 feet. The largest crater is 600 miles across and the	113	46
deepest one extends 14,000 feet below the plain.	122	48

gwam 1′ | 1 | 2 | 3 | 4 | 5 | 6 | 7 | 8 | 9 | 10 | 11 | 12 | 13 | 14 |
5′ | 1 | 2 | 3 |

157c ▶12 Type a report on modified block style

Margins
top: 2″
side: 1″
DS ¶; SS listed items,
DS between them

Modified block, mixed

CS Century Supply Company 219 North Commerce Fort Worth, TX 76102 (817) 871-5640

Current date

Central Electric Company
17 North Meridian
Indianapolis, IN 46204

Attention Purchasing Agent

Ladies and Gentlemen:

Whether it's a single letter or a whole word, you erase it neatly and quickly with the new ERASOMATIC Electronic Eraser.

It's as handy to use as a pencil. Just lift the hand-piece and it starts. Place the handpiece back on the cradle and it stops. And a special lock keeps it from being started accidentally.

When the eraser tip wears down, simply run it across the Trimmer and you have a sharp edge again. Correct tip length is maintained simply by inserting the eraser tip into the built-in Renewer.

Use the handy order card that is enclosed to order your first ERASOMATIC now. After this first tryout, you'll want one for every secretarial work station throughout your company.

Sincerely yours,

CENTURY SUPPLY COMPANY

LeRoy J. Michaels, Manager

xx

Enclosure

PLACEMENT POINTS FOR MODIFIED BLOCK LETTERS
TS

In modified block style, begin the date and closing lines at the horizontal center of the paper. Set a tab stop at the center point to speed alignment. Follow these additional placement points:

1. Type the letter address, attention line, salutation, and paragraphs at the left margin, separated by double spaces. Type the subject line, when used, either at the left margin or centered.

2. When the letter is addressed to a company, the salutation "Ladies and Gentlemen" is acceptable. If directed to the attention of an unidentified person, "Dear Sir or Madam" may be used.

3. When a company name is used in the closing lines, type it in ALL CAPS a double space below the complimentary close.

4. Type the name of the signer of the letter on the fourth line space below the complimentary close (or below the company name when one is used).

5. Type the title of the signer either on the line with the name or on the next line.

6. Type reference initials, enclosure, carbon copy, and other special notations at the left margin, separated by double spaces (in the order given).

157d ▶23 Type a letter in modified block style

plain sheets; 1½″ margins; date on Line 15; proofread and circle errors

Problem 1
Review modified block style
Type the letter to review layout and placement.

Problem 2
Skill building on modified block style

1. Two 1′ writings on opening lines (date through salutation); determine *gwam*.

2. Two 1′ writings on closing lines (complimentary close through enclosure notation); determine *gwam*.

3. A 5′ writing on entire letter; determine *gwam*; circle errors.

	words parts	5′ gwam
Current date Central Electric Company 17 North Meridian Indianap-	13	3
olis, IN 46204 Attention Purchasing Agent Dear Sir or Madam	25	5
(¶ 1) Whether it's a single letter or a whole word, you erase it neatly		8
and quickly with the new ERASOMATIC Electronic Eraser.		10
(¶ 2) It's as handy to use as a pencil. Just lift the handpiece and it		13
starts. Place the handpiece back on the cradle and it stops. And a		15
special lock keeps it from being started accidentally.		18
(¶ 3) When the eraser tip wears down, simply run it across the		20
Trimmer and you have a sharp edge again. Correct tip length is main-		23
tained simply by inserting the eraser tip into the built-in Renewer.		25
(¶ 4) Use the handy order card that is enclosed to order your first		28
ERASOMATIC now. After this first tryout, you'll want one for every		31
secretarial work station throughout your company.		33
Sincerely yours CENTURY SUPPLY COMPANY LeRoy J. Michaels,	12	35
Manager xx Enclosure (137)	16	36

123c ▶30 Measure production skill: tabulation

Time schedule
Planning and preparing .. 6′
Production timing .... 20′
Proofreading; computing *n–pram* .... 4′

full sheet, long side up; SS data; 8 spaces between columns

Note: Longest entry in each column is color underlined for quick identification.

Erase and correct all errors. If you complete the problem before time is called, start over on a new sheet. When time is called, proofread your work.

Determine *n–pram* by deducting 15 words from total words for each uncorrected error; then divide the result by 20. Record rate. Retain paper for use with 129e, Assignment 2, page 215.

			words
	SELECTED BUSINESS FIRMS		5
	Home Offices		7
Name	Street	City, State, ZIP Code	21
Alberto-Culver Company	2525 W. Armitage Ave.	Melrose Park, IL 60164	34
Bausch & Lomb, Inc.	635 St. Paul St.	Rochester, NY 14602	46
Beatrice Foods Co.	120 S. La Salle St.	Chicago, IL 60603	57
Bluebird, Inc.	100 Dayton Ave.	Passaic, NJ 07055	67
Brunswick Corporation	69 W. Washington St.	Chicago, IL 60602	78
Budd Company	2450 Hunting Park Ave.	Philadelphia, PA 19132	91
Burlington Northern, Inc.	176 East Fifth St.	St. Paul, MN 55101	103
CNA Financial	310 S. Michigan Ave.	Chicago, IL 60604	114
Castle & Cooke, Inc.	120 Merchant St.	Honolulu, HI 96802	125
Continental Oil Co.	30 Rockefeller Plaza	New York, NY 10020	138
Crown Zellerback Corp.	One Bush St.	San Francisco, CA 94119	150
Culligan, Inc.	1657 Shermer Rd.	Northbrook, IL 60062	161
Di Giorgio Corp.	One Maritime Plaza	San Francisco, CA 94111	173
Dun & Bradstreet, Inc.	90 Church Street	New York, NY 10007	185
General Mills, Inc.	9200 Wayzata Blvd.	Minneapolis, MN 55426	197
Indian Head, Inc.	111 W. 40th St.	New York, NY 10018	208
Inland Steel Co.	30 W. Monroe Ave.	Chicago, IL 60603	218
Lear Siegler, Inc.	3171 S. Bundy Drive	Santa Monica, CA 90406	231
Purex Corp., Ltd.	5101 Clark Ave.	Lakewood, CA 90712	241
RCA Corporation	30 Rockefeller Plaza	New York, NY 10020	252
Rubbermaid, Inc.	1255 East Bowman St.	Wooster, OH 44691	264
Ryder System, Inc.	2710 S. Bayshore Drive	Miami, FL 33133	275
Stone & Webster, Inc.	90 Broad St.	New York, NY 10004	286
Teledyne, Inc.	1901 Ave. of the Stars	Los Angeles, CA 90067	298

Enrichment material for Unit 19 appears on LM pp. 69, 70.

156d ▶18 Type a letter in block style

plain sheets; 1½" margins; date on Line 15; proofread and circle errors

Problem 1
Review block style
Type the letter to review layout and placement. See Reference Guide, p. iv.)

Problem 2
Skill building on block style letter

1. A 1′ writing on opening lines (date through subject line); determine *gwam*.

2. A 1′ writing on closing lines (complimentary close through enclosure); determine *gwam*.

3. A 5′ writing on entire letter; determine *gwam*; circle errors.

Enrichment material for Unit 26 appears on LM p. 23.

	words parts	5′ gwam
Current date Miss Garnetta Johnson, Supervisor Customer Service	13	3
Division Royal Distributing Company 7300 West 39th Street Little	26	5
Rock, AR 72204 Dear Miss Johnson Subject: Writing Out Loud	38	8
(¶ 1) One of my associates has just written a booklet on the important		10
subject of communication. It is called Writing Out Loud. It contains		14
32 pages of up-to-date, refreshing pointers on one of the most im-		16
portant elements of your job and mine--dictating.		18
(¶ 2) I should like to send you a complimentary copy to see whether		21
you find it as helpful as I did and also whether you agree that most		24
people who dictate could read it with decided profit. The booklet takes		27
only a few minutes to read and will almost certainly help you		29
reduce your dictating time.		30
(¶ 3) Simply fill in and mail the enclosed card, and I shall see that		33
a copy of Writing Out Loud reaches you promptly. Your comments		36
will be most welcome.		37
Sincerely yours WORD PROCESSING SYSTEMS, INC. Alan J. Kent,	12	39
President xx Enclosure	17	40

157

157a ▶5 Conditioning practice

each line 3 times SS (slowly, faster, slowly); DS between 3-line groups

We have checked the six very old quill pens Jan bought from Manzler's.

Joe must sell 35 to 40 tickets for the 19th and 18 to 27 for the 26th.

Strikes in 1977 delayed delivery of 624,350# (or 8% of all shipments).

Did the firm pay a penalty for filing the tax form after the due date?

| 1 | 2 | 3 | 4 | 5 | 6 | 7 | 8 | 9 | 10 | 11 | 12 | 13 | 14 |

157b ▶10 Check word-division skill

1. Set left margin and tab stops according to the key.

2. Center heading on Line 11; type Line 1 as shown.

3. Type remaining lines, showing in Column 2 all syllable breaks and in Column 3 each acceptable word-division point. If a word should not be divided, type it without hyphens in Column 3.

WORD DIVISION

appreciate	ap/pre/ci/ate	ap-pre-ci-ate
conditions		
invoice		
matters		
occasionally		
professional		
referred		
several		
tabulate		
using		

key | 12 | 8 | 16 | 8 | 15 |

unit **20** lessons 124–125

Performance evaluation

Measurement goals

1. To measure and evaluate your typing skill growth.

2. To help you identify areas of needed improvement.

Machine adjustments

Make the usual machine adjustments as required for various activities.

124

124a ▶5 Conditioning practice

each line 3 times (slowly, faster, in-between rate)

alphabet Val bought Jackie a mixed bouquet of zinnias and pretty field flowers.

fig/sym I sold Dot Record Nos. 47-2115-B, 86-2735-A, 92-0413-C, and 64-8015-Z.

continuity Always examine your aspirations and measure them against your talents.

fluency One of the heaviest loads to carry may be a bundle of bad work habits.

| 1 | 2 | 3 | 4 | 5 | 6 | 7 | 8 | 9 | 10 | 11 | 12 | 13 | 14 |

124b ▶15 Measure basic skill: straight copy

two 5′ writings; determine *gwam*; proofread and circle errors; record better rate

all letters used | A | 1.5 si | 5.6 awl | 80% hfw |

	gwam 1′	5′
Any learning worth undertaking is frequently a painful process.	13	3
It requires much time and effort. Learning to typewrite well is no	27	5
exception to this generalized rule. You do not become an excellent	40	8
typist just by copying material from a textbook. The material you type	55	11
must cause you to do something or to react to it if you are to learn.	69	14
If the placement of a letter, or a table, or a report on a page is easy	83	17
to do, you often learn little about how to solve typewriting placement	97	19
problems. In the business office, your employer will expect you to	111	22
type well and to be able to solve difficult typing placement problems.	125	25
It is one of the goals of a good typing book to introduce you to	13	28
typing problems that increase in complexity and difficulty and that	27	30
create some placement problems for you as you type them. Typing appli-	41	33
cations that cause you to think also help you to learn. Less than this	55	36
and you will have been cheated in your typing program; you will be ill-	69	39
prepared to use the typewriter effectively in a work situation. You	83	42
must accept the challenge of a difficult typing problem because it will	98	45
help you reach a new level of typing skill that will greatly enhance	111	47
your job opportunities.	116	48

gwam 1′ | 1 | 2 | 3 | 4 | 5 | 6 | 7 | 8 | 9 | 10 | 11 | 12 | 13 | 14 |
5′ | 1 | 2 | 3 |

unit **26** lessons 156–161

Building letter typing competence

Learning goals

In this unit you will review and practice the placement of letter parts in the three basic letter styles. In addition, you will build letter typing power through intensive timed practice activities.

Machine adjustments

1. Paper guide on *0*.

2. Ribbon control on black.

3. Margin stops: 70-space line for drills and ¶s; as directed for problems.

4. Line-space selector on *1* for drills; on *2* for ¶s; as directed for problems.

156

156a ▶5 Conditioning practice

each line 3 times SS (slowly, faster, slowly); DS between 3-line groups

alphabet Mrs. Joyce Zublick is not quite finished with this expensive training.

figures I ordered 36 desks, 49 chairs, 15 tables, 80 lamps, and 72 file trays.

fig/sym The cost of $6,948 he quoted on Order 30721 included the 5% sales tax.

fluency It is your duty to find a remedy now for each of your typing problems.

| 1 | 2 | 3 | 4 | 5 | 6 | 7 | 8 | 9 | 10 | 11 | 12 | 13 | 14 |

156b ▶15 Improve speed/control

1. A 5′ writing on the ¶s of 155c, page 256.
Goal: High speed.

2. A 5′ writing on the ¶s of 155c, page 256.
Goal: Controlled typing.

156c ▶12 Report on block style letter

Margins
top: 2″
side: 1″

5-space indentions; DS ¶; SS listed items, DS between them

Block style, open

WPS
Word Processing Systems, Inc. 783 Market Street San Francisco, CA 94103 (415) 471-3200

Current date

Miss Garnetta Johnson, Supervisor
Customer Service Division
Royal Distributing Company
7300 West 39th Street
Little Rock, AR 72204

Dear Miss Johnson

Subject: Writing Out Loud

One of my associates has just written a booklet on the important subject of communication. It is called Writing Out Loud. It contains 32 pages of up-to-date, refreshing pointers on one of the most important elements of your job and mine--dictating.

I should like to send you a complimentary copy to see whether you find it as helpful as I did and also whether you agree that most people who dictate could read it with decided profit. The booklet takes only a few minutes to read and will almost certainly help you reduce your dictating time.

Simply fill in and mail the enclosed card, and I shall see that a copy of Writing Out Loud reaches you promptly. Your comments will be most welcome.

Sincerely yours

WORD PROCESSING SYSTEMS, INC.

Alan J. Kent, President

xx

Enclosure

PLACEMENT POINTS FOR BLOCK STYLE LETTERS
TS

In block style, all lines begin at the left margin. These placement points should be followed in typing block style letters:

1. When a subject line is included, double-space above and below it; type the word Subject in ALL CAPS or in uppercase and lowercase, followed by a colon and 2 spaces.

2. When a company name is used in the closing lines, type it in ALL CAPS a double space below the complimentary close.

3. Type the name of the signer of the letter on the fourth line space below the complimentary close (or below the company name when one is used).

4. Type the title of the signer either on the line with the name or on the next line.

5. Type reference initials a double space below the signer's name and/or title. (When the signer's name is typed, only the typist's initials are needed for reference.)

6. Type an enclosure notation (if any) a double space below the reference initials.

7. Type a carbon copy notation (if any) a double space below the reference initials or enclosure notation (if any).

124c ▶20 Check table typing skill

Problem 1

full sheet; DS data; reading position; decide spaces to leave between columns; align Column 2 as shown

DIMENSIONS OF EARTH

Area of surface	196,938,800 sq. miles
Water area	139,500,000 sq. miles
Land area	57,500,000 sq. miles
Equatorial diameter	7,926.41 miles
Polar diameter	7,900.00 miles
Equatorial circumference	24,901.55 miles
Meridional circumference	24,859.82 miles

Source: Columbia Encyclopedia, 1975.

Problem 2

half sheet, long side up; center vertically; DS data

1. Decide spaces to leave between Column 1 and the Column 2 heading and between Column 2 heading and Column 3 heading.

2. Type horizontal lines after table is completed; rule vertical lines with ball-point pen.

AREAS AND DEPTHS OF THE OCEANS

Ocean	Area (Square Miles)	Greatest Depth (Feet)
Pacific	64,186,300	36,198
Atlantic	33,420,000	28,374
Indian	28,350,500	25,344
Arctic	3,662,200	17,880

Source: World Almanac, 1975.

124d ▶10 Check punctuation skill

correct as you type; full sheet; 1" (2.54 cm) top and side margins; DS

1, 3:188 24:194 1. She said Techniques rhythm and continuity are important.
4:188 2. Dr. Pitzer our new teacher knows how to teach typewriting.
2:188 3. He ordered orange juice bread and butter milk and eggs.
5:188 4. Our old school where I learned many things is to be torn down.
6:188 5. I was in Stockholm Sweden on July 4 1976.
8:188 6. The tall redwood trees are indeed beautiful.
1, 7:188 7. A dozen large red white and pink carnations were delivered.
9:190 8. We have 12350 books stored in Room 1352.
10:190 9. What a great day this has been.
11:190 10. Will you cover the typewriter when you are through.
13:190 16:192 11. Spell these numbers 40, 56, and 94.
14:190 12. This is the question Can you go with me tomorrow.
19:192 13. The data see Table 2 were incorrect.
20:192 14. Marilyns report is 1 too long, 2 difficult to read, and 3 poorly typed.
22:192 15. I read the book Typing Speed that was reviewed in the New York Times.
25:194 16. I read the article Toward the Year 2000.
23:119 26:194 17. The words imply and infer have different meanings.
29:194 18. You typed faster however you made more errors.
28:194 19. To be unable to write is a tragedy to be unable to read, a catastrophe.
35:196 20. The boys hockey team will play the mens hockey team.

Use Guide codes to check work.

155c ▶15 Measure basic skill: straight copy

two 5′ writings; determine *gwam*; circle errors

all letters used | A | 1.5 si | 5.6 awl | 80% hfw

	gwam 2′	5′
In the early years of American history, most firms were set up and	7	3
run in an informal way. The owner of a business was, in many cases, the	14	6
only executive; he or she was able to keep in close touch with all phases	22	9
of the day-to-day operations of the firm. Few records were maintained	29	11
and most of the decisions were based on past experiences. However,	36	14
changes in technology and shifts in the buying habits of consumers cre-	43	17
ated a heavy impact on business. Much of this impact was reflected in	50	20
a greater increase in the kinds of office work required. Soon it became	57	23
evident that the informal business practices of the past were no longer	64	26
meeting the needs of our swiftly changing and ever-expanding economy.	71	28
Management has become more and more dependent on the information	7	31
that it can retrieve from data systems with greater speed and ease than	14	34
it has been able to do at any other time in the past. Today, the office	21	37
acts as the memory unit of the firm through the records it keeps. Gather-	29	40
ing, analyzing, and storing this input requires an efficient and well-	36	43
trained staff. As a result, many good jobs exist in the field at the	43	45
present time. Not only are the numbers of jobs increasing rapidly, but	50	48
the values placed by employers on these kinds of duties are increasing	57	51
as well. The future is bright for competent workers who can add to the	64	54
success of their employers.	67	55

gwam 2′ | 1 | 2 | 3 | 4 | 5 | 6 | 7
5′ | 1 | 2 | 3

155d ▶10 Check word-division skill

1. Set left margin and tab stops according to the key.

2. Center the heading on Line 11 and type Line 1 as shown.

3. Type remaining lines in same way, showing in Column 2 all syllable breaks and in Column 3 all acceptable points of word division. If a word should not be divided, type it without hyphens in Column 3.

Enrichment material for Unit 25 appears on LM pp. 5–8.

WORD DIVISION

prefer	pre/fer	pre-fer
willing		
written		
getting		
motions		
personnel		
toward		
into		
enough		
highly		

key | 9 | 8 | 11 | 8 | 11 |

125

125a ▶5 Conditioning practice

each line 3 times (slowly, faster, in-between rate)

alphabet	Exquisite rings were made quickly by the jovial friends on the piazza.
fig/sym	The house located at 23968 Richmond Street sold for $41,750 last year.
shift key	Jack Brown and Don Hutson will visit Chicago, New York, and St. Louis.
fluency	Is life so short that we no longer have time for courtesy and a smile?

| 1 | 2 | 3 | 4 | 5 | 6 | 7 | 8 | 9 | 10 | 11 | 12 | 13 | 14 |

125b ▶15 Measure basic skill: statistical rough draft

two 5′ writings; determine *gwam*; proofread and circle errors

Record better rate and % of transfer: rate of 125b ÷ rate of 124b.

all figures/letters used | A | 1.5 si | 5.6 awl | 80% hfw |

	gwam 1′	5′
Recently, the United States celebrated its 200th birth day. The	11	2
period from 1776 to 1976 was one of great growth. Our population grew	27	5
from about 2,803,000 in 1776 to more than 215,005,859 in 1976. The	40	8
horse was the principle means of transportation in 1776, but the	53	11
automobile quickly replace the horse at the beginning of the 20th	68	14
century. In 1976, there were more than autos, trucks, and buses on	84	17
our highways.	113	23
What can we say has been America's greatest achievement in its	11	25
first 200 years? Perhaps it has been the growth of its system of	25	28
free public education which ex tends all the way from our elementary	38	30
schools to our high schools. Even beyond these levels we find very	53	33
low fees in our highly-rated public universities. In 1976, the total	71	37
school enrollmeth for persons 5 to 34 years old was judged to be	85	39
about 57,763,000, with 32,665 enrolled at the elementary school level,	98	42
14,814,000 enrolled at the high school level, with still another	112	45
10,384,000 enrolled in our post-secondary schools.	124	47

154d ▶15 Improve keystroking technique

1. Type the drill once as shown. Use good techniques and keep the carriage (carrier) moving steadily.

2. Two 1′ writings on each of the last 3 lines. Determine *gwam* on each; then compare rates.

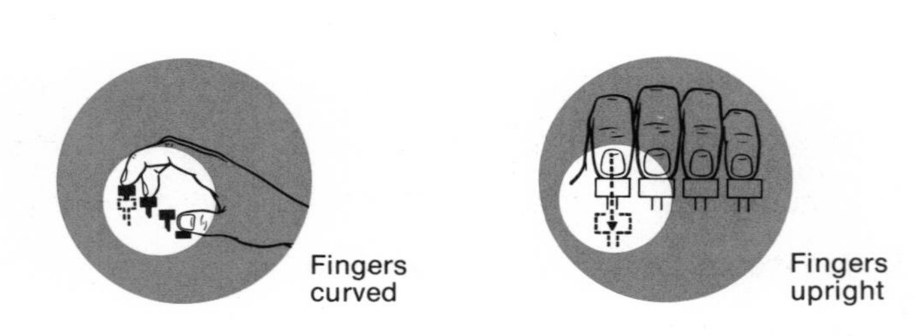

adjacent keys	1	as well as | try our silk | develop new guides | question our pointed answer
	2	Were more sessions necessary before the additional proposal was ready?
direct reaches	3	my brochure | any amounts | grave doubts | obtained payment | many nice pieces
	4	My checking account record served many times as my receipt of payment.
double letters	5	all choose | good books | less effort | accurate account | puzzling suggestion
	6	Cass suggested current matters be recommended to the school committee.
one-hand words	7	my dad | get upon | we are | in my joy | at our age | only base rates | tax on gas
	8	Johnny, were you aware my tax rebate was based only on a minimum rate?
balanced-hand words	9	if he did | to rush | aid us | key goal | both coal and clay | also handy for me
	10	Is it their duty to fight for the amendment and risk their own profit?
one-hand	11	In my opinion, only test case data were stated in rare rate decreases.
balanced-hand	12	A box firm spent the profit for eighty big signs for the island docks.
combination	13	The fifth pay jump in six years was awarded to the union by the firms.

| 1 | 2 | 3 | 4 | 5 | 6 | 7 | 8 | 9 | 10 | 11 | 12 | 13 | 14 |

155

155a ▶5 Conditioning practice

each line 3 times SS (slowly, faster, slowly); DS between 3-line groups

Several people were quietly waiting for Jack and me by the zoo's exit.

I flew 9,486 miles and visited 1,532 stores in 70 cities for the firm.

Knight & Day--as you know--earned $9,000 (15% commission) on the sale.

The goal of this firm is to cut the delay for corn, cocoa, and burlap.

| 1 | 2 | 3 | 4 | 5 | 6 | 7 | 8 | 9 | 10 | 11 | 12 | 13 | 14 |

155b ▶20 Improve keystroking technique

1. Type the lines of 154d, above, twice. Use your best technique and keep carriage (carrier) moving steadily.

2. Two 1′ writings on each of the last 3 lines of 154d. Determine *gwam* on each; then compare rates.

125c ▶30 Check report typing skill

Margins
top: 2″ (5.08 cm) elite
1½″ (3.81 cm) pica
side: 1″ (2.54 cm)
bottom: approx. 1″
Erase and correct errors.

Note: Any insertion in quoted material must be enclosed in *brackets*.
Construct brackets by typing a diagonal before and after the insertion; then type the lower underlines, roll back the platen and type the upper lines.

READING AND WRITING

There is a growing concern in America today that many young persons can neither read nor write well enough to do acceptable work. The statistics on literacy grow more frightening each year. Recently, the Department of Health, Education, and Welfare revealed the results of a special study that showed a steady decline in reading skills among American students since 1965. A rather strong statement, directed to parents, about the writing ability of young people is made in a Newsweek article:

> If [your children] are in high school and planning to attend college, the chances are less than even that they will be able to write English at the minimal college level when they get there . . . . And if they are attending elementary school, they are almost certainly not being given the kind of required reading material, much less writing instruction, that might make it possible for them eventually to write comprehensible English.[1]

Much of the blame for reading and writing weaknesses in young people today is put on the time spent in viewing television. Reading good books seems to have become a lost art.

It seems rather evident that reading and writing must again be stressed, at home and in school, if the downward trend in reading and writing skills is to be reversed. Someone has suggested that a good starting point might be to have students study Strunk's basic book The Elements of Style[2] and encourage them to give renewed emphasis to reading and writing.

---

[1]"Why Johnny Can't Write," Newsweek (December 8, 1975), p. 58.

[2]William Strunk, Jr., The Elements of Style (New York: Macmillan Co., 1972).

154

154a ▶5 Conditioning practice

each line 3 times SS (slowly, faster, slowly); DS between 3-line groups

Zachary and Beckie Maxwell should jog every morning to keep quite fit.
Add 14 meters 25 centimeters, 89 meters 36 centimeters, and 70 meters.
Invoice No. 57-Y included 386# of oats, 495# of rice, and 210# of rye.
The eight girls ran onto the field with their usual and visible vigor.

| 1 | 2 | 3 | 4 | 5 | 6 | 7 | 8 | 9 | 10 | 11 | 12 | 13 | 14 |

154b ▶15 Check rough-draft skill

two 5′ writings; determine *gwam*; circle errors

all letters used | A | 1.5 si | 5.6 awl | 80% hfw |

Text	gwam 2′	5′
There is an office job for you. Firms are always in need of	6	2
qualified work. Eachday many workers quit, retir, transfer and	13	5
or are promoted. Everyday job vacanncies are created and new	19	7
jobs open up. Be ready to make good use of the education and	25	10
trainning you now receive.	28	11
Your enitial job will play a bgi role in designingyours	34	13
appraoch to the world of work. You will pickup many ideas and	40	16
habits that will stay with you for everand greatly affect your	47	19
thinking about any future occupatoins. For these reasons, it	53	21
is extremely important that you choose with great care.	59	23
take time not to think aobut and to analyze the type of job	7	26
you would like to be working at 5 or 10 years from right now.	13	29
Then, be sure to pursue employment opportunities that will serve	19	31
as stepping stones to your over all objective. Apply your educa-	26	34
tion to help you in finally reaching your ultimate goal. Be	32	36
positive your final selection is a job in which you can and should	37	38
make use of your best skills ad abilities. Only in such a manner	44	41
will you acheive satisfaction from yor career, and at the same	50	44
time make your personal contribution to society.	53	45

154c ▶15 Improve skill transfer

1. Two 2′ writings on ¶s 1 and 2 of 154b, above. Push for speed; determine *gwam*.

2. Two 2′ writings on ¶s 3 and 4. Push for speed; determine *gwam*.

3. A 5′ writing on all ¶s combined; determine *gwam*; circle errors.

lessons 126–150

Improving professional typing skills

unit 21 lessons 126–128

Speed/accuracy emphasis

Learning goals

The 25 lessons of Phase 6 continue the emphasis given in the 4 steps of the *Planned Program* to improve your typing skills (see page 125). In addition, you will:

1. Refine and improve your basic typing techniques.

2. Increase your speed and improve your accuracy.

3. Improve your proof-reading skills.

4. Extend and improve your professional typing skills.

Machine adjustments

1. Paper guide at *0*.

2. 70-space line and SS or as directed.

3. Line space selector on *1* or as directed.

4. Ribbon control on black (*R* on Selectric).

126

126a ▶5 Conditioning practice

each line 3 times (slowly, faster, in-between rate)

alphabet	Six women in the valley heard piercing squawks of dozens of blue jays.
fig/sym	The 546 copies, priced at $3.78 each, may be shipped on June 19 or 20.
fingers 3, 4	Aza Waxman sold all six of the popular old quill pens in Oslo, Norway.
fluency	Keep the right thumb close to the space bar in order to space quickly.

| 1 | 2 | 3 | 4 | 5 | 6 | 7 | 8 | 9 | 10 | 11 | 12 | 13 | 14 |

126b ▶10 Evaluate your form patterns: hand-and-finger position

1. Evaluate your hand-and-finger postion.

2. Compose complete sentence answers to each question.

Finger position

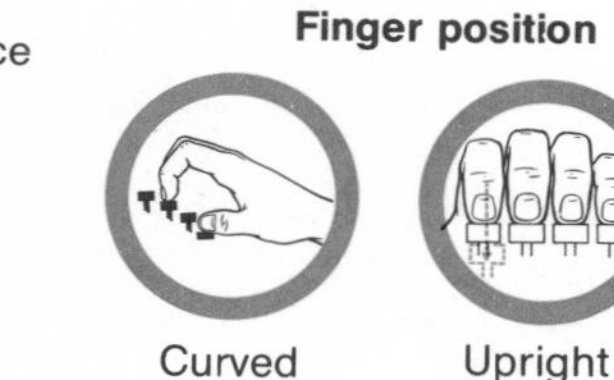

Curved Upright

1. Do you type with your fingers well curved and upright and with little or no curve at the knuckle joint?

2. Do you keep your wrists low and relaxed so that the base of each hand nearly touches the frame of the typewriter?

3. Are both thumbs curved with the right thumb resting lightly on the space bar?

4. If you gave a negative response to any of the questions, what do you plan to do to improve your hand-and-finger position?

126c ▶20 Evaluate your response patterns

each line 3 times (slowly, faster, top speed)

Evaluate your typing in terms of the goals.

Quick, snap stroke

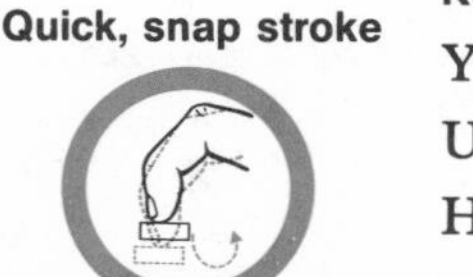

Keystroking goal: quick, snappy keystroking with quiet hands

You will type faster if you keep your fingers well curved and upright.
Use the fingers only and strike each key with a quick, snap keystroke.
Hit a key quickly and then work to reduce the time between keystrokes.

(continued, page 209)

153c ▶10 Improve keystroking technique

each pair of lines twice

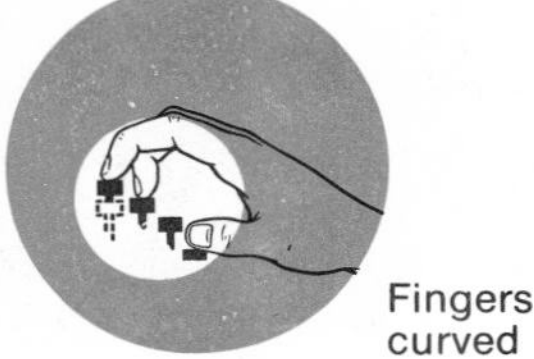
Fingers curved

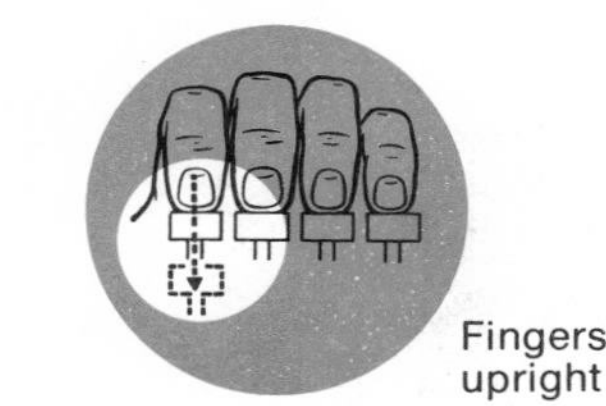
Fingers upright

Upward reach

Downward reach

Goals, line by line

1-2. Fingers curved and upright over home keys.

3-4. Quick, low reaches to third row.

5-6. Direct *finger* reaches to bottom row.

1 add lad ask glad falls hash saga dash fall gash lash salad shall glass
2 Hal has had hash; Al and Sal had a sad dad; a glad lad has had a salad

3 or it pep wit owe you tote rope toot wore pipe type utter queer uproot
4 You were quite right to write your quotes properly prior to your talk.

5 fix ban mix box zoom navy back saved civic brace combine manner circle
6 Manny and Vi found an extra seven dozen scarves in my summer shipment.

| 1 | 2 | 3 | 4 | 5 | 6 | 7 | 8 | 9 | 10 | 11 | 12 | 13 | 14 |

153d ▶20 Check script-copy skill

1. A 5′ writing on all ¶s combined; determine *gwam*; circle errors.

2. Two 1′ writings on each of ¶s 1, 2, and 3; push for speed; determine *gwam*.

3. A 5′ writing on all ¶s combined; determine *gwam*; circle errors.

all letters used | A | 1.5 si | 5.6 awl | 80% hfw |

	gwam 1′	5′
One of the many skills required of new office workers is a	12	2
mastery of office machines. The enormous growth in the volume	24	5
of paperwork has created a need for diverse equipment that is	37	7
capable of doing a variety of tasks; therefore, a full staff of	50	10
workers is required to keep the work flowing smoothly.	60	12
Years ago, nearly all office work was processed by hand;	11	14
and the work was very tedious and not always accurate.	23	17
Today, since older systems just cannot keep up the pace our society	36	19
demands, office machines can be found in firms of all sizes.	48	22
At first thought, it would seem that the trend toward auto-	12	24
mation means fewer jobs in office fields; however, this	23	26
has not been the case. In fact, the change has created many excit-	37	29
ing jobs at various levels by eliminating a lot of work that	50	32
was considered to be boring.	55	33
This trend will be a definite factor in the future of all	12	35
people who are considering office careers. Training now will	24	38
give you leverage when you apply for a position.	34	40

126c, continued

Spacing stroke

Space-bar goal: a fast spacing stroke without waste motion

Strike the space bar with a quick, down-and-in motion after each word.
Keep the right thumb curved and on or near the space bar at all times.
Type a word, strike the space bar, and then start typing the new word.

Shift key reach

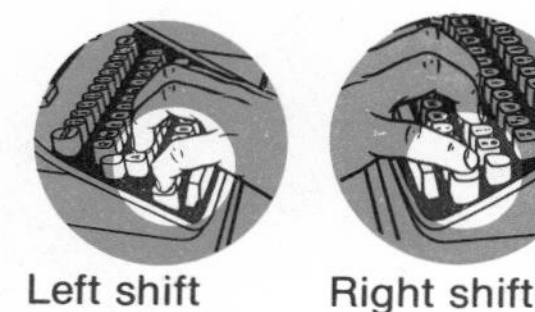

Left shift Right shift

Shift-key goal: quick shift–key reaches without waste motion

Make the Reach to the Shift Keys by Extending Only the Little Fingers.
E. J. Laurie is a Professor of Marketing at San Jose State University.
I read the articles in DAEDALUS on "How Others See the United States."

Return

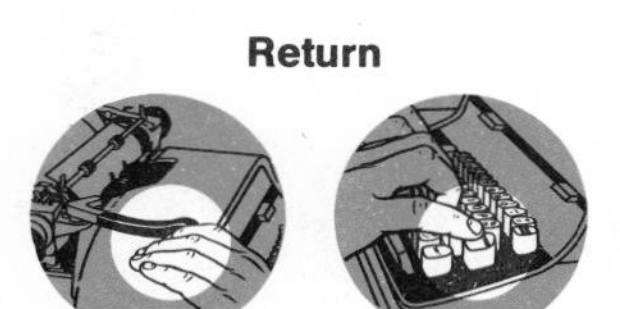

Manual Electric

Return goal: a quick return and start of new line

Tab stop: center + 10

tab → Make the return quickly
and start the new line. — tab → Keep your eyes on this
copy as you make the return. — tab → This is one good way to
increase your speed. — tab → repeat 3 times

126d ▶15 Apply improved techniques: guided writing

1. A 2′ writing at a controlled pace with good keystroking techniques.
2. Determine *gwam*. Add 8 to your *gwam* rate. Set ¼′ goals for 1′ and 2′ writings at your new rate.
3. Three 1′ writings at your goal rate as your teacher calls the ¼′ guides.
4. A 2′ guided writing; try to maintain your goal rate for 2′.
5. A 2′ writing for speed. Try to exceed your goal rate.

all letters used — gwam 2′

As you learn to type with the keystroking action in your fingers 7
and with quiet hands, you will begin to make amazing skill growth. You 14
may recall the importance of having a purpose or a goal for all your 21
typing work. Your skill will improve, too, as you type drill lines at 28
alternating levels of speed. For example, in the activity which you 35
have just completed, you were directed to type the drill lines at gradu- 42
ally increasing speeds as you evaluated your typing in terms of the goals. 49

gwam 2′ | 1 | 2 | 3 | 4 | 5 | 6 | 7 |

127

127a ▶5 Conditioning practice

each line 3 times (slowly, faster, in-between rate)

alphabet Jukebox music puzzled those gentle visitors from a quaint valley town.
fig/sym He borrowed $25,600 at 8 3/4% in 1976 under an FHA mortgage (234-560).
fingers 3, 4 Aza Q. Popolox was asked to escort that popular but plump person home.
fluency An efficient secretary paid the busy clerks for the eighty handy pens.

| 1 | 2 | 3 | 4 | 5 | 6 | 7 | 8 | 9 | 10 | 11 | 12 | 13 | 14 |

152d ▶15 Check statistical-copy skill

two 5′ writings;
determine *gwam*;
circle errors

all letters used | A | 1.5 si | 5.6 awl | 80% hfw

Text	gwam 1′	5′
Between 1972 and 1980, the number of jobs in the United States is	13	3
predicted to jump by about 16 million. From 1980 to 1985, all indicators	27	5
point to an expected gain of 6 million, totaling over 107 million jobs	42	8
in 1985, or 22 million more jobs than there were in 1972.	52	10
The labor force available to fill these jobs is expected to increase	14	13
by 18.7 million persons between 1972 and 1985, reaching a high of 107.7	28	16
million in 1985. The recent and rapid growth due to the postwar "baby	42	19
boom" will begin to taper off quietly in 1978.	52	21
Not only is the size of the work force undergoing change, but its	13	23
composition is being altered as well. Highest growth ratios are pre-	27	26
dicted for the age bracket 25 to 34, which is expected to enlarge its	41	29
sector of the labor market from 19.4 percent in 1965 to 27.6 percent	55	32
in 1985.	56	32
A second factor affecting the labor force and its makeup has been	13	35
the 3.48 percent annual gain in the number of female workers. This rate	28	38
is nearly triple the annual gain made by males (1.28 percent). By 1985,	42	41
females are expected to total 38.7 percent of the labor force.	55	43

gwam 1′ | 1 | 2 | 3 | 4 | 5 | 6 | 7 | 8 | 9 | 10 | 11 | 12 | 13 | 14 |
5′ | 1 | 2 | 3 |

153

153a ▶5 Conditioning practice

each line 3 times SS
(slowly, faster, slowly);
DS between 3-line groups

Six joyful children biked to a party to view an amazing ventriloquist.
The shop is 278.4 meters long, 90.6 meters wide, and 13.5 meters high.
He said, "Policy No. 74381-Y-T (dated 8/7/75) terminated May 4, 1976."
Key firms in both towns may risk a penalty if the fuel profit is down.

| 1 | 2 | 3 | 4 | 5 | 6 | 7 | 8 | 9 | 10 | 11 | 12 | 13 | 14 |

153b ▶15 Improve skill transfer

1. Two 1′ writings on each ¶ of 152d, above. Push for speed; determine *gwam*.

2. A 5′ writing on all ¶s combined; determine *gwam*; circle errors.

127b ▶18 Improve your response patterns

Repeat 126c, pages 208–209.

Goal: Technique refinement.

127c ▶12 Apply improved techniques: guided writing

1. A 2′ writing (at a controlled pace with good techniques).

2. Determine *gwam*. Subtract 4 from your *gwam* rate. Determine ¼′ goals for 1′ writings at new rate.

3. Three 1′ writings at goal rate as your teacher calls ¼′ guides.

Goal: Not over 1 error in each writing.

4. Another 2′ writing for control. Maintain goal rate.

all letters used

	gwam 2′
Here are a few suggestions that may help you reduce your typing	7
errors. First, just be certain that your fingers are in proper typing	15
position, and then keep them in that position by learning to keep your	21
hands quiet. Second, start typing at a lazy, well-controlled pace and	28
gradually increase your speed as you begin to relax. Next, keep your	35
eyes on the copy to be typed. Concentrate on every word. Some typists	42
have found that they can reduce errors by reading the copy for meaning.	49

gwam 2′ | 1 | 2 | 3 | 4 | 5 | 6 | 7 |

127d ▶15 Measure basic skill: straight copy

two 5′ writings; determine *gwam*; circle errors; record better rate

all letters used | A | 1.5 si | 5.6 awl | 80% hfw

	gwam 1′	5′
If you have developed the typing techniques and various other ele-	13	3
ments suggested in this book, you really should be on your way toward	27	5
becoming an expert typist. In the remainder of the lessons of this cycle,	42	8
just make the effort to refine your typing form and response patterns	56	11
even more. You will be amazed at the difference that even a slight	70	14
refinement in this area can make in your typewriting skill. Always	83	17
be sure that your fingers are in the proper position and that they are	97	19
really curved and upright. Keep your wrists low and relaxed, with the	112	22
base of each hand nearly touching the base of the machine.	123	25
Fast keystroking is very important on both the manual and the elec-	13	27
tric typewriters. Reaches to the keys should be made with the action	27	30
in the fingers and with the hands in a quiet and relaxed position. When	42	33
not in use, the fingers should be touching their home keys. Fast down-	56	36
and-in spacing with the right thumb after every word is another element	71	39
contributing to the growth of good typing skill. It is important, too,	85	42
to use proper motions in making capital letters or in making the return.	99	45

gwam 1′ | 1 | 2 | 3 | 4 | 5 | 6 | 7 | 8 | 9 | 10 | 11 | 12 | 13 | 14 |
5′ | 1 | 2 | 3 |

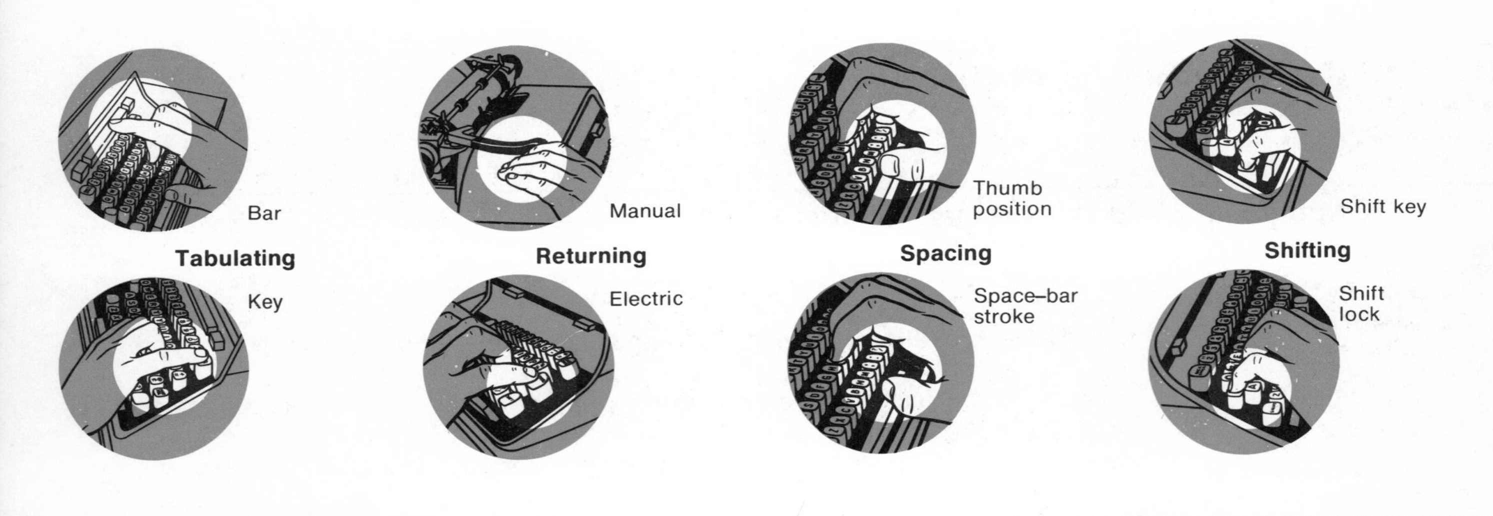

152b ▶15 Improve control of machine parts

exact 60-space line; each pair of lines 3 times

Goals, line by line

1-2. Quick tabulator and return movements.

3-4. Down-and-in motion on space bar.

5-6. Shift, type, and release shift key quickly.

7-8. Efficient use of shift lock.

9-10. Quick use of margin release and backspacer.

Set tab (left margin + 30)

1 Fast and skillful typists have
2 learned to tab, release, and type quickly.

3 my duty | they may fly | try my key | they may try | why buy my copy
4 Ray may enjoy a copy of my survey of the city salary policy.

5 Dody and Alan | Coral and Hank | Rob and Karen | Flip and Betty Jo
6 Pat Quinn will visit Erie, New Haven, El Paso, and St. Paul.

7 KASI, Ames; WWGO, Erie; WIMA, Lima; KRMG, Tulsa; WORK, York;
8 NOTICE: All new CPAs will meet Friday at the downtown YMCA.

9 Your attitude is one factor that determines how well you do your work.
10 Analyze the types of errors you make in order to improve basic skills.

152c ▶15 Check keystroking technique

reset margins for 70-space line; each set of lines 3 times

Goals, line by line

1-3. Fingers well curved over home keys.

4-6. *Finger* reaches to third row.

7-9. *Finger* reaches to bottom row.

1 had fad sad all has gas dash half asks halls gaff flag sash flask glad
2 had a fall | a lass adds a dash | a gala hall | ask all dads | all lads did go
3 Dallas Sahl and Al Falk had a dish of hash. Al had a dish of fig jam.

4 quit pot wire your eye it rope up our your out wiper prior quote quite
5 our error | your trip | we were quiet | route our trip | write to us | our quote
6 Our tour took the proper route; your error was to take the upper road.

7 can man van ban sax cab flaxen zinc box tax minx zebra comb verb amaze
8 in my cab | six moving vans | many women can | name my cabin | any active verb
9 Bobby and Max placed the excess zinc in a box and moved it to the van.

| 1 | 2 | 3 | 4 | 5 | 6 | 7 | 8 | 9 | 10 | 11 | 12 | 13 | 14 |

128

128a ▶5 Conditioning practice

each line 3 times (slowly, faster, in-between rate)

alphabet	A foglike haze developed quickly just as four workmen left the boxcar.
fig/sym	The 6.70 x 15, 4-ply tires (natural rubber) may cost more than $82.39.
fingers 3, 4	Was it Polly who saw Paul quizzing Wally about eating all the loquats?
fluency	The simple way to better our lot in life is to try to do a lot better.

| 1 | 2 | 3 | 4 | 5 | 6 | 7 | 8 | 9 | 10 | 11 | 12 | 13 | 14 |

128b ▶15 Evaluate your response patterns

each line 4 times (slowly, faster, top speed, then in-between rate for control)

Evaluate your typing in terms of the goals.

Goal continuity; no breaks or pauses

1 Did he make the dedication at the old wax museum for economic reasons?
2 My friends may try to get five new butter tubs at the old union store.
3 The economy may improve because of an increase in consumer confidence.

Goal high-speed response

4 They may go with me to the city to sign the forms and pay for the box.
5 If they do a quantity of problems for us, I may pay them for the work.
6 May the men do their work and then go to the city for the eight signs?

Goal variable rhythm response

7 We may ask them to refer the statement to your lawyer for his opinion.
8 Handle the five cases with care so as to reduce breakage to a minimum.
9 Ask them to send a minimum water statement to them at the old address.

128c ▶15 Apply improved techniques: guided writing

1. A 2′ writing at a controlled pace with good keystroking techniques.

2. Determine *gwam*. Add 8 to your *gwam* rate. Set ¼′ goals for 1′ and 2′ writings at your new rate.

3. Three 1′ writings at your goal rate as your teacher calls the ¼′ guides.

4. A 2′ guided writing; try to maintain your goal rate for 2′.

5. A 2′ writing for speed. Try to exceed your goal rate.

all letters used — gwam 2′

All the copy that you type is composed of words which are either (4, 8, 12) — 7
balanced hand, one hand, or a combination of balanced- and one-hand (16, 20, 24) — 13
sequences. A good typist is able to recognize the words which can be (28, 32, 36, 40) — 20
typed at high speed and the words which, because of the mixture of letter (44, 48, 52) — 28
sequences, require an adjustment in keystroking pattern. The good typist (56, 60, 64, 68) — 35
soon learns to type with a variable rhythm pattern, which increases or (72, 76, 80, 84) — 42
decreases in speed according to copy difficulty. (88, 92) — 47

gwam 2′ | 1 | 2 | 3 | 4 | 5 | 6 | 7 |

128d ▶15 Improve basic skill: straight copy

Repeat 127d, page 210.

Goal: Increased speed or improved accuracy.

151c ▶15
Check straight-copy skill

two 5′ writings; determine *gwam*; circle errors

all letters used | A | 1.5 si | 5.6 awl | 80% hfw

	gwam 1′	5′
How often have you been told that to secure a good job you must get	14	3
a good education? Undoubtedly, you have heard these exact words numerous	28	6
times from friends or relatives and over radio or television. Regardless	43	9
of the source, the advice is valid. As a jobseeker today you face a mar-	58	12
ket in which education is one of the most valuable assets you can possess.	73	15
Today you must have a solid education just to be sure that you have	14	17
a chance for a job. Opportunities to embark on an office or a distribu-	28	20
tive career are good, but most of these jobs require a minimum of a high	43	23
school diploma. Even when a diploma is not a specific requirement, em-	57	26
ployers will many times give first preference to high school graduates.	71	29
Of course, a sound education and other benefits go hand in hand.	13	31
For example, most graduates earn almost twice as much money in their	27	34
lifetimes as do workers who have less than a high school education. Many	42	37
economists predict that such a contrast in the earning ability of these	56	40
two groups will grow even wider in the next decade.	66	42
And there are yet other advantages to be realized from a good educa-	14	45
tion. Today many people change jobs a number of times during their	27	47
lives. The ones with limited schooling are finding it very hard to learn	42	50
new skills for new jobs. By establishing a solid academic base from which	57	53
to develop, you will be able to cope better with the challenge of change.	72	56

gwam 1′ | 1 | 2 | 3 | 4 | 5 | 6 | 7 | 8 | 9 | 10 | 11 | 12 | 13 | 14 |
5′ | 1 | 2 | 3 |

151d ▶15
Improve basic skill

1. Two 1′ writings on each ¶ of 151c, above. Push for speed; determine *gwam*.

2. A 5′ writing on all ¶s combined; determine *gwam*; circle errors.

152

152a ▶5
Conditioning practice

each line 3 times SS (slowly, faster, slowly); DS between 3-line groups

Our firm very quickly pressed embezzlement charges against Joe Waxler.
The 105,647 union members voted 98,231 to 7,416 to strike at midnight.
The report by Rose* indicated the base years** (1970-75) were correct.
Eighty firms may bid for the right to make the big signs for the city.

| 1 | 2 | 3 | 4 | 5 | 6 | 7 | 8 | 9 | 10 | 11 | 12 | 13 | 14 |

unit **22** lessons 129–135

Special office applications

Learning goals

1. To develop knowledge of and skill in typing special office applications.

2. To increase basic skill on straight and statistical rough-draft copy.

Machine adjustments

Make the usual machine adjustments as required for various activities.

Procedure

The 7 lessons of this unit are grouped into a series of 11 related job assignments. You will type the assignments during your next 7 class periods. Each time, resume your work after completing the activities listed at the right. Correct errors.

At the start of each class period, type 129a. Then type the activity called for in the schedule below:

Lesson	Class Session	Activity
129	1	129b
130	2	129c
131	3	129d
132	4	129b
133	5	129c
134	6	129d
135	7	129b

129-135

129a ▶5 Conditioning practice

each line 3 times (slowly, faster, in-between rate)

alphabet Jack will help move the boxes of zinc from the gondola cars at Quincy.

fig/sym Order No. 90 (May 23) from Jones & Co. totals $58.60, less 2/10, n/30.

shift key E. N. Salton, of Post, Tryon & McCain Company, met Benson in St. Paul.

fluency They had moved to a new address when the statement was mailed to them.

| 1 | 2 | 3 | 4 | 5 | 6 | 7 | 8 | 9 | 10 | 11 | 12 | 13 | 14 |

129b ▶15 Improve skill transfer (Lessons 129, 132, 135)

1. Three 1′ writings on each ¶; slowly, top speed, in-between rate for control. Record rates; try to improve these rates as you repeat the timings.

2. Compute % of transfer.

Goals: Script, 90–100% of straight-copy rate; statistical rough-draft rate, 75–85%.

¶ 1 straight copy
¶ 2 script
¶ 3 statistical rough draft (see p. 213)

¶s 1–3 | A | 1.5 si | 5.6 awl | 80% hfw

gwam 1′

Which letter of the alphabet would you record as most beneficial? 13
The letter "e" is a possibility because it is the most frequently used 28
letter. As another possibility, the letter "x" is very serviceable. 42
It can be used to x-out words in rough-draft typewriting. It points 55
out the spot, it can express a kiss, it registers a vote, it is used 69
to rate a movie, it has split billing in tic-tac-toe, and at times it 83
even is used for a signature. 89

gwam 1′ | 1 | 2 | 3 | 4 | 5 | 6 | 7 | 8 | 9 | 10 | 11 | 12 | 13 | 14 |

gwam 1′

The art of communicating with another person is 10
to hear what he or she does not say. Often, the things 21
a person does not say are as important as what he 31
or she says. You may have heard the saying that 41
"Actions speak louder than words." You can im- 51
prove your communication skill by developing your 60
power of observation and your listening skill. 69

phase 7 lessons 151–175

Improving typing competence

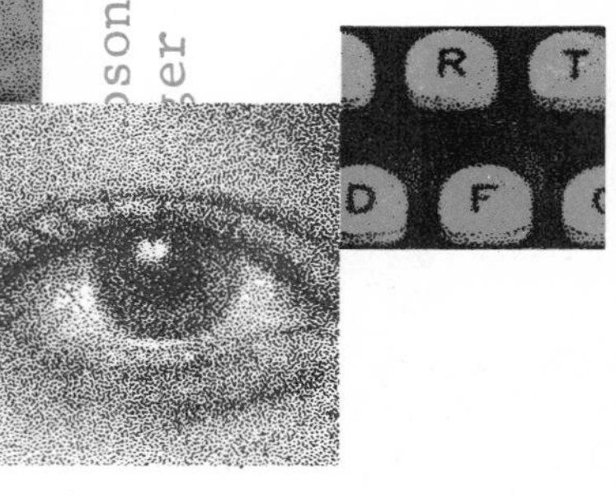

unit 25 lessons 151–155

Improving basic skills

Learning goals

In the 25 lessons of Phase 7 you will:

1. Improve your basic skills on straight copy, script, rough draft, and statistical copy.

2. Review letter formats and build business letter competence.

3. Review table arrangement and develop table typing competence.

4. Review report layout and develop report typing competence.

5. Demonstrate proficiency in typing these three types of business communications.

Machine adjustments

1. Paper guide on *0.*

2. Ribbon control on black.

3. Margin stops: 70-space line for drills and ¶s; as directed for problems.

4. Line-space selector on *1* for drills; on *2* for ¶s; as directed for problems.

151

151a ▶5 Conditioning practice

each line 3 times SS (slowly, faster, slowly); DS between 3-line groups

alphabet Judge Bromwell is expected to penalize the thief quickly and severely.

figures Project 1680X to update Models 24537 and 19330 is due by September 29.

fig/sym The notation must include: *See Footnote 3, Table 711 (Series V 657).

fluency Risk the usual profit for this cycle, or pay the penalty due the city.

| 1 | 2 | 3 | 4 | 5 | 6 | 7 | 8 | 9 | 10 | 11 | 12 | 13 | 14 |

151b ▶15 Check control of machine parts

exact 60-space line; each pair of lines 3 times

Goals, line by line

1-2. Quick tabulator and return movements.

3-4. Down-and-in motion on space bar.

5-6. Shift, type, and release shift key quickly.

7-8. Efficient use of shift lock for ALL CAPS.

9-10. Quick use of margin release and backspacer.

Set tab (left margin + 30)

1 Tab quickly; return the finger
2 to the home-key position at once after striking the tab key.

3 my job | they may pay | try my easy way to pay | only my boys stay
4 Jay and Ivy may really try to fly here today to buy my pony.

5 Glen and Janey | Mary and Toby | Jerry and Elly | Sally and Maurey
6 Mae and Ken will attend the Apple Blossom Festival in April.

7 WCFL, Chicago; WLW, Cincinnati; WJR, Detroit; WBUD, Trenton;
8 Stations WCOP and WEEI will carry the game, not station WBZ.

9 As you finish a unit, take time to review every step you have learned.
10 Remember that different individuals learn new ideas at various speeds.

129b, continued

	gwam 1′
Each year about 15,000,000 foreign tourists come to the	13
United States. About 8,600,000 are from neighboring canada and	28
1,800,000 are from mexico. In a re cent year, 763,000 visitors	40
were form Japan, 450,000 were from great britain, 296,000 were	54
from Germnay. The usual visitor from Japan spends an	65
average of $569; from Britain, $291.	72

129c ▶15 Measure basic skill: straight copy (Lessons 130, 133)

two 5′ writings; determine *gwam*; proofread, circle errors; record better rate

all letters used | A | 1.5 si | 5.6 awl | 80% hfw |

	gwam 1′	5′
The telephone in a business office can be a useful tool of communi-	14	3
cation; but unless it is used correctly, excessive time can be wasted.	28	6
Most business firms have prescribed ways for answering incoming calls,	48	8
but at this point efficient telephone procedures may break down. For	57	11
example, if you get a telephone request for some explicit data, try to	71	14
determine swiftly how long it may take you to assemble the data. If	86	17
it takes more than just a few seconds, rather than keep the caller wait-	100	20
ing it is part of good telephone courtesy to get the name and number and	115	23
to tell the caller that you will ring back soon.	127	25
If an outside caller has been placed on your line in error, you can	13	27
be helpful if you try to ascertain the nature of the call so that it can	28	30
be directed to the appropriate person. The caller may be unfamiliar with	43	33
your organization, so any help you can give will be appreciated. It is	57	36
always frustrating to a caller to be switched to many different exten-	71	39
sions within a business office without results. Such a caller will be	86	42
grateful to anyone within the office being contacted if that person can	100	45
help identify the proper person to whom to speak. Courtesy of this kind	115	47
will help avoid frayed nerves and will enhance company goodwill.	127	50

gwam 1′ | 1 | 2 | 3 | 4 | 5 | 6 | 7 | 8 | 9 | 10 | 11 | 12 | 13 | 14 |
5′ | 1 | 2 | 3 |

150d ▶20 Complete *Typewriting Manual*

1. Arrange the pages for your *Typewriting Manual* in the same order as the table of contents shown here; then number the pages in the upper right corner on Line 4, approximately 1" from right edge of sheet.

2. Type a table of contents for your *Typewriting Manual*.

1½" top margin; 1" side margins; capitalize as shown; DS between major divisions; SS subdivisions under a major title; use leaders

3. Type a title page (follow directions on page 178) for your *Typewriting Manual*.

4. If your teacher so directs, put *Manual* in a special folder.

TABLE OF CONTENTS

Page

RELATED LEARNINGS . . . .
    Grammar Guides . . . .
    Number Guides . . . .
    Capitalization Guides . . . .
    Punctuation Guides . . . .
        Comma . . . .
        Exclamation Mark . . . .
        Question Mark . . . .
        Dash . . . .
        Colon . . . .
        Hyphen . . . .
        Parentheses . . . .
        Underline . . . .
        Quotation Marks . . . .
        Semicolon . . . .
        Apostrophe . . . .

TABLE PLACEMENT SUMMARY . . . .

MINUTES OF MEETING . . . .

APPOINTMENT SCHEDULE . . . .

BUSINESS LETTER STYLES . . . .
    Personal/Business Style . . . .
    Modified Block Style (Block Paragraphs) . . . .
    Modified Block Style with Indented Paragraphs . . . .
    Block Style . . . .

ITINERARY . . . .

TIMED WRITINGS WITH RATES . . . .
     5-Minute Straight Copy . . . .
     5-Minute Rough Draft . . . .
     5-Minute Statistical Copy . . . .
    10-Minute Letter Copy . . . .
    20-Minute Tabulation Production . . . .

LETTER OF APPLICATION . . . .

PERSONAL DATA SHEET . . . .

150e ▶5 Measure spelling skill from dictation

half sheet, short side up; DS columnar items; center heading on Line 11

Left margin setting
elite: 16
pica: 10

Tab stop setting
elite: 38
pica: 32

Arrange words in 2-column table as they are dictated to you by your teacher.

1. Center and type heading.

2. Close book and type words in columns from dictation.

3. Check your spelling with that shown in book.

4. Score spelling skill by deducting 3 ½ points from 100 for each misspelled word.

WORDS FREQUENTLY MISSPELLED

argument mileage | attendance miscellaneous |
beginning misspell | belief ninety |
believe occasion | brief occurred |
calendar planned | campaign privilege |
conferring proceed | copying quantity |
definite receipt | desirable recommend |
enough separate | familiar similar |

129d ▶15 Measure basic skill: statistical rough draft (Lessons 131, 134)

two 5′ writings;
determine *gwam*;
proofread, circle errors

Compute % of transfer on better writing.

Goal: 80% or more.

all figures used

A	1.5 si	5.6 awl	80% hfw

	gwam 1′	5′
On July 4, 1976, *our* American youth *14 to 24 years of age* ~~numbered~~ *totaled* about 44.6 million, or	18	4
~~nearly~~ *approximately* 21 percent of the total population *of the U.S.A.* This figure ~~represents~~ *shows*	35	7
~~an increase~~ *a gain* of 17.3 million, *or about 64 percent,* over the 27.3 million of 1960. Population	52	10
projections ~~indicate~~ *show* that the number of youth will ~~increase~~ *jump* to an all-	65	13
time high of 45.2 million in 1980 *and will then drop to about 42.2 million in 1985.* Over two thirds of our Nation's *lc*	88	18
youth lived in ~~metropolitan~~ *large city* areas in 1976.	96	19
The num ber of persons of ~~high~~ *secondary* school age *(14 to 17 years old)* totaled about 17.2 mil-	18	23
lion in 1976, but the number of this ~~group~~ *throng* will decline to ~~about~~ *approximately* 14.4	34	26
million by 1985. The college-age population *(18 to 21 years old)* totaled 16.3 million in	52	30
1976. *#* It will ~~increase~~ *inflate* to 17.1 million by 1980, and will then deline to	66	32
15.4 million by 1985. *The youth of America are a highly mobile assortment.* One half ofthe population 20 to 21 years old	90	37
and ~~about~~ *virtually* 70 percent of the population 22 to 24 years old moved during	105	40
the ~~period~~ *span* 1970 to 1976.	110	41

129e ▶30 Learn special office applications

Assignment 1: Interoffice memorandum [LM pp. 73, 74]

half sheet;
1″ side margins;
TS after last heading line

INTEROFFICE COMMUNICATION

TO: (Your name)

FROM: (Your teacher's name)

DATE: (Current date)

SUBJECT: Your Office Assignment

TS

In Lessons 129-135, you are to assume the role of special office assistant employed by Contemporary Office Associates, a Los Angeles based firm with offices in key cities of the United States.

At Contemporary Office Associates, you will work directly with Mr. Richard Buchanan, a senior manager. As an employee, you will type the variety of materials presented in these lessons. At times you will be given only minimum directions; in some cases you will be asked to use your judgment in placing materials on the page.

All your typed work will be judged for acceptability for office use. This statement means that you must proofread your work, neatly correcting all errors, and that you must judge whether your work is acceptable before you submit it for final evaluation.

xx

150b ▶15 Measure basic skill: straight copy

two 5′ writings; circle errors; determine *gwam*; record better rate

all letters used | A | 1.5 si | 5.6 awl | 80% hfw

	gwam 1′	5′
Soon you may launch a career in business by accepting a job in an	13	3
office. If you are earnest about your career advancement, you will want	28	6
your work to be superior, not just average. It should be helpful to know	43	9
some of the causes that have been cited for the success or failure of	57	11
younger workers in the business office. Highly successful workers are	71	14
interested in their jobs and understand the function of the job in the	85	17
total office system. They are willing to exert extra effort and carry	99	20
a heavier workload as may be required. They tend to show initiative and	114	23
are flexible and adaptable. They know when to seek advice and do not	128	26
rely needlessly on supervision.	134	27
On the other hand, workers who fail usually do not comprehend their	14	30
jobs or know how a job fits in the office work system. They are unable	28	32
to accept or make positive use of criticism. They may allow their own	42	35
feelings and emotions to affect the work. They are not interested in	56	38
their jobs and have no concern for the office. They let their personal	71	41
affairs take priority over the work of the office. They avoid rather	85	44
than face issues, and, often, they are careless. Strive to emphasize the	99	47
ingredients for success in all your work. Avoid any factors that may	113	49
cause you to fail. If you do these things, you actually enhance your	127	52
chances for success and happiness in your future career.	148	54

Save your copy for *Typewriting Manual*.

gwam 1′ | 1 | 2 | 3 | 4 | 5 | 6 | 7 | 8 | 9 | 10 | 11 | 12 | 13 | 14 |
5′ | 1 | 2 | 3

150c ▶5 Check related learning skill

1. Type the sentence number and the period; space twice, then type the sentences, making any needed corrections or insertions at the points of the color underlines.

2. Mark your errors as your teacher reads the corrections. Record your name and number of errors.

1. the basic colors are red_ yellow_ and blue_
2. i shall meet governor brown at the century club_
3. 9 visitors are here_ twelve or 13 more will arrive soon.
4. The letter _Exhibit A _and the report _Exhibit B _are needed.
5. The boys hat, the mens shirts, and the girls sweaters are lost.
6. Read the articles: _fatigue, _how to relax,_ and _saving energy._
7. _Will he go_ she asked, _this week or next _
8. Everyone (is, are) here.
9. Each of the students (is, are) ready to go.
10. Two thirds of the work (is, are) done.
11. Jan and Jill have lost (her, their) books.

129e, continued

Assignment 2
Index-card mailing list

Mr. Buchanan asks you to prepare a mailing list of prospective clients. Mailing lists are frequently typed on 5" × 3" index cards.

1. From the illustration, type an index card [LM pp. 75–84 or paper cut to that size]. Type a similar card for each firm listed on page 203.

2. Check the alphabetical order of your cards (by firm name).

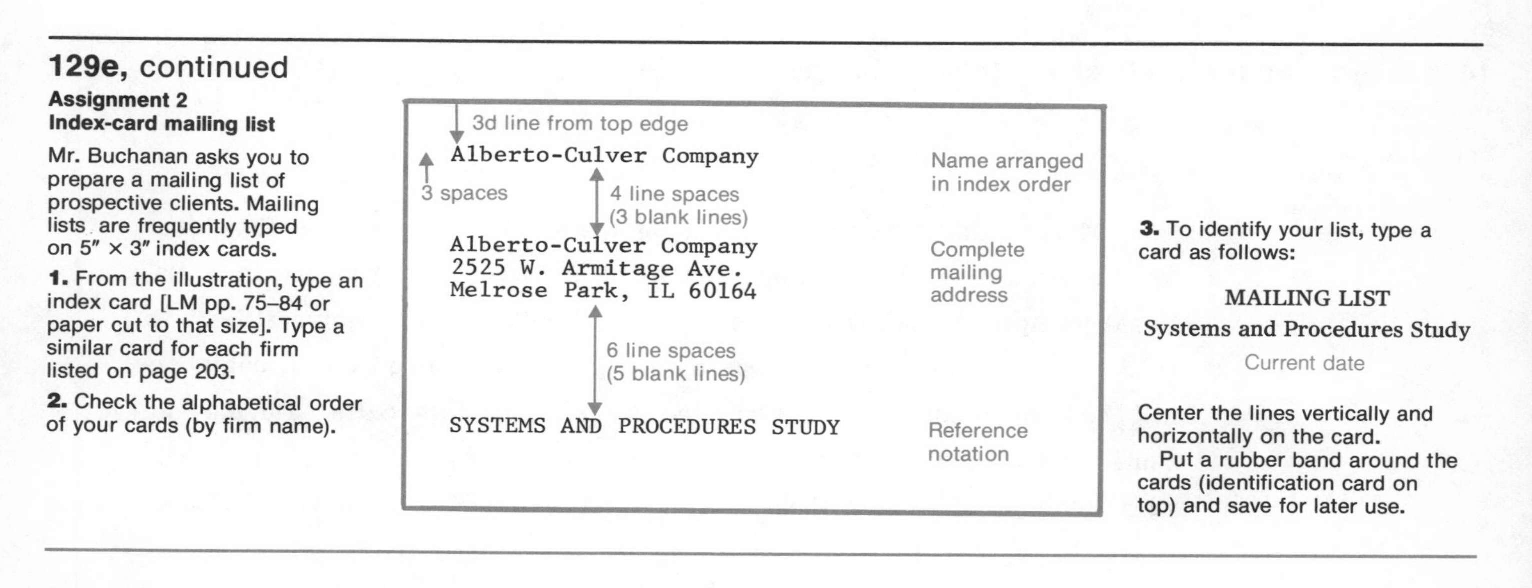

3. To identify your list, type a card as follows:

MAILING LIST
Systems and Procedures Study
Current date

Center the lines vertically and horizontally on the card.

Put a rubber band around the cards (identification card on top) and save for later use.

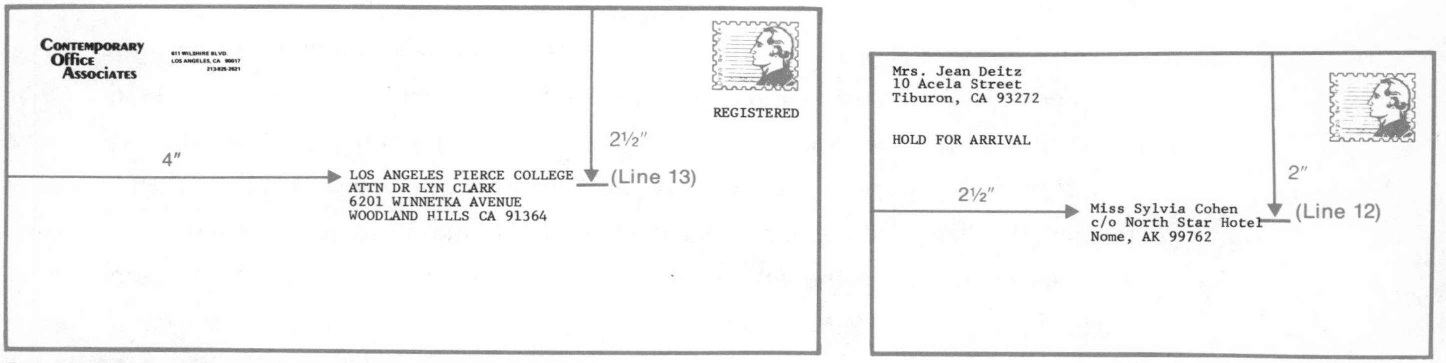

Contemporary
Office
Associates
REGISTERED
2½"
4"
LOS ANGELES PIERCE COLLEGE
ATTN DR LYN CLARK
6201 WINNETKA AVENUE
WOODLAND HILLS CA 91364
(Line 13)
Mrs. Jean Deitz
10 Acela Street
Tiburon, CA 93272
HOLD FOR ARRIVAL
2"
2½"
Miss Sylvia Cohen
c/o North Star Hotel
Nome, AK 99762
(Line 12)

Style used above is that recommended by U.S. Postal Service to aid mechanical mail sorting.

Addressing envelopes

Envelope address placement

Set a tab stop (or margin stop, if a number of envelopes are to be addressed) 2½" from left edge of a small envelope (4" for a large envelope). Start the address at this point on Line 12 (Line 15 for a large envelope).

Use *block style*, SS, as illustrated at right. Type city name, 2-letter state-name abbreviation, and ZIP Code on last address line.

Mailing notations

Type REGISTERED, SPECIAL DELIVERY, and the like, on Line 8 or 9 below the stamp position.

Addressee notations

Type these notations (HOLD FOR ARRIVAL, PLEASE FORWARD, PERSONAL, etc.) a TS below return address and 3 spaces from left edge of envelope.

If an *attention line* is used, type it just below the company name in the address lines.

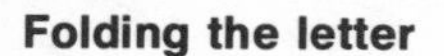

Folding the letter

For large envelopes

Step 1: With letter face up, fold slightly less than ⅓ of sheet up toward top.

Step 2: Fold down top of sheet to within ½ inch of bottom fold.

Step 3: Insert letter into en- velope with last crease toward bottom of envelope.

For procedure for small envelope, see page 85.

149c ▶15 Measure basic skill: statistical copy

two 5′ writings; circle errors; determine *gwam* and % of transfer

Record better rate and % of transfer score.

all figures used | A | 1.5 si | 5.6 awl | 80% hfw

	gwam 1′	5′
More young women are pursuing historic "male" careers than ever	13	3
before, according to a recent survey of 314,069 new students in a na-	27	5
tional sample of 562 two- and four-year colleges and universities. In	41	8
1976, 1 woman in 6 (16.9%) was planning a career in business, engineer-	55	11
ing, law, or medicine. In 1966, the figure was only 5.9%. During the	69	14
same 10-year period, 1966-1976, the ratio of first-year college men who	84	17
were planning to enter these 4 fields fell from 48.9% to 39.4%. Thus,	98	20
the ratio of men to women planning to enter these fields fell from 8:1	112	22
in 1966 to 3:1 in 1976.	117	23
In 1976, the tally of new college students who planned to become	13	26
teachers reached an all-time low. Only 6.5%, compared to 21.7% in 1966,	28	29
planned to become elementary or high school teachers. Election of vari-	42	32
ous fields of study by young men and women continued to show trends	56	34
toward the "applied" areas. Those planning to major in the applied areas	70	37
such as business or the allied health areas grew to 38% in 1976 as com-	85	40
pared to 31.3% in 1966. At the same time, only 10.4% planned to major in	99	43
English, the humanities, fine arts, or math, as compared to approximately	114	46
22% in 1966. The shift is probably due to the hard time students with	128	49
degrees in the nonapplied areas have in finding jobs.	139	51

gwam 1′ | 1 | 2 | 3 | 4 | 5 | 6 | 7 | 8 | 9 | 10 | 11 | 12 | 13 | 14 |
5′ | 1 | 2 | 3 |

Save your copy for *Typewriting Manual*.

150

150a ▶5 Conditioning practice

each line 3 times (slowly, faster, in-between rate)

alphabet	Exquisite lace was found in the Topaz Village Market by the jolly man.
fig/sym	Order 38 of May 7 for 5 files, 48 desks, and 60 chairs totaled $9,210.
speed	If they do the work for us, I may go to the lake and then to the city.
fluency	Ask him to restate the water problem and then set a date for the case.

| 1 | 2 | 3 | 4 | 5 | 6 | 7 | 8 | 9 | 10 | 11 | 12 | 13 | 14 |

129e, continued

Assignment 3
Addressing large envelopes
[LM pp. 85–96]

Type 12 large envelopes from the first 12 cards of your mailing list (Assignment 2). First line of each address:

Office of the President

Note: Beginning office typists should be able to type about 2 envelope addresses a minute. Try to meet this standard.

Position envelopes for easy pickup: Stack at left, *flaps down and away from you* (face up).

Learn quick placement: Observe the amount of space to be left above and to the left of the address. Learn to judge by *eye measurement* the proper starting point.

Assignment 4
Addressing small envelopes
[LM pp. 97–102]

1. Type as many small envelopes as you can in 3′. Use the addresses of your mailing list. Arrange envelopes for easy pickup.

2. Put your addressed envelopes in order.

3. Count them and record this number with your name in the upper left corner of the top envelope. Put a rubber band around the envelopes.

Assignment 5
Interoffice memorandum
[LM pp. 103, 104]

full sheet; 1″ side margins; 1 cc; correct errors

words

TO: All Typists 2

FROM: Richard Buchanan 6

DATE: Current date 9

SUBJECT: Care of Typewriters 13

Because of our increasing typewriter repair costs, we are request- 26
ing that you follow these care-of-typewriter steps: 37

1. End of each day. At the end of each day, please follow these 53
   procedures: 55

   a. Use a stiff brush to clean the typeface. If you use 67
      an element-type machine, remove the element to clean it. 78

   b. Brush away any eraser crumbs, etc., that have fallen 90
      into the typebar segment. (May I remind typists who 100
      use typebar machines to move the carriage to the ex- 111
      treme right or left before erasing an error.) 120

   c. Dust your desk beneath your machine with a dustcloth. 132

   d. Pull the paper release lever forward and leave it in 143
      this position overnight. 149

   e. Finally, center the carriage (typebar machine) and 159
      cover the typewriter. 164

2. End of each week. At the end of each week, do the following: 181

   a. With a soft, lintfree cloth with a corner moistened 192
      slightly with typewriter oil, wipe the carriage rails 203
      of the typebar machine; then wipe them again with the 213
      unmoistened portion of the cloth. 220

   b. Clean the platen with another soft, lintfree cloth 231
      moistened with alcohol. 236

3. Know your operator's manual. Review, as needed, the care and 255
   maintenance steps given in the operating instructions manual 267
   for your typewriter. 271

149b ▶30 Measure tabulation production skill

full sheet; center vertically; DS columnar items; underline column headings; 4 spaces between columns; correct errors

Longest line in each column is color underlined.

Each figure is used a minimum of 15 times.

Time schedule

Preparation .... 5′
Timed production ... 20′
Proofread; compute *n–pram* .... 5′

Arrange problem in proper form as you type it. You will have about 5′ to plan the setup; make notations of the points at which heading lines begin.

Stay ALERT as you type. Proofread; compute *n–pram*: total words minus 15 for each uncorrected error divided by 20.

Main heading: NEW INSTALLMENT ACCOUNTS — 5

Secondary heading: (Spring Quarter) — 9

Column headings: Name | Street Address | City, State, ZIP Code — 25

Name	Street Address	City, State, ZIP Code	words in cols.	total words
Cynthia Bowman	7820 Thurston Circle	Los Angeles, CA 90049	12	36
Ida Cole	848 Allen Street	Hackensack, NJ 07601	21	46
Lucille Faye	63 Sea Cliff Avenue	Sea Cliff, NY 11579	32	56
Marie Gordon	8488 Fenton Street	Denver, CO 80227	41	66
John Hills, Jr.	939 Riverview Drive	Columbus, OH 43202	52	77
Frank B. Johnston	483 Danbury Street	Wichita, KS 67220	63	88
Joseph Long	4659 Portola Drive	San Francisco, CA 94127	74	99
Kevin Maley	5659 E. Upsal Street	Philadelphia, PA 19150	86	110
Wayne McClure, Jr.	8345 Sam Cooper Road	Knoxville, TN 37918	98	122
Peter Mullins	4668 Star Lane, N.E.	Minneapolis, MN 55421	109	134
Darren Paulson	3947 E. Broad Street	Tampa, FL 33610	119	144
Roy W. Roberts	56 Gloucester Street	Boston, MA 02100	130	155
Mark Rogers	3948 W. Elm Street	Greensboro, NC 27406	140	165
Jason Sawatzky	6789 Chicago Avenue	Evanston, IL 60201	151	176
Gary E. Thompson	1391 Fontaine Road	Lexington, KY 40502	162	187
Burt Wieland	4758 Indigo Street	Houston, TX 77035	172	197
Betty Williams	629 - 19th Street	Oklahoma City, OK 73127	184	208
Gary Wolfe	2500 Alaskan Way	Seattle, WA 98121	193	218
Shinji Yoshino	2828 S.W. Corbett	Portland, OR 97201	203	228
Scott Zimmer	3465 Clematis Blvd.	Pittsburgh, PA 15235	214	239

Save your copy for *Typewriting Manual*.

129e, continued

Assignment 6
Two-page form letter
[LM pp. 105–110]

1 cc; plain second sheets; address large envelopes; correct errors; modified block style; open punctuation; center subject line; approximate 1" bottom margin; page 2 heading: horizontal style

1. Study illustrations for placement of special lines.

Note: A subject line may be centered, as illustrated, or typed at the left margin. Also, the word SUBJECT (in all caps or first letter only capped) may be used:

SUBJECT: Systems Study

2. Type the letter to the first addressee on your mailing list. As time permits in these lessons, type the letter to as many of the addressees as possible. For the attention line, use:

Attention Office Manager

For each new letter, type from your copy of the preceding letter; thus you proofread the previous letter as you type a new one.

Note: Before typing any long letter, make a pencil mark 2"–2½" from the bottom of the page. You can then judge where to end page 1 if the letter is too long for one page.

```
April 13, 19--

Alberto-Culver Company
2525 W. Armitage Ave.
Melrose Park, IL 60164

Attention Mr. Frank Dickson, Office Manager

Ladies and Gentlemen

SYSTEMS AND PROCEDURES STUDY

You, too, are no doubt finding it increasingly difficult to cope
with the control of spiraling office costs.  It is in this area
that we can help you.  Our firm has established an international
```

Modified block style; attention line; centered subject line

	words
April 13, 19-- Alberto-Culver Company 2525 W. Armitage Ave. Melrose Park,	15
IL 60164 Attention Mr. Frank Dickson, Office Manager Ladies and Gentlemen	30
SYSTEMS AND PROCEDURES STUDY (¶ 1) You, too, are no doubt finding it	42
increasingly difficult to cope with the control of spiraling office costs. It is in	59
this area that we can help you. Our firm has established an international	74
reputation for its work in resolving problems and reducing costs in the area of	90
office systems and procedures. (¶ 2) Our fundamental purpose is to provide	104
clients with the specialized talent and highly trained personnel that is not	120
readily available within that client's own organization. Our systems and	135
procedures capabilities include studies of information flow-data procedures,	150
clerical work measurement and methods improvement, paperwork controls,	164
records management, and work simplification and time-and-motion study.	179
(¶ 3) How does our service work? The scope and nature of the study is defined	193
in preliminary conferences and is outlined in a written proposal to you, all	209
with no obligation on your part. Once an agreement is reached with a	223
client, our consultants initiate analyses and interviews, both internally and	238
externally, to determine the key factors of the problem. They then thoroughly	254
study these key factors and break them into their component parts for	268
further analysis. They present their findings and conclusions to your man-	283
agement, either in conference or in a formal report. We, then, make rec-	297
ommendations for money-saving resolutions of any problems we have identi-	312
fied. (¶ 4) Relative to the value you will receive, the cost of our service is	326
nominal. A qualified member of our staff will be pleased to discuss your	341
special problems with you at your convenience. We shall then present a	355
written proposal, realistically defining the scope and cost of the assign-	370
ment. We accept only those assignments for which we have qualified staff	385
and only those we believe will be productive for the client. (¶ 5) Don't	398
hesitate to call me collect (213 825-2621) about any special questions you	413
may have. (¶ 6) Just return the enclosed card and we shall take the next	427
steps. Until you decide that we can provide a valuable service to your	441

(continued, page 218)

```
Alberto-Culver Company
Page 2
April 3, 19--

Just return the enclosed card and we shall take the next steps.
Until you decide that we can provide a valuable service to your
```

Page 2 heading, block style

```
Alberto-Culver Company            2            April 13, 19--

Just return the enclosed card and we shall take the next steps.
Until you decide that we can provide a valuable service to your
```

Page 2 heading, horizontal style

Note: Center the page number; dateline ends at right margin

148b, continued

9. **Interviewer: This job doesn't pay too much. Do you mind starting at a low salary?**
Try to give your answer in such a way that the interviewer will know that your primary interest is in the job and the experiences you will gain on the job. You might ask if proving your abilities can lead to an appropriate salary increase after you have been on the job for a while.

10. **Interviewer: What are your hobbies?**
The interviewer is interested in the kinds of things you do during your leisure time. If you have any interesting hobbies, mention them briefly; let the interviewer follow up with other questions.

11. **Interviewer: Thank you. I've enjoyed talking to you. We have several other applicants for this position that I am to interview, so I'll have to let you know what we decide.**
Type what you think is an appropriate response to the interviewer's statement.

148c ▶15 Compose a "thank-you" letter

As soon as possible after an interview, it is a good practice to write a "thank-you" letter to the person who interviewed you.

1. Type a brief rough draft of such a letter to Mr. R. J. Lowe. Include in your letter the points listed at the right.

2. Make any necessary corrections and retype the letter in final form.

Points to include in thank-you letter

Thank Mr. Lowe for the opportunity to meet him and to learn more about the position.

Tell Mr. Lowe of your continuing interest in the job and why.

Close the letter with a statement such as this: If you need any additional information, you can reach me at the address above or by telephone at (give your home telephone number).

148d ▶10 Complete letter of application and personal data sheet

Complete the letter of application and the personal data sheet that you started in 146c, page 239.

Label each paper appropriately and save for *Typewriting Manual*.

149

149a ▶5 Conditioning practice

each line 3 times (slowly, faster, in-between rate)

alphabet	The Aztec jewelry makes an exquisite gift of which everybody is proud.
fig/sym	He bought a rod for $4.79, 3 reels for $52.60, and a creel for $10.85.
space bar	Is it right to make me sign the forms and then go to the city to work?
fluency	Some people never escape from the confinement of their own prejudices.

| 1 | 2 | 3 | 4 | 5 | 6 | 7 | 8 | 9 | 10 | 11 | 12 | 13 | 14 |

129e, continued

organization, there will be no cost or obligation. I shall look forward to hear- 457
ing from you soon. Sincerely yours CONTEMPORARY OFFICE ASSOCIATES 471
Richard Buchanan Senior Manager xx Enclosures Enclosed is a list of 484
firms in your area for whom we have done systems and procedures studies. 499
Feel free to contact them. Satisfied clients are the best recommendation 514
for our services. 517/**540**

Note: Type a postscript (block or indent to agree with ¶ style) without the abbreviation *P.S.*

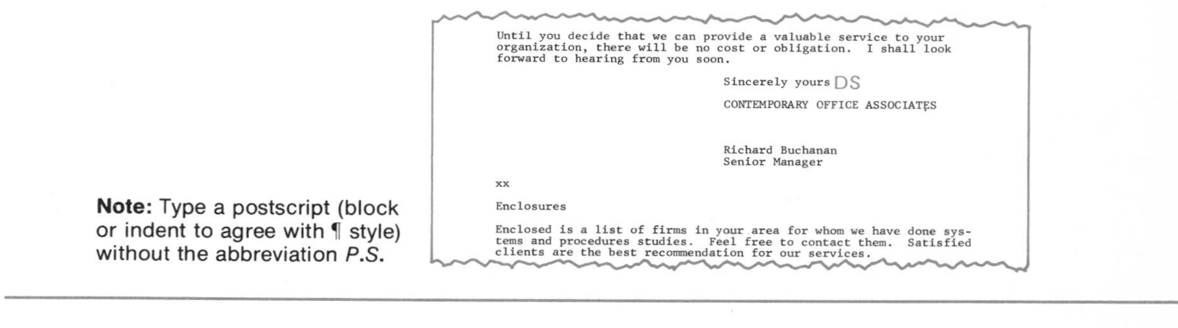
Until you decide that we can provide a valuable service to your organization, there will be no cost or obligation. I shall look forward to hearing from you soon.

Sincerely yours DS

CONTEMPORARY OFFICE ASSOCIATES

Richard Buchanan
Senior Manager

xx

Enclosures

Enclosed is a list of firms in your area for whom we have done systems and procedures studies. Feel free to contact them. Satisfied clients are the best recommendation for our services.

Assignment 7
Invoice
[LM pp. 111, 112]

1. Type an invoice from the data in the illustration. If a form is unavailable, type only the typewritten copy, arranged in the same style as shown on the form.

Set tab stops for typed items. Type across the line, using tab key or bar. In the total column, type last amount, underline; DS; type total amount.

2. Fold the invoice for a window envelope (see RG p. vi).

CONTEMPORARY Office ASSOCIATES

611 WILSHIRE BLVD.
LOS ANGELES, CA 90017
213-825-2621

INVOICE

Margin

California Industries, Inc.
715 S. Broadway Avenue
Los Angeles, CA 90013

Tab

Date April 20, 19--
Our Order No. COA-4310
Cust. Order No. CI-14782

Terms 2/10, n/30

Tab		Tab	Tab
10 days	On-site systems analysis	250.00 da.	2,500.00
1	Study presentation and report	500.00	500.00
			3,000.00

148

148a ▶5 Conditioning practice

each line 3 times (slowly, faster, in-between rate)

alphabet	Jack Culep admired the vivid, waxy sheen of a Guatemalan quetzal bird.
fig/sym	Checks for these amounts were received: $5.28; $6.94; $72.10; $93.10.
variable rhythm	Did he send a statement to the firm at their new address on that date?
fluency	Often, people are lonely because they build walls rather than bridges.

| 1 | 2 | 3 | 4 | 5 | 6 | 7 | 8 | 9 | 10 | 11 | 12 | 13 | 14 |

148b ▶20 Compose answers: interview

Before a job interview, you will usually complete an application form for the company. The questions in an interview may vary.

At the right are some of the questions Mr. Lowe might ask you as he refers to your application form.

Number and type each question; then compose complete answers much as you might give in an interview. Type your response a DS below the question, x-ing out any typing errors.

1. **Interviewer: How are you today?**
   Respond in a brief, friendly way.

2. **Interviewer: Please sit down.**
   A brief "Thank you" is an appropriate response; then be seated.

3. **Interviewer: You're a graduate of** (name of your school)**; how did you like it there?**
   Only a brief response is necessary to this question.

4. **Interviewer: I see you're interested in the office administrative position. Would you tell me something about yourself?**
   Here the interviewer is interested, primarily, in your qualifications for the job. Tell him briefly, why you think you are qualified for the job; include such things as your education and any other special qualifications you may have.

5. **Interviewer: What did you think of the typing courses you took in school? How did these courses qualify you for this job?**
   Recall that the advertisement included the statement: "Must have good typing skill." Emphasize something about your typing skill in your answer.

6. **Interviewer: Why do you think you would like to work here at Contemporary Office Associates?**
   The answer you give may improve your chances for the position if you indicate that you know something about this Company and the kind of work they do. Remember that you learned something about this Company in Lessons 129-135. Tell something you know about the Company and then why you would like to work for them.

7. **Interviewer: What kinds of work experiences have you had?**
   Tell the interviewer about any work experiences you may have had; include any part-time jobs you had while in school; or, if you haven't had any work experience, how you think the classes you took in school prepared you for this job.

8. **Interviewer: Have you ever worked under pressure?**
   Here the interviewer may be indicating that the Company frequently has "rush" jobs that may need to be done in a hurry. You might indicate that in your typing class you frequently worked in situations, such as the 20-minute production writings, that were similar to a "pressure situation in an office."

(continued, page 244)

129e, continued

Assignment 8
Minutes of meeting

page 2: 1″ top margin; page number on Line 4 at right margin; correct errors

1½″ top margin

words

MINUTES OF MEETING OF 4

COMMITTEE ON COOPERATION WITH SCHOOLS 12

Indent 5 → The regular monthly meeting of the Committee on Cooperation 24
with Schools was held in the Conference Board Room of Contemporary 37
Office Associates, 611 Wilshire Blvd., Los Angeles, April 6, 19--. 51

1″ side margins → The meeting was called to order at 9:30 a.m. by Ester Reavis, 63
presiding officer; Jason Ward was the recording secretary. 75

Members present were: 80

Indent 10 → Richard Buchanan, Senior Manager 87
Louis Coppinger, Office Manager 93
Meredith Mota, Vice President 99
Arlene Munsch, Treasurer 104
Ernest Tanner, Industry-Education Council 112

The minutes of the meeting of March 15 were distributed and 124
approved as distributed. 130

Presiding Officer Reavis called on Arlene Munsch for the re- 142
port of the Speakers Panel. Miss Munsch reported that members of 155
the Panel made seven presentations to high school and community 168
college groups in March. Five presentations are scheduled for 180
April. Miss Munsch reported that word processing, tips for begin- 193
ning office workers, office careers, and on-the-job training are 206
some of the topics requested by students. 215

Next, Miss Reavis called on Ernest Tanner for the report of 227
the Industry-Education Exchange Program. Mr. Tanner reported that 240
the Program continues to be well received. The next exchange will 254
take place the first week of May. Elena Johnson, Supervisor of the 267
Communications Center, will exchange jobs for a week with Vernon 280
Munson, Business Communications Instructor, University High School. 294

The Committee then turned to the plans for the Office-Worker- 306
for-a-Week Project. Mr. Coppinger announced that during the last 320
week in April, five senior business education students, selected 333
by teachers in their high schools, will each assume increasing re- 346
sponsibility for a specific job in the offices of Contemporary 358
Office Associates. The employee replaced by the student will help 372
and supervise as needed. The discussion focused on ways to make 385
the Project successful and of most benefit to the students. 397

Mr. Buchanan suggested that the students be given assignments 410
that would offer the maximum opportunity for them to apply basic 423
components of office work in the jobs they assume. He said that 436
careful planning would be needed to accomplish this objective. 448

Approximately 1″

Save sheet for *Typewriting Manual*.

147b, continued

2
Measure rough-draft skill (15′)

two 5′ writings; circle errors; determine *gwam* and % of transfer

1. Record better rate and % of transfer.

2. Save copy for your *Typewriting Manual*.

all letters used	A	1.5 si	5.6 awl	80% hfw

gwam 1′ | 5′

much — and happiness — well

Some of your success in the world of work will depend on how 16 | 3

perform your social role. — of the — young

you get along with others. A recent study reveals some reasons of- 32 | 6

performing — Outstanding

fice workers excel or fail in their social roles. Good workers act 50 | 10

r — en

with matutity and confidnece. They are cheerful and have a harmo- 63 | 13

in the office — ease

nizing effect. They know how to use humor and to lower tension and 79 | 16

tedious — their own

lend enthus iasm to boring work. They are willing to use special 94 | 19

aware of

skills to aid other workers. They are knowledgeable about what is 105 | 21

going on around — and sense the right time to offer necessary help.

in the work area. they meet unkind remarks with positive ones and 131 | 26

are not a party to pettiness. 137 | 27

— qualify — performance

Workers who donot succeed in their social role are insensitive 15 | 30

are

to the needs of otehrs. They may not be aware of the effect their 28 | 33

on the entire office. — and pressures.

behavior has. They tend to react emotionally to job demands. They 48 | 37

#

resent authority and are prone to argue. They are unable to copewith 63 | 40

and lose control of their tempers. — for the job — ed

personality conflicts. They have have no respect and are disappoint 85 | 44

an aid to — social

in themselves. Plan to make positive thinking a rule in your life. 99 | 47

role performance. It will be of value to you as a person 110 | 49

as well as to your career. 116 | 51

3
Measure letter skill (15′)

plain sheet; block style, open; proofread; circle errors; determine *gwam*

1. A 10′ writing on the letter arranged in proper form.

2. Save your copy for *Typewriting Manual*.

words

August 5, 19-- Mr. Michael Halladay 167 South State Street Salt Lake City, UT 84111 Dear Mr. Halladay (¶ 1) If you are one of the rare breed who likes outdoor activity to be self-propelled, then you are bound to like WILDERNESS CAMPING. This bimonthly magazine is devoted exclusively to hiking, back-packing, snowshoeing, canoeing, bicycle camping, and ski-touring. (¶ 2) We offer articles about places to go; but we put much emphasis on equipment--field tests, evaluations, reports from experienced travelers. We'll tell you what's new in backpacking tents, canoes and kayaks, lightweight foods, sleeping bags, and hiking boots. (¶ 3) Many new books are being published for the wilderness camper. We try to review as many of these books as we can squeeze in. There are regular columns on conservation and camping tips. And we have a good share of tasty trail recipes. (¶ 4) Every November there is an annual ski-touring issue with all kinds of information on equipment and technique and a special section on places to go ski-touring. Just return the postagefree card to start your subscription immediately. Cordially yours John R. Fitzgerald Publisher xx Enclosure (200)

Word counts by line: 16, 29, 44, 59, 73, 88, 103, 118, 133, 147, 162, 175, 190, 205, 221, 230/**244**

129e, continued

Assignment 8, continued

Remainder of assignment is in semi-problem form. Follow page 1 style except a 1" top margin and a page number on Line 4 at right margin.

	words
Mr. Ward suggested that luncheon meetings with various members of	462
the office staff be arranged for each student during the week of the	475
Project to encourage exchange of ideas and information about business	489
education and the office.	495
Mr. Tanner suggested that the student participants be furnished a	508
job description of the positions they are to assume at least a week be-	522
fore project implementation.	528
Miss Munsch suggested that a follow-up luncheon meeting with the	541
student participants, teachers, and members of this committee be ar-	555
ranged to discuss the outcomes of the Project.	564
After some discussion, it was the consensus that all suggestions	577
be implemented. Presiding Officer Reavis appointed a committee of three,	592
Louis Coppinger (Chairperson), Arlene Munsch, and Jason Ward, to	605
assume responsibility for the implementation of the suggestions.	618
Miss Reavis announced May 10 as the date of the next meeting of the	632
Committee. The meeting is again scheduled for the Conference Board Room	646
and will begin at 9:30 a.m.	652
There being no further business, a motion for adjournment was made,	666
seconded, and passed. The meeting was adjourned at 11:15 a.m.	679
2DS	
________________________	
Jason Ward, Recording Secretary	691

Save sheets for *Typewriting Manual*.

Assignment 9
Appointment schedule

Mr. Buchanan asks you to prepare his Appointment Schedule.

1. Arrange schedule attractively on full sheet; 1" top, side margins.

2. Center heading lines:

APPOINTMENT SCHEDULE
FOR
RICHARD BUCHANAN
DS

May 10, 19--
TS

3. SS appointment listings; DS after each item.

4. Make accent marks for résumé with pen or pencil.

10:30 a.m. Carlotta Cruz, Media Department. Final selection of materials for slide transparencies.

11:00 a.m. Conference call: Jason Kovack (Chicago office) and Myra Manning (New York office) regarding consulting team for Electronics International proposal.

11:15 a.m. Interview Norman Matsuda, candidate for Industrial Engineering Specialist position. Résumé in folder.

12:15 p.m. Town Hall Luncheon Meeting. Speaker: Hershel Elkins.

2:30 p.m. Meet at Prudential Life Insurance Company with Daniel Widenkopf, Director of Organizational Systems, and Sam Bardokas, team manager.
TS

<u>Special Reminders</u>:

1. Approve final draft of speech for Systems and Procedures Conference.
2. Report for Ormand Industries, Inc., Systems Study, due 5/15.

147

147a ▶5 Conditioning practice

each line 3 times (slowly, faster, in-between rate)

alphabet	Jack executed in oils a small spring bouquet of white azaleas and ivy.
fig/sym	The final payment of $158,367 is due in ninety (90) days or on May 24.
word level	If I do the work, she may spend a day with me and then go to the city.
fluency	He will sign the contract and take title to the eight docks this week.

| 1 | 2 | 3 | 4 | 5 | 6 | 7 | 8 | 9 | 10 | 11 | 12 | 13 | 14 |

147b ▶45 Measure skill: Preemployment testing

Although practice varies, many personnel departments of business firms require an applicant to come for a preliminary interview and to take certain tests as an initial screening device. If the applicant passes these tests, he or she is then considered for the position and may take other employment tests required by the company.

1 Measure straight-copy skill (15′)

two 5′ writings; circle errors; determine *gwam*; record better rate

all letters used | A | 1.5 si | 5.6 awl | 80% hfw |

	gwam 1′	5′
To hunt for a job is a bit of an art. Be sure to organize your	13	3
attack with care. At the outset, get all cogent or pertinent personal	27	5
data, such as your social security number, the names and addresses of	41	8
persons whom you can use for reference, and the dates of your schooling	55	11
and work experiences. Next, prepare a data sheet that lists or sums up	70	14
your personal characteristics, education, and work experiences. If you	84	17
have any useful skills, such as typing or shorthand, be sure to list	98	20
them. Finally, list the names of two or three individuals other than	112	22
relatives who know something about you.	120	24
Now you are ready to hunt for job leads. Inquire among friends,	13	27
relatives, and others who may be in a position to help you. Your school	28	29
may have a placement bureau--be sure to utilize it. Examine the "Help	42	32
Wanted" advertisements in your newspaper. When you locate a promising	56	35
job opportunity, ask by letter or telephone for an interview, unless you	71	38
know that you are to go at once for an interview. If you write a letter	85	41
of application, it should be neatly and correctly typed. When you are	99	44
invited for an interview, dress simply and in good taste; exhibit an	113	47
interest in the company and the job; sell yourself, your skills, and	127	49
your abilities; and you will enhance your chances of getting the job.	141	52

gwam 1′ | 1 | 2 | 3 | 4 | 5 | 6 | 7 | 8 | 9 | 10 | 11 | 12 | 13 | 14 |
5′ | 1 | 2 | 3 |

Save your copy for *Typewriting Manual*.

129e, continued

Assignment 10
Typing a speech

Mr. Buchanan has made extensive changes in a talk he is to give at a conference. He needs the entire speech typed in final form.

Because a typed copy of a speech must be easy to read, do this: Leave 1½" top margin, page 1
1½" side margins
1" bottom margin (approx.)
1" top margin on second and other pages

DS the ¶s with 2 DS between them. Indent ¶s 5 spaces. Number pages (after page 1) on Line 4 at right margin.

Stay alert!

¶1 As a member of this panel, my task is to discuss briefly "Work Measurement in the Office." Perhaps, at the outset, a definition of work measurement is in order.

WORK MEASUREMENT IN THE OFFICE TS

¶3 ~~All~~ most of you are aware that cost of labor ~~comprises~~ is the major expense of the office. ~~Therefore,~~ time-related work measurement techniques are, therefore, needed vital to gather ~~the~~ information in the office for effective planning and control. Information which relates ~~to~~ the accomplishment of a particular task or set of duties to the time it takes to normally perform ~~the~~ that task may be called a "standard." Work measurement provides the information necessary to set standards. Later I shall demonstrate how a standard is set for a common office task. ¶4 Actually, the ability to measure the amount of work required to perform a specific task or job is essential for anyone concerned with improving working conditions and ~~accomplishing work~~ having job tasks completed in the most effective and satisfying manner.

The measurement of work provides ~~a quantitative~~ the means ~~to make~~ for making evaluations and decisions concerning a task which would otherwise be made subjectively.

¶2 Work measurement involves the ~~analysis~~ study of HOW and WHY the job is performed, analysis to determine whether the work is being performed in the prescribed manner with the proper level of quality control, and analysis ~~of~~ to determine whether the work itself is necessary or whether the methods of performing it can be improved.

¶5 Today, several basic work measurement techniques are being used—each ~~with~~ has its own unique place and value when used correctly. Briefly, these techniques are: estimates, historical records, time studies, micromotion studies, work sampling, and predetermined time standards. Predetermined time systems, a term used to include about five or six major systems, are generally considered the most accurate and objective of the techniques available. The basic data have

heading centered 1" from top;
1" side margins; use judgment
in arranging data

PERSONAL DATA SHEET

Daniel Wunsch	Age: 18
1610 Midvale Avenue	Single
Los Angeles, CA 90024	6'2" 175 pounds
(213) 563-4182	Health: Excellent

EDUCATION

Senior at University High School
High school diploma, pending graduation
Major: Business education
Grade average: B+ (upper 15% of graduating class)

SCHOOL ACTIVITIES

Student body treasurer, senior year. Receive and disburse student body funds; keep records; prepare purchase requisitions.

Member of varsity basketball team, junior and senior years.

President of Junior Achievement Club, junior year. Organized University High Products Company which designed and sold personalized T-shirts.

WORK EXPERIENCE

Clerk/typist at NBC Television Studios for two summers. Typed forms and letters; sorted and distributed mail; operated Xerox duplicating equipment; acted as studio guide. Received Idea of the Month Award for work simplification suggestion which resulted in a reduction of errors.

Newspaper route, one year. Delivered 120 papers daily, made monthly collections, and solicited new subscriptions. Was instrumental in increasing circulation on route by 26 percent.

PERSONAL BACKGROUND

Lived first twelve years and attended public schools in Huron, South Dakota. Interests include model building and reading. Enjoy backpacking, volleyball, basketball, and swimming.

REFERENCES (by Permission)

Mr. Donald Click, Boys' Vice Principal, University High School; 11800 Texas Avenue; Los Angeles, CA 90049.

Mrs. Trudy Saffer, Business Instructor, University High School; 11800 Texas Avenue; Los Angeles, CA 90049.

Mr. Paul Guyer, Office Manager, NBC Television Studios; 3000 W. Alameda; Burbank, CA 91503.

Personal data sheet

129e, continued

Assignment 10, continued
Recall: Leave 2 DS between ¶s.

been developed by highly qualified persons; ~~it is~~ consistent; and, in some instandes, ~~it~~ may be used easily and quickly by a person with limited technical knowledge. However, it is important to understand that to ~~properly and extensively~~ use predetermined time satndards, highly specialized training is required.

Predetermined time systems ~~indicate~~ in precise detail well defined tasks. They were developed when ~~engineers~~ asked themselves why the same basic movements were studied when the work remained the same. ~~When all is said and done~~, the human body can only perform so many motions. To insert a sheet of paper in a typeriter in New York requires no more effort than it does in Los Angeles and the time requirements ~~remain~~ the same. In other words, whynot classify activities and measure them <u>once and for all</u>? As a result, predetermined time systems have been estab lished for many ~~times~~ of work. They have been established by ~~very~~ thorough study of the minute movements a person uses in performing a task.

The mtehod of application is the samefor all predetermined time systems. Let's take a simple but repetitive and representative task, such as the typing of an average one page letter and apply a predetermined time system to ~~determine~~ a time for typing a letter. The completed example is projected on the screen to aid you in following the ~~procedure~~.

<u>Step 1</u>. Closely observe the basic movements required to accomplish the task.

<u>Step 2</u>. Briefly describe these movements in the proper sequence of thei performance.

<u>Step 3</u>. Determine through observation, the ~~number of times~~ ~~this~~ element occurs in relation to the task output (in case of this

146c ▶35 Apply for employment

plain sheets

The advertisement shown below appeared in the help wanted section of a newspaper.

OFFICE ADMINISTRATIVE ASSISTANT
Must have good typing skill. Send letter of application and data sheet to: R. J. Lowe, Personnel Director, Contemporary Office Associates, 611 Wilshire Blvd., Los Angeles, CA 90017

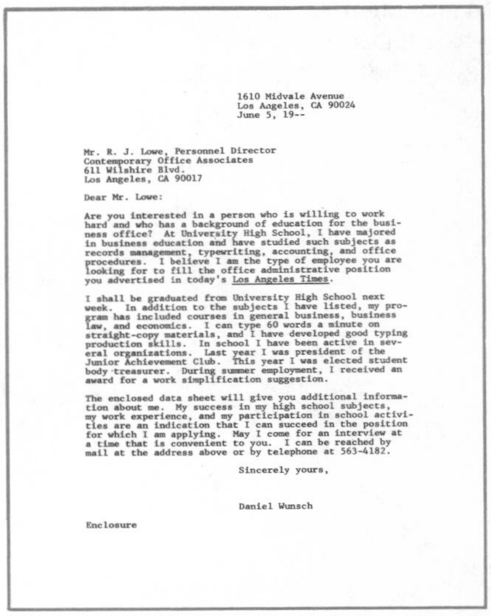

1610 Midvale Avenue
Los Angeles, CA 90024
June 5, 19--

Mr. R. J. Lowe, Personnel Director
Contemporary Office Associates
611 Wilshire Blvd.
Los Angeles, CA 90017

Dear Mr. Lowe:

Are you interested in a person who is willing to work hard and who has a background of education for the business office? At University High School, I have majored in business education and have studied such subjects as records management, typewriting, accounting, and office procedures. I believe I am the type of employee you are looking for to fill the office administrative position you advertised in today's Los Angeles Times.

I shall be graduated from University High School next week. In addition to the subjects I have listed, my program has included courses in general business, business law, and economics. I can type 60 words a minute on straight-copy materials, and I have developed good typing production skills. In school I have been active in several organizations. Last year I was president of the Junior Achievement Club. This year I was elected student body treasurer. During summer employment, I received an award for a work simplification suggestion.

The enclosed data sheet will give you additional information about me. My success in my high school subjects, my work experience, and my participation in school activities are an indication that I can succeed in the position for which I am applying. May I come for an interview at a time that is convenient to you. I can be reached by mail at the address above or by telephone at 563-4182.

Sincerely yours,

Daniel Wunsch

Enclosure

Assignment 1
Type a letter of application
modified block, mixed;
1½" side margins;
start return address at center, Line 10

Assignment 2
Type a personal data sheet
Type the data sheet shown on page 240 to enclose with the letter of application (Assignment 1). The illustration shows one acceptable style.

Assignment 3
Compose a letter of application and prepare a personal data sheet
As time permits, assume that you are applying for the job in the advertisement. Prepare in rough form (x-out errors) a letter of application and a data sheet that are appropriate for you. Save copies for use in Lesson 148.

1610 Midvale Avenue Los Angeles, CA 90024 June 5, 19-- Mr. R. J. Lowe, Personnel Director Contemporary Office Associates 611 Wilshire Blvd. Los Angeles, CA 90017 Dear Mr. Lowe:

(¶ 1) Are you interested in a person who is willing to work hard and who has a background of education for the business office? At University High School, I have majored in business education and have studied such subjects as records management, typewriting, accounting, and office procedures. I believe I am the type of employee you are looking for to fill the office administrative position you advertised in today's Los Angeles Times.

(¶ 2) I shall be graduated from University High School next week. In addition to the subjects I have listed, my program has included courses in general business, business law, and economics. I can type 60 words a minute on straight-copy materials, and I have developed good typing production skills. In school I have been active in several organizations. Last year I was president of the Junior Achievement Club. This year I was elected student body treasurer. During summer employment, I received an award for a work simplification suggestion.

(¶ 3) The enclosed data sheet will give you additional information about me. My success in my high school subjects, my work experience, and my participation in school activities are an indication that I can succeed in the position for which I am applying. May I come for an interview at a time that is convenient to you. I can be reached by mail at the address above or by telephone at 563-4182.

Sincerely yours, Daniel Wunsch Enclosure (277)

129e, continued

Assignment 10, continued

DS ¶s; 2 DSs between ¶s

illustration--the one-page letter), which is used as a consistent and measurable unit.

Step 4. Look up in Predetermined Time Systems Tables the standard time required for each element.

Step 5. Calculate, based upon the frequency with which the element occurs in relation to the final production unit, the total time for the unit.

Step 6. Total elemental times and appropriate personal allowances.

You can see, in the example projected on the screen, that by applying predetermined time standards to a repetitive typing task, a standard time of 8.177 minutes has been established for producing an average single-page letter. Also note that over 40 percent of the time required to produce the letter involves nontyping activity. This information suggests that close attention to methods is required for the most effective performance, and it highlights the importance of methods as one of the valuable uses of quantitative work measurement.

Predetermined time systems, which have been established for many repetitive office tasks, are an excellent and readily available resource for appraising and evaluating job performance in the office since time is the common denominator for establishing office job performance standards. These systems provide the means to make equitable and consistent comparisons of diverse tasks. When attempting to explain to an office worker that a standard minute of his or her work, whether it be 240 keystrokes of typing or one paper sorted and filed, is an absolute measurement, like an ounce, an inch, or a centimeter, and can be used to compare work of different people and departments, you'll be glad to have predetermined time system techniques to support your statements!

That in a nutshell, Ladies and Gentlemen, is what work measurement in the office is all about. In conclusion, I'm tempted to paraphrase a somewhat shopworn joke and say, "Time specialists never die--they continue to measure away."

Enrichment material for Unit 22 appears on LM pp. 113–122.

Assignment 11
Composing letters

The first 2 companies on your mailing list have responded to Mr. Buchanan's letter. Compose brief letters to these companies. Tell them Mr. Buchanan is out of the city until May 25. Tell them that Mr. Buchanan will be pleased to hear from them and that he will answer their questions when he returns. Add any other information you think desirable. In your first draft, x-out your errors. Make needed corrections and retype the letters. Use the date *May 18, 19—*. Address small envelopes.

Letter 1

Mr. Gordon Culver, Vice President
Alberto-Culver Company
2525 W. Armitage Ave.
Melrose Park, IL 60164

Letter 2

Mrs. Ruth Pulumbo, Manager
Bausch & Lomb, Inc.
635 St. Paul Street
Rochester, NY 14602

unit **24** lessons 146–150

Measuring typewriting competence

Measurement goals

1. To measure and evaluate your overall typing skill.

2. To help you develop skill in typing a letter of application and a personal data sheet.

3. To acquaint you with some of the testing procedures which may be used in evaluating your qualifications for employment in an office.

4. To help you prepare for a job interview.

Machine adjustments

Make the usual machine adjustments as required for the various activities.

146

146a ▶5 Conditioning practice

each line 3 times (slowly, faster, in-between rate)

alphabet The new Zula and Jaguar sports cars were moved quickly from a box car.

fig/sym J & B, Inc. sold the store at 14382 Del Mar Drive for $95,760 in 1976.

fingers 3, 4 Sally will poll all politicians about the six bills before the senate.

fluency You can do the seemingly impossible if you have faith in your efforts.

| 1 | 2 | 3 | 4 | 5 | 6 | 7 | 8 | 9 | 10 | 11 | 12 | 13 | 14 |

146b ▶10 Evaluate your posture and typing techniques

Check your typing position (Items 1–3); then type each drill line 3 times (slowly, faster, top speed) as you make the evaluation checks.

Typing position

Evaluation checks

1 Fingers curved and upright?

2 Wrists low and relaxed?

3 Right thumb curved and resting lightly on space bar?

Keystroking

Quick, snappy keystroking

4 Be sure to keep all fingers curved and upright as you strike the keys.

5 Strike each key with a quick snapstroke with the hands and arms quiet.

Spacing

Quick, down-and-in spacing motion

6 Make each spacing stroke quickly; start the next word without pausing.

7 The busy firm may need the map of the city if they are to do the work.

Shift keys

Little-finger reach

8 M. R. McCoy is with the New York firm of Gustin, Gunn, McNeil & Jones.

9 Vice President Berta J. McClellan of Leo A. Daly Co. flew to New York.

Continuity and rhythm

Variable speed pattern; no pauses

10 It is important to type with continuity and a variable rhythm pattern.

11 Please send the statement to them on or before the date of the letter.

Return

tab: center + 10

Quick return; eyes on copy

12 tab ——————→ Make a quick, flick return

13 and start the new line without pausing. (repeat twice)

unit **23** lessons 136–145

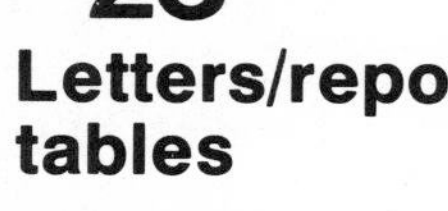

Letters/reports/ tables

Learning goals

1. To increase still more your typing production skills on letters of varying length and letters with tables; on memos, tables, reports, etc.

2. To develop competency in making special error corrections.

3. To learn techniques for justifying the right margin (making it even).

4. To increase basic skills.

5. To review basic letter styles.

Machine adjustments

Make the usual machine adjustments as required for various activities.

Supplies needed

Seventeen envelopes (small or large) for 136c, page 225; 137d, page 226; and 139c, page 230.

136

136a ▶5 Conditioning practice

each line 3 times (slowly, faster, in-between rate)

alphabet	John V. Maze is able to type six words faster by using a quick stroke.
fig/sym	Jerry Trane said, "Dan's Policy 843-756, due in 2019, is for $50,000."
long words	Electromechanical devices and servomechanisms solved systems problems.
fluency	They paid for the gowns with the money she received for her handiwork.

| 1 | 2 | 3 | 4 | 5 | 6 | 7 | 8 | 9 | 10 | 11 | 12 | 13 | 14 |

136b ▶15 Measure basic skill: straight copy

two 5′ writings; determine *gwam*; proofread; circle errors; record better rate

all letters used | A | 1.5 si | 5.6 awl | 80% hfw |

	gwam 1′	5′
If you are employed as a typist, you will frequently be called on	13	3
to choose the appropriate personal title to use with someone's name. Of	28	6
course, there are also occasions when the use of any title is inappropri-	42	8
ate, and you will need to recognize them. A few simple guides are given	57	11
below and represent some of the accepted usages.	67	13
A personal title (Mr., Mrs., or Miss) should precede the name of an	14	16
individual in a letter address or in a salutation that includes a surname.	29	19
When you do not know the marital status of a woman or when she herself	43	22
has used the title, use "Ms." Some professional title (for example, Dr.,	58	25
Professor, or Dean) may replace the personal title in these lines.	71	28
In the closing lines of a letter, a personal or professional title	13	30
is never used with a man's name and needn't be used with a woman's name.	28	33
A woman writer, however, can show consideration for the reader just by	42	36
typing a title before her typed name or by writing it (in parentheses)	57	39
before her script signature.	62	40

gwam 1′ | 1 | 2 | 3 | 4 | 5 | 6 | 7 | 8 | 9 | 10 | 11 | 12 | 13 | 14 |
5′ | 1 | 2 | 3 |

145c ▶25 Type a report with tables

Margins
top: 2" elite
1½" pica
side: 1"
bottom: approx. 1"

DS report; TS after main heading, before side headings; before and after centered table headings. SS columnar items.

Recall: Mark a point 2–2½" from the bottom of first page to alert you to plan for page ending, or use a page line gauge, or both. On page 2, leave space between the table and the footnote divider line so that the bottom margin will be 6 lines (1") deep.

Note: If your typewriter does not have the + symbol, make it by typing the /, then backspacing and typing the hyphen: ⁄-.

RESEARCH SUMMARY

The purpose of the research was to assess the effects of copy difficulty on the typewriting performance of students at the end of their third and fourth semesters of typewriting instruction at the high school level (Typing III and IV).
TS

Speed Comparisons--Typing III and IV

A comparison of mean 5-minute gwam speeds of Typing III and Typing IV students is shown below.
TS

MEAN GWAM SPEED COMPARISONS[1]
TS

Test	Typing III Mean GWAM	Typing IV Mean GWAM	+Increase −Decrease
1	48.30	51.99	+3.69
2	47.97	51.57	+3.60
3	47.79	51.26	+3.44
4	46.22	48.75	+2.53
5	44.60	46.83	+2.23 TS

Typing IV students typed from 2.23 to 3.69 gwam faster than did Typing III students on the various straight-copy tests, which increased in level of difficulty from test to test. The differences in the increase in gwam decreased as the tests became more difficult.

Error Comparisons--Typing III and IV

A comparison of the mean errors of Typing III and Typing IV students is shown on the next page. The comparison indicates that the number of errors made by these students on each of the tests tends to remain relatively constant. On any one of the tests, a difference of less than one error separates these students. From the data shown below, it would appear that Typing IV students typed with less accuracy on Tests 1 and 2 as compared with Typing III students; however, conversion of the error scores to percent-of-error scores refutes this assumption. It should be noted that the average typist makes about 2 errors during each minute of typing.

MEAN ERROR COMPARISONS[2]

Test	Typing III Mean Errors	Typing IV Mean Errors	+Increase −Decrease
1	10.08	10.66	+.58
2	8.83	9.65	+.82
3	10.40	9.52	−.88
4	9.66	9.55	−.11
5	10.83	10.54	−.29

---

[1] Lawrence W. Erickson, "Effects of Straight-Copy Difficulty on the Speed and Accuracy of Second-Year High School Typing Students," NABTE Review (Washington: National Association for Business Teacher Education, 1975), p. 103.

[2] Erickson, p. 103.

136c ▶30
Improve letter production skill

plain sheets; block style, open; standard 6″ line; current date on Line 16; supply appropriate opening and closing lines; use your name as dictator and S-1 as reference

Type letters to as many of the addressees given here as time permits. Address envelopes. As ¶ 1, use the paragraph shown at the right; then use ¶s 2 and 3 of 136b, page 224. Type each letter from your previous one. (Disregard color underlines.)

(¶ 1) The guides given here represent some of the accepted ways to use a personal title with a name. If you have any questions about usage, please let me know.

Addressees

			gwam 3′
Miss Jan Leuthe	2163 Burr Oak Park	Boston, MA 02121	3
Ms. Evelyn Clausen	764 Cumberland Ave.	Portland, ME 04101	7
Dr. Lewis Tarbox	7308 American Ave.	Detroit, MI 48210	11
Mrs. Richard Perry	2433 Lariat Meadows Dr.	Eugene, OR 97401	15
Mr. Emmett Minske	735 Idaho Ave., S.E.	Huron, SD 57350	19
Ms. Jean LaFleur	3310 Fairmount Ave.	Dallas, TX 75201	22

137

137a ▶5
Conditioning practice

each line 3 times (slowly, faster, in-between rate)

alphabet The brown fox jumped very quickly to grab those excited, fuzzy chicks.

fig/sym These fishing boxes (9″ x 8 1/2″ x 4″) with 6/0 reels sell for $23.75.

long words Propulsion system and applied aerodynamics specialists are needed now.

fluency They expect to make the audit of the offices at the end of this month.

| 1 | 2 | 3 | 4 | 5 | 6 | 7 | 8 | 9 | 10 | 11 | 12 | 13 | 14 |

137b ▶10
Check tabulation skill

Two 3′ writings on addresses only, arranged as a SS table. Arrange the addresses given in 136c, above, in 3 columns: Col. 1, name; Col. 2, street; and Col. 3, city, state, ZIP. Leave 4 spaces between columns (longest line is color underlined); leave about a 1″ top margin. If you complete list, DS and start over. Determine *gwam* and % of transfer.

Goal: To try to reach 50% of straight-copy rate on 136b.

137c ▶10
Build high speed

1. Three 1′ writings. Build speed by keeping the keystroking action in your fingers. Note rates.

2. A 2′ writing. Try to maintain your best 1′ rate.

3. Another 2′ writing. Work for increased speed.

4. Record best 1′ and better 2′ rates.

The primary element of high speed typewriting is knowing that you are typing with good form or technique patterns. An individual who can perform at high proficiency levels will be in demand in the world of work. In the busy world of work, personality is another important element of success. If there is one thing of which we can be sure in the world of work, it is the tremendous importance of both of these elements, the element of proficiency and the element of personality.

145

145a ▶5 Conditioning practice

each line 3 times (slowly, faster, in-between rate)

alphabet	Jack Waxlof made amazing progress by using improved typing techniques.
fig/sym	The rates varied from 5 1/2% to 7 1/4% on loans from $300 to $986,250.
continuity	Are you going to send an abstract of the monopoly case to him by noon?
fluency	The full value of happiness is gained through sharing it with someone.

| 1 | 2 | 3 | 4 | 5 | 6 | 7 | 8 | 9 | 10 | 11 | 12 | 13 | 14 |

145b ▶20 Type an itinerary

1 cc; 1" top and side margins; center heading lines; correct errors

An itinerary (a travel schedule) usually includes a chronological listing of departure and arrival times; mode of travel and accommodations; and often a list of scheduled activities.

Type the itinerary as illustrated. SS items but DS between them. Save for *Typewriting Manual*.

Note: Before starting to type a column of figures, check ahead to see if you will need to indent the first item to align with one farther down the column. For example, notice that the first *time* given in the itinerary has been indented 1 space.

ITINERARY OF ROBERT J. LOWE

DS

June 9 to June 12

New York, Chicago, Houston

TS

MONDAY, JUNE 9: LOS ANGELES TO NEW YORK

DS

8:45 a.m. Leave Los Angeles International Airport on United 6 (prepaid tickets at UAL counter at airport). Lunch.

DS

4:45 p.m. Arrive Kennedy International Airport. Guaranteed-arrival reservation at International Hotel.

7:00 p.m. Dinner meeting at hotel with Geoff Runge of New York office. Discuss client promotion program.

TUESDAY, JUNE 10: INTERNATIONAL HOTEL

8:00 a.m. Systems and Procedures Conference at hotel.

1:30 p.m. Deliver speech at Conference. Notes for talk in marked folder; also, copy of speech, marked HOLD FOR ARRIVAL, mailed to you at hotel.

6:00 p.m. Dinner and theater in New York.

WEDNESDAY, JUNE 11: NEW YORK TO CHICAGO TO HOUSTON

10:45 a.m. Leave La Guardia Airport on United 159.
Note: Limousine leaves hotel for La Guardia at 9:00.

12:10 p.m. Arrive O'Hare International Airport. Lunch at airport with Mr. de Kaulb and City of Chicago Records Management Project team for progress report.

5:45 p.m. Leave O'Hare on Braniff 145 to Houston. Dinner.

8:05 p.m. Arrive Houston International Airport. Pick up Hertz car at airport for travel to Continental Hotel (confirmed reservations in travel folder).

THURSDAY, JUNE 12: HOUSTON AND LOS ANGELES

9:00 a.m. Meeting at Texas Instruments Corporation with General Manager Craig Carlson and staff regarding implementation of Work Measurement Program.

5:10 p.m. Leave Houston International Airport on Continental 55 for return to Los Angeles. Dinner.

8:25 p.m. Arrive Los Angeles International Airport. Welcome home!

137d ▶25
Build letter production skill: short letters

plain sheets; block style, open; standard 6″ line

Type these letters, supplying appropriate letter parts as needed. Make 1 cc; address envelopes. Erase and correct errors.

Goal: To complete all letters in 25′ or less.

Stay alert!

Letter 1

Ms. Helen Hustad 1001 N. Natchez Road Chattanooga, TN 37405 (¶ 1) Your subscription to FUTURES DESIGN is due to run out soon. That's why I urge you to tell us to renew your subscription. Just return the enclosed card. (¶ 2) No need to pay until we bill you. All we need for now are your instructions to keep FUTURES DESIGN coming to you. Mary Ellen Oliverio Subscriptions Manager Enclosure (54)

Letter 2

March 25, 19-- Mrs. Mary Handler 6315 San Vincente Blvd. Los Angeles, CA 90057 (¶ 1) Plan to be our guest for an exciting presentation of spring fashions.

Saturday, April 10
Informal Modeling 12:00 to 4:00 p.m.
Mini Show 2:30 p.m.

(¶ 2) Luncheon will be served in the Vista Room. Just return the enclosed card to confirm your reservation. BULLOCK'S WESTWOOD Jerome Nachreiner Fashion Designs Enclosure (50)

Letter 3

Superintendent of Documents U.S. Government Printing Office Washington, DC 20402 (¶ 1) Enclosed is my check for $2.50. Please send me the publications listed below:

Your Federal Income Tax	$1.50
Tax Savings Suggestions	.75
Your Social Security	.25
	$2.50

(¶ 2) Please send these publications to me soon. James Bennett (41)

Letter 4

Mr. Robert Thompson 1135 College Avenue Topeka, KS 66604 (¶ 1) Whether you've got a little money or a lot of money, we invite you to choose a savings plan that is designed to work and to make the most of what you've got. (¶ 2) Our savings plans are described in the enclosed brochure. Study it and then come in and discuss your needs with us. Paul Ambrose Savings Department (55)

Letter 5

Mr. Nicholas Kosikos, President Sports Car Products, Ltd. 900 San Ysidro Lane Santa Barbara, CA 93108 (¶ 1) Thanks for sending us the cutaway carburetor. This carburetor has been very helpful in our sales demonstrations. (¶ 2) I understand that you have prepared a single-loop videotape on the carburetors you manufacture for sports cars. Can you send this videotape so that we can test it at our Divisional Sales Conference next month? Hector Neff Sales Manager (65)

143c ▶30 Type index cards [LM pp. 137-142]

1. From the illustration at the right, type a 5″ × 3″ index classification card. Follow the spacing directions shown in color.

2. Guided by this card, type a card for each additional name on the list of 143b, page 234. Arrange the items appropriately.

3. Sort the cards alphabetically according to skills or experience (for example, SECRETARY in the illustration).

4. Type an identification card using the heading of the table of 143b and the current date. DS. Center the lines vertically and horizontally on the card. Fasten with rubber band.

start on Line 5

```
SECRETARY
                DS
Name:  Bach, Rudolf
                DS
Telephone:  826-5451
                TS

Shorthand 120
Typing 60
```

1″ left margin

144

144a ▶5 Conditioning practice

each line 3 times (slowly, faster, in-between rate)

alphabet	Five kind doctors gazed jubilantly at the new hospital annex marquees.
fig/sym	Call Ocher & O'Brien, 621 St. Louis Street, toll free at 800-574-9365.
space bar	Many of these men and women will pay all union dues today or tomorrow.
fluency	This world is full of good intentions which are waiting to be applied.

| 1 | 2 | 3 | 4 | 5 | 6 | 7 | 8 | 9 | 10 | 11 | 12 | 13 | 14 |

144b ▶15 Improve basic skill: statistical rough draft

two 5′ writings of 138c, page 227

1. In the first 5′ writing, try to type at your best rate.

Goal: Not more than 5 errors.

2. In the second 5′ writing, increase your speed if you made the Step 1 goal; if not, decrease speed slightly and try to type with greater control.

144c ▶30 Review letter styles

plain sheets; correct errors; center name of letter style approximately ½″ from bottom edge

page 73, Style Letter 1
page 83, Style Letter 2
page 150, Style Letter 3
page 157, Style Letter 4

Type as many of the problems listed as you can in the time allowed. Make pencil notations of the problems, page numbers, and general directions so that you will not need to refer to this page.

As you type each letter, evaluate its acceptability: An acceptable letter is attractively placed on the page, is typed with uniform (even) keystroking, has proper word division at ends of lines, and has all errors neatly corrected. It has "eye appeal" and makes a good impression on all who see it.

Save the 4 letters for *Type-writing Manual.*

138

138a ▶5 Conditioning practice

each line 3 times (slowly, faster, in-between rate)

alphabet	The reporters quickly recognized the vexing problems of judging flaws.
fig/sym	A $50 million 12-year 6 3/4% debenture was offered at $98 to yield 7%.
adjacent keys	That popular but wise aquanaut was never careless in any water sports.
fluency	I'll sign a contract by the end of the week, and we can test the case.

| 1 | 2 | 3 | 4 | 5 | 6 | 7 | 8 | 9 | 10 | 11 | 12 | 13 | 14 |

138b ▶10 Improve control: accuracy

Subtract 8 from your best 1' rate on 137c, page 225; then type additional writings on 137c as follows:

1. Type three 1' writings at this new goal rate as your teacher guides your writing by calling the ¼' intervals.

Goal: Not over 1 error each writing.

2. Increase rate by 4 *gwam*; type two 1' guided writings at this new goal rate.

3. Type a 2' writing for control. Try to maintain your goal rate for 2'.

138c ▶15 Measure basic skill: statistical rough draft

two 5' writings; determine *gwam*; proofread and circle errors

Record better rate and % of transfer: rate divided by straight-copy rate on 136b, page 224.

Goal: A 75–80% transfer.

all figures used | A | 1.5 si | 5.6 awl | 80% hfw

	gwam 1'	5'
How much does it cost to own a car? An 8-cylinder, medium-	12	2
size car costs the average American about $3.25 a day. This firm	35	7
cost covers insurance, licence and registration fees, and depreci-	48	10
ation. Gas and oil average about 4.18 cents a mile. Car-mainten-	69	14
ance costs vary from .87 to .93 cents a mile, and tire costs add	82	16
another .65 cents. Thus, the total variable costs jump to an aver-	97	19
age of 5.7 cents a mile. The total general costs vary from 10.6	110	22
cents to 23.2 cents amile.	116	23
How can you reduce these expenses? A 5,000-pound car needs ap-	12	26
proximately twice as much fuel in city driving as does a 2,500-pound	26	28
car. A 4-cylinder job with an 85-cubic-inch engine gets double the	40	31
gas mileage of a 8-cyliner car with a 454-cubic-inch engine. Oper-	54	34
ating airconditioners reduces mileage approximately 9% to 20%, and	68	37
the automatic transmission, approximately 5% to 15%. The best fuel	86	40
economy for all cars occurs at speeds between 30 and 40, with no	101	43
stops and no fast speed changes. "Gunning a car can rob 16% to 17%	117	47
of a car's gas savings.	129	49
	134	50

143

143a ▶5 Conditioning practice

each line 3 times (slowly, faster, in-between rate)

alphabet	Murky haze enveloped a city as jarring quakes broke forty-six windows.
fig/sym	The building at 1473 Bond Street was sold to Jones & Co. for $290,685.
one-hand	Were you aware that the water polo player executed few exciting saves?
fluency	Actions speak louder than words--it is by our deeds that we are known.

| 1 | 2 | 3 | 4 | 5 | 6 | 7 | 8 | 9 | 10 | 11 | 12 | 13 | 14 |

143b ▶15 Improve tabulation skill

full sheet; reading position; DS column data; use judgment as to horizontal placement of columns; correct errors

Goal: To complete typing of table in 15′ or less.

Each figure used 11 times or more.

APPLICANT TALENT INVENTORY

Name	Telephone	Skills or Experience	words
			5
			19
Bach, Rudolf	826-5451	Secretary (120/60)*	27
Bratfish, Gina	393-7274	Stenographer (80/50)	36
Cotton, Carole	550-2730	Typist (50)	44
Dexter, Karen	819-9620	Receptionist (40)	52
Dorsett, Donna	870-4614	Secretary (100/70)	60
Giannini, Peter	398-5612	Accountant (CPA)	69
Kapp, John	478-3159	Bookkeeper (60)	76
McClellan, James	656-3029	Budget Analyst	84
Ostrow, Jack	747-1248	Typist (60)	91
Price, Tracy	686-3910	Custodian	97
Reagan, James	213-7840	Gardener	104
Siegal, Margot	659-0215	Typist (80)	111
Sullivan, Michael	346-7938	General Clerk (50)	120
Van Deran, Ken	475-6210	Accountant	127

______________ 131

* Double numbers indicate shorthand/typing skill; single number, 145
typing skill. 150

Retain sheet for use with 143c, page 235.

138d ▶7 Correct errors by squeezing words

Certain corrections may be made by squeezing letters into half spaces, or by squeezing the letters of an entire word into the available space.

Type the first "As typed" phrase exactly as shown; then follow the "What to do" direction. Check your work with "As corrected" solution. *Repeat, as needed.* Follow same procedure for Items 2–4.

	As typed	What to do	As corrected
1	an omitte letter	Squeeze "d" into the half space.	an omitted letter
2	an omitted etter	Squeeze "l" into the half space.	an omitted letter
3	a leter omitted	Erase "leter" and type "letter."	a letter omitted
4	a lettter added	Erase "lettter" and type "letter."	a letter added

Solutions

If your typewriter has a half-space mechanism, use it as you position the carriage (or element) for typing at the half-space point (the point between the marks on the line-of-writing scale). If not, for **Item 1**, move carriage (or element) to space where letter is omitted. Press your right fingers against carriage (or element) to move it back to half-space point, then type omitted letter.

For **Item 2,** move carriage (or element) to letter following omitted letter; then push carriage (or element) back to half-space point and type omitted letter.

For **Item 3,** move carriage (or element) to second space following last word before erasure. Note number on scale; then push carriage (or element) back to half-space point and type omitted letter. Next, space once, and repeat procedure for other letters.

For **Item 4,** move carriage (or element) to third space following last word before erasure. From this point, follow procedure for typing omitted letters.

138e ▶13 Type copy with right margin justified

line 32; SS;
indent ¶s 3 spaces

You are to type the 2 ¶s in Column 1 with the right margin even; SS between ¶s.

1. Type ¶s 1 and 2 of the WORK COPY with the / to show needed extra spacing for each line.

2. Center and retype the copy on a half sheet (short side up) making the line endings even. Center the heading, COPY WITH EVEN RIGHT MARGIN, above the column. Correct all errors.

Paragraph 1 of the WORK COPY and the final copy is in completed form. To get right margin even, use your judgment and distribute the spaces so that they are least noticeable.

WORK COPY

```
////////////////////////////////
   Copy is justified (typed with
the right margin even) by adding
extra spaces between words to///
fill out short lines and using//
half spaces between words when//
it may be necessary to squeeze an
extra letter on a line.
   School newspapers which may
be produced with the typewriter
are often typed in this manner
sc that the duplicated copies
have the appearance of a printed
page.  First a stencil or spirit
master is typed from the work
copy, and then the desired number
of copies is duplicated.
```

COPY WITH EVEN RIGHT MARGIN

```
   Copy is justified (typed with
the right margin even) by adding
extra  spaces between  words  to
fill out  short lines and  using
half spaces  between words  when
it may be necessary to squeeze an
extra letter on a line.
```

142b ▶15 Measure basic skill: straight copy

two 5′ writings; determine *gwam;* proofread, circle errors; record better rate

all letters used | A | 1.5 si | 5.6 awl | 80% hfw

	gwam 1′	5′
As a consumer, you make a number of decisions each time you enter	13	3
the marketplace. The decisions are related to your funds and your in-	27	5
terests, needs, and wants. Advertising plays a major role in influencing	42	8
the last three factors. The goal of advertising is to convince the con-	56	11
sumer to buy the item. You have an obligation as a member of the consum-	71	14
ing public and as manager of your money to analyze carefully what the	85	17
ad has stated about the item. You need to ask yourself at least three	99	20
vital questions about the ad before you decide to buy.	110	22
First, what promises does an ad make to you? A mouthwash ad, for	13	25
example, might promise fresh breath. Efficient gas mileage for an auto	28	28
under city driving conditions might also be promised. Second, will your	42	30
interests, needs, or wants be satisfied by the promises? Before you buy	57	33
a product, be sure that you have a reasonable idea of what to expect from	72	36
it. Decide whether or not the promises made are relevant to your way of	86	39
life. Third, is the advertiser reputable? One of the best ways to	100	42
verify the integrity of an advertiser is to check with an agency such	114	45
as the Better Business Bureau. The answers to these questions provide	128	48
the data you need to have before you make a purchase. The more facts	142	50
you have, the wiser will be your final decision.	152	52

gwam 1′ | 1 | 2 | 3 | 4 | 5 | 6 | 7 | 8 | 9 | 10 | 11 | 12 | 13 | 14
5′ | 1 | 2 | 3

142c ▶30 Measure production skill: letters [LM pp. 129-136]

modified block, indented ¶s, mixed; 1 cc; address envelopes

1. As you are timed for 20′, personalize the form letter to as many as possible of the names and addresses given on the cc of the 141d memo. Because you are writing for a *local* branch of Promenade, use your city and ZIP Code for each letter and envelope address.

2. Erase and correct errors; proofread; compute *n–pram.*

Time schedule

Planning and preparing .... 4′
Production timing .... 20′
Proofreading; computing *n–pram* .... 6′

	words
May 16, 19-- (Provide address lines and salutation) (¶ 1) Did you overlook our	22
recent statement, (title, last name)? This statement in the amount of (give amount)	36
was sent to you on (give bill date). Your account now appears on our past-due	51
or delinquent list. (¶ 2) The low prices that we are able to offer at our new	65
PROMENADE store are possible because our customers help us keep billing	80
expenses down by making prompt payment. And, of course, we want to avoid	95
the necessity of adding costly service charges on merchandise sold on credit.	110
(¶ 3) Won't you help us by mailing the amount now past due on your account as	126
shown on the enclosed duplicate statement. A return envelope is enclosed for	142
your convenience. If you cannot make full payment now, please contact me.	157
It is important that we hear from you soon. Your credit is one of your	172
most important assets. Sincerely yours, Joseph Picus Account Manager xx	186
Enclosures (161)*	188/200

* The word count is based on the average number of words in the insertions.

139

139a ▶5 Conditioning practice

each line 3 times (slowly, faster, in-between rate)

alphabet	Six juicy steaks sizzle over a big wood fire as the men sleep quietly.
fig/sym	Her check showed 49 men and 26 women on TWA's Flight 718 at 10:35 a.m.
shift key	Jan C. McNeil and Paula O'Brien will speak at the Key West Convention.
fluency	Can we demonstrate to those who would be careless that life is a gift?

| 1 | 2 | 3 | 4 | 5 | 6 | 7 | 8 | 9 | 10 | 11 | 12 | 13 | 14 |

139b ▶20 Build letter typing skill

plain sheets;
block style, open;
1½" margins;
date on Line 18

1. A 3′ writing on the letter to establish a base rate. If you finish before time is called, start over.

2. Determine *gwam*. Add 8 to this rate. Divide goal rate by 4; note ¼′ check points for guided writings.

3. Beginning with the date, type three 1′ guided writings on the opening parts of the letter and ¶ 1. Leave proper spacing between letter parts, but begin letter (dateline) near top of sheet. Start second and third writings a DS below last line of previous writing.

4. Repeat Step 3, using ¶ 2 and the closing lines of the letter.

5. Type another 3′ writing on the letter. Try to maintain your new goal rate. Do this by using good techniques and by typing with continuity. Determine *gwam* and compare it with the rate you attained in Step 1.

	gwam 3′
May 23, 19-- Mr. Christopher Kelford 1800 Bluegrass Avenue Louisville,	5
KY 40215 Dear Mr. Kelford	6
(¶ 1) We share with others in many ways. Let me cite some of the ways.	11
A single person shares his or her income with married persons with chil-	16
dren through the higher income tax rate to which the income of the single	21
person is subjected.	22
(¶ 2) People with large incomes also share with others through higher tax	27
rates on incomes. Businesses, too, share by taxes paid on earnings.	31
Taxes are used to support schools, parks, and other public facilities and	36
services in which we all share and from which we all benefit.	40
Cordially yours Mrs. Melissa B. Thomson Tax Consultant xx	44

gwam 3′ | 1 | 2 | 3 | 4 | 5 |

141c ▶20 Measure tabulation skill

two 5′ writings; proofread; determine *gwam*

full sheet; reading position; 4 spaces between columns; DS data of columns

Each figure used a minimum of 10 times.

Note: When a street has a number as its name, separate the house number from the street number by a hyphen preceded and followed by a space.

Arrange table in proper form. You will have 3′ to 4′ to determine left margin stop and tab stops for columns.

Determine, also, points at which main heading and column headings start. Make notations of these points.

					words
Main heading	DELINQUENT ACCOUNTS				7
Column headings	Name	Address	Bill Date	Amount	18
	Paul A. Alcorn	One Hillside Lane	March 10	$75.60	28
	Mrs. Lillian Block	8 El Dorado Plaza	March 20	$64.49	39
	Jerry Bowen	3889 Constitution Lane	March 15	$73.46	49
	Ms. Karen Crowell	9366 Del Mar Avenue	March 25	$74.20	60
	Miss Betty Field	1927 - 34th St., N.W.	March 15	$47.83	71
	Luis Kabashi	993 North 15th Street	March 15	$62.78	82
	Miss Janis Ready	6347 Driftwood Drive	March 25	$81.90	92
	Martin Stolzoff	10382 Sandwood Drive	March 25	$46.79	103
	Larry Thorpe	2039 Corinthian Walk	March 20	$56.74	113
	Mrs. James Tribbey	37484 Vincent Avenue	March 20	$96.15	125
	John von Coelin	1680 Corso di Napoli	March 15	$47.83	136
	Henry Zwart	26790 Cahuenga Blvd.	March 25	$93.10	146

141d ▶20 Type a memo

[LM pp. 127, 128]

full sheet; 1″ side margins; 1 cc; correct errors; SS table

If a memorandum form is not available, type the heading lines as shown here. Leave 1″ top margin.

Save carbon copy for use in 142c, page 233.

Indent 5 → TO: Mr. Joseph Picus, Account Manager

Indent 3 → FROM: Joy Benedict, Accounting Dept.

Indent 3 → DATE: May 12, 19--

Left margin → SUBJECT: Overdue Accounts

Accounts that are now more than 30 days past due are shown below. These names are being sent to you so that the regular form letter on overdue accounts can be sent to them.

(¶ 2) (Triple-space and type the entire table given in 141c above. Center the table horizontally as directed. SS columnar items.)

142

142a ▶5 Conditioning practice

each line 3 times (slowly, faster, in-between rate)

alphabet The view from the jungle peak was both exciting and amazing to Quincy.

fig/sym They paid the 8 1/4% second mortgage of $12,590 on September 23, 1976.

shift key L. Donald Jeffries is President of Corbett Industries, Inc., of Salem.

fluency No job has a future--the future is with the person who holds that job.

| 1 | 2 | 3 | 4 | 5 | 6 | 7 | 8 | 9 | 10 | 11 | 12 | 13 | 14 |

139c ▶25 Improve letter production skill

plain sheets; block style, open; 1 cc; correct errors; your initials as reference; address envelopes

Type the letter of 139b, page 229, to as many of the addressees given here as time permits. Proofread by typing each letter from the preceding one. Disregard color underlines.

			words
Mr. David Capretz	655 Lake Street	Oak Park, IL 60301	11
Miss Heather Carlson	295 Holiday Road	Detroit, MI 48236	22
Dr. James Deitz	10 Acela drive	Tiburon, CA 94920	32
Ms. Michelle McKay	1305 Hidden Acres Drive	Atlanta, GA 30340	44
Mrs. Kimberly McNaughton	434 Oak Lawn	Waterloo, IA 50701	55
Ms. Lisa Schwartz	8462 Sunset Blvd.	Los Angeles, CA 90069	67

140

140a ▶5 Conditioning practice

each line 3 times (slowly, faster, in-between rate)

alphabet Six flying fish whizzed quickly over my jigs as a big tuna approached.

fig/sym He bought a No. 9572 die for $384.10, taking a 12% discount of $46.09.

shift key Kristy, Adam, Nicole, Robert, and Joseph attend West Coast University.

fluency Some frustration in life may help us develop a better sense of values.

| 1 | 2 | 3 | 4 | 5 | 6 | 7 | 8 | 9 | 10 | 11 | 12 | 13 | 14 |

140b ▶20 Measure tabulation skill

two 5′ writings on the address lines of 139c, above, arranged in table form

1. Use half sheets (long side up); use heading lines given in Column 3; leave 4 spaces between columns.

2. Proofread; determine *gwam*.

Goal: 40% of straight-copy rate of 136b, page 224.

3. You will have 3′ to 4′ to determine the left margin stop and the tab stops for columns. Determine, also, the points at which the main heading and the column headings start. Make notations of these points.

Main heading — words

PROSPECTIVE CLIENTS--TAX SERVICE 7

Column headings

Name Street City, State, ZIP Code 19

140c ▶25 Measure production skill: letters

[LM pp. 123–126]

a 20′ production writing; correct errors; compute *n-pram*

Problem 1
Block style, open, standard 6″ line

Time schedule

Planning and preparing .. 2′
Production timing .... 20′
Proofreading; computing *n-pram* .... 3′

words

Current date Miss Ellen Medley Business Education Department Beverly Hills High School Beverly Hills, CA 90213 Dear Miss Medley (¶ 1) I am glad to respond to your request to describe some of the things we expect from our beginning office typists. In all departments, our typists are expected to be able to type letters, reports, forms, and other copy from rough draft or other source materials. Before they begin the typing task, they are expected to get any special reference materials that may be needed in typing the final copy. (¶ 2) The materials needed to complete typing tasks may originate in a variety of ways: 14 27 41 55 69 83 97 110 125

(continued, page 231)

140c, continued

words

(1) they may be given to the typist by the supervisor; (2) the typist may be asked to refer to the files for needed materials; or (3) the typist may need to go to other offices to secure the source materials or other data. (¶ 3) To perform effectively in an office situation, the typists must have learned to listen to, understand, and follow directions; to make clear notes of directions; to follow such directions without asking unnecessary questions; and to make critical judgments relating to the usability of the copy they have typed. This final comment means that we expect our typists to proofread their completed work and to find and correct all typing errors. (¶ 4) Please let me know if you or your students have other questions or problems with which I might help you. I hope the comments I have made in this letter will be of value to you. Sincerely yours CONTEMPORARY OFFICE ASSOCIATES Richard Buchanan, Senior Manager xx (251) — 139 153 167 181 195 209 223 237 252 265 280 294 307 311/331

Problem 2
Modified block, indented ¶s, mixed
See Placement Table, page 148, for margin setting.

Current date Mr. Frank E. Hughes The Irvine Company 1350 Front Street San Diego, CA 92101 Dear Mr. Hughes: (¶ 1) The costs associated with maintaining a typing station are growing at a staggering rate. One question that should be asked is: — 14 27 42 48

HOW DO I GET THE BEST SERVICE DOLLAR VALUE? — 57

(¶ 2) To help answer this question, we should like to acquaint you with some of the important advantages provided by our Service Agreement Program. This Program is described in the enclosed folder. (¶ 3) One of our representatives will contact you soon to give you more details of the advantages and cost of this service program. You'll be pleased with the savings. Sincerely yours, David Fenwich Service Manager xx Enclosure (105) — 70 84 99 113 128 141/166

141

141a ▶5 Conditioning practice

each line 3 times (slowly, faster, in-between rate)

alphabet The queerly boxed package of zinc mixtures was delivered just in time.

fig/sym The "Old River" Ranch, located at 14678 River Road, sold for $193,250.

shift lock A new book, ILLUSION IN ART, is printed on CARTER-HALL 20# Bond paper.

fluency Regrettably, nuances of techniques may be lost in the drive for speed.

| 1 | 2 | 3 | 4 | 5 | 6 | 7 | 8 | 9 | 10 | 11 | 12 | 13 | 14 |

141b ▶5 Improve response patterns

each line 3 times at top speed

Goal: Quick spacing; no waste motion

pay them | my key city | map room | the busy firm | many men may | then they may

The map of the key city may aid the busy firm when they do their work.

Goal: Variable rhythm pattern; stroking action in fingers

and the date | and the addresses | the statement is | it was an exaggeration

Please be sure the addresses and the dates are correct on the letters.

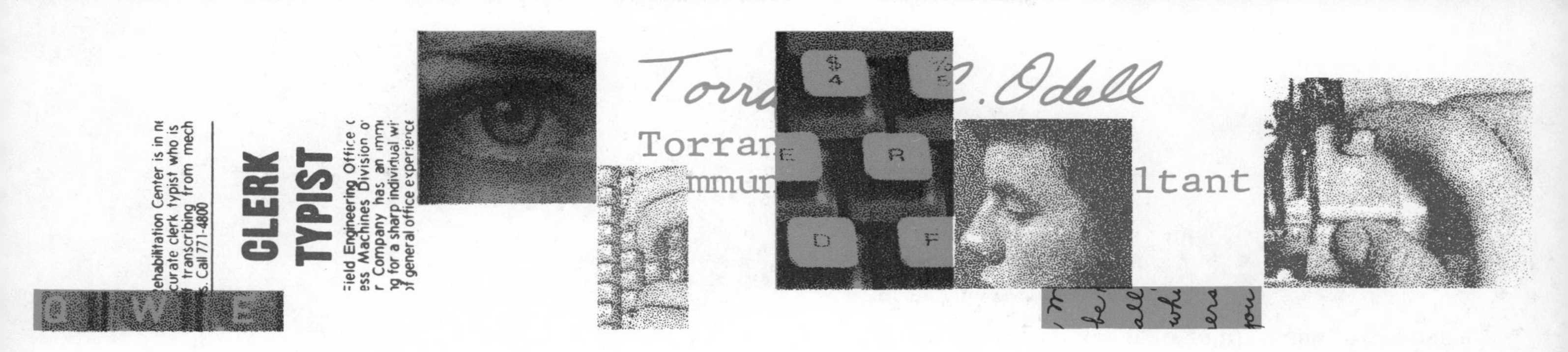

▶ Capitalize

1 The first word of every sentence and the first word of every complete direct quotation. Do not capitalize (a) fragments of quotations or (b) a quotation resumed within a sentence.

She said, "Hard work is necessary for success."
He stressed the importance of "a sense of values."
"When all else fails," he said, "follow directions."

2 The first word after a colon if that word begins a complete sentence.

Remember this: Type with good techniques.
We carry these sizes: small, medium, and large.

3 First, last, and all other words in titles of books, articles, periodicals, headings, and plays, except words of four letters or less used as articles, conjunctions, or prepositions.

Century 21 Typewriting "How to Buy a House"
Saturday Review "The Sound of Music"

4 An official title when it precedes a name or when used elsewhere if it is a title of distinction.

President Lincoln He is the Prime Minister.
The doctor is in. She is the treasurer.

5 All proper nouns and their derivatives.

Canada Canadian Festival France French food

6 Days of the week, months of the year, holidays, periods of history, and historic events.

Sunday Labor Day New Year's Day
June Middle Ages Civil War

7 Seasons of the year only when they are personified.

icy fingers of Winter the soft kiss of Spring

8 Geographic regions, localities, and names.

the South Upstate New York Missouri River

9 Street, avenue, company, etc., when used with a proper noun.

Fifth Avenue Avenue of the Stars Swift & Co.

10 Names of organizations, clubs, and buildings.

Boy Scouts Commercial Club Trade Center

11 A noun preceding a figure except for common nouns such as *line*, *page*, and *sentence*, which may be typed with or without a capital.

Style 34 Catalog 5 page 136 line 7

▶ Type as words

1 Numbers from one to ten except when used with numbers above ten, which are typed as figures.
Note: It is common business practice to use figures for all numbers except those which begin a sentence.

Was the order for four or eight books?
Order 8 typing books and 15 English books.

2 A number beginning a sentence.

Eight persons are here; 25 are at home sick.

3 The shorter of two numbers used together.

ten 50-gallon drums 350 five-gallon drums

4 Isolated fractions or indefinite amounts in a sentence.

Nearly one third of the students are here.
About twenty people came to the meeting.

5 Names of small-numbered streets and avenues (ten and under).

1020 Sixth Street Tenth Avenue

▶ Type as figures

1 Dates and time, except in very formal writing.

May 9, 1976 10:15 a.m.
Ninth of May four o'clock

2 A series of fractions.

Type 1/2, 1/4, 5/6, and 8 7/8.

3 Numbers preceded by nouns.

Rule 6 page 136 Room 1208 Chapter 8

4 Measures, weights, and dimensions.

6 ft. 9 in. tall 5 lbs. 4 oz. 8′ × 10′

5 Definite numbers used with the percent sign (%); but type *percent* (spelled) with approximations in formal writing.

The rate is 7 1/2%.
About 50 percent of the work is done.

6 House numbers except house number One.

1915 - 42d Street One Polk Avenue

7 Sums of money except when spelled for extra emphasis. Even sums may be typed without the decimal.

$10.75 25 cents $500
three hundred dollars ($300)

▶ Use an apostrophe

1 As a symbol for *feet* in billings or tabulations or as a symbol for *minutes*. (The quotation mark may be used as a symbol for *seconds* and *inches*.)

12′ × 16′   3′54″   8′6″ × 10′8″

2 As a symbol to indicate the omission of letters or figures (as in contractions or figures).

can't   wouldn't   Spirit of '76

3 Add *s* to form the plural of most figures, letters, and words. In market quotations, form the plural of figures by the addition of *s* only.

6's   A's   five's   Boston Fund 4s

4 To show possession: Add the *apostrophe and s* to (a) a singular noun and (b) a plural noun which does not end in *s*.

boy's bicycle   women's shoes   a man's watch

Add the *apostrophe and s* to a proper name of one syllable which ends in *s*.

Jones's bill   Bess's Cafeteria

Add the *apostrophe only* after (a) plural nouns ending in *s* and (b) a proper name of more than one syllable which ends in *s* or *z*.

girls' camp   Adams' home   Perez' report

Add the *apostrophe* after the last noun in a series to indicate joint or common possession of two or more persons; however, separate possession of two or more persons is indicated by adding the possessive to each of the nouns.

Lewis and Clark's expedition
the manager's and the treasurer's reports

▶ Use a colon

1 To introduce an enumeration or a listing.

These are my favorite poets: Shelley, Keats, and Frost.

2 To introduce a question or a long direct quotation.

This is the question: Did you study for the test?

3 Between hours and minutes expressed in figures.

10:15 a.m.   4:30 p.m.

▶ Use a comma (or commas)

1 After (a) introductory words, phrases, or clauses and (b) words in a series.

If you can, try to visit Chicago, St. Louis, and Dallas.

2 To set off short direct quotations.

She said, "If you try, you can reach your goal."

3 Before and after (a) words which come together and refer to the same person, thing, or idea and (b) words of direct address.

John, our class president, will give the report.
It was good to see you, Joanna, at the meeting.

4 To set off nonrestrictive clauses (not necessary to the meaning of the sentence), but not restrictive clauses (necessary to meaning).

Your report, which deals with the issue, is great.
The girl who just left is my sister.

5 To separate the day from the year and the city from the state.

July 4, 1976   Philadelphia, Pennsylvania

6 To separate two or more parallel adjectives (adjectives that could be separated by the word "and" instead of the comma).

a group of young, old, and middle-aged persons

Do not use commas to separate adjectives so closely related that they appear to form a single element with the noun they modify.

a dozen large red roses   a small square box

7 To separate (a) unrelated groups of figures which come together and (b) whole numbers into groups of three digits each (however, *policy*, *year*, *page*, *room*, *telephone*, and most *serial numbers* are typed without commas).

During 1976, 1,750 cars were insured under Policy 806423.
page 1042   room 1184   825-2626

▶ Use a dash

1 For emphasis.

The icy road--slippery as a fish--was a hazard.

2 To indicate a change of thought.

We may tour Europe--but I'm getting ahead of my story.

3 To introduce the name of an author when it follows a direct quotation.

"Hitting the wrong key is like hitting me."--Armour

4 For certain special purposes.

"Well--er--ah," he stammered.
"Jay, don't get too close to the --." It was too late.

▶ Use an exclamation mark

1 After emphatic interjections.

What a day! Hey there! Wow!

2 After sentences that are clearly exclamatory.

"I won't go!" she said with determination.
How good it was to see you in Atlanta last week!

▶ Use a hyphen

1 To join compound numbers from twenty–one to ninety–nine that are typed as words.

forty-six fifty-eight seventy-six

2 To join compound adjectives before a noun which they modify as a unit.

five-year period two-thirds majority well-laid plans

3 After each word or figure in a series of words or figures that modify the same noun (suspended hyphenation).

first-, second-, and third-class reservations

4 To spell out a word or name.

s-e-p-a-r-a-t-e G-a-e-l-i-c

5 To form certain compound nouns.

AFL-CIO teacher-counselor WLW-TV

▶ Use the parentheses

1 To enclose parenthetical or explanatory matter and added information.

The contracts (Exhibit A) are enclosed.

2 To enclose identifying letters or figures in lists.

Check these factors: (1) period of time, (2) rate of pay, and (3) nature of duties.

3 To enclose figures that follow spelled–out amounts to give added clarity or emphasis.

The total contract was for five hundred dollars ($500).

▶ Use a question mark

At the end of a sentence that is a direct question; however, use a period after a request in the form of a question.

What day do you plan to leave for Mexico?
Will you mail this letter for me, please.

▶ Use quotation marks

1 To enclose direct quotations.

He said, "I'll be there at eight o'clock."

2 To enclose titles of articles and other parts of complete publications, short poems, song titles, television programs, and unpublished works like theses and dissertations.

"Sesame Street" "The Next Twenty Years"
"Out Where the West Begins" "Living"

3 To enclose special words or phrases, or coined words.

"limited resources" "Gresham's Law"

▶ Use a semicolon

1 To separate two or more independent clauses in a compound sentence when the conjunction is omitted.

To err is human; to forgive, divine.
It is easy to be critical; it is not so easy to be constructive.

2 To separate independent clauses when they are joined by a conjunctive adverb (*however*, *consequently*, etc.).

I can go; however, I must get excused.

3 To separate a series of phrases or clauses (especially if they contain commas) that are introduced by a colon.

These officers were elected: Jon Lane, President; Lisa Schwartz, vice president; Susan Hall, secretary.

4 To precede an abbreviation or word that introduces an explanatory statement.

He organized his work; for example, by putting work to be done in folders of different colors to indicate degrees of urgency.

▶ Use an underline

1 With titles of complete works such as books, magazines, and newspapers. (Such titles may also be typed in ALL CAPS without the underline.)

Century 21 Shorthand New York Times Harper's

2 To call attention to special words or phrases (or you may use quotation marks).
Note: Use a continuous underline unless each word is to be considered separately.

Stop typing when time is called.
Spell these words: steel, occur, separate.

Word-division guides

1 Divide words between syllables only; therefore, do not divide one–syllable words. **Note:** When in doubt, consult a dictionary or a word division manual.

through-out   pref-er-ence   em-ploy-ees
reached   toward   thought

2 Do not divide words of five or fewer letters even if they have two or more syllables.

into   also   about   union   radio   ideas

3 Do not separate a one–letter syllable at the beginning of a word or a one– or two–letter syllable at the end of a word.

across   enough   steady   highly   ended

4 You may usually divide a word between double consonants; but, when adding a syllable to a word that ends in double letters, divide after the double letters of the root word.

writ-ten   sum-mer   expres-sion   excel-lence
will-ing   win-ner   process-ing   fulfill-ment

5 When the final consonant is doubled in adding a suffix, divide between the double letters.

run-ning   begin-ning   fit-ting   submit-ted

6 Divide after a one–letter syllable within a word; but when two single–letter syllables occur together, divide between them.

sepa-rate   regu-late   gradu-ation   evalu-ation

7 When the single–letter syllable *a*, *i*, or *u* is followed by the ending *ly*, *ble*, *bly*, *cle*, or *cal*, divide before the single–letter syllable.

stead-ily   siz-able   vis-ible   mir-acle
cler-ical   but   musi-cal   practi-cal

8 Do not divide figures; try to avoid dividing proper names and dates.

Letter-placement points

Paper-guide placement

Check the placement of the paper guide for accurate horizontal centering of the letter.

Margins and date placement

Use the following guide:

5-Stroke Words in Letter Body	Side Margins	Date-line
Up to 100	2″	20
101–300	1½″	18–12*
Over 300	1″	12

* Dateline is moved up 2 line spaces for each additional 50 words.

Horizontal placement of date varies according to the letter style.

Address

The address is typed on the fourth line (3 blank line spaces) below the date. A personal title, such as Mr., Mrs., Miss, or Ms., should precede the name of an individual. An official title, when used, may be typed on the first or the second line of the address, whichever gives better balance.

Two-page letters

If a letter is too long for one page, at least 2 lines of the body of the letter should be carried to the second page. The second page of a letter, or any additional pages, requires a proper heading. Either the block or the horizontal form may be used for the heading; each is followed by a triple space.

Second-page headings

Block form

```
Mr. J. W. Smith
Page 2
June 5, 19--
```

Horizontal form

```
Mr. J. W. Smith        2        June 5, 19--
```

Attention line

An attention line, when used, is typed on the second line (a double space) below the letter address.

Subject line

A subject line is typed on the second line (a double space) below the salutation. It may be either centered or typed at the left margin.

Company name

Occasionally the company name is typed in the closing lines. When this is done, it is typed in *all capital letters* 2 lines (a double space) below the complimentary close. The modern practice is to omit the company name in the closing lines if a letterhead is used.

Typewritten name/official title

The name of the person who dictated the letter and his official title are typed 4 lines (3 blank line spaces) below the complimentary close, or 4 lines below the typed company name when it is used. When both the name and official title are used, they may be typed on the same line or the official title may be typed on the next line below the typed name.

Unusual features

Letters having unusual features, such as tabulated material, long quotations, or an unusual number of lines in the address or the closing lines, may require changes in the settings normally used for letters of that length.

ZIP Code abbreviations

Alabama, AL
Alaska, AK
Arizona, AZ
Arkansas, AR
California, CA
Canal Zone, CZ
Colorado, CO
Connecticut, CT
Delaware, DE
District of Columbia, DC
Florida, FL
Georgia, GA
Guam, GU
Hawaii, HI
Idaho, ID
Illinois, IL
Indiana, IN
Iowa, IA
Kansas, KS
Kentucky, KY
Louisiana, LA
Maine, ME
Maryland, MD
Massachusetts, MA
Michigan, MI
Minnesota, MN
Mississippi, MS
Missouri, MO
Montana, MT
Nebraska, NE
Nevada, NV
New Hampshire, NH
New Jersey, NJ
New Mexico, NM
New York, NY
North Carolina, NC
North Dakota, ND
Ohio, OH
Oklahoma, OK
Oregon, OR
Pennsylvania, PA
Puerto Rico, PR
Rhode Island, RI
South Carolina, SC
South Dakota, SD
Tennessee, TN
Texas, TX
Utah, UT
Vermont, VT
Virgin Islands, VI
Virginia, VA
Washington, WA
West Virginia, WV
Wisconsin, WI
Wyoming, WY

April 21, 19--

Dr. VierlieAnn Malina, President
Transcontinental Corporation
1005 Ala Lilikoi Street
Honolulu, HI 96818

Dear Dr. Malina

Today many business firms use the block style letter for their correspondence. This letter is an example of that style. You will note that all lines start at the left margin. The advantage of this style is that the mechanical process of indenting opening and closing lines, or paragraphs, is eliminated. This practice saves typing time as well as space.

Open punctuation is used with this letter. Punctuation is omitted after the salutation and the complimentary close. Elimination of these punctuation marks helps to increase letter production rates. Another recommended timesaving feature is to type only the typist's initials for reference when the dictator's name is typed in the closing lines.

As you can see, the block style letter gives good placement appearance. Because many extra typing strokes and motions are eliminated, the use of this style does help to increase letter production rates. It is the letter style I recommend for use in the business office.

Sincerely yours

Torrance C. Odell

Torrance C. Odell
Communications Consultant

tjc

Our new Communications Guide will be sent to you as soon as it comes from the press.

1 Block, open

April 28, 19--

Dr. James E. Deitz
President, Heald Colleges
1101 Van Ness Avenue
San Francisco, CA 94109

Dear Dr. Deitz:

MODIFIED BLOCK STYLE LETTER

This letter is an example of the modified block style. It is one of the most popular business letter styles in use today. As you will observe, it differs from the block style in that the dateline and the closing lines (the complimentary close and the typed name and title) are indented and blocked. Mixed punctuation is frequently used with this letter style: a colon after the salutation and a comma after the complimentary close.

When the modified block style is used, letter production efficiency dictates that the dateline, the complimentary close, and the typed name and title be started at the same point. Actual practice in the business office, however, varies widely. For instance, the dateline may be centered; it may be typed so that it ends at the right margin; or it may be given special placement in relation to the letterhead. Similarly, the closing lines may be started five spaces to the left of center or may be typed so that they end approximately at the right margin.

Although the modified block style gives good placement appearance, it is difficult to account for its popular appeal since, as compared with the block style, additional typing motions are involved in the placement of the various parts. The problem may be that no one has really given serious consideration to the effect of the letter style used on letter production efficiency.

Cordially yours,

Elaine Bronson

Elaine Bronson, Director

lwe

2 Modified block, mixed

May 16, 19--

Blue Hill Industries
255 Blue Hill Avenue
Boston, MA 02187

Attention Office Manager

Dear Sir or Madam:

Thanks for your inquiry about letter styles. This letter is arranged in the modified block style with 5-space paragraph indentions. Business letters are usually typed on 8 1/2- by 11-inch letterhead stationery which has the name of the company sending the letter, as well as other identifying information, printed at the top of the sheet.

The position of the dateline is varied according to the length of the letter. More space is left before the dateline for short letters than for long letters. The address is typed on the fourth line (3 blank lines) below the date. Some business offices use standard margins (a set line length) for all letters; others adjust the margins according to the length of the letter.

Other questions about letter placement are covered in the letter style booklet which is enclosed with this letter. Don't hesitate to write to us if there is any other information you need. Good luck to you in your efforts to improve letter production rates in your office.

Sincerely,

Susan Hunter

Susan Hunter
Communications Consultant

jwr

Enclosure

cc Ms. Ruth Palumbo

3 Modified block, indented ¶s, mixed

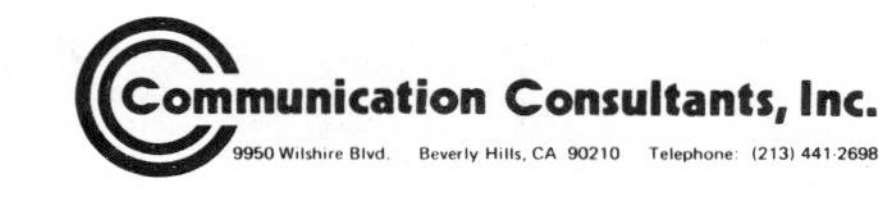

September 20, 19--

Mr. Richard Flamson, III
President, Security Pacific Corp.
510 South Spring Street
Los Angeles, CA 90013

AMS SIMPLIFIED LETTER STYLE

The unique Simplified letter style for business correspondence is sensible, streamlined, and effective. It is a simplified "block style" with all lines beginning at the left margin. Some of its other features are listed below.

1. The address is typed 3 or more lines below the date.
2. The salutation and the complimentary close are omitted.
3. A subject heading in all capitals is typed a triple space below the address.
4. Unnumbered listed items are indented 5 spaces, but numbered items are typed flush with the left margin.
5. The dictator's name and title are typed in all capitals 5 line spaces (4 blank lines) below the body of the letter.
6. Reference initials consist of the typist's initials only.
7. Copy notations are typed a double space below the reference line.

Because of the timesaving features of this AMS Simplified letter style, its use will reduce your letter-writing costs and give your letters a distinctive "eye appeal." Try it. You will like it.

Lee Thompson

LEE THOMPSON, SECRETARY

lrb

Copy to Ms. Davonna Jackson

4 AMS Simplified

Letter styles

1 Addressing procedure

Envelope address

Set a tab stop (or margin stop if a number of envelopes are to be addressed) 2½″ from the left edge for a small envelope or 4″ from the left edge for a large envelope. Start the address here about 2″ from the top edge of a small envelope and 2½″ from the top edge of a large one.

Style

Type the address in *block style*, single–spaced, without punctuation at the ends of lines, except when an abbreviation ends a line. Type the city name, state name or abbreviation, and ZIP Code on the last address line. The ZIP Code is usually typed 1 space after the state name.

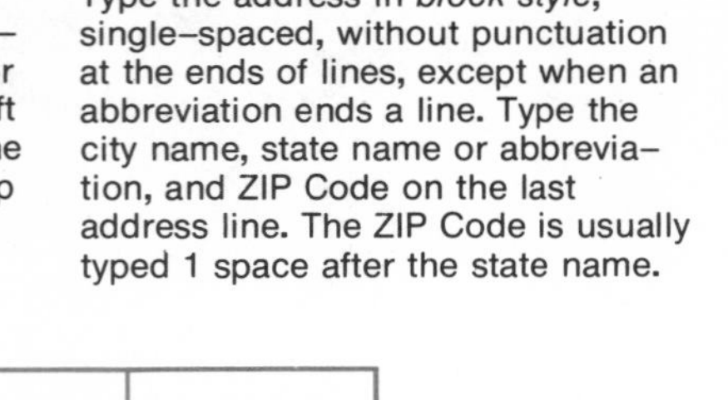
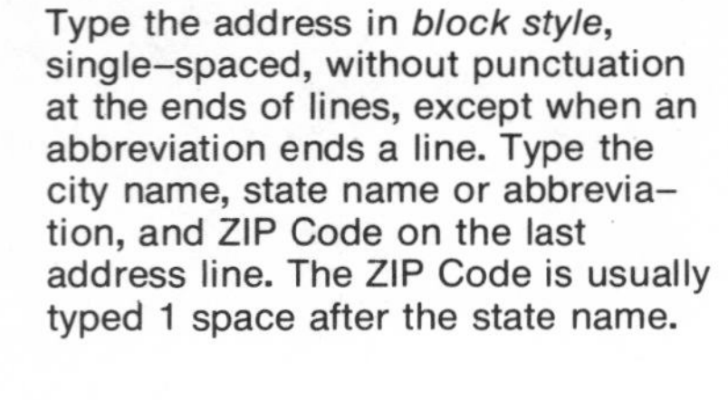
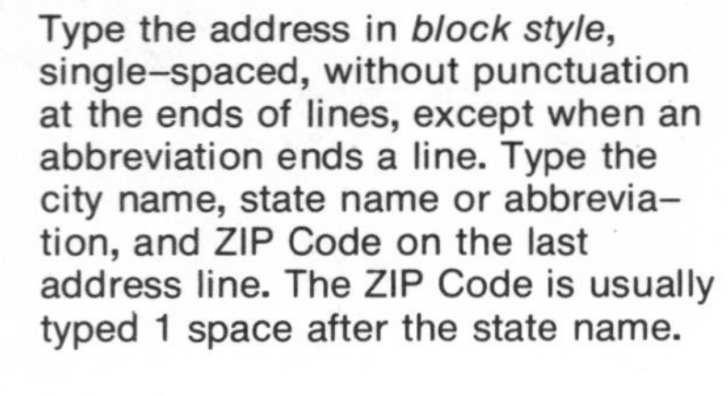
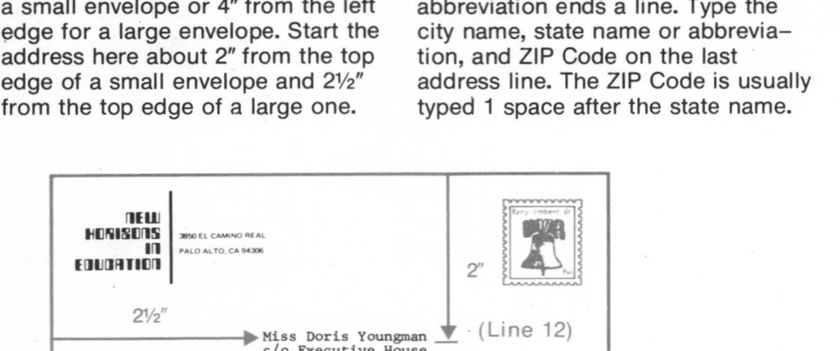
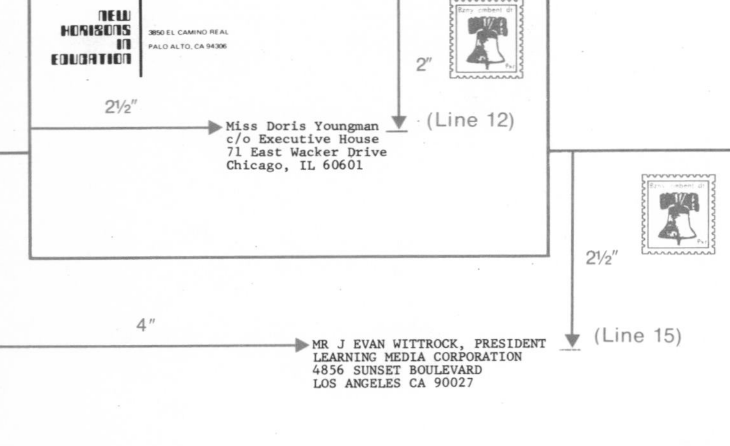

Addressee notations

Type addressee notations, such as *Hold for Arrival*, *Please Forward*, *Personal*, etc., a triple space below the return address and about 3 spaces from the left edge of the envelope. These notations may be underlined or typed in all capitals.

If an *attention line* is used, type it immediately below the company name in the address line.

Mailing notations

Type mailing notations, such as SPECIAL DELIVERY and REGISTERED, below the stamp and at least 3 line spaces above the envelope address. Type these notations in all capital letters.

Gemini International, Inc.
81 BROADWAY•NEW YORK, N.Y. 10006
TS
HOLD FOR ARRIVAL
SPECIAL DELIVERY
Georgia Professional Women's Club
Attention Miss Mary Helen Henninger
100 Edgewood Avenue, SE
Atlanta, GA 30303

2 Folding and inserting procedure

Small envelopes (No. 6¾, 6¼)

Step 1	Step 2	Step 3	Step 4
With letter face up, fold bottom up to ½ inch from top.	Fold right third to left.	Fold left third to ½ inch from last crease.	Insert last creased edge first.

Large envelopes (No. 10, 9, 7¾)

Step 1	Step 2	Step 3
With letter face up, fold slightly less than ⅓ of sheet up toward top.	Fold down top of sheet to within ½ inch of bottom fold.	Insert letter into envelope with last crease toward bottom of envelope.

Window envelopes (letter)

Step 1	Step 2	Step 3
With sheet face down, top toward you, fold upper third down.	Fold lower third up so address is showing.	Insert sheet into envelope with last crease at bottom.

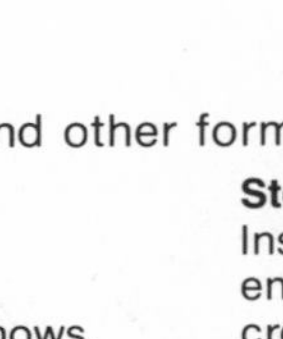

Window envelopes (invoices and other forms)

Step 1	Step 2	Step 3
Place sheet face down, top toward you.	Fold back top so address shows.	Insert into envelope with crease at bottom.

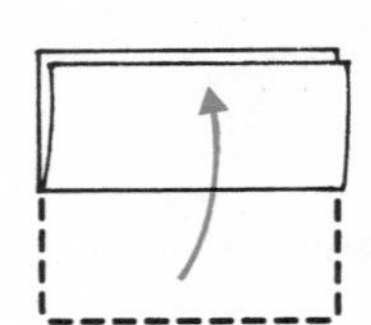
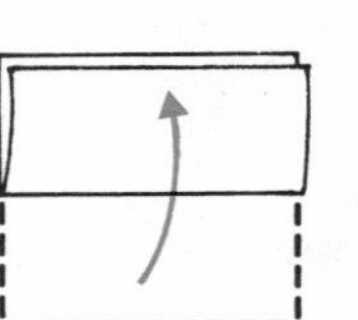
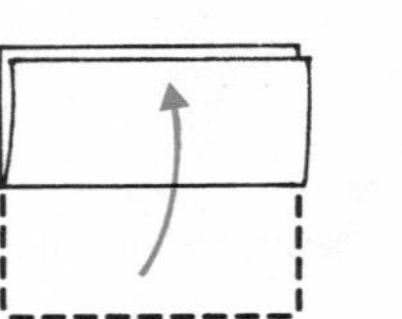

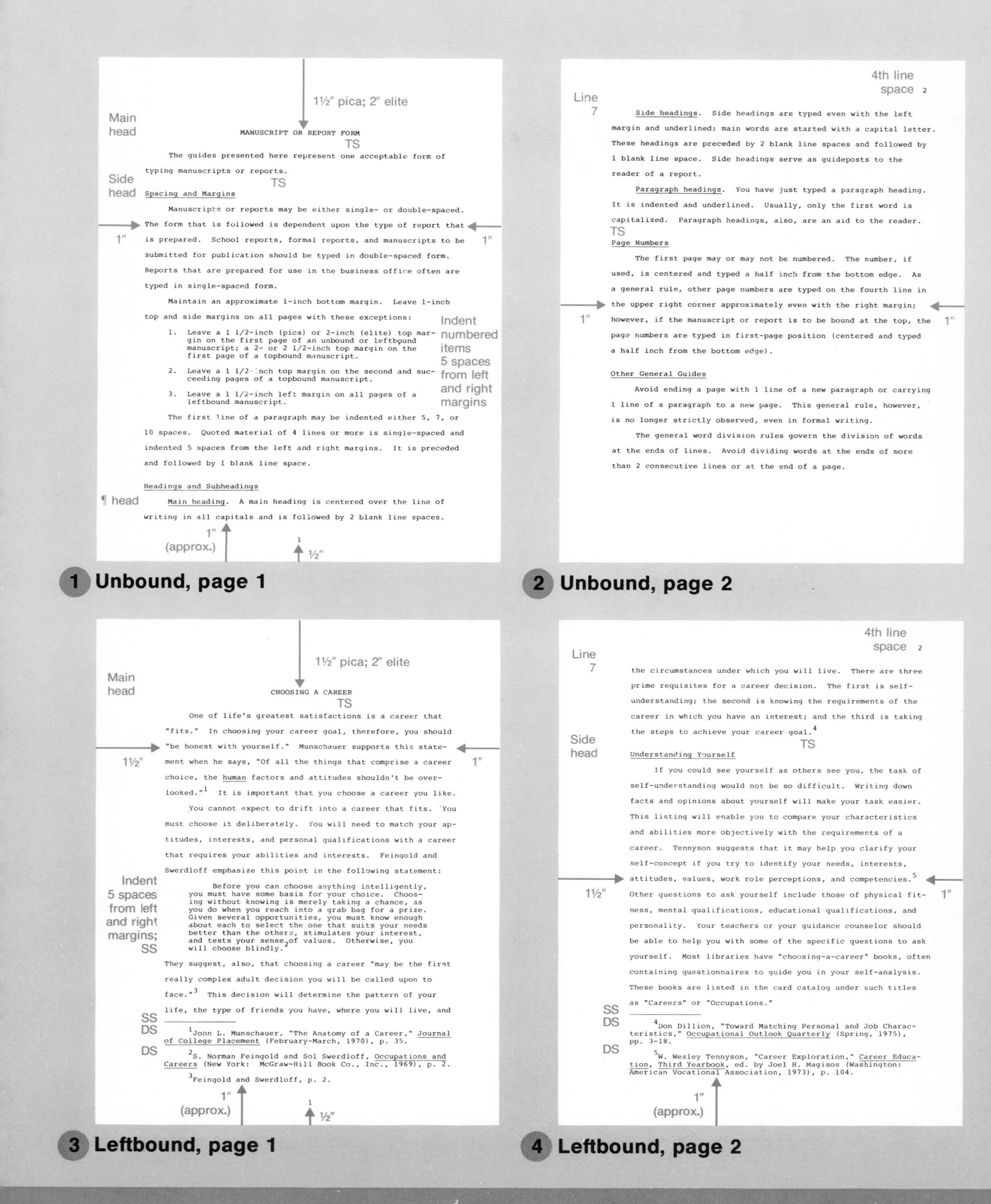

MANUSCRIPT OR REPORT FORM

The guides presented here represent one acceptable form of typing manuscripts or reports.

Spacing and Margins

Manuscripts or reports may be either single- or double-spaced. The form that is followed is dependent upon the type of report that is prepared. School reports, formal reports, and manuscripts to be submitted for publication should be typed in double-spaced form. Reports that are prepared for use in the business office often are typed in single-spaced form.

Maintain an approximate 1-inch bottom margin. Leave 1-inch top and side margins on all pages with these exceptions:

1. Leave a 1 1/2-inch (pica) or 2-inch (elite) top margin on the first page of an unbound or leftbound manuscript; a 2- or 2 1/2-inch top margin on the first page of a topbound manuscript.
2. Leave a 1 1/2-inch top margin on the second and succeeding pages of a topbound manuscript.
3. Leave a 1 1/2-inch left margin on all pages of a leftbound manuscript.

The first line of a paragraph may be indented either 5, 7, or 10 spaces. Quoted material of 4 lines or more is single-spaced and indented 5 spaces from the left and right margins. It is preceded and followed by 1 blank line space.

Headings and Subheadings

Main heading. A main heading is centered over the line of writing in all capitals and is followed by 2 blank line spaces.

1

1 Unbound, page 1

2

Side headings. Side headings are typed even with the left margin and underlined; main words are started with a capital letter. These headings are preceded by 2 blank line spaces and followed by 1 blank line space. Side headings serve as guideposts to the reader of a report.

Paragraph headings. You have just typed a paragraph heading. It is indented and underlined. Usually, only the first word is capitalized. Paragraph headings, also, are an aid to the reader.

Page Numbers

The first page may or may not be numbered. The number, if used, is centered and typed a half inch from the bottom edge. As a general rule, other page numbers are typed on the fourth line in the upper right corner approximately even with the right margin; however, if the manuscript or report is to be bound at the top, the page numbers are typed in first-page position (centered and typed a half inch from the bottom edge).

Other General Guides

Avoid ending a page with 1 line of a new paragraph or carrying 1 line of a paragraph to a new page. This general rule, however, is no longer strictly observed, even in formal writing.

The general word division rules govern the division of words at the ends of lines. Avoid dividing words at the ends of more than 2 consecutive lines or at the end of a page.

2 Unbound, page 2

CHOOSING A CAREER

One of life's greatest satisfactions is a career that "fits." In choosing your career goal, therefore, you should "be honest with yourself." Munschauer supports this statement when he says, "Of all the things that comprise a career choice, the human factors and attitudes shouldn't be overlooked."[1] It is important that you choose a career you like.

You cannot expect to drift into a career that fits. You must choose it deliberately. You will need to match your aptitudes, interests, and personal qualifications with a career that requires your abilities and interests. Feingold and Swerdloff emphasize this point in the following statement:

> Before you can choose anything intelligently, you must have some basis for your choice. Choosing without knowing is merely taking a chance, as you do when you reach into a grab bag for a prize. Given several opportunities, you must know enough about each to select the one that suits your needs better than the others, stimulates your interest, and tests your sense of values. Otherwise, you will choose blindly.[2]

They suggest, also, that choosing a career "may be the first really complex adult decision you will be called upon to face."[3] This decision will determine the pattern of your life, the type of friends you have, where you will live, and

---

[1]John L. Munschauer, "The Anatomy of a Career," Journal of College Placement (February-March, 1970), p. 35.

[2]S. Norman Feingold and Sol Swerdloff, Occupations and Careers (New York: McGraw-Hill Book Co., Inc., 1969), p. 2.

[3]Feingold and Swerdloff, p. 2.

1

3 Leftbound, page 1

2

the circumstances under which you will live. There are three prime requisites for a career decision. The first is self-understanding; the second is knowing the requirements of the career in which you have an interest; and the third is taking the steps to achieve your career goal.[4]

Understanding Yourself

If you could see yourself as others see you, the task of self-understanding would not be so difficult. Writing down facts and opinions about yourself will make your task easier. This listing will enable you to compare your characteristics and abilities more objectively with the requirements of a career. Tennyson suggests that it may help you clarify your self-concept if you try to identify your needs, interests, attitudes, values, work role perceptions, and competencies.[5] Other questions to ask yourself include those of physical fitness, mental qualifications, educational qualifications, and personality. Your teachers or your guidance counselor should be able to help you with some of the specific questions to ask yourself. Most libraries have "choosing-a-career" books, often containing questionnaires to guide you in your self-analysis. These books are listed in the card catalog under such titles as "Careers" or "Occupations."

---

[4]Don Dillion, "Toward Matching Personal and Job Characteristics," Occupational Outlook Quarterly (Spring, 1975), pp. 3-18.

[5]W. Wesley Tennyson, "Career Exploration," Career Education, Third Yearbook, ed. by Joel H. Magisos (Washington: American Vocational Association, 1973), p. 104.

4 Leftbound, page 2

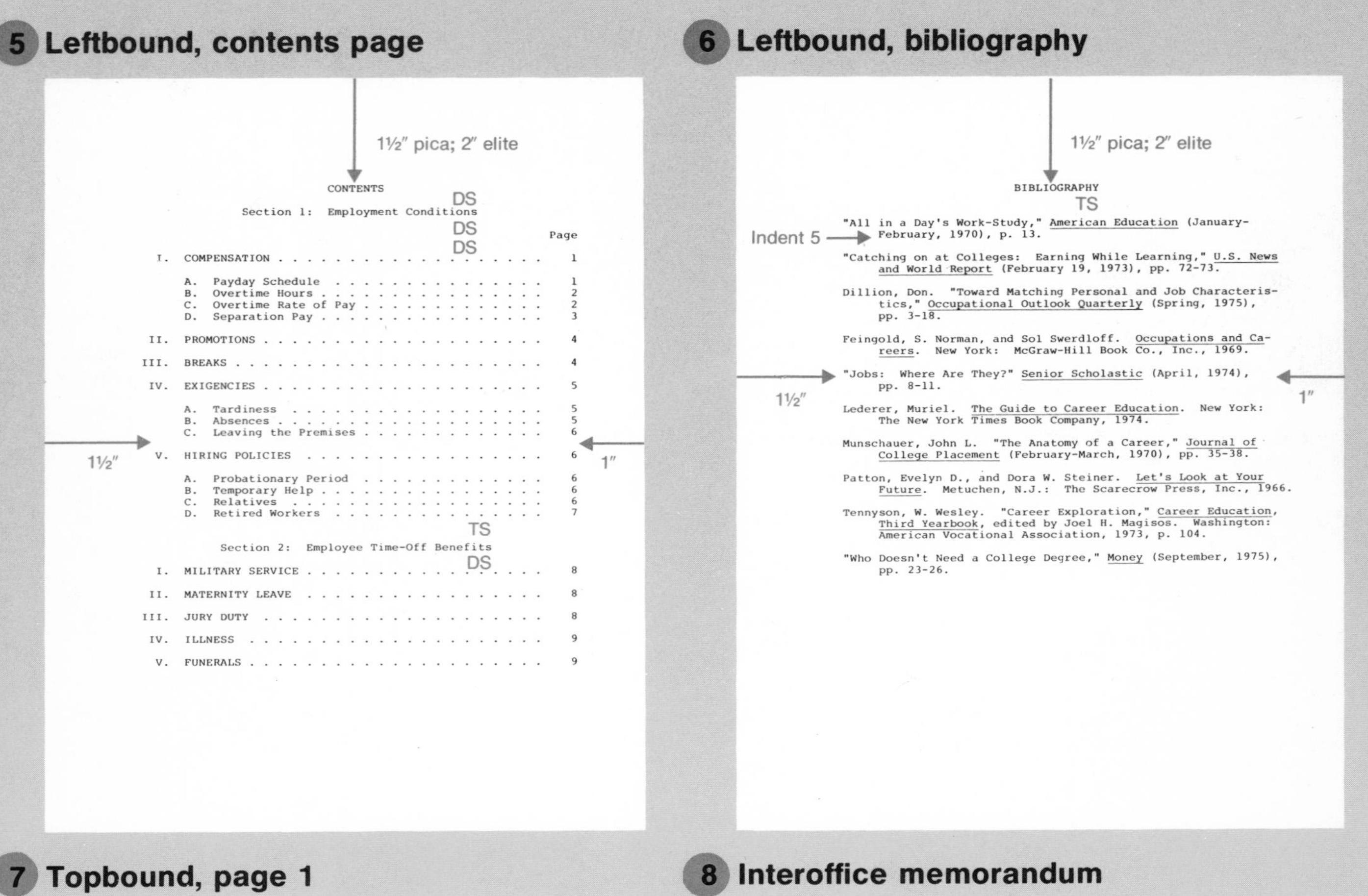

5 Leftbound, contents page

CONTENTS

Section 1: Employment Conditions

Section 2: Employee Time-Off Benefits

6 Leftbound, bibliography

BIBLIOGRAPHY

"All in a Day's Work-Study," American Education (January-February, 1970), p. 13.

"Catching on at Colleges: Earning While Learning," U.S. News and World Report (February 19, 1973), pp. 72-73.

Dillion, Don. "Toward Matching Personal and Job Characteristics," Occupational Outlook Quarterly (Spring, 1975), pp. 3-18.

Feingold, S. Norman, and Sol Swerdloff. Occupations and Careers. New York: McGraw-Hill Book Co., Inc., 1969.

"Jobs: Where Are They?" Senior Scholastic (April, 1974), pp. 8-11.

Lederer, Muriel. The Guide to Career Education. New York: The New York Times Book Company, 1974.

Munschauer, John L. "The Anatomy of a Career," Journal of College Placement (February-March, 1970), pp. 35-38.

Patton, Evelyn D., and Dora W. Steiner. Let's Look at Your Future. Metuchen, N.J.: The Scarecrow Press, Inc., 1966.

Tennyson, W. Wesley. "Career Exploration," Career Education, Third Yearbook, edited by Joel H. Magisos. Washington: American Vocational Association, 1973, p. 104.

"Who Doesn't Need a College Degree," Money (September, 1975), pp. 23-26.

7 Topbound, page 1

2" pica; 2½" elite

Section 1

DS

EMPLOYMENT CONDITIONS

TS

The guidelines provided in this manual do not mean that policies are fixed rules. Policies are simply major guides to help us all follow the same practices under similar circumstances. Individual decisions will have to be made, and many of these are not covered by policies. If we all follow standard practices, however, there will be fewer misunderstandings; and our customers and employees will be happier.

1" 1"

Side head

Compensation

¶ head

Payday schedule. Employees who are not exempt from the overtime provisions of the Fair Labor Standards Act (clerical, shipping, and assembly room personnel) are paid by check every Friday for all time worked for the week ending the previous Saturday.

Employees who are exempt from the overtime provisions of the Fair Labor Standards Act (supervisors, managers, and executives) are paid by check semimonthly on the 15th and the last day of the month unless these days fall on a weekend, in which case payment is made on the preceding Friday, or if Friday is a holiday, on the last workday of the pay period.

Compensation for clerical employees is calculated on a monthly basis, and each week's pay is approximately 4.333 divided into the monthly rate. Exempt employees receive half the monthly rate each

1" (approx.)

1

8 Interoffice memorandum

CONTEMPORARY Office Associates

INTEROFFICE COMMUNICATION

TO: All Typists

FROM: Richard Buchanan

DATE: April 26, 19--

SUBJECT: Care of Typewriters

TS

Because of our increasing typewriter repair costs, we are requesting that you follow these care-of-typewriter steps:

1" 1"

1. End of each day. At the end of each day, please follow these procedures:

   a. Use a stiff brush to clean the typeface. If you use an element-type machine, remove the element to clean it.

   b. Brush away any eraser crumbs, etc., that have fallen into the typebar segment. (May I remind typists who use typebar machines to move the carriage to the extreme right or left before erasing an error.)

   c. Dust your desk beneath your machine with a dustcloth.

   d. Pull the paper release lever forward and leave it in this position overnight.

   e. Finally, center the carriage (typebar machine) and cover the typewriter.

2. End of each week. At the end of each week, do the following:

   a. With a soft, lintfree cloth with a corner moistened slightly with typewriter oil, wipe the carriage rails of the typebar machine; then wipe them again with the unmoistened portion of the cloth.

   b. Clean the platen with another soft, lintfree cloth moistened with alcohol.

3. Know your operator's manual. Review, as needed, the care and maintenance steps given in the operating instructions manual for your typewriter.

 Capitalize

Close up

Delete

Insert

Insert comma

Insert space

Insert apostrophe

Insert quotation marks

Move right

Move left

Move down; lower

Move up; raise

Set in lowercase

Paragraph

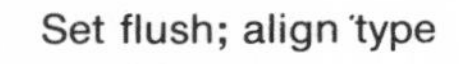 No new paragraph

Set flush; align type

Spell out

Let it stand; ignore correction

Transpose

Underline or Italics

Proofreader's marks

Sometimes typed or printed copy may be corrected with proofreader's marks. The typist must be able to interpret correctly these marks in retyping the corrected copy or *rough draft* as it may be called. The most commonly used proofreader's marks are shown above.

1 Horizontal centering

1 Move margin stops to extreme ends of scale.

2 Clear tab stops; then set a tab stop at center of paper.

3 Tabulate to center of paper.

4 From center, backspace *once* for each 2 letters, spaces, figures, or punctuation marks in the line.

5 Do not backspace for an odd or leftover stroke at the end of the line.

6 Begin to type where back-spacing ends.

Formula for finding horizontal center of paper

	Example
Scale reading at left edge of paper	0
+Scale reading at right edge of paper	102
Total ÷ 2 = Center Point	102 ÷ 2 = 51

2 Spread headings

1 Backspace from center once for each letter, character, and space *except the last letter or character* in the heading. Begin to type where the backspacing ends.

2 In typing a spread heading, space once after each letter or character and 3 times between words.

3 Vertical centering

Backspace-from-center method
Basic rule

From vertical center of paper, roll platen (cylinder) back once for each 2 lines, 2 blank line spaces, or line and blank line space. Ignore odd or leftover line.

Steps to follow:

1 To move paper to vertical center, start spacing down from top edge of paper.

a half sheet
down 6 TS (triple spaces)
− 1 SS (Line 17)

b full sheet
down 11 TS
+ 1 SS (Line 34)

2 From vertical center

a half sheet, SS or DS: follow basic rule, back 1 for 2.

b full sheet, SS or DS: follow basic rule, back 1 for 2; then back 2 SS for *reading position*.

Mathematical method

1 Count lines and blank line spaces needed to type problem.

2 Subtract *lines to be used* from *lines available* (66 for full sheet and 33 for half sheet).

3 Divide by 2 to get top and bottom margins. If fraction results, disregard it. Space down from top edge of paper *1 more than number of lines to be left in top margin.*

For *reading position*, which is above exact vertical center, subtract 2 from exact top margin.

Formula for vertical mathematical placement

$$\frac{\text{Lines available} - \text{lines used}}{2} = \text{top margin}$$

APPROXIMATE DISTANCES BETWEEN NEW YORK
AND SELECTED CITIES

(0.6 Conversion Factor Used from Kilometer to Mile)

City		Kilometers	Miles
Boston	style	315	189
Detroit	for metric measurement	782	469
Houston	omits the comma and	2 265	1,359
Los Angeles	substitutes space	3 925	2,355

1 Vertical placement

1 Vertical centering
Follow either of vertical centering methods explained on page ix.

2 Spacing after heading lines
Double–space (1 blank line space) between *main* and *secondary* headings, if both are used; triple–space (2 blank line spaces) between last line of heading (whether main or secondary) and first line of columns (or column headings). Double–space (1 blank line space) between column headings (when used) and first line of columns.

2 Horizontal placement: backspace-from-center method

1 Preparatory steps

a Clear margin stops by moving them to extreme ends of scale.

b Clear all tab stops.

c Move carriage to center of paper.

d Decide spacing between columns—preferably an even number of spaces (4, 6, 8, 10, etc.).

2 Center heading lines

3 Determine and set left margin stop
Backspace from center of paper 1 space for each 2 letters, figures, symbols, and spaces in *longest line* of each column and for each 2 spaces between columns. Set left margin stop at this point. (If an extra space occurs at the end of the longest line when backspacing, carry it forward to the next column. Ignore an extra space at end of last column.

Note: If a column heading is longer than the longest line in the columns, it may be treated as the longest line in determining placement. The longest columnar line must then be centered under the heading, and tab stops set accordingly.

4 Set tab stops
From the left margin stop, space forward 1 space for each letter, figure, symbol, and space in the longest line in the first column and for each space to be left between the first and second columns. *Set a tab stop at this point for the second column.* Follow similar procedure when additional columns are to be typed.

```
advertisement          efficiency          optimistic
|      13       |   4  |   10   |   4  |   10    |
ad|ve|rt|is|em|en|t1|23|4e|ff|ic|ie|nc|y1|23|4o|pt|im|is|ti|
```

3 Centering column headings

1 Forward-space, backspace method
From point at which column begins, space forward once (→) for each 2 letters, figures, or spaces in the longest line (the line that requires the most strokes to type). From center of column, backspace (←) once for each 2 spaces in heading. Begin to type where backspacing ends. (In both steps disregard an extra space.) The typed heading will be centered over the column.

2 Mathematical method
To the number of the cylinder (platen) or line–of–writing scale immediately under the first letter, figure, or symbol of the longest line of the column, add the number shown under the space following the last stroke of the line. Divide this sum by 2; the result will be the center point. From this point on the scale, backspace to center the column heading.

4 Drawing ruled lines

1 Horizontal rulings
To draw horizontal rulings: Place the pencil point through the cardholder (or on the type bar guide above the ribbon); depress the carriage–release lever to draw the carriage across the line.

2 Vertical lines
To draw vertical lines: Operate the automatic line finder. Place the pencil point or pen through the cardholder (or on the type bar guide above the ribbon). Roll the paper up until you have a ruling of the desired length. Remove the pen or pencil and reset the line finder.

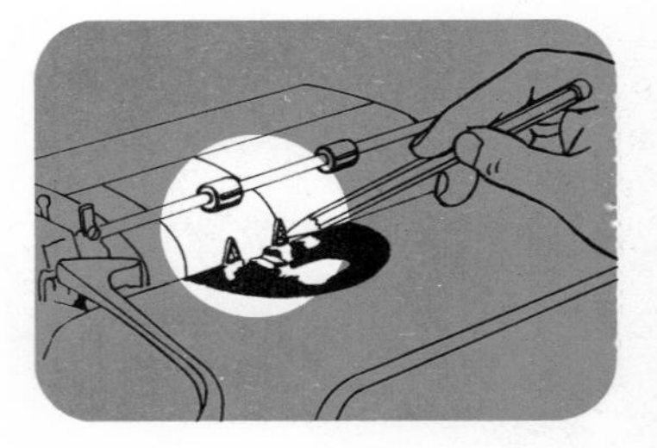

1 Desk-top assembly method

1 Assemble letterhead, carbon sheets (uncarboned side up), and second sheets as illustrated above. *Use one carbon and one second sheet for each copy desired.*

2 Grasp the carbon pack at the sides, turn it so that the *letterhead faces away from you, the carbon side of the carbon paper is toward you, and the top edge of the pack is face down.* Tap the sheets gently on the desk to straighten.

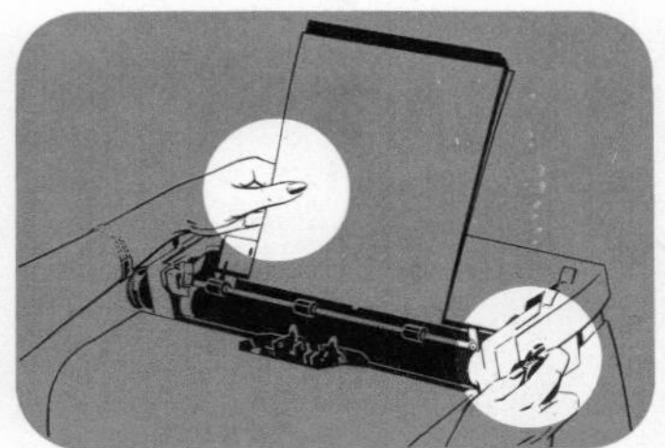

3 Hold the sheets firmly to prevent slipping; insert pack into type-writer. Hold pack with one hand; turn platen with the other.

Tips for wrinkle-free assembly

Start pack into typewriter with paper-release lever forward; then reset the paper-release lever and turn pack into the machine.

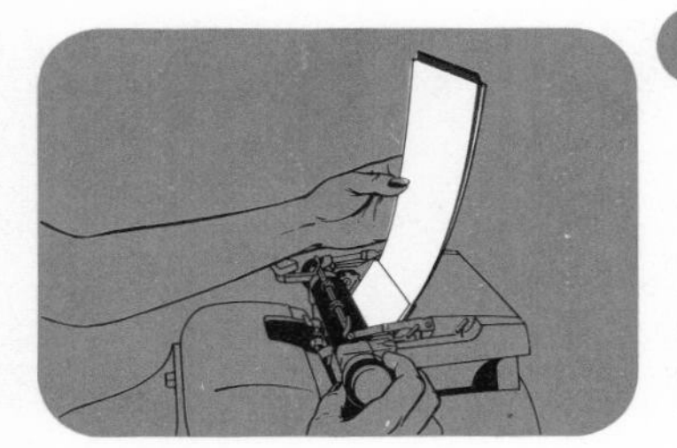

2 Inserting the pack with a trough

To keep the carbon pack straight when feeding it into the typewriter, place the pack in the fold of a plain sheet of paper (paper trough) or under the flap of an envelope. Remove the trough or envelope when the pack is in place.

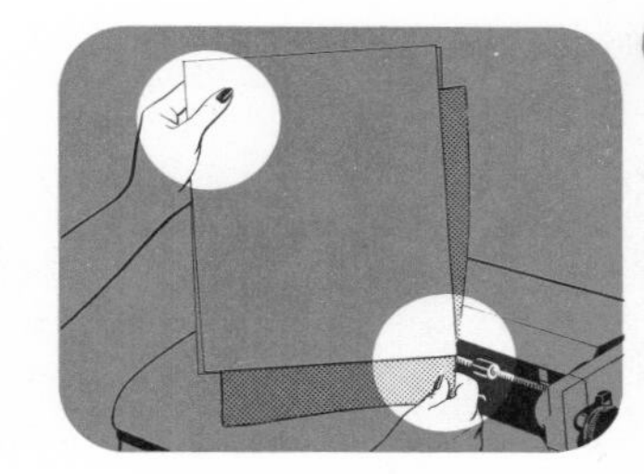

3 Removing carbon sheets

Hold the left edge of the letterhead and second sheets; remove all carbons at one time with the right hand.

4 Machine assembly method

1 Assemble paper for insertion (original on top; second sheets beneath). Turn the "pack" so *original faces away from you* and *the top edge faces down.*

2 Insert sheets until the tops are gripped by the feed rolls; then pull the bottom of all sheets except the last over the top (front) of the typewriter.

3 Place carbon paper between sheets, *carboned side toward you.* Flip each sheet back (away from you) as you add each carbon sheet.

4 Roll pack into typing position.

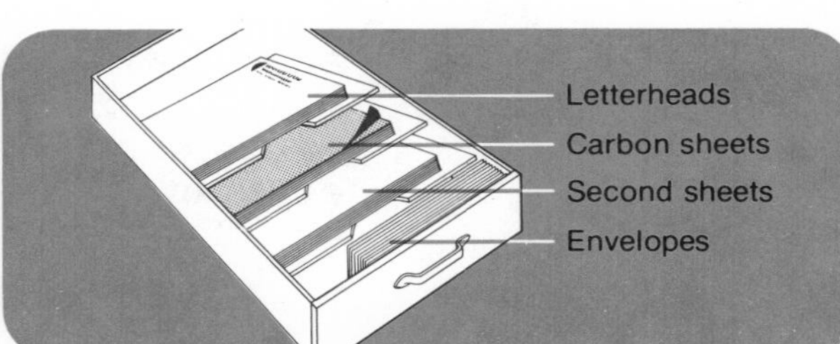

5 Slotted drawer assembly method

1 With sheets correctly arranged in slotted drawer, pick up a let-terhead with left hand, a sheet of carbon paper with right hand; pull sheets slightly forward; grasp both sheets with left hand as right hand reaches and pulls second sheet into position.

2 Pull sheets from slots. Straighten pack by tapping gently on desk as the sides of the sheets are held loosely by both hands.

3 Add extra sheets (a second sheet and a carbon) for any addi-tional copies that may be needed.

4 Insert into typewriter as with desk-top assembly method.

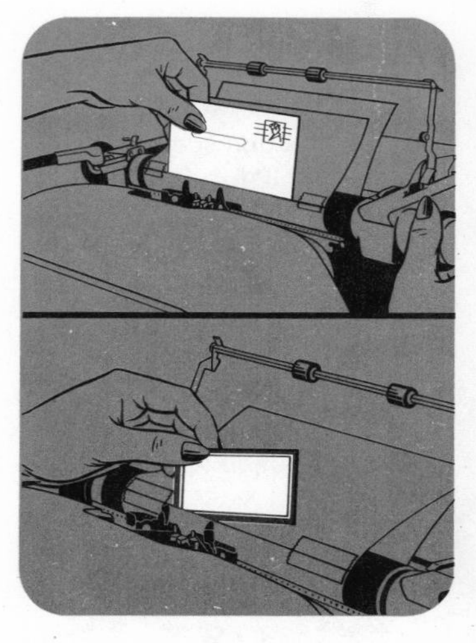

Front feeding small cards and labels

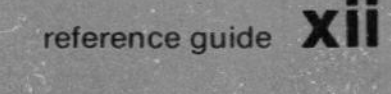

1 Changing typewriter ribbons

The technique for changing ribbons is not the same for all machines, but in no case is it particularly difficult. The basic steps for changing the ribbon are listed here:

1 Wind the ribbon onto one spool, usually the right.

2 Raise and lock the *ribbon carrier* (**23**). Do this by pressing down the *shift lock* (**30**), moving the *ribbon control* (**31**) for typing on the lower portion of the ribbon, and by depressing and locking any two central keys, such as *y* and *u*.

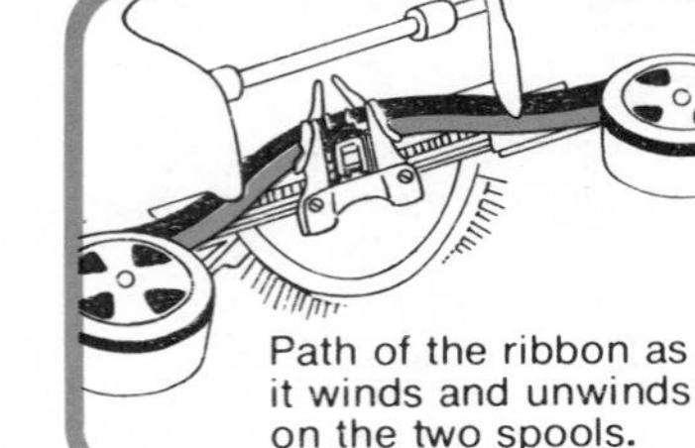

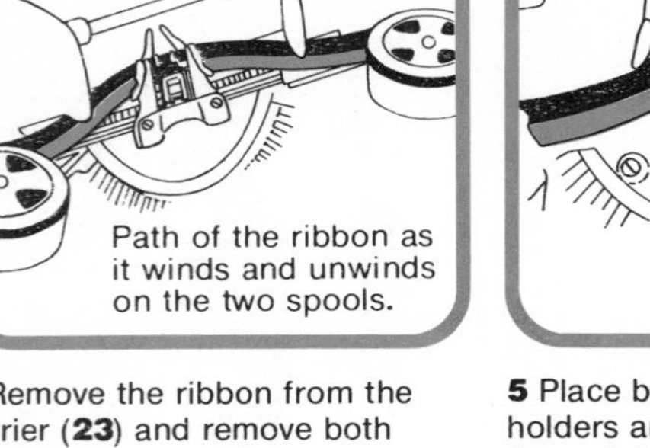

Path of the ribbon as it winds and unwinds on the two spools.

3 Remove the ribbon from the carrier (**23**) and remove both spools.

4 Hook the new ribbon to the empty spool and wind several inches of the new ribbon on it. Be sure that the ribbon winds and unwinds in the proper direction.

Ribbon threaded through the ribbon–carrier mechanism

5 Place both spools on their holders and thread the ribbon through the ribbon carrier.

6 Release the shift lock, and return the ribbon indicator to the position for typing on the upper portion of the ribbon. Unlock the two type bars, and the typewriter will be ready for use.

IBM ribbon

7 Clean the keys, if necessary. When a new ribbon is first used, it may be necessary to clean the keys so that all typed letters will be clear and bright.

Note: Many new typewriters (including the Selectric) use a special ribbon cartridge that makes the foregoing steps unnecessary.

2 How to erase and to correct errors

1 Depress margin–release key and move carriage to extreme left or right to prevent erasure crumbs from falling into the typing mechanism.

2 To avoid disturbing the alignment of the typed copy, turn the cylinder forward if the erasure is to be made on the upper 2/3 of the paper; backward, on the lower 1/3 of the paper.

3 To erase on the original sheet, lift the paper bail out of the way; place a 5″ × 3″ card *in front of* the first carbon sheet. Use an eraser shield to protect the writing that is not to be erased. Brush the eraser crumbs away from the typewriter.

4 If more than one copy is to be made, move the protective card in front of the second carbon. Erase the errors on the carbon copy with a soft (pencil) eraser first, then with the hard typewriter eraser used in erasing on the original copy.

5 When the error has been erased on all copies, remove the protective card, position the carriage to the proper point, and type the necessary correction.

3 Squeezing/ spreading of letters

In correcting errors, it is often possible to "squeeze" omitted letters into half spaces or to "spread" letters to fill out spaces.

Error
an omitte letter

an omitted letter
Correction

1 An omitted letter at the beginning or end of a word

Corrective steps

a Move carriage to the letter *e*.

b Depress and hold down the space bar; strike the letter *d*.

Note: On an electric typewriter, it may be necessary to hold the carriage by hand at the half–space point, or to use the half–space mechanism.

Error
a leter within

a letter within
Correction

2 An omitted letter within a word

Corrective steps

a Erase the incorrect word.

b Position the carriage at the space after the letter *a*.

c Press down and hold the space bar; strike the letter *l*.

d Release the space bar, then press it down again and hold it; strike the next letter.

e Repeat the process for any additional letters.

Note: On the Selectric and some other electrics, use the half–space mechanism.

Error
a lettter within

a letter within
Correction

3 Addition of a letter within a word

Corrective steps

a Erase the incorrect word.

b Position the carriage as if you were going to type the letter *l* in its regular position following the space.

c Press down and hold the space bar; strike the letter *l*.

d Release the space bar; then repeat the process for each remaining letter.

Note: On the Selectric and some other electrics, use the half–space mechanism.

A control of, 7

B control of, 21

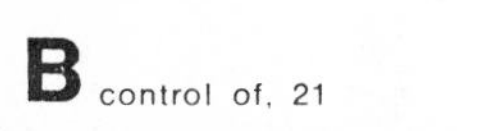

C control of, 16

D control of, 7

E control of, 11

F control of, 7

Special index

Alphabetic sentences [1]

Figure sentences [2]

Figure/symbol sentences [3]

Fluency (speed) sentences [4]

1 An alphabetic sentence appears in every Conditioning Practice, beginning on page 25.

2 A figure sentence appears in most of the Conditioning Practices, beginning on page 43.

3 A figure/symbol sentence appears in many of the Conditioning Practices, beginning on page 59.

4 Beginning on page 19, an easy sentence, designed for speed building or fluency practice, appears in every Conditioning Practice in the book.

Concentration drills

Guided writing copy

Metric activities

Preapplication manipulative drills

Problems in rough draft and script

Related learning drills

Skill-transfer timed writings

Straight-copy timed writings

Technique drills

Keystroking:

Machine parts:

Response patterns:

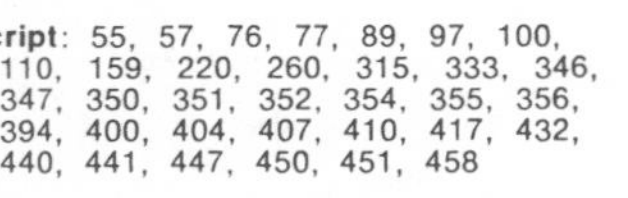